CAMBRIDGE SUF

# NATURAL MONOPOLY REGULATION

# CAMBRIDGE SURVEYS OF ECONOMIC LITERATURE

The literature of economics is expanding rapidly, and many subjects have changed out of recognition within the space of a few years. Perceiving the state of knowledge in fast-developing subjects is difficult for students and time-consuming for professional economists. This series of books is intended to help with this problem. Each book will be quite brief, giving a clear structure to and balanced overview of the topic, and written at a level intelligible to the senior undergraduate. They will therefore be useful for teaching but will also provide a mature yet compact presentation of the subject for economists wishing to update their knowledge outside their own specialism.

# Natural monopoly regulation
## Principles and practice

SANFORD V. BERG
*University of Florida*

JOHN TSCHIRHART
*University of Wyoming*

The right of the
University of Cambridge
to print and sell
all manner of books
was granted by
Henry VIII in 1534.
The University has printed
and published continuously
since 1584.

CAMBRIDGE UNIVERSITY PRESS
CAMBRIDGE
NEW YORK   PORT CHESTER   MELBOURNE   SYDNEY

*To our parents*

Published by the Press Syndicate of the University of Cambridge
The Pitt Building, Trumpington Street, Cambridge CB2 1RP
40 West 20th Street, New York, NY 10011, USA
10 Stamford Road, Oakleigh, Melbourne 3166, Australia

© Cambridge University Press 1988

First published 1988
Reprinted 1989

Printed in the United States of America

*Library of Congress Cataloging-in-Publication Data*

Berg, Sanford V.

Natural monopoly regulation : principles and practice / Sanford
V. Berg and John Tschirhart.

p.   cm. – (Cambridge surveys of economic literature)

ISBN 0-521-33039-4. ISBN 0-521-33893-X (pbk.)

1. Public utilities – Government policy.   2. Public utilities –
Rates – Law and legislation.   3. Monopolies.   I. Tschirhart, John.
II. Title.   III. Series.
HD2763.B445   1988
338.8′2613636′09 – dc19                                          88–10147
                                                                 CIP

*British Library Cataloguing in Publication Data*

Berg, Sanford V.

Natural monopoly regulation : principles
and practice – (Cambridge surveys in
economic literature).

1. Monopolies. Theories
I. Title   II. Tschirhart, John.
338.8′2

ISBN 0 521 33039 4 hard covers
ISBN 0 521 33893 X paperback

# Contents

# Preface

For nearly a quarter of a century, researchers have been responding to a series of path-breaking articles on the economics of public utilities. For example, Stigler and Friedland (1962) examined the effects of regulation on electricity prices, using data from the early 1900s. They found no impact on prices, and an outpouring of additional studies followed. Simultaneously, Averch and Johnson (1962) analyzed the impact of rate-base regulation on a firm's input mix and output. More elaborate models followed on the heels of their seminal contribution. At about the same time, Steiner (1957) and others were establishing the conditions for efficient pricing for a firm that experiences peak and off-peak demands for its output. The field of public utility economics no longer moved at a glacial pace, with case studies composing a substantial portion of its literature. Rather, it became part of the cutting edge of microeconomic theory, with more sophisticated analytical tools being applied to pricing and investment problems encountered in the context of natural monopolies.

Alfred E. Kahn's comprehensive textbook, *The Economics of Regulation* (1971), consolidated the extant literature, but the founding in 1970 of the *Bell Journal of Economics* contributed to the growth in the number of articles on utility topics. As an indication of that journal's impact, one need only note that this relative newcomer quickly became one of the top 10 economics journals. The sustainability of natural monopoly, nonlinear pricing, and regulation under uncertainty are just three of the themes stressed in this literature that have enriched our understanding of complex regulatory issues.

Furthermore, the literature continues to expand. Besides the specialized and more general journals that publish research on public utility topics, there continue to be numerous symposia and conference volumes (such as those edited by Crew and by Danielsen and Kamerschen) that represent important sources of primary material. Keeping up with the burgeoning literature is nearly impossible; so the present survey represents a snapshot of a rapidly changing field of study.

We have tried to pull together the major strands of research, without merely creating an encyclopedic catalogue of the literature. Some themes are treated in an idiosyncratic manner, representing our own views of how the tapestry might be best displayed. We hope that researchers at regulatory commissions can sense the excitement of recent theoretical developments. In addition, we hope that academic analysts will gain an appreciation for the challenges faced by regulators and executives who grapple with problems in the transportation, electricity, gas, and telecommunications industries.

The bounds we have chosen for our coverage reflect both the need to produce a manageable manuscript and our own abilities and interests. Undoubtedly, our survey has missed some important contributions and in some chapters is biased toward our own work. The former is an error, and the latter a natural inclination.

### Prerequisites

The reader is assumed to have a solid grasp of intermediate microeconomics. The material builds on standard consumer and producer theory; the particular applications to public utility issues involve extensions of intermediate theory. We have tried to avoid mathematical elegance for its own sake. However, partial differentiation is used extensively in the context of constrained optimization problems. Similarly, integration is used when deriving consumer surplus and expressing expected values.

Despite the regular appearance of functional notation, the non-mathematical reader will be able to follow the chains of reasoning. The extensive use of figures should assist in the interpretation of key relationships. We have tried to make the material accessible to the technical staffs of regulatory commissions and utilities, but the target audiences are advanced undergraduate and graduate students, in addition to economists wishing to review recent developments in the field.

### Acknowledgments

Any collaboration is a complicated activity. The authors brought different backgrounds and experiences to the enterprise, but the joint work required covering a broad and complicated set of topics. Each author has been surprised and delighted at how various (seemingly dissimilar) concepts have fitted together at times. Each has also despaired at the scope of the themes that, by necessity, have had to be explored. Fortunately, it seems that our moods and our research interests were complementary – enabling balance both in the analytics and in our spirits as the project progressed.

We have benefited greatly from feedback provided by our colleagues and students. We gratefully acknowledge helpful comments on particular sections by Eugene Brigham, Doug Gegax, Jon Hamilton, Douglas N. Jones, John Panzar, Richard Romano, David Sappington, Roger Sherman, H. Sourbis, Steven Slutsky, Linda Stanley, Ingo Vogelsang, and the anonymous reviewers of an earlier draft. Among former students at the universities of Florida and Wyoming we would like to thank Sarmila Banerjee, Charles Bennett, Richard Cabe, Lisa Crone, Louis Gapenski, Martin Grace, Marcie Guira, Cliff Nowell, and Tejaswi Raparla. Colin Day, our editor, provided encouragement and support throughout the project.

The Public Utility Research Center at the University of Florida has provided time and typing support, allowing us to complete needed revisions. Utility executives and regulators have also influenced our work by asking us fundamental questions regarding the nature of regulation of natural monopolies. In an era of change, decision-makers are going to expect academic researchers to contribute to the policy debate. These contributions will require that key concepts be closely linked to their empirical counterparts. Because of data limitations and the fact that disruptions would arise from premature applications of new theories, significant developments in microeconomic theory over the past two decades are only beginning to have an impact on policy. This book provides a comprehensive overview of natural monopoly issues that we hope will stimulate analytical refinements and lead to improved public policies.

S. V. B.
J. T.

# 1

# Introduction to regulatory economics

The regulation of natural monopolies is a fertile field of study for economists. Theoretical developments over two decades call for a consolidation of past research, even as regulators and managers continue to make decisions regarding prices, investments, new products, and possible deregulation. This book attempts to step back from today's headlines to systematically derive principles for efficient public policy toward those firms and industries with natural monopoly characteristics. The first half of the book analyzes why and how we *should* regulate natural monopolies, with some emphasis on actual pricing structures and entry regulations. The second half of the book examines why and how we *do* regulate natural monopolies, as well as the inherent problems that can arise. Throughout, we use current policy issues to illustrate the relevance of the principles for decision-makers.

## 1.1. Historical background

Sometimes causation runs from research results to policy implementation, but economic analysis generally has not had significant impact on regulatory developments. Research has tended to follow rather than to lead policy implementation (Acton, 1982). The institutions of regulation respond primarily to changes in technology, demands, industrial structure, and dominant political ideologies. Nevertheless, the analyses of econo-

1

mists have affected the framing of questions as well as the evolution of regulation in practice (McCraw, 1984; R. H. Nelson, 1987). Theory has contributed to our ability to explain, predict, and evaluate regulatory developments.

A brief overview of natural monopoly or public utility regulation will illustrate how concrete historical developments have influenced economic analysis.[1] Regulatory experience in the United States can be divided into five phases, according to Trebing (1984): (I) Populist/Progressive reform (1877–1920), (II) political inaction (1921–32), (III) New Deal reforms (1933–44), (IV) postwar stability (1945–68), and (V) destabilizing changes in costs and technologies (1969–present). Table 1.1 lists some of the important historical developments associated with each period. Detailed descriptions of current patterns of government intervention and the procedures utilized by regulators must wait until Chapter 8. For now, it suffices to note that issues accompanying the rise of industries have stimulated major analytical developments in the theory of natural monopoly.

In the late nineteenth century, concern over the growing economic power of the railroads placed that industry on the political agenda and spurred economists to examine the implications of this capital-intensive technology. Suspect behavior fell into four groups: (1) prices that were "too high" (reflecting monopoly power), (2) prices that were "too low" (implying predatory pricing, which discouraged economic entry), (3) prices that were "too high" for some, but "too low" for others (involving "undue" discrimination and/or subsidies for some markets), and (4) prices that were "unstable" (making it difficult for producers and consumers to plan ahead). One could argue that today there are few

---

1 "Natural monopoly" and "public utility" are often used interchangeably. We provide a definition of natural monopoly in Chapter 2. If a firm, such as an electricity, gas, or telephone company (which often are referred to as public utilities), satisfies the definition, it is a natural monopoly. Often a firm not satisfying this definition is labeled a public utility. For the most part, we use the term "natural monopoly" and avoid the term "public utility" because it is less precise.

issues that are fundamentally different from those at the turn of the century. Economic analysis has become more rigorous and elegant, but the underlying problems have continued to be addressed and readdressed over the decades. For example, Farrer (1902) catalogued five characteristics of a natural monopolist's product or production process:[2] Products tended

1. to be capital-intensive (having significant fixed costs or scale economies)
2. to be viewed as necessities (or essential to the community)
3. to be nonstorable (yet subject to fluctuating demands)
4. to be produced in particularly favored locations (yielding rents)
5. to involve direct connections with customers

Although that listing illustrates how economists perceived the situation at the time, these characteristics have served as the focus for subsequent analyses. A narrower and more rigorous definition is accepted today (see Chapter 2).

Others also contributed to the early systematic investigation of natural monopolies. J. M. Clark (1923, 1939) and Glaeser (1927) brought together principles of public utility pricing and addressed problems in rate-base regulation. Ely (1937), among others, emphasized the potential for competition to become self-destructive or unstable. Thus, the stability associated with monopoly could be viewed as a positive feature of economic performance. This aspect of the problem anticipated current analyses of the sustainability of natural monopoly in the presence of potential entry (see Chapter 7).

Price-structure issues that emerged in the context of monopoly suppliers attracted the attention of many economists. For example, the Taussig–Pigou (1913) debate on the relationship between railroad costs and the prices of services addressed issues that regulators are still grappling with today. If transportation services

---

2 Lowry (1973) and Sharkey (1982b) have both summarized early attempts to establish the features unique to a natural monopoly.

4

Table 1.1. *Historical phases of U.S. regulation*

| Milestone | Description |
|---|---|
| I. Populist/Progressive reform (1877–1920) | |
| 1877 *Munn v. Illinois* | Tight boundaries drawn about those industries affected with the public interest |
| 1887 Interstate Commerce Commission (ICC) | Regulation of railroad rates and routes |
| 1907–13 | Twenty-nine states create commissions |
| 1920 Federal Power Commission (FPC) | Water projects only |
| II. Political inaction (1921–32) | |
| 1927 Federal Radio Commission (FRC) | |
| III. New Deal reforms (1933–44) | |
| 1934 *Nebbia v. New York* | Property dedicated to "public use" subject to potential regulation |
| 1934 Federal Communications Act | Expands the FRC to include telephones |
| 1935 Federal Power Act | Gives FPC jurisdiction over securities, accounts, combinations, interstate rates and services |
| 1935 Public Utility Holding Company Act | |
| 1935 Motor Act | Expands ICC regulation to modes competing with railroads |
| 1938 Interstate Gas Act | Expands FPC coverage to interstate transportation and wholesale distribution of natural gas |
| IV. Postwar stability (1945–68) | |
| 1946 Atomic Energy Commission | |
| 1947 *Hope Natural Gas* | |
| 1966 FCC computer I inquiry initiated | |

V. Rising costs and destabilizing technological change (1969–present)

1969 FCC MCI decision
1970 Environmental Protection Agency
1973 First OPEC price rise ($4 → $12/barrel)
1974 Nuclear Regulatory Commission
1974 *Madison Gas and Electric* — Marginal-cost pricing supported by Wisconsin PSC

1976 Railroad Revitalization and Regulatory Reform Act
1977 Department of Energy
1978 Public Utility Regulatory Policies Act
1978 Natural Gas Policy Act
1978 Airline Deregulation Act
1979 Second OPEC price rise
1979 Three Mile Island accident
1980 Motor Carrier Act
1980 Staggers Rail Act
1980 FCC Computer II inquiry decision — Basic vs. enhanced services: competition for equipment and enhanced services

1982 IBM antitrust case dropped
1982 AT&T settlement: modified final judgment
1984 AT&T divestiture completed
1985 FERC Order 436 — Pipelines as potential open-access transporters of natural gas
1986 FCC Computer III inquiry decision — Separate subsidiaries for enhanced services waived if comparably efficient connection and open network design

*Source:* Reprinted from the *JEI* by special permission of the copyright holder, the Association for Evolutionary Economics.

for different consumers (say coal and copper) involved the same costs, then different prices would be discriminatory (Pigou). However, if the services were distinct and required a joint input, charging different prices need not be discriminatory (Taussig). Although they did not explicitly examine the cost-allocation procedures implicit in their respective formulations, these economists set the stage for later analyses (see Locklin, 1933, for an extensive overview of this debate). Similarly, Sichler (1928) viewed the telephone network as being characterized by joint costs. He was concerned with the residential and business consumers' use of the local telephone network; the same joint-cost problem he explored arises for local and long-distance access to the local network.

J. M. Clark (1911) was perhaps the first to formally address another pricing issue: time-of-use or peak-load pricing. He noted the attention economists had given to railroad rates, and the lack of analysis of the growing electricity industry. His advocacy of marginal-cost pricing emphasized prices as signals for future cost and usage, in contrast to the rate designers of the day, who focused on cost recovery. Electricity suppliers did not emphasize the efficiency implications of rate structures. However, as Hausman and Neufeld (1984) point out, a number of engineers, utility executives, and economists were sophisticated supporters of time-of-day rates around the turn of the century. For example, long before modern interest in the problem, Bye (1926, 1929) formally derived the analytics of pricing for a shifting peak load.

## 1.2. Regulatory goals

Economists tend to evaluate rate designs in terms of whether or not they provide appropriate price signals leading to efficient allocation of resources. At the same time, regulators tend to emphasize certain attributes that they would like prices or rates to reflect. Bonbright (1961) provides a list of eight traditional rate-making or pricing attributes (Table 1.2) that includes a broad range of criteria, including fairness. At first glance, the list appears to contain many attributes that are in conflict with

Table 1.2. *Eight traditional rate-making attributes*

1. Simplicity and public acceptability
2. Freedom from controversy
3. Revenue sufficiency
4. Revenue stability
5. Stability of rates
6. Fairness in apportionment of total costs
7. Avoidance of undue rate discrimination
8. Encouragement of efficiency

economic rate-making objectives. However, many of the attributes have efficiency components. For example, consumers' information processing costs should be included in the derivation of efficient prices. To economize on these costs, regulators will emphasize simplicity of rates, the first attribute in Table 1.2. Also, the costs associated with regulatory hearings on rate structures will be reduced if policies can be easily understood by the affected parties. Public acceptability contributes to the perceived legitimacy of the regulatory process, which is essential for keeping down the administrative costs associated with regulation.

As will be seen, a shift away from simple rate structures may be desirable in some situations. For example, less weight will be given to simplicity as a rate-making attribute when metering technologies make feasible the introduction of peak-load electricity prices and usage-sensitive local telephone rates. Of course, the acceptability of major changes in rate design depends on the mix of winning and losing customers (see Chapter 3). If there are net benefits from rate redesign, then, conceptually, winners could compensate the losers – facilitating public acceptability.

Freedom from controversy, the second attribute, is closely linked to public acceptability. If there is widespread disagreement regarding the factual basis for prices, then the natural response is to conduct appropriate studies. For example, calculation of opportunity costs and estimation of demand elasticities (and growth) are essential for implementation of the principles developed in this book. A gradual phase-in of new rate structures will also limit controversy. Of course, if some group is being subsidized with current prices, it will fight for the status quo. Most would agree that there is little economic merit in such a position unless there is a consensus that the favored group "deserves" income transfers.

In terms of the revenue-sufficiency attribute, efficient prices equal to marginal costs may not yield total revenues sufficient to cover the costs of production; with inadequate returns, investors will be unwilling to maintain and expand the firm's capital equipment. The issue leading to controversy is how a revenue shortfall is to be made up if marginal-cost prices are used. Economists have suggested increases in flat monthly charges or price increases to consumers with inelastic demands (thus minimizing the distortions resulting from pricing above marginal cost). This revenue-reconciliation problem is nontrivial in practice.

Revenue stability is another of Bonbright's suggested attributes, but, presumably, net revenue (after costs) is the important variable for a firm, because a revenue reduction accompanied by the same cost reduction does not strain the entity's financial resources. Thus, when prices track costs, a reduction in consumption will have less of an impact on utility finances than when they do not. To compare alternative rate structures, regulators must examine how rates, customer responses, and production costs interact to yield revenue stability. Certainly, the cost of capital to a utility increases if it adopts rates that yield highly uncertain net income streams.

Rate stability is one attribute that can conflict with the others. Stability allows consumers to plan ahead; however, if costs are not stable, then unchanging prices provide inefficient signals. For example, when capacity costs are rising over time, average-cost pricing based on historical costs can lead to overinvestment in capacity and overconsumption of output. Rate stability that masks change can be quite inefficient. In the case of electricity, relatively low prices in the 1960s and early 1970s resulted in minimal consumer investments in energy-saving appliances, insulation, and timers for hot-water heaters. Partly to maintain price stability in the 1970s, regulators did not let prices track marginal costs. That policy served as a disincentive for energy conservation. The long-run impacts of such stable, but inefficient, price signals were serious in terms of forgone opportunities.

To avoid imposing hardships on particular consumer classes or on consumers within a class, regulators will tend to prefer a gradual transition to new rates. For example, jumping to peak-load prices that reflect opportunity costs may be very disruptive to those who have made investments based on past pricing policies. Highly disruptive changes are bound to be politically unacceptable and may well be uneconomic.

Fairness in the apportionment of total costs, the sixth rate-making attribute, arises when different consumers benefit differentially from a new rate structure. The economist's observation that the winning group *could* compensate the losing group and leave both better off is not much comfort to the losers when such transfers do not in fact occur. Nevertheless, the efficiency costs of "socially condoned" income transfers should be identified prior to making equity the primary goal of regulation. Also, as is indicated in Chapter 3, the winners and losers may be the same group, and fairness is not an issue.

The seventh attribute, avoidance of undue rate discrimination, also must be balanced against the others. Although charges of discriminatory pricing are often made, the test for whether or not discrimination exists requires information about the cost of service – the standard cost-allocation techniques discussed in Chapter 3 are woefully inadequate for this purpose. Moreover, price discrimination can be beneficial. For example, it may allow a service to be provided that otherwise would not be. As we shall see, relatively higher prices for consumers with low demand elasticities can have positive welfare properties.

Bonbright's final attribute can be broken down into four components. *Technical efficiency* requires that the least-resource-consuming production processes be used to produce a given level of output. Such technical efficiency can be contrasted with *allocative efficiency,* which requires that the economically correct level (and mix) of output be chosen from among the technically efficient outputs. Consumer valuations of various time patterns of consumption also come into consideration for allocative efficiency. Organizational slack or managerial pursuit of goals that are contrary to the owner's interests can lead to what has been labeled *X-inefficiency* (Cross, 1970; Leibenstein, 1966). *Innovative efficiency,* another aspect of this broad attribute, depends on how well firms perform the intertemporal tasks of cost reduction and new product development. Because this book focuses on efficiency considerations, we present detailed discussions of these topics later.

In general, economists have built a strong case for emphasizing efficiency in the rate-making process, although one could argue that the determination of the weight to be given to each criterion when choosing from among alternative rate designs is essentially a political issue. Schmalensee (1979) argues that although the members of society are interested in values other than economic efficiency, the task of balancing efficiency against other goals (such as income distributional concerns) is far too difficult for natural monopoly control mechanisms:

> In short, the political view of appropriate regulatory performance is an inherently unattainable ideal; effective interest group competition on all decisions and effective decision making are incompatible. In order to permit regulators to consider the whole spectrum of collective goals and to respond directly or indirectly to all interest group pressures, they must be given considerable freedom of action. But the relative lack of control that must accompany the delegation of broad authority increases the difficulty of ensuring that desirable trade-offs are made and makes special interest dominance and arbitrary action or inaction more likely. It is simply not possible, desirable though it seems in principle, to use the control of natural monopoly effectively to pursue a number of potentially conflicting social goals. (Schmalensee, 1979, p. 17)

Nevertheless, Bonbright's eight attributes can be viewed as mutually reinforcing up to a point; then the strengths and limitations of alternative structures provide the basis for reaching a final decision. Many economists, including Kahn (1971) and Schmalensee, urge that efficiency be the initial standard for identifying candidate rate alternatives. More detailed analyses of the remaining options may reveal one structure involving reduced efficiency, but improvements in other areas. Then the decisionmaker can make explicit trade-offs among attributes.

The desirability of particular policies depends on how the regulatory instruments relate to the achievement of economic objectives. The expansion of our analytical tool kit has not simplified the regulatory process. If anything, because new analytical tools permit regulatory commissions to ask many more "what if" questions than in the past, additional technical expertise opens up a Pandora's box of regulatory issues. Technical topics such as rating periods, cost allocations, price differentials, appropriate rate incentives, and deregulation have moved to the forefront of natural monopoly discussions, while consideration of complementary (and conflicting) regulatory goals complicates the process.

### 1.3 Overview of *Natural monopoly regulation*

This book is organized to move from principles to practice, although there is substantial overlap. Part I examines why (Chapter 2) and how (Chapters 3–7) we *should* regulate natural monopolies. Although income distributional considerations can be incorporated into price structures, the emphasis is on the implications of alternative rate designs for economic efficiency. Part II examines why and how we *do* regulate natural monopolies (Chapter 8). After this, we turn to inherent problems with the way regulation operates – especially insofar as regulatory constraints (Chapter 9) and technological change (Chapter 10) add to these problems. Next, we examine partial regulation, deregulation, and diversification (Chapter 11), and the concluding chapter considers the pros and cons of alternatives to traditional regulation.

First we focus on the natural monopoly justification of regulation. Chapter 2 considers single-product and multiproduct natural monopolies. The latter, in particular, permit the incorporation of important features of the real-world environment into economic analysis. Multiproduct cost functions, interdependent demands, and more detailed specification of entry conditions now characterize current research. The implications of these structural conditions for regulation have provided one of the most significant themes in microeconomic analysis over the past two decades.

Chapter 3 analyzes market performance when a welfare-maximizing natural monopolist is constrained to using linear prices. After applying the principles to a single-period multiproduct firm and over multiple periods for a single-product firm, we examine the limitations of the approach. Informational requirements, overlapping (and competing) jurisdictional responsibilities, and other factors serve as impediments to the implementation of relatively efficient pricing schemes. However, the limitations of alternative schemes, including various fully distributed cost pricing methods, are so significant that movement toward more efficient pricing can be strongly supported. The cost-allocation procedures traditionally utilized by regulators can involve significant distortions when the natural monopolist is producing some products that are subject to competition. Chapter 3 shows that rate-making in the presence of competition requires trade-offs between the gains and costs of total, partial, or zero regulation. Similarly, if several firms producing partial substitutes have scale economies, regulated outcomes can be compared with the pricing regimes that would emerge under competition. Both individual firms and the industry are analyzed in terms of deviations from optimality.

Next, Chapter 4 expands the natural monopolist's price structures to include nonlinear prices, so that regulators can meet equity (or income distributional) goals without sacrificing economic efficiency to a high degree. One example of a nonlinear price structure used by many natural monopolists is the two-part tariff: a flat monthly fee plus a per-unit charge. More complicated price structures also characterize some utilities. Obtaining revenues via nonlinear prices has a side benefit of increased revenue stability. With marginal prices tracking marginal costs, a reduction in consumption has less of an impact on firm finances. This chapter utilizes some concepts from game theory to illustrate how coalitions of consumers establish bounds on price structures.

Chapter 5 presents models of peak-load pricing for both neoclassical and fixed-coefficient production technologies. Diverse technologies and interdependent demands are also incorporated into the analysis. The peak-load pricing problem is not linked inextricably to the problem of natural monopoly. However, demand fluctuations for nonstorable services like electricity and telephone calls raise a number of pricing and investment issues for these industries. Similarly, water and natural gas present trade-offs between storage and transmission facilities. When intertemporal differences in demand are combined with scale economies, the investment decision becomes even more complicated. Practical considerations affecting implementation include estimating the demands at particular times and the associated marginal costs. Long-run adjustments are also discussed in terms of efficiency impacts.

Chapter 6 extends the pricing analysis to include stochastic demand. After characterizing stochastic demand, we consider rationing, the costs of excess demand, and the need for system reliability requirements. Stochastic demand complicates the revenue-sufficiency considerations and efficient rate-making standards, particularly when reliability is included as a determinant of demand. Interruptible service yields another rate structure available to the natural monopolist facing stochastic demand, and we illustrate how it requires separation of the market into consumer classes, with determination of priority orderings across these classes. Additional rate-design issues include fuses as control devices, the potential for energy storage, and cogeneration as a response to technological opportunities.

Chapter 7 concludes the first part of the book by considering the implications of rate structures for potential entry. Through the use of relatively simple illustrative cost structures, we consider cross-subsidization and situations where no price structure can be found that will both cover total costs and prevent entry. Thus, without entry barriers, no prices that can sustain the natural monopoly market structure may be available. After identifying necessary and sufficient conditions on costs and demands ensuring sustainability, numerical examples are used to illustrate the concepts. Finally, conditions are established under which relatively efficient prices will tend to be chosen by a regulated multiproduct firm.

The second half of the book considers regulation in practice. Chapter 8 examines how and why firms are regulated. After summarizing the public-interest and capture theories of regulation, we present the economic theory of regulation. Like any commodity, regulation can be viewed as having both a supply and a demand, with specific factors influencing the strength of these forces. After describing entry and price regulation, the chapter provides an overview of rate-of-return regulation. Institutional features complicating the regulatory process include determining allowable costs (such as advertising), depreciation expenses, incentives for cost reduction, rate base, and the allowed rate of return. This chapter concludes with a review of theoretical and empirical studies of regulatory behavior, discussing pro-producer and pro-consumer outcomes and the links between the regulatory climate and the cost of capital.

Chapter 9 focuses on theoretical models of regulatory constraint. After analyzing rate regulation for a single-product firm, we consider pricing with multiple outputs. In a sense, rate regulation is a misnomer, because the associated hearings have tended to focus on the total revenues utilities ought to be allowed, rather than on rate design. Empirical evidence is presented regarding the alleged tendency for overcapitalization, a thesis developed by Averch and Johnson (A-J) (1962). Some reasons for not observing a so-called A-J effect include regulatory lag, stochastic demand, and the behaviors of both firms and regulators that violate the A-J assumptions. The chapter concludes with an examination of two other types of regulatory constraints: automatic adjustment clauses and regulation of industry operating ratios.

Innovation under regulation is addressed in Chapter 10, beginning with a survey of the characteristics of technological information complicating the production and application of innovations. We analyze the implications of rivalry and cooperation for technological change in regulated industries. We also consider the determinants of research-and-development (R&D) and multiperiod issues, as well as regulatory reactions to cost-reducing activities. A more comprehensive model of technological change is found in the literature on induced innovations, where capital- or labor-saving technologies may be chosen in response to regulatory constraints. Of course, this more detailed characterization of technological opportunities makes the application of the theoretical models to actual regulation somewhat problematic. In some instances, new technological opportunities are embodied in capital, as with transmission lines for power pooling. These may strengthen the case for regulation. In other cases, technological changes may lead to the restructuring of industry, as single-product or multiproduct economies become exhausted at lower output levels.

Chapter 11 examines how new technological opportunities affect firms' product mixes and the potential gains to deregulation and diversification in some traditional natural monopoly industries. Because partial regulation characterizes current practice in many industries, we analyze issues that can arise when firms have constraints on only some of their price and entry decisions. In addition, cost-allocation regulations pose particularly difficult problems, because such schemes can threaten the firm's financial viability. The efficiency of input and output mixes can be affected by mechanisms for allocating costs.

Given the desirability of a relatively smooth transition to deregulated markets, the process may involve residual regulation of entry, prices, or product quality. For example, price floors may be established to limit predation; price ceilings may be used to limit monopoly power. Because destructive competition has often been a concern of regulators, the potential for such behavior is examined. Expansions in product lines and vertical integration are also analyzed. Chapter 11 concludes with an overview of the potential gains to deregulation.

The principles developed throughout this book conflict with regulatory practice in many industries. In the concluding chapter, we consider alternatives to traditional regulation, dividing them into four categories: (1) movement to public ownership; (2) the possibility of franchising natural monopolies; (3) placing greater emphasis on output quality; (4) adopting new regulatory incentive adjustment processes. Theoretical and empirical studies are analyzed to determine how useful these alternatives might be in supplementing and perhaps supplanting current practices. We emphasize some of the more recent literature on incentives that stresses the asymmetry of information available to the regulator and the firm.

Because the field of government regulation is broader than the material covered in this book, we should briefly indicate what we do not address. Joskow and Noll (1981) divide government regulation into three categories: (1) regulation of natural monopolies; (2) regulation of competitive industries; (3) regulation where there are market failures, including health, environmental, and information issues. We concentrate on category 1, and to a lesser extent category 2. In particular, we concentrate on price and entry regulation within these categories. Quality regulation is discussed, but to a lesser degree. Within categories 1 and 2 we cover many theoretical studies in some detail, with empirical results receiving less scrutiny. We do not cover the sizable empirical literature on demand estimates, responses to peak-load pricing, or production-function estimates. We also do not examine in any detail the finance-theory literature that pertains to natural monopolies.

The field defies summary in some respects. However, there is no doubt that our theoretical understanding of natural monopoly issues has increased dramatically over the past two decades. The key problem is how to translate analytical constructs into usable principles. J. von Neumann (1947) notes eloquently that without closer links between empirical researchers, policy analysts, and theorists,

> . . . there is grave danger that the subject will develop along the line of least resistance, that the stream so far from its source will separate into a multitude of insignificant branches, and that the discipline will become a disorganized mass of details and complexities. In other words, at a great distance from its empirical source, or after much abstract inbreeding, a mathematical subject is in danger of degeneration. At the inception the style is usually classical; when it shows signs of becoming baroque, then the danger signal is up. (von Neumann, 1947, p. 146)

To some extent, the danger-signal flags do wave above the topic of natural monopoly regulation. The goal of this book is to consolidate analytic frameworks and identify those providing insights for decision-makers. The core themes are highlighted by regular reference to actual regulatory issues now facing us in the energy and telecommunications industries. Although we can appreciate the elegant detail of baroque economics, we have tried to restore the crisp outlines of the main models. We hope our blend of rigor and relevance facilitates further additions to the literature and encourages policy implementation of many of the ideas developed here.

# Part I

## Optimal pricing and investment for natural monopolies

# 2

## Natural monopoly and the justification for regulation

Because the need for economic regulation is closely linked with the concept of natural monopoly, we must have a precise definition of a natural monopoly. A recent survey by Sharkey (1982b) describes how our conception of natural monopoly has evolved since the time of Cournot. Although various economists have offered different definitions, all agree that pervasive economies of scale are at the center of the issue, with some noting that production technology is not the only source of efficiency for a single supplier.[1] Consider these statements by Kahn (1971) regarding the essence of natural monopolies:

> . . . their costs will be lower if they consist in a single supplier. (Kahn, 1971, p. 11)
>
> . . . a natural monopoly is an industry in which the economies of scale – that is, the tendency for average costs to decrease the larger the producing firm – are continuous up to the point that one company supplies the entire demand. (Kahn, 1971, pp. 123–4)

---

1 A less technical overview of the concept is available in Lowry (1973). The scale-economies argument was central in many early formulations of the natural monopoly literature. Here, we focus on the *modern* definition of natural monopoly, although the other characteristics further complicate market organization for such products.

Although both statements are familiar, they are not equivalent. We can show that the second implies the first, whereas the first does not imply the second. Recently, the definition of a natural monopoly has been developed in a more rigorous way by Baumol (1977). After reviewing the definition for the single-product firm and deriving implications for price and entry regulation, we extend the definition to a multiproduct firm. Then we show how the financial consequences of efficient pricing complicate the task of regulators.

### 2.1. Natural monopoly in the single-product firm

Two concepts are fundamental for our understanding of single-product natural monopolies: decreasing average cost and subadditivity. The first is very familiar and simply means that unit costs fall with increases in output. The second is less familiar, but very important. A firm with rising unit costs is able to produce a given level of output at a lower total cost than multiple firms if its cost function is subadditive. To be more precise, let $C(q)$ be the firm's continuously differentiable cost function, where $q$ is a measure of the firm's output. A *decreasing average cost* for all positive output less than or equal to $q$ can then be expressed as

$$C(q^i)/q^i < C(q^j)/q^j \tag{2.1}$$

for all $q^i$ and $q^j$, where $0 < q^j < q^i \leq q$. This condition usually is equated with economies of scale in production. Condition (2.1) is sufficient to ensure that production costs will be lowest when there is a single firm supplying the output; however, it is not a necessary condition. That is, the average cost can be rising and production costs may still be lowest with a single firm. To clarify this point, we need to examine the concept of subadditivity. A cost function is *subadditive* at $q$ if and only if

$$C\left(\sum_{i=1}^{m} q^i\right) \leq \sum_{i=1}^{m} C(q^i) \tag{2.2}$$

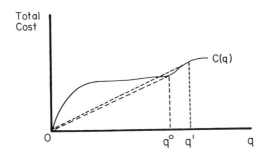

Figure 2.1. A range of output with rising average cost.

for all quantities $q^1, \ldots, q^m$ such that $\Sigma_{i=1}^{m} q^i = q$. Strict subadditivity is associated with strict inequality in (2.2). Condition (2.2) is necessary and sufficient to ensure that costs will be lowest when there is a single supplier. Thus, any firm whose cost function satisfies (2.2) can produce a given output at no greater cost than that incurred by two or more firms whose total productions equal the same given output.

That (2.1) implies (2.2) can be shown as follows. From (2.1),

$$\frac{C(q^i)}{q^i} > \frac{C(q)}{q}$$

where $0 < q^i < q$, $i = 1, \ldots, m$, and $\Sigma_{i=1}^{m} q^i = q$. In turn, this can be written as

$$C(q^i) > \frac{q^i}{q} C(q)$$

and summing both sides over all $i$ yields

$$\sum_{i=1}^{m} C(q^i) > \frac{\sum_{i=1}^{m} q^i}{q} C(q) \equiv C(q)$$

which is the definition of strict subadditivity.

Figure 2.1 illustrates that (2.2) does not imply (2.1). Here, average cost, which is given by the slope of a ray from the origin to the total-cost function, is falling up to $q^0$, rises between $q^0$ and $q^1$, and falls thereafter. Because of the rapidly increasing cost at low output levels, the least expensive method of producing $q^*$, where $q^0 < q^* < q^1$, is with a single supplier, even though average cost is rising in the neighborhood of $q^*$. Thus, subadditivity defined by (2.2) does not imply decreasing average cost defined by (2.1). Baumol (1977) provides a more complete discussion of necessary and sufficient conditions for subadditivity.

We refer to (2.1) as the old definition of natural monopoly, because economists equated natural monopoly with economies of scale for many years, and the definition is still pervasive in textbooks. We refer to condition (2.2) as the new definition of natural monopoly. This new definition is widely accepted, and it seems to be the condition that economists had in mind all along. If a firm's cost function satisfies (2.1) over the relevant range of output, we say that the firm is a *strong* natural monopoly. If a firm's cost function satisfies (2.2), but *not* (2.1) over the relevant range of output, we say that the firm is a *weak* natural monopoly. We shall elaborate on these definitions later, and we shall see that the implications for regulatory policy may differ depending on whether the firm is a strong or a weak natural monopoly. To best see this point, we turn to the dilemmas confronting regulators who deal with natural monopolies.

## 2.2 Regulation for the single-product firm

Continuing with the case of the single-product firm, let us initially assume that the firm is a natural monopoly, either strong or weak. Taking the sum of consumer surplus, CS, and producer profit, $\pi$, as the appropriate measure of society's welfare,[2] and utilizing a single, linear price structure, the welfare-

---

2 Throughout much of this book we use consumer surplus plus profit as our measure of societal welfare. There are potential problems with this, especially with the use of consumer surplus (Silberberg, 1978). Nevertheless, it has been widely used in the literature, it can be readily understood by policy-makers, and, in at least some cases, it provides a useful measure of consumer gains or losses (Willig, 1976). We also use a societal welfare function in some chapters, and when we do, we contrast this function to the consumer-surplus approach. Sherman (1989) provides a good explanation of how the two approaches compare.

maximizing monopolist should choose a price that satisfies the problem

$$\max_{q} W = CS + \pi \tag{2.3}$$

where

$$CS = \int_0^q p(x) \, dx - p(q)q \tag{2.4}$$

$$\pi = p(q)q - C(q) \tag{2.5}$$

and $p(q)$ is the inverse market-demand function. The first-order necessary condition[3] from this maximization problem yields a price equal to marginal cost, or

$$p(q^w) = C'(q^w) \equiv MC(q^w) \tag{2.6}$$

where the prime indicates a derivative, and $q^w$ is the output produced and sold. Of course, this result would be expected in a purely competitive market, and its desirable properties regarding economic efficiency carry over to the natural monopoly market as well.

However, if the firm is left to pursue a pricing policy of its own choosing (still using a single, linear price structure), and if the firm behaves as a profit-maximizer, then the monopolist will simply maximize (2.5). This calculation will yield a price that satisfies

$$MR(q^m) \equiv p(q^m) + q^m p'(q^m) = C'(q^m) \equiv MC(q^m) \tag{2.7}$$

where $q^m$ is the profit-maximizing output, and, again, primes indicate derivatives. This process yields the familiar result that marginal revenue (on the left side) equals marginal cost (on the right side).

---

3 We assume that second-order sufficient conditions for a maximum are satisfied. For brevity, throughout this book we shall assume this without specifying the appropriate convexity conditions on the objective functions and constraints in the optimization problems. In this way, the first-order or Kuhn–Tucker conditions that are shown in the text are necessary and sufficient for an optimum.

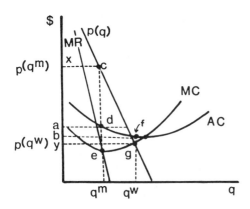

Figure 2.2. The monopoly and the welfare-maximizing
outcomes.

Solutions (2.6) and (2.7) are illustrated in Figure 2.2, where AC
is average cost, the demand curve is labeled $p(q)$, area *xcda* represents the profit enjoyed by the profit-maximizing monopolist,
and area *ceg* represents the increased welfare available to society
by moving from the monopoly output $q^m$ to the welfare-maximizing output $q^w$. Note that the construction of Figure 2.2
implies a strong natural monopoly over the relevant output
range, because AC is falling; however, similar results regarding
the potential for increased welfare when moving from $q^m$ to $q^w$
would hold if the curves were constructed to depict a weak natural monopoly.

### Alternative regulatory policies

In view of the potential welfare gain that a regulator
might achieve by forcing the monopolist to lower the price, is
regulation justified, and, if so, what regulatory forms are called
for? If regulation induced no inefficient responses by firms in
terms of input-mix distortions (see Chapter 9), the gains to regulation would depend on three factors: (1) the extent of the
resource misallocation in the absence of intervention (often
accompanied by large profit); (2) the existence of barriers to entry

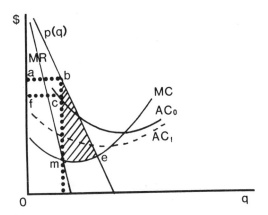

Figure 2.3. Monopoly profits and gains to MC pricing.

into the market; (3) whether the firm is a strong or weak natural monopoly.

Consider the first factor. If the associated resource misallocations are minimal, then regulation may not be justified. Regulation is not costless, and the benefits from correcting minimal misallocations may be less than the cost of running the regulatory agency. If the resource misallocations are significant, however, then the benefits of regulation can outweigh the costs. Large excess profit is an indicator of significant resource misallocations, although it is not a necessary condition for the existence of these misallocations. Suppose Figure 2.3 depicts the market. With average cost $AC_0$, the excess profit given by area *abcf* is relatively small, but the deadweight loss (or misallocation) given by area *bem* is relatively large. If *bem* exceeds the cost of running the regulatory agency, intervention may be justified [depending on factors (2) and (3)]. If a technological change causes fixed costs to fall dramatically, so that average cost drops to $AC_1$, profit will be greater, but the deadweight loss will be unchanged (because MC is assumed unchanged in the relevant quantity range). Thus, the excess profit alone is not an adequate indicator of the need for regulation. The basic efficiency issue is whether or not there is much social welfare to be gained if a regulator restricts the monopolist's pricing policy.

Markets with relatively small misallocations may be quite prevalent. A small town may have only one supermarket, or a larger city may have only one opera house, because the markets are too small to support more than one of either. Yet we would not be inclined to regulate such businesses: Even at the profit-maximizing output level, profit and potential welfare improvements are small. Throughout the remainder of this book, we assume that the market or markets in which the firm operates are large enough to support significant excess profit and resource misallocations, and regulation should be considered. With this in mind, we turn to factors (2) and (3) to examine when regulation is justified and what form it should take.

### Barriers to entry

Suppose that there are barriers to entry into the market. Probably the most common barrier is an incumbent firm with large sunk costs (Baumol, Panzar, and Willig, 1982). In this case, entrants will have to make prohibitively large investments in order to compete at about the same scale of output as the incumbent. If the entrant is successful, expansion of market output, which partly depends on the incumbent's reaction to entry, may so reduce the price that entry will be unprofitable.[4] There are other types of barriers that we need not list here; instead, we simply note that regardless of the pricing policy pursued in this market, entrants do not materialize.

Barriers to entry have significant implications for regulation in the context of strong and weak natural monopolies. For the former, average cost is decreasing throughout the relevant output range. Referring to Figure 2.2, we know that the unregulated monopolist will choose output $q^m$, whereas the efficient output is

---

4 The literature on this topic has grown dramatically as economists have characterized expectations, reactions, and the adjustment process in duopoly markets; see, for example, J. Friedman (1983).

$q^w$. Regulation will be needed to avoid the former result. However, consider what occurs if the regulator attempts to achieve the latter result. Because price is below average cost, a deficit occurs equal to area *bfgy*. The firm is not financially solvent. This simple result captures the fundamental dilemma long associated with natural monopolies. Because average cost is decreasing, society may be better off if the firm is allowed to maintain monopoly status, because this market structure minimizes production costs for any output. However, a deficit results if society forces the firm to price all units at marginal cost; the firm must be subsidized or else shut down. In the latter case, consumers gain *no* consumer surplus, and the result is a reduction in welfare in the long run compared with monopoly pricing. Subsidization, on the other hand, has been a controversial option, as we discuss further in Section 2.5. For now, note that one regulatory option is to force marginal-cost pricing and subsidize the firm.

An alternative to subsidization is to deviate from marginal-cost pricing so that the firm is ensured zero profit. If a single, linear price structure is used, then the solution is to set price equal to average cost. This solution results in an output less than the efficient output $q^w$, but greater than the monopoly output $q^m$. There are other ways, however, in which the firm might deviate from marginal-cost pricing. In particular, the regulator might require a nonuniform pricing structure that would maintain certain efficiency properties, while allowing the firm to be financially solvent. These nonlinear price structures are discussed in detail in Chapter 4.

Next, consider a weak natural monopoly in conjunction with barriers to entry. In Figure 2.4, curve $2C(q/2)/q$ represents average cost when two firms are in the market. The purpose of this curve is simply to locate $q_s$, the output level at which it becomes efficient for a second plant to be built and operated. Average cost for a single firm is falling up to $q_0$ and rising thereafter. Over the range $0 \leq q \leq q_s$, costs will be subadditive. Given demand curve $p(q)$ and marginal cost $C'(q)$, efficient pricing yields output $q^w$, where costs are subadditive; however, average cost is increasing.

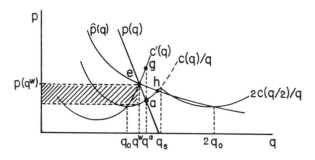

Figure 2.4. Welfare-maximizing output.

Here, the fundamental solvency dilemma does not arise: The firm can set price equal to marginal cost and earn positive profit equal to the shaded area. To ensure this outcome, regulatory intervention is still required to protect consumers, because the firm's incentive still will be to set a price at which marginal revenue and marginal cost will be equal. Nevertheless, the regulator will not be confronted with protecting the monopolist from a deficit.[5]

### Ultrafree entry

Removing barriers to entry will alter the role of the regulator. Suppose that new firms can enter the market and produce at or below the output level at which the incumbent produces. This situation is perhaps extreme, because the entrant will need

---

5 If anything, regulators might be tempted to set price equal to average cost to dissipate profits and lower the price (pleasing consumers). Such a misguided policy would induce overconsumption at $q^a$, as the marginal cost would be greater than price. Consumers value the additional output less than the value of the additional resources in other activities. A deadweight loss of *eag* arises under average-cost pricing. If the market demand can be separated into several submarkets, the misallocation can be reduced by giving price breaks to relatively inelastic demands. This point is developed more fully in Chapter 3. Alternatively, multipart pricing could be used to dissipate excess profits, say via a lump-sum deduction from each customer's monthly bill (considered in Chapter 4).

to duplicate the incumbent's operation and achieve immediate success in marketing the product. Also, this characterization of entry assumes that the incumbent remains idle, rather than temporarily reformulating its prices to thwart this entry. This extreme case, labeled a *perfectly contestable market* by Baumol, Panzar, and Willig (1982), has been criticized for its lack of realism (Shepherd, 1984). Nevertheless, it does provide a polar case for delineating the proper role of the regulator. Moreover, the lack of realism for which it has been criticized becomes less objectionable for a multiproduct firm, because entrants might very well have the ability to attack the incumbent in just one output market. Contestable markets are discussed in Chapter 7; for now, assume that entry into the market is costless and easily reversible via exit.

Under the special case of ultrafree entry, consider first the strong natural monopolist. If the welfare-maximizing output, $q^w$ in Figure 2.2, is to be achieved, then regulation is necessary, because this output will not be chosen by an unregulated monopolist. Under uniform pricing, the regulator will be forced to subsidize the monopolist to avoid the deficit problem. On the other hand, if consumers do not wish to subsidize the monopolist, but would rather have the monopoly cover its costs through revenues, then regulation is unnecessary. The monopolist will be forced to charge a price that will earn zero profits; any higher price that would allow positive profits would attract entrants. Note, however, that without giving further structure to this problem, the monopolist will be indifferent to the type of price scheme used. That is, average-cost pricing or a more elaborate nonlinear scheme that will yield zero profit are equally desirable from the monopolist's point of view. Therefore, regulation still may be required if consumers want a particular zero-profit price scheme invoked.

Finally, consider the weak natural monopoly without entry barriers. Again, refer to Figure 2.4, where the cost function is subadditive at $q^w$, but average cost is increasing. Regulation is needed to ensure the welfare-maximizing price, $p(q^w)$, but not because the monopolist wishes to charge a higher price (as when there were barriers to entry). Rather, a monopoly price invites entry. In fact, a price of $p(q'')$ invites entry as well, because there are positive profits given by the shaded area. Moreover, there is no single price that will thwart all entry, because with ultrafree entry the entrant can always undercut the incumbent's price, take away part of the market, and still enjoy positive profit. For instance, suppose the incumbent's price equaled average cost, and output was $q^a$. An entrant could charge slightly less, sell slightly less (by serving only part of the market), and earn positive profit.

The regulator is now forced into a very different role: protecting the monopolist from entrants. In other words, if the welfare-maximizing output lies between $q_0$ and $q^a$, the regulator must construct a barrier to entry by awarding the incumbent the exclusive right (or franchise) to operate in the market. Without such a mutually beneficial "contract" there might be no incumbent because that firm's managers would recognize that losses would arise under entry.

One form that a regulatory barrier to entry might take would be a requirement that an entrant meet the entire quantity demanded at a price below the incumbent's price. If the incumbent produces where price equals average cost, and the entrant has neither better technology nor access to lower input prices, this policy will bar the entrant from the market. The entrant cannot undercut the incumbent's price, serve the entire market, and make nonnegative profit.

A caveat regarding the policy for weak natural monopolies and Figure 2.4 requires mentioning. Protection from entry is proper when the firm is a weak natural monopoly, and for a firm to be a weak natural monopoly, its cost function must be subadditive over the relevant output range. But what is the relevant output range? After all, output will depend on the price structure. Using simple per-unit prices in Figure 2.4, the firm is clearly a natural monopoly for demand $p(q)$, because $C(q)$ is subadditive over every possible output – even the output associated with a price equal to zero. Consequently, the firm must be a natural monopoly over the relevant output range however this range is defined. Alternatively, suppose demand is given by $\hat{p}(q)$, which intersects the average-cost curve at point $h$ and intersects $2C(q/2)/q$ at quantity $2q_0$, where $2C(q/2)/q$ achieves a minimum. The relationship between demand $p(q)$ and average cost at point $a$ and the relationship between demand $\hat{p}(q)$ and average cost at point $h$ are similar. Both demands intersect a rising average-cost curve where the cost function is subadditive. However, there is an important distinction. For demand $p(q)$, the market is a weak natural monopoly, but for demand $\hat{p}(q)$, the market is a natural duopoly.[6] In the latter case, the relevant output range extends beyond $q_s$, and the natural monopoly definition is not satisfied. The point is that the definition is not independent of the demand side of the market, because the latter is needed to establish the relevant range of output. Accordingly, regulatory policies must account for both cost and demand. In Section 4.4 we shall return to this point in a game-theoretic framework.

Table 2.1 summarizes the appropriate regulatory policies. They allow society to increase allocative efficiency via price regulation and entry limitations. Note that we equate a strong (weak) natural monopoly with marginal-cost pricing causing negative (nonnegative) profit, which is consistent with equating a strong natural monopoly with condition (2.1) and a weak natural monopoly with condition (2.2) and not condition (2.1). We shall use these definitions throughout this book. For a U-shaped average-cost curve, the strong natural monopoly means that average cost is falling, and the weak natural monopoly means that average cost is at its minimum point or rising over the relevant range of output. If price is equal to marginal cost at this minimum point, profit will be zero; otherwise, marginal-cost pricing means positive profit for the weak natural monopoly. If profit is zero for the weak case and there are no barriers to entry, so that we are in

---

6 Baumol, Panzar, and Willig (1983, Chapter 5) examine the cost-minimizing number of firms in an industry.

Table 2.1. *Appropriate regulatory policies*

| Monopoly type | Barriers to entry | No barriers to entry |
|---|---|---|
| Strong natural monopoly (MC pricing creates a deficit) | Enforce $p = $ MC, and subsidize firm or Deviate from MC pricing to eliminate deficit | Enforce $p = $ MC, and subsidize firm or Do not regulate, letting threat of entry force break-even prices |
| Weak natural monopoly (MC pricing allows nonnegative profits) | Enforce $p = $ MC, and address possible "problem" of excess profit | Enforce $p = $ MC, prevent further entry into the market, and address possible "problem" of excess profit |

the lower right corner in Table 2.1, then there will be no need to prevent entry. No firm will have an incentive to enter. However, for the multiproduct firm, U-shaped average-cost curves lose their meaning, and the regulator's role becomes more complex regarding entry. Thus, Table 2.1 applies only to the single-output firm. A similar table for the multiproduct firm will be introduced in Chapter 7.

## 2.3 Natural monopoly in the multiproduct firm

The importance of the new definition of a natural monopoly (subadditivity) becomes more evident when we consider the multiproduct firm. Concepts such as decreasing average cost and economies of scale must be redefined in a multiproduct setting. Equating natural monopoly with decreasing average cost is meaningless when the cost function involves more than one product. Moreover, if economic analysis is to be at all useful, then the multiproduct setting must be addressed. There probably are few, if any, firms in the economy that manufacture only a single product. However, only recently has an extensive literature appeared on the properties and problems of multiproduct natural monopolies. This section introduces a few of the more important properties and illustrates their application. For more detail, see Baumol (1977) and Baumol, Panzar, and Willig (1982).

*Definitions*

Let $q^i = (q^i_1, \ldots, q^i_n)$ be the *i*th vector of *m* output vectors $i = 1, \ldots, m$, where each vector contains one or more of *n* different outputs. We can now generalize the definition of natural monopoly, condition (2.2), to the multiproduct firm. A necessary and sufficient condition for natural monopoly is that the cost function exhibit *strict and global subadditivity* of costs, or

$$C(q^1 + \ldots + q^m) < C(q^1) + \ldots + C(q^m) \qquad (2.8)$$

for any *m* output vectors. If (2.8) is satisfied, then the least expensive method of producing $(q^1_1, \ldots, q^1_n) + \ldots + (q^m_1, \ldots, q^m_n)$ is with a single firm. Note that (2.2) with strict inequality is a special case of (2.8) for $n = 1$.

The multiproduct counterpart to economies of scale for the single-product firm is defined as follows. Consider an input–output vector $(x_1, \ldots, x_r, q_1, \ldots, q_n)$, where $x_k$ is input *k*, $k = 1, \ldots, r$, and scalars $w > 1$ and $\delta > 0$. *Strict economies of scale* exist if $(wx_1, \ldots, wx_r, v_1q_1, \ldots, v_nq_n)$ is a feasible input–output vector, where all $v_i \geq w + \delta$. Thus, an expansion of all inputs by *w* implies a greater expansion of all outputs. Whether or not the firm will ever carry out a proportionate input expansion will depend on the production function and demand conditions.

In the definition of subadditivity given by (2.8), if each vector is associated with only one positive output, and no two vectors have the same positive output in common, then (2.8) will define *economies of scope* [i.e., for any two vectors in (2.8), we have for the dot product $q^i \cdot q^j = 0$, $i \neq j$]. Economies of scope constitute a restricted form of subadditivity, and it captures the essence of multiproduct versus single-product production. It contrasts the cost of producing outputs $q_1, \ldots, q_n$, all in a single firm, with the total cost of producing each output $q_i$, $i = 1, \ldots, n$, in separate

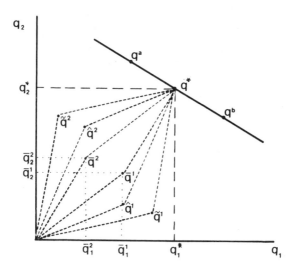

Figure 2.5. Economies of scope, subadditivity, and transray convexity.

firms, each specializing in the production of one product. Many utilities provide examples of the potential for economies of scope. Both long-distance and local telephone services involve the use of joing inputs – receivers and the lines connecting homes to the switched network. Day and night electricity services can be viewed as separate products with strong cost complementarities. Similarly, the provision of natural gas to more than one community may allow efficiencies at the transmission stage.

Figure 2.5 illustrates the distinction between subadditivity and economies of scope in the two-product case. For the cost function to be strictly subadditive at output vector $q^*$, the sum of the costs of separately producing any two output vectors that when added together yield $q^*$ must be greater than the cost of producing $q^*$ in a single firm. The figure illustrates four sets of output vectors that sum to $q^*$: (1) $\bar{q}^1 + \bar{q}^2 = q^*$; (2) $\hat{q}^1 + \hat{q}^2 = q^*$; (3) $\tilde{q}^1 + \tilde{q}^2 = q^*$; (4) $q_1^* + q_2^* = q^*$. For the first set, strict subadditivity at $q^*$ requires the cost of $C(q^*)$ to be less than the cost of $C(\bar{q}^1)$ plus

$C(\overline{q}^2)$. Or the cost of one firm producing $q^* = (q_1^*, q_2^*)$ must be less than the sum of costs of one firm producing $\overline{q}^1 = (\overline{q}_1^1, \overline{q}_2^1)$ and another firm producing $\overline{q}^2 = (\overline{q}_1^2, \overline{q}_2^2)$. Strict subadditivity implies that the same must be true for the other three sets pictured, and also for the infinite other possible vectors with nonnegative outputs that sum to $q^*$. Alternatively, the condition of economies of scope requires that the preceding requirement hold only for set (4); that is, $C(q^*) < C(q_1^*) + C(q_2^*)$. Thus, subadditivity is a more stringent condition than economies of scope.

In the multiproduct firm, we cannot define decreasing average cost in the usual manner because there is no single unambiguously acceptable measure of aggregate output to divide into total cost. However, we can consider proportionate changes in output along a ray from the origin in output space and then observe the shape of the cost function as we move along the ray. The counterpart to decreasing average cost in the single-product firm is for the multiproduct firm to have ray average costs declining. *Declining ray average cost* is expressed as

$$C(vq_1, \ldots, vq_n)/v < C(wq_1, \ldots, wq_n)/w$$

for $v > w$, where $v$ and $w$ are measures of the scale of output along a ray through output vector $q = (q_1, \ldots, q_n)$. A related concept is *ray concavity*, which exists if the marginal costs of output bundles are decreasing along the ray.

Because the firm is not always going to expand or contract output along rays, we need to know something about the behavior of the cost function between rays. For instance, we learn about complementaries in production by moving across rays. A useful concept that looks across rays is transray convexity. Roughly, if a cost function is transray-convex, then it is cheaper to produce outputs in combination rather than separately. In geometric terms, take a cross section of the total cost function through point $q^*$ in Figure 2.5. Costs are lower toward the interior of the cross section than they are toward the edges. The definition is as follows. A cost function is *transray-convex* through $q^* = (q_1^*, \ldots, q_n^*)$ if there exists any set of positive constants $w_1, \ldots,$

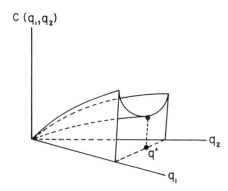

Figure 2.6. Economies to joint production.

$w_n$ such that for every two output vectors $q^a = (q^a_1, \ldots, q^a_n)$, $q^b = (q^b_1, \ldots, q^b_n)$ lying in the same hyperplane $\Sigma^n_{i=1} w_i q_i = w$ through $q^*$,[7] we have

$$C(q^*) = C(kq^a + (1 - k)q^b) \leq kC(q^a) + (1 - k)C(q^b)$$

for any $k$, $0 < k < 1$.

Referring again to Figure 2.5, a hyperplane is shown as the negatively sloped line through $q^*$, and $q^a$ and $q^b$ are two points along this line. They do not have to straddle point $q^*$. Transray convexity requires that a linear combination of the costs of producing $q^a$ and $q^b$ in separate firms be no less than the cost of producing the same linear combination of $q^a$ and $q^b$ in a single firm. Or, on the cost surface, a straight line connecting point $C(q^a)$ with point $C(q^b)$ must not lie below the cost surface anywhere between these points. (See Figure 2.6, where this condition is satisfied for $q^*$.) Note that these conditions need to be satisfied for only *one* negatively sloped line (hyperplane) through $q^*$, even though there is an infinite number of such lines. Also, a function that is trans-

---

7  That is, for

$$\sum^n_{i=1} w_i q^a_i = \sum^n_{i=1} w_i q^b_i = \sum^n_{i=1} w_i q^*_i$$

ray-convex at one point need not be transray-convex at other points.

According to Spence (1983), transray convexity requires that the "cost of producing a weighted average of a pair of output bundles $q^a$ and $q^b$ is not greater than the weighted average of the costs of producing each of them in isolation. That is to say, complementarities in production outweigh scale effects" (p. 985). Spence suggests that this condition is very strong by providing an example of a concave cost function that exhibits strong economies of scope induced by scale economies, but it is weakly transray-convex along one hyperplane and not transray-convex along any other hyperplane. Thus, economies of scope and ray concavity alone are not enough to provide cost advantages for multiproduct production. Transray convexity is an important addition to the conceptual framework because it facilitates rigorous examination of complementarities in production. We now turn to more specific relationships between these concepts to make this clear.

### Relationships for multiproduct cost functions

Here we present just four of the relationships developed by Baumol (1977). First, *declining ray average cost is not necessary for strict subadditivity.* This point is reminiscent of the single-product case, in which decreasing average cost was not necessary for subadditivity. Figure 2.1 applies here as well.

Second, *strict concavity of a cost function is not sufficient to guarantee subadditivity.* In the single-product case, strict concavity would be sufficient, because it would imply decreasing marginal cost. That it does not hold in the multiproduct case can be seen from Figure 2.7. In this two-output situation the cost function is strictly concave, but along any hyperplane between the output axes, cost is greater than on either axis. This general shape does not favor joint production.

Third, *scale economies are neither necessary nor sufficient for subadditivity.* This is another example of a proposition that changes when going from single to multiple products. Scale econ-

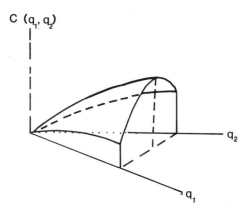

Figure 2.7. Diseconomies to joint production.

omies would imply decreasing average cost in the single-product case; therefore, they would be sufficient but not necessary for subadditivity. For the multiproduct case, consider a production function of one input, $L$, that gives rise to the relationship

$$q_1^{1/2} + q_1^{1/4}q_2^{1/4} + q_2^{1/2} = L$$

This function exhibits scale economies. For instance, a doubling of input $L$ leads to a fourfold increase in both outputs. Now, if $L$ is purchased at a fixed price of 1 then the cost function is

$$C(q_1, q_2) = q_1^{1/2} + q_1^{1/4}q_2^{1/4} + q_2^{1/2}$$

which is not subadditive. This result can be seen by trying $q_1^* = q_2^* = 1$. Here we have $C(q_1^*, 0) = 1$, $C(0, q_2^*) = 1$, and $C(q_1^*, q_2^*) = 3$. Production is less expensive in two separate firms.[8]

---

8 An example of a cost function that has economies of scope and that is derived from a technology exhibiting economies of scale is
$$C(q_1, q_2) = q_1^{1/4} + q_2^{1/4} - (q_1 \cdot q_2)^{1/4}$$
for all outputs. On the other hand, the cost function
$$C(q_1, q_2) = 1 + (q_1 + q_2)^2$$
exhibits economies of scale if and only if $q_1 + q_2 < 1$, and it exhibits economies of scope and is subadditive if and only if $q_1q_2 < \frac{1}{2}$ (Sharkey, 1982b, p. 7).

Fourth, *if a cost function exhibits strictly declining ray average costs and transray convexity along any one hyperplane* $\Sigma_{i=1}^{n} w_i q_i$ = *w, where* $w_i > 0$ *for i* = *1, . . . , n through an output vector q, then the cost function is subadditive for output q.* (See Baumol, 1977, for a proof.) These are not the only sufficient conditions that have been developed, and other weaker conditions may yet be forthcoming. To appreciate these conditions, consider Figures 2.6 and 2.7. In the latter, ray average costs are declining, but transray convexity does not hold. In Figure 2.6, both conditions hold, and the advantages of producing both outputs in a single firm are clear. Figure 2.6 also illustrates economies of scope that follow from subadditivity.

The physical and market conditions that give rise to the desirability of a single supplier are many and varied, and numerous authors have contributed thoughts on the subject (see Gold, 1981, for a survey of scale economies). Sharkey (1982b) dichotomizes the conditions into those that refer to the technical aspects of production processes and those that refer to the advantages of intrafirm transactions over interfirm or market transactions. Considering the technical aspects, the fourth relationship cited earlier indicates that declining ray average costs and transray convexity imply subadditivity. What technical aspects of production might support these properties? The answer is not clearcut. Although some aspects might contribute both technical and transactions savings, a few of the more obvious aspects are worth mentioning.

A declining ray average cost says that the average cost of producing a fixed proportion of outputs falls as the outputs increase. Specialization of inputs may contribute to this property. For example, as the scale of outputs grows, workers can become more specialized and production more efficient. Also, as output grows, the ratio of needed inventory to sales decreases, because the firm can more reliably predict fluctuations in sales. With relatively smaller inventories, unit costs will decrease. Another aspect involves indivisibilities in inputs. Suppose the available electricity-generating units on the market are optimally designed to supply either 1 or 100 consumers. If a firm wants to supply 75 consumers, it purchases the generator designed for 100 consumers and gets excess capacity of 25. If the firm wants to supply 175 consumers, it purchases two generators and still has excess capacity of 25. But the excess capacity is now spread over greater output levels, and unit costs are less than with the smaller output for 75 consumers.

Transray convexity reflects the gains to combining different outputs (products) into a single firm. Here, we would expect that two (or more) outputs could share an accounting, marketing, or other administrative department and incur less cost than if each output utilized a separate department. Or there may be some externality that becomes internalized when two (or more) outputs are brought into the same production process. Producing beef and cowhide is one classic example of shared inputs, and daytime and nighttime uses of electricity provide another example.

Other conditions that give rise to subadditivity have to do with firms being more efficient than the marketplace for conducting certain transactions. This concept dates back to Coase (1937), who argued that firms exist to carry out functions that markets cannot carry out as efficiently. More recently, Williamson (1975) has been one of the leading analysts of the internal organization of firms, and his work is important for appreciating why large and/or multiproduct firms may enjoy advantages over small and/or single-product firms. He also points out that there are limits to increasing firm size that have to do with managerial ability to comprehend complex organizations. Sharkey provides more detail on these conditions of firm organization that support subadditivity, and we shall allude to some of them again in Chapter 8, where we discuss the reasons that regulation occurs.

After developing necessary and sufficient conditions for subadditivity, we would like to test those conditions using data from real firms. Testing for subadditivity is complicated by the fact that this concept is global in nature. For estimation of the cost surface, the econometrician requires data on all levels of output up to the output actually produced. Yet the firm may never have produced at lower levels, or if it did, the plant may not have been optimally designed for those levels. Also useful is information on the cost of producing each output alone rather than in a multi-product firm. If there are no single-product firms, the question is moot.

Evans and Heckman (1984) developed a method of testing for subadditivity, and they applied it to the Bell System for the years 1958–77. They tested for subadditivity locally, so that if it was rejected, then global subadditivity was rejected. Of course, accepting local subadditivity does not imply global subadditivity. On the basis of their findings they rejected local and global subadditivity for the Bell System. For the case of electricity, gas, and combination gas-electricity companies, Mayo (1984) reported diseconomies of scale at large output rates, as well as diseconomies of scope. Chappell and Wilder (1986) reestimated the model, excluding utilities with nuclear facilities, and found economies of scale and scope. Other empirical studies have also begun to address these issues.[9]

### The role of demand conditions

So far, we have equated cost subadditivity with natural monopoly. Product quality has been held constant in our analysis, and we shall continue to do so throughout most of the book (except in Chapters 6 and 12). A new literature has begun to emphasize consumer preferences and the quality of outputs as determinants of a single supplier in an industry. Shaked and Sutton (1982), Sutton (1986), and Gabszewicz and associates (1986) have examined how the nature of demand and the income distribution, in conjunction with the cost of quality improvements,

---

9 Other empirical studies have included railroads (Brown, Caves, and Christensen, 1979; Hasenkamp, 1976b), journals (Baumol and Braunstein, 1977), and electric power (Hayashi, Sevier, and Trapani, 1985; Karlson, 1986; Primeaux and Nelson, 1980).

leads to single-supplier outcomes. Waterson summarizes this line of analysis as follows:

> The traditional theory of natural monopoly implies that particular industries are concentrated, others not, because in some cases fixed costs are high relative to the size of the market. Shaked and Sutton's insight is that in some cases, fixed costs are high because the market is large. This can be seen as a "demand pull" view of technical change: the size of the potential market is what calls forth product improvements.
> (Waterson, 1987, p. 78)

The basic reason the market becomes highly concentrated "is that customers who differ in the horizontal characteristics they prefer may all be captured by one product through significantly large improvements in the vertical quality component" (Waterson, 1987, p. 77). If expenditures on fixed costs lead to quality improvements, and variable costs are relatively unaffected, production will tend to be concentrated in only a few firms, and perhaps monopoly may emerge. From this perspective, quality improvements and demand expansion can lead to reductions in the prices of high-quality products; this process ultimately results in the exit of low-quality producers from the market, leaving consumers with only a single source of supply.

### 2.4. Regulation for the multiproduct firm

In Section 2.2 we discussed the conditions under which regulation is justified and the forms that regulation should take for a single-product natural monopoly. For a multiproduct natural monopoly, the results are similar. With entry barriers, marginal-cost pricing for all outputs is still necessary for economic efficiency, but the profit-maximizing monopolist seeks to equate marginal revenue and marginal cost in each output market. If ray average costs are strictly decreasing, marginal-cost pricing will lead to deficits, and the regulator must either subsidize the firm or deviate in some fashion from uniform marginal-cost prices.

However, if ray average costs are not strictly decreasing, marginal-cost pricing may provide adequate revenues for the firm to be solvent.

Barring entry barriers, if ray average costs are decreasing, the regulator can choose to enforce marginal-cost pricing and subsidize the firm, in which case there will be no incentive for entry unless subsidies are available to all. Or the firm may be allowed to operate free of regulation, in which case the threat of entry will force prices to a level at which the firm will just break even. Finally, if ray average costs are not strictly decreasing, the regulator may be required to protect the monopoly from attack, because marginal-cost pricing can lead to positive profits and the threat of entry.

Interesting complications arise in the multiproduct setting. For example, if prices must deviate from marginal cost to eliminate a deficit, which prices should change, and by how much? What are the redistribution impacts across consumers associated with alternative price structures? Will entry occur across all product lines or just a few? Is partial entry along one or more product lines desirable? Does there exist a set of prices that will deter entry and eliminate any deficits? In recent years, these complications and related problems have been at the forefront of regulatory policy-making in the communications and transportation industries. We provide a more detailed summary of regulatory policies for multiproduct natural monopolies in Chapter 7, where we present a table similar to Table 2.1.

### 2.5. Marginal-cost pricing with subsidies

As noted earlier, when marginal-cost pricing creates a deficit, one regulatory option is to maintain these prices and subsidize the firm to cover the deficit. Early support for this method dates back to Dupuit (1844), a French engineer. He argued, based on consumer surplus, that society's welfare might be better served in some industries if a price-discriminating monopolist were allowed to supplant competition. Almost 100 years later,

Harold Hotelling (1938) modernized the analytical techniques and argued that in decreasing-cost industries, prices should be set equal to marginal cost. The argument for marginal-cost pricing very quickly crosses over into the public-finance literature, and it was in that context that Hotelling presented his case. Marginal-cost pricing can be likened to a tax system in which there are no excise taxes, and deficits that arise are covered by subsidies derived from lump-sum taxes. The alternative is to raise money to cover deficits by levying excise taxes (which amount to deviations from marginal-cost prices).

Hotelling's principal result was the following: If a consumer must pay a particular amount of taxes to the government, her utility will be greater if the levy is made in a lump sum rather than via a system of excise taxes. Or, if a consumer must pay the government $x$ dollars in tax, she is better off if the government collects the $x$ dollars in a lump sum. Then she can arrange her purchases using her remaining budget, rather than having the government arrange her purchases for her by levying differential excise taxes on the commodities she purchases.

Hotelling goes on to discuss candidates for the lump-sum taxes. A tax on land is suggested, provided that the supply of land is perfectly inelastic so that the tax cannot be shifted. He also suggests income and inheritance taxes. Hotelling observes that changing to a marginal-cost pricing system could make everyone better off, thereby making it a Pareto improvement; then he admits that this would require a system of compensation from winners to losers. Because compensation is not realistic, he states that the wealthy would likely lose from the change.

One classic implication of this reasoning concerns toll-free bridges, provided there is no congestion. Although the distribution of wealth will be affected if there are no tolls, total wealth will be maximized. Similar reasoning suggests that more projects like the Tennessee Valley Authority should be undertaken, the outputs being priced at marginal cost, with the lump-sum taxes coming from Tennessee. Other regions could be taxed to the extent that the benefits were not confined to Tennessee, and other projects around the country could balance out any redistributions.[10]

Hotelling's paper led to a spirited debate that came to be known as the marginal-cost controversy, as summarized by Ruggles (1949). A number of objections to Hotelling's thesis appeared. Frisch (1939) pointed out that whereas Hotelling's exercise had been carried out using the Pareto criterion, the fact that some would be made worse off obviously violated the criterion.[11] Some economists might argue in the Hicks and Kaldor tradition that if welfare were to increase with compensation being paid, then it would increase even without compensation. But as Samuelson (1947) pointed out, the compensation must be paid in order to avoid interpersonal comparisons of utility. We can say that if the change is made and compensation paid, there is an increase in welfare, but we cannot say that making the change without compensation is better than not making the change at all.

Other approaches and problems were also discussed. Lewis (1941) and Clemens (1950) advocated price discrimination as an alternative to marginal-cost pricing. For example, a perfectly discriminating monopolist is compatible with Pareto optimality. Meade (1944) pointed out another important flaw in Hotelling's discussion. Because they could distort the work–leisure trade-off, income taxes, which would be needed as a main source of deficit-covering revenues, would not be neutral like lump-sum taxes. Then Wilson (1945) argued that unless the cost of an investment is covered through prices (such as tolls on a bridge), we cannot

---

10 Note that the total benefits from the Tennessee Valley Authority would need to be greater than the total costs if the package of projects were to be justified.
11 Frisch (1939) also argued that prices need be only proportional to marginal cost. However, Samuelson (1947) later indicated that that was incorrect: If final prices are proportional to marginal costs, and payments to factors of production are equal to their marginal costs, distortions will occur. But if factor prices are also in proportion, then nothing has been accomplished. If prices and incomes are doubled, real resource allocation is unaffected.

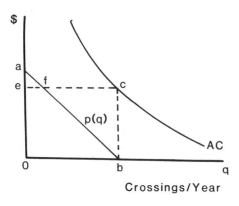

Figure 2.8. The bridge example.

be certain that the initial investment in the bridge is worthwhile. Figure 2.8 depicts this situation: The total benefit when price equals zero marginal cost is area *a0b*, but the total cost is area *ecb*0 > *a0b*. The investment in the bridge does not yield enough benefits to make the project cost-effective. A greater demand or lower average costs would be needed to change the result.

Coase (1946) emphasized equity, noting that unless those who use a good cover its cost, there will be a redistribution in favor of the consumers of products produced by decreasing-cost industries. He advocated price discrimination as a remedy for this problem. For example, a perfectly discriminating monopolist would make the socially efficient decision and *not* build the bridge, given the conditions depicted in Figure 2.8. Furthermore, Coase noted that bureaucracies have little incentive to halt production if subsidies are available. Also, distortions will result unless factors of production have the same price to consumers in all uses. In other words, the steel used to construct a bridge should be as costly to demanders as is the steel used to build a car.[12]

---

12 For subsequent treatments of the practicality of marginal-cost pricing, see Vickrey (1948) and Turvey (1969).

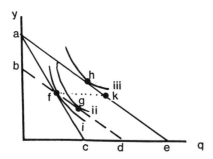

Figure 2.9. Price increase versus lump-sum tax.

Following Hotelling, some authors illustrated the principal result using diagrams. Stigler (1946) and Boulding (1948) used diagrams similar to that in Figure 2.9. Suppose that *q* is the good produced by a decreasing-cost industry, and *y* is a composite good. Figure 2.9 depicts a consumer's indifference mapping over quantities of the two goods. The consumer's starting point is *h*, where indifference curve *iii* is tangent to budget line *ae*. Now suppose the government wishes to tax this consumer, in terms of real resources, by an amount equal to distance *de*. Using a lump-sum tax, the budget line shifts to *bd*, and point *g* represents the new utility-maximizing bundle of goods. Next, instead of using a lump-sum tax, the government levies an excise tax on *q* only. Price (including the tax) is above marginal cost, with the tax designed to again take in an amount of revenue equal to *de*. The new budget line pivots to *ac*, and the consumer gives up in taxes an amount equal to *fk* (= *de*). Given a strictly quasi-concave utility function with indifference curves strictly convex to the origin, the new utility-maximizing point, *f*, must lie on a lower indifference curve than point *g*. Thus, the lump-sum tax is a preferred instrument for covering the deficit.

The problem with the preceding analysis (and with Hotelling's analysis as well) is its partial-equilibrium setting, valid only for an isolated consumer. What happens to the excise or lump-sum taxes collected by the government? A correct diagrammatic pre-

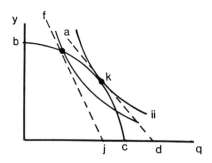

Figure 2.10. Pricing above MC in the *q* industry.

sentation can be found in Rolph and Break (1949) or M. Friedman (1952). In Figure 2.10, curve *bc* is the production possibility frontier showing the goods available to an economy of identical consumers *after* a lump-sum tax has been imposed. Thus, *bc* represents what is available for private consumption after the government has taken its due and covered the deficit. Point *k* is a welfare maximum, where the marginal rate of substitution for consumers is equal to the marginal rate of product transformation for producers, both given by the slope of the price line *ad*. Now introduce an excise tax on *q* (raising the price of *q*) that takes in the same revenue as did the lump-sum tax, so that the production possibility frontier is the same curve, *bc*. The new equilibrium must again fall on *bc*, but the consumers face a ratio of prices given by the slope of price line *fj*. The excise tax is a wedge between marginal cost and price. Thus, a necessary condition for Pareto optimality is not met: The marginal rate of substitution does not equal the marginal rate of product transformation.

The foregoing argument requires that we start from a position of maximum welfare at point *k*, which in turn requires a true lump-sum tax. If we had started at a different point, the excise-tax method could actually lead to a welfare improvement. Silberberg (1978) developed these themes further. He pointed out that Hotelling's original paper was really an exercise in revealed preference: Nowhere in Hotelling's proof is it required that prices be equal to marginal cost. However, as we shall see, a major contribution of Hotelling's work is that it leads to the general area of second best (maximization subject to regulatory or other constraints), which is addressed in the next chapter.

Marginal-cost pricing with subsidies has not been widely applied in the United States, although it has been used extensively in other countries in which many public utility industries are nationalized. For the most part, the United States has followed a policy of private ownership of public utilities, with accompanying regulation. Therefore, in the remainder of Part I, we shall assume that marginal-cost pricing with subsidies is not an option available to the regulator. However, we will return to subsidies in Chapter 12, when we examine new incentive schemes appearing in the regulatory literature that use this approach.

## 2.6. Summary

The new definition of natural monopoly is equivalent to subadditivity of the cost function over the relevant range of output. Natural monopolies can be divided into two types: (1) strong natural monopolies wherein marginal-cost pricing creates deficits and (2) weak natural monopolies wherein marginal-cost pricing does not create deficits. In the single-product firm with a U-shaped average-cost function, a strong natural monopoly exhibits decreasing average cost (which implies strict subadditivity), and a weak natural monopoly exhibits nondecreasing average cost over the output levels where the cost function is still subadditive. Regulation is required for a strong natural monopoly when entry into its market is not feasible, and regulation is required for a weak natural monopoly when entry is feasible. In either case, regulation should be adopted only when the misallocation under nonintervention exceeds the costs of regulation.

The definition of subadditivity also applies to a multiproduct firm. This chapter introduces a number of definitions needed to analyze cost conditions in a multiproduct framework. For example, none of the following is sufficient for subadditivity: declining ray average cost; strict concavity of the cost function; scale economies. However, transray convexity and declining ray average cost together are sufficient for subadditivity. Savings from multiproduct organization can arise from reduced transactions costs or technical features of the production function, including the use of shared inputs or the internalization of an externality. As in the single-product case, marginal-cost pricing again leads to nonnegative (negative) profits for weak (strong) natural monopolies.

The last part of this chapter surveys the debate regarding marginal-cost pricing with subsidies. Such pricing will not be considered further in Part I, because generally it is not available as a regulatory instrument in the United States. Interestingly, we shall revisit the use of subsidies in Chapter 12, because they have resurfaced in recent literature on innovative regulatory incentive schemes. Thus, the debate of the 1930s and 1940s is very relevant to the analyses of the 1980s. Finally, Table 2.1 provides general guidelines regarding entry and price regulation as developed in this chapter. But more specific guidelines are needed to implement regulatory policies. In Chapters 3–6 we develop specific guidelines for optimum price structures, and in Chapter 7 we address entry guidelines.

# 3

## Efficient pricing using linear prices

The marginal-cost pricing rule implies that an allocative inefficiency arises when there is a deviation between the value consumers place on an additional unit of the product and the opportunity cost of producing that additional unit. Constraints on the
price structure of a firm can lead to allocative inefficiencies, as
some consumers face a price that is unequal to marginal cost. The
question then arises how regulators can minimize the misallocations associated with (self-imposed) pricing constraints, particularly because underconsumption and overconsumption both
involve deadweight losses. The design of prices for a multiproduct firm involves balancing the marginal welfare losses across
product markets as prices deviate from marginal costs.

The assumption throughout this chapter is that the firm being
studied is a natural monopoly; therefore, from an efficiency viewpoint, cost minimization requires that it be the only firm in the
market or markets it serves. We also assume that the firm is a
strong natural monopoly, so that marginal-cost pricing of all outputs will create a deficit, and enforcing marginal-cost pricing with
subsidies is not an option. Finally, we assume that there are barriers to entry. We know from Chapter 2 that regulation is justified
in this instance. In this chapter, regulation takes the form of maximizing social welfare subject to a break-even constraint with a
linear price system, that is, a system in which a constant price per

unit is charged in each market, although the prices can vary across markets.

The situation described is essentially the problem of *second-best pricing.* First-best prices (or marginal-cost prices) are non-viable because they do not satisfy certain constraints imposed on the system (the budget constraints that require firms to break even). Therefore, the welfare-maximizing regulator must find an optimum set of prices subject to these constraints. Of course, such prices will necessarily represent departures from marginal-cost prices.

A rich literature has developed on this topic, particularly in the fields of public finance and natural monopoly economics. Baumol and Bradford (1970) provide a brief history and an exposition of the major points in this area. They refer to a number of authors in the 1870s who advocated that the public interest would be best served with public utility prices that would vary indirectly with demand elasticities. The first mathematical treatment was developed by Ramsey (1927), who used a consumer-surplus analysis in a seminal paper on taxation. Hence, second-best prices often are referred to as *Ramsey prices,* and we shall follow that practice here. We discussed Hotelling's (1938) subsequent contribution at length in Chapter 2. In 1951, the French economist Boiteux resolved the basic problem without the use of consumer surplus. He followed that contribution in 1956 with an economy-wide model in which all consumers are maximizing their utilities and all firms in the competitive sector are maximizing their profits. Then, using a Pareto criterion, he solved for a set of prices in the noncompetitive sector that resolves the deficit problems. More recently, Rees (1968) also addressed this natural monopoly, second-best problem in a general-equilibrium framework.

In Section 3.1 we derive the simplest version of Ramsey prices by assuming that there is only one strong natural monopolist, who faces no competition and whose product demands are independent of one another. In the next two sections, we complicate the regulator's problem of deriving Ramsey prices by adding competition and interdependent demands. Section 3.4 covers the interesting case in which there are competing natural monopolies. After deriving Ramsey prices for a variety of situations, we consider some of the practical problems involved with their implementation in Section 3.5. Finally, we analyze the fully distributed cost pricing method often employed by regulators in Section 3.6 in order to compare the results to Ramsey prices. Section 3.7 provides a summary.

### 3.1. Ramsey prices

The intuition behind Ramsey prices is straightforward. Assume that achieving maximum welfare is impossible because marginal-cost pricing results in an unacceptable level of profit (usually negative profit). The firm must adopt prices that deviate from marginal costs in order to reach the target profit level. But how should the deviations be determined? If the problem is negative profit with marginal-cost prices, then prices should be raised above marginal costs for all outputs until the target profit is reached. Prices are not necessarily raised equally, however, They are raised in inverse proportion to the absolute value of the demand elasticities in each market. This minimizes the welfare losses associated with higher prices.

The most simple form of Ramsey prices can be developed as follows. Consider a multiproduct firm producing outputs $q = (q_1, \ldots, q_n)$, with a cost function given by $C(q)$. Demands for the $n$ goods are represented by the inverse demand functions $p_i(q_i)$, $i = 1, \ldots, n$. Both the cost function and demand functions are assumed to be differentiable. In this formulation, cross-elasticities of demand are zero, but this assumption will be relaxed in Section 3.2. Let consumer surplus in the $i$th market be given by

$$CS_i = \int_0^{q_i} p_i(x_i)\,dx_i - p_i(q_i)q_i \tag{3.1}$$

for $i = 1, \ldots, n$, and profit for the firm is

$$\pi = \sum_{i=1}^n p_i(q_i)q_i - C(q) \tag{3.2}$$

Throughout the remainder of this section, $i$ is taken to run from $1, \ldots, n$, and summations are over all $i$.[1] We know from Section 2.2 that if we maximize a measure of welfare ($W$) that is the sum of all $CS_i$ plus profit,

$$W = \Sigma CS_i + \pi$$

the resulting prices will be equal to marginal costs. Because the firm is a strong natural monopoly, these efficient prices will create a deficit (recall that we are considering policies appropriate for the upper left corner in Table 2.1). To eliminate the deficit, we add the constraint that profit must be equal to $\bar{\pi}$, which is non-negative, but less than the profit obtained by the unregulated monopoly. We shall often set $\bar{\pi} = 0$, which is the result we would observe in a perfectly competitive environment. For a single-product natural monopoly, such a constraint will yield the trivial solution that price is set to average cost.

### Break-even constraint for a single period

The multiproduct (or multimarket) problem is to maximize welfare subject to this break-even constraint. Forming a Lagrangian expression, we have

$$\max_q L = W + \lambda(\pi - \bar{\pi}) \tag{3.3}$$

where $\lambda$ is a Lagrange multiplier. The first-order condition for maximization of $L$ with respect of $q_i$ is obtained by partially differentiating (3.3) to yield

$$\partial L/\partial q_i = p_i(q_i) - MC_i(q) + \lambda[p_i(q_i) + q_i p'_i(q_i) - MC_i(q)] = 0 \tag{3.4}$$

---

1 The same framework applies to a single-product firm serving $n$ separable submarkets; so $q = q_1 + q_2 + \cdots + q_n$. In this case, marginal cost is the same for each submarket. However, prices varying across submarkets constitute discriminatory pricing, which usually is illegal. Moreover, the firm could carry out this type of pricing only if it could identify the submarkets, each of which may consist of one or more consumers, and if the good could not be resold easily. We discuss price discrimination again in Chapter 4.

where primes denote derivatives, and $MC_i(q) \equiv \partial C(q)/\partial q_i$, the marginal cost of $q_i$. The Lagrange multiplier has a clear interpretation in this problem. Let profit be constrained to $\pi = \bar{\pi} = 0$, then, using the envelope theorem, we have $\partial L/\partial \bar{\pi} = \partial W/\partial \bar{\pi} = -\lambda$; or, roughly speaking, if the firm's profit is decreased by one dollar, which will mean a one-dollar deficit, then welfare will increase by $\lambda$ dollars. (Note that $\lambda$ is positive.) Rearranging (3.4) to obtain

$$[p_i(q_i) - MC_i(q)][1 + \lambda] = -q_i p_i'(q_i)\lambda \tag{3.5}$$

and then dividing both sides by $p_i(q_i)$ and $[1 + \lambda]$ yields

$$\frac{p_i(q_i) - MC_i(q)}{p_i(q_i)} = \frac{-\lambda}{1 + \lambda} \frac{1}{e_i} \tag{3.6}$$

where $e_i = p_i(q_i)/[q_i p_i'(q_i)] < 0$, the elasticity of demand in market $i$.

The price in (3.6) is called the Ramsey price in market $i$. Because (3.6) is true for all $i$, the formula states that the percentage deviation of price from marginal cost in the $i$th market should be inversely proportional to the absolute value of demand elasticity in the $i$th market. In the unlikely case in which all elasticities of demand are equal at the solution to (3.3), then prices will be proportional to marginal costs. Of course, the value of the marginal cost in (3.6) is not the same as the marginal cost that applies under a first-best pricing policy, because $MC_i(q)$ in (3.6) is evaluated at the vector $q$ that solves (3.3), not at the vector $q$ that would satisfy the unconstrained welfare-maximization problem.

Thus, from (3.6), and for all markets, the percentage deviation of price from marginal cost, times the price elasticity, sometimes called the *Ramsey number,* should be equal to $-\lambda/(1 + \lambda)$. The intuition behind this result is straightforward. If cost and demand parameters yield a $\lambda$ that is very small, the Ramsey number approaches zero, implying that prices will be very close to marginal cost. That is, the deficit under efficient pricing is small: Reducing profit by one dollar and recalculating prices will not increase welfare much in this situation. Alternatively, if the situation is such that $\lambda$ is large (say equal to 10), the Ramsey number is close to 1; such a situation occurs when an unconstrained monopolist barely breaks even. Reducing profit (or increasing the deficit) by one dollar at the solution to (3.3) will increase welfare by approximately 10 dollars. The price–cost deviations are so substantial that large welfare improvements are possible if a subsidy can be transferred to the firm to compensate for negative profit. The zero-profit constraint can be very costly in terms of reduced welfare. These examples illustrate how the profit constraint and Ramsey pricing yield both a *level* and *structure* of prices.

The inverse elasticity pricing rule is evident in (3.6). More inelastic demands mean smaller values of $|e_i|$ and therefore higher percentage price deviations from marginal cost. In elastic markets, the percentage price deviation will be smaller. This point is shown by combining (3.6) for the $i$th and $j$th markets to obtain

$$\frac{[p_i(q_i) - MC_i(q)]/p_i(q_i)}{[p_j(q_j) - MC_j(q)]/p_j(q_j)} = \frac{e_j}{e_i} \tag{3.6a}$$

Given initial Ramsey prices, if $|e_i|$ were to increase, ceteris paribus, $p_i$ and $MC_i$ would have to be brought closer together and/or $p_j$ and $MC_j$ be moved further apart for the Ramsey conditions to hold.

To obtain still further intuition on the sense of the Ramsey prices, we can manipulate (3.5) (by adding $\lambda[p_i + q_i p_i' - MC_i]$ to both sides) for markets $i$ and $j$ to obtain

$$\frac{p_i(q_i) - MC_i(q)}{MC_i(q) - MR_i(q)} = \frac{p_j(q_j) - MC_j(q)}{MC_j(q) - MR_j(q)} \tag{3.7}$$

where $MR_i(q)$ is the marginal revenue in the $i$th market. Suppose we start with prices that yield maximum profit. How should they be lowered to increase consumer surplus and reduce profits to zero? According to (3.7), if we were to increase output by $\Delta q_i$ and $\Delta q_j$ from the profit-maximizing solution, the numerators would be the marginal gain from additional consumption, and the denominators the marginal loss in profit. This marginal-benefit/

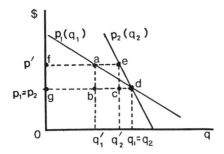

Figure 3.1. Deficit reduction via price increases.

marginal-loss ratio must be equal across markets at the point where profit is down to zero. This relationship implies that the marginal gain to consumers from reducing prices from the profit maximum must be the same across markets per dollar of marginal reduction in profit. Alternatively, starting from a welfare maximum and a deficit, the marginal loss to consumers must be the same across markets per dollar contributed to the budget.

Figure 3.1 provides a rough graphical interpretation of these results for a simple case in which only consumer surplus needs to be considered, because marginal cost, $0g$, is constant. Suppose that two goods, $q_1$ and $q_2$, can both be measured along the horizontal axis, with demand curves plotted as $p_1(q_1)$ and $p_2(q_2)$, respectively. Initially, prices and quantities demanded for both goods are equal at point $d$. If prices must be increased to eliminate a deficit, which market should bear more of the burden in terms of a higher price? If price was raised to $p'$, there would be a deadweight loss of $adb$ in market one and a loss of $ecd$ in market two.[2] The former is larger than the latter, indicating that price should increase more in market two than in market one. Pricing in this way has often been called by public utility practitioners pricing according to "what the traffic can bear" or "value-of-service pricing."

---

2 Note that additional consumer surplus is lost because of the price increase. For example, demanders of $q_2$ also lose *fecg*, but this is only a transfer that is applied to the deficit, thus increasing producer surplus.

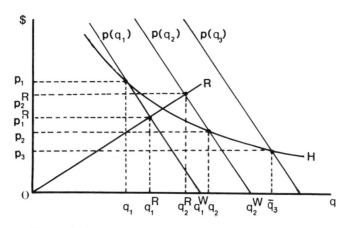

Figure 3.2. Optimal intertemporal pricing for capital recovery.

*Intertemporal Ramsey pricing*

An interesting application of the Ramsey principle arises in the context of pricing in a multiperiod setting. Because physical capital provides services over a period of years, the pattern of covering costs will determine the time pattern of prices. Johnson (1985) presents a simple example, deriving intertemporal Ramsey prices. He assumes that a plant costs $150, has an annual capacity of $\bar{q}_3$, has zero salvage value after three years, and has zero operating costs for the three-year period. Demand is growing, with annual demands for each of the three years shown in Figure 3.2.

The issue is what prices are to be charged in each period so that the discounted sum of consumer surplus will be maximized subject to covering costs and satisfying demands. Assuming zero inflation and interest rates, the revenue collected over the three periods must total $150. If consumers in each period must contribute the same amount, as would be the case if prices reflected straight-line depreciation, the annual revenue will equal $50. The rectangular hyperbola $H$ depicts the combinations of price and output yielding $50; so recovery of capital costs (depreciation) with equal contributions per period uses prices, $p_1$, $p_2$, and $p_3$.

This time pattern of prices is inefficient; it does not maximize discounted consumer surplus. Ramsey pricing will lead to an improved intertemporal allocation of outputs. Given linear parallel demand curves, the price elasticity of $p_1(q_1)$ at $p_1$ is greater than the elasticity of $p_2(q_2)$ at $p_2$. Ramsey pricing will require prices $p_1^R$ and $p_2^R$ for the first two periods (assuming that the final-period price is held at $p_3$). These Ramsey prices can be formed by requiring $e_1 = e_2$, as indicated by (3.6a), because in this particular situation the marginal costs are zero. Because the demand curves are parallel, $e_1 = e_2$ implies $p_1/q_1 = p_2/q_2$; so the Ramsey prices are at the intersections of the demand curves and the ray from the origin, $0R$, with slope $p_1^R/q_1^R = p_2^R/q_2^R$.

Total net consumer surplus is constrained by the predetermined plant capacity, $\bar{q}_3$. To maximize discounted consumer surplus over all periods, we would have allowed an optimum capacity choice given by the intersection of the third price–demand curve and a ray from the origin, where $e_1 = e_2 = e_3$ and the total revenue equals total cost. This socially optimal capacity would have been smaller than $\bar{q}_3$ and would have had lower cost. Furthermore, $p_3$ would have been higher and the other prices lower in our example than when Ramsey pricing is practiced only in two periods. This pattern of rising prices over three periods reduces the amount of unused capacity in the early periods.

The price path described here depends on a number of key assumptions, including indivisibilities in the investment process. Nevertheless, the example illustrates the general applicability of the Ramsey principles to other situations.[3] In Chapter 8 we shall return to actual depreciation policies adopted by regulators and the associated time patterns of cost recovery.

3 Another extension of these principles was proposed by Brock and Dechert (1985) by incorporating dynamic costs into a Ramsey framework. They postulated adjustment costs to adding capacity and set up a dynamic optimization problem in which marginal costs depend on future investment. When investment is expanding, dynamic marginal costs are greater than when investment is contracting. Welfare-maximizing regulators will need to take such factors into account when computing Ramsey numbers for efficient pricing. For a survey of the theory of Ramsey pricing, see Sheshinski (1986).

## 3.2 An application of more complex Ramsey prices

The prices given by (3.6) represent Ramsey prices in their simplest form. They were developed in a partial-equilibrium framework in which only one multiproduct (or multiperiod) firm was considered. There were no competitors in any markets, and all cross-elasticities of demand were zero. We now partially relax these assumptions by examining the following situation involving a multiproduct firm. The firm is still classified as a strong natural monopoly, but it does not enjoy monopoly status in some of its output markets. In particular, some of its outputs are imperfect substitutes or imperfect complements to outputs produced in the private sector. Thus, cross-elasticities of demand are not zero; rather, the market demand for output $i$ depends on the price of good $i$ and on the price of goods other than $i$. These features describe a model developed by Sherman and George (1979) that they apply to the U.S. Postal Service.

### A model with outside goods

Let $q_i^j$ be the amount of the $i$th output consumed by the $j$th individual, $p_i$ be the price for the $i$th output, $y^j$ be the $j$th consumer's income, and $t^j$ be a transfer payment from ($t^j > 0$) or to ($t^j < 0$) the $j$th individual, for $j = 1, \ldots, s$. The transfer payments ensure that everyone will be made better off with the prices determined by the regulatory authorities. Without transfers, a move to the Ramsey prices likely would mean that some consumers would win and some would lose utility relative to the current prices. The transfers allow for compensation to be paid from the winners to the losers so that everyone is made better off. If transfers are infeasible, which is also likely, a move to Ramsey prices might not be Pareto-superior. However, there are valid arguments that we take up in Section 3.5 that still support such a move.[4] Note that firms are ineligible for transfers in this formulation.

4 Feldstein (1972b) derives Ramsey prices with interdependent demands, recognizing that optimum lump-sum transfers are impractical. He explicitly incorporates distributional equity into his model. We take up this approach in Chapter 4.

The *j*th individual behaves as if he maximizes a strictly quasi-concave, twice continuously differentiable utility function

$$U^j(q_1^j, \ldots, q_n^j, q_{n+1}^j, \ldots, q_m^j, q_{m+1}^j) \tag{3.8}$$

subject to his budget constraint

$$y^j - t^j = \sum_{i=1}^{m} p_i q_i^j + q_{m+1}^j \tag{3.9}$$

where there are *n* outputs produced by the multiproduct firm, where $m + 1 - n$ outputs are produced in the private sector, and where the price of the numeraire good, output $m + 1$, is 1. Assuming that the second-order sufficient conditions for the *j*th individual's utility-maximization problem are satisfied, the first-order conditions can be solved to obtain this individual's demand functions,

$$p_i^j = q_i^j(p_1, \ldots, p_m, y^j - t^j) \tag{3.10}$$

for $i = 1, \ldots, n$. The sum over all *s* individuals of the demands for the *i*th output yields the market-demand function for the *i*th output:

$$Q_i \equiv \sum_{j=1}^{s} q_i^j(p_1, \ldots, p_m, y^j - t^j) \tag{3.11}$$

The regulator's problem is to maximize society's welfare by choosing the optimum set of transfers and the prices for the multiproduct firm, given the private-sector prices, market demands, a constraint on the available income in the economy, and the break-even constraint on the multiproduct firm. We denote welfare by an increasing function of individual utilities:

$$W = W(U^1, \ldots, U^s) \tag{3.12}$$

That total income must equal total production costs is given by the constraint

$$\sum_{j=1}^{s} y^j = C(Q_1, \ldots, Q_n) + \sum_{i=n+1}^{m} C_i(Q_i) + Q_{m+1} \tag{3.13}$$

where $C(Q_1, \ldots, Q_n)$ is the total production cost of the multiproduct firm, and $C_i(Q_i)$ is the total production cost for the *i*th firm in the private sector, $i = n + 1, \ldots, m$. All costs are expressed in units of the numeraire good $m + 1$. As implied by the strong natural monopoly assumption, the multiproduct firm's cost function is such that marginal-cost pricing implies deficits; thus, the break-even constraint on the multiproduct firm requires

$$\sum_{i=1}^{n} p_i Q_i = C(Q_1, \ldots, Q_n) \tag{3.14}$$

The regulator chooses $p_1, \ldots, p_n$ and $t^1, \ldots, t^s$ to maximize (3.12) subject to (3.13) and (3.14). Using $\mu$ and $\lambda$ as Lagrange multipliers for the economy-wide constraint given by (3.13) and the firm's constraint given by (3.14), the first-order conditions with respect to $p_i$, $i = 1, \ldots, n$, and $t^j$, $j = 1, \ldots, s$, are as follows:

$$\sum_{j=1}^{s} W_j \sum_{k=1}^{m+1} U_k^j \frac{\partial q_k^j}{\partial p_i} - \mu \left[ \sum_{k=1}^{m} \mathrm{MC}_k \frac{\partial Q_k}{\partial p_i} + \frac{\partial Q_{m+1}}{\partial p_i} \right]$$
$$+ \lambda \left[ Q_i + \sum_{k=1}^{n} [p_k - \mathrm{MC}_k] \frac{\partial Q_k}{\partial p_i} \right] = 0 \tag{3.15}$$

$$W_j \sum_{k=1}^{m+1} U_k^j \frac{\partial q_k^j}{\partial t^j} - \mu \left[ \sum_{k=1}^{m} \mathrm{MC}_k \frac{\partial q_k^j}{\partial t^j} + \frac{\partial q_{m+1}^j}{\partial t^j} \right]$$
$$+ \lambda \sum_{k=1}^{n} [p_k - \mathrm{MC}_k] \frac{\partial q_k^j}{\partial t^j} = 0 \tag{3.16}$$

In these two equations, $W_j = \partial W / \partial U^j$, $U_k^j = \partial U^j / \partial q_k^j$, and $\mathrm{MC}_k$ is the marginal cost of output *k*. When $k = 1, \ldots, n$, $\mathrm{MC}_k$ is a marginal cost for the multiproduct firm, and when $k = n + 1, \ldots, m$, $\mathrm{MC}_k$ is a marginal cost to the *k*th private-sector firm. For convenience, we have omitted the arguments from all functions in (3.15) and (3.16). For example, $\mathrm{MC}_n = \mathrm{MC}_n(Q_1, \ldots, Q_n)$, and the reader should recognize that the marginal cost of one output depends on the level of all other outputs.

### A more general Ramsey rule

Conditions (3.15) and (3.16) can be combined into a convenient form by using both the first-order conditions from each consumer's utility-maximization problem and the derivatives of the consumers' budget identifies with respect to prices and transfers. After some algebraic manipulation,[5] the result is a more general Ramsey rule given by:

$$\frac{p_i - MC_i}{p_i} = \frac{-\alpha}{e_{ii}} - \sum_{\substack{k=1 \\ k \neq i}}^{n} \frac{[p_k - MC_k]Q_k e_{ki}}{p_i Q_i e_{ii}}$$

$$- (1 - \alpha) \sum_{k=n+1}^{m} \frac{[p_k - MC_k]Q_k e_{ki}}{p_i Q_i e_{ii}} \qquad (3.17)$$

for $i = 1, \ldots, n$, where $\alpha = \lambda/(\mu + \lambda)$ and where $e_{ki}$ is the compensate demand elasticity of the $k$th good with respect to the $i$th price. Equation (3.17) can be rewritten as

$$\frac{p_i - MC_i}{p_i} = \frac{-\alpha}{e_{ii}} - \sum_{\substack{k=1 \\ k \neq i}}^{n} \frac{p_k - MC_k}{p_k} \frac{e_{ik}}{e_{ii}}$$

$$- (1 - \alpha) \sum_{k=n+1}^{m} \frac{p_k - MC_k}{p_k} \frac{e_{ik}}{e_{ii}} \qquad (3.17a)$$

by making use of the Slutsky relationship $e_{ik} = e_{ki} p_k Q_k / p_i Q_i$.

First, note that (3.17a) reduces to the simplest form of the Ramsey rule given by (3.6) when (1) all cross-elasticities are zero and (2) $\mu = 1$. For (1), $e_{ik} = 0$, $i, k = 1, \ldots, m$, $k \neq i$, and the second and third terms on the right-hand side of (3.17a) drop out. For (2), $\mu = 1$ implies that the change in welfare with respect to a one-dollar change in exogenous income equals one dollar. This was true in the last section, where (3.6) was derived. In that case, because consumer surplus was measured in dollar units, the change in welfare from a one-dollar change in income did equal one dollar. In the present formulation, $\mu$ may not equal 1, because welfare is given by (3.12), which is not necessarily measured in dollars.

The second term on the right-hand side of (3.17a) accounts for the cross-elasticities of demand between the multiproduct firm's

---

5 The details of this derivation can be found in Sherman and George (1979) or in Chapter 5, where a similar model based on Mohring (1970) is applied to the peak-load pricing problem.

outputs, while the third term accounts for the cross-elasticities of demand between the multiproduct firm's outputs and the outputs of the private sector.[6] Let us consider a two-product case in which outputs by the private sector have zero cross-elasticities with the two outputs of the natural monopoly. The result, which is the counterpart to (3.6a) when demands are dependent, is as follows:

$$\frac{(p_i - \text{MC}_i)/p_i}{(p_k - \text{MC}_k)/p_k} = \frac{e_{kk} - e_{ik}}{e_{ii} - e_{ki}} \tag{3.18}$$

As before, the relative demand elasticities determine the second-best prices. If demand for good $k$ is relatively inelastic, $p_k$ will deviate relatively more from marginal cost. However, in the case of substitutes ($e_{ik} > 0$), if the cross-elasticity is high, the rate designer will have to take into account the outward shift of the demand for good $i$ as $p_k$ increases and the inward shift in the demand for good $k$ as $p_i$ decreases. A high cross-elasticity tends to dampen the second-best-price–marginal-cost markup, as buyers can switch to the other product. The term ($e_{ii} - e_{ki}$) is called the *superelasticity* of good $i$ with respect to changes in its price, because it takes into account the full output response.

Returning to (3.17a), the influence of the private sector depends on $\alpha$, which in turn (given $\mu$) depends on the importance of the firm's budget constraint. As the constraint becomes less binding in the sense that marginal-cost pricing almost covers cost, then $\lambda$ approaches zero, implying that $\alpha$ approaches zero, but as the constraint becomes more binding, $\alpha$ approaches 1. Thus, the influence of the private sector on the multiproduct firm's prices is *greater* when marginal-cost pricing almost allows the firm to cover cost. The less severe the multiproduct natural monopoly's trade-off between marginal-cost pricing and deficits ($\alpha$ approaches zero), the more the private sector influences the optimal prices. The way in which the private sector affects prices

---

6 Mohring (1970) develops an alternative model that highlights the effect of the second term of equation (3.17), and Bergson (1972) does the same for the third term.

depends on its price–cost margins and on whether the private goods tend to be substitutes for or complements to the multiproduct firm's goods. If all private-sector prices are equal to marginal costs, the third term drops out, and the private sector has no influence. Suppose, however, that private prices exceed marginal costs and that, on aggregate, the private goods are substitutes ($e_{ki} > 0$) for the multiproduct firm's $i$th good. Then the price of the $i$th good should be higher than it would be if the private sector were ignored. There is no reason to supplant high-margin output in the private sector with goods of relatively low price from the regulated sector (with relatively high marginal cost). A similar story can be told for complements.

In applying this model to the U.S. Postal Service, Sherman and George note that Postal Service management believes that marginal-cost pricing would yield very large deficits. Accordingly, the budget constraint imposed is strongly binding, approaching 1 in (3.17a), and the private sector can be largely ignored. This, in fact, describes the behavior of the Postal Service, which relies on the simple inverse elasticity rule. Some studies have suggested, however, that marginal costs are much higher than the Postal Service has contended; therefore, more account needs to be taken of the private-sector services that are complements or substitutes for the Postal Service's outputs.[7]

Authors have used multiproduct-firm models to solve analytically for optimum prices in other industries as well. Marchand (1973) models a publicly run telephone industry with multiple outputs and a budget constraint to ensure zero profits. Harris (1979) provides another example by examining hospital prices. Hospitals provide multiple outputs, which if priced at marginal costs would create a deficit. The novelty in this work is the inclusion of insurance availability into the pricing rules. For instance, the author finds that poorly insured outputs should be priced

---

7 Accounting for the effect of private-good cross-elasticities raises the possibility of expanding the natural monopolist's product lines to better take into account such demand interdependencies (assuming costs are unaffected by such changes in industrial structure). Chapter 11 addresses this issue in more detail.

relatively lower. In surface freight transportation, firms may or may not be natural monopolies, depending on the mode of transport. Railroads and pipelines usually are considered to be natural monopolies, whereas motor and air transport are not. Braeutigam (1979) models transport services in which one firm is a natural monopoly in transporting various goods (or multiple outputs) along a route, and all other firms transporting along the same route are not natural monopolies. His model is presented next because it will provide further insight into the nature of Ramsey pricing. Prices for two cases will be derived: (1) cases in which all firms are regulated; (2) cases in which only the natural monopoly is regulated, as in the foregoing Postal Service model.

### 3.3. **More on Ramsey pricing with a competitive fringe**

Natural monopolies often are associated with electricity or natural-gas companies, where the threat of competition is minimal at best. But as the Postal Service application in the previous section illustrated, natural monopolies sometimes face rival firms whose outputs may be substitutes for the natural monopolist's outputs. In this section, we present another model of optimum pricing in the presence of competition to further explore the regulator's dilemma in setting prices when other firms enter the natural monopolist's markets. We shall see in Chapter 7 that a natural monopoly may not be immune to such entry, and zero-profit price vectors can induce competitive investments by rivals.

In the past, the government's response to potential entrants has been to bring competitive services offered by the entrants under regulatory purview. Simons (1948, p. 87) characterized the situation as follows: " ... every venture in regulation creates the necessity of more regulation. . . . The outcome is an accumulation of governmental regulation which yields . . . all the afflictions of socialism with none of its potential benefits." The "tar-baby" process of expanding regulation to include firms that are in no way natural monopolies is exemplified by the trucking regulation exercised by the Interstate Commerce Commission (ICC) beginning in 1935. To protect the price structure of capital-intensive railroads, the ICC regulated prices and entry of trucking firms. In the long run, the results were disastrous for railroads and expensive for shippers. Moore (1978) estimated that the annual impact of regulating railroads, trucks, and water carriers in 1960 was several billion dollars in higher costs for shippers.

The same process, attempting to protect existing firms and to limit the gains of potential entrants, is illustrated by the initial Federal Communications Commission (FCC) regulation of cable television (CATV). In the past, portions of the valuable broadcast spectrum had been given away in the form of FCC licenses. By keeping CATV out of the nation's top 100 markets, the values of these licenses were propped up. The quid pro quo for this protection was (presumably) local news, diversity of information sources, and public-service broadcasting (Bessen, 1974). In retrospect, the many competitive cable offerings (for specialized audiences) have been major spurs to improved programming by the three major networks.

Regulators face an important decision when deciding whether or not to extend regulation to control prices and/or entry of substitute products. In Section 3.2, we saw how substitute products in the nonregulated sector can have an impact on welfare-maximizing prices in the regulated sector. This section presents a model of optimal pricing in the presence of competition when the regulator can control the competitors' prices. Then we relax this control and devise prices similar to those given by (3.17a). The principles apply to telecommunications, transportation, postal service, and other sectors in which alternative technologies permit a competitive fringe or a substitute product to capture market share from a regulated firm.

### *A model of a dominant firm and a competitive fringe*

Braeutigam (1979) uses freight transportation services to examine two regulatory pricing options: (1) totally regulated second best, in which the regulator sets the prices of the natural monopoly goods and all substitute or complementary goods produced outside the natural monopoly; (2) partially regulated second best, in which the regulator can set the prices of the natural monopoly good only. The second option is similar to that presented in the previous section.

To examine the consequences of entry restrictions and pricing rules under these two options, Braeutigam uses the example of a railroad as a strong natural monopoly, and motor carriers and barges as competitively supplied transportation. He generalizes the problem by assuming the following:

1. There are $m$ modes or industries with given technologies providing transportation services between two points, with mode 1 being a strong natural monopoly, whereas other modes have no scale economies and face constant costs.
2. Competition exists in each of the $m - 1$ other modes.
3. Any of the $n$ goods can be transported by any of the $m$ modes, and

   $i$ = modal index, $i = 1, \ldots, m$,

   $j$ = good index, $j = 1, \ldots, n$,

   $q_{ij}$ = amount of good $j$ transported by mode $i$.
4. The service (carriage of $j$) provided by a particular mode is homogeneous; that is, all carriers in mode $i$ provide identical services.
5. The inverse demands for transporting good $j$ via mode $i$ are

   $p_{ij} = p_{ij}(q_{1j}, q_{2j}, \ldots, q_{mj}), \quad i = 1, \ldots, m, j = 1, \ldots, n$

   Here, the demand for transporting good $j$ via any mode is independent of the demand for good $k$ via any mode. Also, consumers of good $j$ view the modes as weak gross substitutes:

   $\partial p_{ij}/\partial q_{kj} < 0, \qquad i \neq k$

   which reflects the idea that modes differ with regard to reliability, speed, and so forth.
6. In addition, $S_{ij}$ is the price of mode $i$ for transporting good $j$, $i = 2, \ldots, m$, and the cost function for mode 1 is $C_1 = C_1(q_{11}, q_{12}, \ldots, q_{1m}; z)$ where $z$ = factor prices.

Each mode, except 1, has a completely elastic supply at price $S_{ij}$.

7. There are zero income effects.[8] So the gross benefits can be defined by $G$, where

$$
\begin{aligned}
G = \sum_{j=1}^{n} \Bigg\{ & \int_{w=0}^{q_{1j}} p_{1j}(w, 0, \ldots, 0) \, dw \\
& + \int_{w=0}^{q_{2j}} p_{2j}(q_{1j}, w, \ldots, 0) \, dw + \ldots \\
& + \int_{w=0}^{q_{mj}} p_{mj}(q_{1j}, \ldots, q_{m-1,j}, w) \, dw \Bigg\}
\end{aligned}
\tag{3.19}
$$

If $G$ were maximized for given $p_{ij}$, the outputs would be chosen such that $\partial G / \partial q_{ij} = p_{ij}$.

Given the foregoing assumptions, the sum of consumer and producer surplus ($W$) for an output mix is

$$
W = G - C_1 - \sum_{i=2}^{m} \sum_{j=1}^{n} S_{ij} q_{ij}
\tag{3.20}
$$

To contrast this model with the one used for the Postal Service in the previous section, note that in the latter the natural monopolist produced $n$ goods. Each of these goods was potentially a substitute for or complement to the other $n - 1$ goods, as well as each of the goods produced outside the natural monopoly. In this section's model, the natural monopoly produces (transports) $n$ goods, each of whose demand is independent of the demands for the other $n - 1$ goods. Thus, in (3.17a), the second term on the right-hand side disappears. However, the natural monopoly faces competition in the production of good $i$, $i = 1, \ldots, n$, from sup-

---

8 Because consumer surplus is being used as a measure of welfare, and demand for shipping good $j$ via mode $i$ is not independent of the demand for shipping good $j$ via mode $k$, a path-dependence problem arises. To avoid the problem in this formulation, income effects are assumed to be zero, so that the compensated and normal demand curves are the same. For more detail on this, see Section 5.3.

pliers who produce a substitute for good $i$. Thus, a term analogous to the third term on the right-hand side in (3.17) will still apply. In this formulation, a railroad shipping, say, coal and freight competes with trucks and barges in the coal market and in the freight market. But coal shipping does not compete with freight shipping.

### *Totally regulated second best*

Under totally regulated second best (TRSB), the regulator's problem is to set output levels for all modes to maximize welfare while just allowing the strong natural monopoly (mode 1) to break even. That is,

$$\max_{q_{ij} \ \forall \ i,j} W \text{ subject to } \sum_{j=1}^{n} p_{1j}q_{1j} - C_1 \geq 0 \qquad (3.21)$$

where the constraint requires that the mode with scale economies breaks even.

Forming a Lagrangian, we have

$$L = G - C_1 - \sum_{i=2}^{m} \sum_{j=1}^{n} S_{ij}q_{ij} + \lambda(p_{1j}q_{1j} - C_1) \qquad (3.22)$$

The Kuhn–Tucker conditions for a maximum of (3.22) with respect to $q_{1j}$ and $q_{ij}$ are

$$\partial L/\partial q_{1j} = p_{1j} - \partial C_1/\partial q_{1j} + \lambda[(\partial p_{1j}/\partial q_{1j})q_{1j} + p_{1j} - \partial C_1/\partial q_{1j}] \leq 0,$$
$$q_{1j} \geq 0, \ q_{1j}\partial L/\partial q_{1j} = 0, j = 1, \ldots, n \qquad (3.23)$$

and

$$\partial L/\partial q_{ij} = p_{ij} - S_{ij} + \lambda(\partial p_{1j}/\partial q_{ij})q_{1j} \leq 0,$$
$$q_{ij} \geq 0, \ q_{ij}\partial L/\partial q_{ij} = 0, i = 2, \ldots, m, j = 1, \ldots, n \qquad (3.24)$$

For $q_{1j} > 0$, (3.23) can be rearranged to obtain the familiar Ramsey pricing rule

$$\frac{p_{1j} - \partial C_1/\partial q_{1j}}{p_{1j}} e_{1j} = -\frac{\lambda}{1 + \lambda} \qquad (3.25)$$

for $j = 1, \ldots, n$, and $e_{1j}$ is the demand elasticity of good $j$ shipped on mode 1. The Ramsey rule for goods shipped by the competitive modes is more complex. For $q_{ij} > 0$, $i = 2, \ldots, m$, $j = 1, \ldots, n$, the rule is

$$\frac{(p_{ij} - S_{ij})/p_{ij}}{(\partial p_{ij}/\partial q_{1j})(q_{1j}/p_{ij}) - (p_{ij} - S_{ij})/p_{ij}} = \frac{-\lambda}{1 + \lambda} \qquad (3.26)$$

where the integrability condition $\partial p_{1j}/\partial q_{ij} = \partial p_{ij}/\partial q_{1j}$ is used. The integrability condition applies because income effects are assumed to be zero. The first term in the denominator on the left-hand side is the cross-elasticity between modes 1 and $i$ for the $j$th good.

To obtain (3.26), we assume that $p_{ij} > S_{ij}$, or that price in the $i$th competitive mode exceeds marginal cost. If it equals marginal cost, then $\partial L/\partial q_{ij} < 0$ in (3.24), because $\lambda > 0$, and the modes are assumed to be weak gross substitutes. But with $\partial L/\partial q_{ij} < 0$, then $q_{ij} = 0$, and the $i$th mode does not ship the $j$th good. Thus, a second-best solution where a positive amount of good $j$ is shipped by the $i$th mode requires that the price exceed marginal cost on that mode. Braeutigam explains this as follows: " ... there is some loss in efficiency which occurs in the markets served by modes $2, \ldots, m$ because price is greater than marginal cost. However, the higher prices in modes $2, \ldots, m$ lead to increased demands (and more consumers surplus) for the services provided by mode 1" (1979, p. 42).

Braeutigam's results for the achievement of totally regulated second best can be summarized as follows:

1. Mode 1 earns zero profits.
2. Prices are set so that modified Ramsey numbers [from (3.25) and (3.26)] in all markets are equal to one another.
3. Entry restrictions in markets served by modes 2 through $m$ are required, because prices exceed marginal costs.

The problems with TRSB are that regulatory authorities must impose and enforce entry restrictions, and they face substantial information requirements pertaining to cost and demand conditions. Consequently, Braeutigam considers a more modest approach that is feasible for regulators.

### Partially regulated second best

Partially regulated second best (PRSB) will allow the modes without economies of scale ($i = 2, \ldots, m$) to clear their respective markets, and regulators will concentrate only on prices set by the natural monopoly mode. Entry control is avoided, because marginal-cost prices and constant costs in the other modes ensure zero profits. More formally, the constraints for the other modes are $p_{ij} - S_{ij} = 0$, $i = 2, \ldots, m$, $j = 1, \ldots, n$. But noting that this system of constraints can be used to derive the $q_{ij}$ ($i \geq 2$) as implicit functions of $q_{1j}$, the PRSB problem becomes the same as the TRSB problem except that the set of decision variables used by the regulators includes only the $q_{1j}$ terms, not all $q_{ij}$.

The pricing rule for PRSB is the same as the basic Ramsey rule given by (3.6a) that applied when the multiproduct firm had a monopoly in all of its markets. Information requirements are limited to price, marginal cost, and demand elasticity in mode 1 only. This result can be related to the concept of second best. If a strong natural monopolist must operate subject to a break-even constraint, and the demand for each of its products is independent of the demand for all other products, then it should deviate from marginal-cost pricing using the Ramsey rule (3.6a). This is a second-best policy; the first-best policy in which prices equal marginal costs is infeasible because we assume a strong natural monopoly. If the demands for its products are not independent of the demands for competitors' products, then the efficiency-minded regulator will require prices of competitive products also to deviate from marginal cost to yield an economy-wide second best. These competitors' prices are given by (3.26) in the TRSB. This outcome implies that if distortions from the optimum are required in the natural monopoly sector, then they will be required in the competitive sector as well.

However, the regulator is unlikely to have the authority or the requisite information to set prices according to a TRSB. One option would be to allow the competitive markets to clear so that the competitors' prices would equal their marginal costs. Then prices would again take the form of the Ramsey rule (3.6a). This situation is equivalent to the more complex Ramsey rule (3.17a), because (3.17a) reduces to (3.6a) when prices equal marginal costs for competing products (and the natural monopolist's products do not compete with one another, which is consistent with Braeutigam's formulation). However, if prices of competing products do not equal marginal costs, then (3.17a) applies again, but now it does not reduce to the simple rule (3.6a). Cross-elasticities between the natural monopoly and the competing products come into play.

The implications of regulatory policy become more clear now. Adopting the simple Ramsey rule is optimal if the demand for the natural monopolist's products is independent of the demand for other products. The rule is also optimal if each of the natural monopolist's products competes with private-sector products, provided the latter are priced at their marginal costs. As Braeutigam points out, the regulator could mistakenly assume independence between product demands, adopt the simple Ramsey rule, and still be correct if competitors' prices equaled their marginal costs. Finally, with demand interdependencies due to the existence of a competitive sector, the more complex Ramsey rule is required.

With the two possible solutions in mind, Braeutigam proceeds to compare the welfare properties of PRSB and TRSB. To facilitate comparison, he assumes only two modes; mode 1 has economies of scale, and mode 2 is competitive. Also, as before, there is intramodal homogeneity and intermodal differentiation.

Suppose the competitive mode has a supply schedule labeled $S_2(q_2)$. As long as the mode-2 market clears,

$$p_2(q_1, q_2) - S_2(q_2) = 0 \tag{3.27}$$

Noting that $q_2$ can be written as an implicit function of $q_1$, as

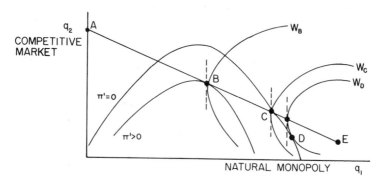

Figure 3.3. Isosurplus and isowelfare.

described earlier, the implicit-function theorem can be used to obtain

$$dq_2/dq_1 = -(\partial p_2/\partial q_1)/(\partial p_2/\partial q_2 - \partial S_2/\partial q_2) < 0 \qquad (3.28)$$

where the inequality follows if $q_1$ and $q_2$ are weak gross substitutes and if the absolute value of the slope of demand for good 2 exceeds that of supply:

$$|\partial p_2/\partial q_2| > |\partial S_2/\partial q_2|$$

The foregoing inequality will follow for constant or decreasing returns in mode 2. Equation (3.28) is the slope of line *AE* in Figure 3.3 that represents the loci of market-clearing outcomes for mode 2, given outputs in mode 1. Below the line, there will be entry by producers of $q_2$; above the line, firms will exit because losses occur, given the output of $q_2$. The sum of consumer and producer surpluses in both the mode-1 and mode-2 markets is

$$W = \int_{w=0}^{q_1} p_1(w, 0) \, dw + \int_{w=0}^{q_2} p_2(q_1, w) \, dw$$
$$- C_1(q_1) - \int_{w=0}^{q_2} S_2(w) \, dw$$

from which we can obtain (3.29) using the implicit-function theorem:

$$dq_2/dq_1 = -(p_1 - C_1')/(p_2 - S_2) \tag{3.29}$$

These isowelfare curves are pictured in Figure 3.3 and labeled $W_B$, $W_C$, and $W_D$.

Along line $AE$, $p_2 = S_2$; thus, the isowelfare curves are vertical when they intersect $AE$, because the denominator of (3.29) goes to zero. Notice also that total welfare $W$ increases along $AE$ as $q_1$ increases up to a level of output in which $p_1$ equals the marginal cost of producing $q_1$. This point follows because, in general, any increase in monopoly output leading to the point where price equals marginal cost will increase the sum of producer and consumer surpluses. In this case, $q_1$ is the monopoly output, and it is increasing as one moves along line $AE$. In terms of the model, the total derivative of welfare is

$$dW = (p_1 - C_1') \, dq_1 + (p_2 - S_2) \, dq_2 \tag{3.30}$$

and along $AE$, $p_2 = S_2$; so (3.30) becomes

$$dW = (p_1 - C_1') \, dq_1 > 0 \tag{3.31}$$

It follows that total welfare is increasing as $q_1$ increases up to the point where $p_1 = C_1'$. If point $E$ in Figure 3.3 is where $p_1 = C_1'$, then $W$ is maximized at $E$ and represents a first-best operating point.

Finally, the rationale for drawing the isoprofit curves for mode 1 as mound-shaped arises out of the profit function for mode 1, written as

$$\pi^1 = p_1(q_1, q_2)q_1 - C_1(q_1) \tag{3.32}$$

Again using the implicit-function theorem, we obtain the slope of the profit curve as

$$dq_2/dq_1 = -[p_1 + (\partial p_1/\partial q_1)q_1 - \partial C_1/\partial q_1]/(\partial p_1/\partial q_2)q_1$$

Because $\partial p_1/\partial q_2 < 0$, the slope of the profit curve is positive if marginal revenue is greater than marginal cost, and negative when the converse is true. Profit is maximized where marginal revenue equals marginal cost. Lower curves yield higher profit because for any given level of $q_1$, profits for mode 1 increase as the level of $q_2$ decreases. Thus, in terms of Figure 3.3, $\pi^1 = 0$ lies above $\pi^1 > 0$.

### Implications of TRSB and PRSB

It is now possible to examine the different points in Figure 3.3 for their welfare and regulatory consequences. Suppose both mode 1 and mode 2 are unregulated. Mode 1 will choose the highest isoprofit contour attainable given that mode 2's market will clear. This is point $B$, with associated welfare $W_B$. The PRSB solution is given by point $C$. Here, mode 2's market is allowed to clear, and so we are along $AE$, and at the same time mode 1 is held to zero profit, and so we are on the $\pi^1 = 0$ curve. In comparing $B$ and $C$, the unregulated solution (dominant-firm price leadership) might be desirable if the mode-1 firm earns only a small profit, with points $B$ and $C$ relatively near each other. This solution would achieve nearly the same efficiency as the PRSB solution, but without incurring the administrative costs of regulation.

Finally, if the regulator controls entry into mode 2, sets the quantity for mode 2, and maximizes welfare subject to mode 1 breaking even, she will achieve point $D$, the TRSB solution with welfare level $W_D$. Because the slope of the isoprofit contour for mode 1 is negative at $D$, then the slope of $W_D$ is also negative; therefore, $D$ lies below $AE$, and mode 2 is not clearing. Taxes and transfers or entry control are needed, along with substantial information.

The main ideas to be gleaned from Braeutigam's discussion are related to the problems of second best when there is competition between regulated modes of service. If all the modes are regulated, the information requirements are enormous, and entry control is necessary. Only if the TRSB solution is costless is it unambiguously better than the PRSB solution.

Here we have investigated a strong natural monopoly producing multiple outputs that faced competition in each of its product markets. The competition came from price-taking firms that did not enjoy scale economies. Welfare-maximizing pricing rules were derived for the natural monopolist, first for the case in which the regulator could choose output quantities for all firms, and second for the case in which the regulator could choose output quantities only for the monopolist. The next section considers a strong natural monopoly facing competition in each of its product markets from other strong natural monopolies. If the regulator's authority extends over all of these monopolies, what pricing rules should she adopt?

### 3.4 Rivalry among strong natural monopolies

Braeutigam (1984) has also examined the problem of competing strong natural monopolies. Such situations arise, for example, where electricity and natural-gas companies compete, where railroads or airlines compete along similar routes,[9] and in telecommunications, where AT&T competes with MCI and US Sprint. The model for competing strong natural monopolies is very similar to the model in the last section, and so we provide only an outline here. Again, there are $m$ firms, each producing any or all of $n$ different goods. Demand for the $j$th product of the $i$th firm, $j = 1, \ldots, n, i = 1, \ldots, m$, is independent of the demand for the firm's other $n - 1$ products; however, each of the other $m - 1$ firms may produce a $j$th product that either is a weak gross substitute or is independent of the $i$th firm's $j$th product. Because the firms are strong natural monopolies, first-best marginal-cost pricing will mean deficits for all of them. Thus, welfare, which is measured in the same way as in Section 3.3 (i.e., consumer plus producer surpluses), is maximized subject to a set of budget constraints. Two different constraint sets are considered: (1) A budget constraint is assigned to each firm separately.

9 Recent evidence (Caves, Christensen, and Tretheway, 1984) suggests that there are economies of scale along city-pair airline routes.

(2) One budget constraint is assigned to the entire industry. If we assume that the budget constraints are break-even constraints, then set 1 implies that each firm's revenues must equal its costs. Alternatively, set 2 implies that the aggregate revenues must equal aggregate costs across all *m* firms. Constraint set 2 is made operational by allowing transfer payments across firms.

### Viable-firm and viable-industry Ramsey optima

Using terminology from Baumol, Panzar, and Willig (1982), Braeutigam terms the solutions to the two welfare-maximization problems as a *viable-firm Ramsey optimum* (VFRO) when constraint set 1 is used and a *viable-industry Ramsey optimum* (VIRO) when constraint set 2 is used. He then derives the following four principles:

> *Principle 1:* At a VFRO, each firm need not have a binding deficit constraint; some strong natural monopolies may earn positive profits. However, at least one firm will have a binding budget constraint.

This principle runs counter to the traditional approach to regulation requiring zero profit for each firm. That there must be at least one binding constraint follows because if all constraints were nonbinding, prices would equal marginal costs, and deficits would result. For the firm or firms with a binding constraint, Principle 2 applies:

> *Principle 2:* The price for every product sold by firm *i* will exceed marginal cost if the budget constraint for that firm is binding at a VFRO.

At a VFRO, at least some prices for every firm must exceed marginal cost to satisfy the budget constraint. Principle 2 states that all prices will exceed marginal costs for a firm whose budget is binding. If all firms have binding constraints, then all prices in the industry will exceed marginal costs. For firms that have a nonbinding budget constraint, the results (indicated in Principle 3) are more involved:

> *Principle 3:* If firm $i$'s budget constraint is nonbinding at a VFRO, then the price for its $j$th product will equal marginal cost if and only if (a) the firm has a monopoly in the $j$th product or (b) no other firm producing a rival product has a binding budget constraint.

Thus, it is possible to have some prices equal to marginal cost at a VFRO, but only in firms that have nonbinding budget constraints. Any firm that has a monopoly in one of its products cannot be earning positive profit if the price of that product exceeds marginal cost. Also, if two firms compete in the same market with one of their products, then a binding budget constraint on either firm implies that neither price is equal to marginal cost.

To better understand the situation, we can ask what causes a firm to have a nonbinding profit constraint. First, consider a firm that has a monopoly in all markets. With no interaction with other firms, this firm is essentially treated like the multiproduct natural monopoly in Section 3.1, where the most basic Ramsey rule (3.6a) applied across all products. (Recall that demands for intrafirm products are independent.) The budget constraint is binding, and all prices deviate from marginal costs. This result is in keeping with Principle 2. But now suppose the firm has a monopoly over all but the $j$th product. Suppose, too, that other firms with binding budget constraints are strong rivals in this $j$th market, selling close substitutes. Then the firm's price in the $j$th market will exceed marginal cost: The stronger the cross-substitution effects, the more this price will exceed marginal cost. It is possible that the price can be sufficiently in excess of marginal cost that the firm will earn positive profit, even with all other prices set at marginal costs. Moreover, these other prices will be set to marginal costs if the goods are monopolized, because there are no cross-substitution effects with other products that would justify higher prices. These interpretations are brought out further with Principle 4:

> *Principle 4:* If firm $i$ has a monopoly in product $k$, but competes against another firm with a binding budget

constraint in selling product *j*, then at a VFRO the Ramsey number for product *k* will exceed the Ramsey number for product *j*.

This principle is reminiscent of the complex Ramsey rules given by (3.17a). Firm *i*'s price for the *j*th product should reflect the cross-elasticities between the *j*th product and any substitute goods produced by other firms. [Recall the right-most terms in equation (3.17).] As Braeutigam points out, if the own-demand elasticities for the *j*th and *k*th products of the *i*th firm are equal, and the firm faces competition in the *j*th but not the *k*th market, then the percentage markup of price over marginal cost is greater in the *j*th market than in the *k*th market. The intuition is straightforward. Some prices must be raised above marginal costs to cover budget deficits, and there is less welfare lost when prices are raised more (in percentage terms) in the competitive market, because consumers have substitutes available.

The second alternative Braeutigam investigates is the VIRO in which there is effectively one budget constraint for all firms. To implement this regulatory scenario, transfer payments (plus or minus) are permitted across firms. The transfer payments are additional regulatory decision variables, and the sum of all transfer payments is zero. At a VIRO, the budget constraint is binding, or, alternatively, each firm's budget constraint is binding when the transfer payment is included. Not surprisingly, then, every price will exceed marginal cost as per Principles 2 and 3. A VIRO will be Pareto-superior to a VFRO as long as the transfer payments are not all zero. This result follows because the regulator has additional instruments (the transfer payments) at a VIRO. Although a VIRO would require a departure from current regulatory practice in many instances, Braeutigam does cite some cases in which transfers are utilized as regulatory instruments (Damus, 1984). Examples include regulators setting prices for wheeling electricity, use of railroad track, or access to local telephone networks.

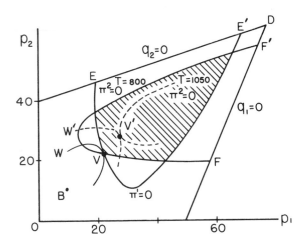

Figure 3.4. Viable-firm Ramsey optimum.

*A numerical example*

Let us turn to a numerical example to illustrate these points. Braeutigam presents the following two-firm example of a VFRO wherein each firm produces a single product, and these products are viewed as gross substitutes by consumers. Demands are given by

$$q_1 = 100 - 2p_1 + p_2 \tag{3.33}$$
$$q_2 = 120 - 3p_2 + p_1 \tag{3.34}$$

and costs are

$$C^1 = 1000 + 10q_1, \qquad q_1 > 0 \tag{3.35}$$
$$C^2 = T + 12q_2 > 0 \tag{3.36}$$

and

$$C^i = 0, \qquad i = 1, 2 \quad \text{for } q_i = 0$$

Here, $T$ is a positive constant that will be varied to make comparisons. Profit and welfare relationships are shown in Figure 3.4, with the axes representing the prices for goods 1 and 2. When $p_2$

= 0, $p_1$ = 50 leads to $q_1$ = 0, and the locus of all prices for good 2 that set $q_1$ = 0 is shown as the straight line that is labeled appropriately. Points to the left (right) of $q_1$ = 0 imply positive (negative) output. A similar story can be told for good 2 and the line labeled $q_2$ = 0 emanating from $p_2$ = 40 on the vertical axis.

The curves labeled $\pi^i$ = 0, $i$ = 1, 2, represent the price combinations where the $i$th firm just breaks even. Inside these curves, the $i$th firm makes positive profit; thus, if both firms produce and make nonnegative profit, they must be in the hatched region. Also, because either firm can shut down and make zero profit, points along $EE'$ and $FF'$ represent viable price combinations, although only one firm is producing positive output.

The regulator's problem is to find the prices that will maximize welfare and allow both firms to survive. Welfare contours are shown by $W$ and $W''$; their shapes follow from a strictly concave welfare function. Point $B$ is the welfare optimum where prices equal marginal costs ($p_1$ = 10, $p_2$ = 12). Without transfers from outside, this first-best outcome is unavailable because the firms are strong natural monopolies. Figure 3.4 shows a unique VFRO at point $V$ when $T$ = 800. Welfare at $V$ exceeds welfare at any other points where both firms are viable, that is, at points in the hatched area and along $EE'$ and $FF'$. At point $V$, both firms have binding budget constraints.

If fixed costs for firm 2 increase from 800 to 1,050, the $\pi^2$ = 0 locus will shift to the right (shown as a dashed curve). Now, a lower level of welfare ($W'$) is achieved at a VFRO that is attained at point $V'$. In addition, firm 1 will be earning positive profit. Finally, if $T$ increases, say $T$ = 1,500, a VFRO yields a different industrial configuration: Firm 2 is eliminated from the market, and firm 1 prices at average cost (point $E$).

The framework also anticipates some of the issues addressed in Chapters 7 and 11: the feasibility of free entry as a substitute for regulation, the efficacy of rivalry compared with regulation for promoting allocative and innovative efficiency, and the strengths and limitations of partial regulation (sometimes called "managed competition"). An alternative to VIRO or VFRO as a regulatory solution would be complete deregulation. The equilibrium prices would then depend on the nature of the rivalry between the duopolists. Under Nash–Cournot behavior, each firm would maximize profits by adjusting its output – assuming that the rival holds its output constant. The process yields equilibrium outputs (and the implied prices). For the demands and costs in the example, firm 1 would have a price of roughly 30, and firm 2 would have a price of about 36. This outcome implies lower welfare than the regulated VFRO at point $V$ (assuming zero costs of regulation). Braeutigam's example illustrates the complexity of the tasks facing regulators, including the selection of appropriate firm and/or industry constraints.

### 3.5. Impediments to Ramsey pricing and second-best considerations

The principles for setting welfare-maximizing prices provide useful guidelines for regulators. However, additional considerations associated with data requirements complicate the actual implementation of these pricing rules, and jurisdictional boundaries limit the prices over which particular regulators have some control. Some economists conclude that these limitations invalidate the use of Ramsey principles in practice.

The argument against Ramsey pricing owing to the problem of second best goes as follows: Suppose the economy consists of one strong natural monopoly and many competitive firms. The latter all take output prices as given, and they equate their marginal costs to these prices in order to maximize profits. To maximize societal welfare, the natural monopoly should also set its prices equal to marginal costs as per Hotelling's recommendation. This is the first-best solution. However, if some of the other firms obtain monopoly power and no longer price at marginal cost, what should the natural monopolist do? Lipsey and Lancaster (1956) showed that the welfare-maximizing course of action for the natural monopolist, given these distortions elsewhere in the economy (i.e., prices not equal to marginal costs), may no longer be to set prices to marginal costs. From our pricing formulas, marginal-cost prices for the monopolist may make things worse. In this case, we say that the economy can now achieve only a second-best solution. Suppose now that there are no distortions elsewhere, but the natural monopolist cannot depend on subsidies to cover a deficit arising from its marginal-cost pricing. Then the natural monopolist can resort to Ramsey prices, but by adopting this policy it also arrives at a second-best solution. That is, Ramsey pricing is necessarily a second-best pricing policy.

Realistically, we can be sure that distortions exist throughout the economy; thus, regulators concerned with socially desirable prices should be taking into account prices elsewhere in the economy, in addition to worrying about the solvency of the natural monopolist. In the preceding three sections, we derived rules that illustrated how natural monopoly prices should be set in order to alleviate at least part of the negative effects of distortions elsewhere. Optimum monopoly prices depended on the magnitude of the distortions; only if the price of a nonmonopoly good was equal to its marginal cost, so that there was no distortion, or if the demand for the nonmonopoly good was independent of the demands for the monopoly goods would the nonmonopoly good not matter in determining optimum prices. But if the regulator does not know the magnitude of the distortions or the degree of interdependence, she cannot be certain that Ramsey prices are an improvement over other sets of prices.

We could complicate things still further, however. Suppose that the natural monopolist's goods are inputs into other firms' production processes. This situation certainly characterizes electricity, communications, and other industries with possible natural monopoly properties. Lancaster (1979) shows that the welfare-maximizing natural monopoly may want to price below marginal cost if the intermediate goods it produces are important inputs into other firms' production processes. Along these lines, Ebrill and Slutsky (1984) show how ICC pricing of coal shipped to electric utilities affects efficiency in the vertical chain of production, especially because coal and electricity directly compete in some markets.

All of these complications leave the regulator with a formidable problem. Information on the natural monopolist's own demand elasticities and costs is difficult enough to obtain, but to obtain information about the cross-elasticities with other firms' outputs and about other firms' short-run (and long-run) marginal costs is virtually impossible. Even if such information is available, we can expect other firms to change their prices once the natural monopoly prices are set. There will be a reaction process, and the conjectures made by the regulator and other firms regarding one another's responses become important. This process has not been examined theoretically, and in practice it increases the informational burden on the regulator.

In addition, the regulator generally can be expected to possess less information than the natural monopolist possesses concerning costs and demand. This asymmetry can cause the regulator to be more cautious in imposing stringent performance standards on the firm. Sappington (1983) models a situation in which a regulator has full information about a firm's demand, but only limited information about costs. Specifically, the regulator knows the firm's cost structure, but does not know what the actual costs will be because information about a crucial technological parameter is missing. The information becomes available only after output prices are set by the regulator. If at a given choice of prices the ex post costs are large, the firm will incur a deficit; if it cannot cover variable costs, the firm will shut down. If the ex post costs are low, the firm makes excessive profit, with a concomitant reduction in consumer surplus. Sappington shows that in this situation the regulator's optimum strategy may be to deviate from Ramsey pricing. Thus, regulators forgo "some surplus under some realizations of the firm's technology to prevent the firm from usurping too much of the total available surplus under other such realizations" (Sappington, 1983, p. 454). (See Section 12.4 for more on asymmetric information between the firm and regulator.)

A related complication is that the long-run own-price cross-price elasticities will be greater than short-run elasticities. The regulator will have to take greater long-run substitutabilities into account, lest the prices induce uneconomic responses elsewhere in the economy, and once induced technological change is included in the list of likely responses, regulators face an even more complicated set of calculations.

One further difficulty that is not brought out in many theoretical models has to do with jurisdictional boundaries and the scope of the regulator's authority. Most models have one regulator overseeing one natural monopoly, but there are actually many regulators overseeing many natural monopolies. In the case of state regulation, there are nearly fifty regulatory agencies, each with a different constituency. If regulators act as if they are welfare-maximizers (see Chapter 8), then each has a different welfare function, whose arguments are the utilities of the consumers and profits of the firms within their political districts. But both the regulated and unregulated firms may operate in one, a few, or all of these jurisdictions. Consequently, the economic forces influencing and resulting from the regulator's decisions will not respect the regulator's political boundaries. Attempts to coordinate the multitude of regulators and firms in order to achieve one consistent second-best policy for the entire economy is beyond reason.

### Applicability to the real world

Critics of both Ramsey prices and marginal-cost prices have used second-best arguments to support the status quo in regulatory proceedings. They point out that because we do not have all the necessary information, and because regulators usually are dealing with only a fraction of the economy and ignoring what happens beyond their political borders, we cannot be sure that any alternative prices will actually increase welfare.

Furthermore, we have assumed that production costs have been minimized. Requiring revenues to match these costs is essential for investors to be willing to supply the capital for capacity replacement and expansion. As we shall see in Chapters 8 and 9, there can be disputes about whether or not some capacity is a "prudent investment." Alternatively, a technological advance may make a plant economically obsolete. Such considerations raise the possibility of regulators punishing firms for past decisions, resulting in negative profit. Although this possibility does not vitiate the Ramsey principle, it complicates the process whereby appropriate Ramsey prices can be determined.

Another consideration in moving to Ramsey prices from existing prices is that there most assuredly will be losers: Some consumers will experience increased utility, but others will experience decreased utility. Although regulators could have the winners compensate the losers (by using the transfer payments in Section 3.2), so that everyone would be made better off, compensation via taxes and transfers is not likely to occur. However, without compensation, the move is not Pareto-superior to the status quo. If the regulator's job were to design prices for a new utility in a new economy, this would not be an issue, and the Ramsey prices would indeed be the preferred second-best prescription. Of course, this situation never confronts the regulator; the real task is always one of pricing reform, not new prices.

The problem of winners and losers is neatly captured by Zajac (1978, p. 48) in a fictitious but enlightening conversation between a policy-maker and an economist. The latter presents the former with a set of Ramsey prices and explains that with these prices, further price changes cannot be made without making someone worse off. The current prices do not have this property. However, a change to the Ramsey prices would mean that some consumers would face higher prices, and some lower. The policy-maker complains that there are no instruments available to her that will allow the winners to compensate the losers. Therefore, if she adheres to the Pareto criteria, the current prices are Pareto-efficient, because a move from them to Ramsey prices would imply that there would be uncompensated losers. The economist then points out that there are situations in which the losers may turn out to be winners as well, and this should be taken into account. In Zajac's economist's words:

> There are some studies that might help you [the policy-maker] decide whether or not you want to change the present prices, even though you can't directly arrange

for compensations. First of all, it may be that the same people subscribe to all the services. If that's the case, the compensations might take place automatically. In effect, consumers would take money out of one pocket and put it in the other. Secondly, [consider a] highly idealized economy with a power company serving only a competitive bakery industry and a residential market. In that situation, the proper compensation [takes] place indirectly by means of the pass-through to residential consumers of the bakeries' lower costs. We could try to determine whether or not such indirect compensations would take place if you moved toward more efficient prices. (Zajac, 1978, p. 48)

The final impediment we mention is that Ramsey prices may not be subsidy-free. Some consumers may be paying more for the good than they would if they were to obtain the good from an alternative supplier. This situation is tantamount to other consumers paying less than the total incremental cost of serving them. These other consumers paying below cost are being cross-subsidized by the first group. (See Chapter 7 for more on cross-subsidies.) In some instances, this outcome may be judged desirable. For example, the regulator may wish to have low-income consumers subsidized by middle- and upper-income consumers. Such welfare weights are incorporated in Chapters 4 and 8. Note, however, that cross-subsidies require that we make ethical decisions that go beyond considerations of economic efficiency. As we shall see in the next section and in Chapters 4 and 7, cross-subsidies can mean instability and can eventually lead to situations in which everyone will be made worse off, even though the regulators intended to help.

For all these reasons, some economists find Ramsey principles unacceptable in practice. For example, Kamerschen and Keenan (1983, p. 200) describe the formulation as "more of a theoretical curiosity than a workable regulatory rule." This defeatist attitude is understandable. Nevertheless, the concern is mitigated in those cases in which the regulated firm is not strongly linked with other sectors in the economy through demand and supply elasticities. Antitrust laws, support of international trade, and many other microeconomic policies are predicated on the presumption that driving prices toward marginal cost leads to resource reallocations that will expand our consumption possibilities. To accept a different presumption for regulated industries would run counter to the broad thrust of policies in other sectors. In addition, the status quo approach would inhibit progress toward improving economic efficiency. It would likely discourage the collection and analysis of the information needed to make better decisions. The principles developed here and in subsequent chapters are based on careful, scientific methods that, if used prudently, should move us in the direction of increased understanding, even if we cannot be absolutely certain that they will always lead toward increased economic efficiency.

### 3.6. Fully distributed cost pricing

We have enumerated a number of impediments to the widespread use of Ramsey prices. But if regulators do not use Ramsey prices, and if marginal-cost prices create deficits, what prices do regulators enforce? In practice, the answer depends on historical developments affecting the industries in question. For instance, we shall see in Part II that in the electric-utility industry, prices typically are formulated after revenue requirements have been established. Marginal costs and demand elasticities may play only minor roles in the formulation. Another approach that has been used by the ICC and the FCC is to enforce *fully distributed cost* (FDC) prices. The idea here is that each output that a multiproduct firm produces and sells should generate at least enough revenue to cover the cost of producing that output. If profit is held to zero, then the generated revenue should exactly cover the incurred cost.

The problem, however, is that much of the firm's total cost may be *shared* or *common costs:* costs that cannot be assigned to any one output. For example, how much of the cost of railway track should be assigned to each of the goods shipped over the track? There are numerous methods for distributing these costs over the various outputs, but they are all arbitrary.[10] There is simply no one cost-allocation method that is consistently superior to the others on efficiency grounds. The purpose of this section is to examine several FDC pricing methods and to compare them to Ramsey prices. What are the likely consequences of FDC prices in terms of possible efficiency loses and biases against certain outputs? The analysis of FDC pricing could be placed in Part II of this book, where we cover actual regulatory practice instead of the ideal regulatory practice covered here in Part I. However, because the problems associated with FDC pricing can be brought out through comparisons to Ramsey prices, we have included FDC pricing in this chapter.

### Determination of FDC prices

The following analysis is taken largely from Braeutigam (1980). He examines three specific methods of FDC pricing: (1) relative output; (2) attributable cost; (3) gross revenue. To define these, we continue with a multiproduct firm producing $n$ goods, $q = (q_1, \ldots, q_n)$. The demands for these goods are assumed to be independent, and we write $R_i(q_i) = p_i(q_i)q_i$ as the revenue for the $i$th good. Suppose the firm's costs can be written as

$$C(q) = \sum_{i=1}^{n} C_i(q_i) + \text{CC} \tag{3.37}$$

where $C_i(q_i)$ is the cost that can be unambiguously attributed to the production of the $i$th output, and CC is the shared or com-

---

10 The presence of shared inputs presents a number of conceptual problems. If the telephone company increases the number of circuits between two points, then the increased capacity is available equally to day and nighttime calls. Thus, the investment involves a joint cost (fixed output proportions). However, the peak circuit capacity provides varying proportions of residential and business calls – so for a given rating period it represents a common cost (attributable by usage). Labeling such a phenomenon as "shared costs" recognizes the possibility that an investment can be both joint (temporally) and common (spatially or by consumer group). Such possibilities greatly complicate the pricing/cost-allocation decisions by regulators. Nevertheless, some costs are unambiguously attributable to one or another good. See Bolter et al. (1984, pp. 349–54) for an overview of these issues.

mon cost. For example, if the common cost is railroad track, then the fuel used to run a coal train over the track can be attributed unambiguously to transporting coal as an output. Similarly, much of the administrative cost of a cable-television company may be common, but the cable attached to a residence is attributable to that residence only.

Because FDC pricing requires each output to generate enough revenue to cover its attributed cost, we have

$$R_i(q_i) \geq f_i CC + C_i(q_i), \qquad i = 1, \ldots, n \qquad (3.38)$$

where $f_i$ is the fraction of common cost assigned to output $i$. What distinguishes the various FDC methods is the determination of $f_i$. For the three methods specified earlier, we have, for $i = 1, \ldots, n$,

$$(1) \quad f_i \equiv q_i \bigg/ \sum_{i=1}^{n} q_i \qquad \text{(relative output)} \qquad (3.39)$$

$$(2) \quad f_i \equiv C_i(q_i) \bigg/ \sum_{i=1}^{n} C_i(q_i) \qquad \text{(attributable cost)} \qquad (3.40)$$

$$(3) \quad f_i \equiv R_i(q_i) \bigg/ \sum_{i=1}^{n} R_i(q_i) \qquad \text{(gross revenue)} \qquad (3.41)$$

The first method, relative output, assigns common cost to each output in proportion to that output's fraction of total output. This method requires some common denominator that allows different outputs to be summed. Weight or volume of freight are possibilities for a railroad. The second method, attributable cost, assigns common costs in proportion to the costs that can be unambiguously attributed to that product. Finally, the third method, gross revenue, assigns common costs in proportion to the revenues generated by all the outputs.

### Limitations of FDC prices

On efficiency grounds, there are some immediate drawbacks to (3.39)–(3.41). Marginal costs do not appear in these identities. Thus, one of the cornerstones of efficient pricing is completely omitted from consideration. There is also circular reasoning applied. For example, revenues will be determined by the prices charged, but according to (3.41), the prices charged are to be determined by previous revenues collected. The acceptance of the resultant prices, then, requires that past prices were acceptable.

Another important drawback is that attempts to detect cross-subsidization become meaningless. The key in detecting cross-subsidies is to have a useful definition of the cost of producing an output. Without being precise, note for now that cross-subsidization occurs when the total revenue generated by one output does not cover the total marginal cost of producing that output. Therefore, the consumers of the output must be receiving subsidies from consumers of other outputs if the firm is financially viable. An important problem with cross-subsidies is that they invite entry from other firms into the markets where the subsidies are being collected. On efficiency grounds, such entry is clearly undesirable if the multiproduct firm is a natural monopoly.

The point is that a proper definition of cross-subsidies, based on marginal cost, will signal a firm or regulator about the possibilities for entry. However, when (3.39)–(3.41) are used in the definition of cross-subsidies, the signal is meaningless. If (3.38) is satisfied for all $i$, then the ICC or FCC may claim that there are no cross-subsidies, but the $f_i$ are chosen arbitrarily, so how can the satisfaction of (3.38) have any bearing, other than by chance, on market conditions and threats of entry? To be sure, Ramsey pricing is not a panacea in eliminating cross-subsidies either; there is no guarantee that a Ramsey price for output $i$ will generate revenue in excess of even the unambiguously assignable costs, $C_i(q_i)$. This problem involving the sustainability of natural monopolies is taken up in Chapter 7.

Returning to the FDC methods, suppose the firm is required to break even, and there are to be no cross-subsidies in the sense that (3.38) must hold. This implies

$$\sum_{i=1}^{n} [R_i(q_i) - C_i(q_i)] = \sum_{i=1}^{n} f_i CC = CC \qquad (3.42)$$

because the sum over $n$ of all $f_i$ must equal 1 for each method. Equation (3.42) and inequalities (3.38) together require

$$R_i(q_i) - C_i(q_i) = f_i \text{CC}, \qquad i = 1, \ldots, n \qquad (3.43)$$

or

$$\frac{R_i(q_i) - C_i(q_i)}{R_j(q_j) - C_j(q_j)} = \frac{f_i}{f_j} \qquad i, j = 1, \ldots, n \qquad (3.44)$$

By substituting (3.39)–(3.41) into (3.44) for the $f$'s, we can obtain expressions for these three FDC pricing methods. The results for all $i$ and $j$ are

(1)  Relative output: $\quad \dfrac{p_i(q_i) - C_i(q_i)/q_i}{p_j(q_j) - C_j(q_j)/q_j} = 1 \qquad (3.45)$

(2)  Attributable cost: $\quad \dfrac{p_i(q_i)}{C_i(q_i)/q_i} = \dfrac{p_j(q_j)}{C_j(q_j)/q_j} \qquad (3.46)$

(3)  Gross revenue: $\quad \dfrac{p_i(q_i)}{C_i(q_i)/q_i} = \dfrac{p_j(q_j)}{C_j(q_j)/q_j} \qquad (3.47)$

Note that methods (2) and (3) yield the same pricing rule in the case with zero profits. The relative-output method requires the markup of price over average attributable cost to be the same across all outputs. The other two methods require that the ratio of price to average attributable cost be the same across all outputs.

Following Braeutigam, these price formulas can be compared to Ramsey price rules. We shall do this for methods (2) and (3), leaving method (1) for the reader. Let

$$A_i = C_i(q_i)/q_i C_i'(q_i) \qquad (3.48)$$

where $A_i$ is the *elasticity of scale* for output $i$, and where the prime indicates a derivative. Assuming that none of the common cost, CC, varies with any output, then $C_i'(q_i) = \text{MC}_i$, which is marginal cost. Substituting (3.48) into (3.46) or (3.47) yields

$$\frac{p_i}{p_j} = \frac{A_i \text{MC}_i}{A_j \text{MC}_j} \qquad (3.49)$$

where function arguments have been dropped for convenience. Rewrite (3.49) as

$$p_i = \frac{p_j A_i \mathrm{MC}_i}{A_j \mathrm{MC}_j}$$

then write

$$
\begin{aligned}
\frac{p_i - \mathrm{MC}_i}{p_i} &= \frac{p_j A_i \mathrm{MC}_i}{p_i A_j \mathrm{MC}_j} - \frac{\mathrm{MC}_i}{p_i} \\
&= \frac{p_j A_i \mathrm{MC}_i}{p_i A_j \mathrm{MC}_j} \frac{p_j - \mathrm{MC}_j}{p_j} - \frac{\mathrm{MC}_i}{p_i} + \frac{A_i \mathrm{MC}_i \mathrm{MC}_j}{p_i A_j \mathrm{MC}_j}
\end{aligned}
\tag{3.50}
$$

The first fraction on the right-hand side equals 1, by (3.49). Thus, multiplying both sides of (3.50) by the price elasticities, $e_i e_j$, yields

$$\frac{p_i - \mathrm{MC}_i}{p_i} e_i e_j = \frac{p_j - \mathrm{MC}_j}{p_j} e_i e_j - \frac{\mathrm{MC}_i}{p_i}\left[1 - \frac{A_i}{A_j}\right] e_i e_j \tag{3.51}$$

Now, from (3.6a), we know that Ramsey prices satisfy

$$k_i = \frac{p_i - \mathrm{MC}_i}{p_i} e_i = \frac{p_j - \mathrm{MC}_j}{p_j} e_j = k_j \tag{3.52}$$

where $k_i$ is the Ramsey number for output $i$. Substituting these Ramsey numbers into (3.51) yields

$$k_j = k_i \frac{e_i}{e_j} - e_i \frac{\mathrm{MC}_i}{p_i}\left[1 - \frac{A_i}{A_j}\right] \tag{3.53}$$

Therefore, (3.53) illustrates that, in general, for the attributable-cost and gross-revenue FDC pricing methods, the Ramsey numbers will not be equal. Consequently, these FDC methods are not efficient in that the prices can be changed, and welfare increased, while maintaining zero profit.

Examining (3.53) reveals the nature of the output biases of FDC prices relative to Ramsey prices. First, if $e_i = e_j$ and $A_i = A_j$, these FDC prices are equivalent to Ramsey prices. Barring this unlikely case, suppose $A_i = A_j$, so that

$$\frac{k_i}{k_j} = \frac{e_i}{e_j}$$

Then we can say that in the market with greater demand elasticity, the absolute value of the Ramsey number will be too large.[11] Accordingly, price should be lowered in the more elastic market. If $A_i \neq A_j$, then (3.53) suggests that if "service $i$ has the more elastic demand and a scale elasticity no less than that of $j$, then $k_i < k_j$. Note that if the absolute value of elasticity of demand is monotonically nonincreasing in each market as output increases, then a lower price in any market will reduce the corresponding Ramsey number. Thus, a relative price change that would improve efficiency without affecting overall profits would be a reduction in $p_i$ relative to $p_j$" (Braeutigam, 1980, p. 189). Generally, for FDC methods (2) and (3), there will be a bias away from producing outputs with more elastic demands. The case of the FDC method (1) is slightly more involved, and a description of the inherent biases can be found in Braeutigam (1980).[12]

### A numerical example

Before leaving this section, we present a numerical example that illustrates the relationship between marginal-cost, profit-maximizing, Ramsey, and FDC prices. Suppose a two-product firm has costs given by

$$C(q) = 6q_1 + 8q_2 - 0.2q_1q_2 + 80 \tag{3.54}$$

The reader can verify that this cost function is subadditive; thus, the firm is a natural monopoly. The demands for the firm's out-

---

11 Braeutigam points out that the method used by the ICC to estimate costs results in $A_i = A_j$, because marginal attributable costs are taken to be constant.

12 Sappington (1983) points out that when the regulator has incomplete information about the firm's costs, Ramsey prices may no longer be optimal (see Sections 3.5 and 12.4). An interesting question is whether or not any of the FDC methods can constitute an optimum regulatory strategy under limited information.

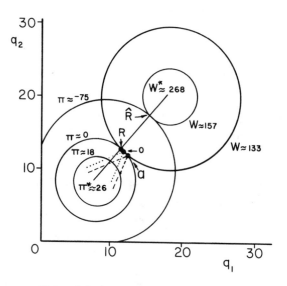

Figure 3.5. An example of Ramsey and FDC outputs.

put are independent and are given by

$$p_1(q_1) = -q_1 + 20 \tag{3.55}$$

and

$$p_2(q_2) = -0.8q_2 + 20 \tag{3.56}$$

Profit is given by

$$\pi = p_1(q_1)q_1 + p_2(q_2)q_2 - C(q) \tag{3.57}$$

and welfare is given by

$$W = \int_0^{q_1} p_1(q_1)\,dq_1 + \int_0^{q_2} p_2(q_2)\,dq_2 - C(q) \tag{3.58}$$

where consumer surplus measures consumers' well-being. Maximizing (3.57) over $q_1$ and $q_2$ yields $\pi^* \cong 26$, which is plotted at $q_1 = 7.8$ and $q_2 = 8.5$ in Figure 3.5. Maximizing (3.58) over $q_1$ and $q_2$ yields $W^* = 268$, which is plotted at $q_1 = 17.9$ and $q_2 =$

19.5 in Figure 3.5. Three isoprofit and two isowelfare contours are also plotted and labeled by the appropriate values of profit and welfare, respectively. The welfare-maximum point represents the marginal-cost pricing solution, and, as expected, profit is negative, so that the firm is a strong natural monopoly.

The line connecting $\pi^*$ and $W^*$ represents those quantities that satisfy the equation

$$e_1 \frac{p_1 - MC_1}{p_1} = e_2 \frac{p_2 - MC_2}{p_2} \qquad (3.59)$$

This has the same form as the Ramsey solution in (3.6a), but the Ramsey solution must also satisfy $\pi = 0$. This occurs only at point $R$ in Figure 3.5. As we move along the line from $\pi^*$ to $W^*$, profit (welfare) monotonically decreases (increases). The line is also the locus of tangency points between the isoprofit and isowelfare contours. This follows from the definition of Ramsey prices: They are prices that maximize welfare subject to a fixed profit. The Ramsey solution will be on the highest isowelfare contour that touches the $\pi = 0$ isoprofit contour: the tangency point $R$. Suppose we calculate Ramsey prices that maximize welfare subject to a fixed profit, not necessarily zero. Then if profit is constrained to, say, $-75$, the Ramsey solution will be on the highest isowelfare contour that touches the $\pi = -75$ isoprofit contour. This is the tangency point $\hat{R}$. The points on the line connecting $\pi^*$ and $W^*$ will be referred to as the set of Ramsey solutions. Clearly, any regulator-mandated solution focusing on allocative efficiency should at least be on this line, if not at $R$.

The FDC pricing solutions can be calculated using (3.38)–(3.41). For example, for the relative-output method, let $i = 1$, and take (3.38) as an equality, with $f_i$ substituted out using (3.39). Then (3.38) is a quadratic in $q_1$ for a fixed $q_2$. Solving this quadratic for $q_1$, given various values of $q_2$, yields the lower dotted curve emanating from point 0 on the $\pi = 0$ isoprofit contour. This curve represents all output combinations that satisfy the FDC relative-output method with revenue from output 1 just equal to its FDC. The upper dotted curve is similar in that it is derived from the relative output method, but has revenue from output 2 just equal to its FDC. Point 0 is where profit is zero and each output generates just enough revenue to cover its FDC. In other words, (3.43) is satisfied for $i = 1, 2$. The area between the two dotted curves represents output combinations for which profit is positive and each output is generating revenue in excess of its FDC. A similar procedure using the attributable-cost method yields point $a$ for zero profit, and the two dashed lines for positive profit. Because (3.46) and (3.47) are identical, the gross-revenue method also yields point $a$ for zero profit, but a different set of lines, not pictured, would emanate from point $a$.

The important observation is that when the firm must break even, all of the FDC methods are inferior to the Ramsey solution, because they are on lower isowelfare contours. In this example, there is a bias toward producing more of good 1 and less of good 2, given the demand and scale elasticities. In general, however, we cannot say where points 0 and $a$ will be relative to point $R$, and they may even be on either side. If the regulator allows positive profit, then there are points in common between FDC pricing and the set of Ramsey prices. Cole (1981) shows that in some special circumstances, a combination of the attributable-cost and relative-output methods can yield Ramsey prices. By allowing variable cost to depend on the level of common costs, Cabe (1988) illustrates that virtually any output vector can be achieved by some FDC method. However, in general, it would seem fortuitous if the regulator, intent on using FDC methods, should happen to select a method or combination of methods that had at least some attractive properties based on efficiency. We shall return to cost-allocation issues in Chapter 11, where we discuss partially regulated firms. Partial regulation complicates the problem when the regulator is intent on allocating common cost to both regulated and unregulated outputs.

## 3.7. Summary

Ramsey pricing by a multiproduct strong natural monopolist involves balancing marginal welfare reductions across products as prices are raised above marginal costs to make the firm financially viable. Such second-best pricing means higher prices for consumers with relatively inelastic demands – raising questions for regulators who are concerned with fairness. By legislative mandate or political persuasion, regulators may sacrifice allocative efficiency through Ramsey prices as they seek to protect consumers from monopoly exploitation; furthermore, Ramsey prices need not be subsidy-free, which further complicates their use. Nevertheless, the application of Ramsey principles across product lines and/or over time at least identifies the losses arising from the introduction of concerns other than efficiency.

When cross-elasticities among the natural monopolist's products and between his products and other products are included in an optimum pricing model, a general but complex Ramsey pricing rule results. It becomes necessary to take into account price-marginal cost deviations for substitute and complementary products. Also, models were presented to develop pricing rules in the presence of competition, where a dominant firm faces a competitive fringe. The role of entry restrictions was shown to be especially important. Under some circumstances, total deregulation comes close to achieving the outcomes of the partially regulated second best – while avoiding the administrative costs of regulation. Next, a model of rivalry among strong natural monopolists allowed us to focus on demand interdependencies. Ramsey-like outcomes need not involve zero excess profits for each firm when cross-elasticities are taken into account. However, transfer payments among firms result in a single Ramsey number for all firms – yielding a Pareto-superior outcome. Design of such transfers represents a challenge for regulatory policy-makers.

Some analysts argue that second-best considerations, jurisdictional boundaries, and information requirements limit the applicability of these Ramsey pricing principles. Nevertheless, we conclude that these principles warrant the thoughtful attention of regulators. Alternatives such as FDC pricing avoid the need to calculate elasticities and marginal costs, but only by ignoring demands and resorting to arbitrary cost-allocation schemes. Neither efficiency nor fairness need be promoted by FDC prices.

In the next chapter, we explore other pricing methods available to regulators to promote efficiency and equity. To do so, however, we abandon linear prices for nonlinear prices, and this introduces new complications as well as opportunities.

# 4

# Efficient pricing using nonlinear prices

The availability of a wider range of price structures can significantly improve resource allocation when the firm is constrained to a particular profit level. As in the previous chapter, we assume that the firm is a strong natural monopoly, so that marginal-cost pricing results in a deficit. Unlike in the previous chapter, however, we allow for more flexibility in the candidate pricing methods by considering nonliner prices. Linear prices now become special cases. Consider the most straightforward and widely studied nonlinear pricing method: the *uniform two-part tariff*. Such tariffs consist of a constant price for each unit purchased and an access (license or entry) fee for the privilege of purchasing any positive quantity. The uniformity refers to the fact that the fee is the same for all purchasing consumers. Thus, the total charge to a consumer purchasing $q$ units is

$$pq + t \tag{4.1}$$

where $t$ is the access fee, and $p$ the unit price. Obviously, if $t = 0$, we are back to linear pricing.

Uniform two-part tariffs and other, more complex nonlinear pricing methods are prevalent in the economy. A consumer may pay a daily charge when renting a car and then a price per mile thereafter. At a ballpark, the consumer might pay a cover charge for entry, followed by a price per each concession good once

103

inside. Or, in the case of public utilities, the electricity, gas, or telephone customer might pay a flat monthly charge in addition to a price per kilowatt-hours of electricity, per cubic foot of gas, or per minute of telephone usage.

Utilities often go further and adopt block tariffs or multipart tariffs. For example, electric utilities have used *declining block tariffs,* where the marginal price paid decreases in steps as the quantity purchased increases. Accordingly, a generalization of (4.1) would be a method using an access fee and multiple unit prices. The consumer purchasing $q$ pays

$$p_1 q + t \quad \text{if } 0 < q \le q_1$$
$$p_2(q - q_1) + p_1 q_1 + t \quad \text{if } q_1 < q \le q_2$$
$$p_3(q - q_2) + p_2(q_2 - q_1) + p_1 q_1 + t \quad \text{if } q_2 < q \le q_3$$
$$\cdot$$
$$\cdot$$
$$\cdot$$

If $p_1 > p_2 > p_3 \ldots$ , then the cost-recovery method involves a declining block tariff. Some variations in this structure, with marginal prices changing nonmonotonically with output, permit the firm to capture additional revenue while approaching universal service. We discuss these types of tariffs in Section 4.6.

Note that nonuniform two-part tariffs, where $t$ varies across consumers, can also be observed, but are less prevalent. For example, some ballparks have ladies day, where the admission for women is reduced. The problem with such two-part tariffs is that they are discriminatory; they may be and sometimes are challenged in court. Thus, they are less attractive to firms. In all that follows, when we discuss two-part tariffs we are referring to uniform two-part tariffs unless otherwise noted. Discriminatory tariffs are taken up in Section 4.3.

The origin of these pricing methods dates back at least to the Hopkinson electricity tariff (1892), which distinguished between costs that were dependent on use and costs that were independent of use. The tariff structure associated with Hopkinson priced usage (kilowatt-hours, KWH) and maximum instantaneous demand (kilowatts, KW) separately. So, in a sense, Hopkinson viewed the two as different products to be priced differently. We now are more aware that price signals for kilowatt-hour usage have implications for kilowatt capacity; so a Hopkinson-like tariff should account for this interplay. Note that the original tariff also contained a separate monthly fee for costs of the distribution system and administration, because these costs are determined by the number of consumers, rather than by usage or capacity.

Lewis (1941) discussed the advantages of two-part tariffs for avoiding the potentially distorting effects of taxes raised to subsidize natural monopolies engaged in marginal-cost pricing, and Coase (1946) suggested setting the unit price equal to marginal cost while letting the access fees cover any deficit. Gabor (1955) also made an important point when he demonstrated that any multipart pricing structure for a given consumer can always be restructured as a two-part tariff without a loss of revenue or consumer surplus. The modern treatment of two-part tariffs begins with Oi's seminal paper (1971), in which he examines an optimum two-part tariff for a profit-maximizing monopolist. Many authors since Oi have generalized his results and, more important for our purposes, applied newly developed analytical techniques to the welfare maximizing firm.[1]

In the first section of this chapter, we cover the basic rationale for two-part tariffs in a welfare-maximizing framework. The second section contains a model that is useful in highlighting the major considerations and results regarding an optimum tariff structure. Section 4.3 addresses discriminatory tariffs, and Section 4.4 examines the concept of stability of these pricing methods. In Section 4.5, a voluntary two-part tariff is introduced that is Pareto-superior to linear pricing methods. In Section 4.6, we extend the Pareto-superiority theme to multipart tariffs. Section 4.7 is a summary.

---

1 A useful survey appears in Lapinski (1974).

### 4.1. The rationale for two-part tariffs

The first-best solution to the public utility regulation problem is to set prices equal to marginal cost and cover the resultant deficit with true lump-sum taxes. These taxes are judged to be elusive at best; so another approach is required. If the regulator is restricted to linear prices, Ramsey pricing, as discussed in the previous chapter, is the answer so long as it does not induce entry (see Chapter 7). If we lift the linear price restriction, what other pricing methods might the regulator consider?

The two-part tariff is one possibility. In fact, it would appear that we can have our cake and eat it too. We can set price equal to marginal cost and then cover the resultant deficit with the access-fee portion of the tariff. The access fee acts as the lump-sum tax in the first-best solution. Pricing becomes nonlinear in the sense that the consumer is paying more than marginal cost for inframarginal units because of the access fee. If no potential consumers are excluded by the fee, this structure does not violate the first-best solution, because only the marginal unit needs to be sold at marginal cost. Indeed, even a perfectly discriminating, profit-maximizing monopolist is compatible with a first-best solution. He charges a lower price for each successive unit sold up to the final unit, which is sold at marginal cost. In this way he extracts all consumer surplus in order to maximize profit. In a similar way, the welfare-maximizing regulator uses the access fee of the two-part tariff to extract consumer surplus. However, she needs to extract only enough consumer surplus to cover the deficit resulting from selling all units at marginal cost; see Figure 4.1, where price equals marginal cost, and declining average cost is linear. The fee ($t$) times the number of consumers ($s$) amounts to area *bcef* or area *aef,* the deficit that arises under marginal-cost pricing.

Unfortunately, designing optimum two-part tariffs is not likely to be as simple as just described. In the first place, the access fee is not a legitimate lump-sum tax, because it does create distortions in the system. It is not levied on all consumers in the econ-

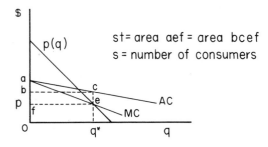

Figure 4.1. Covering the deficit with a fee.

omy, only on those who purchase the natural monopoly good. The size of the fee may affect the final output level, if demand is sensitive to income changes. Basically, Figure 4.1 is drawn assuming a zero income effect. More generally, this is not the case; so the demand curve will not be invariant to different-sized fees. Thus, the location of the marginal unit may change with fee changes, and this possibility must be accounted for by simultaneously solving for an optimum price and access fee. The two then become alternative instruments for manipulating the demand curve in such a way that consumer surplus is maximized after the deficit is covered.

Another problem may arise with two-part tariffs that can complicate an optimum schedule. Some consumers who are willing to pay marginal cost, or even some price higher than marginal cost, may be forced out of the market because the access fee exceeds their remaining consumer surplus. Their gain from trade will be negative under the two-part tariff; therefore, they purchase zero units. This phenomenon means that the optimum price might depart from marginal cost. Perhaps with a slightly higher price, the access fee can be lowered enough to entice some consumers back into the market. To explore the trade-offs between price and the access fee, we need to derive expressions not only for the usual price elasticity but also for elasticities that reveal the sensitivity of market participation to prices and access fees.

Before presenting a model of the two-part tariff, we should discuss in some detail the cost structure of the firm. Unless stated otherwise, we assume that the firm is a single-product, strong natural monopoly. By using a two-part tariff, the firm can cover the deficit resulting from per-unit pricing, where the unit price may not be equal to marginal cost in the two-part tariff. We regard the access fee as an amount that must be paid for the privilege of consuming the firm's output. The cost to the firm of providing this privilege is taken to be zero. Thus, we write the cost function as $C(Q)$, where $Q$ is the firm's output.

This cost structure can be viewed differently, however. Suppose the access fee must be paid for more than just the *privilege* of consuming the firm's output. That is, there may be some physical output that the consumer obtains. Examples include the linkages between the consumer's home and a public utility: Linkages may involve (1) wiring, transformers, and meters for electricity, (2) the pipes and meters for natural gas and water, and (3) access to the telecommunications network via phones, physical lines, and switching units. Now we have a situation similar to that for a two-product firm where one product is purchased in single units only and the other in multiple units. The firm charges two prices for the two products, where one price, the access fee, is a charge per consumer.

Some authors, Schmalensee (1981) and Sherman and Visscher (1982), for example, have presented models in which the cost function for the two outputs is completely separable and the marginal (equal average) costs of both products are constant. If prices are then set at marginal cost, there will be no deficit; yet these authors derive welfare optima in which prices depart from marginal cost. The reason is the special nature of the two products. One of them must be purchased if the other is to be purchased at all. Thus, a consumer who is willing to pay marginal cost for the nonmandatory good, but not for the mandatory good, is priced out of *both* markets. As we shall see in the next section, welfare may be increased by departing from marginal-cost prices and keeping these consumers in the market.

Next, extend the analysis of the two products by dropping constant costs and assuming that setting the per-unit price and access fee to their respective marginal costs creates a deficit. To cover the deficit, we then need to deviate from marginal-cost pricing on one or both of the per-unit charge and access fee. Now it is not only the special nature of the goods that causes the departure from marginal-cost prices but also the deficit dilemma.

This two-product viewpoint adds no additional insights over our single-product presentation, where the consumer will be paying the access charge for a privilege that is costless for the firm to provide. In fact, they are formally identical if the marginal cost of the privilege is zero. Then we are back to a situation where prices depart from marginal cost to cover the deficit, regardless of the consumer exit problem. The two-product viewpoint becomes more interesting if the firm is not a monopoly. In that case there will be strategy involved in setting price and access fees if the firm faces competition. Two-part tariffs in this context have not been fully analyzed, but the general subject of competition and entry is discussed in Chapter 7.

### 4.2. A two-part tariff for a single-product natural monopoly

We assume that a single-product natural monopolist sells his output using a two-part tariff. The monopolist is regulated, and the regulator's objective is to maximize welfare under the constraint that the firm must break even. Again, marginal-cost pricing is a nonviable option because of the resultant deficit. There is a continuous distribution of consumers in the economy who are indexed by $\theta$, where, without loss of generality, $0 \leq \theta \leq 1$.[2] The density function for consumers is given by $f(\theta)$, which the firm is assumed to know. This formulation does not say that the firm can identify particular consumers with a value of $\theta$, but only that the firm knows the distribution of $\theta$ across consumers. The

2 Ng and Weisser (1974) were the first to make the number of consumers a variable in the study of two-part tariffs, and the model presented here is a slightly modified version of their work.

number of consumers of type $\theta^*$ is roughly given by integrating $f(\theta)$ over a small interval around $\theta^*$. Moreover, the total number of consumers in the economy is given by

$$\tilde{s} = \int_0^1 f(\theta) \, d\theta \qquad (4.2)$$

The firm utilizes a two-part tariff of the type given in (4.1). The demand for the firm's output generally will depend on both the unit charge and the access fee, so that we have the demand of consumers of type $\theta^*$ given by

$$q(p, t, y(\theta^*), \theta^*) \qquad (4.3)$$

where $y(\theta^*)$ is the income of consumers of type $\theta^*$. Utility for consumers of type $\theta^*$ will be denoted by the indirect utility function

$$v(p, t, y(\theta^*), \theta^*) \qquad (4.4)$$

and we assume that $\partial v/\partial \theta \leq 0$, so that utility is nonincreasing in the index $\theta$. This simplifies the derivation of the results, because it ensures uniqueness of the marginal consumers, that is, those consumers who are indifferent between remaining in or exiting the market. All marginal consumers will be consuming the same quantities. A $\theta$ value near 1 implies a small demand (for given $p$ and $t$), whereas a $\theta$ value near 0 implies a large demand.

Some authors have assumed that the demand curves for the different consumer types never cross, which is sufficient to ensure uniqueness of the marginal consumers. As the values of $p$ and/or $t$ increase, we expect that some consumer types will exit from the market. If demands do not cross, then an increase in $p$ and a decrease in $t$ that do not cause marginal consumers to exit will also not cause inframarginal consumers to exit.[3] [See Ng and Weisser (1974) for a discussion of the marginal consumers.]

---

3 For example, Renshaw (1985) demonstrated that a two-part tariff (with price greater than marginal cost) could yield less total revenue than a uniform price. His result depends on his demand curves for telephone service crossing at $p =$ MC.

### Derivation of the optimum price and access fee

Given that utility is nonincreasing in $\theta$, consumers with values of $\theta$ above some particular value, say $\hat{\theta}$, will be those who exit the market for a given fee and price. If $\hat{\theta}$ is 1, then no one exits. Because this cutoff value of $\theta$ depends on the price and access fee, we write $\hat{\theta} = \hat{\theta}(p, t)$, and the number of consumers in the market is

$$s = \int_0^{\hat{\theta}(p,\ t)} f(\theta)\ d\theta \tag{4.5}$$

Total output can then be expressed as

$$Q = \int_0^{\hat{\theta}(p,\ t)} q(p, t, y(\theta), \theta)f(\theta)\ d\theta \tag{4.6}$$

and profit for the firm becomes

$$\pi = pQ + ts - C(Q) \tag{4.7}$$

where $C(Q)$ is the cost function. The regulator's measure of consumer welfare is

$$V = \int_0^{\hat{\theta}(p,\ t)} w(\theta)v(p, t, y(\theta), \theta)f(\theta)\ d\theta \tag{4.8}$$

where $w(\theta)$ weights utilities according to their marginal social value. Maximizing (4.8) ensures a Pareto optimum, or any Pareto optimum will maximize (4.8) under a suitable weighting of utilities (Davis and Whinston, 1965). The constrained maximization problem can now be written as

$$\max_{p,t,\lambda} L = V + \lambda\pi \tag{4.9}$$

where $\lambda$ is a multiplier for the break-even constraint.

The first-order necessary conditions for a maximum are

$$L_p = V_p + \lambda[Q + p\partial Q/\partial p + t\partial s/\partial p - \text{MC}\partial Q/\partial p] = 0 \tag{4.10}$$
$$L_t = V_t + \lambda[s + p\partial Q/\partial t + t\partial s/\partial t - \text{MC}\partial Q/\partial t] = 0 \tag{4.11}$$
$$L_\lambda = pQ + ts - C = 0 \tag{4.12}$$

Subscripts in (4.10)–(4.12) denote partials, MC denotes marginal cost of output, and functional arguments have been eliminated to avoid clutter. Referring to (4.5) and (4.6), the partial terms in brackets in (4.10) and (4.11) are

$$\frac{\partial Q}{\partial p} = \frac{\partial \hat{\theta}}{\partial p} q(p, t, y(\hat{\theta}), \hat{\theta}) f(\hat{\theta}) + \int_0^{\hat{\theta}} \frac{\partial q}{\partial p} f(\theta) \, d\theta = \hat{\theta}_p \hat{q} + Q_p \quad (4.13)$$

$$\frac{\partial Q}{\partial t} = \frac{\partial \hat{\theta}}{\partial t} q(p, t, y(\hat{\theta}), \hat{\theta}) f(\hat{\theta}) + \int_0^{\hat{\theta}} \frac{\partial q}{\partial t} f(\theta) \, d\theta = \hat{\theta}_t \hat{q} + Q_t \quad (4.14)$$

$$\frac{\partial s}{\partial p} = \frac{\partial \hat{\theta}}{\partial p} f(\hat{\theta}) = \hat{\theta}_p \quad (4.15)$$

$$\frac{\partial s}{\partial t} = \frac{\partial \hat{\theta}}{\partial t} f(\hat{\theta}) = \hat{\theta}_t \quad (4.16)$$

where, again, subscripts denote partials. Note that $q$ is the quantity consumed by the marginal consumers: those consumers who derive zero utility from consumption. Any increase in $p$ or $t$ will drive them out of the market. The terms $\hat{\theta}_p$ and $\hat{\theta}_t$ represent the changes in the number of consumers in the market as $p$ and $t$ change, respectively.

Next we have

$$V_p = \hat{\theta}_p w(\hat{\theta}) v(p, t, y(\hat{\theta}) f(\hat{\theta}) + \int_0^{\hat{\theta}} w(\theta) v_p(p, t, y(\theta), \theta) f(\theta) \, d\theta$$

which reduces to

$$V_p = \int_0^{\hat{\theta}} w(\theta) v_p f(\theta) \, d\theta \quad (4.17)$$

because the utility of the marginal consumer is zero. From each consumer's utility-maximization problem we can obtain (using the envelope theorem)

$$v_p(p, t, y(\theta), \theta) = -v_y(\theta) q(p, t, y(\theta), \theta) \quad (4.18)$$

where $v_y(\theta)$ is the marginal utility of income to consumers of type

$\theta$. Also, we note that the access fee is equivalent to a reduction in income, so that

$$v_y = -v_t \tag{4.19}$$

Now, if we assume that income distribution problems can be ignored, or that the present income distribution is acceptable, then, following Negishi (1960),

$$w(\theta) = 1/v_y(\theta) \tag{4.20}$$

which states that each consumer's utility in (4.8) is weighted by the reciprocal of his marginal utility of income.[4] Substituting (4.18) and (4.20) into (4.17) yields

$$V_p = -\int_0^{\hat{\theta}} q(p, t, y(\theta), \theta)f(\theta) \, d\theta = -Q \tag{4.21}$$

In a similar fashion, using (4.19) and (4.20), we can obtain

$$
\begin{aligned}
V_t &= \hat{\theta}_t w(\hat{\theta})v(p, t, y(\hat{\theta}), \hat{\theta})f(\hat{\theta}) \\
&\quad + \int_0^{\hat{\theta}} w(\theta)v_t(p, t, y(\theta), \theta)f(\theta) \, d\theta \\
&= -\int_0^{\hat{\theta}} f(\theta) \, d\theta \\
&= -s
\end{aligned}
\tag{4.22}
$$

Substituting (4.21), (4.22), and (4.13)–(4.16) into (4.10) and

---

4 Thus, consumers with high (low) marginal utilities of income are assigned low (high) weights. The result is that if an extra dollar becomes available in the economy to be distributed to some consumer, the additional welfare generated will be invariant to which consumer receives the dollar. The consumer who receives the dollar is better off by his marginal utility of income, but in the social welfare function this marginal utility is weighted by its reciprocal, so that the result is 1. This is true for all consumers. Therefore, income distribution does not matter. Note that when we use consumer surplus (without weights) as a welfare measure, this is again true, because implicitly a dollar to one consumer is valued the same as a dollar to any other consumer. See Sherman (1989), who shows that a market outcome implicitly weights individual utilities in this manner.

(4.11), we can combine the latter two expressions to eliminate terms and obtain

$$[p - \text{MC}][S + \hat{q}[\hat{\theta}_p - \overline{q}\hat{\theta}_t]] + t[\hat{\theta}_p - \overline{q}\hat{\theta}_t] = 0 \qquad (4.23)$$

where $\overline{q} = Q/s$, the average consumption of consumers in the market, and $S = Q_p + \overline{q}Q_y$, the Slutsky term. Next, the first-order condition (4.12) can be rewritten as

$$[p - \text{MC}]Q + ts = C - \text{MC} \cdot Q = D \qquad (4.24)$$

where $D$ can be thought of as a deficit resulting from marginal-cost pricing. Equations (4.23) and (4.24) are two equations in the two unknowns $p - \text{MC}$ and $t$. Letting $Z = \hat{\theta}_p - \overline{q}\hat{\theta}_t$ in (4.23) and solving the two equations yields

$$p - \text{MC} = \frac{-ZD}{s(S + qZ) - QZ} \qquad (4.25)$$

$$t = \frac{(S + \hat{q}Z)D}{s(S + \hat{q}Z) - QZ} \qquad (4.26)$$

### Interpreting the price and access fee

The interpretation of (4.25) and (4.26) is straightforward once we examine the value of $Z$. Applying Roy's identity to the marginal consumers implies $v_p/v_t = \hat{q}$. Thus, to keep the marginal consumers' utility unchanged, the ratio of changes in $p$ and $t$ must equal $q$, or $dt/dp = -\hat{q}$. The minus follows because the changes in $p$ and $t$ must be in opposite directions. Next, holding the number of consumers fixed and totally differentiating $\hat{\theta}(p, t)$ yields $dt/dp = -\hat{\theta}_p/\hat{\theta}_t$. Combining these observations, we obtain for the marginal consumers

$$\hat{\theta}_p - \hat{q}\hat{\theta}_t = 0 \qquad (4.27)$$

The following two results can now be stated.

> *Result 1:* If the marginal consumers are insensitive to changes in the access fee or price, that is, $\hat{\theta}_p = \hat{\theta}_t = 0$, then, for welfare maximization, $p = \text{MC}$, and $t = D/s$.

This follows because $\hat{\theta}_p = \hat{\theta}_t = 0$ implies $Z = 0$. Substituting this into (4.25) and (4.26) provides the stated result. Result 1 captures the basic idea discussed in the introduction of this chapter. With two-part tariffs, we can salvage marginal-cost pricing by covering any deficit with the access fee.

Regulatory concern for equity arises from the possibility that the access fee may be too high and may drive some consumers from the market. Result 1 applies to those situations in which no consumers are driven away; therefore, we can adhere to marginal-cost prices. For a good such as electricity (which is virtually a necessity), where the access fee may not be viewed as too high by almost all consumers, this case probably applies. Certainly, the almost universal use of electricity attests to this. Alternatively, the telephone probably is viewed as a nonnecessity by some consumers, and they will be sensitive to access fees. Not surprisingly, household telephone penetration in the United States in 1980 was about 93 percent, varying across states.

> *Result 2:* Suppose the marginal consumers are sensitive to price and access-fee changes, so that $\hat{\theta}_p < 0$ and $\hat{\theta}_t < 0$. Then the sign of $p - $ MC will be the same as the sign of $\overline{q} - \hat{q}$. Also, if $p - $ MC $\leq 0$, then $t = D/s > 0$, and if $p > $ MC, then $t \geq 0$.

To show the relationship between price and marginal cost, substitute (4.27) for $Z$ in (4.26) and rearrange to obtain

$$\frac{[p - \text{MC}]Q}{D} = \frac{e_\theta \overline{q}[\overline{q} - \hat{q}]}{e_p q \overline{q} + e_\theta[\overline{q} - \hat{q}]^2} \tag{4.28}$$

where $$e_p = S_p/Q < 0 \tag{4.29}$$

is the compensated demand elasticity and $e_\theta = \hat{\theta}_p p/s$ is the price elasticity of the number of consumers in the market. This latter elasticity is also the access-fee elasticity when written $e_\theta = \theta_t p \hat{q}/s$, by (4.29). Thus, $e_\theta$ is a measure of the sensitivity of the marginal consumer to price and access-fee changes, and we refer to it as the *market-participation elasticity*. If the marginal consumers are sensitive, so that $e_\theta < 0$, then the first part of the result follows by (4.29). For the second part of the result, consider that $t > 0$ for $p \le$ MC follows from the budget constraint and the fact that marginal-cost pricing creates a deficit. That $t \ge 0$ for $p >$ MC can be shown by assuming the reverse. If $t < 0$, consumers would be subsidized for consumption, and we would have $e_\theta = 0$, because no one would exit the market. But $e_\theta = 0$ implies $Z = 0$, and then $t = D/s$, from (4.26). This contradicts our premise that $t < 0$.

Result 2 tells us that a necessary condition for deviations from marginal-cost pricing is that increases in either the price or access fee cause some consumers to exit the market. (It is not a sufficient condition, because $p =$ MC when $\bar{q} = \hat{q}$, regardless of the value of $e_\theta$.) To illustrate this, consider a situation in which $p =$ MC, but too many consumers would exit if confronted with the access fee that is needed to cover the deficit. Optimality may require raising price above marginal cost and lowering the access fee to keep consumers in the market. Note the importance here of $\bar{q} = \hat{q}$, average consumption minus the consumption of the marginal consumer. Price can be raised above marginal cost only if $\bar{q} > \hat{q}$, because only then will there be sufficient revenues generated by the higher price on inframarginal consumers to cover the losses incurred from lowering the access fee.

Littlechild (1975b) makes two important points regarding low access fees. First, a profit-maximizer may also have an incentive to charge a low access fee in order to entice more consumers into the market. If so, the loss of profit on the access fee will be more than made up for by the profits from increased sales. Thus, for public utilities that set low access fees, "profit maximization may be a more plausible explanation than the 'social considerations' often adduced" (p. 666). Second, Littlechild adds to the analysis the possibility that consumers may generate positive externalities on entering the market. Telephone consumers provide an example. They enlarge the size of the system on entering and make any one telephone more valuable, because more consumers can be called. In this case, the access fee should be reduced by the value

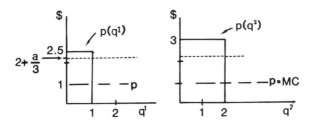

Figure 4.2. Fees and per-unit price.

of the externality generated on entry, where the value will depend on the number of consumers in the system.[5]

In a corner solution, we can have $p >$ MC and $t = 0$. Figure 4.2 illustrates this possibility in a simple case using consumer-surplus arguments and assuming zero income effects. Two consumers, labeled 1 and 2, have perfectly inelastic demand curves, as shown. When $p =$ MC $= 1$, demands are $q^1 = 1$ and $q^2 = 2$, and the deficit equals the fixed cost, which is $3 + a$, where $a$ is a small, positive number. The break-even constraint requires $t = (3 + a)/2$, which will drive consumer 1 out of the market, as the figure makes clear, because $t$ will exceed consumer 1's surplus. Consumer 2 will remain in the market, and welfare will be the area under 2's demand curve minus variable and fixed costs, or $6 - (1)(2) - (3 + a) = 1 - a$. Now suppose that price is raised so that there is no deficit. We will have revenue equal to variable plus fixed costs, or $p^1q^1 + p^2p^2 = 3 + (3 + a)$. Because $q^1 = 1$ and $q^2 = 2$, $P = 2 + a/3$, as shown in Figure 4.2. Welfare has improved to $2.5 + 6 - 3 - (3 + a) = 2.5 - a$ after eliminating the access fee and raising price. Note, too, that $\bar{q} > \hat{q}$, as required by Result 2 for $p >$ MC.

---

5 Oren and Smith (1981) include the demand externality in their comparison of flat rates and three-part tariffs for communications services. The latter facilitate the achievement of a critical mass needed for financial viability; such tariffs can be more efficient both from the standpoint of suppliers and from the standpoint of total welfare.

As Result 2 indicates, there is the possibility that price may be set below marginal cost for optimality. This development can be explained by again starting with a price equal to marginal cost and positive access fees. Suppose that very few consumers can be enticed into the marketplace by lowering the access fee, but many more can be enticed in by lowering the price below marginal cost. These consumers will have flat demand curves with relatively large quantities demanded. A lower price means considerably more surplus, because the additional quantity demanded will be large, with flat demand curves. The revenues lost from inframarginal consumers will not be too great, because $\overline{q} < \hat{q}$. Therefore, the lost revenues can be covered by an increase in the access fee without driving out other consumers. The crucial role of $\overline{q} - \hat{q}$ in this analysis is noteworthy. As Schmalensee (1981) states, "it is interesting to learn that $\overline{q} - \hat{q}$ is a sufficient statistic for general demand patterns." From a policy perspective this is encouraging, because information on $\overline{q}$ and $q$ should be readily available.[6]

### Distributional weights

If the existing income distribution is not considered acceptable and therefore is not treated as a given, then the foregoing results must be modified. Suppose the license fee is viewed as a regressive head tax that places too much burden on low-income consumers. The regulator may choose to remedy the sit-

---

6 Phillips and Battalio (1983) point out that when buyers can purchase from the monopolist more than once per period, they can increase the number of visits and decrease the consumption per visit. The ability to substitute between the visits and consumption reduces the amount of surplus that can be extracted through a two-part tariff. Thus, besides buyer heterogeneity, costs of repeat visits become a determinant of the tariff structure. If visits are perfect substitutes for consumption per visit, the profit-maximizing fixed fee is zero. Alternatively, if visits are insensitive to the per-unit price, a high fee is profitable, with consumers buying a relatively large amount of output per visit. Visitors to Disney World who are vacationers cannot substitute between visits and output per visit; so that price structure involves a high entry fee and zero marginal price. For "local" amusement parks (with repeat buyers), such substitutability implies a low fee and positive price per ride for profit maximization.

uation by balancing pricing efficiency with distributional equity. Feldstein (1972a) demonstrates how this might be accomplished. His model does not allow for a variable number of consumers; however, we can demonstrate his main result using the variable-consumer model. The regulator now differentially weights consumer utilities so that (4.20) need no longer hold. That is, the regulator does not take as given the existing income distribution; instead, she actively pursues a redistribution policy according to some notion of equity. In this case, instead of (4.21) and (4.22), we obtain

$$V_p = \int_0^{\hat{\theta}} w(\theta)v_y(\theta)q(p, t, y(\theta), \theta)f(\theta)\,d\theta \qquad (4.30)$$

and

$$V_t = \int_0^{\hat{\theta}} w(\theta)v_y(\theta)f(\theta)\,d\theta \qquad (4.31)$$

Following the same procedure used earlier to eliminate $\lambda$ from the first-order conditions (4.10) and (4.11), where this time we use (4.30) and (4.31) instead of (4.21) and (4.22), respectively, the new result that replaces (4.23) is

$$[p - \text{MC}][V_p[Q_t - \hat{\theta}_t\hat{q}] - V_t[Q_p - \hat{\theta}_p\hat{q}]]$$
$$- t[V_p\hat{\theta}_t - V_t\hat{\theta}_p] = QV_t - sV_p \quad (4.32)$$

In keeping with Feldstein's fixed number of consumers and zero income elasticity, we set $\hat{\theta}_t = \hat{\theta}_p = 0$ and $Q_t = 0$, respectively, Then, by combining (4.32) with the budget constraint (4.24), we can solve for $p - \text{MC}$ to obtain

$$\frac{p - \text{MC}}{p}$$
$$= \frac{1}{e_p} \frac{\int_0^{\hat{\theta}} w(\theta)v_y(\theta)q(p, t, y(\theta), \theta)f(\theta)\,d\theta - \bar{q}\int_0^{\hat{\theta}} w(\theta)v_y(\theta)f(\theta)\,d\theta}{\bar{q}\int_0^{\hat{\theta}} w(\theta)v_y(\theta)f(\theta)\,d\theta}$$
$$(4.33)$$

This expression for the per-unit price is similar to a Ramsey price. To interpret it, note that the price elasticity, $e_p$, is negative, and the denominator of the complex fraction on the right side is positive, so that the sign of $p - $ MC will be opposite to the sign of the numerator of this fraction. The numerator is the covariance across consumers of the quantity demanded and the social marginal utility of income. If we assume a normal good for which demand increases with income, and if the regulator weights more heavily the utilities of low-income consumers, then the covariance is negative, and $p > $ MC. Consumers with higher incomes pay a larger share of the fixed costs, and the access fee can be lowered. For an inferior good, we obtain $p < $ MC. We can also show that $t > 0$ regardless of the price level.

Thus, in order to achieve an equitable two-part tariff, we have derived a price that departs from marginal cost even though the marginal consumers are not sensitive to price changes, and regardless of the relationship between the quantities consumed on average and by the marginal consumer. Of course, the notion of what is equitable is very problematic, and Feldstein demonstrates just one of many possibilities in his choice of the weighting factor $w(\theta)$ in (4.30) and (4.31). Some would argue, too, that a regulator is not in position to choose between equity and efficiency and should concentrate only on the latter (Schmalensee, 1979). From this perspective, equity should be a concern only at some other, more centralized level, not carried out in a piecemeal fashion through the pricing of natural monopoly goods.

### 4.3. Discriminating two-part tariffs

A more direct method of aiding low-income consumers, or any targeted group, is to charge differing access fees across consumers or groups of consumers. We know that attainment of a Pareto optimum does not imply that all consumers in the economy are consuming the good in question. That is, at the optimum, we may have $s \leq \tilde{s}$ regardless of the value of $e_\theta$. Consumers not in the market are spending their incomes on other goods that are left unspecified in the foregoing model. [In the study of Ng

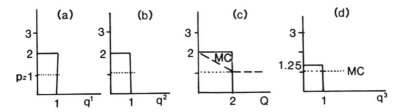

Figure 4.3. Three demanders and a discriminatory fee structure.

and Weisser (1974), a second numeraire good is available.] If consumers are omitted at the optimum, it must be that further reductions in price or the access fee designed to entice omitted consumers into the market are not possible. The lower access fee required for successful enticement may simply be too low to cover the deficit remaining from per-unit pricing. Similarly, the lower per-unit price needed for successful enticement will mean too great a revenue loss from inframarginal consumers, and no access fee that will keep all consumers in the market will cover this loss.

Welfare might be increased, however, if discriminating access fees are used. Through such tariff structures, marginal consumers can be allowed entry, provided they pay a unit price and an access fee that together cover the additional production cost they cause. The price or access fee or both are less than those paid by consumers already in the market; hence, pricing is discriminatory. However, allowing these additional consumers into the market is a Pareto-superior change, because the entrants are better off, and existing consumers no worse off. In fact, it may be possible to make existing consumers better off as well.

This can be illustrated using Figure 4.3, in which demands are perfectly inelastic and income effects are zero. There are two existing consumers, with their demands shown in (a) and (b), and their total demand and marginal-cost curve shown in (c). Price is set at $p = 1$, and access at $t = 0.5$. Both consumers take 1 unit, and each enjoys a surplus of 0.5, for a total welfare of 1.0 (using consumer surplus plus producer surplus as the measure). Note that $p = $ MC, which is constraint with $\bar{q} = \hat{q}$. Obviously, consumer 3 shown in (d) is omitted from this market under a uniform tariff with $t = 0.5$. The most he will pay for access is 0.25. With a uniform fee of $t = 0.25$, all three will pay the same, but the deficit will not be covered. Now allow discrimination, and charge consumer 3 a price equal to marginal cost (1.0) and an access fee of 0.2. This revenue from consumer 3's fee can then be split between consumers 1 and 2 by reducing their fees from 0.5 to 0.4 each. Total costs are covered, consumer 3 is in the market with a surplus of 0.05, and consumers 1 and 2 have enjoyed an increase in their surplus from 0.5 to 0.6. Total welfare has increased from 1.0 to 1.25.

Two-part tariffs are possible only when the good cannot be resold among consumers, although discriminatory tariffs require additional information about consumer demands. To be truly discriminatory, the tariffs must vary across consumers even though the cost of serving those consumers does not. Such discrimination often will be ruled out on legal grounds, although it can certainly be found in business, as, for example, in movie theaters. The cost of serving someone under age 12 years is certainly very close to (perhaps more than) the cost of servicng someone over 12 years; yet the price of admission usually is substantially lower for the former. In public utilities, discrimination is less obvious, but probably there. For example, electric utilities typically have numerous customer classes that partition consumers into groups that face different prices. To determine if such prices are truly discriminatory requires an analysis of the costs of serving various groups. Differing voltage levels, reliabilities of supply, and demand patterns may cause cost differences. Discrimination may also arise with more complicated price structures, as where consumers face different marginal prices, despite equivalent cost consequences of additional consumption. We have more to say about these price structures in Section 4.6.

## 4.4. Examining the stability of two-part tariffs using game theory[7]

Until now we have assumed that consumers are individuals who purchase from a natural monopoly; they act independent of one another and do not have the option to seek alternative supplies. However, there are situations in which these assumptions must be relaxed to more accurately capture the market environment. Consider the case of a large company that consumes electricity from a single-product, strong natural monopoly. Suppose the company decides that because of its size, it is in a position to supply its own electricity at less cost than it is now being charged by the natural monopoly. Or, from a different vantage point, suppose the natural monopoly is overcharging the large company, perhaps through a sizable access fee, and undercharging other consumers by using small access fees. If the large company decides to go it alone by supplying its own electricity, everyone potentially loses relative to what could be achieved under a different pricing policy. The natural monopoly's other consumers can no longer take advantage of the scale economies previously available, because total output decreases. In addition, the large company will pay more for its own electricity than it would have under a different pricing policy with the natural monopolist.

Situations like this are common. Communities and firms, or groups of communities and firms, have at times been dissatisfied with the perceived fairness of the prices charged for electricity and natural gas and have explored the possibility of self-supply. In recent years, these situations have been prevalent in the multiproduct telephone industry, where consumers have sought substitutes for one or more of AT&T's products from new firms entering the industry. More recently, after the breakup of AT&T,

---

7 Most of this section draws from Sorenson, Tschirhart, and Whinston (1978a, 1978b).

the reformulated Bell Operating Companies (BOCs) have complained about bypass, that is, when consumers of BOCs' products turn to unregulated firms for new sources of supply.

We delay the discussion of pricing stability and multiproduct firms until Chapter 7, where we address the concept of sustainability. We confine the presentation in this chapter to a single-product, strong natural monopolist utilizing a two-part tariff. This presentation also allows an introduction to some basic game-theory concepts that will be used in later chapters. Those readers already familiar with the sustainability concept will recognize its features in this section, where there are several consumers of the output of a single-product, strong natural monopoly, and where one or more consumers have the option of seeking an alternative source of supply if they are dissatisfied with the monopolist's pricing policy. Alternatively, a new firm may enter the market and service those dissatisfied consumers by offering a more attractive price structure.

### Game-theoretic concepts

Before constructing a game that is applicable to the natural monopoly problem, we introduce some basic game-theoretic concepts (Schotter and Schwödiauer, 1980). First, we introduce the characteristic function, which is a scalar-valued set function that gives the maximum value attainable by every possible coalition of players in the game. Note that if a game has $s$ players, there are $2^s$ possible coalitions. From this characteristic function we can examine the coalitions that are most likely to emerge. The coalitions will depend on the payoffs received by the players, where a payoff is the net benefit a player obtains by playing. For example, in the natural monopoly game, a consumer's payoff will be the difference between the value he places on the quantity received and the charge levied on him. Because the charge is dependent on the particular tariff structure, each structure results in a different vector of charges to the consumers and, in turn, a different set of payoffs. Some payoff vectors are stable; others are not. A payoff vector is stable when no player or subset of players can improve on their payoffs by withdrawing from the game. If a payoff vector is stable, it is said to be in the core; alternatively, the core consists of all payoff vectors that are stable. Not all games have a core, but for those that do, a reasonable criterion for payoff acceptability is core membership.

An example of a characteristic function for a three-person game is as follows:

$$v(\emptyset) = 0$$
$$v(1) = v(2) = v(3) = 0$$
$$v(12) = v(13) = v(23) = 1$$
$$v(123) = 1.4$$

where the players are labeled 1, 2, and 3. There are $2^3 = 8$ coalitions including the empty set. The value for the empty set is zero. The maximum value that any player acting alone can guarantee himself is also zero. Any two-player subcoalition, however, can guarantee itself a value of 1, and the grand coalition can obtain a value of 1.4.

Now let $x_i$ be the payoff received by player $i$. If each individual behaves rationally, it must be that

$$x_i \geq v(i) \tag{4.34}$$

That is, if a player does not receive a payoff at least as great as what he could obtain by acting independently, then he will drop out of the game altogether. If the grand coalition behaves rationally,

$$\sum_{i=1}^{3} x_i = v(123) \tag{4.35}$$

for a Pareto optimum. Payoffs that satisfy (4.34) and (4.35) are called imputations. The core criterion carries rationality one step further by requiring that every subcoalition behave rationally.

Thus, to be in the core, a payoff vector $(x_1, x_2, x_3)$ must satisfy the foregoing constraints in addition to

$$x_1 + x_2 \geq v(12)$$
$$x_1 + x_3 \geq v(13) \qquad\qquad (4.36)$$
$$x_2 + x_3 \geq v(23)$$

By inspection, it is clear that no payoff will satisfy all of these constraints for this game; therefore, the core does not exist. However, if we change the characteristic function so that $v(123) \geq 1.5$, then a core does exist. For $v(123) = 1.5$, the core is also unique; that is, $x_1 = x_2 = x_3 = 0.5$ is the only core payoff. The number of inequalities that delineate the core increases rapidly with the number of players.

There are numerous solutions or payoff schemes scattered throughout the game-theory literature; see Shubik (1982) for a comprehensive review. One of the most well known is the Shapley value (1953) which has been suggested as a method to address fairness in public utility pricing by Littlechild (1970a) and Loehman and Whinston (1971).[8] Briefly, one interpretation of the Shapley value is as follows. Let $S = \{1, 2, \ldots, s\}$ be the set of players in a game. Consider the sequential construction of the grand coalition by adding one player at a time: $\{1\} \rightarrow \{1, 2\} \rightarrow \ldots \rightarrow \{1, 2, \ldots, s\}$. As player $i$ enters this construction, he is joining a coalition, say coalition $T \subseteq S - i$, and he generates an incremental benefit given by $v(T \cup \{i\}) - v(T)$. A reasonable payoff scheme would be that player $i$ receive this increment, because he is responsible for it. However, this incremental benefit depends on which of the $s$ positions player $i$ occupies as the grand coalition forms. Alternatively, it depends on which of the $s!$ orderings of players actually occurs. In calculating the Shapley value, all of

---

8 One advantage of using the Shapley value to achieve a solution is that it is always in the center of the core for a convex game [see (4.37)]. However, for nonconvex games, the Shapley value may fall outside the core, and it can be computed even when the core does not exist. Another drawback with applying the Shapley value is the computational difficulty for large games.

the $s!$ orderings are assumed to be equally likely to occur, and player $i$ is awarded the average incremental benefit he generates over all orderings. For the first game described earlier, the Shapley value for player 1 is given by

$$x_1 = \tfrac{1}{3}[v(1)] + \tfrac{1}{6}[v(12) - v(2)] + \tfrac{1}{6}[v(13) - v(3)]$$
$$+ \tfrac{1}{3}[v(123) - v(23)]$$

The payoffs for players 2 and 3 are calculated in the same manner, except that 1 is interchanged with 2 and 3, respectively. This game-theory solution and others have been used to allocate costs for electricity (Gately, 1974), aircraft landings (Littlechild and Thompson, 1977), accounting divisions (Hamlen, Hamlen, and Tschirhart, 1977, 1980), and waste-water treatment facilities (Loehmun, Orlando, Tschirhart, and Whinston, 1979).

Another concept used later is convexity. A convex game is one in which the characteristic function satisfied

$$v(T' \cup j) - v(T') \le v(T \cup j) - v(T) \qquad (4.37)$$

for all $T' \subseteq T \subseteq S - \{j\}$. This implies a sort of increasing marginal contribution of players as they join the game. The reader can verify that the three-person game illustrated earlier is convex if and only if $v(123) \ge 2$.

A useful device for comparing these payoff vectors is the fundamental triangle introduced by von Neumann and Morgenstern (1944). To construct this triangle, players 1, 2, and 3 are assigned to axes $x_1$, $x_2$, and $x_3$, respectively, in Figure 4.4. If player 1 receives $v(123)$ and players 2 and 3 receive zero, that is, $x = (v(123), 0, 0)$, the payoffs are represented by point $a$. Similarly, payoff vector $x = (0, v(123), 0)$ is represented by point $b$. Any payoff in which players 1 and 2 divide $v(123)$ and player 3 receives zero can be represented by a point on line segment $ab$ in the $x_1x_2$ plane. If players 1 and 3 divide $v(123)$, the payoff is on line segment $ac$ in the $x_1x_3$ plane; if players 2 and 3 divide $v(123)$, the payoff is on line segment $bc$ in the $x_2x_3$ plane. Finally, if all three players receive a nonnegative payoff and $v(123)$ is totally distributed, the payoff is located on triangle $abc$ in the positive octant.

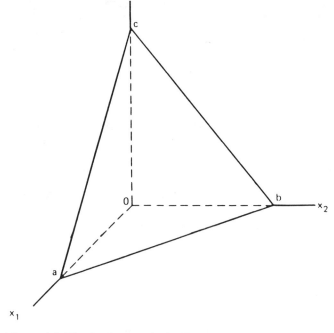

Figure 4.4. The fundamental triangle.

Thus, the fundamental triangle represents the set of imputations, because (4.34) and (4.35) are satisfied.

Recall that to be in the core, a payoff must satisfy (4.36) as well as (4.34) and (4.35). The inequalities of (4.36) can be plotted on the fundamental triangle. Figure 4.5, parts (a), (b), and (c), illustrate the fundamental triangles for the example games with $v(123) = 1.4$, $v(123) = 1.5$, and $v(123) = 2$, respectively. In each case, recall that $v(12) = v(13) = v(23) = 1$. Thus, to ensure a core allocation, we must have $x_1 + x_2 \geq 1$ from (4.36). Because $x_1 x_2 = 1$ is the horizontal line within the triangle in Figure 4.5(c), core allocations must be on or below this line. Plotting $x_1 + x_3 = 1$ and $x_2 + x_3 = 1$ in the triangle as well implies that the

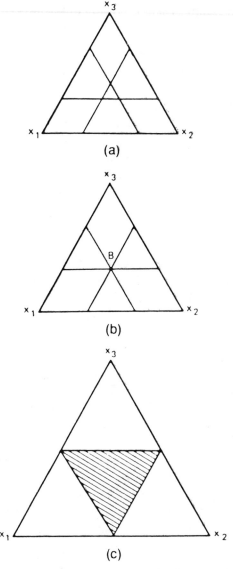

Figure 4.5. Fundamental triangles for example games.

shaded area in Figure 4.5(c) is the core. In Figure 4.5(b), the core consists of point *B* only. There is no core in Figure 4.5(a).

### Producer and consumers

We can now use these concepts to examine a game in which the players are a producer and consumers. The consumers must be in a coalition with the producer in order to obtain the good, and the producer must have consumers in his coalition in order to sell the good. The consumers' payoffs in this game are their surpluses, and the producer's payoff is his profit. The characteristic function for the game is defined as follows:

$$v(T) = \begin{cases} 0 & \text{for } 1 \notin T \text{ or } T = \{1\} \\ \max\{A(T) - C(q), q \geq 0\} & \text{for } 1 \in T \text{ and } T \neq \{1\} \end{cases}$$
(4.38)

where $T$ is the set of players in a coalition, and the firm is indexed by 1. $C(q)$ is the total cost of producing quantity $q$ and is assumed to be continuous. The total value of $q$ to consumers is

$$A(T) = \int_0^q p(q) \, dq = \sum_T \int_0^{q_i} p_i(q_i) \, dq_i$$
(4.39)

where $p(q)$ is the market's inverse demand function, and $p_i(q_i)$ is consumer $i$'s inverse demand function. Let $q^*$ be the quantity that solves (4.38), and allocate it to the members of coalition $T$ so that $\Sigma_{q_i} = q^*$ and $q_i^* = p_i^{-1}(p(q^*))$ for $i \in T$, $i \neq 1$; thus, the characteristic function defines the maximum benefit available to the members of $T$, and this maximum is attained where the total quantity produced and the quantity received by each consumer are those that would occur under marginal-cost pricing.

For simplicity, we assume that income elasticity is zero, so that the ordinary and compensated demand curves are equivalent. This allows us to vary, within limits, the charge to a consumer through changes in the access fee without changing the quantity demanded. Thus, we can increase the fee to one consumer and decrease it to another, again within limits, without changing $q^*$ and therefore without changing the characteristic function. In game terminology, utility is transferable. This assumption allows us to focus on the distributional issue.

If all consumers and the producer form a single coalition, and the core exists, then no subcoalition will have an incentive to withdraw from the game. That is, no subcoalition of consumers will have an incentive to find a new producer, and the firm will have no incentive to eliminate any consumers from the market.

Without proofs, we now state three basic properties of this game; see Littlechild (1975a) and Sorenson, Tschirhart, and Whinston (1978, 1978b) for details.

> *Property 1:* If marginal cost is decreasing on the interval $[0, q^*]$, then the characteristic function given by (4.38) is convex.

If the characteristic function is convex, then the core exists and tends to be "large" in the sense that usually there will be many pricing schemes admitting core solutions.

> *Property 2:* If average cost is decreasing on the interval $[0, q^*]$, then the core of the game is nonempty.

In this case, the core may or may not be convex. Properties 1 and 2 are not surprising, because decreasing costs have always been associated with the natural monopoly concept and the desirability of a single supplier.

> *Property 3:* If average cost is increasing at $q^*$, then the characteristic function may not be superadditive.

Superadditivity is defined for any coalitions $T$ and $T'$ as follows:

$$v(T) + v(T') \leq v(T \cup T'), \qquad T \cap T' = \varnothing \qquad (4.40)$$

This concept is similar to subadditivity applied to cost functions. Property 3 does not rule out the possibility that the characteristic function is superadditive at $q^*$. In this case, the core may exist and no consumer coalition will have an incentive to seek out an alternative producer. Recall that in Chapter 2, a rising average-cost curve was associated with a weak natural monopoly, and entry by new firms was possible. Here, because we do not confine the firm to linear prices, entry may be thwarted. Another possibility, however, is that the characteristic function is superadditive but the core does not exist. Now the consumers will have an incentive to seek out alternative suppliers, which is reminiscent of the weak natural monopoly dilemma in Chapter 2.

When superadditivity does not hold by Property 3, the core does not exist. In this case, there is no justification for a regulator to protect the firm's position as the sole supplier. Welfare will increase if there are multiple suppliers. Property 3 presents the possibility that a firm may have a subadditive cost function at the output where the demand and average-cost curves intersect and yet from a welfare viewpoint should not be the only firm in the market. This was illustrated by point $h$ in Figure 2.4 and by the caveat we mentioned in Chapter 2 of using subadditivity of the cost function as the definition of natural monopoly. The definition refers to subadditivity over the relevant output range, which is a vague way of accounting for the demand side of the market, for welfare, or for the myriad pricing mechanisms that might be employed. By Property 2, superadditivity always holds when average cost is decreasing; therefore, if a natural monopoly is defined in the old manner by decreasing average cost in the single-product case, the same caveat does not apply. Whether or not superadditivity fails to hold depends on the shapes of the consumer-demand functions and the cost function. If consumer demands are perfectly inelastic, then a subadditive cost function implies a superadditive characteristic function, and a single supplier is optimum. But when inelastic and elastic demands are admitted, little can be said without specific information on the demand and cost functions. (This point will be taken up again in Chapter 7 for multiproduct firms.)

Finally, we can examine specific pricing policies within this game. A convenient method for doing this is with an example of

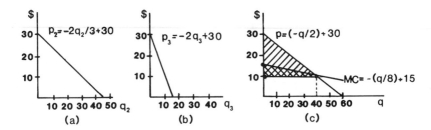

Figure 4.6. One producer, two consumers.

a one-producer–two-consumer game. The two consumers are characterized by the demands depicted in Figure 4.6, parts (a) and (b), and total market demand and marginal cost are depicted in Figure 4.6(c). Because marginal cost is decreasing throughout, the game will have a convex characteristic function, and the core will be "large." The characteristic function defines the optimum output as $q^* = 40$, which will be the output realized with marginal-cost pricing. The firm is a strong natural monopoly, and setting a single uniform price equal to marginal cost will yield a deficit equal to the crosshatched area in Figure 4.6(c). If outside subsidies are infeasible, then the producer must receive at least the crosshatched area as revenues, in addition to the rectangular area of 400. The problem, then, is to distribute the surplus given by the hatched and crosshatched areas in Figure 4.6(c) among the two consumers and the producer in order to determine profit and to provide nonnegative consumer surpluses to the two consumers.

Using various discriminating two-part tariffs with the per-unit price set to marginal cost, we can distribute the areas by awarding (1) all to the producer, (2) all to the consumers, or (3) some combination of (1) and (2). The first case represents the solution obtained by a perfectly discriminating monopolist, and the second case represents a welfare maximum with a break-even budget constraint. These solutions, plus case (3), can be illustrated in the fundamental triangle in Figure 4.7. The firm's payoff is plot-

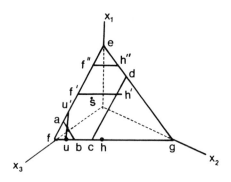

Figure 4.7. Fundamental triangle with two-part tariffs.

ted along axis $x_1$. The consumer's payoffs are plotted along axes $x_2$ and $x_3$. When all three players are in the game and $v(123)$ is obtained, the allocation falls on the *efg* triangle. The Shapley value, for example, is given by point *s,* which is in the center of the core by virtue of the convex characteristic function.

The core is delimited by points *abcde.* Thus, all price mechanisms that yield payoffs within this area are stable. The first case, where the monopolist sets price equal to marginal cost and extracts all consumer surplus via fees, is represented by point *e.* This corresponds to Oi's Disneyland monopolist utilizing a discriminating two-part tariff. Obviously, this solution requires extensive information about consumer demands and substantial entry barriers.

In the second case, the hatched area is awarded to the consumers, and the crosshatched area to the producer, so that profit is zero. For this to occur, there must be either a regulator invoking a break-even constraint or a threat of entry by new firms forcing the producer to zero profits. The producer becomes a passive player in that he will be indifferent to the various distributions among the consumers, as long as profit remains zero. However, the consumers will be concerned with the distribution, and if they are dissatisfied, they may seek out an alternative producer. Two-part tariffs that require zero profit and ensure that each consumer pays no more than what the good is worth to him are indicated by points on line segment *fh* in Figure 4.7. Note that *fh* contains points inside and outside the core, implying that discriminating two-part tariffs do not guarantee stability. Consumers will seek alternative suppliers under certain tariff structures.

In the third case, profit can vary between zero and the maximum possible profit at point *e*. Each profit level corresponds to a line segment parallel to *fh* in Figure 4.7. Two possibilities are given by *f'h'* and *f"h"*, where, again, allocations outside the core are obtained.

The two-part tariffs derived earlier in this chapter utilize uniform access fees and are more realistic for many goods. In our game, we derive uniform two-part tariffs by selecting a particular profit and then calculating the unique license fee for both consumers compatible with that profit. Again, the fees are subject to the criterion that neither consumer pays more than the value of the good. Uniform two-part tariffs yield points along line segment *uu'*. Because some points along *uu'* lie outside the core, uniform two-part tariffs are also potentially unstable.

This instability does not refer to the problem in Section 4.2, in which some consumers may be driven from the market because the access fee is too large. We can solve for a Pareto-optimum two-part tariff, as was done in Section 4.2, which will yield an optimum number of consumers in the market and still have instability. This outcome arises because the Pareto-optimum formulation addresses only one instance in which the two-part tariff may be too large: when it exceeds the value the consumer places on the good. It does not address the instances in which the tariff levied on a consumer, or coalition of consumers, exceeds the total cost of obtaining the good from the least expensive alternative supply, namely, when the outlay exceeds the opportunity cost. Thus, analyzing the core narrows down the set of feasible two-part tariffs in those situations in which coalitions of consumers have the wherewithal to seek new sources of supply.

Referring again to Figure 4.7, these points can be illustrated using line segment *fh,* along which profit is zero and the two consumers share the total consumer surplus. Point *b* represents a distribution in which consumer 2 is indifferent between purchasing from the producer or seeking an alternative supply and in which consumer 3 receives more than enough benefit to continue purchasing from the producer. Point *f* represents a distribution in which consumer 2 receives zero consumer surplus and consumer 3 receives all of it. A similar story can be told for points along segment *ch,* except that the positions of the two consumers are reversed. Models of the type used in Section 4.2 allow solutions along *fb* and *ch,* because the only constraint on any one consumer's benefit is that it be nonnegative (recall the marginal consumers in Section 4.2). In the present formulation, however, we place the more stringent constraint that the benefit to any one consumer (or group of consumers) must be at least as great as the benefit that can be realized in the next-best opportunity. Points along *bc* satisfy this constraint for the two-consumer example.

Finally, although we have referred to the alternative suppliers as other producers, we should not rule out consumer cooperatives as alternative suppliers (Sorenson, Tschirhart, and Whinston, 1978b). Sexton and Sexton (1987) indicate a number of interesting differences between the two supplier types, including that cooperatives will enter more readily than profit-maximizing firms under certain conditions.

### 4.5. Pareto-superior two-part tariffs

When first-best marginal-cost prices are infeasible for a natural monopoly because the requisite lump-sum taxes are impractical, second-best Ramsey prices can be used to maximize welfare subject to the constraints that the firm break even and prices be linear. However, improvements in welfare are made possible by deviating from linear prices and using nonlinear, uniform two-part tariffs. Further improvements are possible if we relax uniformity and permit discriminatory two-part tariffs. But discrimination often is infeasible for legal reasons, and moving from linear to uniform, nonlinear prices may require redistribution of income among consumers if we are to avoid making some consumers worse off. Thus, adopting two-part tariffs may improve welfare in the aggregate, but by using the Pareto criterion as a policy guide, their adoption will not generally lead to an improvement. Willig (1978) demonstrates, however, that if consumers are given the choice of moving to a uniform two-part tariff or continuing with a linear price that exceeds marginal cost, then all consumers and the firm can be made better off.

To demonstrate this point, consider first an individual consumer who has a choice between a linear price schedule and a two-part tariff. The consumer can buy units of output at the uniform price, $p^u$, or can elect to pay the access fee $t = \alpha\beta$, where $\alpha$ and $\beta$ are scalars, for the privilege of buying at the lower price, $p^u - \beta$. If the consumer chooses the linear price, then his maximum utility is given by $v(p^u, p^0, y)$, where $v(\cdot)$ is the indirect utility function, $p^0$ is the price of a composite good, and $y$ is income. If the consumer chooses the nonlinear price, he pays $\alpha\beta$, which is a reduction in his income, and proceeds to maximize utility given the unit price $p^u - \beta$. In this case he achieves utility $v(p^u - \beta, p^0, y - \alpha\beta)$.

### Consumer choice
The two-part tariff is preferred to the linear price if and only if

$$v(p^u - \beta, p^0, y - \alpha\beta) > v(p^u, p^0, y) \tag{4.41}$$

Examining (4.41) reveals that $\beta$ is a reduction in the uniform price and must be a measure of dollars per unit of output. For consistency of units, $\alpha$ must be a measure of output units. Assuming that $\alpha$ is fixed at some positive output level, we can see when the two-part tariff is desirable. Suppose the consumer purchases $\alpha' < \alpha$ units of the good using the two-part tariff. He saves $\alpha'\beta$ relative to the linear price on those purchases, but he pays an additional $\alpha\beta$ as an access fee relative to the linear price. Because $\alpha'\beta < \alpha\beta$ by assumption, the two-part tariff is not an attractive

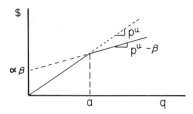

Figure 4.8. Choosing the two-part tariff.

option for this consumer. More formally, we can show that consumers who purchase less (more) than $\alpha$ will choose the linear price (two-part tariff).

For small $\beta$, the consumer prefers the two-part tariff if

$$dv(p^u - \beta, p^0, y - \alpha\beta)/d\beta > 0 \qquad (4.42)$$

evaluated at $\beta = 0$. Taking the derivative yields

$$\left.\frac{dv}{d\beta}\right|_{\beta=0} = -\frac{\partial v}{\partial(p^u - \beta)} - \frac{\partial v}{\partial y}\alpha$$

which, by Roy's identity, becomes

$$\left.\frac{dv}{d\beta}\right|_{\beta=0} = \frac{\partial v}{\partial y}(q - \alpha) \qquad (4.43)$$

where $q$ is the quantity of the good purchased. Because $\partial v/\partial y > 0$, combining (4.42) and (4.43) tells us that consumers prefer the two-part tariff if and only if $q > \alpha$. Figure 4.8 illustrates the situation. The line from the origin with slope $p^u$ represents the consumer's total expenditure on the good under the linear price. The line with intercept $\alpha\beta$ represents expenditure under the two-part tariff. Given a choice, consumers will locate along the lower, solid line segments, so that consumers purchasing less than $\alpha$ choose the linear price, and consumers purchasing more than $\alpha$ choose the two-part tariff.

Figure 4.8 also illustrates the importance of making the two-part tariff optional. If it were mandatory, obviously all consumers who demanded less than $\alpha$ would lose. Moreover, if the good is normal and demand increases with income across consumers, then the losers will be the lower-income consumers. The outputs of regulated natural monopolies usually are considered normal goods; thus, a policy of moving to mandatory two-part tariffs would not be appealing to regulators concerned with equity, because it would benefit upper-income consumers and be more costly to the low-income consumers.

Note, too, that the foregoing observation is consistent with Feldstein's results (1972a) on designing a two-part tariff that reflects distributional equity. If the equitable two-part tariff from Section 4.2 is one that places heavier weights on lower-income consumers, then for normal goods we see that the unit price is higher and the license fee lower than if the weights are equal. This will show up in Figure 4.8 as a counterclockwise rotation of the ray and a downward parallel shift in the two-part tariff line, which together will yield a smaller $\alpha$. Therefore, fewer low-income consumers will suffer under a mandatory policy (where no redistributions are possible).

### Gains from two-part tariffs

Now let us consider the firm's profit to show that not only do consumers with demand greater than $\alpha$ benefit from the optional tariff, but the firm benefits as well. Suppose there are $s$ consumers; $\tilde{s} < s$ have demands less than $\alpha$, and the remaining $s - \tilde{s}$ have demands exceeding $\alpha$. The firm charges the uniform price, $p^u$, which exceeds marginal cost, and profit for the firm is

$$\pi = p^u \sum_{i=1}^{\tilde{s}} q^i + \sum_{i=\tilde{s}+1}^{s} [\alpha\beta + (p^u - \beta)q^i] - C\left(\sum_{i=1}^{s} q^i\right) \qquad (4.44)$$

where $q^i$ is the $i$th consumer's demand. Taking the partial derivative of profit with respect to $\beta$ and evaluating it at $\beta = 0$ yields

$$\frac{\partial\pi}{\partial\beta} = \sum_{i=s+1}^{s} [\alpha - q^i] + [p^u - \text{MC}] \sum_{i=s+1}^{s} \left.\frac{\partial q^i}{\partial\beta}\right|_{\beta=0} \qquad (4.45)$$

The change in $\beta$ does not affect revenues from consumers who do not opt for the two-part tariff. For the $i$th consumer who does opt for the two-part tariff, we expand the last term in (4.45) to obtain

$$\frac{\partial q^i}{\partial \beta} = \frac{-\partial q^i}{\partial(p^u - \beta)} - \alpha \frac{\partial q^i}{\partial(y - \alpha\beta)} = -\left[ \frac{\partial q^i}{\partial(p^u - \beta)} + q^i \frac{\partial q^i}{\partial(y - \alpha\beta)} \right]$$
$$+ \frac{\partial q^i}{\partial(y - \alpha\beta)}[q^i - \alpha] \tag{4.46}$$

The first bracketed term is the Slutsky own-substitution effect, which is necessarily negative. Substituting (4.46) into (4.45) yields

$$\left. \frac{\partial \pi}{\partial \beta} \right|_{\beta=0} = \sum_{i=\tilde{s}+1}^{s} [\alpha - q^i] + [p^u - MC] \sum_{i=\tilde{s}+1}^{s} \frac{\partial q^i}{\partial(y - \alpha\beta)} [q^i - \alpha]$$
$$- [p^u - MC] \sum_{i=\tilde{s}+1}^{s} \left[ \frac{\partial q^i}{\partial(p^u + \beta)} + q^i \frac{\partial q^i}{\partial(y - \alpha\beta)} \right] \tag{4.47}$$

We can ensure that (4.47) is positive, indicating that profit increases if we let $\alpha$ be below, but arbitrarily close to, the largest quantity consumed by any consumer, say $q^s$. As $\alpha$ approaches $q^s$ from below, $\alpha - q^s$ approaches zero, and (4.47) approaches

$$-[p^u - MC] \sum_{i=\tilde{s}+1}^{s} \left[ \frac{\partial q^i}{\partial(p^u + \beta)} + q^i \frac{\partial q^i}{\partial(y - \alpha\beta)} \right]$$

which is positive. Therefore, the firm and the consumer with the largest demand benefit. If we lower $\alpha$ until (4.47) is no longer positive, then all consumers with demands greater than $\alpha$ will benefit. The remaining consumers are unaffected at this point, establishing weak Pareto dominance of the two-part tariff. This result is displayed in Figure 4.9.

$D$ is the demand curve of the consumer with the greatest demand, which is quantity $q^s$ at the uniform price $p^u$. We assume in this diagram that this is the only consumer for whom the quantity demanded exceeds $\alpha$, and we assume that income effects are zero. Under the two-part tariff, the consumer increases his quan-

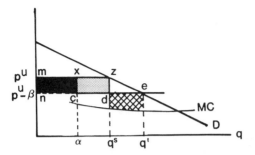

Figure 4.9. Pareto-superior two-part tariffs.

tity demanded to $q^t$ and pays $(p^u - \beta)q^t + \alpha\beta$. Thus, area *mxcn* represents the access fee, and the consumer's gain over the linear price schedule is given by area *xzec*.

The firm sells an additional $q^t - q^s$ units, which adds the crosshatched area to profit, but now the inframarginal units are sold at a lower price, which means the firm loses the dotted area *(xzdc)* as profit. The shaded area is not lost, because it is the access fee. Now, as $\alpha$ approaches $q^s$ from below, the consumer's gain approaches area *zde,* and the firm's increased profit approaches the crosshatched area. Hence, firm profit and consumer surplus both increase for a small enough $\beta$ and an $\alpha$ close to $q^s$. Willig proceeds to demonstrate how the two-part tariff exhibits strong Pareto dominance, wherein all consumers can be made better off.[9] Without providing details, we simply indicate that this is accomplished by feeding some of the increased profit back to the consumers via a lower $p^u$.

Once one Pareto-dominating two-part tariff is found, we might be concerned with the optimality properties of this schedule. Are

9 Ordover and Panzar (1980) show how the absence of perfect competition among firms in the final-product market implies that quantity discounts to large users will shift their final-product supply curves outward – reducing the share of smaller rivals. Such demand interrelationships imply that Pareto improvements (relative to uniform pricing) may not be possible, because some small users will be worse off as they experience reduced revenues and/or exit.

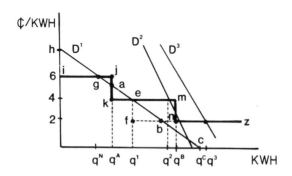

Figure 4.10. Multipart price structures: declining block rates.

there other two-part tariffs that dominate it? Willig demonstrates that any two-part tariff can be strongly dominated itself, unless the uniform price offered to the consumer with the largest quantity demanded equals marginal cost. Moreover, once we recognize that multipart tariffs and declining block rates can be interpreted as two-part tariffs, we can expand on Willig's results and move toward a general theory of nonlinear price structures. Brown and Sibley (1986) accomplish this in an analysis of nonlinear pricing, to which we now turn.

### 4.6. Multipart pricing

At the beginning of this chapter we introduced a general form of a multipart pricing structure that included an access fee and a per-unit price that varied in a stepwise fashion with output. Figure 4.10 displays this type of multipart price structure, with the price varying over blocks of output. Because prices decrease with increases in output, this tariff structure is referred to as *declining block rates*. In this example, the price is 6¢/KWH up to $q^A$, 4¢/KWH between $q^A$ and $q^B$, and 2¢/KWH beyond $q^B$ (traced out by *ijkmnz*). If average cost is above marginal cost, the declining block structure provides one way to cover total cost while the marginal price is near marginal cost.

Historically, covering total costs by having the prices track a falling cost curve has been the justification for the declining block rates used by many electric utilities. Two recent developments have had a significant influence on this rate structure. First, the cost structure in the industry is believed to have changed such that long-run marginal costs may be constant or increasing. Second, the energy crisis of the early seventies led to an emphasis on energy-conservation policies. Consequently, the Public Utility Regulatory Policies Act of 1978 required state commissions to reconsider declining block rates. Most such commissions tried to replace them with linear prices or some type of two-part tariff. As we shall indicate, such replacements may have been premature in certain cases, because, as Brown and Sibley (1986) point out, there is another justification for declining block rates apart from cost considerations. Before examining this point, we briefly return to our example of declining block rates in Figure 4.10 to illustrate consumer behavior when confronting this pricing structure.

Three demand curves are shown in Figure 4.10, representing three consumers. Consumer 1 purchases quantity $q^1$ given the price schedule. To see why, note that the consumer's outlays for consumption between $q^N$ and $q^A$ are greater than the consumer surplus received by area *gja*. The outlays to expand consumption beyond $q^A$ to $q^1$ are less than consumer surplus by area *eak*. So consumer surplus is maximized at $q^1$ units (*eak* > *gja*). In contrast, consumer 2 does not expand consumption into the final block, because additional benefits would be less than additional costs (beyond $q^2$).

Brown and Sibley's study of block rates and nonlinear pricing develops these points further and makes the theoretical issues accessible. They show how declining block rates can be interpreted as two-part tariffs; this allows us to develop results similar to those of Willig for a wider range of price structures. The interpretation is illustrated in Figure 4.11 where we have duplicated in panel (b) the declining block rates shown earlier in Figure 4.10. Panel (a) can be likened to Figure 4.8, except that here we have two two-part tariffs instead of only one. Line segment 0*a* is panel (a) shows the total outlays of a consumer who purchases all output at the uniform price of 6¢. Line segment *bc* in panel (a) shows

144    *Optimal pricing and investment*

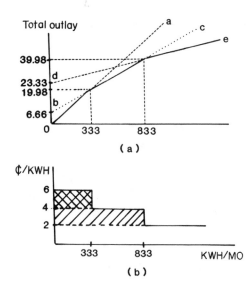

Figure 4.11. Declining block rates as two-part tariffs.

the total outlay of a consumer who purchases all output at the uniform price of 4¢ after paying an access fee of $6.66. Similarly, line segment *de* corresponds to a uniform price of 2¢ and an access fee of $23.33. The slopes of the three line segments correspond to the three block rates in panel (b); the total-outlay schedule appears in (a), and the marginal-outlay schedule in (b). The access fees for the two two-part tariffs associated with segments *bc* and *de* are given by the vertical intercepts at 6.66 and 23.33, respectively. The $6.66 is shown by the crosshatched area, and the $23.33 is shown by the sum of the hatched and crosshatched areas in panel (b).

### Self-selecting two-part tariffs

Given a choice among the three pricing options displayed in panel (a), that is, the linear price or one of the two two-part tariffs, a consumer will choose one such that his total outlays are somewhere along the undominated or least-cost schedule

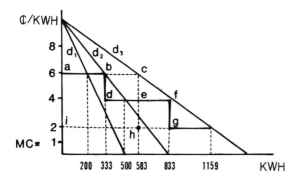

Figure 4.12. Self-selecting two-part tariffs.

(shown as the solid line segments). In this way, each consumer can select the tariff that best fits his own demand. This pricing structure is referred to as a *self-selecting two-part tariff,* and in comparison with a single uniform price for all consumers, it can be shown that there exists a self-selecting two-part tariff that is strongly Pareto-dominant.

To illustrate this point, we can construct a diagram similar to Figure 4.9, in which we showed how a single consumer and the firm are better off when a two-part tariff is introduced. Now, reproducing the block rates from Figure 4.11(b) in Figure 4.12, and adding three demand curves, we can demonstrate how the block rates are superior to a single uniform price, while at the same time interpreting the block rates as a system of two-part tariffs. Suppose marginal cost is 1¢/KWH, and the firm initially charges the single uniform price of 6¢/KWH. Three consumers have demands given by

$$p_1 = -0.0200q_1 + 10$$
$$p_2 = -0.0120q_2 + 10$$
$$p_3 = -0.0069q_3 + 10$$

which are shown in Figure 4.12 along with the block rate schedule from previous figures. At the initial uniform price of 6¢, the consumers' demands are $q_1 = 200$, $q_2 = 333$, $q_3 = 583$. Now introduce the declining block rates, so that the quantities demanded become $q_1 = 200$, $q_2 = 500$, and $q_3 = 1,159$. We continue to assume zero income effects for simplicity. This same set of new demands will be realized by offering the following self-selecting two-part tariffs:

$$p = 0.06 \quad \text{and} \quad t = 0$$
$$p = 0.04 \quad \text{and} \quad t = 6.66$$
$$\text{or} \quad p = 0.02 \quad \text{and} \quad t = 23.33$$

The Pareto-dominance story can be told in the same way it was for Figure 4.9. For consumer 1, nothing changes; he is no better or no worse off, and the firm's profit remains the same. For consumer 2, the picture is virtually identical with that in Figure 4.9 if point $\alpha$ from Figure 4.9 is set equal to 333 in Figure 4.12. For consumer 3, the picture is also identical if $\alpha$ is now set equal to 583. The quantity 583 follows because the access fee under the two-part tariff, area *achi,* must equal the premiums paid for inframarginal units under the declining block rates, area *abdefgi.* Thus, consumers 2 and 3 can both be made better off, and the firm's profit will increase by the same reasoning applied earlier in Figure 4.9. Also, consumer 1 can be made better off if some of the increased profit is fed back to him in the form of a price below 6¢.

Obviously, the particular two-part tariffs in this example were tailor-made for these demands. In practice, we do not expect to achieve such ideal results, given the limitations on demand information. Also, we need to be sure that a tariff designed for a particular consumer, or consumer class, is actually chosen by that consumer. For instance, if the demand curve for consumer 3 pivots inward, we may find that he opts for the second tariff instead of the third, even though the third is still superior to the single-price tariff for this consumer. This result can create significant profit losses for the firm. Brown and Sibley (1986, p. 86) show how tariffs can be made incentive-compatible, thereby avoiding this problem.

When there are more than three consumers, this method of designing self-selecting tariffs can be extended to construct additional tariffs. In the limit, intuition suggests that each consumer should have a two-part tariff designed specifically for him. This, too, is demonstrated by Brown and Sibley, who show that if there are $s$ consumers and a multipart tariff that can be interpreted as $m$ two-part tariffs, $m < s,$ then a multipart tariff with $m + 1$ two-part tariffs can be shown to be Pareto-superior.[10]

### Optimum nonlinear prices

The two-part tariffs in Figure 4.12 were chosen to be Pareto-superior, but not optimizing. Tariffs that optimize a welfare objective, with a profit constraint on the firm, require more analysis. Not surprisingly, however, the same pricing principles that apply to the single, welfare-maximizing two-part tariff also apply for multipart tariffs. We still need to be concerned with demand elasticities and elasticities associated with consumer participation in the market. Increasing the per-unit prices will have the effect of decreasing consumption more when demands are more elastic, whereas increasing the access fees will have the effect of decreasing consumers in the market more when participation elasticities are more elastic. Brown and Sibley demonstrate how optimum tariffs can be derived; in more general contexts, optimum nonlinear prices have been studied by Spence (1977b), Roberts (1979), and Katz (1983). These latter authors generalize multipart pricing by looking at a nonlinear price schedule in which the marginal price can change over all output levels. Such a schedule is shown in Figure 4.13. Each unit is priced differently, as shown by the marginal-price schedule $p$.

An optimum schedule must take into account all consumer demands by noting when rising portions of $p$ will force consumers out of the market versus not forcing them out and gathering more revenues to cover fixed costs. As Brown and Sibley indicate, the optimum $p$ is similar in form to a Ramsey rule. That is,

10 This point is also made by Leland and Meyer (1976).

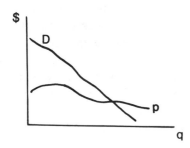

Figure 4.13. General nonlinear prices.

if we interpret each unit of output along the horizontal axis in Figure 4.13 as a distinct good, then the price of that good is given by a formula in which $(p - MC)/p$ is inversely related to the elasticity of consumer participation.[11] Roughly, when participation is elastic (inelastic), price should be low (high). There are obvious similarities between this and the Ng and Weisser pricing rule given by (4.28) for the single two-part tariff, where market-participation elasticity played an important role.

An optimum nonlinear price, or, in the discrete case, optimum block rates, will fall or rise with the elasticity of market participation. This fact is the other justification for declining block rates apart from the cost considerations that we alluded to earlier in this section. For example, if market participation is inelastic for small outputs, declining block rates may be justified even if marginal cost is not decreasing. One empirical study of declining block rates for 30 electricity firms found that only 27 percent

11 The technique whereby each unit of output is interpreted as a distinct good, so that a different price can be charged for each unit, is also employed by Mirman and Sibley (1980) to derive nonlinear prices for a multiproduct monopolist. Their analysis represents one of the few efforts to merge the pricing literatures on multiproduct linear and nonlinear pricing. Those authors find that the welfare-maximizing monopolist, selling $n$ outputs, offers for sale only those vectors of outputs along a one-dimensional path in $n$ space. Consumers must choose a point along the path and pay the price associated with that point.

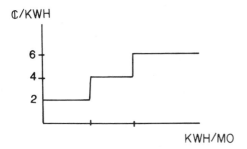

Figure 4.14. Inverted block rates.

reached the final block (Crockett, 1976). Although the author concluded that the impact on allocative efficiency was significantly negative, he did not take into account the possibility of inelastic market participation as justifying such a structure. Alternatively, if market participation is elastic for small outputs, increasing block rates may be called for.

An example of the use of increasing block rates, which are referred to generally as *inverted rates* (Figure 4.14), is the recent attempt to aid low-income demanders who consume relatively small quantities of electricity.[12] These rates have been labeled *lifeline rates* to reflect the view that basic needs are being met. Low-income consumers presumably cause very elastic market participation at low levels of individual consumption. Some authors have argued, however, that unless the rates are available only to truly needy consumers, for example, by using a signal, such as food stamps, that will identify the needy, the benefits will be spread relatively indiscriminantly across the population (Dahl, 1978; Howe, 1976).

---

12 A second example is energy conservation. Meyer (1975a) uses data from New York, California, and Illinois to design optimum nonlinear price structures that show increasing marginal prices when conservation is a goal. He also finds that for most other objectives, optimum designs will entail higher access fees than are typically·used.

Dimopoulos (1981) compared average-cost pricing, two-part tariffs, and declining block and inverted rates using data based on the Wisconsin Power and Light Company. He finds that even if the correlation between electricity consumption and income and the benefits to low-income demanders are weighted relatively heavily, lifeline pricing may not increase total welfare. This result is particularly true if marginal cost is less than average cost, if the variation in income is small, if income elasticity is small, and if the price elasticity of demand is large.

Berg and Roth (1976) compare lifeline rates to other techniques that can benefit target groups. They show that direct cash subsidies and forms of electricity stamps (similar to food stamps) can yield greater benefits for the same program costs. Furthermore, those benefits are concentrated on those families considered most in need of assistance. The results illustrate the importance of carefully specifying goals not associated with efficiency considerations.

### 4.7. **Summary**

The possibility of using nonlinear pricing expands the range of options available to regulators and to firms. In one common form, the two-part tariff, a uniform price can be set to marginal cost, and any resulting deficit can be covered with an access fee. In this way, the price structure retains the efficiency properties of marginal-cost pricing.

However, a number of complications arise in designing optimum two-part tariffs. The access fee reduces the consumer's income; so the quantity of output consumed will depend on the size of the fee. We noted that the uniform price and access fee are alternative instruments for manipulating demand. Some consumers may be driven from the market if the access fee is too large; therefore, relative to linear pricing, the number of consumers becomes an additional decision variable for the regulator. An optimum two-part tariff will have price above, below, or equal to marginal cost as the average quantity consumed is above, below, or equal to the quantity consumed by the marginal consumer. If the access fee is determined to be too burdensome for some consumers, income distributional weights can be used to design tariffs that will balance equity and efficiency. Also, discriminating two-part tariffs in which access fees vary over consumers can improve welfare, but usually they are disallowed by law.

When consumers or coalitions of consumers have the option of obtaining the good from a source other than the natural monopolist (through self-production or alternative suppliers), then the two-part tariffs should meet a stability criterion. Stability implies that no coalition of consumers will abandon the natural monopolist as a supplier; consequently, the advantage of having a single producer is retained, and welfare is maximized. Game theory can be used to determine stable two-part tariffs.

Moving to two-part tariffs from linear prices can improve welfare in the aggregate. However, in general, the move will not be Pareto-superior, because some consumers will be made worse off. By making the tariffs voluntary, it is possible that all consumers, and the producer, can be made better off. This process ensures Pareto improvements with two-part tariffs. Further improvements are possible with self-selecting two-part tariffs in which consumers are offered a menu of tariffs to choose from.

In the limit, nonlinear pricing takes the form where each output unit may be sold at a different price. The optimum price need not be monotonic in output; instead, it varies with the elasticity of participation in the market. Such pricing may be a justification for declining block rates, which have been abandoned by many electric utilities in recent years because prices have not tracked marginal costs.

Nonlinear prices in the form of two-part tariffs and block rates have been used for many years and for a wide variety of goods. When used properly, they can benefit both producer and consumer. In the electricity industry, they sometimes take the form of kilowatt demand charges, whereby separate charges for energy consumption (kilowatt-hours) and capacity (maximum kilowatts) are levied. The latter is similar to the access fee, except that it is not completely insensitive to usage. Often it is based on the maximum quantity of electricity demanded by the consumer during the month or year. However, admitting time into the analysis creates additional complications. For example, we can show that the demand charge should be based on the consumer's demand during the time interval when system-wide demand is at its peak; it should not be based on the consumer's maximum demand regardless of time.[13] Although admitting time complicates the analysis, it is essential because of the cyclic demand pattern and nonstorability of output that characterize many natural monopolies. The next chapter addresses these complications by examining time-dependent optimum pricing structures.

13 Wenders and Taylor (1976) and Henderson (1983) conclude that current kilowatt demand pricing policies create serious misallocations because of the non-coincident-demand problem. Neufeld (1987) points out that the demand charge was not instituted as a form of peak-load pricing, but as a device enabling price discrimination – given competition from self-production between 1905 and 1915. Costs at such isolated (competitive) plants depended on maximum power consumption and total energy consumption; so a rate structure that included a kilowatt demand charge allowed the utility to undercut self-production (so long as the per-unit charge was low enough).

# 5

## Peak-load pricing

Goods produced by natural monopolies often have two characteristics that further complicate optimum pricing strategies: (1) cyclic demand and (2) nonstorability. Cyclic demand is typical of goods such as roadways and entertainment facilities, as well as public utility goods such as electricity, natural gas, water, and telephone service. For example, at a given price, the quantity of electricity demanded depends on the season, on whether it is day or night, and on the time of day or night. The demand pattern tends to be cyclic in that winter demand always exceeds summer demand in colder climates, whereas the reverse is true in warmer climates, where daytime demand exceeds nighttime demand, late afternoon demand often exceeds early morning demand, and so on.

Of course, many other goods experience cyclic demand. The demand for ice skates is high in winter and low in summer, whereas the reverse holds for swimsuits. But these goods do not possess the second property of nonstorability; therefore, production levels can be uniform year-round, with in-season sales matched by inventories accumulated during the off season. This pattern of production is not possible with electricity and the other goods cited earlier. Electricity is produced when it is demanded; inventories are impossible or impractical in most instances because of the high cost of storage.

The dilemma, then, is this: Should the firm acquire adequate capacity to meet peak-period demands, thereby being burdened with significant excess capacity during off-peak periods, or should the firm acquire only enough capacity to meet off-peak demands, thereby allowing a significant portion of peak demand to go unsatisfied? We shall see that the answer is crucially linked to the marginal-cost pricing rules already developed. However, now marginal cost must be carefully defined, because it varies over the cyclic period depending on the extent to which capacity is being utilized.

We begin with a general model of peak-load pricing in Section 5.1 and compare the pricing rules to those in earlier chapters. Then in Section 5.2 we contrast this general model to a more restrictive model that has become the standard in the literature on peak-load pricing. Section 5.3 covers two other complications often associated with peak-load models: diverse technology and interdependent demands. Section 5.4 addresses some practical difficulties encountered when applying the peak-load models to public utilities. A summary of the chapter follows in Section 5.5.

### 5.1. A model of peak-load pricing

The following model draws on the work of Mohring (1970) and Panzar (1976). Both authors examine the peak-load problem in a welfare-maximization framework, and neither author requires the firm to be a natural monopoly. Their work differs from most of the literature on peak-load pricing in that a neoclassical production technology is employed instead of the less general, fixed-proportions technology usually assumed. As we shall see in this section and the succeeding section, the different assumptions about technology create interesting differences in the implications for pricing and outputs.

#### *Neoclassical assumptions*

We assume that the firm experiences a peak-load problem; demand varies over a given time period, and the good produced is nonstorable.[1] For simplicity, we assume two time periods of the same length. The market demands in these periods are given by $Q_j(p)$, $j = 1, 2$, where $p = (p_1, p_2, p_3)$ is a vector of prices that includes the prices for the firm's two outputs, $p_1$ and $p_2$, and the price of a composite good, $p_3$. We shall at times refer to period 1 as the peak period, and period 2 as the off-peak period, which we formally define in the following manner:

$$Q_1(p_1', p_2'', p_3''') \geq Q_2(p_1', p_2'', p_3''') \tag{5.1}$$

for all $p_1', p_2'', p_3''' \geq 0$ and $p_1' \leq p_2''$. Thus, for prices as defined, demand for the firm's output in period 1 is never less than the demand in period 2. The restriction to two equal-length time periods can easily be extended to more periods and unequal lengths with additional notation.[2]

The firm's, or regulator's, objective is to maximize consumer welfare given by the general welfare function:

$$W(U^1, \ldots, U^s) \tag{5.2}$$

where $U^i$ is the utility of consumer $i$, $i = 1, \ldots, s$. To carry out this objective, the firm must choose the level of inputs used in its production process, as well as linear output prices in both periods. Additionally, to ensure an actual (as opposed to potential) increase in welfare when moving to the prices prescribed by the maximization problem, income redistribution will, in general, be required. To effect this redistribution, the regulator chooses $s$ lump-sum transfers, one for each consumer.

Before describing the firm's technology and maximization problem further, we focus on an individual consumer. The results from the consumer's individual utility maximization will

---

1 Storage in some form is sometimes possible. For example, in the production of hydroelectric power, water can be pumped into reservoirs during off-peak hours and then released during peak hours to produce electricity. Gravelle (1976) presents a model in which storage is feasible.

2 See Williamson (1966) for an early model with unequal-length time periods, and Takayama (1974) for a model with continuous time.

be used to interpret the solution to the welfare problem. Consumer $i$, $i = 1, \ldots, s$, behaves as if he maximizes the twice continuously differentiable, strictly quasi-concave utility function

$$U^i(q_1^i, q_2^i, q_3^i) \tag{5.3}$$

where $q_j^i$ is the $i$th consumer's consumption of the $j$th good, $j = 1, 2, 3$. Goods 1 and 2 are the peak and off-peak outputs, and good 3 is the composite good. The consumer is a price-taker in all three markets, with a budget constraint given by

$$y^i - t^i = p_1 q_1^i + p_2 q_2^i + q_3^i \tag{5.4}$$

where $y^i$ is income, $t^i$ is the lump-sum transfer, and the price of the composite good is 1. Letting $\tau$ be the multiplier for constraint (5.4), the first-order necessary conditions for a maximum of (5.3) subject to (5.4) are

$$U_j^i - \tau^i p_j = 0, \qquad j = 1, 2 \tag{5.5}$$
$$U_3^i - \tau^i = 0 \tag{5.6}$$
$$y^i - t^i - p_1 q_1^i - p_2 q_2^i - q_3^i = 0 \tag{5.7}$$

where subscripts on $U^i$ represent partial derivatives. Assuming that second-order sufficient conditions are satisfied for a maximum, we can solve (5.5)–(5.7) to obtain demand functions for the three goods. Substituting these demands into (5.7) and differentiating the resulting identity with respect to $p_1$, $p_2$, and $t^i$ yields

$$q_j^i + p_1 q_{1j}^i + p_2 q_{2j}^i + q_{3j}^i = 0, \qquad j = 1, 2 \tag{5.8}$$
$$1 + p_1 q_{1t}^i + p_2 q_{2t}^i + q_{3t}^i = 0 \tag{5.9}$$

where the second subscript on the $q^i$ represents partials with respect to prices in (5.8) and the tax in (5.9). Finally, we can sum (5.8) over all $s$ consumers to obtain

$$Q_j + p_1 Q_{1j} + p_2 Q_{2j} + Q_{3j} = 0, \qquad j = 1, 2 \tag{5.10}$$

Equations (5.5), (5.6), and (5.8)–(5.10) will be used later.

The firm employs one variable input in each period, $L_j$, $j = 1$, 2, and a fixed input for both periods, $K$. Thus, whereas the amount of $K$ available for production is the same in both periods (for example, the size of the entertainment facility or the electricity-generating plant), it can be used with varying intensity in that the $K/L_j$ ratio can vary between periods. The firm is a price-taker in the input markets, paying $b$ per unit of variable input and $\beta$ per unit of fixed input. Setting up the welfare-maximization problem, we have

$$\max_{p_j, t^i, L_j, K} W(U^1, \ldots, U^s)$$
$$j = 1,2; i = 1, \ldots, s \tag{5.11}$$

subject to

$$(\mu) \qquad bL_1 + bL_2 + \beta K + Q_3 \leq Y \tag{5.12}$$
$$(\gamma_j) \qquad Q_j \leq f^j(L_j, K), \qquad j = 1, 2 \tag{5.13}$$
$$p_j, t^i, L_j, K, Q_j, \mu, \gamma_j \geq 0, \qquad j = 1, 2; i = 1, \ldots, s$$

Constraint (5.12) requires that total expenditures not exceed total income, $Y = \Sigma_{i=1}^s y^i$, and constraint (5.13) requires that consumption in each period not exceed the firm's output in each period given by the production function $f(L_j, K)$. The production function is assumed to have the usual properties of differentiability and strict quasi concavity. Multipliers are shown in parentheses to the left of each constraint.

Assuming nonsatiation for at least one consumer, which implies that the multipliers are positive,[3] and also assuming positive inputs, prices, and transfers, the Kuhn–Tucker conditions for a maximum reduce to constraints (5.12) and (5.13) written as equalities and to (5.14), (5.15), (5.16), and (5.17) corresponding to variables $p_j$, $t^i$, $L_j$, and $K$, respectively:

$$\sum_{i=1}^{s} W_i \sum_{k=1}^{3} U_k^i q_{kj}^i - \mu Q_{3j} - \gamma_1 q_{1j} - \gamma_2 Q_{2j}$$
$$= 0, \qquad j = 1, 2 \tag{5.14}$$

3 By nonsatiation, $W_1 U_k^i$ is positive for some $i$, $i = 1, \ldots, s$, for some $k$, $k = 1$, 2, 3, and for some $j$, $j = 1, 2$. Therefore, from (5.14) and downward-sloping demands, at least one of $\mu$ or $\gamma$ is positive, but if one is positive, then both must be positive, from (5.16).

$$W_i \sum_{k=1}^{3} U_k^i q_{kt}^i - \mu q_{3t}^i - \gamma_1 q_{1t}^i - \gamma_2 q_{2t}^i$$

$$= 0, \qquad i = 1, \ldots, s \quad (5.15)$$

$$-\mu b + \gamma_j f_L^j = 0, \qquad j = 1, 2 \quad (5.16)$$

$$-\mu \beta + \gamma_1 f_K + \gamma_2 f_K^2 = 0 \quad (5.17)$$

Again, subscripts on $W$ and $U$ represent partials, as do the second subscripts on $Q$ and $q$. Also, $f^j \equiv f(L_j, K)$, $f_L^j \equiv \partial f^j / \partial L$, and $f_K^j \equiv \partial f^j / \partial K$, $j = 1, 2$.

### Interpreting the efficient prices

These conditions can be interpreted after some manipulations. First, for (5.14) we can eliminate the $U_k^i$ using (5.5) and (5.6) to obtain for the first term on the left side

$$\sum_{i=1}^{s} W_i \tau^i \sum_{k=1}^{3} p_k q_{kj}^i$$

This becomes, after substituting (5.8),

$$- \sum_{i=1}^{s} W_i \tau^i q_j^i$$

Finally, using (5.10) to eliminate $Q_{3j}$ in (5.14), the latter can be written as

$$- \sum_{i=1}^{s} W_i \tau^i q_j^i + [\mu p_1 - \gamma_1] Q_{1j}$$

$$+ [\mu p_2 - \gamma_2] Q_{2j} + \mu Q_j = 0 \quad (5.14')$$

Similar substitution of (5.5), (5.6), and (5.9) into (5.15) yields

$$- W_i \tau^i + [\mu p_1 - \gamma_1] q_{1t}^i + [\mu p_2 - \gamma_2] q_{2t}^i + \mu = 0 \quad (5.15')$$

Multiplying (5.15') by $q_j^i$, summing over all $s$ consumers, and then subtracting the result from (5.14') yields

$$[\mu p_1 - \gamma_1][Q_{1j} - Q_1 Q_{1t}] + [\mu p_2 - \gamma_2]$$

$$[Q_{2j} - Q_2 Q_{2t}] = 0, \qquad j = 1, 2 \quad (5.18)$$

Let $S_{kj} = [Q_{kj} - Q_k Q_{kt}]$, which is the Slutsky substitution effect: the rate of change in market demand for good $k$ when the price of good $j$ changes, given that income is redistributed in such a way that consumers' utilities are unchanged. If (5.16) is substituted into (5.18), we can write an expression that characterizes prices as

$$\begin{bmatrix} S_{11} & S_{21} \\ S_{12} & S_{22} \end{bmatrix} \begin{bmatrix} p_1 - b/f_L^1 \\ p_2 - b/f_L^2 \end{bmatrix} = 0 \qquad (5.19)$$

As noted by Mohring, second-order conditions for utility maximization ensure that the left-hand matrix has an inverse, so that we obtain $p_j - b/f_L^j = 0$, $j = 1, 2$. Finally, using these prices and (5.16) to substitute into (5.17), we have

$$p_1 f_L^1 = b, \qquad p_2 f_L^2 = b \qquad (5.20)$$

and

$$p_1 f_K^1 + p_2 f_K^2 = \beta \qquad (5.21)$$

An unconstrained, welfare-maximizing firm not facing cyclic demands will set price equal to marginal cost, which is equivalent to employing each input until the value of the marginal products equals their prices, or $pf_L = b$ and $pf_K = \beta$. With a peak-load problem, the firm still employs the variable input in this fashion; however, the fixed input is employed until the sum of the value of marginal products over both periods is equal to the fixed input's price. This is because the fixed input is utilized in both periods and contributes to output and value in both periods. If the firm contemplates employing one more unit of $K$ at a cost of $\beta$, then additional output and value are generated in both periods. It is the sum of these marginal-value products that must be weighed against the marginal cost of $\beta$. The fixed input is similar to a public good, in that once it is available in one period, it is available in all periods at no additional cost. In general, for $m$ time periods, we have

$$\sum_{j=1}^{m} f_K^j / f_L^j = \beta / b$$

Thus, the peak-load problem adds this interesting modification to results in earlier chapters. Price equal to marginal cost is still required for an unconstrained welfare maximum, but marginal cost now must be defined more carefully. The cost of employing an additional unit of the variable input is confined to a single period, but the cost of employing an additional unit of fixed input is spread over all periods. Consequently, marginal cost can vary across periods, implying that optimum prices should be time-dependent as well.

### Implications of the model

We now derive several implications from this model that will be useful when exploring alternative production technologies in Section 5.2. First, we note that in neither period does output press on full capacity. That is, given the fixed input $K$, then full capacity is defined as

$$\max_{L_j} f^j(L_j, K)$$

The necessary condition for a maximum is $f^j_L = 0$, which contradicts Kuhn–Tucker condition (5.16) in the welfare-maximization problem. (Recall that $\mu$ and $\gamma$ are positive by nonsatiation.) Hence, full capacity is never reached. This simply says that an input with a positive price should not be employed to the point where its marginal product is zero.

Next, we note that consumers in both periods contribute to the cost of the fixed input; that is, the total revenue in period $j$, $j = 1, 2$, exceeds the cost of the variable input employed in that period:

$$p_j Q_j - bL_j > 0$$

We have

$$p_j Q_j - bL_j = p_j f^j(L_j, K) - bL_j = bf^j/f^j_L - bL_j > 0$$

The first equality holds by nonsatiation in the welfare-maximization problem, because nonsatiation implies $\gamma > 0$;[3] so (5.13) is satisfied as an equality. The second equality holds by substituting for $p_j$ from (5.20), and the inequality follows from diminishing marginal productivity.

Another implication is that the peak-period price exceeds the off-peak-period price. From (5.20), $p_1 f_L^1 = b = p_2 f_L^2$; thus, a higher price in one period implies a lower marginal product in that period, which in turns implies higher output in that period by diminishing marginal productivity. Combining this with (5.1), which requires the off-peak demand curve to lie inside the peak demand curve, confirms this implication. This result is intuitively appealing because meeting the demands of peak-period consumers is the cause of the larger capacity that lies idle during off-peak periods. Compared with a single price in both periods, the prices derived here provide consumers with the appropriate signals. The higher peak price suppresses peak demand and permits less idle capacity, and the lower off-peak price encourages consumers to take advantage of the excess capacity.

Finally, we examine whether or not charging the optimum prices will result in a deficit. As in the single-period problem, this hinges on the production technology. Write total revenue minus total cost as

$$p_1 Q_1 + p_2 Q_2 - bL_1 - bL_2 - \beta K \tag{5.22}$$

Substituting the optimum prices from (5.20) and (5.21) into (5.22) yields

$$p_1 f^1 + p_2 f^2 - p_1 f_L^1 L_1 - p_2 f_L^2 L_2 - p_1 f_K^1 K - p_2 f_K^2 K$$

which, after rearranging, becomes

$$p_1 [f^1 - f_L^1 L_1 - f_K^1 K] + p_2 [f^2 - f_L^2 L_2 - f_K^2 K] \tag{5.23}$$

Total revenue will be greater than, equal to, or less than total cost as (5.23) is positive, zero, or negative. If the production function is homogeneous of degree 1, then by Euler's theorem the bracketed terms are zero, and costs are exactly met. In this case, we have constant returns to scale, and we obtain the not very surprising result that marginal-cost pricing allows the firm to break even. Alternatively, if the firm's production function is homogeneous of degree greater than 1, the bracketed terms are negative, and the firm runs a deficit. This is the result we would normally associate with a natural monopoly; the peak-load problem does not alter the deficit problem associated with marginal-cost pricing.

The situation is complicated, however, by the multiple periods. There is no guarantee that the production function is homogeneous, in which case a more general analysis along the lines of Panzar is required. He defines scale economies using elasticities of scale and indicates that a firm may very well have increasing returns over small outputs (off-peak period) and decreasing returns over large outputs (peak periods), so that the firm may experience a deficit in the off-peak period and a surplus in the peak period. In this case, an overall deficit becomes dependent on demand patterns as well as the production technology.

### Pricing with a budget constraint

To complete this model, let us suppose that with marginal-cost prices, the firm does run a deficit. Furthermore, the firm cannot expect a subsidy, but must cover any deficit by charging a different set of linear prices. In other words, we are again in the subject matter of Chapter 3, where the firm must append a budget constraint to the welfare-maximization problem in order to break even. In the present context, the firm appends the constraint

$$(\lambda) \qquad p_1 Q_1 + p_2 Q_2 - bL_1 - bL_2 - \beta K = \bar{\pi} \qquad (5.24)$$

to the problem defined by (5.11)–(5.13). Here, $\lambda$ is the multiplier, and $\bar{\pi}$ is the targeted profit level. If $\bar{\pi}$ is zero, the firm breaks even.

Carrying out an analysis similar to the preceding, in which the marginal-cost prices were derived, we can show that the solution to our appended problem is

$$\begin{bmatrix} S_{11} S_{12} \\ S_{21} S_{22} \end{bmatrix} \begin{bmatrix} p_1 - b/f_L^1 \\ p_2 - b/f_L^2 \end{bmatrix} = \frac{-\lambda}{\mu + \lambda} \begin{bmatrix} f^1 \\ f^2 \end{bmatrix} \qquad (5.25)$$

Or, solving (5.25),

$$p_1 - b/f_L^1 = \left[ \frac{-\lambda}{\mu + \lambda} \right] \left[ \frac{S_{22}f^1 - S_{12}f^2}{S} \right] \qquad (5.26)$$

$$p_2 - b/f_L^2 = \left[ \frac{-\lambda}{\mu + \lambda} \right] \left[ \frac{S_{11}f^2 - S_{21}f^1}{S} \right] \qquad (5.27)$$

where $S = S_{11}S_{22} - S_{12}^2$ is the determinant of the Slutsky matrix. These price equations represent a form of the Ramsey pricing rules developed in Chapter 3. In fact, if we assume that cross-elasticities of demand are zero, we obtain the simplest form of the Ramsey pricing rules. Zero cross-elasticities imply $S_{12} = S_{21} = 0$, and substituting this into (5.26) and (5.27) and dividing both sides by the appropriate price, we obtain

$$\frac{p_j - b/f_L^j}{p_j} = \left[ \frac{-\lambda}{\mu + \lambda} \right] \frac{1}{e_j}, \qquad j = 1, 2 \qquad (5.28)$$

where $e_j$ is the compensated demand elasticity. This is very similar to our first Ramsey rule derived in equation (3.6). The principal difference is the presence of $\mu$ instead of 1: The former is associated with a general welfare formulation, and the latter with consumer surplus. This difference was explained in Section 3.2.

Because capacity is a shared input, the capacity choice depends on consumer valuations in both periods. Thus, utilizing the first-order condition with respect to $K$ from the appended problem, we can obtain

$$\frac{p_1 f_K^1 + p_2 f_K^2 - \beta}{p_1 e_1 + p_2 e_2} = \left[ \frac{-\lambda}{\mu + \lambda} \right] \frac{1}{e_1 e_2} \qquad (5.29)$$

which illustrates the importance of the capital input in both periods.

Expressions (5.26) and (5.27), however, allow for nonzero cross-elasticities of demand between the peak and off-peak periods ($S_{12} \neq 0$), which is important in most peak-load pricing environments. We would expect the daytime demand for electricity, for telephone service, or for other public utlity goods to be dependent on the nighttime price. Indeed, this dependence, as we discuss later, is part of the impetus for movements to peak-load pricing in recent years, because such pricing is expected to shift at least some consumer demands from peak to off-peak periods.

The prices given by (5.26) and (5.27) or by (5.28) no longer guarantee that peak price will not fall below off-peak price. If peak demand is very elastic and off-peak demand very inelastic, a reversal in peak and off-peak prices cannot be ruled out. Bailey and White (1974) explore this possibility for a firm with increasing returns to capacity and a budget constraint.

The reader should recognize the formal similarity between the model developed here and the one developed in Chapter 3, where complex Ramsey rules were derived. Both are welfare-maximization problems utilizing transfer payments and constrained by budget requirements. In the former model, we allowed for any number of goods produced by the natural monopolist and any number produced by other firms in the economy. In this way we were able to highlight the influences of private substitutes and complements on the optimum prices charged by the natural monopolist. In the peak-load model, we ignore the possibility that there may be substitutes or complements; however, we do highlight the production side by adding capital and labor inputs. This treatment allows a greater appreciation for the way capital inputs typically are shared across periods, whereas variable inputs are confined to single periods.

Nevertheless, the equivalence between the multiproduct natural monopoly pricing problem and the peak-load pricing problem is evident. Although there is a time element implied in the latter, it does nothing to change the formal presentation. Indexing applies merely to time periods, not to goods in different markets (where time is not introduced). However, the production process is one area in which differences may arise between the two problems when specific industries are being analyzed. Is there a difference between the way inputs are shared across time periods, on the one hand, and the way they are shared across multiple outputs, on the other hand? (See footnote 10 in Chapter 3.) The answer requires scrutiny of production processes for the various properties of multiproduct cost functions discussed in Chapter 2.

To summarize, our presentation of the peak-load problem assumes that the capital input is shared across periods, and the variable inputs are confined to single periods. Because this is just one possibility among many, our peak-load natural monopoly can be considered a special case of the more general multiproduct natural monopoly.

### 5.2. Fixed-coefficient production technologies

Much of the early literature in the development of peak-load pricing theory utilized a fixed-coefficient production technology. Examples of this literature include papers by Boiteux (1960), Steiner (1957), Williamson (1966), and Littlechild (1970b). This technology is a limiting case of the general neoclassical technology presented in the previous section; not surprisingly, the pricing prescriptions derived under a fixed-coefficient technology tend to be polar cases.

For example, consider that with this technology, optimum marginal-cost pricing implies (1) that total revenue equals total cost, (2) that only peak consumers contribute to capacity costs, and (3) that during peak periods, output is equal to capacity. All three are at variance with the general results derived earlier. Nevertheless, fixed-coefficient technologies are still used to study the peak-load problem by both academics and practitioners. Such models are easily understood, and the basic principles can be easily explained with simple diagrams. More important, however, a fixed-coefficient technology, or its variants, may be an accurate description of the actual technologies employed by some public utility industries. This point is particularly true for electricity (Scherer, 1976), which we shall explore in more detail later, and for the telephone industry, for which Littlechild (1970c) uses this technology to examine peak-load pricing.

### The fixed-coefficient technology

The form of a fixed-coefficient technology with capital ($K$) and labor ($L$) inputs is captured by the production function

$$h = f(K, L) = \min\left\{\frac{K}{a_1}, \frac{L}{a_2}\right\} \tag{5.30}$$

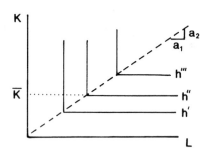

Figure 5.1. Fixed-coefficient technology.

where $a_1$ is the number of capital units needed for one unit of output, and $a_2$ is the same for labor (or fuel or maintenance or other variable input). Isoquants for three output levels are illustrated in Figure 5.1. The reader can verify that (5.30) implies a long-run cost function given by

$$C(h) = h[a_2\hat{b} + a_1\hat{\beta}] \qquad (5.31)$$

where $\hat{b}$ and $\hat{\beta}$ are the prices of $L$ and $K$, respectively. This cost function is obtained by moving along the long-run expansion path in Figure 5.1, where each additional unit of output requires $a_1$ additional units of $K$ and $a_2$ additional units of $L$. For brevity, let $b = a_2\hat{b}$ and $\beta = a_1\hat{\beta}$, so that b and $\beta$ are the costs of the $a_2$ labor units and $a_1$ capital units needed for one additional unit of output, respectively. In the short run, where $K = \overline{K}$ in Figure 5.1, movements in output take place along the horizontal expansion path emanating from $\overline{K}$. The short-run total cost of output along the dotted portion of the path is

$$C_s(h) = \hat{\beta}\overline{K} + bh \qquad (5.32)$$

but along the solid portion the cost is

$$\hat{\beta}\overline{K} + \hat{b}L \qquad (5.33)$$

Note that in (5.33), cost will continue to increase as we move out the solid portion of the short-run expansion path, but output

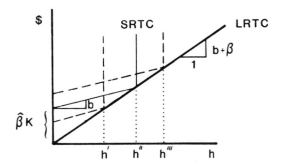

Figure 5.2. Long-run and short-run total costs.

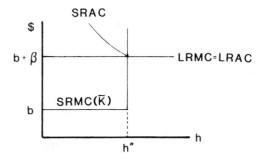

Figure 5.3. Short-run and long-run marginal and average costs.

does not increase. Obviously, it would not be cost-minimizing in the short run (a fortiori in the long run) if a firm were to be in this region of production in the isoquant space. Putting (5.31), (5.32), and (5.33) together, we have the long-run and short-run cost functions exhibited in Figure 5.2. Similar to the neoclassical case, the long-run cost function is the envelope of the corner points of the short-run cost functions. Finally, we can use Figure 5.2 to derive a picture of marginal and average costs in Figure 5.3. With $K = \overline{K}$, $h''$ is the maximum output obtainable, and from (5.32) the short-run marginal cost equals $C'_s(h) = b$ up to $h''$. The long-run marginal and average cost, from (5.31), is $C'(h)$

$= b + \beta$. We shall use the cost curves in Figure 5.3 along with demand curves to develop the basic peak-load pricing rules for a fixed-coefficient technology.

### Welfare maximization

We continue to assume two equal-length time periods in which the quantity demanded in the first period, the peak, equals or exceeds the quantity demanded in the second period, the off-peak, for any uniform price across periods. In conforming with most of the literature, we ignore all other goods, and we use consumer surplus as a measure of welfare. However, using consumer surplus becomes more complicated when there is more than one good, because this measure depends on the precise way in which prices are changed. Changing $p_1$ first and $p_2$ second may produce a different measurement than if the order of change is reversed. We shall have more to say about this later; for now, we can do away with this complication by assuming that demands in the two periods are independent. This is a strong assumption for the peak-load problem, but it has been used repeatedly because it greatly simplifies the analysis.

The objective function for a welfare-maximizing firm is

$$W = \int_0^{Q_1} p_1(Q_1) \, dQ_1 + \int_0^{Q_2} p_2(Q_2) \, dQ_2$$
$$- bQ_1 - bQ_2 - \hat{\beta}\overline{K} \quad (5.34)$$

where all notation should be familiar. Because output cannot exceed capacity in either period, we have the two constraints

$$Q_1 \leq \overline{K}/a_1 \qquad (\gamma_1) \qquad\qquad (5.35)$$
$$Q_2 \leq \overline{K}/a_1 \qquad (\gamma_2) \qquad\qquad (5.36)$$

where the multipliers are shown in parentheses. The form of these constraints follows from the production function in (5.30). Finally, we have the usual nonnegativity constraints for the choice variables and multipliers:

$$Q_1, Q_2, \gamma_1, \gamma_2 \geq 0 \qquad\qquad (5.37)$$

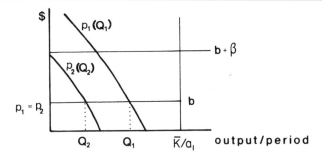

Figure 5.4. Peak-load prices with excess capacity.

Notice that we have not made $\overline{K}$ a variable, which means that we are in a short-term situation. Capacity is fixed, and we must set optimum outputs and prices given the peak and off-peak demands. We shall consider the choice of an optimum $K$ shortly.

The Kuhn–Tucker conditions for this problem are

$$Q_i[p_i - b - \gamma_i] = 0 \tag{5.38}$$
$$p_i - b - \gamma_i \leq 0 \tag{5.39}$$
$$\gamma_i[\overline{K}/a_1 - Q_i] = 0 \tag{5.40}$$
$$\overline{K}/a_1 - Q_i \geq 0 \tag{5.41}$$
$$Q_i, \gamma_i \geq 0 \tag{5.42}$$

for $i = 1, 2$. There are numerous cases that can be examined with these conditions, but we shall consider only three.

*Case 1:* $0 < Q_1 < \overline{K}/a_1$ and $0 < Q_2 < \overline{K}/a_1$

With positive output less than capacity in both periods, $\gamma_1 = \gamma_2 = 0$ and $p_1 = p_2 = b$, from (5.38)–(5.42). Figure 5.4 illustrates the situation. The demand curves are drawn with period 1 as the peak period. At no nonnegative prices will capacity be reached. The rectangular area given by $\beta\overline{K}/a_1 = \hat{\beta}\overline{K}$ is a cost that cannot possibly be recouped by the firm. Raising price above $b$ will simply eliminate some consumer surplus while converting other consumer surplus to revenue, which has an offsetting effect on welfare. Thus, there is no gain in raising price above $b$.

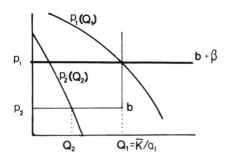

Figure 5.5. Peak-load pricing with optimum capacity.

That this case cannot be an optimum in the long run can be seen if we allow capacity to be adjusted. Using the envelope theorem, the change in optimum welfare in Case 1 for a small change in capacity is

$$\frac{\partial W}{\partial \overline{K}} = -\hat{\beta} + \gamma_1/a_1 + \gamma_2/a_1 \tag{5.43}$$

Because $\gamma_1 = \gamma_2 = 0$ in Case 1, $\partial W/\partial \overline{K} = -\beta < 0$, which states that a decrease in capital will increase welfare. This is evident in Figure 5.4. At optimum capacity, $\partial W/\partial \overline{K} = 0$, which we now incorporate into the second case.

*Case 2:* $0 < Q_1 = \overline{K}/a_1$ and $0 < Q_2 < \overline{K}/a_1$

Period-2 output is still less than capacity, and so $\gamma_2 = 0$; but period-1 output equals capacity, and $\gamma_1 \geq 0$. However, with optimum capacity, $\partial W/\partial \overline{K} = 0$ and $\gamma_1 = \beta$, from (5.43). Then, from (5.38) and (5.39), $p_1 = b + \beta$ and $p_2 = b$. This case is illustrated in Figure 5.5. Peak price equals long-run marginal cost, and off-peak price equals short-run marginal cost. Capacity is optimal, and peak output equals capacity. Total revenue, given by area $p_1Q_1 + p_2Q_2$, equals total cost, given by area $(b + \beta)Q_1 + bQ_2$. Off-peak consumers cover only the operating cost of serving them; they contribute no revenues to cover the capital cost $\hat{\beta}\overline{K}$.

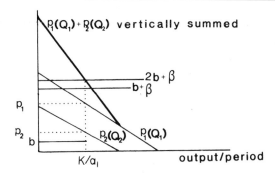

Figure 5.6. Shifting-peak case.

Finally, peak price exceeds off-peak price, and given the position of the peak and off-peak demands, this will always be the case at the optimum.

*Case 3:* $0 < Q_1 = Q_2 = \overline{K}/a_1$

Demand in both periods is pressing against capacity, and $\gamma_1 \geq 0$ and $\gamma_2 \geq 0$. With capacity at the optimum, we have $\gamma_1/a_1 + \gamma_2/a_1 = \beta$. If both $\gamma_1$ and $\gamma_2$ are positive, we have $p_1 = b + \beta - \gamma_2 < b + \beta$ and $p_2 = b + \gamma_2 > b$. This case is depicted in Figure 5.6 and is referred to as a shifting-peak situation. The "shift" refers to what would occur if prices were $p_1 = b + \beta$ and $p_2 = b$, for then off-peak quantity demanded would exceed the peak quantity demanded. To avoid this undesirable result, off-peak price is raised, and peak price lowered by equivalent amounts ($\gamma_2$), until demand in both periods equals capacity. Total costs are still exactly covered in the shifting-peak case; however, off-peak consumers cover some of the capacity costs instead of having the entire cost fall on peak consumers.

Figure 5.6 is constructed by first noting that the shifting-peak situation applies. Peak quantity demanded would fall below off-peak quantity demanded if prices were set to long-run and short-run marginal costs; that is, $p_1 = b + \beta$ and $p_2 = b$. Correct prices can be found by constructing a new demand curve that is the vertical sum of the peak curve and the off-peak curve. The sense of this is that users in both periods are going to be using the available capacity; therefore, the marginal unit is justified by comparing revenues and consumer surpluses from both periods with the marginal cost. The vertical summation of demands allows us to compare the joint valuation of the incremental unit of output in each period with the marginal running costs in both periods, $2b$, plus the marginal-capacity cost, $\beta$. The intersection of the summed demand curve and long-run joint marginal cost, $2b + \beta$, determines optimum capacity. Price in each period is that given by the intersection of each demand curve and a vertical line drawn at the capacity output. The marginal "deficit" by not pricing the peak demand at $b + \beta$ is just met by the additional contribution above $b$ from off-peak demanders (reflecting the valuation placed on the additional output). This construction is reminiscent of the general problem of pricing for joint products outlined by Samuelson (1969), where joint valuations equal joint marginal cost.

Much of the literature on peak-load pricing developed around this basic fixed-coefficient model. Whether or not this framework has been too restrictive is an empirical matter that requires analysis of the particular industries in question. In Section 5.4, we refer to the diagrams developed in this section to address some of the practical considerations that arise when applying the principles. First, however, we address two important modifications to this model: (1) introduction of a diverse technology that is intermediate between the fixed-coefficient and neoclassical technologies; (2) allowance for interdependent demands.

### 5.3. Diverse technology and interdependent demands

Because the results of the fixed-coefficient model are at odds with the general neoclassical model, applying the results requires care. We should not prescribe, for instance, a set of prices whereby off-peak consumers contribute nothing to capacity cost if the industry is not properly characterized by a fixed-coefficient technology. Turvey (1968) questioned the appropriateness of the fixed-coefficient technology, particularly for electric utilities, and Crew and Kleindorfer (1975, 1979a) and Wenders (1976) have adopted an alternative technology for electricity that is more general than the fixed-coefficient technology, is less general than the neoclassical technology, and is a reasonable description of electricity production: the diverse technology.

### Diverse technology

To illustrate, suppose a firm has three production techniques available: (1) peak load, (2) intermediate load, and (3) base load. Base load may be a coal-burning or nuclear plant, intermediate load may be an oil-burning plant, and peak load may be an internal-combustion engine. The distinction between the three is in the capacity and operating costs. Capacity cost refers to the cost of a kilowatt, and operating cost refers to the cost of producing a kilowatt-hour *for one year*. If there is no downtime for maintenance, a 100-KW plant will be capable of producing at a rate of 100 KWH around the clock, or 1 KW of capacity, fully utilized, produces 8,760 KWH of electricity each year (24 hours/day × 365 days/year). In keeping with previous notation, we let $\beta_i$ and $b_i$ be the unit capacity cost for a kilowatt and the unit variable cost of operating a kilowatt for a year using technique $i$, $i = 1, 2, 3$, respectively. All three techniques are potentially employable if $b_1 > b_2 > b_3$ and $\beta_1 < \beta_2 < \beta_3$; if a technique does not fit this pattern, it can be discarded as inefficient, because it is dominated by an existing technique. Thus, the base-load technique entails high capacity costs and low operating costs, and the reverse is true for the peak-load technique. The intermediate-load technique falls between these extremes.

We can illustrate these concepts by defining the marginal cost of using any technique. If $\alpha_i$ is the percentage of a year that capacity $i$ is utilized, then the marginal cost of using technique $i$ is $MC_i(\alpha_i) = \alpha_i b_i + \beta_i$. Again, this is the marginal cost of adding 1

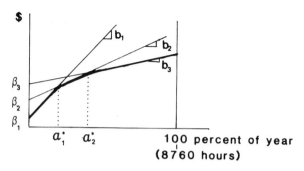

Figure 5.7. Cost in a diverse technology.

KW of capacity $i$, which is operated for $\alpha_i$ percent of the year. All three marginal-cost curves are plotted in Figure 5.7, where $\alpha_1^*$ is obtained by setting $MC_1(\alpha) = MC_2(\alpha)$ and solving for $\alpha$ to obtain

$$\alpha_1^* = [\beta_2 - \beta_1]/[b_1 - b_2] > 0$$

Similarly, $\alpha_2^*$ is found by setting $MC_2(\alpha) = MC_3(\alpha)$ to obtain

$$\alpha_2^* = [\beta_3 - \beta_2]/[b_2 - b_3] > 0$$

Because any increase in output should be accomplished at minimum marginal cost, the darkened piecewise-linear curve represents the least-cost means of the increase. And any new technique is discarded unless it fits the pattern of $b$'s and $\beta$'s in the sense that if $(b_0, \beta_0)$ represents a new technology and $\beta_0 > \beta_i$ $(b_0 > b_i)$, then we must have $b_0 < b_i$ $(\beta_0 < \beta_i)$ for $i = 1, 2, 3$. Otherwise, the marginal-cost curve for the new technology will lie everywhere above the envelope (the darkened piecewise-linear curve).

Figure 5.7 reveals the technique that should be employed for increases in output; here, $\alpha_1^*$ and $\alpha_2^*$ are the dividing points between techniques that define the supply periods. Suppose that at current prices, capacity is fully utilized, and demand increases by 1 KW, which is used $\alpha_0$ percent of the year, where $\alpha_1^* < \alpha_0^* < \alpha_2^*$. Using the figure, intermediate-load capacity should be employed. Or, algebraically,

$$MC_1(\alpha_0) - MC_2(\alpha_0) = \alpha_0[b_1 - b_2] + \beta_1 - \beta_2 \qquad (5.44)$$

Because $\alpha_0 > \alpha_1^* = [\beta_2 - \beta_1]/[b_1 - b_2]$, (5.44) must be positive, indicating that intermediate-load expansion will be less costly than peak-load expansion in meeting the increased demand. In a similar fashion, we can show $MC_3(\alpha_0) - MC_2(\alpha_0) > 0$, indicating that intermediate-load expansion is also less costly than base-load expansion. The greater the portion of the year a given demand must be met, the more advantageous base-load capacity becomes. Because base load has high capacity cost and low operating cost, the larger the proportion of the year a given demand must be served, the more attractive the low operating cost becomes. Alternatively, for demands that must be met for short periods, in particular less than $\alpha_1^*$, operating cost is less important. A least-cost solution calls for using the peak-load technique with its low capacity cost.

Wenders demonstrates the derivation of welfare-maximizing prices in a model with three time periods, independent demands, and base, intermediate, and peak production techniques. The solution requires that base-load capacity be operated in all time periods, intermediate-load capacity during the peak and shoulder peak periods, and peak-load capacity during the peak period only. Prices are

$$p_1 = b_1 + \beta_1/\alpha_1 \tag{5.45}$$

$$p_2 = \frac{[\alpha_1 + \alpha_2]b_2 - \alpha_1 b_1 + \beta_2 - \beta_1}{\alpha_2} \tag{5.46}$$

$$p_3 = \frac{b_3 - [\alpha_1 + \alpha_2]b_2 + \beta_3 - \beta_2}{\alpha_3} \tag{5.47}$$

where the subscripts on prices are 1 for the peak period, 2 for the shoulder peak (intermediate) period, and 3 for the off-peak period. Also, $\alpha_i$ refers to the portion of the year that technique $i$ is utilized. Note that capacity costs enter into all three prices, although there are special cases in which this does not occur. Consider, for instance, the should peak price $p_2$. The right side of (5.46) is the marginal cost of increasing shoulder peak demand. Additional intermediate-load capacity is needed for a demand increase, but less peak-load capacity is needed, because the new intermediate-load capacity can replace some of the existing peak-load capacity. Therefore, only the difference between the intermediate and peak costs, $\beta_2 - \beta_1$, enters (5.46). There is also a saving in operating cost, because intermediate load is less costly to operate than the replaced peak load. This enters as $[\alpha_1 + \alpha_2]b_2 - \alpha_1 b_1$.

A special case arises when the pricing periods coincide with the supply periods defined in Figure 5.7. In this event, $\alpha_1 = \alpha_1^*$ and $\alpha_2 = \alpha_2^*$. Substituting the values of $\alpha_1^*$ and $\alpha_2^*$ into (5.46) yields $p_2 = b_2$; shoulder peak price equals operating cost only. This is because the increase in marginal-capacity cost needed to meet the expanded shoulder peak demand exactly offsets the savings in operating cost from running intermediate-load capacity instead of peak-load capacity. A similar result holds for the off-peak period in this case, and we can obtain $p_3 = b_3$.

The diverse-technology model is useful for deriving optimum electricity price structures, because it captures important features of the underlying technology of electricity generation. We know, for example, that utilities do use varying production techniques over the course of the demand cycle. The derived prices are complex forms of the marginal-cost prices derived with the fixed-coefficient technology. The frequently cited result that off-peak consumers do not contribute to capacity cost is modified, although it is still possible in special cases. Like the constant-returns fixed-coefficient technology, the diverse technology ensures prices that allow total revenue to equal total cost. Of course, in practice, derived prices may require adjustments if the underlying technology is such that marginal-cost prices still result in a deficit.

### Interdependent demands

In Section 5.1, welfare-maximizing peak-load prices were derived in a model in which demands were interdependent. In Section 5.2, the same prices were derived in a model in which demands were independent. The reason for the difference was that consumer surplus was used as a measure of welfare in Section 5.2, and to avoid complications that arise with consumer surplus and interdependent demands, we assumed independence. These complications did not arise in Section 5.1, because a general-welfare function was used, and welfare measurements were made using compensated demand curves.[4] Making welfare measurements with consumer surplus implies that market-demand curves are used, and this can result in nonunique measurements.

The nature of the complications with consumer surplus and interdependent demands is as follows. Recall that for independent demands, consumer surplus in a two-period model [from (5.34)] is

$$\int_0^Q p_1(Q_1) \, dQ_1 + \int_0^{Q_2} p_2(Q_2) \, dQ_2 - p_1(Q_1)Q_1 - p_2(Q_2)Q_2 \quad (5.48)$$

With interdependent demands, the inverse demand functions are $p_1(Q_1, Q_2)$ and $p_2(Q_1, Q_2)$, but in general we cannot simply rewrite (5.48) as

$$\int_0^{Q_1} p_1(Q_1, Q_2) \, dQ_1 + \int_0^{Q_2} p_2(Q_1, Q_2) \, dQ_2$$
$$- p_1(Q_1, Q_2)Q_1 - p_2(Q_1, Q_2)Q_2 \quad (5.49)$$

to obtain a measure of consumer surplus. The reason is that for the first integral, where integration is over $Q_1$, $Q_2$ is held constant at some value. The value of the integral will depend on the constant value of $Q_2$, because the demand curve for good 1 shifts because of changes in $Q_2$. But what constant value of $Q_2$ is appropriate? After all, the second-integral $Q_2$ is being varied over the designated limits. Of course, the same problem occurs with the second integral: where to hold $Q_1$ constant. The correct formulation is to use a line integral and change $Q_1$ and $Q_2$ in a specific

---

4 The complications also did not arise in Chapter 3, where interdependent demands were assumed for a multiproduct firm's products, because a general-welfare function was used.

manner; or, in $Q_1Q_2$ space, if $(Q_1^0, Q_2^0)$ is the starting point and $(Q_1^1, Q_2^1)$ the terminal point, then a particular path is chosen between these points. The line integral is written as

$$\oint_{C \atop Q_1^0, Q_2^0}^{Q_1^1, Q_2^1} [p_1(Q_1, Q_2) \, dQ_1 + p_2(Q_1, Q_2) \, dQ_2] \tag{5.50}$$

where $C$ is the path chosen.[5]

The problem, however, is that the value of (5.50) will depend, in general, on the chosen path. There is not a unique measure of consumer surplus for given price changes. Consider that as peak quantity $Q_1$ changes, then off-peak inverse demand changes at the rate $\partial p_2 / \partial Q_1$. And as off-peak quantity changes, then peak inverse demand changes at the rate $\partial p_1 / \partial Q_2$. In general, $\partial p_1 / \partial Q_2 \neq \partial p_2 / \partial Q_1$; so the order in which the quantities are changed will determine the consumer-surplus areas. There are, however, situations in which the path does not matter, in particular, when

$$\partial p_1 / \partial Q_2 = \partial p_2 / \partial Q_1 \tag{5.51}$$

This occurs, for instance, when income effects are zero. In that situation, the total effect of a price change, which can be broken into the substitution and income effects, is equal to the substitution effect only, and by symmetry of the Slutsky matrix, (5.51) holds. Zero or small income effects often are used as a justification for using consumer surplus. In Section 5.1, where interdependent demands are not a problem, welfare measures are made in terms of compensated demands, and (5.51) holds if the $Q_i$ are compensated demands.

Because consumer surplus is so often used in applied peak-load pricing problems, where demands are typically interdependent, the analyst should be aware of its shortcomings. There is a large literature on consumer surplus and how it relates to the compensating and equivalent variations. These are well-defined amounts

---

5 Pressman (1970) presents this formulation, which he credits to Hotelling (1935), in a rigorous development of peak-load pricing.

of money that consumers would pay or would need to be paid in order to face certain price changes. Silberberg (1978) provides a lucid presentation of consumer surplus in a general context, and Just, Hueth, and Schmitz (1982) discuss the error introduced into the estimation of compensating and equivalent variations using raw consumer-surplus measures when the problem of path dependence arises. The latter authors also provide formulas that allow an estimation of compensating and equivalent variations using an adjusted consumer-surplus measure. In addition, they derive a necessary and sufficient condition for uniqueness of consumer surplus when only some subset of prices changes: namely, that all income elasticities for the subset of goods with changing prices must be equal.

### 5.4. Practical considerations for peak-load pricing

In the war being fought to translate microeconomic theory into public policy, economists have had disappointingly few victories. For this reason, the adoption of peak-load pricing (PLP) in the electric-power industry over the past decade has been gratifying. A number of progressive state public service commissions were studying PLP during the early seventies, but these commissions also found themselves increasingly involved in hearings on electricity rates as utilities requested rate hikes in response to increasing production costs. The 1973 oil shortage added to these costs, and the energy crisis in general led to a greater public awareness of the potential for energy shortages and the need to allocate existing supplies efficiently. Increased attention was paid to electricity and natural gas as prices rose and shortages actually materialized. Environmental groups were interested in slowing the growth of the electricity industry and decreasing its adverse effects on the environment, and they found cost-based pricing principles in accord with their objectives.

All of these events culminated in the federal Public Utility Regulatory Policy Act (PURPA) of 1978; see Joskow (1979) for an evaluation. That act required state commissions to consider

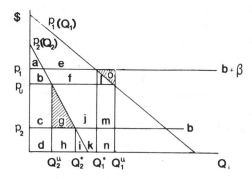

Figure 5.8. Benefits of peak-load pricing.

adopting more efficient pricing policies and production techniques within their states. Millions of dollars were awarded to support benefit–cost analyses of implementing rate structures for PLP, seasonal pricing, cogeneration of power, lifeline rates, load management, interruptible service, and other policies. The benefit–cost analyses drew heavily on the theoretical studies of pricing policies developed over the previous two decades.

### Benefit–cost analysis

To introduce some of the practical considerations that arise when adopting PLP, we outline the more important elements that need to be considered in a benefit–cost analysis. The major sources of benefits can be illustrated in a simple diagram. Figure 5.8 depicts a firm peak situation, with two independent demand curves and a fixed-coefficient technology. Again, the peak (off-peak) period is indexed by 1 (2), and $b$ and $\beta$ are the marginal operating and capacity costs, respectively. We shall identify the benefits of moving from a uniform price, $p_u$, to an optimum peak price, $p_1$, and off-peak price, $p_2$. Initially, total revenue equals total cost.

The uniform price implies that $Q_2^u$ is demanded in the off-peak period, and $Q_1^u$ in the peak period. As before, welfare is measured by consumer surplus plus revenue minus cost, which for the off-peak period equals area $a + b + c$, and for the peak period equals area $e + a - o$.[6] Although these calculations allocate all of the capacity cost to the peak period, the aggregate welfare is not affected by the allocation. After moving from the uniform price to the optimum prices, the quantities demanded become $Q_1^*$ and $Q_2^*$ for the peak and off-peak periods, respectively. Welfare for the off-peak period now equals area $a + b + c + g$, and for the peak period it equals area $a + e$. Comparing the pre-price-change area with the post-price-change area reveals a net welfare gain with PLP equal to area $g + o$, which is hatched in Figure 5.8.

We should note that there may be both winners and losers in this process. In our example, off-peak consumers are winners because their consumer surplus has increased by area $c + g$, the firm is indifferent because profit is still zero, and the peak consumers are losers because their consumer surplus has decreased by $b + f + l$. Therefore, although the peak-load prices represent a Pareto optimum, the move toward PLP is not Pareto-superior to the uniform price. There is a net welfare gain from the move (area $g + o$), but unless that gain is redistributed to compensate the losers, the Pareto criterion is violated. Although this line of reasoning constitutes an argument against change, there are counterarguments that support the change, as outlined in Section 3.5. There we discussed how a move toward Ramsey pricing may not be Pareto-superior, and the same considerations apply here.

The hatched areas in Figure 5.8 may understate benefits, because demands are assumed to be independent. If demands are interdependent, we expect the off-peak demand curve to shift to the right and the peak demand curve to shift to the left in response to changes in the price of a substitute, thereby increasing the shaded areas. These shifts occur as peak-period consum-

---

6 For example, at the peak, consumer surplus is area $a + e + b + f + l$, total revenue is area $c + g + j + m + d + h + i + k + n$, and total cost is area $b + f + l + o + c + g + j + m + d + h + i + k + n$. Therefore, consumer surplus plus total revenue minus total cost is area $a + e - o$.

ers shift their consumption from peak to off-peak hours to take advantage of the lower price. Naturally, not all consumption will shift. A residential consumer, for instance, may be able to shift the electricity used to wash and dry clothes from the peak to the off-peak period, whereas electricity used to operate the television set during the peak cannot be shifted.[7]

In order to charge different prices for peak and off-peak consumption, the firm must be able to determine the time of day that electricity is demanded. The cost of meters that are capable of recording the time of day, in excess of the cost of simple meters that do not record time, is the principal cost of adopting PLP. If the benefits determined earlier exceed these metering costs, PLP is justified. The typical finding of most benefit–cost analyses in the United States is that PLP is justified for large consumers, but not for small consumers. For the latter, the capacity savings and increased off-peak consumer surplus do not match the extra cost of the sophisticated meter. The total cost of these meters was between $150 to $200 in 1985.

Typically, demands for electricity are cyclic over seasons of the year as well as over each day. This pattern suggests that prices should vary with the seasons in addition to varying over the day. Wenders and Taylor (1976) use the analysis of Figure 5.8 to illustrate the benefits of seasonal pricing, while pointing out that the metering costs are zero because the more sophisticated meters are unnecessary. Thus, in any benefit–cost study of implementing new prices, the benefits from seasonal prices should be exhausted first, and only the remaining benefits from daily PLP should be compared with metering costs. We now turn to some of the practical considerations that complicate the benefit–cost analyses.

---

7 See Wenders and Taylor (1976) for a diagrammatic explanation of the benefits and costs when demands are interdependent. High cross-elasticities complicate the selection of rating periods and appropriate prices. The avoidance of "needle peaking" due to demand shifts under PLP is one motivation for kilowatt demand charges. If users' demands are correlated, the kilowatt demand charge makes economic sense (Veall, 1983).

*Selecting the length of the periods*

Unfortunately, daily demand patterns do not exhibit nice, discrete jumps at convenient intervals. The peak demand is stochastic, dependent on weather conditions and economic factors; furthermore, it may not be unique. Load-duration curves are used to show the relationship between quantity demanded and time, and they are useful in the process of trying to select rating periods for pricing purposes. Of course, the selection is complicated further by the very prices adopted, because quantities demanded during an interval (and the associated load curves) will shift in response to prices.

Consider a simple example with three 8-hour periods that must be classified either as peak or off-peak periods. We assume that demands in the periods are easily distinguished and that they are independent. In Figure 5.9(a), a narrow 8-hour peak rating period is selected and applied to $p_1(Q_1)$. Compared with a uniform price of 40, a higher peak price of 50 causes a cutback in peak-period consumption from 240 megawatt-hours (MWH) per 8 hours to 200 MWH per 8 hours. This shift implies a peak megawatt demand of 25 MW (200/8), compared with 30 MW under uniform pricing. Figure 5.10(a) displays this shift on the hourly load curve as the movement from the solid to the dashed lines. In the other two periods, reflected in megawatt-hour demand functions $p_3(Q_3)$ and $p_2(Q_2)$, a lower off-peak price of 20 induces additional consumption. With a narrow 8-hour peak period, total megawatt-hour consumption for the complete 24 hours actually increases.

In contrast, Figure 5.9(b) shows a price of 50 applied to both period 1 and period 2 for a 16-hour peak period. Total megawatt-hour consumption is reduced, and the load factor (ratio of average consumption to peak consumption) is lower than in the (a) case. The new load shape could be more expensive to meet than in the (a) case, depending on the production techniques available. Of course, the calculation of the appropriate peak price will also depend on the length of the rating period – with the longer period having a lower price than the 50 applied in the (a) situation, if 50

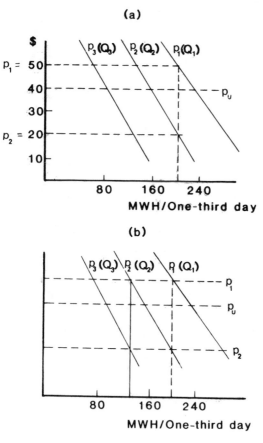

Figure 5.9. Three periods.

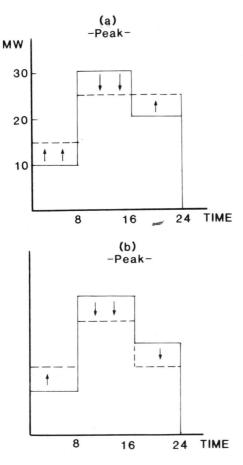

Figure 5.10. Hourly load curves for different rating periods.

was appropriate for 8-hour peaks. However, the analytical point is the same: The duration and specification of the rating periods affect the load-shape changes, and the load curves are important in determining the mixture of production techniques among base-load intermediate-load and peak-load capacities.

### Demand elasticities

The actual reduction of peak-period consumption and stimulation of off-peak consumption depend on their respective elasticities and cross-elasticities of demand, given the new PLP structure. Key features of the structure include the peak/off-peak ratio, the presence or absence of shoulder rates, the starting times, and the durations of the periods. Aggregate responses are also influenced by features of the consumer population: income, education, family size, and appliance mix. Other factors include characteristics of a geographic area, such as climate and housing density. These variables often are included in studies of the determinants of kilowatt-hour consumption. The shape of the daily load curve, as influenced by the foregoing factors *and* as it changes over time, will determine the costs and benefits experienced by consumers and utilities.

A primary step in evaluating a new rate structure is the estimation of load curves as accurately as possible – before and after changes in rate structures. Incorporating complex consumption interdependencies and long-run adjustment processes into the framework involves making assumptions if no quantitative studies exist for the local population. Because many empirical issues are not as yet fully resolved, sensitivity tests for variables must be conducted prior to the implementation of new rates. For example, daily load curves, as directly observed, are complicated. Individual load curves (for a single household) are quite variable over time (either hour by hour or across households), but aggregate or system-wide load curves are somewhat more regular, because *demand diversity* can smooth individual behavior. However, instantaneous kilowatt demand is still highly variable on an hourly and daily basis. To use these hourly load curves in any modeling effort, researchers must discover the sources of systematic variation in instantaneous residential demand and project these into the future to determine the expected aggregate load curve for a particular utility.

The importance of consumer knowledge and perceptions is illustrated by some simple examples. In a study sponsored by the Department of Energy (DOE) in Edmond, Oklahoma, PLP was largely ineffective in changing load shapes because consumers typically were ignorant of the rate itself and the cost savings made possible by switching some consumption to off-peak hours. However, utilities can affect consumer behavior through educational and marketing campaigns. Some companies conduct detailed, in-house presentations to consumers in order to secure understanding of and participation in innovative rate programs. Others have failed to secure adequate participation in PLP studies because their consumer-contact materials have been confusing or misleading. Regulators and managers are learning more about how to handle the psychological factors critical to the success of innovative rates.

Other studies of PLP funded by the DOE have appeared in a number of reports. Basically, the conclusion that can be relied on from these studies is simple: PLP does produce shifts in the time patterns of consumption. Unfortunately, because of numerous flaws in the design and analysis of these studies, it is difficult to be more precise. Inappropriate sampling strategies, less than optimal consumer education, arbitrary rate selection, and other problems leave us with very little basis for computing elasticity estimates. The usefulness of utility-funded studies is, if anything, worse. Very few studies offer anything like the necessary basis for estimating impacts that might be transferable to other populations.

The statistical techniques used to draw inferences from DOE-sponsored and other experiments are complicated. Analysis of variance is used to quantify changes in the average customer's hourly load curve caused by PLP. The statistical significance of changes in mean kilowatt-hour usage is calculated and is controlled for the influence of other variables (such as household size) so that the effect of the PLP can be identified with greater precision. Besides these *comparative* studies (pre vs. post PLP for a set of customers, or control vs. PLP households), economists have specified more complete demand models to estimate price elasticities (Acton and Mitchell, 1983; Caves and Christensen, 1980). Thus, besides determining that there is an impact, such specifications allow researchers to identify load shifts for a wide range of alternative PLP structures. The gain in precision sometimes comes at the expense of additional complexity.

### Estimates of marginal costs

The technical features of any utility environment generally are complex and constantly changing, and electric-power systems are no exception. In our examples, the production technology has been simple, and we have implicitly assumed constant input prices. Rate designers at utilities and regulatory commissions have to deal with much more detail in determining price structures. Furthermore, in actual rate cases, practitioners have shunned marginal-cost-based rates, partly because of the conceptual difficulties in calculating costs. Although the existing non-time-differentiated pricing schemes are replete with arbitrary cost allocations, the prospect of opening debate over a host of issues places a heavy burden on those advocating change.

How does one go about calculating marginal cost? A number of methods, which will be briefly reviewed here, have been suggested by researchers. Some aspects of these methods, in fact, are currently used by utilities. The major conceptual problem in calculating marginal costs is how capacity costs are to be handled. The Electric Utility Rate Design Study (EURDS), sponsored by the Electric Power Research Institute (EPRI) and other organizations, identified several techniques:

1. Base-load perturbation method
2. Peaker perturbation method

3. Production function
4. Linear programming

The base-load perturbation method assumes that marginal-capacity costs are the costs of shifting future generating units (already planned) forward or backward in time. The peaker method assumes that because peaking units are the most economical way of meeting peak loads only, they represent the marginal generating capacity. Production-function methods attempt to model the input–output relationship for utilities using Cobb–Douglas or similar functions. In this way, changes in variables such as load can be used to determine analytically the changes in costs. Linear-programming models essentially re-create the system in an optimal way, based on given constraints, and determine the cost of re-creating the last optimal unit of capacity.

Let us review one difference in approaches:

> One school of thought defines long-run marginal cost as the cost incurred when producing one more unit of output from a theoretical firm that has been designed de novo. This definition is labeled the "static" long-run marginal cost. . . . The other school of thought defines long-run marginal cost as the cost incurred when producing one more unit of output from an actual firm that alters its existing plant optimally over time. This definition is labeled the "dynamic" long-run cost.
> (Temple, Barker & Sloan, 1978, p. 3)

National Economic Research Associates (NERA) has promoted the "static" definition and takes the cost of the least capital-intensive unit that would be added to the optimal system to meet peak-period demands. An alternative formulation by Cicchetti, Gillen, and Smolensky (CGS) (1976) is closer to a "dynamic" definition of long-run marginal cost. CGS assert that

> the cost of capacity is the cost of advancing or delaying units in the construction schedule to meet a change in demand. The cost of this change is equal to the annualized capital cost of the plants being advanced,

adjusted for the operating savings which may occur as a result of the new plants in the dispatch order. The marginal cost of capacity is allocated equally across all hours in the peak period using loss of load probability and judgment to determine the peak period. (Cicchetti et al., 1977, p. 4)

Thus, NERA usually has peaking units (combustion turbines) represent marginal generating capacity, whereas CGS may take the next movable base-load unit (or units) as the marginal capacity.

Can both be "correct" or reasonable? Whether one should consider peaking or base-load units marginal capacity depends on many factors, and most practitioners qualify their results. The CGS perturbation method takes the system's previously planned generating unit, if any, as the marginal capacity the system planners will advance to meet an increase in demand. This is a different view of marginal generating capacity that places greater weight on the potential nonoptimality of present systems. If the utility is not in long-run equilibrium, a peaker might not be advanced to meet peak load. Nonoptimality and expectations about input prices are two key areas where methods can yield different "answers," because they depend on the time horizon and other assumptions.

Other approaches parallel the NERA and CGS differences in the definitions of long-run marginal cost. Some draw more heavily on econometrics and optimization via computer modeling. For example, production functions have been used to derive a total-cost function. Drawing from neoclassical economic theory, the marginal cost is just the change in total cost caused by a change in output.

Others make a short-run marginal-cost calculation that explicitly considers the price needed to limit the quantity demanded if the reliability criterion is not to be exceeded. Thus, instead of developing a *long-run* capacity charge on the cost of planned capacity additions (as with CGS), they calculate a short-run capacity charge necessary to ration demand. In equilibrium, when input prices are stable, the short-run marginal cost calculated using this technique will yield the same results as the NERA or CGS perturbation approaches.[8]

### 5.5. Summary

Cyclic demand and nonstorability complicate the pricing and capacity decisions for many natural monopolies. Much of the previous literature is couched in terms of the fixed-coefficients model. With a neoclassical production function, optimal capacity depends on both off-peak and peak demands. Increased capacity can lower the unit cost of providing both peak and off-peak service, and in contrast to the situaion with the fixed-coefficient technology, efficient pricing involves off-peak consumers being priced above variable cost. Thus, they may make some contribution to covering capacity costs. Furthermore, a diverse-technology formulation provides a reasonable approximation of electricity generation – providing a less restrictive characterization than the fixed-coefficient technology. The basic conclusions from the more general neoclassical formulation also apply.

If charging optimum prices results in a deficit, a Ramsey rule can be applied, taking into account both cross-elasticities between time periods and production-cost interdependences. Thus, the peak-load natural monopoly is a special case of the more general multiproduct natural monopoly. Demand elasticities for peak and off-peak periods and the associated marginal costs determine the second-best prices.

Practical considerations complicate the implementation of these pricing principles. Compared with uniform pricing, peak-load pricing involves additional metering investment; so improvements in resource allocation stemming from implementation must be greater than metering costs. In addition, selecting the number and length of the time periods requires information

---

8 For estimates of peak and off-peak marginal operating costs for an electric utility, including spatial considerations associated with line losses, see Scherer (1976). In his example, the imposition of the most restrictive pollution standards raises system average total costs by 25%.

about cross-elasticities and hourly marginal costs. Deriving appropriate opportunity-cost information from historical accounting data is impossible, given the forward-looking nature of marginal costs.

Thus far, we have examined three basic pricing structures: (1) linear prices in Chapter 3, (2) nonlinear prices in Chapter 4, and (3) time-varying prices in this chapter. Before leaving the topic of optimum pricing policies for a regulated firm, we shall add one more level of reality by examining optimum prices under stochastic-demand conditions. This provides the subject matter of Chapter 6.

# 6

## Pricing and capacity under stochastic demand

In Chapters 2–5, we assumed that demand for the firm's output was known with certainty, so that the firm or regulator knew precisely the quantity that would be demanded once a price was set. In reality, a more complicated situation faces decision-makers. At a given price, the quantity demanded is essentially a random variable. Based on experience, the firm may have knowledge of the parameters that define the distribution of this random variable, where these parameters may be functions of the price set. However, the firm will not know the exact quantity needed to satisfy demand.

Stochastic demand can be attributed to changes in various parameters: preferences, competing technologies, incomes, prices of other goods, or the weather. Extreme weather conditions can cause unanticipated swings in the demands for electricity and natural gas, as well as transportation and communications services. How stochastic demand complicates the firm's pricing decision will depend on the nature of the product and the institutional setting in which it is produced. Although most of the examples used in this chapter are drawn from the literature on electric-power utilities, the principles that are developed apply to the other regulated sectors as well. We shall often refer to the natural monopoly firm in this chapter as a public utility.

The introduction of stochastic demand raises a number of

important issues related to pricing and capacity. Leland (1972) suggests that public utilities are good examples of price-setters: firms that set prices before demand is known and then adjust output to meet demand. However, if demand exceeds capacity, then some demand will go unsatisfied. If some demand goes unsatisfied, we must consider reliability of service as a characteristic of the good. When demand is known with certainty, reliability is always 100% and therefore can be omitted from analysis.

Reliability will be determined by the price and the capacity selected by the firm. High prices and a large capacity will contribute to high reliability, but they may also result in significant excess capacity and a deficit. As we shall show, if there is demand uncertainty, then a deficit is possible even with a constant-cost, fixed-coefficient technology and marginal-cost prices. Moreover, the firm's problem may be further complicated if demand is also dependent on reliability. In this case, the firm must quote a price and a degree of reliability of service to the consumers, as well as provide adequate capacity to ensure the quoted reliability.

We assume throughout the chapter that there is no uncertainty on the supply side; the public utility's equipment does not break down. Of course, this characterization of the environment is not true, because power outages, downed telephone lines, ruptured water mains, and so on, are not uncommon, and they do represent another source of uncertainty. But adding uncertain supply would further complicate the following analysis and obscure the major issues we wish to discuss. For an analysis that derives prices when supply is random but demand is not, see Vardi, Zahavi, and Avi-Itzhak (1977), and for an analysis that considers both random supply and demand, see Chao (1983).

Among the complications introduced by random elements on the demand side, we shall emphasize the firm's choice of reliability, its relationship to budget deficits, and its feedback effects on consumer demand. The derivation of marginal benefits and marginal costs is less straightforward when additional dimensions of product quality affect the choices made by producers and consumers. Thus, some of the analysis will differ from that used in earlier chapters, but the expanded framework is necessary if we are to understand these complications. Many derivations of results are omitted, but references are made to where they can be found. Uncertainty will be reintroduced in Chapter 9, and a knowledge of the techniques in this chapter will be useful for that chapter as well.

### 6.1. Stochastic demand in a peak-load model[1]

We introduce stochastic demand by again analyzing a PLP situation. For simplicity, we assume a fixed-coefficient technology, which will allow us to isolate those complications attributable only to the stochastic elements. We also assume that there are $n$ periods of equal duration and that the firm must choose capacity and $n$ prices to maximize the expected value of social welfare. Because welfare depends on demand, which is random, welfare itself is random and can be maximized only in an expected-value sense; here, society is viewed as risk-neutral. The welfare level actually achieved will depend on the value of demand actually realized. As in the previous chapter, $\overline{K}/a_1$ is capacity, which is determined by the choice of capital, owing to the fixed-coefficient technology. For brevity, we let $Z = \overline{K}/a_1$, and prices are again denoted by $p = (p_1, \ldots, p_n)$, where $p_i$ is the price in period $i$. Throughout, subscript $i$ will run over all periods from 1 to $n$.

Demand in each period is subject to random fluctuations, so that a unique relationship does not exist between $p_i$ and the quantity demanded, given by $Q_i$. The firm cannot choose a particular price and be certain as to what the demand response will be. Instead of the riskless relationship $Q_i = Q_i(p_i)$, the firm is confronted with $Q_i = Q_i(p_i, u_i)$, where $u_i$ is a random variable. The firm is assumed to know the density functions of the random variables, given by $f_i(u_i)$. This knowledge may stem from historical records of weather patterns, changing consumer tastes, and

---

1 Sections 6.1–6.4 are largely taken from Tschirhart (1980). Other overviews of this material can be found in Finsinger (1980) and Gellerson and Grosskopf (1980).

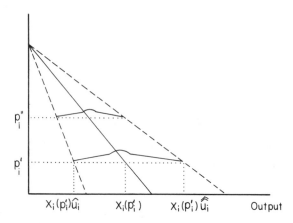

Figure 6.1. A multiplicative stochastic-demand curve.

so on. Thus, although the firm does not know what demand will be, it does know the range of values of demand and the probability attached to each interval of values within that range. This assumption does not seem to be too strong for goods such as electricity, natural gas, and telephone service, for which historical records are readily available.

Brown and Johnson (1969) were the first to explore the problem of random demand and public utility pricing. They examined two specific forms of the demand function, namely, the additive and multiplicative forms. Similar results are obtained for both forms; so our analysis will be confined to the latter. The multiplicative form is written as

$$Q_i(p_i, u_i) = X_i(p_i)u_i$$

where $X_i$ is the mean demand function for period $i$. The distribution functions for the $u_i$ are given by $F_i(a) = \int_0^a f_i(u_i)\, du_i$, and the expected value of $u_i$ by $\int_0^\infty u_i f_i(u_i)\, du_i = 1$.

Figure 6.1 provides an illustration of a multiplicative demand function, where $X_i(p_i)$ is linear. The solid line represents the mean or expected demand curve, where $u_i = 1$. As $u_i$ takes on values from 0 to $\infty$, the demand curve pivots about the vertical intercept, moving from the vertical axis to a horizontal line. When

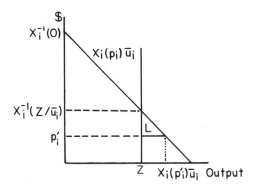

Figure 6.2. Consumer surplus and stochastic demand.

price is set at $p_i'$, the figure shows three possible values of output: (1) $X_i(p_i')\hat{u}_i$ when $u_i = \hat{u}_i$; (2) $X_i(p_i')$ when $u_i = 1$; (3) $X_i(p_i')\hat{u}$ when $u_i = \hat{u}_i$. For a different price, say $p_i''$, we could write the three quantities associated with the same three values of $u_i$, but note that they would be less in each case. For this reason, the price is a parameter in the distribution of demand; that is, the value that demand, a random variable, takes on depends on the price selected. The density functions sketched above the horizontal price lines provide the probability of demand falling in any particular interval, given that price.

The expected value of welfare is

$$E[W] = E[\text{consumer surplus (CS } - L)\\ + \text{ total revenue (R)} - \text{total cost } (C)] \qquad (6.1)$$

The term CS in (6.1) is the usual consumer-surplus triangle under the demand curve. But when demand exceeds capacity, the entire triangle is not attained. Assuming efficient rationing, as explained later, the lowest valuations are not met; any portion of the triangle beyond the capacity level is lost, because demand in this region is not satisfied. This lost portion, denoted $L$, must be subtracted from CS. Figure 6.2 depicts $L$ for a demand curve where $u_i = \bar{u}_i$. The value of $L$ will be positive when there is excess demand, and zero otherwise. Equations (6.2) and (6.3) represent the summations over all periods of $E[CS]$ and $E[L]$, respectively, where $X_i^{-1}$ is the inverse demand function:

$$\sum_{i=1}^{n} \left[ \int_0^\infty f_i(u_i) \int_{p_i}^{X_i^{-1}(0)} X_i(p_i)u_i \, dp_i \, du_i \right] \tag{6.2}$$

$$\sum_{i=1}^{n} \left[ \int_{Z/X_i(p_i)}^\infty f_i(u_i) \int_{p_i}^{X_i^{-1}(Z/u_i)} [X_i(p_i)u_i - Z] \, dp_i \, du_i \right] \tag{6.3}$$

The upper limit on the second integral in (6.2) is the intercept of the demand curve with the price axis, and the lower limit is the selected price. The lower limit of the first integral in (6.3) represents the value of $u_i$ such that demand exactly equals capacity [i.e., $X_i(p_i)u_i = Z$, or $u_i = Z/X_i(p_i)$]. The upper limit on the second integral of (6.3) is the price that will clear the market when there is excess demand. These limits are also illustrated in Figure 6.2. For example, at price $p_i'$ there is excess demand equal to $X_i(p_i')\overline{u}_i - Z$. To clear the market, price must be raised so that $X_i(p_i)\overline{u}_i = Z$, or $p_i = X_i^{-1}(Z/u_i)$.

The efficient-rationing assumption in this formulation of $L$ implies that consumers are costlessly ranked according to their willingness to pay. When demand exceeds capacity, those consumers with the highest valuations are served first. This follows from the location of $L$. In reality, ranking consumers is not a costless operation, suggesting that the cost of ranking should be included in the objective function (which is done in the next section).

Total revenue includes revenue when there is excess supply plus revenue when there is excess demand. $E[R]$ is given by (6.4), where the first integral is associated with excess supply, and the second with excess demand:

$$E[R] = \sum_{i=1}^{n} \left[ \int_0^{Z/X_i(p_i)} f_i(u_i)X_i(p_i)u_ip_i \, du_i + \int_{Z/X_i(p_i)}^\infty f_i(u_i)Zp_i \, du_i \right]$$

$$\tag{6.4}$$

Total cost is the sum of operating costs and capacity costs. From the fixed-coefficient technology, both are constant per unit of output and are given by $b$ and $\beta$, respectively. Equation (6.5) is the $E[C]$ that includes operating costs when there is excess supply in the first integral and excess demand in the second integral:

$$E[C] = \sum_{i=1}^{n} \left[ \int_{0}^{Z/X_i(p_i)} f_i(u_i) X_i(p_i) u_i b \, du_i \right.$$
$$\left. + \int_{Z/X_i(p_i)}^{\infty} f_i(u_i) Z b \, du_i \right] + \beta Z \tag{6.5}$$

As demonstrated by Brown and Johnson (1969), when $E[W]$ is maximized over all $p_i$ and $Z$, the first-order necessary conditions[2] yield the prices

$$p_i = b \tag{6.6}$$

There are two fundamental problems with these prices: First, they will result in excess demand in periods when $u_i$ is large. Second, there is no possibility that revenue will cover costs. Both of these problems are of great concern to public utilities, and they are discussed in detail later.

The reason that price equals operating cost only in the Brown–Johnson model can be seen in Figure 6.3, where four demand curves are drawn for four values of $u_i$, and $X_i(p_i) = 30 - p_i$. These four $u_i$ values are 0.5, 0.71, 1, and 2. Because capacity is chosen ex ante, total-capacity cost, $\beta Z$, is essentially a fixed cost when demand becomes known. For demand curve $0.5X_i$ in Figure 6.3, $p_i = b$ is clearly the welfare-maximizing price, because operating cost is covered, and consumer surplus is at a maximum. This price also applies for any demand up to curve $0.71X_i$,

2 To obtain this result, it must be the case that the probability that demand is less than capacity is nonzero. Clearly this is true in the Brown–Johnson formulation, because the lower bound of $u$ is zero, and there is always a chance that demand is less than capacity (except for the uninteresting case where $Z = 0$). However, Crew and Kleindorfer (1976) show that if the range and variance of $u$ are small, the probability that demand is less than capacity may be zero. In this case, price is indeterminate.

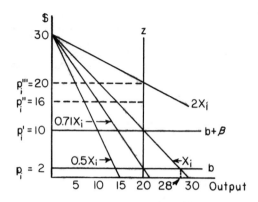

Figure 6.3. An example demand function.

for which demand at price $p_i$ equals capacity.[3] For demand curve $2X_i$, any price between zero and $p_i'''$ will yield the same maximum welfare, although the distribution of welfare between revenue and consumer surplus will vary. Prices near zero for demand curve $2X_i$ will require more rationing, but because rationing is costless in the model, no problems arise. This reasoning also applies for any demand beyond curve $0.71X_i$. Thus, $b$ is the unique optimum price for all demands up to curve $0.71X_i$, and $b$ is an optimum but not unique price for all demands beyond $0.71X_i$. Therefore, $p_i = b$ is selected. This argument holds for all positive $Z$, and it crucially relies on the assumptions (1) that those who value the service least are the first to be cut off when rationing is necessary and (2) that rationing is costless.[4]

This result for pricing is similar to the result obtained under certainty in Section 5.2 and illustrated in Figure 5.4. In that case, capacity was much larger than demand at any price; so capacity

3 The value $u_i = 0.71$ is obtained by noting that $X_i(p_i)u_i = Z$ or $(30 - p_i)u_i = 20$; therefore, if $p_i = 2$, then $u_i = 0.71$.

4 Visscher (1973) points out that the Brown–Johnson results are dependent on the type of rationing system used. For example, when consumers with the highest willingness to pay are served first, as in Brown–Johnson, price equals short-run marginal cost. But when consumers with the lowest willingness to pay are served first, the efficient price equals long-run marginal cost.

cost was a fixed cost that could not be recovered. Optimization called for prices equal to operating cost, so that consumer surplus would be maximized. With stochastic demand, Figure 5.4 is a possibility, because demand may fall short of capacity.

### 6.2. Accounting for excess demand and deficits

In the stochastic setting, the following relationships hold:

$$Q_i(p_i, u_i) \leqq Z \to Q_i(p_i, u_i) = \text{output}$$
$$Q_i(p_i, u_i) > Z \to Z = \text{output}$$

The latter case gives rise to excess demand and rationing. This problem was avoided under riskless demand by simply adding the constraint $Q_i \leqq Z$, but this is now impossible because $Q_i$ is random. Moreover, the problem of excess demand will be exacerbated by a PLP policy that calls for the low prices given in (6.6). Brown and Johnson (1969) acknowledged the cost of rationing in a reply to comments by Salkever (1970) and Turvey (1970). As Turvey stated, "there is thus a tradeoff between the sacrifice of consumer surplus on the one hand and the stringency of rationing on the other hand" (1970, p. 485).

The problem of unsatisfied demand and rationing can be particularly acute for public utilities providing goods considered to be necessities. The loss of power or natural gas is at least an inconvenience and may jeopardize the lives of some consumers who rely on these services for heat or medical needs. Furthermore, rationing is costly because of both the technical requirements and the difficulty of classifying consumers according to their willingness to pay. We shall have more to say about rationing policies later, when we discuss interruptible service. For now, we show how to deal with the excess-demand problem in the preceding model in two different ways: (1) by adding a rationing cost and (2) by including reliability constraints.

### *Penalty costs of excess demand*

Suppose a penalty cost of $\phi$ is assessed for each unit of excess demand; $\phi$ can be thought of as the cost of rationing, including the cost of ranking consumers (Crew and Kleindorfer, 1976). To account for this cost, the following terms, one for each period, are subtracted from the right-hand side of (6.1):

$$\phi \int_{Z/X_i(p_i)}^{\infty} f_i(u_i)[X_i(p_i)u_i - Z] \, du_i$$

The necessary conditions for optimum prices now yield

$$p_i = b + \frac{\phi I_i}{1 - I_i} \tag{6.7}$$

where $I_i = \int_{Z/X_i(p_i)}^{\infty} u_i f_i(u_i) \, du_i$ is the truncated expected value of $u_i$ when there is excess demand.

Clearly, prices now exceed operating cost $b$. The value of the integral expressions will depend on the capacity, $Z$, and $f_i(u_i)$. Accordingly, $0 \leq I_i \leq 1$, because as $Z$ approaches zero, the value of the integrals monotonically approach $E[u_i] = 1$. Thus, the smaller the level of capacity, the higher the price; of course, the higher price mitigates potential rationing costs. Also, if $\phi$ increases, indicating higher rationing costs, then prices increase in response. For example, if rationing costs are $1/KWH, the short-run marginal cost ($b$) is 10¢/KWH, and $I_i = 0.20$, the ex ante (risk-neutral) welfare-maximizing price for this period is

$$p = \$0.10 + \frac{0.20}{0.80} (\$1.00) = \$0.35$$

### Chance constraints and system reliability

The second approach to the problem of excess demand that also admits higher prices is to introduce chance constraints on demand. This approach is used by Meyer (1975a, p. 331) to obtain prices that are "sufficiently high to meet specified standards of system reliability." Thomas, Whinston, and Wright (1972) use a similar approach to allocate uncertain water supplies. The procedure is to add the following constraints to the problem:

$$P\{X_i(p_i)u_i \leq Z\} \geq \epsilon_i > 0 \tag{6.8}$$

where $P$ indicates probability. The value of the $\epsilon_i$ reflects the stringency of system reliability requirements: Larger $\epsilon_i$ imply more stringent requirements. Letting $\gamma_i$ be the Lagrangian multipliers, the appended problem is

$$\max E[W] + \sum_1^n \gamma_i \left( \int_0^{Z/X_i(p_i)} f_i(u_i) \, du_i - \epsilon_i \right)$$

From the necessary conditions for a maximum, prices are

$$p_i = b + \gamma_i \frac{\theta_i f(\theta_i)}{X_i(p_i)[1 - I_i]} \tag{6.9}$$

where $\theta_i = Z/X_i(p_i)$. Because the $\gamma_i$ are nonnegative, prices equal or exceed short-run marginal cost. As Meyer (1975a, p. 334) points out, "a higher price using risk constraints implies capacity could be reduced over what would have been required to meet the constraints while charging a price of $b$."

This chance-constraint approach to excess demand is representative of current practice in some countries. For instance, in the United States, electric-power-generating systems use a "1-day-in-10-years" loss-of-load probability as a reliability target.[5] Crew and Kleindorfer (1976, 1978) use the rationing-cost approach, arguing that establishing safety margins (i.e., the chance-constraint approach) becomes very complex under a diverse technology. Also, the chance-constraint approach does not account for the cost of ranking consumers in order of willingness to pay. Of course, the rationing-cost approach is not without disadvantages; in particular, there is the problem of measuring rationing costs. If this proves to be a difficult and costly task, then using large values of $\epsilon_i$ in the chance-constraint approach becomes more attractive. The large $\epsilon_i$ imply that excess demand occurs less frequently, and the simplifying assumption that consumers are ranked properly is less troublesome.[6]

5 See Telson (1975) for U.S. standards. Standards for other developed countries are also high (Webb, 1977).

6 A more reasonable assumption about how capacity is rationed might be the one suggested by Visscher (1973), where capacity is rationed randomly.

### Revenue sufficiency

Although prices given by (6.7) or (6.9) maintain excess demand at acceptable levels, they do not ensure nonnegative revenues.[7] A deficit problem is important if the utility cannot expect to be subsidized. Under risk, prices that will always produce nonnegative revenues may be nonexistent, just as always eliminating excess demand may be impossible. Thus, here again is a place for some form of risk constraints to replace the standard riskless budget constraints introduced in Chapter 3.

Sherman and Visscher (1978) address the revenue problem by utilizing the following constraint:

$$E[R] = E[C] \tag{6.10}$$

When expected welfare is maximized subject to (6.10), the deficit will equal zero, on average; or, more precisely, the average revenue will equal the average cost. Of course, for any particular values of the $u_i$, we may still have a deficit or surplus. Recall that in the world of certainty, a fixed-coefficient technology implied that costs would be exactly covered at the optimum. But with stochastic demand, deficits are possible even with the fixed-coefficient technology. Under certainty, we added a budget constraint to the strong natural monopolist's problem to obtain Ramsey prices. When we add constraint (6.10) to the utility's problem in the world of uncertainty, we arrive at a stochastic version of the Ramsey prices.

Because the problem is to maximize *expected* welfare by setting *expected* revenues and costs equal, it follows that *expected* elasticities are needed. That is, the monopolist is interested in an elasticity of expected sales, instead of the usual elasticity of demand, because sales do not always equal quantity demanded in the stochastic case. Let $S_i$ be sales in period $i$, and define elasticity of expected sales as

---

7 Using an additive disturbance term, Nguyen (1978) shows that for very high reliability levels (large $\epsilon_i$), price will be close to $b + \beta$. But this does not rule out large deficits. See footnote 10.

$$E[\eta_i] = -\frac{(\partial E[S_i]/\partial p_i)p_i}{E[S_i]} \tag{6.11}$$

where

$$E[S_i] = \int_0^{\theta_i} X_i(p_i)u_i f(u_i)\,du_i + \int_{\theta_i}^\infty Z f(u_i)\,du_i \tag{6.12}$$

and, again, $\theta_i = Z/X_i(p_i)$. The two terms in (6.12) represent sales when there is excess supply and excess demand. The partial derivative of (6.12) with respect to $p_i$ is

$$\frac{\partial E[S_i]}{\partial p_i} = X_i'(p_i)\int_0^{\theta_i} u_i f(u_i)\,du_i \tag{6.13}$$

Using this definition of elasticity, expected-welfare maximization subject to (6.10) yields prices of the form

$$\frac{p_i - b}{p_i} = \frac{\lambda}{1 + \lambda}\frac{1}{E[\eta_i]} \tag{6.14}$$

where $\lambda$ is a Lagrange multiplier; see Tschirhart (1980) for more detail. These prices are identical with welfare-maximizing Ramsey prices in a nonstochastic framework, as derived in Section 3.1, except that $E[\eta_i]$ replaces the usual definition of price elasticity; moreover, (6.14) is a generalization of the Ramsey pricing rule that illustrates the robustness of the Ramsey theory.

We should also point out that with prices given by (6.9) or (6.14), consumers in both peak and off-peak periods must cover part of capacity cost, because $p_i > b$. Thus, in spite of the fixed-coefficient technology, the frequently cited result that only peak users should bear capacity costs (see Section 5.2) does not follow under stochastic demand. Indeed, the very definition of peak and off-peak periods is somewhat obscured, given that the demand curves can pivot in and out depending on the value of $u_i$.

A second way of dealing with the revenue problem is to use a chance constraint. A certain probability distribution for $R$ and $C$ is associated with each choice of $Z$ and $p$. With some probability distributions, the probability that $R$ equals or exceeds $C$, $P\{R \geqq C\}$, will be higher than with other probability distributions.

Because the utility is now confronted with a budget constraint, values of $p$ and $Z$ must be selected such that $P\{R \geqq C\}$ will be as great as possible, or at least as great as some minimum value, say $\alpha$. Therefore, the budget constraint for the utility is

$$P\{R - C \geqq 0\} \geqq \alpha \tag{6.15}$$

The form of the pricing rules that follow after appending (6.15) to the expected-welfare-maximization problem can be found in Tschirhart (1980). The next section presents a numerical example that allows for a graphical interpretation of all the pricing rules discussed so far.

### 6.3. A comparison of pricing rules

For clarity in our diagrams, only a single period is used, and subscripts are dropped. Let demand be given by

$$X(p)u = (30 - p)u$$

and assume that capacity is fixed at $Z = 20$.[8] Also, let $b = 2$, let $\beta = 8$, and let the random disturbance be continuous on the interval $(0, 2)$. Figure 6.3 depicts the situation. The mean-demand curve is labeled $X$, and three other demand curves are drawn as previously indicated. The capacity cost is $\beta Z = 160$ and is enclosed by lines $b$, $b + \beta$, $Z$, and the price axis. The operating cost will depend on price and $u$. Four prices are labeled: $p = 2$, $p' = 10$, $p'' = 16$, and $p''' = 20$.

*Welfare and profit*

Figure 6.4 illustrates welfare and profit for the four prices as the disturbance term varies between 0 and 2. In Figure 6.4(b), a simple density function for $u$ is given where the expected value of $u$ is 1. Consider, first, price $p = 2$, which is equal to short-run marginal cost $b$ in Figure 6.3. As $u$ varies, the short-run operating cost will be covered, but there will be a constant deficit equal to

---

8  Fixing $Z$ allows a diagrammatic presentation of the partial effects from changes in price. The optimum prices discussed are optimum relative to the fixed capacity. Conceptually, to obtain the optimum price for the complete welfare problem, a separate set of diagrams could be constructed for each possible capacity level.

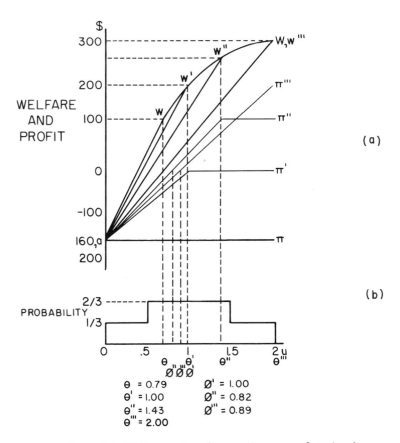

Figure 6.4. Welfare and profit over the range of stochastic demand.

the long-run capacity cost $\beta Z = 160$. This deficit is represented by the solid horizontal profit curve $a\pi$ in Figure 6.4(a). Welfare for price $p = 2$ is given by the heavy curve $awW$. This is derived by evaluating welfare for each value of $u$. For example, when $u = 1$, satisfied demand at $p = 2$ is 20, with an excess demand of 8 (Figure 6.3). Welfare is $CS(392) - L(32) + R(40) - C(200) = 200$. The heavy linear segment $aw$ in Figure 6.4(a) represents values of $u$ for which there is excess supply, and the heavy nonlinear segment $wW$ represents excess demand. The $u$ value at point $w$

on this heavy curve is obtained[3] by noting that at $w$, $X(p)u = Z$ for $p = 2$. The $awW$ curve becomes nonlinear at point $w$, where $L$ becomes nonzero.

Next, consider price $p' = b + \beta = 10$. Profit is given by the solid kinked curve $a\pi'$. As $u$ increases from 0 to 1, profit increases from $-160$ to 0. At $u = 1$, demand is exactly equal to capacity, as depicted in Figure 6.3. Because price equals long-run marginal cost, and demand equals capacity, profit is zero. For $u > 1$, total revenue and total cost are the same as for $u = 1$, because no additional demand can be served. Thus, the kink in curve $a\pi'$ occurs where demand equals capacity. From a profit standpoint, price $p'$ obviously dominates price $p$. Welfare for $p'$ is given by the heavy curve $aw'W$, which is linear to the point $w'$, where demand equals capacity. At point $w'$, $u = 1$, and welfare, from Figure 6.3, is $CS(200) - L(0) + R(200) - C(200) = 200$. From a welfare standpoint, price $p$ obviously dominates price $p'$. Note that the welfare curves do not level off after demand equals capacity as the profit curves do, because consumer surplus continues to increase when demand exceeds capacity.

Individual derivations of the profit and welfare curves for profit $p''$ and $p'''$ are left to the reader. The prime notations on the prices in Figure 6.3 correspond to the primes used in Figure 6.4 for $\pi$ and $w$. The reliability of service and the probability of covering costs are indicated on the density function. Price $p'$ allows a 50 percent reliability, given by the area to the left of $\theta'$, and a 50 percent probability of covering costs, given by the area to the right of $\phi'$. For price $p''$, a 79 percent reliability is obtained, given by the area to the left of $\theta''$, and a 62 percent probability of covering costs, given by the area to the right of $\phi''$.[9] There is zero

9 These figures are calculated as follows: At $\theta''$, demand equals capacity; so $(30 - p'')u = 20$, or $u = 1.43 = \theta''$. To find the area to the left of $\theta''$, note that the area to the left of $u = 1$ is 50%, and the area between $u = 1$ and $u = 1.5$ is $33\frac{1}{3}\%$. We want 43/50 of this latter area, or $(43/50)(33\frac{1}{3}\%) = 28.7\%$. The total area is then $50\% + 28.7\% \cong 79\%$. Point $\phi''$ is found by noting that $R = C$, so that $X(p)up = X(p)ub + \beta Z$. Therefore, $(30 - p'')up'' = (30 - p'')ub + \beta Z$ at $p'' = 16$, $b = 2$, and $\beta Z = 160$, which implies $u = 0.82 = \phi''$. The area to the right of $\phi''$ is calculated in the same manner as the area to the left of $\theta''$ was calculated.

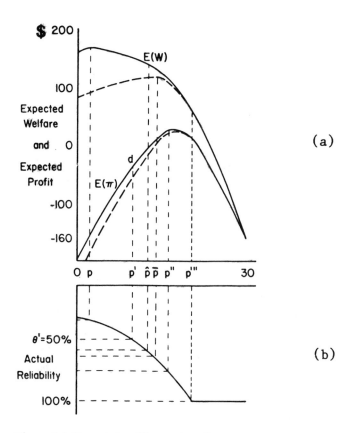

Figure 6.5. Expected welfare and profit.

probability of covering costs with price $p$; so there is no corresponding $\phi$ along the density function. Naturally, values of $\theta$ on the extreme right and values of $\phi$ on the extreme left are desirable. The reliability constraint (6.8) sets the positions of the $\theta$ values, and the chance budget constraint (6.15) sets the positions of the $\phi$ values.

### Properties of solution concepts

To illustrate the trade-offs and properties of the various solution concepts. Figure 6.5 is constructed using Figure 6.4. For

Table 6.1

| Interval | Average profit over interval | Weight of interval from density function (%) | Expected profit over interval |
|---|---|---|---|
| $0 < u < 0.5$ | $-120$ | $16\frac{2}{3}$ | $-20.0$ |
| $0.5 < u < 1.0$ | $-40$ | $33\frac{1}{3}$ | $-13.3$ |
| $1.0 < u < 1.5$ | $0$ | $33\frac{1}{3}$ | $0$ |
| $1.5 < u < 2$ | $0$ | $16\frac{2}{3}$ | $0$ |
| Total | | | $-33.3$ |

each price in Figure 6.4, the profit and welfare curves are weighted by the density function to obtain the expected profit and expected welfare plotted in Figure 6.5(a). Thus, each profit (welfare) curve in Figure 6.4(a) corresponds to one point on the expected-profit (welfare) curve in Figure 6.5(a). In addition, Figure 6.5(b) shows the reliability for each price obtained from the values in Figure 6.4(b). For example, consider price $p'$. To obtain $E[\pi]$ from Figure 6.4(a), the kinked segment can be broken into four intervals as shown in Table 6.1. The expected profit of $-33.3$ is at point $d$ in Figure 6.5(a). Tracing point $d$ down to Figure 6.5(b) reveals that the actual reliability of service for $p'$ is $\theta' = 50$ percent. Each point on the $E[W]$ and $E[\pi]$ curves can be derived geometrically in like fashion. For an alternative derivation of Figure 6.5(a), (6.1) can be used to determine $E[W]$ and $E[\pi] = E[R - C]$, for each value of price, and where $Z = 20$. The density function used is

$$\begin{aligned} f(u) &= \tfrac{1}{3}, & 0.0 \leq u < 0.5 \\ &= \tfrac{2}{3}, & 0.5 \leq u < 1.5 \\ &= \tfrac{1}{3}, & 1.5 \leq u \leq 2.0 \end{aligned}$$

The various pricing solutions discussed in the last two sections appear in Figure 6.5 for the fixed capacity $Z = 20$. Expected-welfare maximization, the Brown–Johnson approach, is attained at $p = b$, but expected profit at this price indicates a deficit of $-160$, and reliability is only 30 percent. Expected-profit maximization is attained at $p''$. The Sherman–Visscher solution is $\hat{p}$, where expected welfare is maximized subject to (6.10), the expected break-even constraint. Reliability in this case is about 60 percent. To obtain Meyer's solution, where the reliability constraint in (6.8) is used, a reliability must be specified. Suppose a 1-day-in-10-years loss-of-load probability is required, so that reliability is virtually 100 percent (i.e., $\epsilon_i \cong 1.0$). This requires that price $p'''$ be levied.

The alternative method in which rationing costs are used without constraints can also be illustrated. Suppose that rationing costs consist of two parts, as suggested by Crew and Kleindorfer (1978): (1) the costs of organizing and administering the program and (2) the inconvenience of being cut off, which will depend on willingness to pay. The former costs must be subtracted from expected profit, and both costs must be subtracted from expected welfare for each possible price below $p'''$. Prices above $p'''$ do not require rationing, as Figure 6.3 indicates. Suppose the former cost is $b$ per unit to be rationed, and the latter cost is $L$. The dashed curves in Figure 6.5(a) represent the revised expected welfare and expected profit given these costs. Optimum price is then $\bar{p}$, with a reliability of about 65 percent.

A comparison of all these prices indicates that $p$ will yield the largest expected welfare, the largest expected deficit, and the lowest reliability. The relationships among the other prices will depend on the particular example used; clearly, trade-offs among expected welfare, expected profit, and reliability are apparent. In particular, neither a budget constraint nor rationing costs alone will ensure high reliability levels, and a stringent reliability constraint alone will not ensure a nonnegative $E[\pi]$.[10]

10 Nguyen (1978) discusses the case of a stringent reliability constraint under additive stochastic demand. Combining the conditions for optimum price and capacity yields a pricing rule, using the foregoing notation and an additive disturbance term, as follows:

*Demand dependent on reliability*

In all of the preceding analysis, demand has been assumed independent of the reliability of service. Figure 6.5(b) illustrates that as price varies between zero and $p'''$, reliability varies between 28 percent and 100 percent. Yet, in spite of this wide reliability variation, the mean-demand curve is stationary. This unrealistic assumption needs to be recognized. A reliable product is certainly of higher quality than an unreliable product, and demand should reflect this important point.

Figure 6.5 brings out this shortcoming very clearly. Setting a high reliability via the constraints should have some payoff in terms of welfare. Otherwise, utilities will not strive for or be forced to strive for the high reliabilities between $p$ and $p'''$. Thus, the models discussed, with the exception of the Crew and Kleindorfer (1976, 1978) model (the dashed curve), do not recognize any welfare payoff to high reliabilities: Maximum expected welfare is where $p = b$ and reliability is low. Crew and Kleindorfer allow a payoff to high reliabilities by adding the rationing cost, which includes the inconvenience of being cut off. However, the inconvenience should be reflected in the demand function itself, so that greater inconvenience means lower consumer surplus.[11]

In other words, a price of, say, $p = b$, with a 30 percent reliability, is likely to have feedback effects on $X(p)$, because consumers may seek an alternative supply to ensure greater reliability.

$$p = b + \beta - \int_{2/X}^{\infty} [X^{-1}(Z - u) - p]f(u)\,du$$

The last term is the expected-welfare gain from an increase in capacity, and with a stringent reliability this term is approximately zero. Therefore, price is approximately equal to long-run marginal cost. A multiplicative disturbance term gives similar results. But if price is about $b + \beta = 10$ and reliability is about 100%, then optimum capacity must be about $Z = 40$ (Figure 6.3). At these values, calculations yield $E[\pi] = -160$; therefore, a reliability constraint alone does not eliminate deficits.

11 Carlton (1977, 1978) criticizes consumer surplus as a measure of welfare benefits when demand is uncertain because it does not reflect consumers' preferences regarding the interaction between price and probability of obtaining the good. The formulation presented later addresses this criticism.

To allow for this dependence, rewrite mean demand as $X(p_i, \rho_i)$, where $\rho_i$ is the reliability of service quoted to the consumers in period $i$. Also, assume that $\partial X_i(p_i, \rho_i)/\partial \rho_i > 0$, so that higher reliabilities imply greater demand. The expected-welfare problem is still given by (6.1), except that $X_i(p_i, \rho_i)$ replaces $X_i(p_i)$. To ensure that the actual reliabilities are consistent with quoted reliabilities, $n$ constraints are needed:

$$P\{X_i(p_i, \rho_i)u_i \leqq Z\} \geqq \rho_i \tag{6.16}$$

Constraint (6.16) is very similar to (6.8). The important difference is that with (6.16), the *optimum* reliabilities are chosen given that demand depends on reliabilities. In the formulation characterized by (6.8), reliabilities are arbitrarily imposed and have no effect on demands.

The addition of $\rho$ in the demand function allows for a better assessment of the welfare implications of pricing and capacity choices under stochastic demand. Reliability is an important aspect of utility service that is not always appreciated. For example, although Meyer's method of adding reliability constraints covered an important omission in the Brown–Johnson analysis, the model was inconsistent in the following sense: High reliability levels were said to be required by regulatory agencies, where these agencies presumably had the consumer's well-being in mind. But the welfare function did not bear out the regulatory decision to require high reliabilities, because welfare decreases with increased reliabilities, as seen in Figure 6.5(a). Also, maximizing the Brown–Johnson welfare function constrained by (6.8) for various values of $\epsilon$, and then selecting the maximum of the maximum, still will yield $p = b$ and, most likely, a low reliability. Only when reliability is allowed as an argument in the demand function can there be improvements in welfare due to higher reliabilities.

### Reliability as a choice variable

Expected welfare must now be maximized with respect to $n$ prices, capacity, *and* $n$ reliabilities. The condition for prices is identical with that given in (6.9), and the condition for optimum capacity does not change, except that again the new demand function must be inserted [see equation (13) in Meyer (1975a)]. However, there are $n$ new first-order conditions corresponding to the $n$ quoted reliabilities. The condition for an optimum $\rho_i$ is

$$\frac{\partial X_i}{\partial \rho_i}[p_i - b][1 - I_i] + \int_0^\infty f_i(u_i) \int_{p_i}^{X^{-1}(0)} \frac{\partial X_i}{\partial \rho_i} u_i \, dp_i \, du_i$$
$$- \int_{Z/X_i}^\infty f^i(u_i) \int_{p_i}^{X_i^{-1}(Z/u_i)} \frac{\partial X_i}{\partial \rho_i} u_i \, dp_i \, du_i = \gamma_i \left[ \frac{\partial X_i}{\partial \rho_i} \frac{\theta_i f(\theta_i)}{X_i(p_i, \rho_i)} + 1 \right]$$

$$(6.17)$$

Substituting (6.9) for the first term and simplifying yields

$$\int_0^{Z/X_i} f_i(u_i) \int_{p_i}^{X_i^{-1}(0)} \frac{\partial X_i}{\partial \rho_i} u_i \, dp_i \, du_i$$
$$+ \int_{Z/X_i}^\infty f_i(u_i) \int_{X_i^{-1}}^{X_i^{-1}(0)} \frac{\partial X_i}{\partial \rho_i} u_i \, dp_i \, du_i = \gamma_i$$

$$(6.18)$$

Equation (6.18) states that the Lagrange multiplier, which is the marginal-welfare cost of requiring that actual reliabilities are as great as those quoted, is equal to the marginal-welfare benefits from a change in reliability, $\rho_i$. The first term on the left side is the marginal benefit when there is idle capacity, and the second term is the marginal benefit when there is excess demand. The left side of (6.18) is obviously positive, so that $\gamma_i > 0$, and the constraints are binding. For a binding constraint, the actual reliability equals the quoted reliability. The producer does not provide a greater reliability than what was promised, because reliability is costly.

The numerical example illustrates these results. Rewrite demand as

$$X(p, \rho)u = \frac{(30 - p)\rho}{0.8} u$$

The 0.8 is arbitrary, and the implication is that the previous example depicted in Figures 6.3 to 6.5 is now a special case, where quoted reliability is 80 percent, or $\rho = 0.8$. Obviously, $\partial X / \partial \rho > 0$, as assumed. The expected-welfare curve and reliability curve in Figures 6.5(a) and 6.5(b) are duplicated in Figures 6.6(a) and 6.6(b) and labeled as 80 percent. This entire $E[W]$ curve in Figure 6.6(a) [or Figure 6.5(a)] is derived given that the consumer is quoted an 80 percent reliability level. However, only one point on this curve is actually compatible with an 80 percent reliability, because only at one point is the constraint satisfied. The compatible point can be found by locating an actual reliability of 80 percent on the curve labeled 80 percent in Figure 6.6(b) (point $b$) and then tracing this point vertically to the curve labeled 80 percent in Figure 6.6(a) (point $a$). Point $a$ then is the only pertinent point on the 80 percent curve in Figure 6.6(a).

Conceptually, the entire procedure used to derive the curves in Figure 6.5, as duplicated in Figure 6.6, must be repeated for all values of $\rho$ between 0 percent and 100 percent. This gives rise to a family of curves. In Figure 6.6, six sets of curves from this family are sketched for $\rho$ values of 30, 53, 60, 70, 80, and 100 percent. The dashed lines connecting Figures 6.6(a) and 6.6(b) show the compatible points, such as point $b$ in Figure 6.6(b) and point $a$ in Figure 6.6(a). The resulting curve, *cdrae,* in Figure 6.6(a) illustrates the expected welfare over all prices. Any point on this curve can be thought of as the solution to an expected-welfare maximization problem, where $\rho$ is fixed at $\bar{\rho}$ and demand is $X(p, \bar{\rho})u$. This is the equivalent to Meyer's problem where $\bar{\rho} = \epsilon$ in (6.8), except that with each different specification of $\bar{\rho}$, mean demand is different.

The linear segment $cd$ of curve *cdrae* in Figure 6.6(a) reveals that for quoted reliabilities between 0 and 53 percent, the optimum price is $p = b = 2$. This is because values in this range (e.g., $\rho = 30$ percent is illustrated) yield demands that are very small, and actual reliability exceeds quoted reliability. The reliability constraint is nonbinding ($\gamma = 0$), and from (6.9), $p = b$. Essentially, the Brown–Johnson result is obtained for the reasons cited

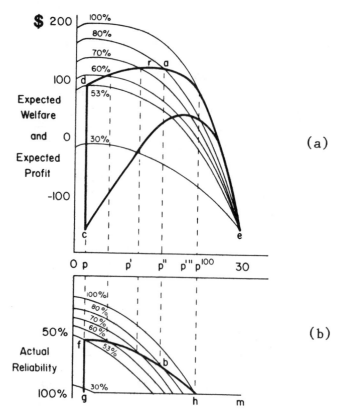

Figure 6.6. Expected welfare and profit when demand depends on reliability.

in Section 6.2. Note that welfare increases with increases in quoted reliabilities between 0 and 53 percent, although price remains at *b*. Above 53 percent, a price of *b* will cause actual reliabilities to fall short of quoted reliabilities. To avoid this constraint violation, price is raised above *b* as quoted reliabilities increase. In spite of the increase in price, however, welfare continues to increase up to its maximum at point *r*, where quoted reliability is about 75 percent and price is slightly less than $p''$. Thus, for segment *dr*, the gains in welfare due to higher reliabilities outstrip the losses in welfare due to higher prices. The reverse occurs for segment *rae*, where welfare declines. For completeness, curve *ce* illustrates expected profit in Figure 6.6(a).

Figure 6.6(b) shows the relationship between actual and quoted reliabilities. Curve *gfbh* represents the actual reliabilities. For quoted reliabilities between 0 and 53 percent, the actual reliabilities are greater, giving rise to the linear segment *gf*. As an example, consider the quoted reliability of 30 percent and the line segment labeled the same. The intersection of this segment and *gf* is at an actual reliability of about 97 percent. As quoted reliabilities are raised above 30 percent, actual reliabilities fall from 97 percent, until the two merge at 53 percent. Finally, as quoted reliabilities are raised above 53 percent, actual reliabilities keep pace via price increases.

The advantage of formulating the problem with $\rho$ as a variable is reflected in curve *cdrae,* because there is now a trade-off among prices, reliability, and welfare that did not exist previously. As price increases and reliability increases, there may be gains in welfare that are not recognized in formulations of the problem in which demand is independent of reliability.

The numerical example indicates that optimum reliability is about 75 percent. Of course, this is entirely dependent on $Z$, the specific demand function, and on the way in which $\rho$ enters this function. Empirical work on demand estimation with reliability as an argument would be difficult in the United States, because historically reliability has been on the order of 99 percent, with little variation. The analysis here, however, indicates that there may be welfare gains available through decreases in reliability. Consumers, if given a chance, may opt for lower reliabilities if accompanied by lower prices. A reliability of 75 percent would undoubtedly be unacceptably low, but according to some economists, a 1-day-in-1-year (99.73 percent) or a 1-day-in-5-years (99.95 percent) loss-of-load probability may be a better target than 1-day-in-10-years (99.997 percent).[12] For example, in a study of a Brazilian city, Munasinghe and Gellerson (1979) found that an optimally designed system, accounting for the benefits and costs of power outages, would have about a 1-day-in-1-year loss-of-load probability.

Provided that consumers desire less than 100 percent reliability, rationing is still required. Therefore, rationing costs that include the costs of organizing and administering the program could be incorporated into the formulation. The result would be that the $E[W]$ curve in Figure 6.6(a) would be lower in the same way that rationing costs lowered the $E[W]$ curve in Figure 6.5(a). Note that including willingness to pay in the rationing costs is unnecessary, because these costs are now reflected in the demand function.

### 6.4. **Monopoly determination of interruptible rates**

One of the important assumptions in the models developed so far in this chapter is that when demand exceeds capacity, the available supply can be rationed to those consumers with the greatest willingness to pay. In practice, the public utility's ability to identify these consumers is limited. Typically, voltage is reduced by 5 or 10 percent. If this tactic is inadequate, utilities implement load-shedding, where service to some consumers is interrupted to avoid a total blackout. Although industrial consumers usually are the first to be interrupted, there is a notable lack of specific criteria for establishing an interruption ordering. Operators in charge of load-shedding may simply rely on ease of implementation for establishing an order.

The New York State Public Service Commission has addressed

---

12 Alessio, Heckerman, and Wenders (1976) analyze the benefits and costs of generation reliability, and they cite several studies concluding that reliability can be lowered without welfare losses. Webb (1977) discusses optimal reserve-capacity levels and suggests that current standards are arbitrarily imposed and too high. He states that optimum reserves should be established by measuring the associated benefits and costs. Some economists have interpreted the relatively high reliability levels in the United States as reflecting incentives to pad the rate base.

this issue for natural-gas supplies by attempting to classify consumers: "When such emergencies arise, the [planned order of curtailment] is obviously pertinent, since it embodies our conception of those customers for whom the continued availability of gas is relatively more and relatively less important, from the standpoint of the welfare of the people of the State" (State of New York Public Service Commission, 1977). The commission's curtailment plan for natural gas distinguished 15 classes of consumers. The first classes to be interrupted would include consumers with alternative sources of energy, whereas residential consumers would be the last to experience interruptions.

The models discussed here incorporate several approaches to curtailment plans in order to highlight some of the important considerations that arise. Marchand (1973) was the first to derive welfare-maximizing prices in an interruptible-service framework. In his model, consumers are free to choose their probability of service, and prices are levied on both the maximum demand and the mean demand of each consumer. Dansby (1979) examined PLP with "ripple" control, whereby consumers are limited to prespecified levels of service during instances of excess demand. Harris and Raviv (1981) take the pricing method as endogenous and show how the selection of a method is related to the capacity constraint. In another paper, Tschirhart and Jen (1979) develop a model of interruptible service that is closer in formulation to those illustrated in previous sections. Although it utilizes a profit-maximizing instead of welfare-maximizing monopolist, it does provide a useful point of departure for introducing the complications that arise from rationing available supplies.

### Separation into consumer classes

Suppose a monopolist sells a good to consumers arranged in distinct classes according to some observable characteristics. These groups may simply be residential, commercial, and industrial classes. The monopolist practices both price discrimination and reliability-of-service discrimination among these various classes; however, in a strict sense, "price discrimination" may not be an accurate term, because the differences in reliability of service imply a nonhomogeneous good.

For simplicity, we divide the consumer classes into two categories: (1) the stochastic class, or that class whose demand is subject to random disturbances, and (2) the contractual classes, or those classes whose demands are nonstochastic in that they have contracts with the monopolist for specified levels of service at a given price and reliability of service. In the public utility context (with residential, commercial, and industrial consumers), the latter two classes may be viewed as having specified contracts with the utility. The contracts state that their demands will be constant and fully satisfied as long as supply is available; the diverse nature of small residential consumers makes contracts unmanageable for this group. The use of specified contracts naturally eases rationing problems and other problems brought about by stochastic demand. The situation is not unlike a utility establishing levels of service that certain consumers cannot exceed. Usually, these levels are based on a percentage of the consumer's usage over some past time period.[13]

Because the monopolist can provide output only until production capacity is reached, a large demand from the stochastic class may mean that total demand from all classes cannot always be satisfied. This situation calls for a rationing policy. An essential feature of a rationing policy is the order of service interruption to the various classes. Expected profit will depend on the ordering, and the monopolist must treat the ordering as a decision variable.

The classes whose service is eligible for interruption include the stochastic class and any nonstochastic, or contractual, class that has a lower priority in the ordering. If any contractual classes have higher priorities than the stochastic class, then the monop-

---

13 During the harsh winter of 1977, National Fuel Gas of New York informed certain industrial and commercial customers that their usage could not exceed 75% of their previous year's usage. In the Northwest, Bonneville Power Administration has reduced electric power to some industrial consumers by 25%.

olist simply treats their demands as deterministic, and their service is never interrupted. In this case, the problem with regard to these contractual classes simply reduces to the standard nonstochastic monopoly situation. In keeping with the public utility setting, however, it is assumed here that the stochastic or residential class has the highest priority. Therefore, all other classes are eligible for interruption. This may not be in accordance with the monopolist's preferred ordering, but he is free to order the contractual classes in any fashion.

### Priority orderings

Let $X_i(p_i, \rho_i)$ be the desired demand of contractual class $i$, $i = 2, \ldots, n$, and let $X_1(p_1, \rho_1, u)$ be the desired demand of class 1, the stochastic class, where again $p_i$ and $\rho_i$ are the price and quoted reliability of service for class $i$, $i = 1, \ldots, n$, and $u$ is a random variable. $X_i(p_i, \rho_i)$ represents the contracted maximum quantity that class $i$ can receive, and the actual quantity received is min$[X_i(p_i, \rho_i)$, available supply]. The reliability levels $\rho_1$ and $\rho_i$ are defined as the quoted minimum probabilities of full service; that is, the consumer is informed that the probability is at least $\rho_1$ that $X_1(p_1, \rho_1, u)$ will be supplied to group 1, and the probability is at least $\rho_i$ that $X_i(p_i, \rho_i)$ will be supplied to group $i$, $i = 2, \ldots, n$. The assumption here is that a reliability level and a price provide the consumer with adequate information for him to make his decision regarding demand.

When $X_i(p_i, \rho_i)$ is supplied, class $i$ is said to be fully served. The available supply, on the other hand, can be anywhere between zero and $X_i(p_i, \rho_i)$, depending on class 1's demand. Available supply is determined as follows. Given the priority ordering 1, 2, $\ldots$, $n - 1$, $n$ during periods of excess demand, the supply to class $n$ is reduced below $X_n(p_n, \rho_n)$ until the demands of classes 1 through $n - 1$ are met. If this is impossible, then the supply to class $n$ is completely curtailed, and the supply to class $n - 1$ is reduced below $X_{n-1}(p_{n-1}, \rho_{n-1})$ until the demand of classes 1 through $n - 2$ is met. If this, too, is impossible, then the supply to classes $n$ and $n - 1$ is completely curtailed, and the supply to class $n - 2$ is reduced below $X_{n-2}$ $(p_{n-2}, \rho_{n-2})$ until the demand of classes 1 through $n - 3$ is met. This process of interrupting the lower-priority users first is repeated until there is adequate supply for the remaining users. If excess demand persists after all the contractual classes are interrupted, then the available supply will be rationed among class-1 consumers only. The upshot is that class 1 causes stochastic-demand conditions for the monopolist and stochastic-supply conditions for the remaining classes.

Given the interruption ordering specified, the monopolist's problem is to choose the $n$ prices, the $n$ quoted reliabilities, and the capacity denoted by $Z$ that will maximize expected profit. The random variable $u$ is assumed to be an additive disturbance term, so that class-1 demand is $X_1(p_1, \rho_1) + u$.[14] The monopolist is assumed to be cognizant of the distribution function of $u$ given by

$$F(a) = \int_{-X_1(p_1,\rho_1)}^{a} f(u) \, du$$

where

$$\int_{-X_1(p_1,\rho_1)}^{\infty} uf(u) \, du = 0$$

Again using the fixed-coefficient technology, an operating cost of $b$ is incurred for each unit of output produced, and capacity has a cost of $\beta$ for each unit of output it can deliver. With this information, the expected value of profit is given by (6.19), where function arguments are dropped for convenience and

$$h(k) = Z - \sum_{i=1}^{k} X_i, \qquad k = 1, \ldots, n$$

14 The results from this model hold for the case of a multiplicative disturbance term as well. Because demand is always assumed nonnegative, $u_i$ must not take on values less than $-X_i(p_i, \rho_i)$. Therefore, the lower bound on $u_i$ depends on $p_i$. In keeping with other models using additive disturbances, it will be assumed that this dependence does not hold and that $-X_i(p_i, \rho_i)$ is a good approximation for the lower bound.

$$E[\pi] = \int_{-X_1}^{h(1)} [p_1 - b][X_1 + u]f(u)\,du + \int_{h(1)}^{\infty} [p_1 - b]Zf(u)\,du$$

$$+ \sum_{i=2}^{n} \left[ \int_{-X_1}^{h(i)} [p_i - b]X_i f(u)\,du \right.$$

$$\left. + \int_{h(i)}^{h(i-1)} [p_i - b][Z - u - \sum_{j=1}^{i-1} X_j]f(u)\,du \right] - \beta Z$$

$$(6.19)$$

The first and second integral terms are the expected operating revenue from class 1 when this class is fully served and when its demand exceeds capacity, respectively. The two terms under the first summation are the expected operating revenues from the other classes. The first term is revenue from class $i$ for full service, and the second term is revenue from class $i$ for partial service. The last term in (6.19) is capacity cost. Because this formulation represents only one particular order of interruptions on the $n = 1$ contractual classes, and because the monopolist is free to choose the order, he must consider $(n - 1)!$ different formulations of (6.19). This, then, is a two-stage problem for the monopolist: first, to determine the maximum profit for each ordering; second, to select the ordering yielding the largest maximum.

We now specify the actual as opposed to the quoted reliabilities of service for the contractual classes. Given the definition of $h(k)$, $F(h(k))$ is the actual probability that the demand for the first $k$ classes will not exceed capacity. Clearly, $F(h(i)) > F(h(j))$ for $i < j$ and $i, j = 1, \ldots, n$, $i \neq j$, provided all contracts are written for positive supply. Let $S_i$ denote the available supply to class $i$, and let $P$ denote probability. Then

$$P\{S_i \geqq X_i(p_i, \rho_i)\} = F(h(i))$$
$$P\{0 < S_i < X_i(p_i, \rho_i)\} = F(h(i - 1)) - F(h(i)) \qquad (6.20)$$
$$P\{S_i = 0\} = 1 - F(h(i - 1))$$

for $i = 2, \ldots, n$. Implicit in (6.20) is the reliability-of-service discrimination mentioned earlier. The situation is one in which product quality is controlled by the monopolist. Class $n$ receives the poorest quality of service, because it is the first to be interrupted; class $n - 1$ receives the next poorest quality of service, because it is the second to be interrupted; and so on.

To ensure that the actual reliability levels comply with those quoted to the consumers, $n$ chance constraints must be satisfied, one constraint for each class. The chance constraints take the form

$$F(h(i)) \geqq \rho_i \qquad (6.21)$$

for $i = 1, \ldots, n$. The left side and right side of (6.21) are the actual and quoted probabilities of full service, respectively. Manipulating the $\rho_i$ in (6.21) has the effect of changing the excess-demand riskiness to consumers, and in turn consumers adjust their demands. Thus, we allow for demands that depend on reliability, following our arguments in Section 6.3. The constraints are satisfied at a given capacity only when the firm quotes prices and reliabilities that will result in demands that will yield a compatible set of actual reliabilities.

### Solutions for prices and reliabilities

Without providing detailed conditions for an optimum, we shall discuss the more important conclusions regarding the prices and reliabilities derived from this model. If class $n$ is quoted a positive reliability of service, then all classes are quoted positive reliabilities, and the actual and quoted reliabilities are equal. Furthermore, price exceeds operating cost for all classes, and price for class 1 exceeds operating cost plus capacity cost. This holds for any ordering. Thus, no class is permitted a reliability of service higher than the one it was quoted. This is not surprising, because providing higher reliabilities is costly. Also, the monopolist ensures a positive contribution to profits from all classes, and price for at least one class exceeds capacity cost plus operating cost. Of course, if no price exceeds capacity cost plus operating cost, losses will be certain.

This result contrasts with the nonstochastic version of a multiproduct, profit-maximization problem, where price exceeds operating cost plus capacity cost for all classes, but it is similar to the nonstochastic peak-load problem, where off-peak prices may exceed operating cost only. This outcome follows from the fact that the monopolist can increase profits by having idle capacity utilized by either the contractual consumers in the stochastic case or the off-peak consumers in the nonstochastic peak-load case. Idle capacity is a result of periodic demand fluctuations in the peak-load problem or random demand fluctuations in the stochastic problem, and it is these demand fluctuations that account for prices less than $b + \beta$.

As stated earlier, there are $(n - 1)!$ orderings available to the monopolist. He must search for the particular ordering that will yield the largest profit maximum. We can gain insight into an optimum ordering by considering two cases: (1) Demands are independent of reliability; that is, $\partial X_i / \partial \rho_i = 0$. (2) Demands depend positively on reliability; that is, $\partial X_i / \partial \rho_i > 0$. Furthermore, we define the set of $n$ prices as being either sequential or nonsequential. Sequential prices have the property that classes receiving a lower quality of service are charged lower prices. From the consumer's viewpoint, this would seem to be the only justifiable approach to price discrimination. Nonsequential prices are not sequential, and they follow no particular pattern regarding prices and reliabilities.

For case (1), the optimum set of prices will be sequential. This result is not surprising; if the monopolist must curtail service to some consumers, it should be to those consumers for whom the revenue loss is the smallest. This will be the consumers enjoying the lowest price. Hence, low prices are associated with low reliabilities. And because demand is independent of reliability, the monopolist need not worry that the low quoted reliability will affect demand. This result changes in case (2). Now, a low quoted reliability may affect demand. Consequently, a consumer group whose demand is very sensitive to reliability might be quoted a high reliability of service, but at the same time enjoy a low price – depending on the price elasticity of demand. Accordingly, in case (2), there is no guarantee that optimum prices will be sequential.

In other words, there are now two types of elasticities to be considered: price elasticity and reliability elasticity, $(\partial X_i/\partial \rho_i)(\rho_i/X_i)$, which is the percentage change in quantity demanded with respect to the percentage change in reliability of service. These elasticities are inversely related; furthermore, there is a trade-off between ordering classes to take advantage of price elasticities and ordering classes to take advantage of reliability elasticities. A class that has a high price elasticity in case (1) should have a low priority and relatively low price. In case (2), if this same class has a high reliability elasticity, it may be advantageous to give it a higher priority.

The role of price elasticities under interruptible service warrants a further note. In the nonstochastic case, the relationship between prices and elasticities for profit maximization is given by

$$p_i \left[ 1 + \frac{1}{e_i} \right] = p_j \left[ 1 + \frac{1}{e_j} \right] \tag{6.22}$$

where $i$ and $j$ are two products in a multiproduct firm. This inverse elasticity rule implies that if and only if $p_i < p_j$, then $e_i < e_j$; or, products whose demands are more elastic are priced lower.

The analogous expression for interruptible-service pricing with reliability-dependent demands and adjacent classes $i$ and $j$, where $i = j - 1$, is

$$p_i \left[ F(h(i)) + \frac{w_i}{e_i} \right] = p_j \left[ F(h(i)) + \frac{w_j}{e_j} \right] + \gamma_i \tag{6.23}$$

Here, $w_k \equiv E[S_k]/X_k$ for $k = i, j$ is the expected supply received divided by desired demand, and $\gamma_i$ is the Lagrange multiplier for the reliability constraint. A comparison of (6.22) and (6.23) indicates that the inverse elasticity rule will hold only for particular values of the actual reliabilities and $w$ values. In particular, for nonsequential prices, $e_i < e_{i+1}$ if $p_i < p_{i+1}$. The result is intuitively appealing. Sequential prices are desirable because services to the consumers paying the lower prices are interrupted first. However, some orderings may lead to nonsequential results, because the monopolist may find it more profitable to price according to the inverse elasticity rule than according to reliability elasticities. When prices for adjacent classes deviate from a sequential price structure, then it must be the case that the monopolist is holding to the inverse elasticity rule between these classes. One pricing rule is abandoned to take advantage of another.

This model illustrates that the monopolist must consider an elaborate system of trade-offs among the decision variables. Prices should be chosen to (1) be sequential, (2) conform to the inverse elasticity rule, (3) clear the market of excess demand, (4) be compatible with the quoted reliabilities for service, and (5) allow adequate supply to lower-priority classes, so that their prices can conform to the inverse elasticity rule. The ordering is a variable that is relevant only in the stochastic setting, and the optimum ordering is one that tends toward low priorities for classes with price-elastic demands and high priorities for classes with reliability-elastic demands. However, these may be conflicting goals.

### 6.5. Fuses for load management and rate design

Interruptible service offered by a welfare-maximizing monopolist is more complex. To use consumer surplus, demand curves must be specified for all classes, so that when service is interrupted, we can calculate the loss. An ordering in which class A's service is totally curtailed before any curtailment to class B begins will not yield an optimum unless class A's willingness to pay for the last unit of service to be curtailed is less than class B's willingness to pay for the first unit to be curtailed. This situation seems unlikely. Consequently, an optimum will require rotating interruptions across classes.

Hamlen and Jen (1983) define a curtailment procedure for electricity that makes the modeling more tractable. Consumers have "limiter" fuses that allow the utility to curtail service to all within a class simultaneously. These authors also distinguish between the probability of interruption and the extent of the interruption (number and duration of episodes). The two affect demand differently. Their results are that for consumers in a class that is never interrupted, a high-priority class, $p = b + \beta$. If a break-even constraint is imposed, then $p \geqq b + \beta$. For consumers in a class for which curtailments occur, $p \leqq b + \beta$, and higher prices are associated with greater reliability elasticities.

Kay (1979) eschews consumer surplus and uses a detailed model of the individual consumer's choice problem when confronting uncertain demand. He distinguishes between cases in which the utility cuts back some service for all consumers and cases in which all service is cut back to some consumers. The Postal Service practices the former, with delivery in peak periods, and telephone utilities practice the latter, when some consumers cannot get a call through. In Kay's formulation, the addition of uncertainty leads to higher prices and probably higher capacity, with smaller profits.

### Fuses as control devices

An interesting variant of the foregoing procedure, one that is practiced in Europe, is to have each consumer purchase his own fuse. In this way, each consumer is selecting his individual capacity, and if his demand exceeds that capacity, the fuse blows. The beauty of this system is that the consumer is directly involved with the capacity decision, and no one is in a better position to decide the needs of the consumer than the consumer himself. Presumably, consumers with greater willingness to pay and/or those who are more risk-averse to power losses will purchase larger fuses. Once the fuses are purchased, the utility knows with certainty that the maximum possible demand on the system is simply the sum of the fuses. This transfers the burden of uncertainty from the firm to the consumer.

Panzar and Sibley (1978) have modeled this system, with each consumer purchasing a fuse from the utility and paying a per-unit price for the fuse size in kilowatts. In addition, the consumer pays a per-unit price for each kilowatt-hour purchased from the utility. The utility has a fixed-coefficient technology, with sufficient capacity to serve the maximum possible demand: the sum of all fuse sizes. This is a simplification, because a utility would not expect to have to serve all fuses at capacity at any one time. Therefore, it would reintroduce uncertainty into its problem by choosing a plant capacity less than the sum of all the fuse sizes based on loss-of-load probabilities and the costs of excess demand. Similarly, as these authors demonstrate, consumers do not choose those fuses that would provide them 100 percent reliability. Ensuring against service interruptions under the most extreme conditions would be too costly, just as it would be for the utility aiming for 100 percent reliability. An interesting question is whether or not consumers who have participated in a fuse system have chosen the stringent 99.997 percent reliability typically sought by utilities in the United States.

A welfare maximum under the fixed-coefficient technology calls for a fuse price per kilowatt equal to $\beta$ and an energy price equal to $b$. Because the uncertainty has been shifted to the consumers, these prices exactly cover total cost. One of the major advantages of this system is the relatively small amount of information required by the utility. In particular, the utility needs no information about consumer preference regarding loss of power; the consumers choose their own levels of insurance against power losses through their fuse selection.

In comparing this solution to the Brown–Johnson solution, in which price is equal to $b$, Panzar and Sibley point out that it will yield lower welfare. Recall that in the Brown–Johnson solution, excess demand requires that consumers with the least willingness to pay have their service curtailed first. There is no guarantee with the fuse system that consumers pressed against their fuse capacity have the least willingness to pay. Furthermore, situations likely will arise in which one consumer's fuse blows, whereas another consumer's fuse has excess capacity. Transferring the excess capacity from the latter to the former consumer would improve welfare, but no market exists to effect such a trade. Of course, judging this solution against the Brown–Johnson solution is unfair, because the latter is infeasible, and its demands are independent of reliability. The fuse system is feasible and is a constructive approach to the problem of selecting optimum reliability levels.

### Backup capacity for solar heating

The fuse system also has been proposed by Hamlen and Tschirhart (1980) for use when consumers purchase solar-powered heating systems for their dwellings or businesses. Solar energy is collected during the day and heats a water-filled storage tank, from which heat is drawn during the day and night. When solar energy is unavailable for extended periods, the consumer heats with electricity from the local public utility. With conventional pricing policies, the addition of solar-heated buildings to the public utility system can exacerbate the utility's problem in dealing with uncertain demand. The solar user's peak demand for electricity will occur during cold, cloudy weather, when storage provides little heat. But this peak demand will be the same as for a comparable nonsolar building. Therefore, if the utility must supply all the electricity that is demanded, then the same generating capacity must be available for solar users as is available for nonsolar users. Hence, the solar user will demand fewer kilowatt-hours of electricity than the nonsolar user, but both will have the same peak demand. Solar users, in other words, exhibit low load factors.

This situation is unsatisfactory from the utility's viewpoint and from that of nonsolar users, who would be subsidizing the solar users. Some suggested remedies for this problem have included (1) fixed demand charges for solar users only, reflecting backup-capacity costs, and (2) increases in the early blocks of declining block tariffs. Neither of these approaches really addresses the key issue: The burden of uncertainty continues to lie with the utility. The fuse system, however, shifts at least some of the burden to the consumer. If solar consumers were required to use fuses, decentralized solar energy might be more palatable to public utilities.

Another interesting alternative for energy use arises when PLP (with or without kilowatt demand charges) is mixed with storage at the consumer's location. If the off-peak price for electricity is significantly lower than the peak price, then heating storage with electricity in the off-peak period may be economically attractive. With a larger storage capacity, the solar user could ensure that heat in storage obtained from either solar radiation or off-peak electricity would be adequate to get through the peak period without using electricity. The greater the discrepancy between peak price and off-peak price, the greater the incentive to use larger storage to avoid the peak price. Similarly, the presence of kilowatt demand charges provides additional incentives for storage.

In a sense, solar heating is now forced to compete with inexpensive off-peak electricity, making solar heat a less competitive alternative. In determining the competitiveness of solar versus conventional heating, the possibility of heating storage with off-peak electricity underscores an important point. The solar heating system should not be compared with a conventional electric heating system; instead, the solar heating system should be compared with a conventional electric heating system that has a storage component. For example, Asbury and Mueller (1977) contend that "most of the electricity supply savings claimed for solar energy systems stem from the storage, rather than the solar, component of the systems."

### Cogeneration

Consumer production of electricity, a logical alternative to storage, further complicates the pricing, reliability, and capacity decisions of electricity utilities. Heat is a by-product of many production processes, and the utility's consumers who run these processes have the option of using the heat to produce steam, run turbines, and produce electricity. They can use this electricity themselves and, in some cases, sell it to the utility.[15] Under PURPA, alluded to in Chapter 5, cogeneration was strongly promoted, and in some states utilities were forced to purchase cogenerated electricity. However, utility planning is complicated by the contractual terms governing payments by the utility for electricity purchased from cogenerators. Regulators may require payments far in excess of the utility's opportunity costs. Furthermore, as with solar heating, the provision of backup capacity requires the development of prices that will signal this cost to cogenerators. Incorrect prices will encourage uneconomic bypass, whereby cogenerators will cease purchasing power from the public utility. This can mean higher prices to the utility's remaining consumers as the same fixed costs must be spread over smaller output.

### Power-factor adjustments

Economic analyses of electricity demand have submerged much of the richness of present electricity pricing structures into an average price per kilowatt-hour and sometimes a simple kilowatt demand charge. Yet other contractual conditions of rate structures for large industrial customers warrant more attention, including voltage levels, interruptibility conditions,

---

15 Joskow and Jones (1983) discuss cogeneration and note that it is an economical investment only if the value of the self-produced electricity exceeds the incremental capital and operating costs of self-production. The topic is receiving much attention from economists. Braeutigam (1986) derives second-best buy and sell rates for electricity utilities. Milon (1981) underscores the importance of using the utility's marginal cost as a basis for determining buy and sell rates that the utility uses to purchase and sell power to a cogenerator. Barclay, Gegax, and Tschirhart (1987) examine the possibility that cogenerators will dump steam while producing electricity, which makes them appear to be producers of electricity instead of producers of their primary product. Zweifel and Beck (1987) argue that under rate-base regulation (Chapter 9), electric utilities have a disincentive to purchase electricity from cogenerators.

and power-factor adjustments. As regulators continue to examine the efficiency implications of rate structures, these components will begin to be investigated.

A discussion of utility approaches to power-factor adjustments in the United States is available in Berg (1983a). Two loads involving the same kilowatt demand and kilowatt-hour energy consumption can have different electric-current requirements. One way to characterize the issue is to envision a bucket of water. If the bucket is rocked, waves are created; so higher sides are needed for the bucket to have the same effective capacity as a stable bucket. Some uses of electricity create similar instabilities, requiring additional capacity to deliver the same kilowatt-hours and the same effective instantaneous power as more stable uses require. *Resistive* loads (such as a light bulb or an electric heat strip) are such that electric current remains in phase with voltage in an alternating-current (AC) power system. Application of the voltage to an *inductive* load (such as an unloaded transformer) causes the consumption of reactive power (measured in kilovolt-ampere reactive, KVAR). As more reactive power is consumed, less real power (measured in kilowatts) can be produced. Thus, more kilowatt capacity will be needed to serve a demand with a large inductive load.

Utilities charge industrial customers for KVARs through penalty prices for low power factors. However, the levels and structures of the charges have not been systematically analyzed by regulators. The current industry "standard" reflects cost and materials constraints present 70 years ago. Given present costs of additional investments by utilities, regulatory analysts ought to be deriving prices from economic principles, under *today's* technological constraints. This example illustrates the usefulness of applying economic principles to what are often viewed as purely engineering issues.

## 6.6. **Summary**

Admitting uncertainty into the analysis of optimum price structure is important, because natural monopolists usually confront problems of random demand and supply. In this chapter, uncertainty takes the form of a stochastic demand for the monopolist's output. Choice variables are delineated into ex ante and ex post: Are they selected before or after the state of nature is known? For the natural monopolist, price and capacity typically are chosen ex ante, but quantity demanded is known only ex post, which implies that it may fall short of or exceed capacity. These possibilities complicate the choices of optimum prices and capacity, because the regulator or monopolist must trade off between ideal capacity and excess demand. Thus, reliability becomes a new choice variable.

To determine optimum reliability, penalty costs can be included in an expected-welfare-optimization problem. The penalty cost is assessed on each unit of excess demand. An alternative approach, which is more in keeping with practice, is to use a chance constraint. This approach requires the monopolist to satisfy all demand with a specified probability. The more costly excess demand is, the higher the probability is set. Neither approach assures that there will be sufficient revenue to cover costs. An additional budget constraint must be appended to the model that requires revenue to equal costs either on average or with a specified probability, allowing the derivation of a stochastic form of the Ramsey rule.

Because consumers will be concerned with the reliability of service, we can expect demand to reflect whatever reliability is quoted to them. This is a further complication, because demand must be specified as a function of reliability. The reliability quoted to consumers must be at least as great as the reliability set by the producer, and the reliability that is set determines consumer demand. Chance constraints are used to specify the probability of service, except now the probability is endogenously determined.

If reliability is less than 100 percent, then some mechanism must be used to determine which consumers go without service when there is excess demand. For electricity, one method is to use interruptible rates, whereby consumers are grouped by some characteristic and a predetermined ordering of groups is specified. Each group is quoted a reliability of service and price, which then determine demand. Profit maximization may or may not require quoted prices to be monotonically increasing with quoted reliabilities when demand is sensitive to reliability.

Fuses are another means of setting reliability standards. Consumers choose fuses for their own consumption, and if a consumer's demand exceeds the capacity of the fuse, it blows. This mechanism has the advantage of shifting some of the burden of uncertainty to consumers, who are in the best position to determine their preferred trade-off between price and reliability. An example is given in which fuses are used as a backup to a solar heating system. Without an innovative approach like fuses, solar consumers can create low load factors for the utility, because they require the utility to provide backup. Cogeneration creates similar problems. In short, the production and distribution of electricity are complicated processes, and our pricing models have only begun to address such complexities as reliability, voltage levels, interruptible services, and power-factor adjustments.

Another possibility raised by cogeneration is the entry of new firms into the electricity industry. Entry, in fact, is an issue for other regulated industries, including telecommunications, and it is crucially linked to the prices set by the monopolists or regulators. To these issues we now turn.

# 7

# Sustainability of natural monopolies

In Chapter 2 we stated the fundamental dilemma facing a strong natural monopoly: Efficient marginal-cost prices result in a deficit. Historically, this dilemma has been the principal justification for government regulation of natural monopolies. As Schmalensee (1979, p. 18) has stated, "control of natural monopoly is another policy area where a single clear objective can be productively adopted . . . that objective should be economic efficiency." Throughout Chapters 3–6 we examined pricing policies designed to make the natural monopoly financially solvent while simultaneously adhering as closely as possible to efficient pricing principles.

Recent developments in the theory of natural monopoly and industrial organization, however, justify broader regulations for some natural monopolies, whereas for other monopolies they have suggested that there is no need for any regulation. Table 2.1 indicated which possibility applied in the single-product case. Table 7.1 extends the taxonomy to the multiproduct case. Sector (1.1) in Table 7.1 represents the subject matter in Chapters 3–6. The purpose of this chapter is to explore in detail the remaining sectors, all of which represent different roles for regulators. In doing so, we develop the concepts of cream-skimming, cross-subsidization, and sustainability. This chapter addresses a number of questions, including the following:

236

Table 7.1. *Policies toward multiproduct natural monopolies*

| Type of monopoly | Barriers to entry | No barriers to entry | |
|---|---|---|---|
| | | Sustainable | Not sustainable |
| Strong natural monopoly (MC pricing creates deficits) | (1.1) Regulate to deviate from MC pricing to eliminate the deficit and to avoid monopolistic prices. | (1.2) Do not regulate. Allow threat of entry to force break-even prices. | (1.3) Regulate to deviate from MC pricing both to eliminate deficits and to avoid monopolistic prices, while disallowing entry. |
| Weak natural monopoly (MC pricing allows nonnegative profits) | (2.1) Regulate to enforce MC pricing and address "problem" of excess profits. | (2.2) Do not regulate. Allow threat of entry to force MC prices. | (2.3) Regulate to enforce MC pricing and address "problem" of excess profits, while disallowing entry. |

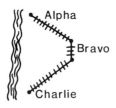

Figure 7.1. Railroad lines for Alpha, Bravo, and Charlie.

If the multiproduct natural monopolist adheres to the
   pricing principles developed in Chapters 3–6, will it
   be free from infringements on its markets by potential entrants?
Will entrants tend to infringe on only a subset of the
   product markets? Should the regulator allow such
   entry?
Can the natural monopolist thwart entry when entry
   would be beneficial?
Should the regulator allow some consumers to be
   undercharged at the expense of others?

Our framework for posing and answering these questions will be
a somewhat stylized numerical example in the spirit of Kahn's
railroad-and-barge scenario (Kahn, 1971, Vol. 1, pp. 166–8). The
example is presented in Sections 7.1 and 7.2. In Section 7.3 we
summarize some of the recent technical results in this area and
indicate some of the remaining difficulties. Section 7.4 points out
that Ramsey prices need not be sustainable, and Section 7.5 provides a summary. First, we consider the case of a strong natural
monopoly.

### 7.1. Pricing and sustainability in a strong natural monopoly

Alpha, Bravo, and Charlie are three towns, and the citizens of these towns would like to promote intertown trade. The
three towns are depicted in Figure 7.1, which is a map of the area
containing the town locations, a river, and proposed railroad
lines. Citizens in Alpha would like to ship goods to the north end
of Bravo, and this would be possible if rails connecting Alpha

with northern Bravo were constructed at a cost of $C(ab)$. Bravo citizens would like to ship from the south end of town to Charlie, and this would be possible if rails connecting southern Bravo to Charlie were constructed at a cost of $C(bc)$. Finally, Charlie citizens would like to ship to Alpha, and this would be possible if rails connecting Alpha and Charlie were constructed through Bravo, including a link between the north and south ends of Bravo. The cost of connecting Charlie with Alpha, via Bravo, is $C(ca)$. A direct link between Alpha and Charlie is far too costly for consideration owing to the rugged terrain along the river. For convenience, we shall now refer to the citizens in Alpha, Bravo, and Charlie collectively as user $a$, user $b$, and user $c$, respectively.

### A cost structure

Suppose the costs for all the rail lines are given by

$$C(ab) = 10, \qquad C(bc) = 10, \qquad C(ca) = 25 \qquad (7.1)$$

These costs would apply if each town constructed and operated a separate railroad, implying that there would be two tracks between Alpha and Bravo and Bravo and Charlie, and one track through Bravo. This arrangement would be a wasteful duplication of resources, however, because sharing rail lines in cooperative ventures would be less costly. For example, consider the costs for any two users together. Users $a$ and $b$ would incur costs $C(ab, bc)$, users $a$ and $c$ would incur costs $C(ab, ca)$, and users $b$ and $c$ would incur costs $C(bc, ca)$. Because a railroad that serviced user $c$'s needs would also serve user $a$'s and user $b$'s needs, the costs for any two towns acting jointly would be

$$C(ab, bc) = 20, \qquad C(ab, ca) = 25, \qquad C(ca, bc) = 25 \qquad (7.2)$$

Finally, if all three towns cooperated, only one railroad would be needed, for a total cost of

$$C(ab, bc, ca) = 25 \qquad (7.3)$$

We can think of this situation as follows. There are three distinct products: transporting user $a$'s goods, transporting user $b$'s goods, and transporting user $c$'s goods. If one railroad served all three users, it would be a multiproduct monopolist. Would it be a natural monopolist? Yes. The least expensive way of serving all three users would be with a single railroad firm; or, the cost function for the railroad would be subadditive. This result can be seen by applying the definition of subadditivity from Chapter 2, which in this context requires that the following inequalities hold:

$$C(ab) + C(bc) + C(ca) \geq C(ab, bc, ca) \tag{7.4}$$
$$C(ab, bc) + C(ca) \geq C(ab, bc, ca) \tag{7.5}$$
$$C(ab, ca) + C(bc) \geq C(ab, bc, ca) \tag{7.6}$$
$$C(bc, ca) + C(ab) \geq C(ab, bc, ca) \tag{7.7}$$

Because (7.4)–(7.7) all hold as strict inequalities for our railroad, this three-product firm would be a natural monopoly. For example, (7.4) implies that three independent railroads would cost $C(ac) + C(bc) + C(ca) = 45$, which would exceed the cost of a single railroad, $C(ab, bc, ca) = 25$. Furthermore, two independent railroads in (7.5) would cost $C(ab, bc) + C(ca) = 45$, which again would exceed the cost of a single railroad. Inequalities (7.6) and (7.7) also pertain to two independent railroads.

Next, we determine whether this is a strong or weak natural monopoly. Recall that this distinction hinges on whether or not marginal-cost pricing will cover cost. We define marginal cost to a user as the cost of adding that user to a system that already serves the other two users. Thus, marginal cost (MC) for users $a$, $b$, and $c$ will be

$$MC_a \equiv C(ab, bc, ca) - C(bc, ca) = 0 \tag{7.8}$$
$$MC_b \equiv C(ab, bc, ca) - C(ab, ca) = 0 \tag{7.9}$$
$$MC_c \equiv C(ab, bc, ca) - C(ab, bc) = 5 \tag{7.10}$$

Letting $p_a$, $p_b$, and $p_c$ be the prices charged by the natural monopoly to users $a$, $b$, and $c$, respectively, and noting that in this example we interpret each user's consumption as one unit of output, then marginal-cost pricing will yield total revenue equal to

$$p_a + p_b + p_c = 5 < C(ab, bc, ca)$$

Thus, the railroad is a strong natural monopoly.

*Barriers to entry*

The scenario to this point places us in the first row of the "matrix" that is Table 7.1. To proceed further, we initially assume that there are barriers to entry perhaps owing to the sunk costs of the roadbed. This places us in sector (1.1). Again, the pricing methods developed in Chapters 3–6 are appropriate for this situation. In our simple example, however, those principles will not provide us with much guidance. Most of those methods rely on demand elasticities to arrive at optimum departures from marginal-cost prices. In our example, demands are perfectly inelastic. Therefore, based on efficiency alone, the regulator will be indifferent as to how the three users' prices can be increased above marginal clost to cover the deficit. Suppose the railroad charges

$$p_a = 0, \qquad p_b = 0, \qquad p_c = 25 \qquad (7.11)$$

which will be equivalent to charging each user 500 percent of his marginal cost. These prices will exactly cover costs. As a profit-maximizer, the railroad will want to charge higher prices to enjoy positive profits, but we assume that regulation holds the railroad to zero profits [part of the regulator's task in sector (1.1)]. There appears to be an asymmetry in how the users are treated in (7.11), because user $c$ is being charged much more than its marginal cost relative to the other users. Yet, based on efficiency, these prices are as acceptable as, say,

$$p_a = 20/3, \qquad p_b = 20/3, \qquad p_c = 35/3 \qquad (7.12)$$

where each user pays marginal cost plus 20/3, and again profit is zero. There is, in fact, an infinite number of price vectors that will cover costs and be equally acceptable based on efficiency. In game terminology, the users are participating in a game with a nonempty core possessing infinite solutions.

The range of acceptable price sets will be narrowed if users' total willingness to pay is less than what the railroad might charge. In effect, this adds the demand side of the picture. Suppose users $a$, $b$, and $c$ are not willing to pay more than 10, 8, and

15, respectively. This is equivalent to perfectly inelastic demand curves at quantity 1 and heights of 10, 8, and 15. Then prices such as

$$p_a = 9, \qquad p_b = 9, \qquad p_c = 7 \qquad (7.13)$$

which will yield zero profits, will be unacceptable to user $b$, and he will withdraw from the market. He can no longer transport, because we assume that no other railroads can enter the market. In addition, users $a$ and $c$ now must cover the cost

$$C(ab, ca) = 25$$

which is greater than what they needed to pay before $b$ withdrew. All users potentially lose by the withdrawal of $b$. The range of acceptable price vectors is narrowed after the demand curves are admitted. The pricing rules derived for the *stability* of two-part tariffs (see Section 4.4) should be applied here.

### Cross-subsidization with entry barriers

Next, we consider prices that involve *cross-subsidization*. We also assume that willingness to pay will not be a constraint; that is, let the willingness to pay for users $a$, $b$, and $c$ be large, say $w_a = 30$, $w_b = 30$, and $w_c = 30$. Suppose the prices are

$$p_a = 11, \qquad p_b = 11, \qquad p_c = 3 \qquad (7.14)$$

In this case, users $a$ and $b$ can be said to be subsidizing user $c$. Following Faulhaber (1975), we define cross-subsidization as a situation in which a user or group of users is paying more than its stand-alone costs. In our example, the stand-alone costs are given by (7.1) and (7.2). This definition is equivalent to the definition of the core in Section 4.4; thus, the presence of cross-subsidies implies that the prices are not in the core. Note, too, that cross-subsidies imply that some user or group of users is not covering its marginal cost. This is easily shown in our example, where users $a$ and $b$ are paying more than their stand-alone costs separately or jointly, given prices in (7.14). Considering the latter,

$$p_a + p_b > C(ab, bc) \qquad (7.15)$$

Moreover, by zero profit,

$$p_a + p_b + p_c = C(ab, bc, ca) \tag{7.16}$$

Combining (7.15) and (7.16) gives us

$$p_c < C(ab, bc, ca) - C(ab, bc) \equiv \mathrm{MC}_c$$

Based on efficiency, there is no justification for charging the prices in (7.14). But a regulator may have other objectives in mind. User $c$ may represent a low-income or otherwise disadvantaged group that could benefit through subsidies from other users. This decision is distributional in nature; the regulator implicitly applies a set of unequal welfare weights for the users.

### *No barriers and sustainable prices*

Now suppose that barriers to entry are removed. Other railroads can freely enter these markets by duplicating one or more of the rail lines currently operated by the natural monopoly. The same technology used by the natural monopoly is available to entrants. This moves us into either sector (1.2) or sector (1.3) in Table 7.1, depending on whether or not there is at least one sustainable price vector available to the natural monopolist. We define a sustainable price vector as one such that the natural monopolist makes nonnegative profits, and no firm can succeed in entering any subset of markets served by the natural monopolist by undercutting the latter's price(s).[1] Success for a potential entrant will imply positive profit. Thus, a sustainable price vector prevents entry. In our example, sustainable price vectors exist, so that we are in sector (1.2) of Table 7.1. Price vectors (7.11), (7.12), and (7.13) are all sustainable, provided that none of the prices exceed users' willingness to pay.

However, price vector (7.14) is not sustainable, because it involves a cross-subsidy. An entrant could undercut the natural monopoly's price for either user $a$ or user $b$ by charging less than 11, but no less than 10. The latter charge is, of course, the break-even price. The prices in (7.14) are therefore not sustainable,

1 A formal definition can be found in Section 7.3.

because they invite entry and cause the existing railroad to lose business. Yet there are infinite sustainable prices for the railroads. Any prices that satisfy

$$p_a \leq C(ab), \qquad p_b \leq C(bc), \qquad p_c \leq C(ca)$$
$$p_a + p_b \leq C(ab, bc), \qquad p_a + p_c \leq C(ab, ca),$$
$$p_b + p_c \leq C(bc, ca) \ p_a + p_b + p_c = C(ab, bc, ca)$$

$$(7.17)$$

are candidates, because no entrant can profitably enter and take away business. (We ignore ties; that is, a railroad will not enter and charge the same as the natural monopoly, only to break even.) Note that because nonsustainability applies when new railroads can successfully enter and serve any combination of one, two, or all three users, any price vector that awards the natural monopolist positive profit is nonsustainable. With positive profit, an entrant could duplicate the entire operation, charge slightly lower prices, and make positive profit (assuming no reaction from the initial firm).

Consider now a second scenario in which the river flowing between users $a$ and $c$ is navigable, and user $c$ has the option of transporting by barge instead of rail. This changes user $c$'s cost to

$$C(ca) = 15 \tag{7.18}$$

and all other costs remain the same. The railroad retains its natural monopoly status, because the rail cost for all three users is 25, but the cost of users $a$ and $b$ using the railroad and user $c$ using the barge is 35. What this does is to narrow the sustainable price vectors. Whereas prices

$$p_a = 4, \qquad p_b = 4, \qquad p_c = 17 \tag{7.19}$$

were sustainable without the navigable river, they are no longer sustainable, because the barge can serve user $c$ at less cost than 17. This price vector now represents cross-subsidization, this time from user $c$ to users $a$ and $b$. The new technology forces the railroad to abandon these nonsustainable prices or face entry. There remain infinite sustainable price vectors, and by adopting one of them, the railroad will prevent the barge from entering.

Suppose the railroad is forced to charge the prices in (7.19), because a regulator believes that the cross-subsidy is justified. Such a scenario is not farfetched; familiar examples can be found in regulated industries.[2] In our example, the market for user $c$ will appear very attractive to entrants, and they will attempt to *cream-skim;* that is, the barge will attempt to skim the net revenues in the market of user $c$. If the regulator successfully prevents entry, the cross-subsidy prices can survive. But the lesson from real-world markets is that the pressure to enter, including self-production by coalitions, can be great enough to overcome the efforts of powerful natural monopolies.[3]

Another possibility is that the railroad is not a natural monopoly at all, and cross-subsidies with entry prevention are protecting a very inefficient means of production. Suppose the barge can serve user $c$ at a cost of $C(ca) = 4$. The railroad will no longer be a natural monopoly, because the total cost of the barge and a

2 For years, long-distance users in the AT&T system have made contributions for services provided by local networks that have partially covered the costs of local networks. A division of the savings that arose from cooperation between long-distance and local-exchange carriers was viewed by many as benefiting only local users. However, this contribution to local users need not have involved a cross-subsidy if the available technologies had not in the past made long-distance connections directly to customers financially feasible. Today, developments in computer, satellite, and microwave technologies have lowered the cost of serving portions of the market, altering the extent to which the contribution can be recovered from some long-distance users. Of course, if part of the contribution from long distance used to go toward covering excessive costs incurred locally because of pricing calls *below* marginal cost, then that part of the contribution *can be* viewed as a subsidy. Thus, contributions from long-distance customers that are less than the stand-alone costs of directly accessing local subscribers (and do not cover inefficient local costs) are in the core of a cost-sharing game between local and long-distance users of the local loop. Given the dramatic technological changes of recent decades, the past price structures induced entrants into the lucrative high-density long-distance markets.

3 For our railroad, moving to prices that do not reflect cross-subsidies will be sufficient to keep out the barge. Whether or not such prices existed for AT&T prior to divestiture is not clear. The answer would require extensive studies of the company's cost structure and demand functions. An interesting note, however, is that AT&T made attempts to lower long-distance rates, but sometimes was prevented from doing so by regulators or antitrust authorities on the grounds that *predatory pricing* would occur.

smaller railroad for users *a* and *b* alone will be $C(ab, bc, ca) = C(ab, bc) + C(ca) = 24$. The monopoly railroad in this case can survive only with the help of a regulator who will protect the cross-subsidizing prices through legal entry barriers.

Returning to the original railroad and the barge case in (7.18), the definition of cross-subsidy can be examined in the context of the prices in (7.19). We said earlier that cross-subsidies occur when any user or group of users is paying more than its stand-alone cost. Prices in (7.19) exhibit no cross-subsidies when we consider just rail costs. However, they do exhibit cross-subsidies when the barge cost is included in the opportunity set. Thus, if we want to use cross-subsidies to signal when the natural monopolist's prices are nonsustainable, then all relevant technologies must be accounted for, not just that of the monopolist.

Note that without barriers to entry, the threat of entry will force the natural monopolist to charge sustainable prices. Any nonsustainable price vectors imply that an entrant can undercut one or more natural monopoly prices and make a positive profit. Thus, for an entry threat to be viable, the potential entrant must believe that the natural monopolist will not immediately react to a sustainable price vector upon his entry. This hit-and-run entry, as described by Panzar and Willig (1977b), requires potential entrants to adopt a Bertrand–Nash point of view. That is, the entrant anticipates nonnegative profit, given the announced prices of the natural monopolist. But if the latter is unregulated, we expect it to meet entry threats by lowering prices in the threatened markets. We know that this is possible when a sustainable price vector exists. The importance of there being no barriers should be underscored here. Indeed, as Shepherd (1984) has argued, entry must be ultrafree. Any positive entry cost will mean that the natural monopolist has some leeway in charging prices in excess of sustainable prices. The greater the entry costs, the more the natural monopolist can charge in excess of sustainable prices.

Knieps and Vogelsang (1982) have examined the sustainability concepts under behavioral assumptions other than Bertrand–

Nash. They have found that sustainability results are very sensitive to the behavior of the incumbent. For example, if the incumbent behaves in a Cournot fashion and reacts to entrants through quantities rather than prices, then the incumbent's vulnerability to attack is reduced. This result can be seen by referring back to Figure 2.4. We showed there that a firm producing $q^a$ and charging a price equal to average cost is a weak natural monopoly, and another firm can enter, charge a slightly lower price, and take away much of the incumbent's market. However, if the incumbent maintains output $q^a$ regardless of entry, the entrant's residual demand curve is $p(q) - q^a$, which may be everywhere to the left of the average-cost curve, and entry is not feasible. Thus, allowing the monopolist to react reduces the sustainability problem (Baseman, 1981). Knieps and Vogelsang also show that Stackelberg (leadership) behavior guarantees sustainability, but not necessarily efficient prices.

In sector (1.2) of Table 7.1 we have implicitly assumed costless entry and Bertrand–Nash behavior by claiming that there is no need for regulation. That is, we have assumed contestable markets, as developed by Baumol, Panzar, and Willig (1982). To believe that the markets are perfectly contestable, so that the threat of entry will force break-even prices, is a sanguine view. Shepherd (1984) has strongly criticized contestability theory because of its extreme assumptions on costless entry and exit and because it ignores the market power of the incumbent firms. Also, he finds the Bertrand–Nash behavior of the incumbent untenable. An entrant will virtually have to duplicate the incumbent firm's entire operation to take advantage of scale economies, but no incumbent will stand idly by while this occurs.

In spite of these criticisms, contestability (no barriers to entry in Table 7.1) provides a benchmark for analyzing the regulator's role. In no industry is entry costless, but costs do vary across industries. In the electric-power industry, barriers currently are significant because of the large initial investment required (although cogeneration alters the picture in some regions of the country). Thus, sector (1.2) of Table 7.1 is not applicable; gener-

ally, regulators will be developing policies in the context of sector
(1.1). However, in the case of the airline industry, barriers to
entry along particular routes are relatively small, and sector (1.2)
may be applicable (presuming that there is a natural monopoly
along the route). Of course, even here, entry costs will not be
zero, and the incumbent airlines have some ability to charge
prices at least slightly in excess of sustainable prices. This situation is likely to arise if there is unequal access to airport facilities
(including landing/take-off slots). But does this situation mean
that regulation is needed? The answer is no if the efficiency losses
from the excessive prices are smaller than the costs associated
with regulation: both direct administrative costs and the costs of
inefficiencies that might arise due to regulation. For example, inefficient work rules may evolve in a protected environment. Furthermore, antitrust policy can address issues of access to essential
facilities. In sum, the remedies in the sectors of Table 7.1 may be
polar cases, but they do provide guidance for problems that usually fall between these extremes.

### No barriers and nonsustainable prices

Next, consider sector (1.3). In this simple example with
inelastic and independent demands, we cannot generate a situation that will yield nonsustainability in a strong natural monopoly. It is instructive to explain at some length why this is so. First,
without bringing in demands (willingness to pay), the railroad's
problem for charging sustainable prices is equivalent to finding a
solution in the core of a cost game. The game is that the players
(or users $a$, $b$, and $c$) must share the cost of a single railroad. The
incentive to play is the saving they can enjoy from having a single
railroad, as opposed to multiple railroads. For instance, the saving for users $a$ and $b$ is

$$C(ab) + C(bc) - C(ab, bc)$$

The conditions for sustainability of prices given earlier are
identical with the conditions for core existence in Chapter 4. Fur-

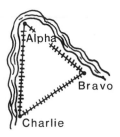

Figure 7.2. Symmetric railroad lines.

thermore, a core will exist in our three-user game if and only if (Shapley, 1967)

$$C(ab, bc) + C(bc, ca) + C(ab, ca) \geq 2C(ab, bc, ca) \qquad (7.20)$$

From the definition of marginal cost, (7.8)–(7.10), the foregoing is equivalent to

$$MC_a + MC_b + MC_c \leq C(ab, bc, ca) \qquad (7.21)$$

If (7.21) holds as an inequality, we are in sector (1.2), because the natural monopoly is strong (marginal-cost pricing yields a deficit) and sustainable (the core exists). If (7.21) holds as an equality, we are in the lower row of Table 7.1, because the natural monopoly is weak.

Next, we introduce demands in an attempt to create a nonsustainable, strong natural monopoly. For specificity, suppose that the geography has changed, and the map in Figure 7.2 pertains. The costs for the railroad are now

$$\begin{aligned}
C(ab) &= C(bc) = C(ca) = 10 \\
C(ab, bc) &= C(ab, ca) = C(bc, ca) = 18 \qquad (7.22) \\
C(ab, bc, ca) &= 24
\end{aligned}$$

The river is *not* navigable; the reader can verify that the railroad is a natural monopoly. If the railroad charges

$$p_a = p_b = p_c = 8 \qquad (7.23)$$

costs will be covered, and prices apparently are sustainable, because no entrant railroad can offer lower prices and make a positive profit. But suppose that users' willingness to pay is

$$w_a = 5, \qquad w_b = w_c = 10 \tag{7.24}$$

Prices in (7.23) no longer work, because user $a$ is not willing to pay 8. To ensure that user $a$ is served, he must be charged no more than 5, or

$$p_a = 5, \qquad p_b = p_c = 19/2$$

But these prices are nonsustainable, because an entrant railroad can profit by serving users $b$ and $c$ at lower prices. A necessary condition for the natural monopoly railroad to be sustainable is that user $a$ be willing to pay at least the marginal cost of serving him, which is 6. But if he is willing to pay 6, the natural monopoly becomes sustainable.

Are we in sector (1.3), with a nonsustainable natural monopoly, when user $a$ is willing to pay only 5? After all, the least expensive means of serving all three users is with a single railroad. The key question is whether or not all these users should be served. The only way to achieve universal service is to cross-subsidize from users $b$ and $c$ to $a$, and then bar entry by other railroads. The total net benefit of serving all three users is $w_a + w_b + w_c - C(ab, bc, ca) = 1$. The total net benefit of serving users $b$ and $c$ only is $w_b + w_c - C(bc, ca) = 2$. A three-user railroad is not justified under the criterion of economic efficiency. A two-user railroad is a strong, sustainable natural monopoly. The lesson here is that we might be misled if after determining that a firm is a natural monopoly, we conclude that its outputs must be protected from entry. The presence of cross-subsidies may imply that current output levels are unjustified.

An example of a strong, nonsustainable natural monopoly can be found in Panzar and Willig (1977b, p. 10). They present a numerical example with two outputs, two consumers, and elastic interdependent demands.[4] Prices that cover costs are unique and

---

4 Their example is presented later in the context of Figure 7.5.

lie above marginal costs, which are zero. However, at these prices, an entrant can make a positive profit by offering one of the goods. The policy prescription in sector (1.3) of Table 7.1 is appropriate: Minimize pricing distortions, cover costs, and do not allow entry.

## 7.2. Pricing and sustainability in a weak natural monopoly

We can change the railroad to a weak natural monopoly by simply changing the total cost in (7.22). In particular, suppose that

$$C(ab, bc, ca) = 27 \tag{7.25}$$

The railroad is a weak natural monopoly, because the marginal cost for serving each user is 9, and pricing at marginal costs exactly covers total cost. There is no deficit problem. With barriers to entry, we are in sector (2.1). A regulator is needed to prevent the railroad from charging prices that will generate monopoly profits. However, there is no need to deviate from marginal-cost prices, as in sector (1.1), because these prices are efficient and create no deficits or surplus.

> *Barriers to entry with positive profits*
> Suppose we change the costs slightly to
>
> $C(ab) = 10, \qquad C(bc) = 10, \qquad C(ca) = 11$
> $C(ab, bc) = 17, \qquad C(bc, ca) = 18, \qquad C(ca, ab) = 18$
> $C(ab, bc, ca) = 27 \tag{7.26}$

This situation is still a natural monopoly; the least expensive way to serve all these users is with a single railroad. But now marginal costs are

$$MC_a = C(ab, bc, ca) - C(bc, ca) = 9$$
$$MC_b = C(ab, bc, ca) - C(ca, ab) = 9$$
$$MC_c = C(ab, bc, ca) - C(ab, bc) = 10$$

and their sum exceeds total cost. Marginal-cost pricing creates a surplus. This situation is in sharp contrast to the traditional dilemma of public utility regulation. The regulator can dictate marginal-cost pricing and do no more, in which case the railroad enjoys positive profit. If we judge the performance under regulation against the two results we expect from competitive markets (that is, prices equal to marginal costs and zero profits), then the regulator is successful in duplicating one competitive result. Of course, regulation can duplicate the other competitive result by charging each user 9. Then profit will be zero, but one price will be below marginal cost. Another alternative is to charge marginal-cost prices, and then tax away any positive profit. The railroad, however, will have no incentive to hold down costs, which will force the regulator to become a watchdog for waste. In subsequent chapters, we go into these incentive problems in more detail.

### No barriers with sustainable prices

We now remove barriers to entry and return to the costs given by (7.22) for one and two users and (7.25) for all three users, placing us in sector (2.2) of Table 7.1. Marginal-cost prices are sustainable. They exactly cover total cost, and no entrant can undercut these prices and enjoy a positive profit. There is no need for regulation, because the threat of entry will compel the railroad to maintain these prices. Moreover, the reader can verify that marginal-cost prices are the only prices that are sustainable in our example.

This last observation turns out to be true in general. We pursue this by noting the distinction between the two middle sectors. In sector (1.2), the threat of entry forces the railroad to break-even prices, but not marginal-cost prices. The latter would mean a deficit. In the lower sector, the threat of entry forces the railroad to break-even price, but these can be only marginal-cost prices. In other words, a natural monopoly in sector (2.2) is weak, but barely weak. Marginal-cost pricing yields zero profit, never positive profit. If it yielded positive profit, the natural monopoly would not be sustainable, and we would move to sector (2.3). Alternatively, if prices below marginal cost produced zero profit, we would lose sustainability because of the cross-subsidization inherent in such prices.

This result follows in our examples with inelastic demand by recalling (7.20) and (7.21). Together they imply that if marginal-cost prices yield a surplus, then the condition for core existence is violated. Without a core, the natural monopoly is nonsustainable. More generally, Panzar and Willig (1977b) show that prices no less than marginal cost and zero profits are two of the necessary conditions for sustainability. Thus, sustainability is possible for weak natural monopolies only if prices set to marginal costs create zero profit. Accordingly, we can be sure that the break-even prices in sector (2.2) must be marginal-cost prices.

### No barriers and no sustainable prices

Finally, we can study sector (2.3) and a nonsustainable situation by adopting the costs given in (7.26). Recall that now marginal-cost pricing will yield a surplus, and this is the source of the nonsustainability. Because sustainability requires zero profit, one or more prices will have to be below marginal cost. But this will imply cross-subsidization, which in turn produces nonsustainability.

The railroad might charge

$$p_a = p_b = p_c = 9 \tag{7.27}$$

to break even, but an entrant can charge less than this to users $a$ and $b$ and still make a profit. If the railroad attempts to check this by charging 8.5 to both users $a$ and $b$, it will have to charge 10 to user $c$ to break even. But this will encourage an entrant to undercut prices and serve either users $a$ and $c$ or $b$ and $c$. In short, there does not exist a set of prices that will always thwart entry. A regulator will have to protect this natural monopoly from entrant railroads in order to ensure that users will be served at least cost.

This same problem can arise from an outside source. Suppose we return to the cost structure in (7.22), except that $C(ab, bc, ca)$ = 27. Recall that this situation represents a sustainable, weak

natural monopoly. Prices given by (7.27) will allow the railroad
to break even and deter entry. Suppose further that a barge can
navigate the river in Figure 7.2, thereby serving users $a$ and $c$.
The cost for the barge's service is $C_B(ab, ca) = 17.5$. The railroad
is still a natural monopoly and represents the least expensive way
of serving the three markets. And even though the railroad will
be safe from entrant railroads that have the same technologies, it
is not safe from an entrant barge. The railroad's prices in (7.27),
the uniquely sustainable prices prior to the barge, are now vulnerable to attack. The barge can profitably serve users $a$ and $c$.
Again, the regulator will have to protect the railroad from
entrants to preserve the natural monopoly.

### 7.3. Conditions for sustainability

The literature on the sustainability of natural monopolies has grown dramatically, with able summaries available in
Baumol, Panzar, and Willig (1982) and Bailey and Friedlaender
(1982). This growth has been timely, because over the last two
decades the problems of entry into and pricing for multiproduct
natural monopolies have been at the forefront of economic policy
debates. The transportation, communications, and energy industries have undergone significant structural changes involving new
firms and product mixes. However, the literature prior to the
mid-1970s had not formally examined multiproduct natural
monopolies and associated pricing principles; thus, earlier work
did not provide guidance for evaluating entry and technological
changes in these industries.

Much work still remains to be done in developing the pricing
principles in Chapters 2–6 for multiproduct natural monopolies
and then relating the resultant prices to sustainability and the
potential gains from regulation. An even greater need exists for
empirical analyses of cost and demand structures in key industries. As we demonstrated in the previous section, regulatory policy prescriptions differ significantly depending on the structural
properties of the industry. Quantitative studies can help identify
the industries that are true natural monopolies, including

whether they are strong or weak. However, empirical analysis is difficult and often inconclusive. For example, Evans and Heckman (1984) develop tests of necessary conditions for subadditivity that do not require global information on outputs. One can reject subadditivity for an industry failing these tests, but one cannot accept subadditivity if the tests are passed.

Joskow and Noll (1981) are apprehensive about taking the types of policy prescriptions derived in Table 7.1 too seriously, given the difficulties of measuring subadditivity and thereby determining which sector in the table is applicable for any particular firm. If a firm incorrectly classified as a nonsustainable weak natural monopoly is protected from entry, that firm's prices will be inefficient, and the output can be produced with lower costs by multiple suppliers. The flip side is that a natural monopoly, incorrectly thought to be sustainable, will endure unwarranted entry if it is not protected. Perhaps even more problematical is the introduction of innovation into our models of multiproduct industry structure. Although a natural monopoly may require protection for allocative efficiency, such limitations on entry dramatically reduce the number of independent centers of initiative, potentially limiting the exploitation of technological opportunities (discussed in Chapter 10). The promotion of innovative efficiency may conflict with static-efficiency considerations.

We know that incorrect policy decisions can waste society's resources. Because our techniques for classifying firms into the sectors of Table 7.1 are still primitive, we should be careful in drawing definitive policy recommendations from the theory (especially in terms of structures that promote technological advance). However, at least we now have the outlines of a theory that will allow us to frame the right questions, even if we do not always have enough information to derive the right answers.

### A formal definition of sustainability

Before surveying some necessary conditions and sufficient conditions for a natural monopoly to be sustainable, we present a formal definition of sustainability. Let $q^m =$

$(q_1^m, \ldots, q_n^m)$ be an output vector for a natural monopoly producing $n$ goods. Costs are given by $C(q)$, $p^m = (p_1^m, \ldots, p_n^m)$ are the prices charged by the natural monopolist, and $q_i^m = y^i(p^m)$, $i = 1, \ldots, n$, are the market demands. If we replace $m$ by $e$ in the foregoing expression, then we refer to an entrant's quantities, prices, and costs. An entrant might consider producing any subset $S \subseteq N = \{1, \ldots, n\}$ of the products and need not serve the entire market demand. When making an entry decision, the potential entrant can be viewed as taking a Bertrand–Nash approach toward the natural monopoly: He assumes that the monopolist will not change the prices $p^m$.

Panzar and Willig (1977b) define a sustainable price vector as follows: *The price vector $p^m$ is sustainable if and only if $p_S^e q_S^e - C(q_S^e) < 0$ for all $S \subseteq N$, $p_S^e \leq p_S^m$, $q_S^e \leq y^s(p_S^e, p_{(S)}^m)$, with $q_S^e \neq y(p^m)$. It is also required that $\pi(p^m) \equiv p^m y(p^m) - C(y(p^m)) \geq 0$.* A natural monopoly is said to be sustainable if and only if there exists at least one sustainable price vector. The definition indicates that if an entrant charges prices no greater than the natural monopolist for a subset of the $n$ goods, he will make negative profit, while the natural monopolist will enjoy nonnegative profit. The possibility that the entrant will exactly duplicate the entire operation of the natural monopolist is ruled out by $q_S^e \neq y(p^m)$, and the maximum demand for the entrant's goods is given by $y^s(p_S^e, p_{(S)}^m)$, where $p_S^e$ is a vector of entrant prices for $i \in S$, and $p_{(S)}^m$ is a vector of incumbent prices for $i \in (S) = N - S$. If the entrant charges the same price as the natural monopolist for any good, there is a question of how the market will then be split. After all, the entrant's good is a perfect substitute for that produced by the natural monopolist. These authors point out that taking $p_S^e \leq p_S^m$ to mean $p_S^e \leq p_S^m - \epsilon$ (for $\epsilon$ a small number) makes no substantive difference in their analysis.

Their definition of sustainability is set in a framework that obviously is more general than the railroad-and-barge examples in the previous two sections. Demands are not restricted to be perfectly inelastic, consumers are not restricted to one unit of output, cross-elasticities of demand may be nonzero, and the cost function allows for varying degrees of substitutability in production. As a result, the relationships between the core, the prices that are free of cross-subsidies (subsidy-free prices), and sustainability are more complex. For instance, in the railroad example, subsidy-free prices and sustainable prices were equivalent, whereas now we see that subsidy-free prices are necessary (but not sufficient) for sustainability.

### *Weaker versions of sustainability*

Several researchers have made progress in identifying more precise conditions on cost and demand functions that will allow either for sustainable prices or for some weaker version of sustainability. These weaker versions of sustainability are worth noting. The weakest is *subsidy-free prices* for outputs. To reiterate, no consumer or group of consumers pays more than its stand-alone costs for producing an output or output mix. Next weakest is *supportability,* as introduced by Sharkey and Telser (1978). Here, the revenue collected for any part of the total output must not exceed the stand-alone cost of producing that output. It is not required that the part of total output in question correspond to the output taken by any consumer or group of consumers, nor is it required that prices be market-clearing, so that $q_i = y^i(p)$ for all $i = 1, \ldots, n$. *Anonymously equitable prices* are supportable prices such that demands at these prices are market-clearing. Anonymously equitable prices reflect an absence of consumer subsidies, as opposed to product subsidies. This distinction can be very important in the context of regulatory decision-making, where the concern may be with industrial versus residential consumers, urban versus rural groups, or high-income versus low-income residents. Finally, *sustainable prices* involve the strongest condition, because they are anonymously equitable prices that allow for entry at lower prices that may not be market-clearing.

The reader is referred to papers by Sharkey (1981), Faulhaber and Levinson (1981), ten Raa (1984), and Mirman, Tauman, and Zang (1985) for details on the relationships between these various versions of sustainability. For example, if each good exhibits declining average incremental cost, subsidy-free prices imply anonymously equitable prices. We shall concentrate here on a general description of sustainability, which is ultimately the pertinent concern for the regulator. But we note that these other versions provide insights into the technical properties of demand and cost functions that permit sustainability.

### Necessary conditions for sustainability

Panzar and Willig (1977b) offer necessary conditions for sustainability of a monopoly in a world with no entry barriers. One of the conditions is that the monopolist's cost function be subadditive, so that it is indeed a natural monopoly. Other conditions are

1. output $q^m$ is produced at least cost
2. $p^m$ is undominated
3. declining ray average cost
4. $\pi(p^m) = 0$
5. prices not less than marginal cost
6. for all $S \subset N$, $\Sigma_{i \in S} \, p_i^m q_i^m < C(q_S^m)$, where $q_i^m = y^i(p^m)$

Condition 1 follows because a natural monopolist not producing at least cost and making nonnegative profit will be vulnerable to an entrant charging the same or slightly lower prices and producing at least cost, because the entrant will enjoy positive profit. Condition 2 simply states that there does not exist a price vector $p^e \leqq p^m$, $p^e \neq p^m$, available to the entrant such that $\pi(p^e) = 0$ (shown graphically later). Condition 3 requires declining ray average cost (defined in Section 2.3), which eliminates situations like that in Figure 2.4. In such situations, the natural monopolist charges a break-even price equal to average cost, but an entrant can charge a lower price, serve a portion of the market, and realize positive profit.

We illustrated conditions 4, 5, and 6 in the railroad example in the last two sections. Regarding condition 4, positive profit will invite entry, because a competitor can charge slightly lower prices and enjoy positive profit. We saw that condition 5 follows because prices below marginal costs involve cross-subsidies and therefore vulnerability to entrants. Formally, an entrant can attempt to market

$$q^e = (q_1^m, \ldots, q_{i-1}^m, q_i^m - \Delta^i, q_{i+1}^m, \ldots, q_n^m) \equiv q^m - \Delta^i \text{ at } p^m$$

For sustainability,

$$p^m(q^m - \Delta^i) < C(q^m - \Delta^i)$$

But $C(q^m) \leqq p^m q^m$; so it is necessary that $p_i^m \Delta^i > C(q^m) - C(q^m - \Delta^i)$ and

$$p_i^m > \frac{C(q^m) - C(q^m - \Delta^i)}{\Delta^i}$$

Taking the limit as $\Delta^i \to 0$,

$$p_i^m \geqq \frac{\partial C(y^m)}{\partial q_i}$$

Condition 6 is the analogue to the requirement in Section 7.1 that the prices must be subsidy-free or in the core of an appropriately defined game. Of course, if the core is empty, the natural monopoly is not sustainable.

### Cost games and benefit games

Defining the game can be an involved problem in itself. The railroad-and-barge example primarily dealt with a cost game and perfectly inelastic and independent demands – the simplest type of game. We can also define benefit games, and we can allow for elastic and interdependent demands. The characteristic function for a cost game is based on costs alone.[5] If $S = \{1, \ldots, s\}$ is a coalition of consumers that is a subset of all consumers in the game, then the value of participation in this coalition is

$$v(S) = \sum_{i \in S} C(q_i) - C(q_1, \ldots, q_s) \tag{7.28}$$

5 The characteristic function for a game was defined in Section 4.4.

which is the cost savings enjoyed through single-firm production, as opposed to multifirm production. Each consumer is associated with a single output in this formulation. Obviously, a strictly subadditive cost function ensures that (7.28) is nonnegative and positive for $s > 1$. The game defined in Panzar and Willig (1977b) is a cost game in which demands are elastic. They show that this game has a nonempty core if the cost function exhibits weak cost complementarities. A differentiable cost function exhibits weak cost complementarities if $\partial^2 C / \partial q_i \partial q_j \leqq 0$, $i \neq j$.

Examples of benefit games can be found in Littlechild (1975a) and Sorenson, Tschirhart, and Whinston (1976, 1978a). A formulation of a characteristic function is given by (4.38). We saw in the railroad-and-barge example how the core of a benefit game is a subset of the core of a cost game, although this is not always the case. Using the numbers from our example (7.1)–(7.3), the characteristic function for a cost game will be

$$v(a) = C(ab) - C(ab) = 10 - 10 = 0$$
$$v(b) = C(bc) - C(bc) = 10 - 10 = 0$$
$$v(c) = C(ca) - C(ca) = 25 - 25 = 0$$
$$v(a, b) = C(ab) + C(bc) - C(ab, bc) = 10 + 10 - 20 = 0$$
$$v(b, c) = C(bc) + C(ca) - C(bc, ca) = 10 + 25 - 25 = 10$$
$$v(c, a) = C(ca) + C(ab) - C(ca, ab) = 25 + 10 - 25 = 10$$
$$v(a, b, c) = C(ab) + C(bc) + C(ca) - C(ab, ca, ca)$$
$$= 10 + 10 + 25 - 25 = 20$$

The payoff to user $a$, $B_a$, of playing the game is the cost of going it alone minus the price he pays (recall that there is only one unit in the railroad-and-barge game), or $B_a = C(ab) - p_a$. Users $b$ and $c$ have similarly defined payoffs. To be in the core, the sum of payoffs to a subset of users must be no less than the characteristic-function value for that subset, a condition equivalent to subsidy-free revenue. For users $b$ and $c$, for instance, this simply says $B_b + B_c \geqq v(b, c)$, or

$$p_b + p_c \leqq C(bc, ca) = 25 \tag{7.29}$$

which is one condition for a price vector to be in the core. All the conditions are displayed in (7.17).

To change this situation to a benefit game, recall the willing-ness-to-pay numbers $w_a = 10$, $w_b = 8$, and $w_c = 15$ used at one point in the railroad-and-barge example. The characteristic function using (4.38) is

$$v(a) = \max\{0, w_a - C(ab)\} = 0$$
$$v(b) = \max\{0, w_b - C(bc)\} = 0$$
$$v(c) = \max\{0, w_c - C(ca)\} = 0$$
$$v(a, b) = \max\{0, w_a + w_b - C(ab, bc)\} = 0$$
$$v(b, c) = \max\{0, w_b + w_c - C(bc, ca)\} = 0$$
$$v(c, a) = \max\{0, w_c + w_a - C(ca, ab)\} = 0$$
$$v(a, b, c) = \max\{0, w_a + w_b + w_c - C(ab, bc, ca)\} = 8$$

The payoff to user $a$ is his willingness to pay minus his total payment, $B_a = w_a - p_a$, and to be in the core still requires the sum of payoffs to a subset of users to be no less than the characteristic value for that subset. In the example, for users $b$ and $c$, this now requires

$$p_b + p_c \leqq w_b + w_c = 23 \tag{7.30}$$

Comparing (7.30) with (7.29) shows that the core restriction for these two users is more stringent in the benefit game versus the cost game. For the other coalitions, the core restrictions are at least as stringent in the benefit game.

A comparison of cost and benefit games can be found in Sharkey (1982a). He provides conditions on the demand and cost functions that will guarantee core existence. He also defines a more general benefit game that avoids using consumer surplus. Similarly, Salas and Whinston (1982) define a benefit game in which utility is nontransferable. They examine the welfare properties of subsidy-free prices and also derive conditions that guarantee core existence.

### A sufficient condition for sustainability

An illuminating sufficient condition for sustainability is derived by Panzar and Willig (1977b) (see the Appendix to this chapter for the derivation). It shows that cost complementarities favor sustainability, whereas product-specific scale economies will tend to promote entry. Their sufficient condition for sustainability of a two-product natural monopolist is

$$
\begin{aligned}
\frac{\partial y^2}{\partial p_2} &\left[ \frac{\partial C(y^1, y^2)}{\partial y^2} - \frac{\partial C(0, y^2)}{\partial y^2} \right] \\
+ \frac{\partial y^1}{\partial p_2} &\left[ \frac{\partial C(y^1, y^2)}{\partial y^1} - \frac{C(y^1, y^2) - C(0, y^2)}{y^1} \right] \geqq 0
\end{aligned}
\tag{7.31}
$$

where the price arguments are omitted for convenience.

The first term in (7.31) is the product of the own-price effect and the reduction in marginal cost attributable to complementarities in production. The second term is the product of a positive substitution effect and the rate of change of average incremental cost, where average incremental cost is a generalization of ray average cost, defined in Chapter 2.[6] In the present context, declining average incremental cost holds if

$$
C(q_1, q_2) - C(0, q_2) < \frac{C(\lambda q_1, q_2) - C(0, q_2)}{\lambda}
\tag{7.32}
$$

for $q_1 \neq 0$ and $0 < \lambda < 1$. The average cost of producing good $\lambda q_1$ declines with its output level $\lambda$ when a fixed level of $q_2$ is also being produced. This condition says, for example, that if there are two firms producing the fixed quantity $q_2$, then the least expensive method of adding the production of $q_1$ is to have one of the firms produce all of it rather than having both firms produce half of it. Taking the derivative of the right-hand side of (7.32) with respect to $\lambda$ and evaluating the result at $\lambda = 1$ yields

---

6 Declining average incremental cost is defined as

$$
C(q_S, q_T) - C(q_S) < \frac{C(q_S, \lambda q_T) - C(q_S)}{\lambda}
$$

for $0 < \lambda < 1$, $S, T \subseteq N$, $S \cap T = \phi$, and $q_T \neq 0$. It implies that the average cost of a composite good $\lambda q_T$ declines with the output level $\lambda$, when $\lambda q_T$ is combined with a constant level of other goods, $q_S$. The derivative of the right-hand side of the definition with respect to $\lambda$ evaluated at $\lambda = 1$ is the rate of change of average incremental cost.

$$q_1 \frac{\partial C(q_1, q_2)}{\partial q_1} - C(q_1, q_2) + C(0, q_2) \leqq 0$$

which is the rate of change of average incremental cost. A strict inequality implies declining average incremental cost. Moreover, a strict inequality implies that the second bracketed term in (7.31) is negative; or, declining average incremental cost implies that this second bracketed term is negative.

Using this information to examine the sufficient condition in (7.31) reveals that the cost complementarities favor sustainability, whereas declining average incremental cost does not. The two-product natural monopolist may be vulnerable to an entrant who enjoys extensive economies of scale in producing good 2 only. This entrant may charge a price for good 2 less than the natural monopolist's price, thereby taking sales of good 2 *and* good 1 away from the natural monopolist (because $\partial y^1/\partial p_2 > 0$). Matching the entrant's lower price for good 2 may be impossible if the average incremental cost of producing good 1 increases significantly. Also, for a given declining average incremental cost (second bracketed term nonpositive), strong substitution effects will decrease the possibility that the natural monopoly will be sustainable, for then, as prices are lowered in one market to take advantage of the falling average incremental cost, demand is reduced in the other market, and the advantage of a falling incremental cost there is lost. A firm specializing in a single output will not have this problem. Of course, strong cost complementarities may dominate this effect, leaving the natural monopolist invulnerable to entry.

### Numerical examples

At this point, several numerical examples and a graphical representation like those used by Panzar and Willig should be instructive. Suppose a two-product firm's cost function is given by

$$C(q_1, q_2) = 5q_1 + 4q_2 - 0.3q_1q_2 + 24 \tag{7.33}$$

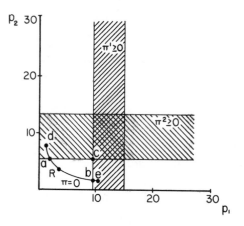

Figure 7.3. Sustainability and independent demands.

The market demands for these two goods are independent and are given by

$$y^1 = -0.5p_1 + 10 \tag{7.34}$$

and

$$y^2 = -1.4p_2 + 20 \tag{7.35}$$

A firm that specializes in good 1 only will have profit

$$\pi^1 = p_1y^1 - C(y^1, 0) \tag{7.36}$$

where we use $y^{1'}$ in the cost function instead of $q_1$ to ensure that output is demand-compatible. Substituting (7.33) and (7.34) into (7.36) yields

$$\pi^1 = -0.5p_1^2 + 12.5p_1 - 74$$

and if we set $\pi^1 = 0$ and solve the quadratic for $p_1$, we obtain two values for $p_1$ such that the firm breaks even. These values are approximately 9.6 and 15.4, as plotted along the horizontal axis in Figure 7.3. For values of $p_1$ in the range $9.6 < p_1 < 15.4$, the firm makes positive profit. Thus, the hatched area between the vertical lines represents the set of all $(p_1, p_2)$ such that a firm specializing in good 1 makes nonnegative profit.

Similarly, a firm specializing in good 2 will have profit

$$\pi^2 = p_2 y^2 - C(0, y^2) \tag{7.37}$$

Substituting (7.33) and (7.35) into (7.37), setting the result equal to zero, and solving for $p_2$ yields values for $p_2$ of 12.2 and 6.1, which enclose the region in Figure 7.3 labeled $\pi^2 \geqq 0$. The cross-hatched region represents the set of prices such that both firms can operate profitably. Point $c$ represents the lowest set of prices such that both firms break even.

How can sustainability be represented in this figure? We can consider those points in $p_1 p_2$ space where a firm producing *both* products makes zero profit. If any such point lies southwest of point $c$, it will represent a sustainable price vector, because neither specialized firm can undercut the multiproduct firm's prices and make nonnegative profit. To determine if sustainable prices exist, write the two-product firm's profit as

$$\pi = p_1 y^1 + p_2 y^2 - C(y^1, y^2) \tag{7.38}$$

Substitute (7.33)–(7.35) into this expression and set it equal to zero to obtain a quadratic in $p_1$ for a fixed $p_2$. We need consider only zero-profit prices, because zero profit is necessary for sustainability. Then, with $p_2$ fixed at different values, solve the quadratic for $p_1$. The result is an ellipse in $p_1 p_2$ space. We plot only the southwest portion of the ellipse in Figure 7.3 as segment *de*, because only points on this segment represent undominated-price vectors. Recall that undominated prices are a necessary condition for sustainability.

Along segment *de*, only points along *ab* represent sustainable prices for the two-product firm. Neither single-product firm can undercut the two-product firm's prices and make nonnegative profit. Accordingly, a necessary condition for the two-product firm to be a sustainable natural monopolist is that segment *ab* lie southwest of point *c*. When demands are independent, as in this example, this condition is also a sufficient one, although this is not true in general (as we show in the following examples). Points along *de* but not *ab* are not sustainable, which can be easily seen by considering point *d*. If the natural monopolist charges prices represented by point $d$, then a firm specializing in good 2 only can undercut the natural monopolist's price by charging a price less than the $p_2$ associated with $d$. A price above 6.1 and below point $d$ will give the specialized firm nonnegative profit. Should this threat of entry unfold, we expect an unregulated natural monopolist who is free to change prices to simply move into the $ab$ portion of the line segment. However, recall that the entrant is assumed to exhibit Bertrand–Nash behavior and does not anticipate price changes in retaliation to this entry.

We can determine whether or not the demand and cost functions in this simple example satisfy the sufficient conditions for sustainability given by (7.31). The second term in (7.31) is zero, because $\partial y^i/\partial p_j = 0$, $i$, $j = 1, 2$, $i \neq j$, by independent demands. The reader can verify that the second bracketed term is zero as well, implying that average incremental costs are constant. Thus, if there are cost complementarities of the type given by the first bracketed term, the sufficient condition will be satisfied. That is, because $\partial y^2/\partial p_2 < 0$, from (7.35), we need the first bracketed term to be nonpositive. Using (7.33) in (7.31), we obtain

$$\frac{\partial C(y^1, y^2)}{\partial y^2} - \frac{\partial C(0, y^2)}{\partial y^2} = 4 - 0.3q_1 - 4 < 0$$

Therefore, we conclude that a two-product firm with a cost function given by (7.33) and facing demand conditions given by (7.34) and (7.35) is a sustainable natural monopolist. The complementarities in production give the natural monopolist a significant advantage over specialized firms, and there are no offsetting disadvantages that can occur through dependent demands and declining average incremental costs. Figure 7.3 illustrates this conclusion.

### Interdependent demands

Next, consider an example with interdependent demands, where the market demands for the two products are given by

$$y^1 = -0.2p_1 + 0.1p_2 + 10 \tag{7.39}$$

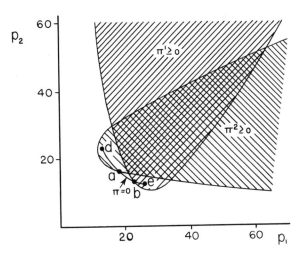

Figure 7.4. Sustainability and interdependent demands.

and

$$y^2 = -0.3p_2 + 0.1p_1 + 12 \tag{7.40}$$

The cost structure is

$$C(q_1, q_2) = 0.8q_1 + q_2 + 270 \tag{7.41}$$

for positive $q_1$ and $q_2$, and

$$C(0, q_2) = 1.2q_2 + 140 \tag{7.42}$$

and

$$C(q_1, 0) = q_1 + 150 \tag{7.43}$$

Clearly, there are complementarities in production, because both the constant marginal costs and fixed costs are less when a single firm produces both outputs. Proceeding in the same fashion as in the previous example, we solve for the values of $p_1$ and $p_2$ that yield zero profit in (7.36) and (7.37), using the new demand and cost functions, for the case of two specialized firms. This situation generates the hatched areas in Figure 7.4, where the sets of prices labeled $\pi^1 \geqq 0$ and $\pi^2 \geqq 0$ show all those prices at which firms 1 and 2 make nonnegative profits, respectively. The boundaries of the sets represent zero profit for the respective specialized firm. Again, the crosshatched area represents the prices at which both firms can make nonnegative profits. Note that these areas do not extend to the axis as was the case for independent demands, because there are values of $p_1$ ($p_2$) that are so low that firm 2 (firm 1) cannot possibly make a profit, because it sells a substitute good.

For a single two-product firm, we substitute (7.39)–(7.41) into (7.38) and obtain values of $p_1$ and $p_2$ that yield zero profit. The undominated prices that do this are given by segment *de* in Figure 7.4, and again only points along segment *ab* on *de* represent sustainable prices. As in the previous example, this natural monopoly is sustainable.

However, unlike the last example, here the sufficient condition for sustainability, (7.31), is not satisfied at any points along line segment *ab*. If we use (7.39)–(7.43) in (7.31), we obtain

$$-0.3[1 - 1.2] + 0.1\left[0.8 - \frac{0.8y^1 + y^2 + 270 - 1.2y^2 - 140}{y^1}\right]$$

which reduces to

$$0.06 + \frac{0.02y^2 - 13}{y^1} \tag{7.44}$$

Using the quantities generated by the prices along segment *ab* reveals that (7.44) is negative, and this sufficient condition does not hold. The first term in (7.44) is derived from the cost complementarities and the own-price effect, whereas the second term is derived from the price-substitution effect and declining average incremental cost. The disadvantages of the latter for sustainability (as discussed earlier) outweigh the advantages of the former, and this sufficient condition is not strong enough to verify that sustainable prices exist in this particular example. [This result still holds if we reverse the indices 1 and 2 in (7.31).]

In the previous section, we pointed out that with the inelastic,

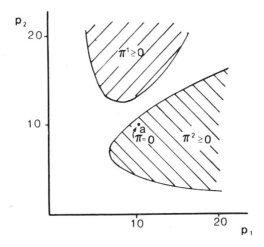

Figure 7.5. A nonsustainable strong natural monopoly.

independent demands in the railroad-and-barge framework, constructing an unsustainable, strong natural monopoly was not possible. It is possible with elastic, dependent demands. We now present an example of this situation, taken from Panzar and Willig (1977b), and incorporate it into the graphical techniques used earlier. Demands are given by

$$y^1 = 20 - 2p_1 + p_2 \quad \text{and} \quad y^2 = 20 - p_2 + p_1 \quad (7.45)$$

Costs are subadditive and are given by

$$C(q_1, q_2) = 200, \quad q_1 > 0, q_2 > 0; \quad C(0, 0) = 0$$
$$C(0, q_2) = 90, \quad q_2 > 0; \quad C(q_1, 0) = 130, \quad q_1 > 0 \quad (7.46)$$

Marginal cost for both products is zero, so that marginal-cost prices create a deficit; hence, the two-product firm is a strong natural monopoly.

We proceed in the same manner as the previous examples by calculating the set of prices that will yield nonnegative profit for two specialized firms, and then for a single two-product firm. The results are displayed in Figure 7.5. Because the two hatched areas

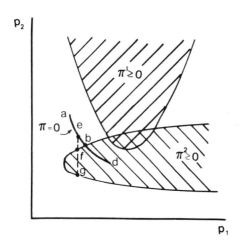

Figure 7.6. Another case of nonsustainability.

do not intersect, two specialized firms cannot operate simultaneously. At least one of them would be making a loss. For a two-product firm, $p_1 = p_2 = 10$ are the only prices that will yield zero profit. But this point (point $a$) falls within the $\pi^2 \geq 0$ set, and these prices are not sustainable. A firm specializing in good 2 can charge $p_2 < 10$ and make positive profit.

Finally, without providing a numerical example, we illustrate another, slightly different, case of a nonsustainable natural monopolist. In Figure 7.6, a segment of the undominated-price locus for the natural monopolist lies between the crosshatched set and the origin (which is necessary for sustainability). However, this situation does not protect the natural monopolist from entry. If he tries to charge prices given by point $e$, where single firms cannot operate, a firm specializing in good 2 can charge a price on segment $fg$ and take away all the natural monopolist's sales of good 2.

### 7.4. Ramsey prices and sustainability

In examining sustainability when demands are not perfectly inelastic, we have confined the analysis to linear prices only. Recall that linear prices were the subject of Chapter 3. Combining questions of sustainability with nonlinear pricing, peak-load pricing, and pricing under stochastic demand, which were examined in Chapters 4, 5, and 6, respectively, represents a fertile area of research. When we allow for nonlinear prices, say in the form of two-part tariffs, a natural monopoly has more flexibility in allocating the cost of its output across consumer groups. But if competitors can use two-part tariffs as well, does this mean that the natural monopolist will be more or less vulnerable to entry?[7] In peak-load problems, where capital inputs are shared across periods, does the nature of sustainability change significantly? Under what conditions might we observe an entrant taking business away from an incumbent in only the peak or off-peak period? What influence do random fluctuations in demand have on an incumbent's vulnerability to entrants? How will differences in risk attitudes between entrants and incumbents affect sustainability?

### *Implications of unsustainable Ramsey prices for regulators*

In confining our examination to linear prices, we find that if a natural monopoly is found to be sustainable and there are no barriers to entry, then there is no need for a regulator, as indicated in Table 7.1. The market will ensure that the firm charges break-even prices, and production will be at least cost. However, we now add a caveat to this result. The particular sus-

---

7 The efficiency and stability of market equilibrium depend on price structures utilized by firms. For example, if duopolists were constrained to offer only one entry-fee/marginal-price combination per period, a stable Nash–Cournot equilibrium could emerge, with each firm catering to different types of consumers: large demanders paying a high fee and low price to one firm, with small demanders paying a low fee but high price to the other. Calem and Spulber (1984) and Oren, Smith, and Wilson (1983) analyze multiproduct two-part tariffs and competitive nonlinear tariffs, respectively. These papers begin to lay the foundations for sustainability comparisons in which nonlinear pricing can be used by a multiproduct natural monopolist. All the analyses of this chapter consider only linear pricing schemes. The efficiency implications of sustainability may change when nonlinear pricing is introduced.

tainable prices charged by the natural monopolist may not be the best choice from the set of all sustainable prices based on welfare considerations. Ideally, the prices should maximize welfare subject to a zero-profit constraint. In other words, they should be Ramsey prices, because Ramsey prices maximize welfare subject to a profit constraint. Sustainable prices ensure zero profit, but can we be certain that the set of sustainable prices includes the Ramsey prices?

We can easily calculate Ramsey prices for the numerical example in Section 7.3, where demands were independent. We know from (3.6a) that Ramsey prices will satisfy

$$e_1 \frac{p_1 - \partial C/\partial y^1}{p_1} = \frac{p_2 - \partial C/\partial y^2}{p_2} e_2 \tag{7.47}$$

where $e_i = (\partial y^i/\partial p_i)(p_i/y^i)$, $i = 1, 2$. Using (7.34) and (7.35) in (7.47) yields an ellipse in $p_1 p_2$ space, and the intersection of this ellipse with the $\pi = 0$ locus in Figure 7.3 represents the Ramsey prices. Point $R$ in Figure 7.3 is this intersection where $p_1 \cong 4.0$ and $p_2 \cong 3.8$. Thus, in this example, the figure reveals that Ramsey prices are sustainable, because $R$ lies along segment $ab$.

Unfortunately, this result is not guaranteed in general. Ramsey prices may or may not be included in the set of sustainable prices. The implications for regulation are noteworthy. If we take Ramsey prices as the second-best outcome and assume that welfare declines monotonically as we move away from these prices along the zero profit contour, the following holds: If the set of sustainable prices is small, regulation may be unwarranted, as indicated in Table 7.1, regardless of whether or not Ramsey prices are included in the set. The potential gain of determining the welfare-maximizing prices from among the sustainable prices may not be justified by the costs of operating a regulatory authority that will perform the task. Alternatively, if the set of sustainable prices is large, then the gains of determining and enforcing the welfare-maximizing prices may justify regulatory intervention. If Ramsey prices are not included in the sustainable-price set, then the regulator is, in effect, enforcing prices that maximize welfare sub-

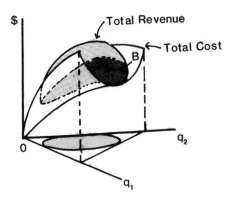

Figure 7.7. Revenue and costs for a natural monopolist.

ject to sustainability. No entry regulation is required, but it could increase welfare. If Ramsey prices are included in the sustainable-price set, then the welfare-maximizing regulator should move the natural monopolist to those prices. The firm, of course, may charge the welfare-maximizing prices from the sustainable set without regulatory intervention, although there is no apparent reason why this would be so, because all prices in the set yield zero profit. The firm may then be indifferent among price structures.

### A weak invisible hand

Results from Baumol, Bailey, and Willig (1977) suggest that if the Ramsey prices are sustainable, there is some hope that they will be the prices selected by an unregulated monopolist. These authors refer to this possibility as a weak invisible hand at work. Their analysis can be shown graphically by augmenting Figure 2.7, which illustrated a two-output cost function exhibiting decreasing ray average cost and transray convexity. In Figure 7.7, the cost function is duplicated, and a revenue hill for a single firm is added. We assume that barriers to entry are absent, so that there are zero entry costs into these markets for the two goods

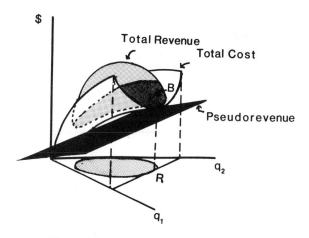

Figure 7.8. Sustainable prices for a natural monopolist.

currently served by the natural monopolist.[8] Recall that decreasing ray average cost and transray convexity are sufficient for subadditivity; hence, this firm is a natural monopoly. The darkest shaded area represents the intersection of the cost surface with the revenue hill. We refer to this as area $B$. The shaded area on the $q_1 q_2$ plane represents all those output combinations for which the natural monopolist makes nonnegative profits. On the boundary of this area, profit is zero.

In Figure 7.8, a pseudorevenue hyperplane is added. The hyperplane is given by the inner products of all output vectors and a set of fixed prices; that is, pseudorevenue is

$$q_1 h_1 + q_2 h_2 \qquad (7.48)$$

where the $h$'s are the fixed prices. The term "pseudorevenue" is used because the $h$'s are not market-clearing prices, except for values of $q$ in (7.48) such that $q_i = y^i(h_1, h_2)$, $i = 1, 2$. This occurs

---

8 We can allow for entry costs by adding them to the cost surface. This addition implies that the natural monopolist can make profit slightly less than entry costs and not be confronted with entrants.

at those points held in common between the pseudorevenue hyperplane and the total-revenue surface. Figure 7.8 is constructed so that the area B is tangent to the pseudorevenue hyperplane, which we shall call $H$, and one point that is projected down to the $q_1 q_2$ plane as point $R$. This tangency represents a sustainable-output vector. If the fixed prices were lowered proportionately so that $H$ was everywhere below $B$, then the natural monopolist would earn negative profits at these new fixed prices. Alternatively, if the fixed prices were raised proportionately from their values at the tangent point, $H$ would slice through $B$ in a way that would leave points on the revenue hill's surface below $H$ but above the total-cost surface. These points on the revenue hill would represent opportunities for entry, because entrants could undercut the natural monopolist's prices and make positive profits by virtue of being on the revenue hill, but above $B$.

Baumol, Bailey, and Willig show that the point of tangency between $H$ and $B$ in Figure 7.8 is the Ramsey pricing solution. This elegant result relies on the point that "with prices held fixed at their market levels, the derivatives of profit with respect to quantities are proportional to the corresponding derivatives of consumer's plus producer's surplus" (1977, p. 358). The important roles of decreasing ray average cost and transray convexity are evident in the figure. Together they ensure a unique tangency between $H$ and $B$. These authors present a set of sufficient conditions on the cost and revenue functions for Ramsey pricing to be sustainable; these are actually weaker than decreasing ray average cost and transray convexity.[9]

Why might the natural monopolist be more inclined to choose Ramsey prices over other sustainable prices? These authors point out that at any non-Ramsey prices, the natural monopolist requires global information about demand and cost functions to assess sustainability, and such information is likely to be outside

9 Mirman et al. (1986) argue that the weak-invisible-hand theorem requires "very restrictive" conditions on cost.

the range of historical data. Whereas the sustainability of Ramsey prices relies on global properties of the cost function, only local information is needed to assess sustainability. Consequently, whether or not the natural monopolist chooses Ramsey prices from among the sustainable set of prices may hinge on the amount of information available. Limited information would tend to promote a Ramsey outcome.

### 7.5. Summary

The pricing principles in Chapters 3–6 provide guidance for the regulator whose goal is to achieve economic efficiency. However, the regulator's role does not always stop once efficient prices are in place. If the prices invite entry, the regulator will have to protect the incumbent firm, and if entry is not possible, the regulator will have to ensure that the incumbent firm adheres to the prices. Alternatively, there may be cases in which the regulator can abandon market controls, letting the threat of entry ensure efficient prices.

These points have been made in the context of a simple example in which a railroad serves three towns or users. If this three-product railroad is a strong natural monopoly and there are barriers to entry, the regulator's task is to protect the users from monopolistic prices by ensuring zero profit. There can be many different prices that will ensure zero profit, although acceptable prices are bounded by the users' willingness to pay. The presence of cross-subsidies implies nonacceptable prices, because a group of users (or a single user) is paying more than its stand-alone cost. However, the regulator may allow cross-subsidies in order to benefit a perceived disadvantaged group.

When entry barriers are dropped, cross-subsidies invite entry into the market. But if the railroad is a strong natural monopolist, it can find a set of prices that will avoid cross-subsidies and discourage entry. Such prices are labeled sustainable. Moreover, if the threat of entry is significant, regulation may be unnecessary; The market will force the railroad to charge efficient, sustainable prices. The possibility also exists, however, that the railroad may be a strong natural monopoly and there may not exist a sustainable price vector. The railroad then must be protected from entry to ensure that output is produced by a single supplier.

If the railroad is a weak natural monopoly and there are barriers to entry, the regulator's task is to enforce marginal-cost prices and/or to monitor any positive profits. Without entry barriers, prices are sustainable only if they equal marginal cost *and* produce zero profit. If they allow positive profit, entry will occur unless the regulator intervenes.

These policy prescriptions are hampered by the empirical difficulties associated with classifying firms as strong or weak natural monopolies and determining whether or not sustainable prices exist. Economists continue to search for testable necessary and sufficient conditions for sustainability. We know that cost complementarities favor sustainability, whereas declining average incremental cost does not. Several two-output numerical examples are provided to relate the sufficient conditions with the properties of demand and cost functions.

Finally, because Ramsey prices have been shown in previous chapters to have important efficiency properties, they are related to sustainability. Assuming that sustainable-price vectors exist, we cannot guarantee that Ramsey prices are in the set. If the set of sustainable-price vectors is small, regulatory enforcement of Ramsey prices may be unwarranted: The cost of determining whether or not Ramsey prices are in the sustainable set may not justify the welfare gains of using Ramsey prices versus other sustainable prices. If the set is large, regulatory intervention may be warranted to enforce Ramsey prices if they are in the set, because the firm may not choose Ramsey prices on its own. The weak-invisible-hand theorem offers hope, however, because it suggests that firms may choose Ramsey prices over other sustainable prices when there is limited information about demand and cost functions.

This result ends Part I of this book on an optimistic note. We have examined many pricing methods that can be used to promote efficient outcomes, and Ramsey pricing, with its positive efficiency properties, is found to be a method that firms might adopt even without regulatory guidance. In Part II, however, the note begins to turn sour. The view of a benevolent, welfare-maximizing regulator in Part I is an overly sanguine view of the regulatory process. We shall see that regulation often comes about for reasons quite unrelated to economic efficiency, and the inherent problems with actual regulatory practices often place principles of economic efficiency in a secondary role.

### Appendix

Panzar and Willig (1977b) derive a sufficient condition for sustainability. Suppose that a natural monopolist produces two outputs at the undominated-price vector $p^m = (p_1^m, p_2^m)$. The outputs are substitutes in demand. Suppose an entrant firm markets good 2 at price $p_2^e < p_2^m$ and makes profit

$$\pi^e(p_1^m, p_2^e) = p_2^e y^2(p_1^m, p_2^e) - C(0, y^2(p_1^m, p_2^e)) \qquad (7A.1)$$

Assuming that $p^m$ is undominated, which is one of the necessary conditions for sustainability from above, the natural monopolist's profits must be negative at $(p_1^m, p_2^e)$, or

$$\pi^m(p_1^m, p_2^e) = p_1^m y^1(p_1^m, p_2^e) + p_2^e y^2(p_1^m, p_2^e) \\ - C(y^1(p_1^m, p_2^e), y^2(p_1^m, p_2^e)) < 0 \qquad (7A.2)$$

Adding and subtracting $C(0, y^2(p_1^m, p_2^e))$ to the right-hand side of (7A.2) yields

$$[p_2^e y^2(p_1^m, p_2^e) - C(0, y^2(p_1^m, p_2^e))] + [p_1^m y^1(p_1^m, p_2^e) \\ - C(y^1(p_1^m, p_2^e), y^2(p_1^m, p_2^e)) + C(0, y^2(p_1^m, p_2^e))] < 0 \qquad (7A.3)$$

The first bracketed term is the entrant's profit from (7A.1). If the second bracketed term in (7A.3) is nonnegative, then the entrant's profit must be negative. Thus, a sufficient condition for sustainability of $p^m$ is that the second bracketed term be nonnegative, or, after rearranging,

$$\frac{C(y^1(p_1^m, p_2^e), y^2(p_1^m, p_2^e)) - C(0, y^2(p_1^m, p_2^e))}{y^1(p_1^m, p_2^e)} \leq p_1^m \qquad (7A.4)$$

We now transform (7A.4) into a more usable formulation. The foregoing necessary condition 6, which requires subsidy-free prices for sustainability, implies in the present context that

$$p_2^m y^2(p_1^m, p_2^m) < C(0, y^2(p_1^m, p_2^m))$$

Subtracting this from the nonnegative profits of the monopolist at $p^m$ implies that

$$p_1^m y^1(p_1^m, p_2^m) > C(y^1(p_1^m, p_2^m), y^2(p_1^m, p_2^m)) - C(0, y^2(p_1^m, p_2^m))$$

or

$$\frac{C(y^1(p_1^m, p_2^m), y^2(p_1^m, p_2^m)) - C(0, y^2(p_1^m, p_2^m))}{y^1(p_1^m, p_2^m)} < p_1^m \qquad (7A.5)$$

The left-hand sides of both (7A.4) and (7A.5) can be viewed as values of the function $G(p_2)$, where

$$G(p_2) = \frac{C(y^1(p_1^m, p_2), y^2(p_1^m, p_2)) - C(0, y^2(p_1^m, p_2))}{y^1(p_1^m, p_2)} \qquad (7A.6)$$

If $G(p_2)$ were nondecreasing in $p_2$, so that $\partial G(p_2)/\partial p_2 \geqq 0$, then $p_2^c < p_2^m$, and (7A.5) would assure the derived sufficient condition in (7A.4). Taking this partial of $G(p_2)$ and rearranging yields the sufficient condition for sustainability:

$$\frac{\partial y^2}{\partial p_2} \left[ \frac{\partial C(y^1, y^2)}{\partial y^2} - \frac{\partial C(0, y^2)}{\partial y^2} \right]$$
$$+ \frac{\partial y^1}{\partial p_2} \left[ \frac{\partial C(y^1, y^2)}{\partial y^1} - \frac{C(y^1, y^2) - C(0, y^2)}{y^1} \right] \geqq 0 \qquad (7A.7)$$

where the arguments $p_1^m$ and $p_2$ are omitted for convenience. This inequality is (7.31) in the text.

# Part II

## Natural monopoly regulation in practice

# 8

## Regulation in practice:
## Why and how are firms regulated?

In this and subsequent chapters, we turn our attention from the principles underpinning why and how we *should* regulate price and entry in natural monopolies to examine the realities that dictate why and how we *do* regulate natural monopolies. As we shall see, on the one hand, realities often lead to compromised principles, and on the other hand, realities may sometimes be so complex that the principles seem to fall short of supplying adequate guidance to policy-makers.

This chapter provides an overview of the regulatory process, and Chapter 9 presents formal models that capture important features of that process. There we show how rate-base regulation for single-product and multiproduct firms can affect both the input and output mixes. Moreover, uncertainty, strategic behavior, and other features of the institutional environment further complicate outcomes in regulated industries. For example, automatic adjustment clauses and industry-wide regulatory constraints create incentives that lead to inefficiencies in levels of output and numbers of firms.

The remaining chapters also expand on points developed here in Chapter 8. The role of research and development in lowering costs and altering industrial configurations is surveyed in Chapter 10. In the context of a theoretical model of innovative activity, the chapter considers whether or not rate-base regulation biases the choice of technology toward capital-using techniques. Given the significant technological opportunities in energy and telecommunications, maintaining incentives for innovation is a key issue facing regulators. A further complication is that technological change can either reinforce or destroy the underlying justification for regulation.

Chapter 11 picks up this theme by examining partial regulation, deregulation, and diversification. Issues explored here are examined in the context of recent regulatory developments; these issues include sustainability, cost allocation, predation, and cross-subsidization. The final chapter examines whether or not inefficiencies induced by current regulatory practices might be mitigated through alternative policies toward these industries. It surveys public ownership, franchising, quality-of-service regulation, and new incentive schemes. Although these approaches emphasize economic efficiency, their applicability is limited by the fact that current regulatory practices give significant weight to issues of "fairness."

This chapter on regulation in practice is divided into five sections. In Section 8.1, we discuss several broad theories that attempt to explain why firms are regulated. In particular, why, starting with the late 1800s, have more and more industries become part of the regulators' domains? Next, in Sections 8.2 and 8.3, we take up the primary instruments used to regulate firms. We refer to a number of specific commission decisions and court rulings to illustrate how these instruments have been applied.[1] Then, in Section 8.4, we examine some theoretical and empirical investigations that have attempted to explain the behavior of regulatory agencies. Section 8.5 summarizes the theories and quantitative studies of regulatory motivations and impacts.

## 8.1. Why are firms regulated?

Economists and political scientists have written an extensive literature attempting to explain why firms are regu-

---

1 The court cases can be found in Morgan, Harrison, and Verkuil (1985).

lated. Because there are summaries of this literature elsewhere (Schmalensee, 1979; Wilcox and Shepherd, 1975), we do not present one here. Instead, we briefly outline two major themes in this earlier literature and then describe them as special cases of a more general theory. The two themes usually are referred to as the public-interest theory and the capture theory. In the former, regulation is said to come about in order to protect the consumer from powerful monopolies, whereas in the latter, regulators are eventually captured by the firms they regulate.

### The public-interest and capture theories

Part I of this book described the circumstances justifying intervention and discussed appropriate regulatory techniques, using welfare criteria. The public-interest theory takes the sanguine view that these reasons for why firms should be regulated are indeed the motivations for regulation. Although early writers did not discuss subadditive cost functions and similar technical concepts, they were well aware of the potential abuses associated with monopolistic power, and they saw regulation as the guardian against those abuses. In the public-interest framework, the regulator performs the task of maximizing social welfare through proper pricing and entry policies, as described in Chapters 2–7.

Some proponents of the approach have identified administrative shortcomings over the regulatory life cycle that result in inefficiencies. During periods of rapid change, reformers call for structural improvements in the regulatory process. For example, a public-interest critique of regulation may stress improved procedures, the addition of technical staff, greater accountability to legislative oversight committees, and integration of consumer interests into the hearings process.[2] Unfortunately, squaring this

2 Many views of regulatory practice suggest changes in the regulatory process. See Noll (1971) for an evaluation of the Ash Council proposals, one such set of recommendations. That presidential advisory council was critical of independent regulatory commissions – raising questions regarding legal procedures, regulatory lags, and policy development in the context of collegial organizations. Noll argues that organizational issues are not the main problem; rather, the regulatory process is intrinsically flawed.

theory of regulation with actual practice and decisions only serves to point out its lack of explanatory power. If the public-interest theory were supported by the data, we could conclude this book here; there would be no need to have a Part II, where actual regulatory policies are covered.

The capture theory describes regulatory agencies as beginning their existence with the public interest in mind, but eventually succumbing to the interests of the firms they regulate. Thus, the agency has a life cycle: The commission begins with youthful energy and protects consumers, and it ends up a calcified agency that protects producers (Bernstein, 1955). One way in which this capture is alleged to occur is via the movement of personnel between regulatory agencies and firms, thereby creating close ties and a desire for cooperation.

Neither of these theories can claim strong support from observation of actual regulatory behavior. The problem is that both are one-sided. Either the consumers or the firms eventually win in the struggle for government favors, but "economics is a theory of balance, not of all-or-nothing, as implied by the 'capture' theory of legislation" (Becker, 1976, p. 245). We should expect to see government favors awarded to more than one group, provided that more than one group has sufficient interest and concentrated power to influence regulatory decisions. In addition, Jarrell points out that neither the public-interest theory nor the capture theory explain how or why regulators are motivated to behave as the theories hypothesize:

> The mechanism that transforms the demand for regulation into regulatory behavior is largely neglected by both theories. The public interest theory asserts that regulation corrects private market failures, and the capture theory asserts that this noble goal is consistently thwarted so that regulation serves the regulated industry. Although actual regulatory behavior is often counter to the public interest, it is not uniformly proproducer either. Neither theory explains the widely

observed tendency for regulating agencies to selectively help and harm certain interest groups. (Jarrell, 1978, p. 277)

### Economic theory of regulation

To explain these mixed results of regulatory behavior, Stigler (1971) developed a theory wherein regulation comes about because there is a demand and supply for it. In this economic theory of regulation, groups demand government favors that will result in their receiving transfers of wealth. The particular producing firm and coalitions of consumers compete for influence.

The government has the power to transfer wealth privately by controlling entry into a market and fixing prices, although it can grant direct subsidies to groups as well. The government, via the political process, provides the supply of regulation in the form of these favors. Legislators will be responsive to their constituencies in order to be reelected; therefore, they will grant favors to the most influential constituents. Influence may take the form of votes, campaign funds, or future political favors.

A regulatory policy that means a transfer of wealth from a large group to a small group will be lobbied for heavily by members of the small group, because members have much at stake per capita. However, the large group has little at stake per capita, and so its lobbying efforts will be less forceful. Generally, small, concentrated groups will be more successful in satisfying their demands than will large, diffuse groups. Because firms usually are associated with small groups and consumers with large groups, Stigler's theory has been described as a producer-protectionist view of regulation. However, this description is incorrect, because any group that has influence can potentially be the victor in the struggle for favors.[3]

---

3 Cross-subsidization, as described in Chapter 7, is one means by which groups can be helped or hurt through the regulatory process. See Posner (1971), who described this as taxation by regulation.

Peltzman's work makes this clear as he develops a formal model of Stigler's theory:

> Stigler's work provides a theoretical foundation for this "producer protection" view. However, its scope is much more general. It is ultimately a theory of the optimum size of effective political coalitions set within the framework of a general model of the political process. Stigler seems to have realized that the earlier "consumer protection" model came perilously close to treating regulation as a free good. In that model, the existence of market failure is sufficient to generate a demand for regulation, though there is no mention of the mechanism that makes that demand effective. (Peltzman, 1976, p. 212)[4]

In Peltzman's development, regulation comes about as a means of transferring wealth from one group to another. Thus, the recipient group is a winner, and the donor group a loser, in this competition for government regulation. This analysis does not imply an all-or-nothing game. If the competition is between a natural monopoly and consumers, the final result is neither a profit-maximizing price nor a welfare-maximizing price; rather, it is somewhere between these extremes. Lee (1980) takes this theory one step further and argues that regulation can involve a positive-sum game: There can be winners and winners in this competition for legislation and regulatory policies. The key to this possibility is the saving that can be realized when the government assumes enforcement duties previously carried out by private concerns.

By way of example, consider a multiproduct natural monopoly that is unregulated. This firm cannot charge monopoly prices, because that would invite entry. But it does charge prices that

---

4 For a critique of Stigler's economic theory of regulation, see Trebing (1976, 1984). Hirschleifer (1976) amends Peltzman's formal model to include regulators as an interest group. Peltzman's characterization of political competition is severely criticized by Goldberg (1982). The latter author argues that the support function that regulators maximize depends crucially on which parties are included in the analysis.

allow positive profit, while at the same time expending real resources in protecting itself from entrants. Thus, consumers will demand regulation to obtain lower prices and profits, and the firm will demand regulation that will protect it from entrants. Because the "state has coercive powers such as imprisonment and the imposition of fines and taxation, which private industries could create only at greater costs ... the social mode of cartel enforcement may be much cheaper than the private mode" (Lee, 1980, p. 849). Consequently, there exists a bargaining game in which both consumers and the firm can be made better off. After regulation, prices are lowered, and consumers are winners. The firm also wins, however, because the loss in profits owing to the lower prices is more than made up for by having the state assume the burden of policing entry.

The state's coercive power places it in an advantageous position for enforcing cartels or price structures, as Lee suggests. The state may also be in a better position to enforce contracts between private concerns. Consider that in most natural monopoly public utility situations, there is a physical link between the producer and consumers. The link may be a telephone or power line, a gas-distribution pipeline, or water pipe. Thus, there will be an ongoing relationship between producer and consumer, and typically this relationship is defined by an explicit or implicit contract. How should this contract be arrived at? If each consumer contracted separately with the producer, the transactions cost would be enormous. Consumers as a group probably are best served by employing a single agent to represent them and protect their interests. Likewise, the producer, having incurred the sunk costs of establishing the links with consumers, will want his right to serve the market protected from entrants. A regulator has the ability to protect the producer's right to serve, as well as to protect the consumer's interests. Furthermore, there are transactions-cost savings from having a single regulator acting as the contract-enforcer between consumers and producers, instead of having individual bargaining between the two groups. There appears to be a justification for regulators as contract-enforcers, and both producers and consumers may be winners as a result of this institutional arrangement.

This novel view of regulation as an efficient method to enforce contracts was developed by Goldberg (1976). He stated that "in searching for a rationale for regulation we should not look at the shape of the long-run average cost curve, but instead at the complexities involved in devising and administering ... a private contract for the right to serve" (p. 431). Regulation can be viewed as the administration of a long-term flexible contract between the producers and consumers. The agency resolves the division of rents (arising from uncertain developments) via bargaining rather than through the introduction of new suppliers.

Goldberg's view of the situation provides a noteworthy addendum to the justification for regulation in Chapter 2. It reminds us that the definition of natural monopoly should include the market-transactions costs of trade that are avoided by a firm's internal organization, as well as the technical production costs for the goods. Chapter 2's discussion of conditions that give rise to subadditivity underscored this point. The importance of including physical links, in particular, depends partly on how many industries will be classified as natural monopolies with and without considering such costs in the definition. Because producers having physical links with consumers often are found in industries that are natural monopolies solely because of production technologies, including transactions costs in the definition of natural monopoly may not substantially change the number of industries that are classified as such. Still, studies of the efficiency of regulation should not ignore any benefits accruing from lower transactions costs.

The demand-and-supply theory for the existence of regulation goes a long way in explaining the diversity among observed regulatory practices. That there is diversity is not surprising when we consider how many different groups play roles in regulatory decisions: the consumers, who are likely to be divided into competing coalitions; the producers; the regulatory agencies, which may have overlapping jurisdictions; the state and federal legislatures. We have only briefly touched on the interactions among these groups, and the literature on the subject is vast and growing. One of the more promising avenues of research involves exploring the link between the legislatures and agencies. Weingast and Moran (1983) present an interesting empirical analysis of the relationship between the U.S. Congress and the Federal Trade Commission (FTC). In the late 1970s, Congress took strong action against the activist FTC, almost shutting down the agency, on the grounds that it was overstepping its bounds in regulating the economy. According to Weingast and Moran, traditional theory would suggest that this was an example of an agency run amok that the legislature had to reel in. However, they provide evidence suggesting that the FTC was merely following congressional demands; it was Congress that moved from an activist role in the early 1970s to a more passive role in the late 1970s. Thus, regulatory agencies are not insulated from state and national political climate.

In recent years, the movement toward deregulation of certain industries has been met with opposition, sometimes from particular consumer groups, sometimes from industries, and sometimes from both. We would expect the source of this opposition to be those receiving the government transfers. Much of Part II is devoted to the examination of specific regulatory policies and how particular favored groups obtain transfers.

## 8.2. How are firms regulated?

Control of entry and control of prices are the primary means by which natural monopolies are regulated by state and federal agencies. We examined ideal approaches to these regulatory instruments in Part I, and now we turn to actual practice. Note, however, that regulating price is fruitless if quality is not maintained at some specified level. Degradation of product quality (e.g., unsatisfied excess demand for electricity) must be addressed by regulators. Such quality regulation has received little attention in the economics literature. We implicitly hold quality constant in most of this book, although Chapter 12 does contain analyses in which quality is also a concern of the regulator.

### Entry: MCI and the FCC

Entry restrictions represent an important regulatory instrument; they may be quite visible, as when regulators issue a limited number of licenses permitting firms to operate. Less obvious are rules specifying certain safety or hiring requirements that merely limit the number of firms interested in entering. Such limitations can be justified on economic-efficiency grounds only if there is an unsustainable natural monopoly; even in such situations, restrictions may be necessary only when entry barriers can be overcome. However, the natural monopoly argument often has not been the primary factor in commission hearings concerning entry regulation.

Consider Microwave Communications, Inc. (MCI), which filed an application with the FCC to provide small businesses with limited communications service between Chicago and St. Louis, MCI claimed that its subscribers would enjoy substantially lower rates than those charged by established carriers. These established carriers, including Western Union, General Telephone of Illinois, Illinois Bell, and Southwestern Bell, all opposed the application. The hearings commenced in early 1967, and a decision in favor of MCI was reached in 1969. The chief issues raised by the established carriers and considered by the FCC revolved more around questions of MCI's financial and technical qualifications than around questions of natural monopoly and economic efficiency. There was some question whether or not MCI's service was needed by the public, although what constituted need was not clear. The established carriers pointed out that MCI's services would be of lower voice quality; so it should be considered unacceptable. But the commission indicated that it had never specified what constitutes a minimum degree of quality.

The primary economic issue here was whether or not the established carriers were natural monopolies; if so, MCI should not have been allowed entry. But could the established carriers find and set sustainable prices and not worry about entry? This question was never debated, because the FCC and state commissions had always encouraged cross-subsidies from high-density to low-density routes. Thus, MCI may have been cream-skimming, where the cream was a result of past regulatory pricing policies. The FCC chairman, Rosel Hyde, articulated this viewpoint in a dissenting statement to the commission's decision:

> How is it that applicant is able to propose lower rates than the existing common carriers? . . . For no reason [other] than that it is proposing a typical "cream skimming" operation. Thus, it has selected a major route, Chicago to St. Louis, with heavy traffic density characteristics and the concomitant lower unit costs. The existing common carriers, on the other hand, have been encouraged by the Commission, primarily for social reasons, to base their rates . . . on nationwide average costs. . . . The evidence in this record tends to show [that the established carrier] could offer lower rates . . . than those proposed by MCI, were they to base such rates on their costs for that rate alone. (1969, 18 F.C.C.2d 953, 16 R.R.2d 1037)

Other commissioners were not persuaded by these arguments; so the United States took its first halting steps toward deregulation of long-distance telecommunications. Entry regulation continues to be a very active area in telecommunications and energy; so we shall return to this issue in Chapter 11.

### Pricing and cost allocation

Turning now to prices, we first note that entry and price regulation are really inseparable. In the preceding FCC case, price regulations involved cross-subsidies, which may have invited MCI to seek entry in the first place. In Chapter 3, other examples of cross-subsidization were shown that were based on FDC pricing. When following FDC pricing, a multiproduct firm will assign to each output any directly attributable costs. Then the firm will apportion the remaining costs, or common costs, to each output according to the output's relative share of (1) past revenues, (2) total directly attributable costs, or (3) total output (to note just three of many possibilities). As was pointed out, all of these methods are arbitrary; so identifying cross-subsidization on the basis of such arbitrary cost allocations is inappropriate. In formulating a proper definition of cross-subsidization, we need to define the costs that must be covered by revenues, but these costs must be defined independent of the pricing method used to raise revenues. The stand-alone test from Chapter 7 accomplishes this task.

We have already mentioned the ICC as an agency that has utilized FDC pricing methods.[5] Although this cost-allocation approach can lead to cross-subsidization, sometimes other factors are brought into the decisions regulating pricing and entry that will override arguments for economic efficiency. An example is a case involving a railroad line serving a rural area in North Carolina and Georgia. The Louisville and Nashville Railroad (L&N) requested abandonment on the grounds that it was losing $200,000 annually to operate the line. The ICC initially permitted the abandonment, but the decision was appealed by the Georgia Public Service Commission, the North Carolina Department of Transportation, and a number of city and county governments. In 1983, the U.S. Court of Appeals (Eleventh Circuit, 704 F.2d 538) reversed the ICC's ruling. In the court's decision there was no mention of whether or not the rural area was being subsidized by other users of the L&N. No analysis was presented as to what the marginal costs of serving the rural area were and whether or not the railroad was covering those costs. Instead, the court's decision was based on the harm that would be done to the businesses in the rural area, because they would no longer be able to ship their goods. Harm to rural communities was the overriding concern in this instance. Barke and Riker (1982) argue that the ICC's railway abandonment policy runs counter to the Stig-

5 Recently, the ICC has also been receptive to Ramsey pricing concepts and stand-alone cost tests for cross-subsidies. See Damus (1984) for a discussion of the ICC and Ramsey pricing for railroads.

ler–Peltzman model. However, Dougan (1984) finds that "subsidization of low density customers by their high density counterparts is . . . to be expected in those regulated industries with cost structures similar to [those of railroads]" (p. 301).

In another case involving cross-subsidies, *National Association of Greeting Card Publishers* v. *U.S. Postal Service* (1976), the U.S. Court of Appeals for the District of Columbia ruled against the Postal Service's Rate Commission's method of allocating costs. Initially, the Rate Commission determined what costs could be directly attributable to each class of mail, and because of lack of data, it attributed common costs by the volume of mail in each class. Eventually, as data and costs were gathered, the Rate Commission was able to increase the directly attributable cost, using estimates of long-run variable costs, to 52.5 percent of the total costs. But the Court of Appeals found this approach unacceptable and required the Rate Commission to allocate all costs on the basis of "cost accounting principles." For example, costs should be assigned by the weight or cubic volume of the mail, "notwithstanding a lack of proof that such factors play an accurate role" in costs.[6] In 1983, the Supreme Court remanded the matter of rate marketing to the Rate Commission and concluded that the commission is not bound to any particular "cost accounting principles" for establishing prices. The decision opens up the possibility of more efficient pricing, possibly along the lines of the Sherman–George model of Ramsey pricing for postal services (see Chapter 3). Their prices were based on demand elasticities, marginal costs, and cross-elasticities between postal services and substitute services in the private sector.

The FDC provides one method of determining the structure of prices. Other elements of price structures that commissions may consider include nonlinear and multipart tariffs, variations in prices by time of use, and variations in prices by reliability of service. In Part I, we developed the principles of optimum prices that incorporate these elements; however, these principles are not

---

6 See *National Association of Greeting Card Publishers* v. *U.S. Postal Service*, Supreme Court of the United States, 1983, 462 U.S. 810, 103 S.Ct. 2717, 77 L.Ed.2d 195.

consistently followed in practice. For example, we can find price structures in which consumers are charged a price per kilowatt-hour of electricity in addition to a fee that is based on the consumer's maximum demand. This would be a reasonable way of implementing time-of-use or peak-load pricing if the consumer's maximum demand was coincident with the system's peak load, but if the consumer's maximum demand is in an off-peak period, then the principles of optimum prices are being violated.

Many economists argue that past pricing practices in telecommunications have promoted inefficiency. Long-distance has been priced on the basis of usage only; so revenue for the contribution to the local network has essentially been collected as a usage surcharge. Based on data from Southwestern Bell and AT&T, Wenders and Egan (1986) find the ratio of price to marginal cost in interstate service to be greater than 3 in 1983. The zero access charge and high marginal price induce underconsumption of long-distance and encourage uneconomic bypass.

Several authors have estimated the magnitude of the resulting welfare losses. Griffin (1982) estimated the loss at $1.55 billion for 1975, slightly less than the National Telecommunications and Information Association estimate of $1.7 billion for 1978 (reported in the Congressional Budget Office study, 1984). Wenders and Egan (1986) calculated a $5.3 billion loss for 1983, using a more elastic residential demand elasticity than Griffin ($-0.8$ vs. $-0.6$). Also, they expanded the market to include business demand, and the more recent year implies higher quantities. Such losses partly explain the FCC's shift to access charges, so as to de-load the markup on usage.

The reverse problem arises in local service. Most consumers do not face usage-sensitive pricing for local calls. Here, the two-part tariff has a high flat fee and a zero marginal price. We know that even if marginal cost were zero, the optimal two-part tariff would, in general, have a positive marginal price to bring some small demanders onto the system. If there is a network externality to having a larger number of subscribers, a lower flat fee is also justified. Mitchell (1978) estimated that the net gain from moving to usage-sensitive pricing of local service could be as large as 9 percent of current net benefits. He also found the possibility of a net loss if the metering costs are very high and marginal costs very low. For the case most favorable for usage-sensitive pricing, the net welfare gain was about $250 million in 1975. Wenders and Egan (1986) estimated the welfare gain at $685 million (without peak-load pricing). Even greater gains arise under peak-load pricing – doubling or tripling the gains. The reason these gains are low relative to long-distance is the low marginal cost of a local call (2–4 cents per minute); so the deviation between price and marginal cost is low. Also, the demand is relatively inelastic (about $-0.1$). If distributional weights are incorporated into the analysis, usage-sensitive pricing receives additional support because of the heavier usage by high-income consumers and exclusion of very low income customers under the flat-fee system.

In spite of the extent of the deadweight losses caused by inefficient pricing, there is room for optimism. There is evidence of progress toward more efficient pricing in several industries with regulated natural monopolies. The divestiture of the regional telephone companies from AT&T and increased competition in long-distance telecommunications have forced cost-based pricing in this industry. Similarly, new technologies for cogeneration and escalating fuel prices (and PURPA) have brought about pressures for pricing reform in the electric-power industry. Natural-gas deregulation and greater attention to rate design by distribution systems illustrate further pricing adjustments induced by competitive pressures.

### Rate-of-return regulation

In deriving optimum prices, we assumed full knowledge of costs, and we required prices to generate enough revenue to exactly cover these costs. Once prices were derived, we knew output, revenue, and costs (or probable outcomes in the case of stochastic demand). In other words, prices, revenues, output, and costs were determined simultaneously to maximize welfare.

However, regulation does not take place in a world of full information, with economic efficiency as the key goal.

In practice, prices often are determined in a more stepwise fashion. Under cost pressures, a firm will apply to the appropriate regulatory agency for permission to raise its prices. A hearing will be held, at which the commissioner(s) will listen to the firm's arguments as to why the increase is necessary. Typically, a test period will be selected, such as the past 12 months, for which the firm will gather data on costs and revenues. There may also be intervenors in the hearing, including consumer advocates or environmental groups, who will argue, sometimes through outside experts, why prices should not be raised. The commission also has a staff that will study the arguments and data and make recommendations.

The process can be divided into three basic steps: (1) The firm's costs are reviewed, and costs deemed to be unnecessary are eliminated. (2) A rate-of-return judged to be fair for the firm is specified. (3) Prices and their structure are set to generate enough revenue to cover costs and provide a fair rate of return. This process is referred to as rate-of-return regulation, and it is widely used by state and federal regulatory commissions. Rate-of-return regulation probably has been studied more than any other form of regulation. Although the next chapter will analyze it in detail, a general description of the rate-of-return process and problems inherent in that process will be useful.[7]

Consider a regulated firm that uses two inputs to produce a single output. Profit for the firm is

$$\pi = R - wL - rK - d - T \tag{8.1}$$

where $L$ is a variable input such as labor or fuel (for a power company), and $K$ is the capital stock. The prices of $L$ and $K$ are $w$ and $r$, respectively, and the firm takes these prices as given. $R$

---

7 The presentation here should be viewed as a description of what regulators who impose a rate-of-return constraint must consider, rather than as a description of the regulatory process. Joskow (1974) criticizes what he believes is an overemphasis on models with a rate-of-return constraint. We discuss this further in the next chapter.

is revenue, which is price times quantity, or $p(f(K, L))f(K, L)$, where $f(K, L)$ is the firm's production function. Depreciation of the capital stock is $d$, and $T$ is the firm's tax bill. Assuming profit-maximizing behavior, the firm's objective is to maximize (8.1). However, regulation imposes a constraint on the firm's behavior, requiring the firm's rate of return to be no greater than a specified allowed rate of return. The rate-of-return constraint takes the form

$$\frac{R - wL - d - T}{K - D} \leq s \tag{8.2}$$

where the left-hand side is the rate of return, and where $s$ is the allowed rate of return specified by the regulator. The numerator is the net operating income, and the denominator is the firm's rate base.

Note that the rate base is the capital stock less depreciation, where $D$ is the sum of all past periods' depreciations (i.e., the sum of past $d$'s). A more detailed description would specify time periods and would subscript the $d$'s, but for now, (8.2) is sufficient to capture the important elements. To impose this constraint, regulators require a uniform system of accounting for public utilities. This framework is important in order to maintain consistency across firms in categorizing operating expenses, capital outlays, depreciation, and taxes. Without a uniform system, the regulator would be faced with the time-consuming task of interpreting accounting procedures that vary from firm to firm. This formulation takes the price of physical capital as one dollar per unit; so the rate base, $K - D$, is measured in dollars, and $r$ is a percentage – reflecting the cost of financial capital, which is then used for the acquisition of physical capital.

### 8.3. Problems with rate-of-return regulation

There are inherent problems with imposing the rate-of-return constraint on a firm's behavior. We divide the problems into four classes: (1) allowable costs; (2) depreciation expense; (3) incentives; (4) the rate base and allowed return.[8] Each of these

---

8 For more detail on these problems, see Kahn (1971) or Phillips (1984).

areas will be considered in the context of specific models later. However, the implications of regulatory discretion in enforcing (8.2) are outlined here to provide an overview of the issues.

### *Allowable costs*

Operating costs raise two basic problems. First, the firm may have incentive to exaggerate its costs. By claiming that operating costs ($wL$) are greater than they actually are, the firm is in a position to increase its revenue and still remain within the allowed rate of return. Second, the firm can incur costs that are not necessarily in the best interest of consumers. Examples include advertisements that are intended to promote goodwill, instead of providing information, and charitable contributions also meant to provide goodwill. The idea is that the firm can acquire this goodwill and include the cost of acquisition in its operating expenses, thereby passing these costs on to the consumers. A firm regulated in this manner is unlike an unregulated firm, which generally will not incur non-revenue-enhancing expenses. Because the regulated firm typically is charging a price below the profit-maximizing level, it has the ability to raise prices and cover the costs without lowering profit.

The courts have been split on the question whether or not all advertising and charitable contributions are allowable expenses. In a 1971 case, the Massachusetts Supreme Judicial Court overturned the Department of Public Utilities decision to disallow $300,000 of advertising expenses incurred by New England Telephone.[9] The department had allowed another $500,000 of advertising expense because it was informative. But the $300,000 was related to an "attempt to improve the climate of public opinion toward the Company [and therefore] the cost of the advertising should be borne by the stockholders." The court said that "as a business corporation engaged in selling an important service, the

---

9 *New England Telephone and Telegraph Co.* v. *Department of Public Utilities*, Supreme Judicial Court of Massachusetts, 1971, 360 Mass. 443, 275 N.E.2d 493. Note that advertising directed at both conservation and promotion can be profitable if the timing of consumption can be changed – reducing only peak consumption. Kaserman and Mayo (1985) find that advertising in the 1974–9 period reduced electricity demand.

Company is entitled to take all reasonable means to promote and to seek to enlarge that business. One of the means used by almost all business corporations is advertising. [The Company] is no less entitled to advertise by reason of the fact that it is a regulated public utility than is the ordinary business corporation." The Supreme Court of California came to the opposite conclusion in a 1972 case[10] in which it upheld the Public Utility Commission's ruling to disallow $1.4 million of advertising expense from Pacific Telephone's total of $12.9 million of advertising. One judge indicated that advertising should be informative if it is to do more than create a good public image, concluding that to be an allowable expense, advertising should result in a reduction in operating costs and more efficient service.

These same two courts ruled in the same way regarding charitable contributions.[11] On the one hand, the Massachusetts court overturned the Department of Public Utilities decision to disallow charitable contributions by New England Telephone on the grounds that they were vital in the effort to establish and improve public relations. On the other hand, the California court upheld the Public Utility Commission's ruling that charitable contributions were not allowable expenses for Pacific Telephone. It added to the commission's statement that "contributions, if included as an expense for rule making purposes, become an involuntary levy on ratepayers, who, because of the monopolistic nature of the utility service, are unable to obtain service from another source and thereby avoid such a levy. Ratepayers should be encouraged to contribute directly to worthy causes and not involuntarily through an allowance in utility rates."

Similar issues arise with R&D expenses. Some states have disallowed portions of funds given to research consortia on the grounds that some of the projects (e.g., studies of nuclear power) did not benefit customers of the utility. In addition, R&D may

10 *City of Los Angeles* v. *Public Utilities Commission,* Supreme Court of California, 1972, 7 Cal.3d 331, 102 Cal.Rptr. 313, 497 P.2d 785.
11 The Massachusetts case is the same as in footnote 8. The California case is *Pacific Telephone and Telegraph Co.* v. *Public Utilities Commission,* Supreme Court of California, 1965, 62 Cal.2d 634, 44 Cal.Rptr. 1, 401 P.2d 353.

be allowed as an expense in one state, but treated as a capital outlay in another – thus becoming part of the rate base, $K$. We make no attempt to catalogue the different (and changing) policies of various state commissions. However, regulatory policies will influence the patterns of outlays made by companies.

Sometimes state commissions follow federal precedents in the treatment of particular types of expenses. But as the Massachusetts and California examples illustrate, state commissions (and courts) can follow very different philosophies. The portfolio of policies in a state is considered by investors when evaluating the riskiness of utility stocks, and indices of state regulatory climates are published regularly by a variety of organizations. These rankings reflect different approaches to depreciation and taxation, rate-base determination, and allowed rates of return, and they have been used in empirical studies of regulatory behavior, as illustrated in Section 8.4.

### Depreciation expense

Depreciation expenses raise a number of important issues. Depreciation can be a real cost in the sense that it represents wear and tear on capital and therefore should be included as an allowable expense. Depreciation can also reflect economic obsolescence; the capital will become outdated before it wears out physically. In such situations, depreciation represents an imputed cost that firms distribute over the projected life of the capital, so that consumers pay the capital costs. Because there is no completely reliable way to determine what the economic life of a particular capital input will be, there may be considerable leeway in just how rapidly an item in the rate base may be written off. As was shown in Section 3.1, the intertemporal pattern of capital cost allocations has significant implications for efficient pricing. Economic depreciation will be equal to straight-line depreciation under a narrow set of circumstances (Joskow and Schmalensee, 1986, pp. 6–7). Furthermore, inadequate depreciation can lead to disincentives to adopt new technologies, as discussed in Chapter 10.

Depreciation plays a dual role in calculating the rate of return, because it appears in both the numerator and denominator of (8.2). Obviously, the regulated firm would like to see a small deduction for depreciation in the denominator and a large deduction in the numerator, but this would be inconsistent. But not all commissions act consistently. Some states do not deduct the full depreciation in the denominator, thereby keeping the rate base larger. This method may approximate a replacement-cost approach (as opposed to an original-cost approach) to rate-base determination. During periods of rising equipment costs, the utility is allowed to revise upward the value of its rate base.

In addition, the tax bill depends on depreciation and interest expenses. Typically,

$$T = t[R - wL - iB - d]$$

where $t$ is the tax rate, and the term in brackets is net income before taxes. The term $iB$ represents interest expense. Although it was omitted from equation (8.2) for simplicity, the mix of financial capital (equity stocks and corporate bonds) will affect the revenue requirements of the utility. The role of depreciation is such that depreciation will lower the tax bill. Firms can choose to use accelerated depreciation, a method that yields large depreciation expenses in the early years of an asset's life, rather than straight-line depreciation, which involves equal deductions per time period. When the tax savings from accelerated depreciation for a single year are passed on to consumers that year, regulators are following a flow-through approach to distributing the tax benefits of accelerated depreciation. Alternatively, regulators can "normalize" the savings – passing on the savings over a number of years. Normalization is equivalent to the utility obtaining an interest-free loan from the government. Some regulatory jurisdictions using this procedure include such funds in their calculation of the allowed rate of return – lowering $s$, because some capital is available at zero interest.

In a 1980 case before the Missouri Court of Appeals,[12] this interest-free loan was debated. A consumer group argued that the

---

12 *Utility Consumers Council of Missouri* v. *Public Service Commission,* Court of Appeals of Missouri, Western District, 1980, 606 S.W.2d 222.

state Public Service Commission was wrong when it allowed Union Electric Company to use as part of its operating expenses an amount of tax [$T$ in (8.2)] that was more than the actual taxes paid. The taxes paid were calculated using accelerated depreciation, whereas the taxes used as expenses were calculated using straight-line depreciation. The consumer group argued that prices should be based on actual costs incurred. (Of course, if the test year used in the original hearing was such that the actual taxes were *greater* than the taxes used as operating expenses, a situation that would arise in later years, then presumably the consumer group would have been receptive to this procedure.) At any rate, the court ruled in favor of the commission. Judge Kennedy argreed that the deferred taxes amounted to an interest-free loan, but he believed that it was beneficial to ratepayers because it was "a cost free addition to capital." About half the states have adopted flow-through accounting, accepting the argument that a growing company never fully pays off its deferred taxes. On the other hand, there is an intergenerational transfer from future customers to present customers under such a scheme, because the time pattern of revenue requirements is affected by regulatory policies. Furthermore, utility cash flows are reduced – leading to higher cost of capital for such utilities. Thus, current customers pay at least part of the cost through higher allowed rates of return (Brigham and Tapley, 1986).

### Incentives for cost reduction

Undesirable incentives constitute a third class of problems arising when there is a rate-of-return constraint. Many analysts have concluded that there is very little incentive for a firm to hold down its operating costs if they can be passed on to the consumer. For example, a firm operating in a competitive environment will have strong incentive to search for the least-cost inputs to be used in its production process. The regulated firm, say an electricity company, may not have this strong incentive to seek out the least-cost fuel supply or to bargain with a union over wages. These analysts conclude that the regulator not only must be a watchdog on waste but also must monitor the firm's effort in seeking least-cost solutions. However, effective monitoring is virtually impossible short of duplicating the firm's managerial functions.

Another, less obvious, undesirable incentive is that firms subject to rate-of-return regulation have been hypothesized to operate with too much capital for the output being produced. This non-cost-minimizing activity is due to the asymmetry of constraint (8.2). Because allowed revenue, net of operating costs, depends on the rate base (capital), there is an incentive to increase the level of capital beyond what is needed for economically efficient production. This phenomenon, known as the Averch–Johnson effect (Section 9.1 contains a formal model of this effect), has a number of theoretical extensions. However, empirical findings regarding this hypothesis have been mixed, and alternative characterizations of the regulatory process have yielded very different implications for capital intensity. The strengths and limitations of this model are discussed in the next chapter.

### Rate-base determination and the allowed return

The fourth class of problems with a rate-of-return constraint has to do with the difficulty in measuring the firm's rate base. As is evident from equation (8.2), the firm's capital stock, or rate base, is instrumental in determining the firm's total profit. The calculation of the rate base is particularly critical for natural monopolies such as electric utilities and local telecommunications companies with very high capital-to-sales ratios. In *Smith* v. *Ames*,[13] a landmark case for regulation heard before the Supreme Court in 1898, Justice Harlan delivered the opinion that the rate base should be the fair value of the capital; in calculating the fair value, the original cost of the capital, its market value, and its replacement (present) cost should all be considered.

13 *Smith* v. *Ames,* Supreme Court of the United States, 1898, 160 U.S. 466, 18 S.Ct. 418, 42 L.Ed. 819.

Because these three measures individually will yield different results, almost 50 years of controversy followed that ruling.

During inflationary (deflationary) periods, consumers will favor using original (present) cost, whereas firms will favor the reverse. Using market value to determine the rate base leads to circular reasoning, because market value depends on anticipated earnings, which depend on the prices set, which depend on the regulator's decision, which depends on the market value. Because of the vast time and effort that would have to be expended to determine present value, most state commissions use the original cost to estimate fair value. Original cost less accumulated depreciation is easier to calculate and provides stability in the determination of revenue requirements. This approach is also in keeping with the Supreme Court decision in the *Hope Natural Gas* case (1944),[14] in which Justice Douglas delivered the opinion that whatever is necessary to keep the firm operating is fair.

Besides the problem of determining the value of the rate base, there are fundamental questions concerning what should be included as capital. Should excess capacity be included, since equipment is idle? If the Nuclear Regulatory Commission shuts a unit down for safety reasons, should the unit be included in the rate base? Should working capital in the form of cash be included, or should units under construction be included? This latter question has been particularly controversial in recent years, with state commissions coming down on both sides of the issue.[15] Note that regulatory policies toward such issues (and the associated regulatory climate) will affect the utility's cost of capital.

Once the value of the firm's rate base is determined, the regulator still must decide on the allowed rate of return. Constraint (8.2) makes clear that determining $sK$, not $K$, is the ultimate objective. Thus, if regulators increase $s$, but decrease what is permitted in the rate, revenue requirements may remain stable. Determining $s$ is essentially a bargaining process, with the regu-

---

14  *FPC* v. *Hope Natural Gas Co.*, Supreme Court of the United States, 1944, 320 U.S. 591, 64 S.Ct. 281, 88 L.Ed. 333.

15  See, for example, *Legislative Utility Consumers' Council* v. *Public Service Co.*, Supreme Court of New Hampshire, 1979, 119 N.H. 332, 402 A.2d 626.

lator as an arbitrator between the firm and the consumers. The lower bound is the minimum return required to attract investors, and the upper bound is what the firm would earn as an unconstrained profit-maximizer. The difficulties have to do with measuring the cost of capital, *r,* and then judging whether the firm should be allowed a return equal to *r* or perhaps slightly above it. Of course, when *s* equals *r,* economic profit is zero; so one argument is to set *s* slightly above *r* to provide some incentive. Measuring the cost of capital is complex, however. Should the regulator look at other firms or the entire industry to determine the cost of capital for a particular firm? Should only regulated or unregulated firms be considered when calculating comparable returns? Should it be a historical cost of capital or a projected cost? Is there some optimal mix of equity and debt that will minimize *r* – and if so, how does one take the tax advantages of interest payments into account? How does risk get measured when risk depends on the regulator's actions? In addition, very efficient firms may have lower capital costs, but then if they are allowed a lower return, their efficiency will be punished. An extensive finance literature has developed on measuring firms' costs of capital, and the technical methods used have found their way into regulatory hearings.[16]

### 8.4. Regulatory behavior

From Chapter 2, a necessary condition for *justifying* price and entry regulation of a firm is that the firm must be a natural monopoly. From Section 8.1, a sufficient condition for *observing* price and entry regulation is that there exist a demand for the wealth transfers that such regulation can provide and that there exist a political body able to supply the wealth transfer via regulation. Taken together, what do these statements imply? To answer, first consider that where there is a natural monopoly, there will exist a demand for and supply of regulation. Consumer

---

16 The reader is referred to Jensen (1972), Davis and Sparrow (1972), Breen and Lerner (1972), Myers (1972), Morin (1984), Kolbe and Read (1984), and Brigham and Tapley (1986) for examples of this literature, particularly as it applies to regulated firms.

groups will seek low prices, and firms will seek high profits and protection from entrants. Moreover, in many cases of natural monopoly, some type of price and entry regulation will be justified. The exceptions are those markets in which there are no barriers to entry and the natural monopoly is sustainable (recall Table 7.1). Second, there will exist a demand for and supply of regulation in many markets in which natural monopoly is not present. Accordingly, we are likely to observe regulation that is wholly unjustified by natural monopoly arguments.

Although there will be cases of unjustified regulation, there will also be cases of justified regulation. Unfortunately, price and entry regulation need not follow guidelines like those presented in Chapters 3–7 – guidelines that will promote efficient price and output choices. The economic theory of regulation suggests that it stems from the existence of a demand for and supply of regulation. It does not result from a societal quest for economic efficiency. Thus, where we observe firms that are justifiably regulated, we cannot expect that we shall consistently find efficient outcomes. Valid economic goals may be supplemented by political concerns and the appeasement of groups competing for transfers.

The purpose of this section is to review some of the theoretical and empirical literature that attempts to explain regulatory outcomes by recognizing that goals other than economic efficiency influence policy. Given that regulation may evolve for the wrong reasons, how does this affect economic efficiency? Given that regulators may not view economic efficiency as their primary goal, how will they behave, and what will be the results of their behavior? How do regulators use the instruments at their disposal (described in the previous section) to formulate decision criteria?

### Theoretical studies

In Part I, welfare maximization was assumed to be the objective of regulators; efficient prices and outputs were derived under this assumption. However, if we are to formulate a positive model of regulatory behavior that captures political influences, social welfare maximization must be discarded. Welfare may enter into a regulator's preferences, but it need not be the overriding concern. Attempts to model a general preference ordering or utility function for a regulatory agency have been scarce. Most studies have observed actual behavior in specific industries and then compared that with what would be predicted by the capture, public-interest, or economic theories.

Owen and Braeutigam (1978) credit this absence of regulatory objective functions in theoretical models to the lack of convincing arguments that would justify them. Perhaps regulatory agencies are passive, without any objective, and simply respond to their constituents within the constraints set up by legislative bodies. These authors argue that agencies are endogenous forces whose behavior can be manipulated by the regulated firms. They also argue that regulation represents the institutionalization of the status quo. Regulatory delays and the role of precedent are both designed to prevent the sudden capital losses that consumers and investors incur under a market system. Essentially, participants are viewed as having property rights in existing price structures; highly choreographed hearings are like charades, designed to preserve prices and output mixes. The benefit of such a regulatory orientation is that planning by consumers and producers is facilitated by the reduction of uncertainty. The burden is borne by those who would gain by changes in the status quo. Although markets might be efficient without intervention, the political process can establish institutional arrangements promoting fairness, social values, and stability.

Posner (1971) has emphasized regulation as a means of facilitating transfers via cross-subsidies, except that the legitimacy and efficiency of the transfer make the process resemble taxation. Even while noting the deadweight losses that accompany cross-subsidization, Posner notes that the alternative, taxes, will also induce distortions and involve administrative costs. From this perspective, public utility regulation can be viewed as a branch of public finance. Because fairness is an explicit goal expressed in legislative mandates, using prices as tax and transfer devices has broad public support. Of course, a major objection to such practices is the absence of public scrutiny; hidden subsidies are not reviewed to determine if alternative means to the same end might be more cost-effective. However, this complaint applies to many other government programs. Just because careful comparisons of benefits and costs are not routinely made is no reason to eliminate this particular instrument of taxation. Nevertheless, one can still question whether or not the instruments available to regulators allow adequate degrees of freedom. Furthermore, the indirect, long-term impacts of limiting entry and underpricing a service can be especially damaging to efficiency.

Russell and Shelton (1974) model regulators as self-interested individuals intent on building coalitions that will allow them to survive and expand their authority. They list several reasons why regulators can behave in this way with relative impunity. First, the impacts of a single decision will not be known with certainty. Second, decisions are judgment calls, because there are few objective standards on which they can be based. Third, regulators have flexibility because legislators typically have not provided regulators with objective standards. Fourth, judicial review of decisions is related more often to matters of due process than to matters of fact. Therefore, given the wide range of choices available to regulators, behavior may not be uniform enough to model and to derive predictable actions.

If regulators do grant preferential treatment to certain consumer groups, because of a group's political influence or simply because of regulatory attitudes about social justice, then this preferential treatment may be observable. Ross (1984) suggests a method based on Ramsey pricing that will uncover a regulator's social-welfare weights. For example, he shows that if the regulator enforces linear prices and maximizes an objective function that is a weighted sum of consumer surpluses for different consumer groups, and if the profit of the firm being regulated is constrained to some fixed amount, then the pricing rules obtained reduce to

$$\frac{\beta_A}{\beta_B} = \frac{\dfrac{q_2^B}{q_2^T}\left[1 - \dfrac{p_1 - \text{MC}_1}{p_1}e_1\right] - \dfrac{q_1^B}{q_1^T}\left[1 - \dfrac{p_2 - \text{MC}_2}{p_2}e_2\right]}{\dfrac{q_1^A}{q_1^T}\left[1 - \dfrac{p_2 - \text{MC}_2}{p_2}e_2\right] - \dfrac{q_2^A}{q_2^T}\left[1 - \dfrac{p_1 - \text{MC}_1}{p_1}e_1\right]}$$

This formula applies to a two-good (1 and 2), two-consumer ($A$ and $B$) situation. As usual, $q$'s, $p$'s, $e$'s, and MC's represent quantities, prices, own-price elasticities, and marginal costs, respectively. Also, $q_i^T$ is the total amount of good $i$ consumed by groups $A$ and $B$, so that, for instance, $q_2^B/q_2^T$ is group $B$'s share in consumption of good 2. On the left-hand side of (8.3) are the weights given to the two groups' surpluses.[17] The information required to determine these weights includes prices, marginal costs, shares of consumption, and elasticities. Of course, even if all this information were known by regulators, we could not conclude that the regulators had weights $\beta_A$ and $\beta_B$ in mind; rather, we could conclude only that they behaved as if they had these weights in mind.

This method is limited to linear prices, and certain adjustments must be made if the number of goods does not equal the number of consumer groups and if demands are interdependent. Also, the regulator's treatment of the regulated firm is passive. The firm is not included in the groups competing for favors from the regulator; favors simply mean lower prices with constant profit. Thus, the framework does not consider how the regulator balances the claims of all the competing groups.

Recent literature on regulatory behavior has focused on the importance of information. In particular, central to an understanding of the regulatory process is knowledge of who has what information and when, and who has the right to take actions and when. Sappington and Stiglitz (1986) provide a survey of this literature. The problems usually are cast in a principal–agent framework where, typically, the principal receives an output or

17 Feldstein (1972b) derives optimum prices by weighting consumer utilities with weights based on income distribution. This formulation is similar to his optimum two-part tariffs in Chapter 4.

desires some actions to be taken by an agent in her employ or under her authority. The agent's raison d'être is that he possesses better information than the principal about production or feasible actions. The principal's problem is to design incentives that will encourage the agent to do her bidding. In a regulatory setting, a natural interpretation is that the regulator is the principal, who wants the firm, or agent, to set prices and capacity at levels that will optimize some regulatory objective. The firm has better information regarding its technology of production and demand structure. But the regulator cannot rely on the firm to divulge the truth. Much of the literature involves devising methods whereby the firm will make truthful revelations. Section 12.4 provides a review of these incentive schemes.

One example of an informational problem that arises in the context of rate-of-return regulation is studied by Baron and Taggart (1980). They show that unless the regulator possesses the same information as the firm about production technology and demand, there will be welfare losses owing to strategic behavior by the firm. In the context of their model, if the regulator sets an output price that depends on the firm's choice of inputs, then the firm will have an incentive to choose an inefficient combination of inputs. Alternatively, if the regulator sets an output price that depends on an ideal level of inputs, and the price does not change even if the firm chooses different inputs, the incentive for strategic behavior is eliminated, and the firm will choose an efficient combination of inputs. As these authors indicate, the informational requirements for the latter approach are substantial, which may explain why the former approach is used in practice.

### Empirical studies of the economic theory of regulation

Stigler and Friedland's study (1962) of state commission regulation of electric utilities represents an early attempt to measure the effectiveness of regulatory agencies. Their conclusion is that regulation between 1907 and 1937 had no measurable impact on prices or market value of utility stocks. Since their work, numerous authors have derived methods to determine the impact and behavior of regulatory agencies.[18] Jordan (1972) summarized these and other analyses in an attempt to explain the mixed results of regulation. By studying a broad range of regulated industries, he noted that regulation sometimes appears beneficial to the producers, and sometimes to the consumers, which seems to support (or not support) both the consumer-protectionist and producer-protectionist theories. However, his mixed results *are* explained by the economic theory of regulation that Stigler developed at about the same time as Jordan's work. For instance, Jordan concluded that regulation has had modest success in lowering price levels for electricity, but most of the benefits are enjoyed by commercial and industrial consumers. Because these consumers have more at stake per capita than residential consumers and probably are more easily organized (with less free-rider problems), this result is precisely what the economic theory would predict.[19]

In a subsequent study, Jarrell (1978) was able to draw upon the economic theory of regulation to explain the beginnings of state commission regulation of electric utilities. Jarrell presented a graphical interpretation of the theory, showing how regulation will evolve to favor either the producers or consumers, depending on who has more at stake, their political effectiveness, and the distribution of market surplus (i.e., profits and consumer surplus) in the absence of regulation. His data were from the 1900s, before and after state regulation. Before state regulation, there was municipal regulation, which, the author argued, created a relatively competitive environment among utilities. Prices and profits, therefore, tended to be low: The lower they were in a particular state, the earlier we would expect to have seen municipal regulation give way to state regulation in that state, as utilities sought relief from a competitive environment. Jarrell's results

18 Extensions by Jackson (1969) and Moore (1970) introduced other variables and corrected data limitations in the original Stigler–Friedland study.
19 See Stigler (1971) for a discussion of the free-rider problem in this context.

support a pro-producer view of the beginnings of state regulation of electric utilities. The historical pattern is consistent with the economic theory.

Meyer and Leland (1980) also examined electric utilities by comparing prices across states. They pointed out that Moore's empirical finding (1970) that regulation has lowered prices by 3 percent is in contrast to the Callen, Mathewson, and Mohring (1976) pseudoempirics that the gains from regulation can be substantial (this latter study is discussed further in the next chapter). Meyer and Leland concluded that the effectiveness of regulation across states is extremely irregular, and the different political climates may contribute to this. They found that in 1969, prices reflected cross-subsidies from residential to commercial-industrial users, but that had changed substantially by 1974. Finally, they found that prices were lower than what an unconstrained profit-maximizer using linear prices would have charged, but prices could have been lowered further for an improvement in welfare.

In another paper dealing with electric utilities, Nelson (1982) failed to find evidence supporting the economic theory of regulation. Gathering price, marginal-cost, and demand-elasticity data, he examined the degree to which 78 privately owned utilities employed Ramsey pricing. In support of the Ramsey approach to pricing, his results indicated that prices roughly reflected differences in demand elasticities across consumer groups. Regarding political influence, however, prices did not reflect either differences in potential per-capita benefits of lower prices to consumer groups or the relative numbers of consumers in various groups. A study by Primeaux and Nelson (1980) concluded that price discrimination did exist in the rate structures of private electric utilities, with industrial customers being favored over residential and commercial customers. Whether such an outcome involves political favoritism or merely reflects elasticity differentials is unclear.

Thus, the tests of the economic theory of regulation yield mixed results. It is even unclear who the beneficiaries might be.

Some have found a pro-industrial-consumer bias, whereas others have observed a pro-residential-consumer bias. Both results can be in keeping with the economic theory of regulation if the levels of political influence of these groups change over time. The economic theory of regulation is somewhat flexible in its application to industries, because quantifying the determinants of the supply of and demand for regulation is problematic. The economic theory suggests that, all other things being equal, the few benefit at the expense of many. However, Wenders (1986a,b) notes that all other things are not equal: Residential electricity and telephone consumers are well aware of how the industry affects their well-being; the itemized monthly bill serves as a regular reminder. Furthermore, they are aware of the link between regulation and prices. Thus, given the potential for political backlash, the seemingly unorganized many still weigh heavily in the regulatory process.

Using a sample of five electric utilities, Wenders (1986a) calculates the price-to-marginal-cost ratios for residential, commercial, and industrial consumers as 0.612, 0.853, and 0.623, respectively. Commercial customers pay relatively high prices, but price is less than marginal cost for all three customer classes. These calculations ignore fixed customer costs. Wenders also computes the incremental share of total costs covered by revenues from the consumer classes, with the residential class paying 82.8 percent and commercial and industrial customers paying 111.5 and 112.0 percent, respectively. He concludes that regulation has a pro-consumer bias, with the rents from non-marginal-cost pricing captured by residential consumers. He observes that failure to implement peak-load pricing is consistent with a pro-consumer bias on the part of regulators. However, he also notes that further modification of rate design could have reduced misallocations, with the savings being passed on to the consumers.

The mixed results from the tests of the economic theory of regulation may be explained by the theory's narrow focus. It implicitly assumes that regulators are maximizers of political support and that the public welfare does not come into play. A hybrid theory would have regulator preferences defined over both political support and the public welfare. This is the approach taken by Nowell and Tschirhart (1988), who argue that the hybrid theory is more useful in predicting regulatory decisions than are theories that depict the regulator as a maximizer over either political support or the public welfare, but not over both. They also argue that empirical tests that find support for the economic theory of regulation are often inconclusive, because they cannot rule out the hybrid theory as an alternative explanation. This is because political support and the public welfare, as functions of a regulatory decision, may exhibit high positive correlation, and it is impossible to determine whether the regulator was concerned with the former or the latter. The authors derive a set of necessary conditions that regulatory decisions must satisfy before being used to test regulatory behavior, and then they apply these conditions to regulatory decisions in the context of PURPA (see Chapter 5). We next consider some other analyses of specific regulatory decisions.

### Empirical studies of regulatory decisions

Joskow (1972) presented an interesting econometric approach to examining regulatory behavior. In the context of rate-of-return regulation, he sought the determinants of the return allowed by public service commissions. If the regulators know the cost of capital, their task would seem to be straightforward, and we would expect the cost of capital to be the principal determinant. But economists cannot agree on an exact measurement of this cost, and regulators typically have less expertise in these matters than economists. Consequently, the regulators may proceed on a general feeling that the firms request too much, consumer groups recommend too little, and some compromise must be reached.

Using a two-equation, recursive econometric model, Joskow examined decisions made by the New York Public Service Commission in rate-increase hearings for electricity and natural-gas companies. In one equation, the firm's actual request is expressed as a function of its embedded cost of debt, whether or not it is a wholly owned subsidiary of a holding company, and whether it is a gas-and-electicity company or just an electricity company. The residual term from this equation is a measure of the firm's aggressiveness: Does it ask for more than it would be expected to receive? This residual term is used as an independent variable in the second equation, which estimates the regulator's allowed returns. Other variables used to explain the allowed returns include the firm's actual request, whether or not the firm presents testimony in support of its request, whether or not there are intervenors (e.g., environmental or consumer groups) opposing the firm's request, whether it is a natural-gas or electricity hearing, and whether or not the firm is efficient. This latter variable is measured by whether or not the regulator has commended the firm for efficiency.

Joskow found that all of the signs on the coefficients were as expected, and only the coefficient for the efficiency variable was insignificant. These results suggest that regulators respond to firm testimony, but also are influenced by intervenors. Aggression on the firm's part does not pay, and gas companies apparently believe that they are more risky, leading them to ask for a risk premium, but being denied by the regulators. Finally, the coefficient on the firm's actual request exceeded 1.0, which is troublesome, because it suggests that these firms receive more than they request. Joskow attributed this to the regulator attempting to delay future hearings by granting a premium for inflation.[20]

In a similar study, Hagerman and Ratchford (1978) asked what political as well as economic variables might be determinants of the rate of return allowed by regulators. These authors obtained

20 Roberts, Maddala, and Enholm (1978) find fault with Joskow's econometric approach. They use probit and tobit two-stage least-squares analysis applied to data from public service hearings in Florida. Their method explains the Florida data better than does Joskow's method, which they credit to their taking into account selectivity and simultaneity problems. Hajiron, Kamerschen, and Legler (1986) present estimates of Joskow's model for Georgia, 1970–81. Georgia has elected commissioners; only 2 of 27 rate-increase requests were filed during preelection periods. The firms' requests and intervenors' recommendations were given different weights by regulators in the granted rates of return, with the former being much more important for telephone companies, and the latter more important for gas and electricity companies.

data on 79 utilities from 33 states. The economic variables used to explain the allowed return included measures of risk for each utility (debt–equity ratios and $\beta$ coefficients). If these measures capture risk, they should be related positively to the allowed return. The size of the utility was included in case larger firms have more expertise in dealing with regulators and are allowed larger returns, or in case their size makes them more noteworthy in the public eye and they are granted smaller returns. Market interest rates were also included, because equity investors who expect a risk premium will require a higher return when interest rates are high. The final economic variable was whether the state commission regulating the utility uses the book value or fair (market) value for determining the rate base. Book-value states may adjust the allowed return upward to allow for smaller rate bases during inflationary periods.

The political explanatory variables used were novel, representing a direct test of whether or not commissioners were politically influenced. The salary of the commissioners was included because a higher salary can be associated with a more desirable job. In trying to keep the job, the commissioners may want to please the public and allow lower returns. The number of commissioners was included because more commissioners may mean more buck-passing and less responsiveness to the public. The term of office for commissioners was also included, with a positive impact expected, because longer terms mean greater insulation from public pressure. A variable was included to distinguish between elected and appointed commissions, because the former could be more responsive to the general consuming public.

More economic variables than political variables were significant, suggesting that politics may not play an overriding role. The term of office was the only significant political variable, and it had the expected sign.[21] The significant economic variables, all of

21 The impact of elected vs. appointed regulators has been examined by Costello (1984), who critiqued previous studies and reestimated earlier models. Using data from 1980, he concluded that the method of selecting commissioners did not have a statistically significant effect on electricity prices. In the area of

which had the expected signs, included the interest rate, the size of the utility, the debt–equity ratio, and whether the regulator used the book value or fair value to determine the rate base.

This latter result is supported by the findings of Primeaux (1978), who examined 127 electricity companies to determine how realized rates of return depend on the use of book value versus fair value. He found no significant differences in the earnings of utilities subject to these two different regulatory practices. Like Hagerman and Ratchford, he credited this to the fact that both the rate base and allowed returns are regulatory instruments, and any downward bias in the rate-base valuation caused by the book-value approach is offset by regulators allowing a larger rate of return.

As commissions behave in somewhat predictable fashions, their decisions give rise to a regulatory climate. A given state may get a reputation as having either a favorable or unfavorable climate for regulated industries. The financial community concerns itself with these climates, and numerous research and investment firms have developed ways to measure them. Measurement typically is by an index that weights various criteria, such as the allowed rates of return granted by the commissions, regulatory lag (the time between regulatory hearings), the use of a historical or future test year, the allowance for construction work in progress in the rate base, the treatment of tax benefits from accelerated depreciation (flow-through vs. normalization), and the extent to which automatic adjustment clauses are in effect (allowing utilities to pass on increased operating costs to consumers

relative prices for various consumer classes, he did not find differential treatment by elected or appointed commissions. Primeaux and Mann (1986) found evidence of appointed commissioners restraining prices relative to elected regulators for 1967, with slight reversals for 1973 and 1979. The mixed (and weak) results are explained by three factors. First, external constraints (administrative procedures, statutes, and judicial review) limit regulatory flexibility. Second, direct election may reduce citizen involvement in the regulatory process. Third, staff resources were significantly lower in a sample of states with elected commissioners; five of seven had expenditures per capita less than one dollar in 1980, whereas five of seven states with appointed commissioners had expenditures per capita in excess of two dollars.

without formal hearings). On the basis of such criteria, states are listed as having very favorable, favorable, or unfavorable climates.

Using this measure, Dublin and Navarro (1982) investigated the influence of regulatory climate on the cost of capital to utilities. They found that unfavorable climates substantially increased the cost of equity capital, and moving an otherwise average utility from a very favorable climate to an unfavorable climate resulted in a bond-rating drop of several steps. Hence, self-proclaimed "pro-consumer" commissions may be doing more harm than good for the consumers. By enforcing tight constraints on utilities, they make raising capital for new investment more difficult. In another study, Gegax and Tschirhart (1984) examined whether or not regulatory climates influenced electric utilities' choices to construct jointly owned plants within power-pooling arrangements.[22] Their results suggest that a favorable climate is a disincentive for joint ownership. They concluded that because joint ownership is a way to reduce capital expenditures at the expense of losing some autonomy in operating the company, firms operating in favorable climates have less pressure to seek this cost savings.

### 8.5. Summary

No single theory of regulatory behavior has been able to explain fully the motivations for and the impacts of regulation. The phenomenon is far too complex to be characterized by a set of equations. Furthermore, the competing theories are not always mutually exclusive. In particular, Stigler's economic theory of regulation identifies important determinants of the demand for and supply of regulation. The capture and public-interest theories can be viewed as special cases – taking into account the costs of organizing to obtain wealth transfers via the political process. Both producer protection and consumer protection can occur in this competition for legislative favors. A general theory of rent-seek-

---

22 See Chapter 9 for more on power pooling.

ing activity has emerged from these early studies, with rent creation (Tollison, 1982) and rent extraction (McChesney, 1987) often resulting in misallocations. However, the possibility of a positive-sum game has been stressed by Lee, whereas Goldberg has emphasized resource savings and reduced transactions costs. Regulators can be viewed as monitoring long-term contracts between customers and the utility – with rights and obligations for both parties.

The regulatory instruments available include entry, price, and direct or indirect constraints on profit. Although regulatory decisions often sidestep or ignore fundamental economic issues, the decisions have significant impacts on industrial organization and economic performance. For example, regulators may force an unsustainable natural monopoly to face cream-skimming entry or to allocate costs in such a way as to promote uneconomic entry. Economic analysis is beginning to assume greater importance in regulatory deliberations, however.

Rate-of-return regulation, in particular, raises numerous issues as regulators grapple with allowable costs, appropriate depreciation expenses, incentives for efficiency, and determination of the rate base. Treatments of advertising, charitable contributions, and R&D expenses can differ widely across regulatory jurisdictions, influencing utility behavior. Similarly, treatment of deferred taxes raises some intertemporal fairness issues. Financial considerations also loom large in the hearing process, as the market-determined cost of capital depends on the set of regulatory policies. If the allowed rate of return is below the cost of capital, the efficient level of new investment will not be forthcoming – lowering the quality of service and leading to higher-cost production.

Formal theories of regulatory behavior have attempted to capture these dimensions of the process by specifying regulatory objective functions. The common thread is that the firm operates in a particular environment (market demands, substitutes, and a production technology), and regulatory commissions can place additional constraints on this environment. These constraints may include maximum prices, a maximum rate of return, a minimum quality of service, a minimum number of customers, limited entry, or a particular product mix (disallowing exit). In some of the models, self-interested regulators maximize their own utility; in other models, views of social justice result in differential weights being given to gains obtained by producers and different consumer groups. Because the information sets available to regulators are not known to researchers, analyses claiming to explain behavior must be carefully hedged.

Empirical studies have enriched our understanding of particular situations. Nevertheless, there still is much debate whether pro-consumer or pro-producer outcomes characterize particular industries. Even within a particular sector, such as the electric utility industry, economists have not reached consensus whether residential, commercial, or industrial customers gain the most from regulation. There is strong evidence, however, that the regulatory climate affects the firm's cost of capital, which influences the price consumers ultimately pay for the service.

In the remaining chapters, we look at the ways in which regulation provides incentives or disincentives for firms to operate efficiently. In the next chapter, we discuss regulatory constraints and illustrate how even the best-intentioned nonpolitical regulators enforcing these constraints can induce serious inefficiencies.

# 9

# Models of regulatory constraints

A disproportionately large share of the literature on regulation has involved models of regulatory constraints on a firm's choice set, in particular, models of the rate-of-return constraint. Many theoretical and empirical studies have examined how regulatory instruments in the form of constraints on profits, rates of return, operating ratios, and so on, might affect a firm's choices regarding outputs, factors of production, and, to a lesser extent, prices. This chapter reviews the major results emerging from the literature and points out where additional work is needed. Additional work is important because, for the most part, the literature on regulatory constraint has not crossed over into other topics, such as price structures, sustainability issues, and the expansion of regulated firms into unregulated markets.

Also absent from this literature is an analysis of why one particular regulatory instrument is chosen over another. For instance, why do some regulatory agencies use a rate-of-return constraint and others use an operating ratio as a measure of restricting firm profit? The informational approach discussed in Chapter 8 offers some insights here, but this area is largely untouched. Examining the issues will mean exploring the links among several factors: why regulation is adopted in the first place, what types of instruments are used, and how the instruments affect industry performance. Future research should provide a better understanding of how the demand for regulation and the behavior of regulators (see Chapter 8) give rise to specific instruments and lead to particular outcomes (Chapters 9–11).

The first three sections of this chapter cover the rate-of-return constraint – the issue that dominates the literature on regulatory constraints. We present the major result, known as the Averch–Johnson (A-J) effect, and discuss extensions and empirical evidence. Then we examine factors that may mitigate this effect, or at least make difficult the search for evidence. In the fourth and fifth sections of this chapter, we cover two other constraints often imposed on regulated firms: automatic adjustment clauses and restrictions on operating ratios.

### 9.1. Rate-base regulation: the A-J effect in a single-product firm

Averch and Johnson (1962) were concerned with the input bias that can result when a firm confronts a rate-of-return constraint, and they analytically demonstrated how this bias comes about. Numerous papers followed that elaborated on and extended their work,[1] although the bias has become known as the A-J effect.[2]

### Structure of the model

The basic treatment involves a regulated firm producing a single output using two inputs. Let $K$ be the capital input, and let $L$ be the variable input, which we refer to as labor. The firm is a price-taker in the two-input markets, paying the per-unit prices $r$ and $w$ for capital and labor, respectively. Output is produced according to a well-behaved production function

---

1 For some of the earlier mathematical and geometric treatments, see Wellisz (1963), Westfield (1965), Takayama (1969), Kafoglis (1969), Sherman (1972), Bailey (1973), Zajac (1970), Baumol and Klevorick (1970), and McNicol (1973). See Sherman (1985) for a critical survey of this literature.
2 Because Wellisz's paper appeared at about the same time as the paper of Averch and Johnson, the bias is sometimes referred to as the A-J-W effect. Wellisz, however, placed more stress on a bias on output prices in the context of peak and off-peak demands.

$$q = f(K, L) \tag{9.1}$$

and the inverse demand function for the firm's output is

$$p(q) \tag{9.2}$$

Both (9.1) and (9.2) are twice continuously differentiable, and we combine them to write revenue as

$$R = p(f(K, L))f(K, L) \tag{9.3}$$

The problem for the firm is to

$$\max_{K,L} \pi = R - rK - wL \tag{9.4}$$

subject to

$$\frac{R - wL}{K} \leqq s \tag{9.5}$$

where (9.4) is profit, and (9.5) is the rate-of-return constraint, with $s$ being the return allowed by the regulator. Note that this constraint is a simplification of the rate-of-return constraint given by (8.2), because taxes and depreciation are omitted in (9.5). Furthermore, no distinction is made between debt and equity financial capital.

It is important that the assumptions in this formulation be made explicit. The firm is choosing inputs that in turn determine output and price. Thus, the firm is a price-setter – which is not consistent with the regulatory process as described in Chapter 8. We shall have more to say about this inconsistency in Section 9.3. The allowed return is assumed to satisfy

$$r < s < r^m \tag{9.6}$$

where $r^m$ is the return that an unregulated monopolist would receive. If $s$ were set at $r$, then the firm would make zero economic profit: The owners of capital would just be earning the market rate of return. This situation would yield an indeterminate solution to (9.4) and (9.5), because the firm would be indifferent to the levels of $K$ and $L$ chosen. Thus, (9.6) allows the firm positive profit, but not so much as it would obtain if it were unregulated. In other words, constraint (9.5) will be a binding constraint, satisfied as an equality. Also, the model abstracts from time, so that (9.5) is always met as an equality; there is no period when the rate of return exceeds or falls below $s$. This assumption will be modified when we discuss regulatory lags and a stochastic environment.

The Lagrangian for the problem is

$$R - rK - wL + \lambda(sK + wL - R) \tag{9.7}$$

where $\lambda$ is a multiplier. Assuming that at the optimum $K > 0$, $L > 0$, and $\lambda > 0$, where the latter implies that constraint (9.5) is binding, the Kuhn–Tucker conditions are

$$K: \qquad \mathrm{MR}f_K - r + \lambda[s - \mathrm{MR}f_K] = 0 \tag{9.8}$$

$$L: \qquad \mathrm{MR}f_L - w + \lambda[w - \mathrm{MR}f_L] = 0 \tag{9.9}$$

$$\lambda: \qquad sK - R + wL = 0 \tag{9.10}$$

where $\mathrm{MR} \equiv (\partial p/\partial f)f + p$ is the marginal revenue, and subscripts represent partials. Conditions (9.8) and (9.9) can be written as

$$\mathrm{MR}f_K(1 - \lambda) = r(1 - \lambda) - \lambda(s - r) \tag{9.11}$$

$$\mathrm{MR}f_L(1 - \lambda) = w(1 - \lambda) \tag{9.12}$$

From (9.11), $\lambda \neq 1$; otherwise, $s = r$, which would contradict our earlier assumptions; hence, we can divide (9.11) by (9.12) to obtain

$$\frac{f_K}{f_L} = \frac{r}{w} - \frac{\lambda(s - r)}{(1 - \lambda)w} \tag{9.13}$$

Cost minimization requires $f_K/f_L = r/w$, but because the second term on the right-hand side of (9.13) is not zero (by $\lambda > 0$ and $s \neq r$), the firm is not minimizing the cost of production. There is a bias in the choice of inputs. To determine the nature of the bias, we need to evaluate $\lambda$. This can be done by analyzing the second-order conditions for a maximum, which involve the bordered Hessian

$$H = \begin{bmatrix} (1 - \lambda)R_{KK} & (1 - \lambda)R_{KL} & s - R_K \\ (1 - \lambda)R_{LK} & (1 - \lambda)R_{LL} & w - R_L \\ s - R_K & w - R_L & 0 \end{bmatrix} \quad (9.14)$$

where $R_K \equiv MRf_K$, $R_{KK} \equiv \partial R_K / \partial K$, and the remaining notation should be obvious. Because $w = R_L$, from (9.12), the determinant of (9.14) is

$$-(s - R_K)^2(1 - \lambda)R_{LL} > 0 \quad (9.15)$$

where the sign follows by second-order sufficient conditions for a maximum. Assuming $R_{LL} < 0$, by diminishing revenue returns to labor, we obtain $\lambda < 1$, which, combined with previous assumptions, means

$$0 < \lambda < 1 \quad (9.16)$$

Combining (9.16) and (9.13) yields

$$\frac{f_K}{f_L} = \frac{r}{w} - \frac{\lambda(s - r)}{(1 - \lambda)w} < \frac{r}{w} \quad (9.17)$$

Given a diminishing rate of substitution between capital and labor, (9.17) states that the firm is using a capital–labor ratio that is too large for minimizing the cost of the output produced. This overcapitalization bias is the crux of the A-J analysis that pertains to input use.

The bias does not say that the regulated firm will choose to use more capital or to produce more output than if it were unregulated. If rate-of-return regulation did result in increased output over what a profit-maximizing monopolist would produce, the bias might be considered an advantage. However, that result is not guaranteed, although Baumol and Klevorick (1970) describe conditions under which we can expect greater output. Also, the bias does not imply that the firm is necessarily technologically inefficient in production; however, it is economically inefficient

in production. This point is important, because utilities sometimes are accused of "gold-plating" or "rate-base padding,"
meaning that they acquire useless capital to enlarge the rate base.
Provided the firm operates in the elastic portion of the demand
curve, which we would expect, and can satisfy the rate-of-return
constraint without moving into an irrational region of production, then there is no gold-plating. However, there is a possibility
that the firm cannot meet the rate-of-return constraint and, in
order to operate in the elastic range, will gold-plate by acquiring
capital to the point at which $f_K \leqq 0$ (Sherman, 1972; Westfield,
1965; Zajac, 1972). Equations (9.11) and (9.12) do not rule out
this possibility, which would represent a particularly unfortunate
consequence of this form of regulation.

Kafoglis (1969) raised the possibility of another potential distortion, this time associated with an expansionary output effect.
When the regulated firm can price-discriminate among consumers, the rate-of-return constraint induces the firm to sell some
output at prices below marginal cost. Thus, a price-discriminating firm expands its rate base while dissipating excessive profits.
Such behavior leads to overproduction – affecting both allocative
efficiency and equity – because other consumers are paying
greater than marginal cost. Even though Kafoglis applies the
point to the output-maximizer, the implications of the analysis
also apply to the A-J profit-maximizer. As Needy (1975) notes,
an extreme form of price discrimination – with negative marginal
prices – is theoretically possible if the firm reaches market satu-
ration prior to eliminating excess earnings.

Is there anything to be said in favor of rate-of-return regulation, given these biases? Klevorick (1971) and Sheshinski (1971)
address the issue of optimum rate-of-return regulation. That is,
if a rate-of-return constraint is to be the instrument used for constraining a monopolist's profits, at what level should the allowed
return be set? Pursuing this question further, Callen, Mathewson,
and Mohring (1976) examine conditions under which the constraint leads to welfare gains. Using an example with a Cobb–

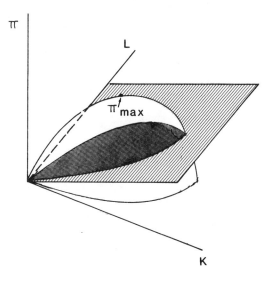

Figure 9.1. Profit hill and rate-of-return constraint.

Douglas production function, they find that an allowed return in excess of the firm's cost of capital causes minimal misallocation when demand elasticity is low, increasing returns are modest, and the exponent on capital in the production function is small. In this case, the potential welfare gains over an unregulated profit-maximizing environment are substantial. However, these authors point out that generalizations of their results are needed and that the cost of the regulatory process itself is not considered.

*A geometric presentation*

The A-J bias can be captured nicely in a graphical presentation (Baumol and Klevorick, 1970; Zajac, 1970). In Figure 9.1, profit as a function of capital and labor is represented by the hill. The top of the hill represents maximum profit: the point that would be chosen by an unregulated monopolist. Slicing through the hill is a plane emanating from the $L$ axis. The plane repre-

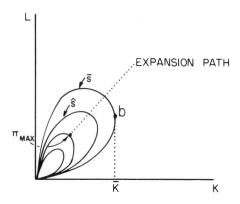

Figure 9.2. The A-J bias.

sents the rate-of-return constraint for a particular allowed return, $s$. To see this, write the constraint as $R - wL = sK$, then subtract $rK$ from both sides and get $R - wL - rK = sK - rK$, or

$$\pi = (s - r)K \qquad (9.18)$$

which is the equation of the plane. The plane can be thought of as a door that is hinged on the $L$ axis. As we move along the plane in the $K$ direction, profit increases, but the rate of return stays the same. When $s = r$, profit is zero, and the door is shut, lying on the $KL$ plane. As $s$ increases, the door opens, slicing through the profit hill at varying heights. The shaded region in Figure 9.1 represents points that are both on the door and on or within the profit hill. If a firm were operating on the border of the shaded region, it would be satisfying the constraint; if a firm were operating on the shaded region, but not on the border, it would be satisfying the constraint, but operating inefficiently.

Next, we shift to Figure 9.2, where the border of the shaded region is projected down to the $KL$ plane. In addition, three other borders corresponding to three other doors and values of $s$ are also projected. These projections are iso-rate-of-return contours. Consider the contour labeled $\hat{s}$, which corresponds to the regulator setting $\hat{s}$ as the allowed return. At every point along the con-

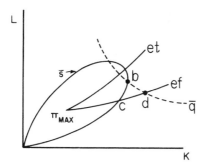

Figure 9.3. Proof of the A-J bias.

tour, the firm is making exactly the allowed return, $\hat{s}$. Inside the contour, the firm is making a return greater than $\hat{s}$, which violates the constraint. Outside the contour, the firm is making less than $\hat{s}$, and the constraint is nonbinding. The top of the profit hill is projected as the point labeled $\pi_{max}$. As we move away from $\pi_{max}$ in any direction, profit decreases. Finally, the expansion path is pictured, showing the economically efficient combinations of $K$ and $L$ for varying output levels; $\pi_{max}$ must lie on this path.

To locate the point at which the regulated firm operates, suppose that the regulator sets $s = \bar{s} < \hat{s}$, so that the firm must not operate strictly inside the contour labeled $\bar{s}$. The firm will not choose to operate outside contour $\bar{s}$, because it can always do better moving up the hill toward the $\bar{s}$ contour. Where on the contour will the firm locate, or, subject to staying on the contour, what point maximizes profit? Referring to (9.18), the answer must be where $K$ is at a maximum along the contour: point $b$, or the extreme right-hand point on contour $\bar{s}$, where capital is $\overline{K}$. Because $b$ is not on the expansion path, the firm is not minimizing cost. Moreover, because $b$ is below the expansion path, the firm is overcapitalizing.

The A-J bias states that point $b$ must lie below the expansion path. We show that this must be the case in Figure 9.3. Again, the regulator sets $s = \bar{s}$, and the firm chooses to operate at point

$b$ on contour $\bar{s}$. The firm produces output $\bar{q}$, shown by the iso-quant labeled $\bar{q}$. We prove that $b$ must lie below the expansion path, by contradiction. The true expansion path is given by $et$, but we assume that the expansion path is $ef$, which lies below point $b$. Now consider the firm's profits at points $b$, $c$, and $d$, which we label $\pi_b$, $\pi_c$, and $\pi_d$, respectively. We have

$$\pi_b > \pi_c \tag{9.19}$$

because on the contour, profit attains a maximum at $b$. We have

$$\pi_c > \pi_d \tag{9.20}$$

because $c$ and $d$ are both on the expansion path, but, by conti-nuity (and a well-behaved profit hill), profit is greater the closer we are to $\pi_{max}$. Finally, we have

$$\pi_d > \pi_b \tag{9.21}$$

because both points lie on the same isoquant, and so outputs are the same, but output at point $d$ is produced at minimum cost. Putting (9.19)–(9.21) together gives us $\pi_b > \pi_c > \pi_d > \pi_b$, which is a contradiction. Thus, our assumption that the expansion path lies below point $b$ must be false.

We noted earlier that the A-J bias does not imply that the over-capitalizing firm will produce more output than if it were unreg-ulated. This is easily shown graphically. In Figure 9.3, the curves are constructed such that rate-of-return regulation causes greater output. Clearly, output $\bar{q}$ exceeds output at point $\pi_{max}$. In Figure 9.4, however, the opposite case is constructed. Regulated output at point $b$ is less than the output chosen without regulation.

There is little to be said regarding how regulated output com-pares with welfare-maximizing output. We know that the wel-fare-maximizing output lies somewhere along the expansion path. If the firm has increasing or constant returns to scale, then setting price equal to marginal cost to maximize welfare (or to average cost as a Ramsey price) will mean an output along the expansion path and an isoquant representing greater output than

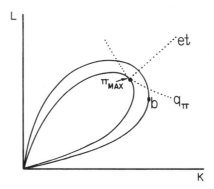

Figure 9.4. Output and the A-J bias.

point $b$. This result follows because the regulated firm is making positive profit and is charging a higher price than the welfare-maximizer. As will be seen in the next section, the analysis becomes more complicated with multiple outputs.

### 9.2. Pricing and multiple outputs

Price structures have not received much attention in the literature on the rate-of-return constraint. The basic model has the firm selecting one linear price for a single output. The selected price maximizes profit subject to the regulator's constraint on the return. Yet natural monopolies and other regulated firms frequently use more elaborate price structures, as covered in Chapters 3–6; therefore, it is important to obtain an understanding of how the rate-of-return constraint influences these structures.

*Peak-load pricing*

Several authors have studied how rate-of-return regulation influences a firm's peak-load pricing policies. Early on, Wellisz (1963) argued that peak-load pricing will be distorted by firms such that peak prices will be too low, and off-peak prices too high. This point was later brought out by Bailey (1972), who constructed a peak-load model with a fixed-coefficient production technology and a rate-of-return constraint. The firm's objective was to set peak and off-peak prices that would maximize profits subject to the constraint. She found that the monopolist's off-peak price was not affected by the regulatory constraint, but the peak price was lower than what it would have been absent the constraint. This follows because in a firm-peak case, only peak users press against capacity, and lowering the price to these users means more capacity and a greater rate base. Off-peak users do not contribute to capacity, and the firm's best strategy is to charge these users a monopoly price.[3] Because of the fixed-coefficient technology, overcapitalization does not occur, owing to the lack of substitutability between inputs. The A-J input bias follows from a distortion of input prices that causes an inefficient capital–labor ratio to be chosen. Without substitutability, there will be no change in the ratio. The A-J bias usually means technological efficiency, but not economic efficiency; in the fixed-coefficient framework, a technologically efficient firm will also be economically efficient in production, although the mix between peak and off-peak outputs will be inefficient.

Waverman (1975) pointed out that the pricing prescription and lack of an A-J input bias in the Bailey model stemmed from the fixed-coefficient technology. He modified a neoclassical technology that was more in keeping with the original A-J framework and, not surprisingly, obtained results similar to those derived in Section 9.1. In his model, the firm can choose any capital–labor ratio ex ante, but ex post it must use only the chosen ratio. Thus, the capital–labor ratio is a long-run decision variable whose value cannot be altered in the short run.[4] The firm turns out to produce inefficiently in both peak and off-peak periods, with the expected overcapitalization bias. Also, under reasonable assump-

---

3  Sherman and Visscher (1979) point out that because the firm has an incentive to charge a lower peak price and a higher off-peak price than it would without regulation, there may be a tendency to simply abandon peak-load pricing and charge a single price.

4  A more general formulation of the technology can be found in Marino (1978).

tions, both peak and off-peak prices are lower than what the unconstrained profit-maximizing monopolist would charge.

### Two-part tariffs

Sherman and Visscher (1982) attack the problem of how rate-of-return regulation influences a firm's decision to adopt two-part tariffs. They employ a fixed-coefficient technology, and so they do not address the A-J bias regarding input choices, but they do derive interesting results concerning the price structure. The model is not unlike that in Chapter 4 used to derive an optimum two-part tariff. Consumer utility functions are the measures of welfare, and the number of consumers in the market is a variable. Unlike the situation in the previous model, however, capital inputs are dichotomized into those used to provide access to the consumer (e.g., the electricity wires and gas pipes connecting the consumer to the producer) and those used to produce output (e.g., the electricity-generating plant or natural-gas-processing plant).

Sherman and Visscher's main conclusion is that rate-of-return regulation may encourage the use of two-part tariffs, which emphasize the access fee over the per-unit price. In particular, the access fee will exceed the marginal cost of servicing the consumer relatively more than the per-unit price will exceed the marginal cost of output. Consequently, the declining block pricing structures used by many public utilities may be in part a consequence of rate-of-return regulation. There are two primary reasons for this result. First, the firm must consider the sensitivity of the number of consumers in the market to the access fee and per-unit price. Because public utility goods such as electricity, natural gas, and water are virtual necessities, the elasticity of market participation with respect to the access fee will be small. Consumers will tend to participate in the market in spite of high access fees, and the firm will take advantage of this by levying high fees. Of course, this behavior will apply to an unregulated profit-maximizing monopolist as well. Second, if connecting consumers to the system is capital-intensive on the margin, the firm will overcapitalize by stressing universal service, which can still be attained with high access fees if the participation rate is insensitive to such charges. Otherwise, the fees will tend to be set below cost to encourage connections.

### Ramsey pricing versus A-J prices

As we have seen, output and price biases due to the rate-of-return constraint arise in the peak-load problem, but they also arise in the general case of a multiproduct firm (Sherman, 1981). Braeutigam (1981) demonstrates this result by comparing the prices selected by a regulated, profit-maximizing, multiproduct firm with the prices selected by a welfare-maximizing firm that is subject to a constraint on profit. Essentially, this comparison is between the regulated firm's prices and the second-best, Ramsey prices. To illustrate Braeutigam's results, we can use a diagram like Figure 3.2, which was used to compare Ramsey prices and FDC prices. Figure 9.5 displays five isowelfare and three isoprofit contours for a two-product firm, where $\pi_m$ and $W_m$ are the points chosen by the unregulated profit-maximizer and the welfare-maximizer, respectively. At $W_m$, prices equal marginal costs, and we assume that the firm is a strong natural monopoly; so profit is negative. The line connecting $\pi_m$ and $W_m$ is the locus of tangencies between isoprofit and isowelfare contours and represents those points that solve the problem of maximizing welfare subject to a constraint on profit [i.e., points that satisfy equation (3.41)]. Ramsey prices satisfy (3.41) and lie along this line at point $R$, where the line intersects the $\pi = 0$ contour.

The contours labeled $h^1$, $h^2$, and $h^3$ are essentially production possibility frontiers for the firm. Along any $h$ curve, the regulated firm is using a fixed amount of inputs in a technically efficient manner to produce varying combinations of the two outputs. This is a special case in which all inputs are shared. Line $\pi_m\pi_r$ represents the locus of points along which a profit-maximizer will locate when subject to a rate-of-return constraint. The tighter the constraint, the farther from $\pi_m$ the firm operates. Note that $\pi_m\pi_r$ is also the locus of tangencies between the $h$ curves and isoprofit

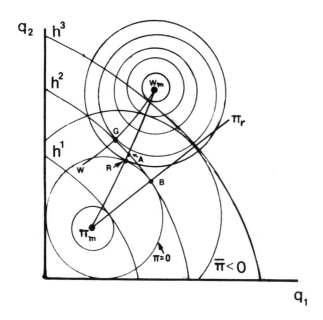

Figure 9.5. Rate of return and multiple outputs.

contours, because points on that line solve the problem of maximizing profit subject to a fixed amount of inputs. According to Braeutigam, line $WW_m$ represents the locus of points along which a welfare-maximizer will locate when subject to a fixed amount of inputs. Also, $WW_m$ is the locus of tangencies between the $h$ curves and isowelfare contours.[5]

Braeutigam shows that the three lines $WW_m$, $W_m\pi_m$, and $\pi_m\pi_r$ will occupy the relative positions shown in Figure 9.5 when the demand for product 1 is more elastic than the demand for product 2. For example, let $h^2$ denote the level of inputs at a regulated equilibrium point $B$. Along $h^2$, point $G$ represents maximum welfare, and point $A$ represents efficient second-best prices whose

---

5 Marino (1981) analyzes a different version of the multiproduct problem by deriving the prices for a welfare-maximizing firm subject to a rate-of-return constraint.

profit is constrained to be slightly negative. The regulated firm operates at point $B$, which implies a bias toward producing too much of good 1, whose demand is relatively more elastic than that of good 2, which is underproduced. Alternatively, price for the elastic (inelastic) good is too low (high) for economic efficiency.

Moving from point $B$ to, say, point $R$, profit will stay the same, while welfare will increase. Thus, $B$ cannot represent an efficient outcome. We can understand why the regulated firm chooses points along $\pi_m \pi_r$ by comparing points $B$ and $R$. Profit is the same at both points; so the firm is indifferent between them. However, suppose $R$ is not permitted because the rate of return is higher than allowed. The firm can achieve the same profit by moving to $B$, which is permitted: More inputs are hired, increasing the rate base and reducing the realized rate of return. To use the additional inputs in a technically efficient manner, the firm lowers price in the elastic market to realize a large increase in quantity demanded, and it raises price in the inelastic market to realize a small decrease in quantity demanded.

A number of other complications for the regulated firm arise in the multiproduct setting. In Braeutigam's formulation, a single-product firm will not operate in an inelastic region of the demand curve. This result can change in a multiproduct setting if there are complementarities among the demands for the products. Also, in a single-product firm, where capital is a normal factor of production, changes in the allowed rate of return will cause output changes in the opposite direction. This result does not hold generally in all markets of a multiproduct firm. The direction of output changes will depend on cross-elasticities of demand and common costs.

Using a similar approach, Baumol, Fischer, and ten Raa (1979) derive the price vectors yielding the permitted rate of return and examine the properties of the price–iso-rate-of-return locus for the regulated multiproduct firm. In a more general framework, Cabe (1988) provides a diagrammatic representation of the input and output bias in a multiproduct setting. He also derives conditions under which a rate-of-return-regulated firm will expand into unregulated markets. By doing so, he formalizes one of the major concerns raised by Averch and Johnson, but which has been largely neglected.

Cowing (1976) applies the A-J model in a multiproduct setting by examining a regulated monopoly producing two outputs: a good and an effluent. He analyzes the effect of rate-of-return regulation on the level of effluent. Determining appropriate effluent charges for a constrained firm is shown to be a much more difficult task than depicted in standard derivations of externality taxes. The use of effluent charges can have a perverse impact on allocative efficiency, in terms of both the effluent and the firm's primary output. Such modeling efforts illustrate the importance of determining the underlying production relationships prior to the implementation of particular constraints.

### 9.3. Complications in the search for an A-J effect

There are benefits and costs that result from the prominent position in the literature occupied by the A-J effect. Sherman (1985) presents a compelling account of some of the costs. Primarily, he argues that because of the heavy emphasis on the input bias, other inefficiencies caused by the rate-of-return constraint have been ignored. In particular, he cites the works of Wellisz and Westfield as having been severely understudied, whereas Averch and Johnson's contribution has been overstudied. Wellisz directed his research toward the potential peak-load pricing distortions arising from rate-of-return regulations, and Westfield concentrated on capital waste in the form of gold-plating. Both of these problems are potentially important and deserve more attention than they have received in the literature described in the previous section. Also, Joskow (1974) criticizes the overemphasis on the A-J model on the grounds that it is not an adequate description of the regulatory process; we postpone further discussion of Joskow until later, when regulatory behavior and the rate-of-return constraint are covered in detail.

One benefit of the A-J analysis is in its potential for improving public policy. Too often, theories become intractable and untestable, and/or data are unavailable, so that the ultimate goal of improved public policy is lost. However, the A-J analysis addresses an important regulatory problem with an accessible theoretical model. It yields clear hypotheses that can be tested with available data. Statistical results permit the economist to make useful recommendations about future public policy. Yet, in spite of these benefits, the A-J model has lost ground as an influence in academic studies of the regulatory process. The reason probably is twofold: (1) Empirical support for the A-J bias has been mixed, and (2) the model is too simplistic as a description of regulation and regulated firms. We briefly describe the mixed quantitative results, and then, in the next five subsections, we offer reasons for the mixed results that essentially revolve around the simplistic nature of the model.

### Empirical tests of the A-J model

Various methods have been used in empirical studies to test for the A-J effect in the electric-power industry. Courville (1974) estimates the marginal productivities of inputs directly and compares them to input prices. Spann (1974) estimates the Lagrange multiplier, $\lambda$ in (9.13), to determine if it lies between 0 and 1. Petersen (1975) derives and tests comparative static properties of a regulated firm's minimum cost function. Hayashi and Trapani (1976) employ input demand functions for capital and labor in a manner consistent with McNicol's theoretical development (1973). Boyes (1976) also employs input demand functions for fuel and maintenance in addition to capital and labor. Using duality theory, Atkinson and Halvorsen (1980) devise a means of testing for an A-J effect and other inefficiencies simultaneously. Consequently, we shall refer to their approach again when automatic adjustment clauses are covered in Section 9.4. Baron and Taggart (1977) modify the A-J model by having price set by the regulator and by introducing investor preferences. Their model draws upon work by Leland (1974a,b), who combines the firm's production decisions with stock-market equilibrium. They estimate a Cobb–Douglas production function, demand elasticity, and a price-anticipation effect by shareholders that allow them to detect regulatory bias. Finally, Smithson

(1978) does not test for evidence of an A-J effect directly, but does test a corollary proposition derived from the A-J model (Baumol and Klevorick, 1970) that lowering the allowed rate of return will cause increased overcapitalization.

The data for all those tests came from the 1950s, 1960s, and 1970s. Because the various studies used different time periods, that in itself may explain some of the differences in results, as the regulatory environment and economic conditions changed over those decades. At any rate, studies by Boyes and Baron and Taggart found no evidence of an A-J effect, with the latter finding evidence of undercapitalization. Smithson's results could not be used to provide support for the corollary proposition. In contrast, Courville, Spann, Petersen, Hayashi and Trapani, and Atkinson and Halvorsen all found evidence of an A-J overcapitalization bias, and in some cases these authors suggested that the dollar losses due to the bias were substantial. Boyes offers a number of reasons why, a priori, the bias might not be found. These reasons and others will now be considered in detail.

### Regulatory lag

The basic A-J effect is based on a static model wherein the firm's rate of return is equal to the allowed return. Time is ignored; so there is no possibility that the actual return will sometimes deviate from the allowed return. Yet, in a world of changing prices, technologies, and input levels, such deviations are inevitable. Situations will arise in which, subsequent to a regulatory hearing, a firm will acquire new capital. This investment will alter the rate base, and different price and output levels will be warranted in order to achieve the allowed return. But prices will not change until another regulatory hearing is requested, scheduled, and held – these requests are almost always made by the firms. This process takes time; so there will be a lag between the time price changes are warranted and the time prices are actually allowed to change by the regulator. The key question is whether or not the regulatory lag will have a significant effect on the firm's incentive to overcapitalize.

Bailey and Coleman (1971) augment the A-J model to address

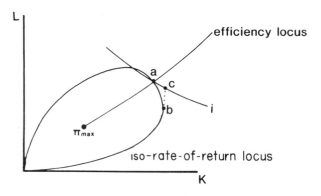

Figure 9.6. Regulatory lag.

this issue. Their fundamental result can be readily derived. Figure 9.6 shows a single isoquant labeled *i*, a single iso-rate-of-return locus representing the allowed return, and the efficiency locus. Suppose the firm is initially at the efficient point *a* after a regulatory hearing is held. We know the firm would prefer to be at point *b*, where profit would be greater. Moving to *b* requires hiring additional capital and reducing labor inputs. Because less output is produced and sold at *b*, the move cannot be made without a price increase, and a price increase cannot be initiated until a regulatory hearing is held and the new rate base recognized by the regulator. Thus, while waiting for the hearing, that is, during the lag, the firm will operate at *c*, where the new capital is employed, but labor is not fully reduced. Again, operating at *c* is necessary because output cannot be reduced until after the hearing.

The trade-off for the firm is clear. It can continue to operate at point *a*, or it can plan to move to point *b* after the next hearing and make greater profits than at *a*. However, while waiting for the hearing at point *c*, it will make less profit than at point *a*. Obviously, the length of time spent at *c*, the lag time, will be crucial to the firm's decision. Let $\pi$ be the profit earned at point *a* in each time period, so that the present value of future profits without a move is

$$\pi_0 = \pi \sum_{j=0}^{\infty} d^j = \pi/(1 - d) \tag{9.22}$$

where $d = 1/(1 + r)$ is the discount factor. The cost of capital, $r$, and other notations used in the following are consistent with Section 9.1.

If the firm chooses to move to point $b$ via point $c$, production at $c$ will be given by

$$F(L_c, K_c) = f(L_a - \Delta L, K_a + \Delta K) \tag{9.23}$$

where $L_i$ and $K_i$, $i = a, c$, are labor and capital used at point $i$ in producing output. Also, $\Delta L$ is the change in labor needed to move to point $c$, and $\Delta K$ is the change in capital needed to move to point $c$ and point $b$. The change in cost of moving to $c$ is then

$$r \, \Delta K - w \, \Delta L > 0 \tag{9.24}$$

where the inequality follows because moving from $a$ to $c$ entails moving from efficient to inefficient production. This cost change is a loss that must be incurred in each period until the hearing. After the hearing, profits will increase to

$$\pi + (s - r) \, \Delta K \tag{9.25}$$

which is realized in each post-hearing period. Hence, the discounted future profit of moving to $b$ via $c$ is given by combining (9.24) and (9.25) to obtain

$$\begin{aligned}
\pi_1 &= [\pi - (r \, \Delta K - w \, \Delta L)] \sum_{j=0}^{T-1} d^j + [\pi + (s - r) \, \Delta K] \sum_{j=T}^{\infty} d^j \\
&= \pi/(1 - d) - [r \, \Delta K - w \, \Delta L](1 - d^T)/(1 - d) \\
&\quad + (s - r) \, \Delta K d^T/(1 - d)
\end{aligned} \tag{9.26}$$

where $T$ is the period in which the hearing is held. If (9.26) exceeds (9.22), overcapitalization is beneficial to the firm; that is, the A-J effect arises if

$$\begin{aligned}
\pi_1 - \pi_0 = (s - r) \, \Delta K d^T/(1 - d) - [r \, \Delta K \\
- w \, \Delta L](1 - d^T)/(1 - d)
\end{aligned} \tag{9.27}$$

is positive. The first term on the left side is the additional profit the firm makes by the move to point $b$, and the second term is

344 Natural monopoly regulation in practice

the initial loss incurred at point $c$. Expression (9.27) will be positive if

$$[s \, \Delta K - w \, \Delta L]d^T > r \, \Delta K - w \, \Delta L > 0 \qquad (9.28)$$

where the right-most inequality follows by (9.24). Inspection of (9.28) reveals the factors that will encourage the firm to make the move and overcapitalize. They include a larger allowed rate of return, a smaller cost of capital, a smaller wage rate, and a shorter regulatory lag (smaller $T$).

Bailey and Coleman determine the optimum $\Delta K$, which, if positive, says that at least some overcapitalization will occur. Because (9.27) represents the gains from overcapitalization, maximizing it with respect to $\Delta K$ determines the optimum. Noting that the change in labor needed for the move is a function of the change in capital, $\Delta L = g(\Delta K)$, differentiating (9.27) yields

$$(s - r)d^T/(1 - d) - (r - wg')/(1 - d) \qquad (9.29)$$

where $g' = d \, \Delta L/d \, \Delta K$, the slope of the isoquant at point $a$. For a very small $\Delta K$, we obtain $r \cong wg'$, because point $a$ is on the efficiency locus. Hence, the second term will be close to zero, and we can expect (9.29) to be positive, indicating that some positive $\Delta K$ is desirable and overcapitalization will occur.

This result requires that we start at point $a$. If we start at a point on isoquant $i$ to the left of $a$, (9.29) will be positive, and the firm will acquire more capital until it is at some point to the right of $a$. And if we start at a point on the isoquant to the right of $a$, (9.29) may not be positive, but the firm is already overcapitalized. Consequently, regardless of the starting point, overcapitalization occurs. Note that an optimum $\Delta K$ is found by setting (9.29) equal to zero and obtaining

$$g' = \frac{r}{w} - \frac{d^T}{1 - d^T} \frac{s - r}{w} \qquad (9.30)$$

This is basically the A-J effect, except that $d^T$ has replaced the Lagrange multiplier. Again, some overcapitalization will occur, but as $T$ becomes larger, the magnitude of overcapitalization diminishes.

Thus, regulatory lag mitigates the A-J effect. Used judiciously, such lags may provide an effective tool for discouraging regulated natural monopolies from production inefficiencies. To the extent that lags, whether planned or random, mitigate the A-J effect, empirical studies will be less likely to find evidence of production inefficiency.

### Stochastic environment

If a random element enters into the regulated firm's demand or cost functions, will the A-J bias still exist? Because the actual regulatory environment is fraught with uncertainty, a negative answer to this question will mean that empirical studies may fail to detect the bias. If uncertainty alters the A-J results in a predictable manner, then this should be accounted for in these studies. A number of authors have examined theoretically the A-J effect under uncertainty. Although Das (1980) finds the A-J thesis to be robust, given uncertainty in demand, Peles and Stein (1976), Perrakis (1976), Meyer (1979b), Chapman and Waverman (1979), and Perrakis and Zerbinis (1981) all find the A-J thesis to be sensitive to the introduction of uncertainty.

These papers differ in the way uncertainty enters the models. For example, whether labor and capital are treated as ex ante or ex post variables (i.e., they are chosen before or after the state of nature is known) differs across authors, and in some cases the firm sets quantity, whereas in others it sets price and quantity. Furthermore, the treatment of the rate-of-return constraint varies. The actual rate of return will not be known to the firm until after the state of nature is known. Therefore, this return may not equal the allowed return ex post. Some authors force the two to be always equal by making inputs ex post variables, whereas others require that the constraint be satisfied on average. Rather than explore the advantages and disadvantages of these approaches, we offer an alternative model that can be closely related to the A-J model under certainty. We let uncertainty enter through the demand function, and we use the graphical analysis developed earlier.

In the A-J model developed in Section 9.1, capital and labor are the only decision variables, and a constrained, profit-maximizing selection of $K$ and $L$ yields the optimum quantity $f(K, L)$ and, in turn, the optimum price $p(f(K, L))$. However, in a stochastic version of the A-J model, if the firm is to exhibit price-setting behavior, then price must be selected ex ante. In addition, because regulated firms usually are characterized by large capital investments, the most reasonable formulation is to have $K$ also selected ex ante. On the other hand, labor is a more flexible input and can be adjusted relatively quickly to meet demand conditions. Accordingly, $L$ is selected ex post. This behavior is consistent with Leland's suggestion (1972) that electric utilities are good examples of firms that set price and then adjust quantity to meet actual demand, although for other regulated firms, such as, say, natural-gas companies, this formulation may be less accurate, because shortages occur more frequently than with electricity. Nevertheless, here the firm will select price and capital, then observe the state of nature, which reveals the quantity demanded, and finally hire the amount of labor needed to produce this quantity.

A problem with introducing stochastic demand is the notion of how the firm deals with the regulatory constraint. In the nonstochastic case, the regulatory constraint was given by (9.5). Optimum values of capital and labor, $K^*$ and $L^*$, yielded the certain revenue $p(f(K^*, L^*))f(K^*, L^*)$ and the certain operating cost $wL^*$. With stochastic demand, however, actual output may not be $f(K^*, L^*)$, and the labor hired may not be $L^*$. Instead, both of these terms are random, and the firm cannot predict with certainty the rate of return that will actually be realized. But if the distribution function for the random variable in demand is known, the firm can determine the probability of meeting the constraint for particular values of price and capital that it selects ex ante. This characterization permits a chance-constrained programming approach to the problem. Let the firm attempt to satisfy the regulatory constraint with a certain probability, say $\gamma$.

The more severe the consequences of not satisfying the constraint, the larger the value of $\gamma$ we expect the firm to use.[6]

The quantity demanded depends on the price and a random variable $u$ that has a distribution function given by $F(\overline{u}) = \int_0^{\overline{u}} f(u)\,du$. A multiplicative version of stochastic demand is assumed, so that quantity demanded is $q(p, u) = X(p)u$, where $X(p)$ is the riskless demand curve.[7] After $p$ and $K$ are chosen and $u$ is known, the firm must adjust its labor supply to meet demand. Thus, labor is flexible ex post and is not a decision variable; it is dictated to the firm once $K$ is chosen and the value of $u$ is known. Therefore, the required labor function can be written as $L(q(p, u), K)$. With the usual assumptions on the production function (positive marginal products and diminishing returns to $K$ and $L$), it can be shown that

$$\frac{\partial L(q, K)}{\partial q} > 0, \qquad \frac{\partial L(q, K)}{\partial K} > 0$$
$$\frac{\partial^2 L(q, K)}{\partial q^2} > 0, \qquad \frac{\partial^2 L(q, K)}{\partial K^2} > 0 \tag{9.31}$$

where $q(p, u)$ is written as $q$ for brevity.

Given this labor-requirement function, the firm seeks to maximize the expected value of profits, given by

$$E[\pi] = E[pq(p, u) - wL(q(p, u), K) - rK]$$

Maximization is subject to satisfying the rate-of-return constraint

$$P\left\{ \frac{pq(p, u) - wL(q(p, u), K)}{K} \leqq s \right\} \geqq \gamma \tag{9.32}$$

6 A chance-constrained programming approach does not imply risk neutrality. For a given reaction by the regulatory agency toward not satisfying the constraint, firms that are more risk-averse will work with higher values of $\gamma$. The firm is risk-neutral among the set of decision variables that satisfy the chance constraint, and it selects from among this set those values that maximize expected profit. Meyer (1975a) points this out in his discussion of a monopolist who must choose $p$, $K$, and $L$ (in this case, $K$ and $L$ are implicit in capacity level $Z$) ex ante, but must meet demands with a specified reliability. His use of a chance constraint in a different setting was shown in Chapter 6.

7 Stochastic demand is presented in more detail in Chapter 6.

where $P$ denotes probability. Thus, both revenue and operating costs are random. We should emphasize that this form of the constraint allows the actual return to be above, below, or equal to the allowed return. Admitting these possibilities is realistic, as revealed by data from regulated industries.

To proceed with the maximization problem, (9.32) must be manipulated into a usable form. Let

$$h(u{:}p, K) = \frac{pq(p, u) - wL(q(p, u), K)}{K}$$

that is, $h$ is a function of $u$, with parameters $p$ and $K$. The values of these parameters are set by the firm, and once this is done, the return to capital, $h$, depends on the value that $u$ assumes. Because the firm knows the distribution function of $u$, it also knows the distribution function of $h$ and the probability that $h \leqq s$. Its goal is to select $p$ and $K$ to maximize expected profit, while keeping this probability above $\gamma$.

A graphical interpretation of the regulatory constraint may serve to clarify the problem. Figure 9.7(a) depicts $h$ as a strictly concave function of $u$ for a given selection of price, $\bar{p}$, and capital, $\bar{K}$. The implications of $h$ being a strictly concave function of $u$ with an interior maximum, as depicted in Figure 9.7(a), can be seen from the first and second derivatives:

$$\frac{dh}{du} = \frac{\partial q}{\partial u}\left(\bar{p} - w\frac{\partial L(q, \bar{K})}{\partial q}\right) \bigg/ \bar{K} = 0 \qquad (9.33)$$

$$\frac{d^2h}{du^2} = \frac{1}{\bar{K}}\left(\frac{\partial^2 q}{\partial u^2}\left(\bar{p} - w\frac{\partial L(q, \bar{K})}{\partial q}\right) - w\left(\frac{\partial q}{\partial u}\right)^2\frac{\partial^2 L(q, \bar{K})}{\partial q^2}\right)$$

$$= \frac{-1}{\bar{K}}w\left(\frac{\partial q}{\partial u}\right)^2\frac{\partial^2 L(q, \bar{K})}{\partial q^2} < 0 \qquad (9.34)[8]$$

From (9.33), a necessary condition for a maximum is that price be equal to marginal cost for some value of $u$. Strict concavity

8 To obtain this result, note that $\partial^2 q/\partial u^2 = 0$. This follows from the multiplicative formulation of risky demand; i.e., $q(p, u) = X(p)u$. This result is also consistent with the additive formulation where $q(p, u) = X(p) + u$.

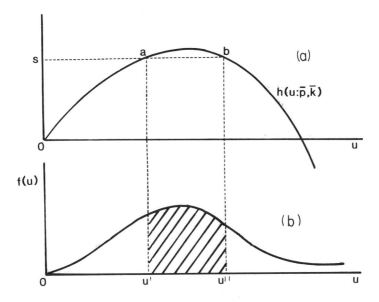

Figure 9.7. Rate-of-return constraint under uncertainty.

follows from the sign of (9.34), which in turn follows from (9.31), where diminishing returns to labor was assumed. [For increasing returns to labor, the sign of (9.34) is reversed, and $h$ is convex in $u$, with an interior minimum, and for constant returns to labor, equality holds in (9.34), and $h$ is linear in $u$.]

Figure 9.7(b) is the probability density function of $u$. Note that the $u$ axes in both figures are vertically aligned. The allowed rate of return, $s$, is located along the vertical axis in Figure 9.7(a), and $a$ and $b$ indicate the points for which the allowed and realized returns are equal ($s = h$). For a different selection of $p$ and $K$, $a$ and $b$ will shift to the right or left, and in some instances the entire $h$ curve may lie below $s$. In any case, $a$ and $b$ are traced down to points $u'$ and $u''$, respectively, in Figure 9.7(b). Thus, $u'$ and $u''$ are the values of the stochastic variable that will exactly allow the fair return, given the firm's ex ante choice of $\bar{p}$ and $\bar{K}$.

The regulatory constraint requires that the shaded area in Figure 9.7(b) between $u'$ and $u''$ be less than $\gamma$. Consequently, (9.32) can be written as

$$1 - P\{u' < u < u''\} \geqq \gamma$$

where $u' = u'(p, K)$ and $u'' = u''(p, K)$.[9] Using $\gamma$ as a multiplier, the constrained maximization problem becomes

$$\max_{p, K, \lambda} E[\pi] + \lambda\left(1 - \int_{u'}^{u''} f(u)\, du - \gamma\right)$$

and assuming that a solution exists for $K > 0$, the first-order condition with respect to $K$ is

$$E\left[-w\frac{\partial L}{\partial K}\right] - r + \lambda\left(\frac{\partial u'}{\partial K} f(u') - \frac{\partial u''}{\partial K} f(u'')\right) = 0 \qquad (9.35)$$

For the regulated firm that is not constrained, or for the regulated firm for which the constraint is inactive ($\lambda = 0$), condition (9.35) implies that expected costs are minimized. In this case, the expected marginal rate of substitution is equal to the ratio of input prices, or

$$E\left[-\frac{\partial L(q, K)}{\partial K}\right] = \frac{r}{w} \qquad (9.36)$$

Therefore, a reasonable interpretation of the A-J effect in a stochastic setting is that the firm does not operate according to (9.36). Instead, it expects to overcapitalize and operates where

$$E\left[-\frac{\partial L(q, K)}{\partial K}\right] < \frac{r}{w} \qquad (9.37)$$

From (9.35), this is equivalent to

$$\frac{\partial u'}{\partial K} f(u') - \frac{\partial u''}{\partial K} f(u'') > 0 \qquad (9.38)$$

9 For increasing (constant) returns to labor, $y$ is convex (linear) in $u$, so that the constraint becomes
$$P\{u' < u < u''\} \geqq \gamma(P\{u \leqq u'\} \geqq \gamma)$$
Figure 9.7(a) will then be changed appropriately.

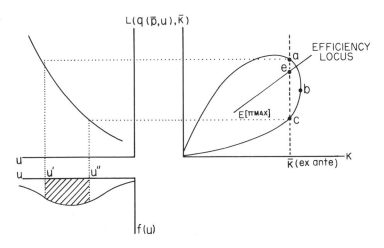

Figure 9.8. The A-J effect under uncertainty.

assuming $\lambda$ is positive and the constraint is active. The extent of the A-J effect is a function of the actual marginal rate of technical substitution and the ratio $s/w$ when the firm is making exactly the allowed rate of return (see the Appendix to this chapter).

In Figure 9.8, this stochastic A-J effect is shown using the familiar graphical analysis. The right-hand diagram shows an iso-rate-of-return locus in capital–labor space. In this problem, however, capital is selected ex ante, and labor ex post. The firm selects a value of $K$, say $\overline{K}$ in the figure, before demand is known; then, after demand is known, it must use the value of $L$ on the vertical axis that will satisfy demand. Thus, once $\overline{K}$ is chosen, the firm must operate on the dashed line. The efficiency locus represents those points satisfying (9.36). The lower left diagram is the probability density function (reoriented from Figure 9.7), and the upper left diagram translates values of the random variable, $u$, into the labor required to satisfy demand.[10]

---

10 Another distinction between this figure and the nonstochastic figures used earlier is that here, output price is fixed at $\bar{p}$. Output varies over $K$–$L$ space, but these output changes are a result of the random element. In the nonstochastic figures, output varies as price changes.

Figure 9.8 reveals that if the firm chooses $\overline{K}$ and $\overline{p}$, the probability of violating the rate-of-return constraint is the shaded area under the density function. Or, using the upper right diagram, the figure shows that the probability of operating between points $a$ and $c$ within the rate-of-return locus is the shaded area. Ex post, the firm can end up at point $e$ and operate efficiently, or it can be undercapitalized or overcapitalized, depending on whether it operates above or below point $e$, respectively. If the firm hired more capital and operated to the right of $\overline{K}$, so that point $b$ was on the dashed line, then the probability of violating the rate-of-return constraint would be zero. Points $u'$ and $u''$ would coincide. This result might occur if the regulator's penalty for violators was substantial and/or the firm was so risk-averse that $\gamma$ was set to 1.

Depending on the density function, the production technology, and demand, the input bias may be consistent or inconsistent with the A-J effect, as Figure 9.8 reveals. Our goal is to show that the A-J effect may not hold in a stochastic environment; so we need only show a counterexample. Using a uniform probability density function and the Cobb–Douglas production function $f(K, L) = K^{1/2}L^{1/2}$, we need to obtain a contradiction to (9.38). This production function implies that $h$ is concave in $u$, because there are diminishing returns to labor. In the following, it is assumed that the regulatory constraint is binding and that both $u'$ and $u''$ exist, as per Figure 9.7.

A uniform probability density function implies $f(u') = f(u'')$; therefore, obtaining a contradiction to (9.38) is equivalent to showing

$$\frac{\partial u'}{\partial K} - \frac{\partial u''}{\partial K} \leq 0 \tag{9.39}$$

Now, when $u$ takes on a particular value, output is given by $X(p)u$, and from the production function, the labor required to produce this output is

$$L = \frac{X(p)^2 u^2}{K}$$

Substituting this value in the regulatory constraint (9.32) and evaluating (9.32) at $h = s$ yields a quadratic in $u$, as follows:

$$s = \left( pX(p)u - \frac{wX(p)^2u^2}{K} \right) \Big/ K$$

or

$$\frac{wX(p)^2}{K} u^2 - pX(p)u + sK = 0$$

Solving this quadratic for $u$ yields

$$u = \frac{p \pm (p^2 - 4ws)^{1/2}}{2wX(p)/K}$$

where the plus and minus correspond to $u''$ and $u'$, respectively. Thus, taking the partial derivatives of these values for $u''$ and $u'$ with respect to $K$ and substituting into (9.39) results in

$$\frac{\partial u'}{\partial K} - \frac{\partial u''}{\partial K} = \frac{-(p^2 - 4ws)^{1/2}}{wX(p)} < 0$$

Consequently, the inequality in (9.38) is reversed, and the firm uses less capital than the expected cost-minimizing amount for the output produced. This result is the opposite of the A-J effect in a stochastic setting, and it lends support to the point that stochastic conditions may result in a lack of empirical evidence of the A-J bias.

There is another difficulty implicit in the stochastic A-J model that may result in an empirical lack of support for the A-J effect. Ex ante, the firm has a probability of $\gamma$ that it will satisfy the regulatory constraint. If the firm hires precisely the minimum amount of labor needed to produce the quantity demanded ex post, then the actual rate of return may be greater or less than the allowed return. In the latter case, the firm is in good standing with the regulator (although not with its stockholders). But in the former case, the firm can expect to be reproached by the regulator, and therefore it has an incentive to depart from hiring the minimum amount of labor. In particular, a form of featherbedding will ensue in order to bring the actual return in line with the allowed return. Thus, featherbedding can act as a sort of safety valve that will encourage the firm to use a small value of $\gamma$. In the extreme, the firm can ignore the constraint ex ante and use its labor supply as a means of satisfying the constraint ex post.

### Aggregation problems: power pools

Our discussion in this subsection is confined to the A-J effect within the electric-power industry. In particular, we show that the A-J effect may be manifested in the form of overreliability of service at a regional level as opposed to firm level – again making empirical detection difficult. To examine this issue, we must investigate power pools, which are groups of two or more electric utilities that are coordinated with respect to the generation and transmission of electricity.[11] Coordination can occur along several dimensions, including the connection of generation facilities with transmission lines, joint planning for the construction of new facilities and lines, and meeting demands for electricity by dispatching from the least-cost generating source across member utilities at any given time. Utilities participating in pools will enjoy benefits and incur costs that generally depend on the degree of coordination. Loose coordination will mean low costs, but few benefits, whereas tight coordination means high costs, but greater benefits.

Coordination in U.S. power pools runs from moderately tight to very loose. Overall, however, there is a tendency toward looseness.[12] In 1964, the Federal Power Commission (FPC) issued the National Power Survey, which indicated that closer coordination could produce substantial savings in the cost of energy production. A decade later, Breyer and MacAvoy (1974) concluded that

---

11  For more on power pools, see Berkowitz (1977), Christensen and Greene (1978), Cramer and Tschirhart (1980, 1983), Joskow and Schmalensee (1983), and Herriott (1985). Much of the discussion here draws on Gegax and Tschirhart (1984).

12  This point is argued by Cramer and Tschirhart (1983), who examine the contractual agreements for 17 major U.S. power pools.

pooling had not grown substantially since the commission's report and that "there should be considerably more coordination at this time than now exists." They based their assertion on calculations of potential cost savings. The magnitude of these savings is impressive, with estimates running as high as several billion dollars annually. More recently, the 1979 National Energy Act exempted utilities from state laws that prevent voluntary coordination where such coordination is designed to obtain economic utilization of resources. The Federal Energy Regulatory Commission (successor to the FPC) was also instructed by the act to submit a report to the president and Congress on the opportunities for future pooling. The lack of progress toward achieving a highly integrated electric-power industry reflected in these reports is the key to understanding how utilities are overcapitalized at the regional level.

Gegax and Tschirhart (1984) explain the lack of coordination by augmenting the A-J model to account for reliability of service and the benefits and costs of pooling. The benefits are chiefly the cost savings available through constructing new facilities that account for all pool members' needs, the cost savings available from reduced reserve generating capacity needed to maintain a particular service reliability, and the dispatching of energy from the least-cost generating source available across all pool members. The costs of pooling are capital outlays for transmission lines and generating units and a variety of transactions costs, including the loss of an individual member's flexibility in decision-making.

The germane result from their model for this discussion is how rate-of-return regulation can bias pool members away from achieving reliability of service levels at least cost. The intuition is straightforward. For an individual electric utility, obtaining reserve capital via a pooling arrangement is less costly for satisfying a given reliability constraint than is capital acquired outside the pool that achieves the same reliability. However, the pool capital contributes less to the utility's rate base than does the nonpool capital. Consequently, the utility is biased away from pooling by rate-of-return regulation, and pools tend to be more loosely coordinated. Also, if two utilities are in neighboring states, and one is more stringently regulated, then both are influenced by the stringent regulator. The bias against pooling means that each utility is not minimizing the cost of maintaining reserve requirements. This is not to say that each utility is being overly reliable because it is maintaining a level of reserves that presumably is optimal when it is viewed in isolation. However, the pool as a whole composed of the utilities in a particular region *is* being overly reliable. Costs can be decreased without a loss in reliability if each utility acquires its reserves through the pool. This bias is a more subtle result of rate-of-return regulation than is the traditional A-J bias, because it is observable only at the regional level, not at the firm level. Empirical studies that do not account for reliability at the regional level are less likely to detect overcapitalization.

### The firm's behavior

Like most models in the theory of the firm, the A-J model has a single decision-maker acting as a profit-maximizer. But firms can be more intricate, having complex hierarchies and multiple decision-makers whose goals depart from profit maximization. Williamson (1964) has been a long-time proponent of highlighting managerial discretion in the theory of the firm. The hypothesis that managers will behave as profit-maximizers in accordance with owner objectives is not beyond question, given separation of management from ownership in firms. A large body of literature has revolved around the search for alternative hypotheses and around incentive mechanisms that will encourage managers to do the bidding of owners.[13]

In fact, managers of regulated firms may have even more incentive than their unregulated counterparts to depart from profit-maximizing behavior. If the rate-of-return constraint per-

---

13 The principal–agent literature deals with incentive mechanisms. See Sappington and Stiglitz (1986).

mits a guaranteed profit, and if this profit is satisfactory to management, then nonprofit goals can be pursued more vigorously. Alternatively, because the constraint puts a cap on profit, profit-minded managers may be discouraged from vigorously pursuing profit in the same way that a taxpayer may eschew additional work because of high marginal tax rates. Also, managers must deal with regulators, rather than with competitors, depending on whether or not the firm is a monopoly. Such an adversary may promote goals and behavior that differ from those of managers in the unregulated sector.

Authors who have studied alternative behavioral hypotheses for regulated firms have concentrated on revenue-maximizing and expense-preference behavior.[14] In either case, the A-J results are altered. Consider revenue maximization first. Suppose the firm maximizes revenue instead of profit, but the regulatory constraint is still binding, so that the firm makes at least enough profit to attain the allowed return. Then, instead of the Lagrangian expression given by (9.7), the firm maximizes the Lagrangian

$$R + \lambda(sK - R + wL) \tag{9.40}$$

over $K$, $L$, and $\lambda$. The first-order necessary conditions for this problem with respect to $K$ and $L$ are

$$
\begin{aligned}
K: &\quad \mathrm{MR}f_K(1 - \lambda) = -\lambda s \\
L: &\quad \mathrm{MR}f_L(1 - \lambda) = -\lambda w
\end{aligned}
$$

from which we obtain

$$\frac{f_K}{f_L} = \frac{s}{w} > \frac{r}{w} \tag{9.41}$$

The firm hires inputs according to (9.41), which shows an inequality opposite that of (9.17); hence, the bias is in the opposite direction, and the revenue-maximizing firm undercapital-

---

14 See Bailey and Malone (1970), Baumol and Klevorick (1970), Crew and Kleindorfer (1979a), and Arzac and Edwards (1979).

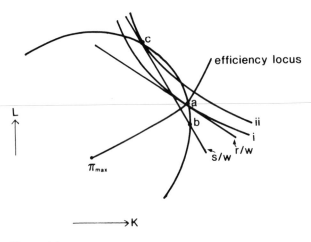

Figure 9.9. Revenue-maximizing behavior.

izes.[15] Diagrammatically, this is shown in Figure 9.9, where a single iso-rate-of-return locus has been blown up. Point *b* is the A-J point, as in Figure 9.2, and point *a* is on the efficiency locus where isoquant *i* is tangent to the input price line labeled *r/w*. All points along the efficiency locus represent similar tangencies, and the slopes at all the tangencies must be *r/w*. The revenue-maximizing firm operates on the iso-rate-of-return locus by assumption, and at a tangency between an isoquant and a pseudoprice line with slope *s/w*. With convex-to-the-origin isoquants, this tangency must occur above the efficiency locus, at a point such as *c*. This result implies undercapitalization.

Expense-preference behavior posits that managers have preferences for goals other than (or in addition to) profit. For example, managers may channel funds into managerial emoluments,

15 Bailey and Malone (1970) show that the output-maximizing firm also undercapitalizes. Atkinson and Waverman (1973) criticize the model, because it does not include a minimum-profit constraint. If the minimum profit required by the revenue-maximizing firm is below the profit earned when the actual return equals the allowed return, the regulatory constraint is nonbinding, and the firm's behavior is not affected by regulation.

large staffs, or a plush working environment beyond the levels consistent with profit maximization. More pertinent for regulated industries, Williamson hypothesizes that firms in less competitive environments will have larger staffs and pay higher wages. Along these lines, Crew and Kleindorfer (1979a) develop a model of a firm subject to rate-of-return behavior. Rather than maximizing profit, management maximizes a utility function whose arguments are profit and total expenditure on the staff. A minimum amount of staff expenditure is required to support each output level. These authors' results show that this firm will make less profit and still exhibit an A-J bias, but the extent of overcapitalization is less severe than in a rate-of-return-constrained profit-maximizing firm. They state that for the expense-preference firm, regulation has "the effect of substituting inefficiency in the use of staff for the A-J type inefficiency."

How important revenue-maximizing or expense-preference behavior is for explaining a firm's decisions depends on the prevalence of such behavior, and this is an empirical issue. Edwards (1977) finds evidence of such behavior in the regulated banking industry, whereas Rhoades (1980) does not. Awh and Primeaux (1985) fail to find evidence of this behavior in the electric-power industry. Thus, the question remains open regarding how important alternative firm behaviors are for empirical investigations of the A-J effect.

### The regulator's behavior

Perhaps the most telling blow against the A-J model as an acceptable description of the regulatory process is the argument that it is too simplistic to capture the intricacies of this environment. Joskow (1974) has been a leading proponent of this point. He notes that what began as a neoclassical model of the firm subject to a particular regulatory constraint wrongfully evolved into a model that was too often accepted as a description of the regulatory process. However, because the model does not characterize the regulatory process adequately, he argues that the implications are not very useful.

Joskow views the regulatory process as having three sets of actors: firms, regulators, and consumers. The firm's objective is to maximize profit, and it is subject to periodic hearings at which prices are set by the regulators, not by the firm, as in the A-J model. There is also a less formal regulatory process outside the hearings at which the firms and regulators establish a working relationship, and personnel often transfer among regulatory agencies and the firms they regulate. The objectives of the regulators are not clear. Although they have a mandate to ensure "quality" service at "reasonable" rates, these terms are nebulous and leave the regulators with little direction: No specific sets of instruments are prescribed to carry out the mandate. In addition, although the legal statutes compel the regulators to ensure that the firms survive, this requirement merely places a lower bound on the rate of return; it suggests no particular return or rate structure. Although the regulators appear to have considerable flexibility, some observers maintain that regulators merely try to minimize conflict and criticism subject to the legal constraints.

Joskow argues that nominal prices, not the rate of return, were the primary concerns of regulators during the 1950s through the early 1970s. Hearings on the rate of return were held when firms requested price increases, but if they kept prices constant or falling, then the realized rate of return went uncontested. Consequently, no allowed return was monitored during this period. This depiction of the regulatory process leads to several propositions for which Joskow finds some empirical support. Over periods when firms' average costs are falling, we should observe (1) few, if any, hearings, (2) constant or falling prices, and (3) rising or constant rates of return. This scenario differs from the A-J framework, in which falling average costs will mean a rising rate of return, followed by a hearing. Also, when average cost is rising, we should expect more hearings as firms seek higher returns. During these periods, the A-J bias may be present, because firms want large rate bases applicable for the hearing. But when average cost is falling, the A-J bias is less likely, because when firms can keep all of their profits, they have an incentive to minimize cost. Thus, detecting an A-J bias in empirical work will depend on the study period and the behavior of average cost over the period.

Finally, Joskow discusses the changing regulatory environment from the 1950s to the 1970s, a factor not captured by the simple A-J model. Early on, average costs were falling, and hearings were infrequent. However, as realized rates of return began to fall because of inflation and the exhaustion of economies of scale, firms were requesting frequent hearings. The tremendous increase in the caseload was burdensome on the regulators, with the situation becoming further complicated when consumer and environmental groups became active as intervenors. According to Joskow, the regulators were simply unprepared for dealing with the new issues. They began to adopt new instruments to avoid conflict and criticism, including the following: (1) temporary price increases that could be levied before a formal hearing to avoid lags, and then rescinded after a hearing if judged to be unjustified; (2) automatic adjustment mechanisms that allowed price increases for variable inputs to be passed on without a formal hearing (see the next section); (3) the use of future test years instead of the historical approach for setting prices.

Joskow's description of the regulatory process is more complex than the A-J framework, and some authors have attempted to formalize certain aspects of this richer environment. Prior to Joskow's work, Klevorick (1973) and Davis (1973) both developed dynamic models of the regulatory process to capture more dimensions of reality. Klevorick advanced many of the same arguments as Joskow regarding the A-J model's simplistic nature. In his model, the firm's capital stock can grow over time, and it is combined with labor and knowledge in any one period to produce output. The regulator sets the price, and the firm must meet all output at that price. The price does not change until the next hearing, but the timing of the hearing is random. Thus, the firm does not know when the next hearing will occur, but when it does, the current rate base will be used to determine prices.

Unfortunately, the complexity of the model precludes specific results regarding the A-J bias. Nevertheless, the generality of the A-J results was brought into question.

In the Davis model, hearings are not random, but when they occur, the price set by the regulator depends on the difference between average cost and the current price. If average cost is greater (less) than the current price, the dictated change in price is positive (negative). Davis is able to show that the stationary point of his dynamic model is not the traditional A-J solution. The stationary point does exhibit overcapitalization, but not to the extent of the A-J bias. Moreover, the regulator can move the firm toward an efficient solution by being slow in its price adjustments. This conclusion is similar to the result that regulatory lag will discourage overcapitalization.

More recently, Bawa and Sibley (1980) have used a dynamic model of the firm subject to stochastic regulatory review that adds still more realism. As in the models of Klevorick and Davis, the regulator sets the price. The probability of review, however, is endogenous (as opposed to Klevorick's exogeneity assumption) and is an increasing function of the absolute deviation between the firm's actual return and the allowed return. Because the actual return can be greater than, less than, or equal to the allowed return, this feature overcomes a shortcoming in the standard A-J analysis, where they are always equal. Also, in the standard analysis, recall that when the regulator sets $s = r$, the solution is indeterminate, and as Baumol and Klevorick (1970) showed, as $s$ approaches $r$, the capital stock approaches infinity. This result suggests that when regulators do a better job of measuring the cost of capital in order to lower the allowed return to capital, inefficiency may be exacerbated. In Bawa and Sibley's model, the firm will initially overcapitalize, be efficient, or undercapitalize, depending on whether the allowed return exceeds, equals, or is less than its cost of capital. However, after many time periods, even with $s \neq r$, the firm converges to cost minimization. Thus, again the generality of the A-J effect is brought into question.

Using a very different approach, Burness, Montgomery, and Quirk (1980) studied the electric-power industry's acquisition of nuclear plants. To explain the industry's actions, they contrasted the predictive power of the A-J model with that of what they referred to as a Joskow-type model. The setting was in the "turnkey era," 1963–6, when nuclear-reactor manufacturers were offering turnkey contracts to electric utilities. Under these contracts, the cost to the utility of a nuclear facility was fixed. The burden of inflation and cost overruns was borne by the manufacturer. Yet only two-thirds of the contracts during that period were turnkey contracts, the rest being more conventional types of contracts. Following the turnkey era, there was a significant increase in orders for new nuclear plants. Was there something inherent in the regulatory process that encouraged utilities to avoid these seemingly low-risk turnkey contracts?

To work risk into the A-J model, these authors assume that the price of capital is random. Under a turnkey contract, the nuclear-plant manufacturer sells capital to the utility at a guaranteed price equal to the manufacturer's expected costs. The utility then maximizes profit subject to a rate-of-return constraint, and because there is no uncertainty for the utility, the standard A-J model is applicable. Under a conventional contract, the utility knows only the distribution function for the price of capital, and it chooses its capital input before the actual price is known. Once the price is known, the utility chooses its variable input either to maximize profit, if the rate-of-return constraint is not binding, or to achieve exactly the allowed return, if the constraint is binding. Low (high) ex post capital prices will mean that the constraint is (is not) binding. Their principal result is that the utility will order more capital under a turnkey contract than under a conventional contract. The reason is that under a turnkey contract, where there is no uncertainty to the utility, the allowed rate of return is always attained, along with the corresponding profit, $\pi^T$. Under a conventional contract, there are two possibilities. Either the allowed return is not attained, so that profit is less than $\pi^T$, or the allowed return is exactly attained, so that profit is $\pi^T$. Obviously, the turnkey contract is more attractive, because profit never falls below $\pi^T$, as it can with the conventional contract. The rate-of-return constraint creates an asymmetry in the range of profit under a conventional contract: Profit can be high or low, but never too high. Because the standard A-J model requires the actual return to be less than or equal to the allowed return, the Burness, Montgomery, and Quirk adaptation is consistent with it. Of course, in the standard analysis of the turnkey decision, the utility is always able to make the constraint binding, because there is no uncertainty.

Turning to their Joskow-type model, risk is handled again through the random price of capital. However, the regulator now sets output price, and the utility must meet all demand at that price. Also in keeping with Joskow's observations of the regulatory environment in the late 1960s and 1970s, the regulatory constraint is assumed nonbinding. The utilities initiate all the hearings, and the regulator enforces a nonnegativity constraint on profit. This model is consistent with those periods in which average costs are rising, and firms are concerned with losses, as opposed to attaining an allowed return. These authors' results here are that the utilities prefer conventional contracts to turnkey contracts. Moreover, if output demand is inelastic, the firm will employ more capital under a conventional contract. If demand is elastic, the result is ambiguous. The intuition centers around the idea that now the nonnegative-profit constraint, rather than the rate-of-return constraint, is binding. Under a turnkey contract, the firm can attain the certain profit $\pi^T$. Under a conventional contract, the firm can attain more or less than $\pi^T$ ex post, but there is a limit to how much less. If the ex post price of capital is high enough to yield negative profit, the nonnegativity constraint will become active and save the utility from this loss. Again, there is an asymmetry in the range of profit under a conventional contract. But in the Joskow-type model, it is the nonnegative constraint that causes the opposite asymmetry: Profit can be high or low, but never too low. The upshot of this work, then, is that a Joskow-type model is a better predictor of utility behavior than the standard A-J model, at least during the mid-1960s.

With these models, we conclude our discussion of complications in the search for an A-J effect. Complications have included factors that may mitigate the bias (regulatory lag, regulatory behavior), that may reverse the direction of the bias (stochastic conditions, firm behavior), or that may cause the bias to occur at a more aggregate level (power pools). All this suggests the difficulty of finding evidence to support the bias and indicates additional factors that empirical studies might consider. Also, for public policy, the A-J bias should continue to be recognized as a potential source of inefficiency inherent in rate-of-return regulation.

### 9.4. Automatic adjustment clauses

In the preceding section, we cited the difficulties that regulators had in coping with the increased numbers of regulatory hearings beginning around 1970, and we mentioned that automatic adjustment clauses were instruments adopted to alleviate this burden. However, the origin of these instruments dates back to World War I, when rapidly rising fuel prices prompted their adoption.[16] They work by allowing regulated firms to adjust their output prices in response to changes in their variable input prices, without going through a formal regulatory hearing.[17] The regulator, however, does have control over the formula used to make the adjustment. Almost all state commissions allow adjustment clauses for industrial and commercial consumers, and about two-thirds of state commissions allow them for residential

16 Kendrick (1975) provides a brief historical and institutional perspective of automatic adjustment clauses and argues that efficiency incentives should be built into them. He concentrates on their use in the telecommunications industry.

17 The types of inputs that are covered by adjustment clauses vary across state commissions. Examples of the inputs for power companies include fossil fuels, nuclear fuels, hydroelectric power, geothermal power, transportation fees, taxes, fuel-related labor, wheeling, purchased power, line losses, and uncollectable expenses. See Baron and DeBondt (1979).

consumers. They accounted for increases of over $5 billion in electricity revenues in 1974 alone.

### Arguments for and against automatic adjustment clauses

Baron and DeBondt (1979) outline the arguments for and against automatic adjustment clauses in the context of a model of a profit-maximizing firm subject to the clauses. The primary argument on the positive side is that adjustment clauses can maintain the financial viability of the firm in times of rapidly rising input prices. Without them, the inevitable lags in the regulatory process would not allow the utilities to adjust output prices fast enough, and ultimately this could result in a lower quality of service and financial crises. In addition, adjustment clauses relieve the pressure on regulators during times of rapidly rising prices, because utilities need not continually seek price increases in formal hearings. As the New Mexico commission pointed out, this process allows them to channel their efforts into their other, sometimes neglected responsibilities.[18]

Among the arguments against adjustment clauses is the availability of better methods for alleviating the financial burden on the utilities, methods that would not abdicate regulatory responsibility. In particular, lags can be reduced and future test years can be used in formal hearings to establish prices, instead of using data on historical costs. Undoubtedly, regulators would argue that the possibility of shorter lags is remote without additional resources, and current lags simply reflect their burdensome responsibilities. And although the use of future test years might allow expected increases in input prices to be recognized, so that adjustments might not be necessary, this procedure requires regulators to predict the increases. The uncertainty in making such predictions has often discouraged this approach.

Another criticism of adjustment clauses is that they may allow pass-through of endogenous as well as exogenous costs. Their

---

18 Case number 1196, April 22, 1975, before the New Mexico Public Service Commission.

purpose is simply to pass through the latter costs, because only these are beyond any control of the utility. But regulators often include a wide range of costs in the clauses,[17] over many of which the utility will have some control. A good example of this is the situation in which a utility is allowed to pass through increases in the cost of fuel or transportation, and then does not expend reasonable search and bargaining efforts to find the least-cost suppliers. In this case, increases in fuel or transport costs are only partially exogenous, because the utility could have lowered them through additional search and bargaining.

Perhaps the most frequently cited argument against adjustment clauses is that they encourage inefficient production. The idea here is identical with the idea behind the A-J bias. If the regulator imposes a constraint on the utility that is asymmetric, in that it favors one type of input over others, then the utility will respond by using an inefficiently large amount of the favored input. In the A-J model, the favored input is capital. With adjustment clauses, the favored input usually is fuel, although other inputs may also be favored. Thus, if the price of a fuel input that is not covered by an adjustment clause increases, we should expect the cost-minimizing utility to switch to other fuels and, in the long run, to adopt less-fuel-intensive technologies. The presence of an adjustment clause can mitigate the utility's incentive to switch fuels or adopt different technologies, because the increased price can be simply passed on in higher output prices.

### A theoretical model of adjustment clauses

Baron and DeBondt (1979) construct a detailed theoretical model of a utility operating under an automatic adjustment clause. They point out that an important aspect of such a model is that it should reflect the regulatory environment in which it is embedded. Because utilities that operate under adjustment clauses typically operate under rate-of-return constraints as well, some care must be taken to recognize any possible interactions. Baron and DeBondt argue that the adjustment clause is automatic, and when it is executed there is no consideration of how output price increases will affect the rate of return. But the rate of return can be expected to change, implying that either before or after execution of the adjustment clause, but not both, the allowed and actual rates of return are unequal. Consequently, the standard A-J analysis with constant equality between the rates of return is inappropriate. In the Baron and DeBondt model, the regulator sets an initial price in keeping with an allowed return, but the adjustment clause changes that price and the return.

The form of the adjustment clause is as follows. Suppose the utility uses capital, $K$, and fuel, $F$, in producing output according to the production function

$$f(K, F) \tag{9.42}$$

For fuel adjustment clauses, output prices typically are allowed to increase in order to match increases in average cost due to the higher fuel price. Let $p_1$ ($p_2$) and $w_1$ ($w_2$) be the pre-adjustment (post-adjustment) output and fuel prices, respectively. When the fuel price changes, the change in average cost is $(w_2 - w_1)F/q(p_1)$, where $F$ is the initial amount of fuel used, and $q(p_1)$ is output. The post-adjustment output price is then

$$p_2 = p_1 + (w_2 - w_1)F/q(p_1) \tag{9.43}$$

where production of $q(p_1)$ is according to (9.42).[19]

The major features of the Baron and DeBondt model are as follows. First, there are three periods over which the firm maximizes expected discounted profit. In the first period, the output and fuel input prices are $p_1$ and $w_1$, respectively. The first period ends when the fuel price changes to $w_2$. However, output price does not change according to (9.43) until the end of period 2 (beginning of period 3). This lag between the time the fuel price changes and the adjustment clause takes effect reflects actual practice. It is referred to as a "collection lag," and proponents of

---

19 Some have argued that multiplying the right-hand side of this formula by a positive constant less than 1 would increase the firm's incentive for efficiency; see Kendrick (1975) for an example. Baron and DeBondt show in their model that this constant has more ambiguous effects on efficiency than the use of a lag in enforcing the formula.

adjustment clauses argue that this lag diminishes any incentives for the utility to be inefficient. Finally, period 3 begins with the new output price and has an infinite horizon. No rate-of-return constraint is invoked during the latter two periods. The second major feature is that both the second fuel price and the time of its change are independent random variables, with the latter being distributed exponentially. Third, the utility must satisfy all demand using a capital/fuel ratio chosen ex ante in a homothetic production process. This ratio is the utility's sole decision variable.

The results of this model yield some support for the position that adjustment clauses may promote inefficiency. If the probability of an increase in the fuel price is 1, then the firm will choose an inefficiently small capital/fuel ratio. (Decreases in the fuel price with probability 1 imply too large a ratio.) The firm can pass along the increase via (9.43) and overutilize fuel in its choice of technology. These authors point out that past energy-crisis legislation requiring conversion of power plants from oil to coal may have been justified, because adjustment clauses would have discouraged conversion. When the fuel price is expected to be stable, no definitive result emerges regarding the capital/fuel ratio. Also, the collection lag may be a useful instrument for the regulator. Comparative statics reveals that the capital/fuel ratio chosen by the utility decreases as the lag increases. However, the efficient capital/fuel ratio also decreases; so no definitive result emerges regarding the magnitude of the bias. Nevertheless, the influence of this collection lag is not unlike the effect that regulatory lag had on the optimum capital/labor ratios in Section 9.3.

Because the model assumes that the period-1 price is equal to average cost, in period 2 the new price will mean a new output level. Unless production is subject to constant returns to scale, the new price will no longer equal average cost. In particular, a utility with increasing returns to scale, which we expect for strong natural monopolies, will have the adjusted price below average cost, and the return to the utility will no longer be adequate. Baron and DeBondt indicate that this outcome could encourage the firm to file for a hearing, which is precisely what the adjustment clause was designed to avoid.

In another theoretical treatment of adjustment clauses, Isaac (1982) uses a Joskow-type model similar to that employed by Burness and associates (1980), as discussed in the preceding section. The regulator sets output price and does not continually monitor the utility's rate of return. If the utility's profit becomes negative, it will request a rate hearing. Therefore, the operable constraint requires nonnegative profit, rather than a particular rate of return. Isaac assumes that the future price of fuel is random and that the utility must choose capital before the price is known. Ex post, the utility is a price-taker in the input market, so that there is no endogenous component of the fuel price, and the utility is risk-neutral, so that it maximizes the expected value of profit. Two types of fuel adjustment clauses are considered: the first is identical with that in (9.43); the second uses the change in total fuel expenditures from period 1 to period 2, instead of the change in expenditures necessary to purchase period 1's fuel, as in (9.43).

Isaac's results indicate that the utility will adopt an inefficiently low capital/fuel ratio when the future fuel price is known with certainty. But with uncertainty, the result is ambiguous. The ambiguity arises because the expected marginal rate of substitution between capital and fuel depends on the realized future price of fuel, because this price determines whether or not the nonnegative constraint on profit becomes binding. Moreover, the price of fuel that makes the constraint binding depends on whether or not there is a fuel adjustment mechanism. Consequently, the ex post marginal rates of substitution, with and without an adjustment clause, cannot be compared. These results are similar to those of Baron and DeBondt in that definitive conclusions about the chosen capital/fuel ratio emerge only when the fuel price increases with probability 1. In fact, the Baron–DeBondt formulation is essentially a Joskow-type model as well, in that output price is fixed by the regulator, and there is no rate-of-return constraint. However, their model does not enforce a nonnegativity constraint on profits after the future price of fuel becomes known.

### Empirical tests of automatic adjustment clauses

Kaserman and Tepel (1982) test for two of the negative effects credited to automatic fuel adjustment clauses: that utilities covered by clauses (1) may not expend reasonable search and bargaining efforts to obtain the least-cost fuel supplies and (2) will have less incentive to switch their production processes to lower-cost fuels. These are referred to as the search and switching effects. The search effect, of course, assumes that utilities do not take the price of fuel as given, but that the price depends on the quantity purchased, the sulfur content of the fuel, and the utility's search effort. As stated earlier, this implies that fuel costs are not exogenous, in spite of the raison d'être for adjustment clauses: exogenous input price shocks.

These authors estimate utilities' demands for fuel, where these demands are derived from a Cobb–Douglas production technology and constant elasticity output demands. The analytically derived demands differ depending on whether or not the utilities are covered by an adjustment clause. Using data from 121 U.S. utilities, their results suggest that utilities covered by adjustment clauses pay more for fuel and that the magnitude of the overpayment is substantial. However, whether the overpayment implies that utilities covered by the adjustment clauses are paying higher fuel prices or are not switching to cheaper fuels is unclear.

State commissions differ in their treatment of purchased power. Some allow the cost of a utility's purchased power to be covered by adjustment clauses; others do not. Here, again, we would expect to see a bias; this time, utilities not covered by purchased-power adjustment clauses would be making too few purchases. Blair, Kaserman, and Pacey (1985) demonstrated this with a nonstochastic theoretical model in which the firm chooses between satisfying demand with purchases or with self-generation. They tested this model using data from 113 electric utilities, 82 of which were covered by purchased-power adjustment clauses. As predicted, utilities not covered by adjustment clauses used less purchased power, ceteris paribus. Also, because purchasing power is one indication of cooperative efforts among electric utilities, these authors inferred that purchased-power clauses provide another explanation for loosely organized power pools. This point is in addition to those explanations discussed in Section 9.3 and Chapter 11.

Other authors who have tested for the impact of fuel adjustment clauses include Gollop and Karlson (1978), Stewart (1982), and Atkinson and Halvorsen (1980). Gollop and Karlson estimated a translog cost function that depended in part on whether or not the utility was covered by an adjustment clause. Using data from the early 1970s, they found little evidence of an input bias. However, as they and Stewart pointed out, their specification was based on long-run equilibrium conditions, and because fuel prices did not begin escalating drastically until the early 1970s, utilities may have been in transition with respect to their capital/fuel ratios. Alternatively, Stewart did find evidence of a bias toward fuel use, by using more recent data and estimating a function describing the technology choice of the utility. Those utilities covered by fuel adjustment clauses chose more-fuel-intensive new plants. Because the collection lag was incorporated into his explanatory variable for the fuel clause, Stewart was able also to infer that longer collection lags led to smaller input biases.[20] This result is consistent with one of Baron and DeBondt's theoretical propositions.

We alluded to Atkinson and Halvorsen's work in Section 9.3 because their econometric method simultaneously tests for an A-J bias and a fuel bias. Their method is to note that production efficiency between inputs $K$ and $F$, using (9.42), can be expressed as

---

20  Actually, Stewart (1982) and Gollop and Karlson (1978) both use an index developed by the latter authors to measure whether or not the utility is covered by a fuel adjustment clause. The index depends on the percentage of fuel costs that can be passed on, the percentage of total sales that the clause can be applied to, and the difference between the regulatory lag and the collection lag.

$$\frac{\partial f/\partial K}{\partial f/\partial F} = k\,\frac{r}{w} \tag{9.44}$$

where $k$ is a constant. If $k \neq 1$, the marginal rate of substitution is not equal to the input price ratio, and there is relative price inefficiency. These authors use three $k$'s to represent the input ratios between capital/fuel, capital/labor, and fuel/labor. The $k$'s are then estimated in a translog profit function and its associated demand functions. The data are from 1973, which may have allowed for utilities to adjust to escalating fuel prices. Atkinson and Halvorsen's results show input inefficiency between capital and labor in the manner of the A-J bias and input inefficiency between fuel and labor in the manner of the bias induced by fuel adjustment clauses. They find no evidence of inefficiency with capital and fuel, which may be a result of the A-J bias and the fuel-adjustment-clause bias offsetting one another.

### 9.5. Industry-wide regulatory constraints

Most of the analyses cited thus far have focused on the individual firm. However, some regulated industries, such as motor carriers until 1980 and insurance, are subject as a group to regulatory constraint based on an industry-wide aggregate performance measure. To some extent, long-distance telecommunications prices prior to divestiture were based on national average costs rather than on the actual costs of high-density and low-density routes. This type of regulation, as opposed to case-by-case review, reflects an attempt to reduce the administrative costs of dealing with a large number of firms and the concomitant lack of information about costs and profits of individual firms. In addition, rate-of-return regulation as an alternative for the motor carrier industry has been judged inappropriate by the ICC, because the relatively small capital bases for trucking firms would mean volatile rates. Daughety (1984) examines the effects of industry-wide regulation on firm behavior and industry structure and finds that when regulators set price according to an average performance measure of the industry, inefficiencies can arise not only in the input use of an individual firm (i.e., an A-J bias) but also in the number of firms in the industry. Specifically, prices can be set high enough to maintain inefficient firms because of an incentive to inflate costs. As a result, this type of regulation confers benefits both on inefficient firms, by allowing them to operate profitably, and on efficient firms, by protecting their profits.

### The classic oligopoly problem

Before examining Daughety's results in more detail, let us review outcomes under Cournot rivalry and Stackelberg leadership behaviors in an unregulated two-firm industry.[21] For simplicity, we assume a linear market demand and declining average costs. Inverse demand is written

$$p = a - b(q_1 + q_2), \qquad a, b > 0 \qquad (9.45)$$

where $p$ is the industry price, and $q_1$ and $q_2$ are the outputs of firms 1 and 2, respectively. Total costs of $q_i$, $i = 1, 2$, are

$$C_i(q_i) = \begin{cases} c_i q_i + f_i, & q_i > 0 \\ 0 + f_i, & q_i = 0 \end{cases} \qquad (9.46)$$

where $f_i$ are the fixed costs of firm $i$, and $c_i$ is a per-unit variable cost of producing $q$. Under Cournot behavior, each firm takes the other's output as given in selecting its profit-maximizing output. First-order conditions define the reaction function for the firm that gives the profit-maximizing output for each level of the competitor's output. The reaction functions for firms 1 and 2 are denoted $\phi_1$ and $\phi_2$, respectively, in Figure 9.10. Point $C$ represents the equilibrium Cournot outcome.

Under the assumption of Stackelberg behavior, one firm acts as a leader in choosing output, and the other acts as a follower, or acts according to Cournot behavior. Firm 1, assumed here to be the output leader, incorporates firm 2's reaction function directly into its profit-maximization calculation. Firm 1's highest profit contour tangent to firm 2's reaction function determines

21 A good explanation of duopoly outcomes can be found in Intriligator (1971).

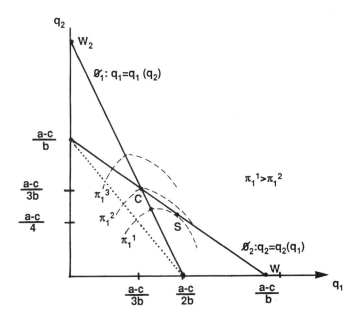

Figure 9.10. Cournot and Stackelberg outcomes.

the equilibrium output of the industry. The equilibrium is represented by point *S* in Figure 9.10. Now let us turn to decision-making under regulatory constraint.

### Constraints on average costs and operating ratios

Two types of regulatory constraints, the average-cost (AC) constraint and the operating-ratio (OR) constraint, have been used to regulate prices on an industry-wide basis. The AC constraint uses the average of individual average costs of production to restrict the allowed price via a proportionality constant. This constraint can be written for the two-firm industry as

$$\frac{1}{2} \sum_{i=1}^{2} \frac{C_i(q_i)}{q_i} \geqq \alpha_A p(q_1 + q_2) \tag{9.47}$$

where $\alpha_A$ is set between 0 and 1 by the regulator. The OR constraint requires that the ratio of operating costs to operating rev-

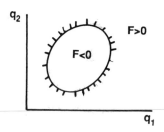

Figure 9.11. The average-cost constraint.

enues equal or exceed some fraction $\alpha_0$, between 0 and 1, specified by the regulator. It can be denoted

$$\sum_{i=1}^{2} C_i(q_i) \Big/ \sum_{i=1}^{2} p(q_1 + q_2)q_i \geqq \alpha_0 \tag{9.48}$$

Note that if $C_1 \neq C_2$, the OR and AC constraints are not the same, because the OR constraint is a market-share-weighted average-cost constraint.

What does the average-cost constraint look like for the two-firm industry? Using (9.45) and (9.46), equation (9.47) can be rewritten for $q_1, q_2 > 0$ as

$$\begin{aligned} F \equiv (c_1 + c_2 - 2\alpha_A a)q_1q_2 + f_1q_2 \\ + f_2q_1 + 2\alpha_A b(q_1 + q_2)q_1q_2 \geq 0 \end{aligned} \tag{9.49}$$

The constraint is nonlinear, and an example of (9.49) is depicted in Figure 9.11 as $F$. Output mixes inside $F$ are not feasible under regulation, whereas those on or outside $F$ meet the regulatory constraint. Daughety notes that under an AC constraint like that in Figure 9.11, any price or aggregate output is feasible under regulation; the constraint instead restricts potential distributions of total output over firms for some prices.

To analyze the effects of a constraint such as $F$ on firm and industry performance, Daughety postulates the following regulatory scenario: (1) Regulators specify the group constraint and $\alpha$. (2) Firms agree on how to share the market and on the proposed price. (3) Regulators accept the proposal. (4) The regulated price becomes the ceiling price. Although unusual, step (2) of this scenario is realistic, as firms under regulation often are given antitrust immunity, leading to an official institution in which price proposals can be developed by the industry.

Because of the interdependence of firms in the industry, as seen in step (2), the analysis must be approached as a problem of regulating an oligopoly. Daughety employs a Stackelberg model in which the leader, firm 1, uses the reaction function of the follower, firm 2, and the regulatory constraint to choose its output level and thus the distribution of output for the industry. The leader is assumed to have power during step (2) of the regulatory process, but not after the price ceiling, $\bar{p}$, is set. After $\bar{p}$ is set, firms act in a Cournot manner by taking $\bar{p}$ and the output of the other firm as given in maximizing profits.

With these assumptions, we can examine the price ceiling and output that will be chosen in step (2) and compare these to the price and output in an unregulated environment. Under regulation, in step (4) the follower will maximize profits subject not only to the leader's output but also to the ceiling price that will be established in step (2).

The reaction function for the follower under regulation, denoted $\psi(q_1, \bar{p})$, will be equal to its reaction function $\phi_2$ in the unregulated environment for those output levels at which the constraint is nonbinding, and it will be equal to $q(\bar{p}) - q_1$ for output levels at which the constraint is binding, where $q(\bar{p})$ is the demand function. When the constraint is binding, the reaction function gives $q_2$ that solves $p(q_1 + q_2) = \bar{p}$. An example of $\psi$ is illustrated in Figure 9.12. Note that the slope of $q(\bar{p})$ is $-1$, and outputs that satisfy the price ceiling lie on or above this line. Knowing $\psi$, the leader in step (2) can choose an equilibrium industry output and thus a price ceiling such that its profit is maximized and the regulatory constraint is satisfied. The leader's problem can be expressed as

$$\max_{q_1, \bar{p}} \pi^1(q_1, \psi(q_1, \bar{p}))$$

subject to $p(q_1 + \psi(q_1, \bar{p})) \leq \bar{p}$ and $F(q_1, \psi(q_1, \bar{p})\alpha) \geq 0$.

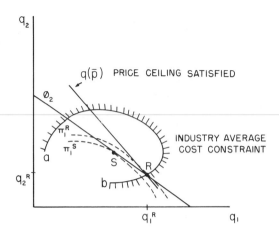

Figure 9.12. Regulation increases output.

The first constraint requires that industry output satisfy the price ceiling proposed. The second constraint requires that aggregate output and the price ceiling satisfy the regulatory constraint $F$.

The solution to the leader's problem provides the following relationship between regulated industry output, $q^R$, and unregulated (Stackelberg) industry output, $q^S$:

$$q^R \lessgtr q^S \quad \text{if and only if } (F_1 + F_2\phi')|_{q=q^R} \lessgtr 0 \qquad (9.50)$$

where subscripts denote partial derivatives. This condition states that whether or not regulation results in lower aggregate output depends on the relationship between the marginal rates of output substitution along $F$ and $\phi$. Figures 9.12 and 9.13 illustrate two examples of condition (9.50), the former in which $q^R > q^S$, and the latter in which $q^R < q^S$.

Consider first Figure 9.12. The leader maximizes its profits by choosing $q^R$ as the industry output. This results in a price ceiling $\bar{p} = p(q_1^R + q_2^R)$; $q^R$ is an equilibrium because at $q^R$, the regulatory constraint and price ceiling are satisfied, and $q^R$ lies on firm 2's reaction function. Firm 1 cannot increase its profits without rais-

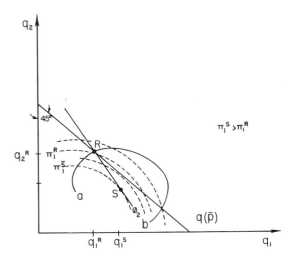

Figure 9.13. Regulation decreases output.

ing price, and that is not possible if the regulatory constraint is to be met. In this case, regulation works in that aggregate output is increased and price is lowered relative to the unconstrained solution (denoted by point $S$). This situation might occur when firms have constant average costs and the industry faces AC regulation.

Figure 9.13 illustrates the case in which regulated output is lower and price is higher than in the unconstrained solution: $q^R$ is the equilibrium solution, because firm 1 can raise its profits only by moving along $\phi$, but this will violate the regulatory constraint. Note that the output of firm 2, $q_2^R$, has increased, and $q_1^R$ has decreased, relative to $q^S$. This scenario can occur if both firms face constant average costs of production and the regulation is an operating-ratio constraint. If firm 2 has higher costs than firm 1, output under regulation will be lower and less efficiently produced than output in the unregulated environment. Indeed, if firm 1's costs are low enough, for efficiency it should choose to face the constraint alone by choosing a price that would eliminate firm 2. But it has an incentive to share the market with a high-cost firm to maintain higher profits. There are also cases in which the regulated output is less than the monopoly output, and hence the regulated price exceeds the unregulated monopoly price.

Likewise, $q^R < q^S$ can occur under both OR and AC constraints if the industries are not structurally competitive. Suppose firm 1 is subject to economies of scale, whereas firm 2 has constant returns to scale. Under no regulation, firm 1 will be a natural monopoly. Under regulation, firm 1 will prefer to share the market with a higher-cost firm, that is, inflate the costs of the industry, in order to keep the regulated price and profits high and avoid facing average-cost pricing alone at a lower price. Thus, although the leader can produce output more efficiently than the follower, "it has an incentive to distribute output so as to keep an inefficient firm operating, thereby padding the average" (Daughety, 1984, p. 947). Note that entry controls are needed if the output leader is to benefit from this type of regulation.

To the extent that additional constraints emphasize a particular input, distortions in input use analogous to an A-J bias can also occur. The bias will occur only in the leader's choice of inputs, because it is only the leader that observes the regulatory constraint. Followers face only the output of firm 1 and the price ceiling in choosing their input mix; they never directly observe the constraint. Therefore, they have no incentive to produce inefficiently. As output is shifted more to the leader, the degree of the input distortion becomes more significant.

### 9.6. Summary

Models of regulatory constraint contain highly stylized characterizations of the instruments available to regulators, the timing of their use, and the responses of firms. Nevertheless, these models shed light on the potential side effects of attempts to limit rates of return or prices. We have learned from macroeconomic models that when the number of instruments is less than the number of targets, goals will not be achieved. The same principle applies to regulators. When firms can adjust input mixes, product quality, price structures, and output mix, the potential for misallocation is present.

The rate-of-return constraint for the single-product firm illustrates the input-mix bias, in which the firm is technologically efficient (operating on an isoquant), but not economically efficient. The overcapitalization bias examined by Averch and Johnson spawned a multitude of analyses. Concurrent with Averch and Johnson, Westfield pointed out the potential for capital waste, and Wellisz, followed by Kafoglis, indicated the output effect of regulation (for the multiproduct firm and single-product firm). The work of these latter authors has, until recently, not received the same amount of attention, although the associated impacts are just as important from the standpoint of allocative efficiency. Incentives for pricing below marginal cost most certainly hurt consumers.

Despite input and output biases, rate-of-return regulation can improve welfare relative to the monopoly situation. The net impact will depend on the elasticity of substitution between inputs, demand elasticities, and scale economies. If the elasticity of substitution is low, there are limited opportunities for moving to higher capital–labor ratios. Also, inelastic demand increases the potential impacts of cost distortions, as consumers cannot switch to substitutes. Finally, the gains to expanding output (via regulation) are greater when scale economies are greatest. A number of issues have been examined in the context of the multiproduct firm: peak-load pricing, two-part tariffs, and the relationship between Ramsey pricing and A-J prices.

Tests for the A-J effect have yielded mixed results.[22] Zimmer (1978) presents a critical review of the early studies and finds them "defective in the measurement of the cost of capital as well as in the assumptions made in the empirical implementation of

22 For example, Callen (1978) has examined the impact of rate-of-return regulation on the U.S. interstate natural-gas-transmission industry. His empirical investigation of 28 firms compared the actual outputs under regulatory constraint with the profit-maximizing outputs and marginal-cost outputs, using detailed production-function information. He concludes that the total actual net benefits with regulation are within 5.2% of those obtained under marginal-cost pricing – so potential input distortions and output-mix distortions are relatively small when compared with the absence of regulation.

the tests" (p. 167). Furthermore, modifications to the static A-J framework yield different conclusions regarding input biases. Regulatory lag and the introduction of uncertainty both alter the standard results. Institutional arrangements complicate the analysis – as with the possibility of power pools. For example, an A-J effect may be reflected in overreliability of service at a regional, rather than firm, level. In telecommunications, prior to divestiture, the impact of A-J biases on AT&T depended on jurisdictional rate-of-return differences. Non-profit-maximizing behavior has been postulated for regulated firms; so revenue or output maximization, or expense-preference behavior, could explain negative tests for A-J. In addition, as Joskow has emphasized, regulatory behavior differs from the A-J characterization: Prices, not allowed rates of return, are often the key regulatory instruments.

Automatic adjustment clauses have also been surveyed as important features of the regulatory environment. There is some evidence that although such mechanisms alleviate utility financial burdens and better allow prices to track costs, they can reduce incentives to economize on fuel. Atkinson and Halvorsen suggest that the A-J effect may be offset by such a bias.

The last part of this chapter has introduced industry-wide regulatory constraints to illustrate how a multifirm environment complicates the regulatory process. The prevalence of firm adjustments to such constraints will be highlighted again in Chapter 11 when we discuss the transition to deregulation. Some aggregate performance measures or specific behaviors are likely to remain under regulatory purview. Daughety has shown how such constraints may provide an umbrella – expanding the output of high-cost firms, while allowing a dominant firm with scale economies to restrict output. Thus, the potential for distortion is associated with all of the regulatory instruments examined.

### Appendix

We can obtain additional insight into the firm's expected profit-maximization problem when subject to a chance constraint on its rate of return by returning to (9.38) in the text. When (9.38) holds, the firm overcapitalizes; when the equality is reversed, the firm undercapitalizes; when the bracketed term is zero, the firm is efficient. Therefore, the values of $\partial u'/\partial K$ and $\partial u''/\partial K$ are crucial to the presence of an input bias. From Figure 9.8 we can see that $u'$ and $u''$ are determined by the intersection of the dashed line and the iso-rate-of-return locus. Also, as $\overline{K}$ changes, $\partial u'/\partial K$ is positive, while $\partial u''/\partial K$ may be positive or negative, depending on the position of $\overline{K}$. More generally, these terms can be examined as follows. Recalling the definition of $h(u : p, K)$, the implicit-function theorem can be used to obtain

$$
\begin{aligned}
\frac{\partial u}{\partial K} &= \frac{\partial h}{\partial K} \bigg/ \frac{\partial h}{\partial u} \\
&= \left( h + w \frac{\partial L(q, K)}{\partial K} \right) \bigg/ \left[ \frac{\partial q}{\partial u} \left( p - w \frac{\partial L(q, K)}{\partial q} \right) \right]
\end{aligned}
\tag{9A.1}
$$

Assume that $u'$ and $u''$ exist and that a unique interior extremum for $h$ exists at $u^*$ such that $u' < u^* < u''$. From (9.33) in the text, this extremum occurs where price equals marginal cost, so that the denominator of (9A.1) is zero when evaluated at $u^*$, but nonzero otherwise. Thus, evaluating (9A.1) at $u'$ and $u''$ implies (1) a nonzero denominator and (2) $h = s$, by definition of $u'$ and $u''$. Therefore, (9.38) in the text may be written as

$$
\frac{s + w \dfrac{\partial L(q(p, u'), K)}{\partial K}}{\dfrac{\partial q}{\partial u} \left( p - w \dfrac{\partial L(q(p, u'), K)}{\partial q} \right)} f(u')
$$

$$
- \frac{s + w \dfrac{\partial L(q(p, u''), K)}{\partial K}}{\dfrac{\partial q}{\partial u} \left( p - w \dfrac{\partial L(q(p, u), K)}{\partial q} \right)} f(u'')
\tag{9A.2}
$$

Noting that $\partial q/\partial u = X(p)$, so that this term can be factored out, and after simplifying notation, (9A.2) is rewritten as

$$\frac{s + wL'_K}{p - wL'_q} f(u') - \frac{s + wL''_K}{p - wL''_q} f(u'') \qquad (9A.3)$$

The denominators in the fractions in (9A.3) indicate that the input bias depends on the difference between marginal revenue and marginal cost when actual output is $X(p)u'$ and $X(p)u''$. The numerators indicate that the A-J effect depends on the difference between the actual marginal rate of technical substitution and the ratio $s/w$ when actual output is $X(p)u'$ and $X(p)u''$. Of course, when actual output is $X(p)u'$ or $X(p)u''$, the firm is making exactly the allowed rate of return. Also, the fractions are weighted by $f(u')$ and $f(u'')$, the values of the density function when the firm is making exactly the allowed rate of return.

# 10

# Technological change under regulation

The resource-allocation issues considered so far have taken the technology as given; so the regulated natural monopoly has had no choice in the nature of its production function. However, some of the most important policy issues of the day involve incentives for innovative activity by natural monopolies and how regulation affects the pace and pattern of technological change. Although there are no simple answers in such matters, a number of models have been developed that offer insights into how the incentives facing the regulated firm help determine the introduction of new products, the tendency to improve the quality of various production inputs, and the rate of cost reduction.

First, we need to characterize technological change and identify the firm's decision variables and the instruments available to regulators. Because the sources and impacts of innovation have been surveyed by Kamien and Schwartz (1982), Section 10.1 provides only a brief review of how the characteristics of new knowledge complicate the analysis of its production and application. Then we examine the impact of competitive pressures on the incentive to engage in research and development (R&D). In addition, because cooperative ventures are significant suppliers of innovations in electricity and telecommunications, we consider how regulatory policies affect these joint R&D activities. Section 10.2 presents a model of cost-reducing R&D programs. The model allows us to examine the interrelationships among technological opportunities, regulatory lag, and R&D activity.

Specifying the precise nature of the technological changes underlying cost reductions allows additional inferences regarding the potential impacts of regulation. After exploring how regulated and unregulated firms respond to factor-augmenting technological change in Section 10.3, the degree of factor augmentation is made endogenous, so that firms choose the nature of the technological change. In Section 10.4, issues associated with multiproduct natural monopolies are explored, including regulatory impacts on the price and pattern of innovation. Section 10.5 discusses different institutional features of regulation that affect the development and adoption of new technologies. Finally, Section 10.6 provides a summary of the chapter.

## 10.1. **Characteristics of technological change**

Just as regulatory activity can be explained in terms of the supply and demand for regulation, innovative activity can be viewed as resulting from the interaction of supply and demand for innovations. Figure 10.1 depicts the factors influencing the supply of inventive activity and the determinants of its demand.[1] The various boxes in the figure represent aspects of the innovation process, with steps 1, 3, and 6 showing how the state of the industry drives the demand for inventive activity. The expected profit from a particular invention provides a strong incentive to devote resources to the project. Ceteris paribus, a given cost reduction will be worth more in a large, growing industry than in a small, stagnant industry. Of course, the net profitability depends on the cost of R&D activity, which in turn is a function of R&D input prices (box 2) and the state of scientific knowledge (box 4). Until fundamental scientific and engineering relationships are understood, technical breakthroughs are likely to be

---

1 Here, we take "inventive activity" to be synonymous with R&D; however, much cost-reducing activity is performed in the context of production – ways to save resources are identified and applied by workers. We focus on inventive inputs and outputs, but the principles apply to other programs as well.

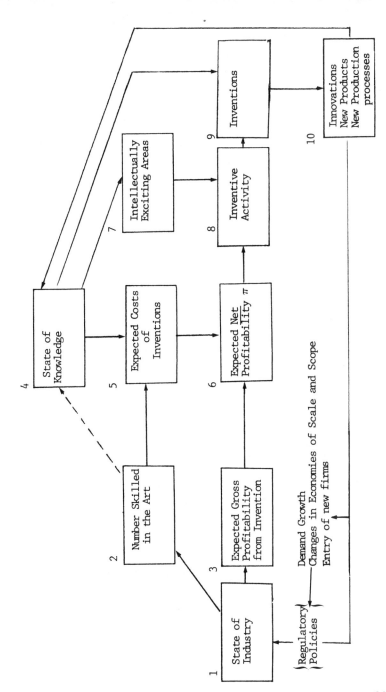

Figure 10.1. Determinants of inventive activity (adapted from Schmookler, 1962).

very costly. Note that fundamental advances in scientific knowledge are not likely to arise from market-driven activity, partly because of absence of patent protection. Thus, the funding for basic research comes primarily from governments, and that research generally is performed at universities and research institutes.

Some inventive activity arises because the particular field of research is intellectually exciting (box 7). However, most applied research arises in the pursuit of profit, taking into account the cost of R&D. Additional heavy expenditures accompany the scaling-up and prototype testing required prior to the introduction of the new production process or commercial product. Whether the invention is due to deliberate investment activity or is only incidental to other activities, and whether it is compatible or incompatible with previous technologies, not all inventions are exploited. Product-demand conditions, as well as current and expected relative input prices, may make additional development expenditures uneconomic. Thus, even if the pattern of new technological information is exogenous, the innovation-selection process involves economic decisions.

### *Technological information and efficiency*

Regulatory policies influence the inventive activity of the natural monopolist through incentive effects. Pricing and other policies also influence the R&D behavior of potential entrants into the industry and the behavior of input-supplying industries. Chapter 7 examined the sustainability issues associated with potential entrants. The recommended policy of entry restrictions to protect the multiproduct natural monopolist with nonsustainable price vectors promotes allocative efficiency. However, that policy may conflict with the goal of innovative efficiency if promising avenues of R&D are left unexplored because of reduced rivalry. The focus here is on the natural monopolist's incentives to innovate, but these can be related to the incentives for an external firm supplying a cost-reducing invention to the regulated firm.

Regulated industries depend on both internal and external R&D for the promotion of technological change. For example, a substantial amount of the R&D that promotes technological change in regulated industries is funded by input-suppliers, such as General Electric (GE) developing new electricity-generating units to be sold to the industry. On the other hand, vertical integration has characterized much of telecommunications, with Western Electric manufacturing the equipment embodying new technologies for AT&T and its regional subsidiaries. These technologies, such as the transistor, were developed at Bell Laboratories. In general, technological opportunities, developmental capabilities, and the profit incentives established by regulators will influence the level and mix of inventive activity by the suppliers of technology. From the standpoint of consumers, innovative efficiency (reflected in the rate of technological change) represents a key indicator of performance.[2]

Since Arrow's classic discussion (1962) of resource allocation for invention, economists have tried to determine how various market structures promote innovative efficiency by influencing the level and mix of R&D. Arrow argued that efficient production and dissemination were complicated by three aspects of new technological information: risk, appropriability, and indivisibilities. The first characteristic, risk, also applies to other investments, but the capacity to bear risk (or diversify against acceptable losses) varies across firms and organizations. In the case of natural monopolies, regulation itself can be a major source of uncertainty. Furthermore, whereas regulation may reduce downside risk, it also tends to eliminate gains from successful R&D, unless regulatory lag is substantial.

The appropriability problem results because once a new idea is

---

2 Here, we view "inventions" simply as a subset of all technical discoveries that are characterized as being patentable. The first actual commercial application is an important phase in the implementation of new technological information and is labeled "innovation." Technological change, then, can be a change in the coefficients of production (relating inputs to outputs) resulting from a *discrete* Schumpeterian innovation or from *continuous* minor resource savings.

available, others may be able to benefit from it without compensating the discoverer. This externality dampens the incentive to engage in inventive activity in both regulated and unregulated industries. Although the patent system exists to correct this problem, there still can be "free-riders" who benefit from a discovery. Even without violating a patent, other firms can gain useful information from the inventing firm. Without compensation, less R&D will be performed by firms than otherwise. If the potential gainers would have been willing to pay for the "lost" discoveries, then we can say that there was underinvestment in innovation.

The third characteristic affecting R&D is the indivisibility of information, which implies that once information has been discovered, it is socially inefficient to withhold it from others: The incremental cost of letting others use it is zero, while the benefits they receive are positive. Thus, some form of collective funding of R&D projects may make sense, especially if the results are expected to have wide applicability and could reduce the costs of a group of firms. However, rivalry can increase the benefits to "being first" – thus encouraging R&D. The case for joint R&D organizations is stronger if the firms do not compete with one another, so that cooperative R&D cannot dampen competitive incentives to beat out rivals. Regulators need to take these characteristics of new technological information into account when establishing incentives for R&D.

### Size and R&D performance

Another issue is the relationship between the size of the firm and the cost of conducting R&D (box 5, Figure 10.1). If R&D scale economies associated with research laboratories are significant, innovative efficiency may require either mergers or joint R&D activity. An example of the latter is the Electric Power Research Institute (EPRI), with an annual budget of $250 million, supported by individual utilities. EPRI performs a significant proportion of the total R&D funded by electric utilities in the United States. Similarly, after the 1983 AT&T divestiture, about 14 percent of Bell Laboratories' employees were transferred to Bellcore; funding came from the former Bell (regional) operating companies. With an annual budget exceeding $900 million in 1986 (Noll, 1987), a cooperative organization like Bellcore represents a major commitment of resources to R&D. One important policy question is whether or not EPRI and Bellcore will survive new competitive pressures within their respective industries. US West has questioned its Bellcore relationship, partly because the group research has not yielded technologies that would give that firm a unique advantage in the new competitive environment. As of early 1987, Bellcore planned to have proprietary projects supported by and benefiting individual firms – forestalling withdrawals from this R&D joint venture.

Divestiture created a smaller AT&T, with assets dropping from $148 billion in 1982 to $40 billion in 1984. The loss of the regional holding companies reduced revenues from $65 billion to $33 billion over that period (excluding $21 billion collected and paid as access charges in 1984). M. Noll (1987) reports that the reduction in size has actually been associated with an increase in R&D. The Bell Labs budget was $2.02 billion in 1984, and total AT&T expenditures for R&D rose to $2.37 billion in 1985. Competitive pressures plus the desire to enter new markets have stimulated R&D, although it appears to be more applications-oriented than in the past. It will be years before we will be able to have a comprehensive evaluation of size, R&D performance, and deregulation in telecommunications.

Studies relating individual firm size to inventive activity and innovative outcomes have attempted to determine whether larger or smaller research laboratories tend to promote technological advance in particular industries. For example, Wilder and Stansell (1974) showed that R&D expenditures by electric utilities rose rapidly with size. On the other hand, Link (1978) purported to show a negative relationship between R&D activity by electric utilities and the size of the firm. He found that R&D divided by operating revenue fell off beyond a fairly modest size ($142 million in operating revenue for 1972). This finding could have important policy implications, because it could lead one to "advocate normalizing firms to this optimal size." However, his sample consisted of relatively small firms, because it was limited to those that had only fossil-fuel generation; he omitted many larger firms with nuclear generating units, which were responsible for a substantial share of the R&D expenditures by electric utilities. In another empirical analysis, Delaney and Honeycutt (1976) used a larger sample, and their findings supported the earlier study by Wilder and Stansell. Forty-one firms (some with operating revenues of over $1 billion) were added to the initial sample of 12 in the large-size class. These additions suggest that the maximum size of $360 million in the Link sample is not representative of the industry, thus bringing into question his results.

Of course, R&D expenditures are only the means to an end. Policy-makers are ultimately interested in the innovations (cost reductions and quality improvements) stemming from these expenditures. Research on this topic has been sparse. In the area of electric utilities, the effectiveness of R&D was investigated by Smith (1974), who concluded that technological productivity and firm size were inversely related, but more work will be needed to estimate indices of innovative output. In the area of telecommunications, the basic and applied research associated with Bell Labs in the past has been viewed by many as stemming from the scale of activity and a natural monopoly position of AT&T in long-distance communications. The post-divestiture alterations in the Bell Labs R&D program are sources of concern to many industry observers. Others view the growth of multiple centers of initiative as promoting even more technological change. They note the difficulty of determining the relative contributions of technological opportunities and market structures to rapid technological advances in telecommunications.

### Market structure and innovation

The debate whether monopoly or competitive market structures will yield appropriate investments in developing new production technologies and new products is of some relevance to how regulation affects innovative activity. We have to understand the incentives in the absence of regulation and then determine how regulation affects (1) the risk associated with successful and unsuccessful projects, (2) the ability to capture the gains to innovation when entry is prohibited, and (3) the cost of R&D under various alternative treatments of outlays.

Earlier discussions that were directed at ascertaining whether monopoly leads to more research than do competitive environments were limited in two critical respects. First, they failed to distinguish between competition in the existing product market and competition in R&D. Second, they failed to recognize that the market structure itself (box 1 of Figure 10.1) was an endogenous variable. Thus, a natural monopoly can influence both the inventive activity of potential entrants and its own production function.

Dasgupta and Stiglitz (1980) studied the nature and consequences of competition in R&D and the relationship between this form of competition and competition in the product market. They focused on comparisons among the timing (speed) of research, the efficiency in R&D (as determined by the number of independent research laboratories), and the level of risk undertaken. Four issues were addressed:

1. the effect of the product-market structure on R&D activity
2. the effects of competition in R&D on the level of research
3. the impact of R&D competition on product-market competition
4. the determinants of the number of firms (laboratories) engaged in R&D at any given time

Their findings indicate the strengths and limitations of competition and monopoly. For example, if the existing product market is dominated by a monopolist, there is likely to be more R&D than there would be if the product-market structure were competitive; the reason is simply that after an invention, there still will be less competition and therefore more profits for the sup-

plier of the innovation. Their conclusion that monopoly stimu-
lates R&D depends on whether or not the successful inventor can
enter the output market (Romano, 1987). Of course, competition
in R&D leads to more research than does the presence of only a
single supplier of R&D. With free entry, expected average returns
must equal average costs, leading to a potential divergence
between marginal benefits and marginal costs. Thus, competition
may result in *excessive* expenditures on R&D relative to the
social optimum, even with partial appropriation of returns.

The impact of R&D competition on product-market competition depends on potential entry. If there are no barriers to entry
in the R&D activity, R&D competition can be expected to lead
to entry of new firms into the product market, thereby reducing
the duration of monopoly power. Nevertheless, under certain
conditions, a monopoly may persist. If the R&D technology is
also available to the existing product-market monopolist, he can
adopt an entry-deterrent strategy. The incentive of potential
entrants to engage in R&D is reduced if the monopolist speeds
up his research program. Under these circumstances, monopolies
will not be short-lived, although the threat of competition may
lead the monopolist to engage in significantly more research than
he would otherwise. AT&T's speedup of microwave-relay
research in the early 1950s fits this conclusion of Dasgupta and
Stiglitz. They also underscore the crucial role played by uncertainty in determining the number of firms engaged in R&D.
Within their model, only one firm will engage in R&D under certainty, whereas uncertainty with respect to the results of R&D
can induce several firms into the R&D market.

Whether there is an insufficient or an excessive number of
research units depends critically on the product's elasticity of
demand, which determines the ratio between private profits and
social returns. A relatively elastic market demand implies relatively higher social returns to the price cut accompanying a cost-
reducing innovation. The demand elasticity also affects the size
of the invention. Dasgupta and Stiglitz bring into question the

view that competition in R&D is a substitute for competition in the product market, or that it will eventually give rise to competition in the product market. The contestable-market framework offers some promise for extensions along these lines.

Regulated markets do not always fit neatly into the Dasgupta–Stiglitz framework. Typically (at least under rate-of-return regulation), we have a single supplier; yet there may be competition in R&D among input-suppliers. Two factors complicate this story: regulatory lag and treatment of intercompany sales (for a vertically integrated firm with an R&D/manufacturer component). As we shall see, incentives for engaging in innovative activity can be reduced to zero in certain circumstances.

Also, if the regulated firm is a monopsonist (the only buyer of innovative output), it will purchase too little of the new equipment in which the new technology is embodied. The combination of this possibility plus entry restrictions in the output market reduces incentives for innovation by the input-supplier. On the other hand, if the innovation removes the justification for regulation, and regulators permit entry, then incentives remain for input-suppliers to invest in R&D, supply entrants, or become entrants.

In addition, a dramatic innovation may create a natural monopoly. If regulation occurs, for the reasons discussed in Chapter 8, it can reduce the rents to the innovation if the short-run interests of consumers are served. Alternatively, regulation can increase the rents if the innovator is protected from subsequent entry. Thus, the incentive to conduct R&D is affected by the likelihood and nature of post-invention regulation.

Schumpeterian technological advances may create new products, new production processes, and new markets – all of which may remove the justification for regulation. Furthermore, substitute products may alter demand elasticities, thus limiting the market power of a natural monopolist. Also, new production technologies may reduce scale economies, making entry feasible. As new markets are developed, more firms of large scale can be sustained, limiting the market power of existing firms. The disruptive nature of innovation complicates the task of regulators.

The question facing regulators is how to structure incentives to take advantage of scientific and technological opportunities. Without some regulatory lag, the utility's reward structure would seem to be asymmetrical: A poor decision (ex post) is punished, but a good decision (e.g., one that reduces cost) is not rewarded. Even early adoption of cost-reducing technology involves some risks. Clearly, regulatory treatment of R&D expenses will influence the utility's behavior. Two major issues arise: (1) incentives for R&D by the natural monopoly, once regulated, and (2) incentives for R&D by potential entrants. The next two sections develop models for examining the first issue, but we do not explore the impact of regulation on potential entrants.

### 10.2. Incentives for cost-reducing innovative activity

Let us turn to incentives for a firm to reduce its cost through R&D investments, without considering the relative reductions in input usage yielding the resource savings. The model, developed by Bailey (1978), draws from the theory of optimal patent life, wherein the patent establishes a lag between the time of the invention and the time that rivals can imitate the new technology. The patent provides an incentive for the performance of R&D. In Bailey's model, the profit-maximizing firm faces known opportunities for cost reduction, and the patent lag is replaced by the regulatory lag. The latter is an instrument for promoting innovation.

#### Cost reduction and regulatory lag

Bailey characterizes a single-product firm as investing in cost-reducing activity and earning excess profits until regulators require that output price be equal to average cost. Thus, the assumed regulatory behavior is along the lines of Joskow's characterization: The price ceiling and the lag are the instruments under regulatory control. Bailey assumes that R&D costs must be covered by revenues greater than production costs; so a zero

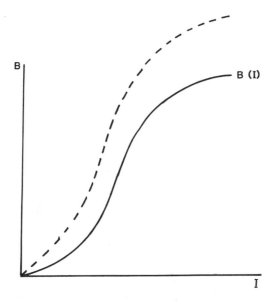

Figure 10.2. Cost reduction and innovative outputs.

lag leads to zero incentives for R&D. If the firm is forced to reduce price as soon as costs fall, then the firm cannot ever cover the cost of R&D.

Alternatively, if R&D is viewed as a risky activity whose precise outcome is uncertain, then regulators may disallow expenditures on unsuccessful R&D projects when establishing revenue requirements. Gains from successful projects are passed on to consumers after some regulatory lag. Under either interpretation, shorter lags lead to less R&D. An important feature of the model is the relationship between innovational outlays and the associated cost reduction. Figure 10.2 shows increasing and then diminishing returns to R&D. R&D is depicted here as innovative inputs, $I$; the investment has a total payoff to the firm measured on the vertical axis by $B$. Bailey postulates a situation in which a firm makes expenditures on innovation ($cI$, where $c$ is the per-unit cost of innovative inputs). These outlays lower costs by $B(I)$,

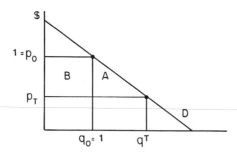

Figure 10.3. Impacts of a cost reduction.

where the benefit to the firm is a function of $I$. Initial price and output are normalized to unity, so that $B(I)$ corresponds to the cost saving per time period. The market demand and illustrative cost reduction are depicted in Figure 10.3.

Constant marginal cost equals 1 prior to the innovation and falls by $B$ afterward. A discount rate or $r$ is used to compare present with future dollars. At time $T$, regulators set price ($p_T$) equal to the new marginal cost; so no positive profit is earned after this point. The firm has as its goal the maximization of the present value of its net revenue stream, where the term to be integrated in equation (10.1a) is the cost saving per unit of time, and the investment in the innovation ($cI$) is subtracted from these savings:

$$\max_{I} V = \int_{0}^{T} \{p_0 - [p_0 - B(I)]\}q_0 e^{-rt}\, dt - cI \quad (10.1a)$$

Note from (10.1a) that if $T = 0$, then $I = 0$: There is no incentive to invest in innovation if there is no time lag. We normalize by setting $p_0 = q_0 = 1$. Thus,

$$V = \int_{0}^{T} B(I)e^{-rt}\, dt - cI$$

$$= \left(\frac{1}{r}\right)(1 - e^{-rT})B(I) - cI = 0$$

Differentiating $V$ to find the maximum with respect to changes in innovative investment ($I$), we obtain

$$\frac{dV}{dI} = V' = \frac{1}{r}(1 - e^{-rT})B'(I) - c = 0 \qquad (10.2)$$

The firm's value is maximized when the present value of a stream of $B'(I)$ dollars just equals the marginal cost of additional investment, $c$. $B'(I)$ is the marginal-value product of additional investment in $I$. The additional cost savings are captured by the firm until time $T$; then price is forced to $p_T$ by the regulators. At this point, the firm loses $B$, but consumers gain $A + B$, shown in Figure 10.3.

Assuming that second-order sufficient conditions for a maximum are satisfied, so that $B'' < 0$, we can determine the impact on the optimum $I$ from a change in parameters by totally differentiating (10.2) with respect to $I$ and $T$, setting the resulting equation to zero, and rearranging. We obtain

$$\frac{dI}{dT} = \frac{-re^{-rT}B'}{(1 - e^{-rT})B''} > 0 \qquad (10.3)$$

As the lag increases, additional investment in innovation occurs. By totally differentiating (10.2) with respect to $I$ and $r$, the impact of a change in the discount rate is

$$\frac{dI}{dr} = \frac{[1 - (1 + rT)e^{-rT}]B'}{r(1 - e^{-rT})B''} < 0 \qquad (10.4)$$

A higher interest rate decreases investment. Similarly, higher costs of inventive input reduce the quantity of R&D:

$$\frac{dI}{dc} = \frac{r}{(1 - e^{-rT})B''} < 0 \qquad (10.5)$$

Furthermore, Bailey shows how the shape of the $B(I)$ function affects innovation. For example, the dotted line in Figure 10.2 represents an increase in the ease of innovation. If $B(I) = ib(I)$, where $i$ is an ease-of-innovation parameter, then

$$\frac{dI}{di} = \frac{-b'}{ib''} > 0 \qquad (10.6)$$

That is, a larger $i$ results in greater innovation.

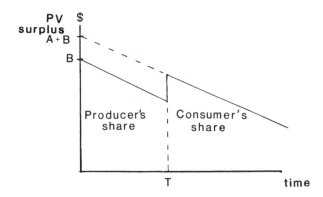

Figure 10.4. Time pattern of surplus.

The trade-off facing regulators is illustrated in Figure 10.4. The firm captures the cost reduction until time $T$; thereafter, consumers gain the benefit ($A + B$) of a lower price. The question is what the regulator's objective function looks like. The firm is already maximizing its portion of the perpetuity of $B$ (less the present cost $cI$); so Bailey takes the regulatory objective function as the discounted flow of benefits to consumers: $A + B$ after $T$. As will be seen shortly, this formulation takes the firm to be a follower in a Stackelberg duopoly problem, which implies that other behavioral assumptions could be used that would result in a different choice of $T$. The firm maximizes its net revenue stream over $I$ given time $T$, and the regulator maximizes the discounted flow of benefits to consumers over $T$, given innovation $I$:

$$\max_T W = \int_T^\infty \{B[I(T)] + A[I(T)]\}e^{-rt}\, dt$$
$$= (1/r)\{B[I(T)] + A[I(T)]\}e^{-rT} \tag{10.7}$$

The first-order condition for problem (10.7) is

$$W' = -r(B + A) + (B' + A')\frac{dI}{dT} = 0$$

Another comparative-statics analysis shows how regulators change $T$ in response to parameter changes in the discount rate

($r$), the ease of innovation ($i$), and the elasticity of demand. For example, as $r$ increases, the firm spends less on innovative inputs; so $T$ needs to be increased to maximize welfare. The associated gain in resource savings more than outweighs the reduction in benefits arising from delaying consumer gains. Also, when innovation becomes easier, the regulator can reduce the lag and still achieve high marginal benefits. Similarly, as demand becomes more elastic, area $A$ becomes larger, and the additional deadweight loss that accompanies longer lags (greater $T$) becomes greater.

### Regulator–firm interaction

The assumption in Bailey's model that regulators set the lag and firms respond to it implies very naive firm behavior. Wendel (1976) argues that the regulatory lag is not exogenous to the firm. Rather, the firm's actions influence regulatory behavior. Thus, the problem moves from profit maximization subject to a constraint to a problem involving game-theoretic concepts. Because the firm can influence regulatory lag, the chosen level of cost-reducing effort becomes dependent on the strategies followed by the two players. In Wendel's extension, a firm influences regulatory lag through its choice of R&D expenditures ($cI$) and through bargaining with the regulator.

As depicted in Figure 10.5, zero profit follows from zero lag and zero R&D. Zero profit also can occur with a positive lag, $T$, if R&D outlays are large enough. For a higher level of profits, say $\pi_1 > 0$, at lower levels of $cI$, the benefits from the cost savings must outweigh the cost of innovation. At low levels of investment, an increase in $I$ must be accompanied by a decrease in $T$ to hold $\pi = \pi_1$. However, at higher levels of R&D outlays, due to diminishing returns, the cost of additional innovative outputs outweighs the benefit; so an increase in $cI$ will require a longer regulatory lag to keep the firm on a given level of profit. The minimum point on each of the higher isoprofit curves lies successively to the right, because higher profits mean that at relatively higher $cI$, the benefits of incremental R&D cease to outweigh the incremental cost.

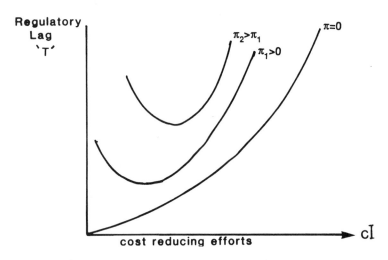

Figure 10.5. Isoprofit map.

The regulator's task is again taken to be maximization of welfare measured by the sum of producers' profits and consumer surplus. We can define various combinations of $cI$ and $T$ for which consumer surplus is constant. Consumer surplus will rise with increased R&D because the cost reduction is greater. To keep levels of consumer surplus constant, the lag, $T$, must be increased. Figure 10.6 depicts the isobenefit map. For a given $T$, surplus increases for larger $cI$. The slope reflects the fact that cost decreases involve diminishing returns. For a given combination of $T$ and firm investment, if $T$ were to increase, a proportionally larger outlay on R&D would be required to bring the present value of consumer surplus back to the initial level.

From isoprofit and isosurplus curves we can derive isowelfare curves. Point $f$ in Figure 10.7 identifies the maximum level of profits that can be achieved for a given level of consumer surplus, $A + B$. However, the level of welfare ($W$) associated with $f$ can also be achieved by other combinations of $T$ and $cI$. The isosurplus line passing through $f$ cannot be in the shaded area of Figure 10.7, because both profits and consumer surplus are lower than at $f$. The isowelfare curve is concave from below and lies inside

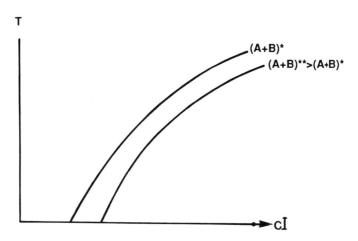

Figure 10.6. Isobenefit map.

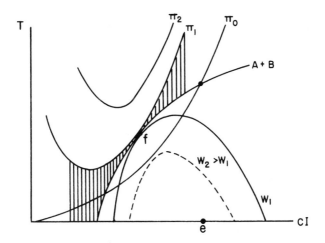

Figure 10.7. Isosurplus map.

the consumer-surplus curve. There is a family of welfare curves that increase in value as they converge on *e*.

Wendel combines the previous three figures into one figure, and the result is Figure 10.8. The locus $0A$ is obtained by joining the minimum points of the isoprofit curves, and the locus $De$ is

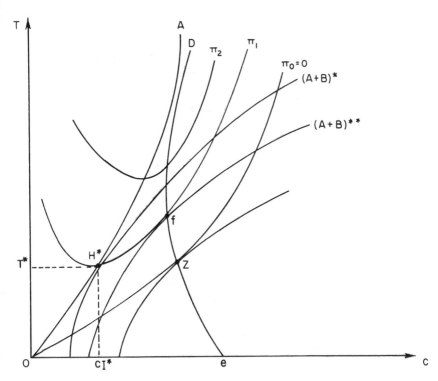

Figure 10.8. Firm–regulator interaction.

obtained by joining the points of tangency between the isosurplus curve and the isoprofit curve. The $0A$ curve is the combination of points representing the Cournot reaction function of the firm. It shows the profit-maximizing levels of R&D chosen, given the regulatory lag. Thus, it represents the Cournot equilibrium points.

Let us assume that the length of lag chosen by the regulator is $T^*$; then the firm chooses the level $cI^*$ to maximize its profits, which results in point $H$. This outcome (from the Bailey framework) yields $(A + B)^*$ as the level of consumer surplus. Given $0A$, point $H^*$ represents the highest point of welfare. But if we allow bargaining between the firm and regulator, Pareto improvements are possible. Consider point *f* in Figure 10.8. This point has the same profit level for the firm as at *H,* but the benefits to consumers increase to $(A + B)^{**}$ (i.e., the move from *H* to *f* represents a Pareto improvement). Wendel argues that with firm–regulator interaction, the level of R&D will be chosen along curve *De,* which represents Pareto-optimal combinations of regulatory lag and inventive investments. Which particular allocation is chosen depends on the bargaining powers of the two parties. The bliss point *e* is welfare-maximizing, but leaves the firm with negative profit. Point *Z* involves zero profit, with consumers covering the cost of R&D.

Note that this formulation assumes that regulators will not just allow any amount of R&D as an allowed cost – like fuel costs. First cost-reducing effort may be unobservable to the regulator – while it represents an added burden to managers. Managerial utility is then taken to be a function of firm profits and effort, with the latter being a negative factor. In addition, the issue of commitment arises within the bargaining model, because the firm might question whether or not the commission will follow through on the sharing of realized surplus gains.

### Markup regulation and cost-saving technologies

In some settings, price regulation can delay the introduction of cost-saving technologies. Sweeney (1981) develops a model in which the firm produces a nonstorable product, with the price set by the regulator. In the Sweeney model, unlike the Joskow and Bailey approaches, at the start of each time period, price is set equal to the average cost of the previous period plus a markup, which can be plus or minus. The firm is required to meet the demand at the fixed price. The model is not used to address the question of incentive to invest in cost-reducing activity. Rather, Sweeney examines the speed with which a technological innovation is actually adopted by a firm under markup regulation.

At the beginning of period 0, a costless innovation appears

that, if adopted, will lower the cost of production throughout the relevant output range. If the firm takes full advantage of the innovation immediately, and demand is unchanged from the previous period, then profit is earned in excess of that earned previously. At the next rate review, the lower costs are identified, and a new markup price is established. Partial adoption of the innovation would yield lower profit in period 0, but would result in the possibility of greater profits in periods 1 and 2.

Turning to Figure 10.9(a), we find the regulated firm producing $q_0$, with average cost $AC_0 = C(q_0)/q_0$. Price, $p_0$, reflects a markup of $m$ ($>1$) over average cost. The example uses constant returns to scale to illustrate the impact of a one-period lag on the firm's incentives to adopt a cost-saving technology, which lowers average cost to $AC_1 = C(q_1)/q_1$. If the firm totally adopts the innovation in period 0, it earns profit ($P_0CBA$) that period and earns the standard "markup profit" ($P_1FEA$) in period 1, when the markup is applied to the new average cost.

A different outcome arises if the firm partially adopts the innovation in period 0. Assume that the production cost for any output level can be reduced to anywhere between the cost at which there is zero implementation and the cost at which there is total implementation of the innovation. Let the average cost of partial implementation be $\frac{1}{2}(AC_0 + AC_1)$. Now, the firm earns profits ($P_0CIH$) in period 0, as seen in panel (b). It is still allowed a relatively high markup price in period 1 (at the beginning of which, complete adoption of the innovation occurs). Thus, profit is $P_1KJA$ in period 1. Finally, the standard markup is applied to historical costs in period 2, and profit drops to $P_2FEA$.

Depending on the length of the regulatory review period and the discount rates, the delayed-adoption scenario may maximize the present value of profits. Thus, under markup regulation, regulatory lag (allowing one period of excess profits) can actually retard the adoption of new technologies relative to the optimal timing. Note that even with a one-period lag, the markup-regulated firm has no incentive to innovate if demand is inelastic, because profits would be lower after the innovation. The partial-

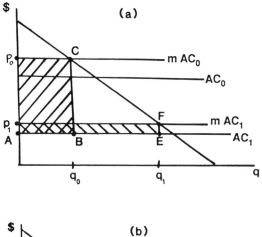

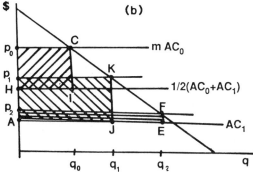

Figure 10.9. Phasing-in a cost-saving innovation under markup pricing.

implementation scenario could actually encourage R&D, because the payoff to innovation can be greater than with immediate, complete implementation. Of course, the regulator is extremely myopic in this model, neither rewarding nor penalizing firms for productivity advance.

The Bailey and Sweeney models both illustrate how lags and the nature of regulation affect incentives for innovation. Neither of the models explores whether or not the nature of technological change is affected by regulation. Nor do they examine how alternative treatments of R&D and depreciation affect incentives for innovation. The next section turns to the first question.

## 10.3. **Input bias and induced technological change**

So far, the models have focused on production-cost reductions without specifying the nature of the associated changes in the underlying production function. Here, we specify the implications of the technological change for the input mix. Not surprisingly, rate-of-return regulation is shown to influence the direction of technological change under certain assumptions.

### *The nature of technological change*

Technological change has many features worthy of analysis. It can be continuous or discontinuous, patentable or nonpatentable; it can involve a cost reduction or the introduction of a new product; it can be embodied in particular inputs or can affect the productivity of all inputs. Given the vast literature on the subject and the narrowness of our focus, we shall not attempt to examine exhaustively every combination and permutation of the preceding features. We do note, however, the highly stylized nature of these characterizations. In practice, any new technological development is likely to involve a blend of these features.

When technological change reduces the cost of production, this alters the parameters of the production function.[3] Four characteristics that can be changed are (1) elasticity of substitution, (2) input intensity, (3) returns to scale, and (4) efficiency. First, changes in the relative ease of input substitution along a given isoquant can save resources – as when a fixed-factor-proportions technology becomes variable proportions. Second, for a given input price ratio, the equilibrium capital–labor ratio can change. Third, returns to scale can increase – increasing output for any

---

3 The literature on production functions is substantial, and the functions have been estimated for many utilities. In Section 9.3, for example, they were used to test for the existence of A-J impacts.

given input combination. Fourth, the overall efficiency of resource utilization can increase. Technological change can alter any of these parameters for a firm, leading to lower cost for a given output.

### Factor-augmenting technological progress

Innovations have been labeled labor- or capital-augmenting, depending on whether $a_1$ or $a_2$ changes in the production function

$$q = f(a_1 L, a_2 K)$$

Such changes increase the "effective" labor and capital, respectively.[4] Thus, $a_1 L$ can be interpreted as the quality-adjusted labor input, with total costs equal to $wL + rK$. Changes in $a_1$ and $a_2$ affect output via the production function. We assume that the change is disembodied; that is, it applies to all units of capital and/or labor. A labor-augmenting technical change increases $a_1$, so that at the given input price ratio, the capital–labor ratio increases (for an elasticity of substitution less than 1). After such a change, a higher share of total cost will be accounted for by capital. Thus, one can see the potential link between some regu-

---

4 Technical change has been classified according to a number of schemes (Kamien and Schwartz, 1982). Hicks (1932) defined labor- and capital-saving changes on the basis of whether the relative labor share decreased or increased, holding the original factor supplies fixed. Solow (1957) and Harrod (1961) used other criteria for evaluating the neutrality of technical change. The factor-augmentation framework has the following equivalency. Labor-augmenting technical progress is Hicks labor-saving if the elasticity of substitution is less than 1. Note that for the neoclassical production function, $q(t) = f(K(t), L(t))$, the rate of technical change at time $t$ is conventionally measured as follows:
$$R = \frac{dq/dt}{q} - \alpha_K \frac{dK/dt}{K} - \alpha_L \frac{dL/dt}{L}$$
where $\alpha_K$ and $\alpha_L$ are the elasticities of output with respect to capital and labor, respectively. If $q(t) = f(a_1(t)K(t), L(t))$, then $da_1(t)/a_1(t)$ is the rate of capital augmentation, and $\alpha_K(da_1(t)/dt)/a_1(t)$ is the rate of technical change. See Brown (1966) for a thorough discussion of theoretical and empirical issues associated with technological change. The use of $R$ in calculating price caps is discussed further in Section 12.4.

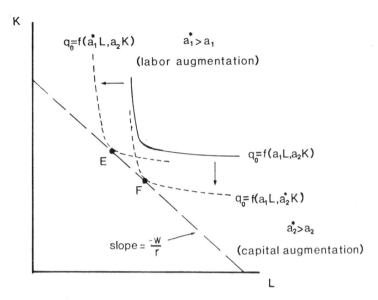

Figure 10.10. Factor-augmenting technological changes.

latory incentives and choices between "comparable" innovations. Referring to the isoquants pictured in Figure 10.10, suppose that the firm is initially operating on isoquant $q_0 = f(a_1L, a_2K)$. If an unregulated firm had a choice between labor-augmenting and capital-augmenting technological change, that is, a choice between points $E$ and $F,$ it would be indifferent. For the given input prices, production costs would be the same (but lower than initially). However, for an A-J rate-base-regulated firm, with the allowed rate of return ($s$) greater than the cost of capital ($r$), the incentive to overcapitalize carries over to the adoption of labor-augmenting innovations.

In the first comprehensive examination of the effects of technological change on the regulated firm, Westfield (1971) considers the effects of technological progress on the firm's use of inputs and on its profits. He examines how three types of regulation affect a firm's incentives to adopt different types of exogenously determined technological advances. Under ceiling-price regulations, the firm maximizes profits subject to $p \leq m$. With markup regulation, $R \leq h(rK + wL)$, where $h > 1$. The rate-of-return constraint is the third type of regulation explored by Westfield, and it has already been discussed. In the absence of uncertainty, firms initially choose efficient input mixes for the first two types of regulation, but with $s > r$, an A-J bias holds for the third, and so the firm is initially overcapitalized. Westfield then considers how firms adjust to exogenously given technological change. For "neutral" advances ($a_1^*/a_2^* = a_1/a_2$), the three types of regulation yield different outcomes.

Ceiling-price (or price-cap) regulation permits the firm to capture the entire cost saving, providing an incentive for adopting the innovation; this result is in keeping with Bailey's model, in which the regulatory lag is infinite. Westfield asserts that capital-input-suppliers will have reduced incentive to create the innovation, because under ceiling-price regulation, product output is unaffected by the technological change. However, whereas the quantity of inputs used is reduced, the individual inventor can certainly capture much of the cost savings. The incentives attributed to price-cap regulation will be evaluated further in Section 12.4.

In the case of markup regulation along the lines of Sweeney's model (1981), the firm has no incentive to adopt the innovation unless demand is elastic or regulatory lag is present. Thus, a very elastic demand leads to an expansion of output and input use. Input-suppliers have a strong incentive to promote such technological changes, although the gain in profits to the firm will be less than under ceiling-price regulation. The impact of factor-augmenting neutral technological change is more complicated for the rate-base-regulated firm. With the initial A-J input mix, and the same initial output levels as under the other two forms of regulation, the profit increment is lower than under markup regulation. Westfield shows that the effect on the demand for $L$ can be positive or negative, with the amount of capital increasing if output demand is elastic.

In the case of capital- or labor-augmenting innovations, comparing the gains to the rate-base-regulated firm with the gains to firms under the other two regimes depends on parameters of the production function and on the average-revenue function. Under markup regulation, the stimulus for innovation is greater the higher the share of the augmented factor in its total cost. As shown in Figure 10.10, "equivalent" labor- and capital-augmenting changes for given input prices will be valued differently by a rate-of-return-regulated firm. Thus, in theory, the incentive to engage in R&D (to produce an inward shift in the production isoquants) depends on the regulatory constraint. The difference between $s$ and $r$ will affect the net gain to changes in $a_1$ and $a_2$.

Of course, these characterizations of choices under different regulatory regimes do not capture the disruptive nature of technological change that permits firms to enter markets that had been dominated by natural monopolies. Similarly, the likely reactions of regulators to the availability of new technologies strongly influence decision-making by current input-suppliers. For example, if a regulated firm is unable to recover the depreciated book value of assets that have become economically (if not technically) obsolete, then the firm will be less willing to adopt a new technology that is embodied in new capital equipment. Alternatively, disembodied factor-augmenting changes can leave capacity underutilized, raising questions about regulatory treatment of the rate base.

### Induced innovations

In Westfield's analysis, the changes are exogenous, rather than endogenous. However, the analysis of regulation's impact on input choice has been extended to the type of technological changes fostered by regulation. One line of research examines incentives for differential factor augmentation, wherein the firm can allocate its resources devoted to innovation toward expanding the effective amount of labor or capital. The question, then, is whether or not the decision rule for a rate-of-return-regulated

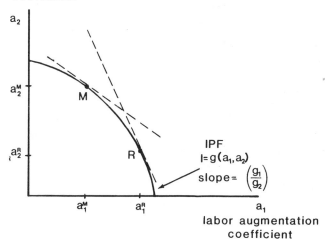

Figure 10.11. Innovation possibilities frontier: innovational choices.

firm is the same as for an unregulated monopolist. Let the monopolist have the production function

$$q = f(a_1 L, a_2 K), \qquad \partial f/\partial L > 0, \partial f/\partial K > 0$$

where $a_1$ and $a_2$ again represent augmentation coefficients. The coefficients are related by the innovation possibility frontier (IPF) depicted in Figure 10.11. Concavity reflects diminishing returns to innovation: For given R&D expenditures, additional augmentation of capital (larger $a_2$) can be obtained only by less augmentation of labor. Thus,

$$I = g(a_1, a_2)$$

where $I$ is the total innovational effort.

The firm is assumed to select $L, K, a_1,$ and $a_2$, given the output demand, the production function, and the IPF. The marginal rate of substitution in innovation (MRSI) of $a_1$ for $a_2$ equals $g_1/g_2 \equiv -da_2/da_1$, which is the slope of $I$ in Figure 10.11. An unregulated cost-minimizing firm chooses the mix of augmentation factors such that the MRSI times the relative share of a given input equals the relative rate of augmentation ($a_2/a_1$):

$$\frac{a_2}{a_1} = \text{MRSI} \cdot \frac{rK}{wL}$$

That is, relatively more capital augmentation is selected if outlays on capital ($rK$) are high relative to outlays on labor ($wL$). Thus, for the IPF depicted, a firm that is very capital-intensive can be expected to choose to augment capital at point $M$.

To see the choice for the regulated firm, we form the Lagrangian function for the profit-maximizing firm under the rate-of-return constraint:

$$G \equiv R - wL - rK - cI$$
$$- \lambda[R - wL - cI - sK] \quad (10.8)$$

where $R = p(q)q$. In this formulation, which differs slightly from equation (9.7), expenditures on $I$ are treated as a cost of service by regulators, and the rate-of-return constraint is assumed binding. Following Smith (1974) and Okuguchi (1975), the first-order conditions are

$$\partial G/\partial L = (1 - \lambda)(\partial R/\partial L - w) = 0 \quad (10.9)$$
$$\partial G/\partial K = (1 - \lambda)\partial R/\partial K - (r - \lambda s) = 0 \quad (10.10)$$
$$\partial G/\partial a_1 = (1 - \lambda)(\partial R/\partial a_1 - cg_1) = 0 \quad (10.11)$$
$$\partial G/\partial a_2 = (1 - \lambda)(\partial R/\partial a_2 - cg_2) = 0 \quad (10.12)$$
$$\partial G/\partial \lambda = -\{R - wL - cI - sK\} = 0 \quad (10.13)$$

where $g_i = \partial g/\partial a_i$, $i = 1, 2$. The marginal products of augmented labor and augmented capital are defined as

$$q_1 \equiv \partial q/\partial (a, L), \qquad q_2 \equiv \partial q/\partial (a_2K)$$

At the optimum, from (10.9) and (10.10) we obtain

$$(a_1/a_2) \cdot (q_1/q_2) = (1 - \lambda)w/(r - \lambda s) \quad (10.14)$$

As in the standard A-J model, the marginal rate of substitution between capital and labor along the production isoquant [the left-hand side of (10.14)] does not equal the ratio of input prices – implying production inefficiency. Also, from (10.11) and (10.12) we find

$$\text{MRSI} \equiv g_1/g_2 = (L/K) \cdot (q_1/q_2) \tag{10.15}$$

Okuguchi (1975) gives an example with constant returns to scale in which the elasticity of substitution between capital and labor is less than 1. In such a situation, the selection of the point on the IPF will tend to reinforce the static A-J input distortions in this situation – moving the choice to, say, point $R$ in Figure 10.11. This idea is essentially the same as that derived in the previous section using Figure 10.10. Note that this result depends on the parameters of the production function and the initial equilibrium for the regulated firm.[5]

In general, we can conclude that ceiling-price regulation results in a more rapid rate of technological change than would occur without regulation. However, as Okuguchi (1975) shows, compared with the no-regulation outcome, rate-of-return regulation may increase or decrease the degree of labor augmentation. In the special case of a constant elasticity of substitution (less than 1), there is a bias toward labor augmentation. Magat (1976) examines homothetic production functions with increasing or decreasing returns to scale and demonstrates that the degree of labor augmentation can be greater or less than would occur for an unregulated firm. Thus, conjectures regarding distortions in the patterns of technological change actually induced by regulation await careful empirical analysis.

### 10.4. Innovations and the output mix

So far, we have considered the behavior of a single-product firm. An extension to the multiproduct enterprise is some-

---

5 Link (1977) applies the model to a regulated monopoly facing a union. Depending on the nature of the union constraint, the firm may try to augment capital relative to labor. Such theoretical exercises remind us how the complexity of institutional settings can affect the outcome of maximizing activity.

what complicated, but it yields insights into the incentives facing such firms and the associated issues addressed by regulators, including potential impacts on the pattern of technological change and on the sustainability of current price structures.

### Factor intensities

Although we do not present formal models of regulatory impacts, we indicate how different types of regulation (rate base, price, or entry) may have implications for both the input mix and output mix that arise under different forms of regulation. For example, we have seen how rate-base regulation affects incentives to augment labor and capital in a single-product firm. In general, a multiproduct firm will be producing goods with different factor intensities. All other things being equal, there will be an incentive to apply more of a fixed R&D budget to labor augmentation for the labor-intensive good because of rate-base regulation. Over time, this behavior will affect the rates of cost reduction differentially: affecting the shape and position of the zero-profit locus in price space. The relatively more labor-intensive good will tend to experience greater technological advance – in the form of labor augmentation. Arbitrary cost-allocation mechanisms, such as fully distributed cost algorithms, will also be expected to affect the mix of labor and capital augmentation. Such effects are discussed more fully in Section 11.2.

Another issue is whether entry regulation needs to be tightened or loosened in the face of new technological developments that alter economies of scale and scope. As was noted in Chapter 2, changes in either can alter the optimal industry configuration, possibly changing it from a multiproduct natural monopolist to two specialized natural monopolists. Alternatively, the innovation can create competitive markets for one or both goods. Thus, depending on the initial situation, the existing firms will be threatened to different degrees by innovations. The cost reductions that actually result from R&D outlays will depend on the underlying technological opportunities, the production functions for the goods, and the net expected revenue streams associated with lowering the production cost for each of the products.

### Potential entry and shared inputs

The fixed-proportions model used in the peak-load pricing problem can be used to illustrate these points. Recall that capital (capacity) is essentially a shared input, with peak demand (and price) determining capacity requirements. A wide range of peak and off-peak price combinations can yield zero profits for the multiproduct firm. How will labor (variable input) augmentation and capital augmentation affect the shape and position of the zero-profit locus? Consider the case of dramatic capital augmentation: Units of capital are now much more productive.

$$q_i = f_i(a_1 L_i, a_2 K), \qquad i = 1, 2$$

In the foregoing production-function characterization, suppose that the $a_2$ coefficient increases substantially. The proportion of capital costs in total cost will greatly decrease. The new efficient peak and off-peak prices are closer together than before. The zero-profit locus in price space shifts inward for the multiproduct firm, and if the new technology is available to specialized firms, a firm specializing in the off-peak good will just earn zero profit at a price equal to its average cost. This price constrains the sustainable price offerings of the multiproduct firm. After the capital-augmenting innovation, capital (the shared input) becomes less important in terms of costs. With the relative advantage of the multiproduct firm reduced, the range of sustainable prices is also reduced.

Such a technological change is highly stylized, because there are no substitution possibilities, and the change cannot be patented. However, the point is still valid. A multiproduct firm facing the threat of entry will tend to emphasize labor augmentation (rather than capital augmentation) in its R&D program: increasing the relative importance of the shared input and reducing the possibility that technological change will induce specialized firms

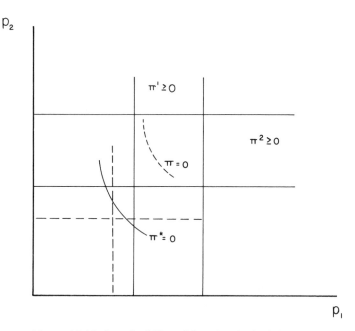

Figure 10.12. Sustainability with technological change.

to threaten its markets. Stolleman (1987) finds that rate-base regulation reinforces this tendency to increase productivity by expanding the nominal rate base rather than by investing in productivity-enhancing innovations (increasing $q_2$). For example, with regulation, AT&T may have had inadequate incentives to enhance the efficiency of the local loop. The possibility of inducing regulators to erect entry barriers has implications for the nature of innovations. Sappington and Shepherd (1982) examine incentives for a regulated firm to "choose its technology so as to appear deserving of protection on those product lines most susceptible to entry" (p. 44). They depict the firm as having a strategic motivation: behaving so as to increase the likelihood that regulators will limit entry. However, expected profits could be greater if the regulated firm invested in technologies that reduced the likelihood of entry, for example, those that could increase the relative importance of a shared input. In addition, cost-allocation schemes, such as the separations and settlements procedures under which AT&T operated, will also affect R&D incentives to augment one factor relative to another.

We can illustrate some of these points by using Figure 10.12, which depicts the zero-profit contour for the multiproduct firm and the price ranges yielding positive profits for firms specializing in products 1 and 2. The figure shows a shift from $\pi = 0$ to $\pi^* = 0$ for the two-product firm. If the straight solid lines bound the profitable prices for firms that specialize in each of the products, the multiproduct firm is not sustainable until the zero-profit locus becomes $\pi^*$. Alternatively, the dashed straight lines illustrate how cost reductions for specialized firms can make the multiproduct firm nonsustainable. The example shows how innovations from inside or outside the industries can force regulatory responses: limiting (or permitting) entry, and determining whether or not the input involves an *essential facility* (affecting competition in other output markets). As will be seen in the later discussion of sunk costs and the regulatory transition (Section 11.6), a finding of the latter generally will result in changing the terms for accessing that facility and revising the cost-allocation formulas used to determine prices in the two markets.

### 10.5. Institutional structures for innovation

Several issues remain regarding how regulation affects the creation and application of new ideas. Some of the impacts of regulation on technological change that have not been examined with mathematical models warrant our attention. Regulatory depreciation practices certainly influence the adoption of new technologies embodied in capital equipment. Similarly, alternative organizational forms can be used to coordinate decisions regarding new technologies – as they affect system compatibility, reliability, and new service offerings. Cooperative R&D

presents a particularly complicated set of trade-offs, especially to the extent that government-funded basic and applied research influences the technological opportunities available to firms.

### Depreciation and technological change

As shown in Section 3.1, depreciation can be viewed in the context of intertemporal capacity cost allocation. To cover a fixed capacity cost over a period of years with an outward-shifting linear demand involves the adoption of a pattern of rising prices. These Ramsey prices and the less efficient equal-allocation-per-period cost-allocation scheme both presume a given economic life for the equipment. However, it sometimes becomes clear that the choice of fewer years of use makes more economic sense than was originally assumed in allocating capacity costs over several periods. The change in perception occurs because entry will drive price far down or because the average total cost with a new technology will be less than the average variable cost of using the current equipment. Now the firm and regulator face a dilemma. The current price is too low to allow full capital recovery; so price must increase to provide the cash flow (depreciation) to maintain the financial viability of the firm.

The implications of economically obsolete equipment for utility depreciation practices and rate-base treatment are significant. For example, scrapping equipment that has not been fully depreciated will force stockholders to take a loss, unless regulators allow an adjustment (permitting unused equipment to remain in the rate base, or allowing extra depreciation). Regulated telephone companies found themselves in this situation with customer-premises equipment whose rate-base value was greater than its economic value (replacement cost) because of dramatic technological changes. The problem arose in the context of deregulation and competitive entry in this line of business. Firms had to write off equipment that had been underdepreciated, which meant that the product had been priced artificially low in the past. Depending on the regulatory jurisdiction, the unusual charges either were spread out over several years or were borne by companies.

Valuing AT&T's assets in the divestiture proceedings involved similar problems: Past depreciation practices had not adequately reflected technological change; asset lives of 5 to 10 years should have been used for depreciation purposes instead of the 20 to 30 years used to allocate capacity costs over time. Furthermore, some expenses had been capitalized to keep prices down, and owner recovery of those outlays also raised regulatory issues. When firms are not price-takers, regulatory decisions determine intertemporal allocations of financial burdens and therefore intertemporal price patterns. Once competition and dramatic technological opportunities perturbate the system, the resulting adjustments can raise many policy issues.

### *Coordination and technological change*

Three alternative organizational arrangements can be used to coordinate the decision-making in an industry: (1) competition within the market, (2) full financial and managerial integration, and (3) voluntary cooperation among independent entities. The first structure, the competitive price system, facilitates the resolution of disagreements regarding the sharing of benefits that arise from specialization and the division of labor. Without government intervention, price signals alert entrepreneurs to commercial opportunities, with the division of benefits based on competitive outcomes. Not only are resources drawn into and out of markets in accordance with private gains and losses, but also new products and production processes arise in response to technological opportunities. The coordinating features of this system are well known and appreciated by economists.

The other two organizational arrangements, integration and cooperation, also have strengths in certain situations. Integration may be called for when there are production and demand interdependencies. The literature on transactions costs provides numerous examples of situations in which unitary management may be most efficient for organizing resources when the cost of using the price system is relatively high (Williamson, 1975). Voluntary cooperation represents a mix of integration and independence. Entities may give up some independence in order to gain cost savings or an expansion of sales. The example of power pooling perhaps best illustrates this point in the context of regulated natural monopolies. However, that example also underscores the need to separate the levels of cooperation. Some industry analysts view electricity generation as being potentially competitive – with local regulated distribution systems contracting for service, and regulated transmission companies serving as common carriers. In the case of telecommunications, the cost-separation and revenue-sharing procedures that arose prior to divestiture represented one division of benefits from the sharing of facilities. Now, new arrangements are evolving as competition replaces cooperation in some market segments.

The same organizational alternatives are available for the creation and dissemination of entirely new technologies. Rivalry, integration, and cooperation represent different institutional formats for promoting innovation. This chapter stresses that the choice of the format that will be most efficient depends on the costs and incentives associated with each. In some cases, voluntary cooperation proves to be a cost-effective way of achieving economies. Alternatively, regulatory (or other) intervention may reduce transactions costs incurred by producers and consumers, enhancing social welfare. In such circumstances, the question then becomes one of regulatory rules versus regulatory discretion. The latter can stimulate rent-seeking activity by groups seeking "favorable" treatment.

Power-pooling arrangements, municipal and cogenerator access to electricity-transmission facilities, and access to local telephone networks by long-distance firms are just three regulatory issues currently in the headlines. They all illustrate the dilemma of establishing the best organizational mechanisms for promoting coordination. To what extent is regulation needed to ensure that efficiency-enhancing activities are promoted? When can independent firms be left to make the best deals they can with other firms and final consumers? In the area of technological change, we are only beginning to appreciate the complexity of the issues.

### Cooperative R&D ventures

Given the significant opportunities for innovation in several of the regulated industries, it is useful to consider the pros and cons of cooperative R&D ventures. Katz (1986) shows that industry-wide cooperation tends to promote efficiency "when the degree of product market competition is low, when there are R&D spillovers in the absence of cooperation, when a high degree of sharing is technologically feasible, and when the agreement concerns basic research rather than development activities" (p. 527). He also analyzes royalty-free cross-licensing agreements and finds that although this reduces the equilibrium level of innovative activity, it promotes efficiency in the use of R&D: There is no duplication of efforts, and the output of R&D is shared.

MacAvoy (1979) asked which organizational structures were best suited for developing promising but unproven technologies in energy. He focused on major (large and complex) technological changes (such as magnetic-hydrodynamic generators, breeder reactors, and superconductivity), rather than minor innovations. The alternative institutional structures can include a consortium of buyers, a group of producers, or the government as possible organizations for bringing together the necessary financial resources and technical expertise.

Innovations can so disturb the basis for existing cooperative arrangements that profits are threatened, which establishes an incentive for bringing R&D into a collusive arrangement. To the extent that the pace of technological change is determined by R&D strategies, firms can reduce competitive pressures by limiting the amount or coordinating the character of such expenditures. To the extent that R&D sponsored by industrial associations becomes an important factor in an industry, the potential anticompetitive effects warrant ongoing scrutiny by antitrust authorities.

There are disincentives for truly innovative (especially disruptive) research through cooperative efforts. Firms in a position to contribute the most to the joint research program are unlikely candidates for upsetting the status quo. They will prefer low-risk projects that are narrow in scope; such projects are unlikely to alter the existing market structure to any great extent. For example, improvements in larger-scale generating units may strengthen the market position of established electric utilities, whereas improvements in small generating units may invite entry. Furthermore, although firms within the industry are familiar with existing production technologies, this may be analogous to wearing blinders. Instances in which major breakthroughs have come from outside the industry testify to the physical and psychological ties to existing technologies and products. For example, talking pictures, jet engines, and instant cameras all came from new entrants. Note that these observations apply whether the cooperative effort involves producer R&D or the specification of product characteristics by producers.

Having government conduct the R&D raises other issues, because various agencies have historically been linked to certain constituencies. For example, putting all the effort in energy research under the Department of Energy umbrella does not necessarily yield a coherent program. In fact, given the uncertainties involved, strong competitive pressures among governmental departments are probably desirable. Another issue is when to halt a project that has proved to be unpromising: Momentum and budgetary inertia tend to favor "trying harder." Unfortunately, sunk costs tend *not* to be ignored by officials who would like to justify their past R&D budget allocations. Perhaps the United States would not have rejected subsidizing the development of the ill-fated supersonic transport (SST) had the Civil Aeronautics Board (CAB) been funding aircraft R&D. The slow death of federal funding for shale-oil research and demonstration projects illustrates how another multi-billion-dollar program finally fell to changes in market conditions. Competition in the "legislative capital market" (appropriations) may reveal losers more quickly than when there is a unified energy plan. This description of issues associated with innovation suggests that multiple centers of initiative should be retained in the regulated industries. Heterodoxy offers a good counterbalance to the pulls and pressures of industry consortia, dominant suppliers, consumer groups, large producers, and government agencies.

So far, we have not emphasized the disruptive nature of technological change. However, a study by Ekelund and Higgins (1982) extends Goldberg's regulated-contract theory of regulation to a situation in which existing suppliers face a potential innovation that will impose capital losses on them. In their model, a firm's willingness to commit resources to current capacity (and its associated technology) depends on anticipated contingencies regarding future losses. Furthermore, incumbents can, to a degree, reduce the likelihood of entry by choosing an output closer to the competitive level. Potential entrants calculating the benefits and costs resulting from an innovation will find a relatively greater reduction in the benefits as initial output is greater. In the Ekelund–Higgins model, regulation is not designed to economize on transactions costs, but to restrict entry to those producers using the current technology. Regulation esssentially forecloses entry – reducing the incentives for outsiders to conduct R&D. When existing suppliers experience capital fixity, the welfare consequences of entry regulation may be very negative in terms of reduced innovation by suppliers.

## 10.6. Summary

Regulation often has been characterized as being passive-reactive. In such a characterization of regulation, commissions wait for events to perturbate the system, and then respond to the developments. Government agencies may take the initiative with respect to many emerging problems, forcing firms to consider new rate structures, changing the tax treatment of depreciation, disallowing particular items from rate-base calculations, imposing energy-conservation programs, and forcing divestiture and vertical dis-integration. However, regulators probably are unable to force technological change. Compared with creating incentives for economic efficiency, it is even more difficult to design and implement programs for encouraging innovative efficiency.

For example, Nelson (1984) estimated the rate of technical change in the electric-power industry from 1951 to 1978: 3.3 percent annually until 1970, and 2.6 percent annually thereafter. More stringent environmental regulations account for part of the latter drop-off. He concluded that tighter regulation (a 1-point reduction in the allowed rate of return) would have reduced the rate of technological advance by only about 1.5 percent. So encouragement of innovative activity might be best handled by instruments other than rate of return.

Clearly, technological innovation raises many problems in government–corporate interactions. Regulators may establish incentives, but ultimately it is up to utility managers to determine the level and mix of R&D expenditures and the rate at which new technologies are adopted. This chapter primarily focuses on theoretical relationships. However, the reader's attention is drawn to case studies such as those found in Capron (1971) and Khanna (1982), who provide specific examples of how regulation influences the pace and pattern of technological change.

In order to explore how regulation affects the incentives for innovation, we have had to understand how the characteristics of new technological information influence decisions made in unregulated sectors of the economy. We have considered how the size of the firm, market power, and cooperation affect R&D activity. After delineating the determinants of R&D, we have examined several models of incentives for cost reduction under regulatory lag and under markup pricing. Regulator–firm interactions have been important in these analyses.

Then we turned to issues of potential biases in technological change – whether toward capital- or labor-augmenting technologies. These models contain characterizations of the IPF that make the choice of factor augmentation endogenous. A-J-like results emerge, although they are dependent on the stability of the IPF and the absence of uncertainty and regulatory lag. In the context of uncertainty regarding technological opportunities, regulation may have more of an impact on the level than on the mix of R&D. Also, note that Schumpeterian technological change may outweigh the effects of smoothly continuous, cumulative cost reductions. Although multiproduct functions have been estimated, the impact of R&D on underlying cost structures has not been fully explored. We have seen how incentives to insulate products from rivals or to take advantage of joint inputs can influence the pattern of technological change.

Technology is held constant in the next chapter. However, technological change is a major source of changing market structures, as regulated firms move into unregulated markets, and vice versa. Regulators have responded to such developments by limiting entry or by partially deregulating some markets. Firms have responded to new technological opportunities by diversifying into new markets. To these topics we now turn.

# 11

## Partial regulation, deregulation, and diversification

In Part I of this book, we carefully delimited the conditions that justify natural monopoly regulation. Using concepts of subadditivity, contestability, sustainability, and whether the natural monopoly was strong or weak, the conditions were summarized in Table 7.1. Applying these conditions to formulate public policy is problematic, because they represent polar cases, involve difficult empirical examinations of industry cost and demand functions, and can require projections of technological developments. Nevertheless, the ultimate goal of economists working in this arena is to translate these conditions into recommendations concerning which industries should be regulated and which industries should be deregulated because contestable markets and sustainability will ensure relatively efficient outcomes.

Unfortunately, the real world does not always wait for economists to make recommendations. In the late 1970s and the 1980s, policy-makers made many changes in the extent of the regulator's domain, without necessarily waiting for widespread agreement among economists (admittedly an elusive goal) as to the efficacy of such policies. On the one hand are the trucking and airline industries, which have been largely deregulated. Here, there probably is widespread agreement among economists that this policy was proper, because either firms in these industries are not natural monopolies or else the markets are contestable. In fact, deregulation of the airlines probably is one of the crowning achievements of regulatory economic analysis, particularly because it was orchestrated by CAB commissioner Alfred Kahn under the constant scrutiny of the public (McCraw, 1984).

On the other hand are the telecommunications, railroad, and natural-gas industries, which have been partially deregulated. The need for deregulation, or at least particular mixes of deregulation activity, was less clear. For instance, deregulation of telecommunications by permitting entry may prove to be wise if technological advances are spurred as a result. But if entry occurs only from bad regulatory policies to begin with, namely, regulated prices that involve cross-subsidies, then deregulation may prove costly. The important point is that economists must continue to improve their methods for determining where regulation is justified and where deregulation can yield efficiency gains. These determinations seldom will be obvious or will go unchallenged, and where deregulation is implemented, it must be assessed for its success or failure with the same vigor often used to analyze regulation.

In Section 11.1 we illustrate a number of the issues that arise when firms become partially regulated or diversify into potentially competitive markets. Whether or not these partially regulated firms are sustainable is covered in Section 11.2, along with a discussion of separation procedures, which are common regulatory methods for dealing with partially regulated and diversified firms. Section 11.3 covers some of the pricing considerations under residual regulation. There is also the possibility that regulation will create incentives for mergers between firms, as addressed in Section 11.4, or that individual firms will have incentives to integrate vertically, and this is covered in Section 11.5. In either case, product mixes may be altered. Section 11.6 covers some of the expected and observed benefits of deregulation. The last section provides a summary of the chapter.

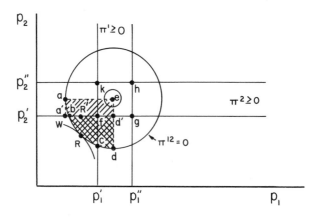

Figure 11.1. Sustainability under partial regulation.

## 11.1. **Issues under partial regulation**[1]

To introduce the nature of pricing and entry issues under partial regulation, consider a two-product case in which demands for the products are independent. Figure 11.1 depicts the price combinations available to a two-product profit-maximizing monopoly and to two single-product profit-maximizing firms, each specializing in one of the products. For two single-product firms, if firm $i$, $i = 1, 2$, sets price $p_i$ such that $p_i' \leq p_i \leq p_i''$, it will be assured of nonnegative profit. Either $p_i'$ or $p_i''$ will yield zero profit. Consequently, rectangle *fghk* contains all price vectors $p = (p_1, p_2)$ such that both firms enjoy nonnegative profits. Alternatively, a monopolist producing both products can realize profit $\pi^{12}$ designated by the isoprofit contours shown. Maximum profit for the monopoly is attained at point *e*.

Figure 11.1, of course, is the same type of diagram as those used in Chapter 7 to analyze sustainability issues. Figure 11.1 shows a sustainable, two-product natural monopoly. Sustainability requires that the monopolist earn zero profit and charge

1 Some of the points raised in this section are also raised in Baseman (1981), Baumol (1981), and Panzar (1981).

undominated prices, and these conditions are satisfied along arc *ad*. In addition, sustainability requires that there be no cross-subsidies, which narrows the eligible prices to those along arc *bc*. No firm specializing in either product alone, and no firm producing both products, can earn positive profit by undercutting the monopolist's prices if they are along arc *bc*.

### The role of contestability

Consider next the following three scenarios. First, suppose a monopolist produces both products in noncontestable markets; there are barriers to entry into either market, perhaps because of sunk costs. Without deregulation, the monopolist, using undominated prices, can opt for any price vector in the crosshatched and hatched areas, with point *e* being the preferred price vector. According to the policy prescriptions in Table 7.1, the regulator's task in this case is to dictate prices that will maximize a welfare criterion (say consumer plus producer surplus) subject to a break-even constraint on profit. Given the welfare contour *W* in Figure 11.1, the dictated prices are given by point *R*. This point represents the Ramsey prices, which are sustainable in this example. (As pointed out in Chapter 7, however, in general there is no guarantee that Ramsey prices are sustainable; point *R* need not lie on arc *bc*.)

In the second scenario, suppose entry barriers are removed, and both markets are perfectly contestable. The monopolist is then compelled by market forces to prices along *bc*. Moreover, the monopolist may even choose point *R*, owing to information problems (see Section 7.4). At any rate, in either scenario one or two, which are referred to as the totally regulated and the totally unregulated cases, respectively, either an optimum regulatory policy or market forces will result in a price vector along *bc*.

In the third scenario, suppose that market two is contestable, and market one is not. Further, the regulator eschews all price and entry regulation in the second market; that is, market two is deregulated relative to scenario one. This becomes a case of partial regulation. The monopolist, again using undominated prices, is free to choose any price vector in the crosshatched area (*bd′d*). But now there are neither market forces nor regulatory policies to move the monopolist to *bc*. Market forces are not present provided the monopolist chooses price in market two no greater than $p_2'$; no firm specializing in product 2 can undercut him and earn nonnegative profit. And regulatory policies will not be useful, because we assume that the regulator can dictate prices for product 1 only. If the regulator can do more than this, then deregulation is not genuine. The upshot is that any prices in the crosshatched area are *sustainable under partial regulation.* A formal definition of this concept is given later.

To be more specific about the prices a two-product monopolist will choose within the crosshatched area, assumptions about regulatory behavior are needed. For example, suppose that initially the monopolist is protected from entrants in both markets by the regulator, and prices are given by point *R*, the Ramsey prices. Then suppose that only market two is totally deregulated; that is, the regulator abandons both price and entry regulation in market two, while maintaining what was a Ramsey price in market one. The monopolist will move from *R* to point *R′*, where profit is at a maximum subject to the market-one price. At *R′* there is no cross-subsidy, and the monopolist is safe from entrant firms, although profit is positive. Regulators could require that a portion of the windfall profit from partial deregulation be applied to writing down overvalued assets, where past depreciation did not adequately take into account the rate at which technological change made the assets economically obsolete. Such write-offs strengthen the natural monopolist vis-à-vis future entry by new technologies in the first market as the multiproduct zero-profit locus shifts inward.

Alternatively, financial problems can be exacerbated by partial deregulation. Suppose that prior to deregulation in market two, the monopolist operates at point *d*, where profit is zero and there is a cross-subsidy from product 1 to product 2. Pricing product 1 above stand-alone cost is viable owing to regulatory entry barriers. Under the same form of deregulation, the monopolist will move to point $d'$, where the cross-subsidy persists but profit now is positive. The cross-subsidy remains viable owing to entry regulation in market one, although instead of the subsidy going from product 1 to product 2, it is now going from product 1 to the firm.

On the other hand, a cross-subsidy from product 2 to product 1 cannot persist after deregulation of market two. If point $a$ represents the initial pre-deregulation prices, then after deregulation, if the monopolist moves along a vertical line below point $a$, he cannot thwart entry into market two. In fact, without a change in regulatory policy allowing a higher price for product 1, the multiproduct monopoly cannot survive.

### Expansion of product lines

Finally, Figure 11.1 suggests possibilities for monopoly expansion. If initially there are two independent firms, and the first is regulated by being both barred from entering competitive markets and held to zero profit, whereas the second is unregulated, the starting point lies along segment $fk$, where firm 2's profit is at a maximum. If the first firm is then allowed to enter unregulated markets, it can operate just below point $f$ and drive firm 2 out of business. Regulators are concerned that regulated firms will enter unregulated markets and use revenues from the regulated sector to subsidize their unregulated operations. Some might mistakenly view point $f$ as reflecting such behavior. However, having a two-product monopolist operating at point $f$ is superior to having two independent monopolists. That is, point $f$ is on a higher welfare contour than any point within area $fghk$ where independent firms can survive. Thus, the regulator's fear that firm 1 might drive out the other and lower overall welfare is unfounded. The fear is based on a policy that was misguided at the outset, because the two-product firm is a natural monopoly and should have been operated as such.

When evaluating the introduction of new product lines by regulated firms, regulators must consider at least four issues: (1) the potential for cross-subsidization, (2) the effects on other firms, (3) the extent of the economies associated with the new product, and

(4) the dilution of managerial attention and maintenance of utility incentives. The first issue, cross-subsidization, can stem from inappropriate allocations of fixed or variable costs or from inefficient investments in joint facilities (see Section 11.2). Also, transfer pricing, which increases the reported costs of the regulated firm, might be used to shift profits from the regulated firm to an unregulated subsidiary. Yet when regulators mandate complete separation among business units, the firm may not achieve economies of scope.

The second issue, the impact on other firms, raises similar regulatory trade-offs. If high-cost suppliers are driven from the market because of entry by a natural multiproduct monopoly, resource allocation is improved. However, these suppliers may claim predatory pricing if the output is produced by an unregulated subsidiary or by the regulated firm. Producers of substitute products can argue that revenues from the utility's captive consumer groups (or regulated products) cover costs associated with products subject to competition. Another scenario is illustrated by Daughety's model of industry-wide regulation (see Section 9.5), which demonstrated how the presence of high-cost firms could increase the profits of efficient suppliers. The removal of such regulation would reduce prices and lead to bankruptcy or consolidation of inefficient firms, again bringing forth charges of predation.

Multiproduct economies, the third issue, have already been discussed at length. Economic gains can arise from underlying technological factors or from demand interdependencies. In the latter case, the addition of a substitute or complement will expand the potential application of Ramsey pricing by a regulated firm. If entry barriers can be erected, switching a product from outside to inside the firm's set of offerings can improve welfare. The data requirements for such fine tuning are substantial, however. Similarly, determining how to share the benefits of jointly used facilities requires that regulators have full information on demand and cost interdependencies. Often, the core of the cost-sharing game will be quite large, so that a wide range of alternative divisions of benefits is possible.

Regarding the fourth issue, those concerned with recent trends toward diversification argue that managerial attention may be diverted from regulated areas, that the financial position of the regulated firm can be weakened, or that regulators lack the resources to exercise adequate supervision over cost allocation and transfer pricing. Kahn (1983) notes that the logic of the first point is backward: Vigorous, enterprising managers will not be "protected" from exploring commercial and technological opportunities if they are legislatively barred from such activity. If strict boundaries are drawn, managerial talent probably will not flow into potentially declining regulated firms. To those arguing that these firms are trying to diversify out of their regulated markets, Kahn (1983) notes that a successful unregulated operation will not be more valuable separated from the regulated utility unless the latter is being held to a return less than its cost of capital. If regulators are motivated by this concern, they will be limiting the firm's alternatives – holding its capital captive.[2] Finally, Kahn views this fourth objection to diversification as reflecting "the conservatism and compulsive tidiness of the regulatory mentality. . . . That is a ridiculous way to make public policy – 'if we can't watch it, we won't let you do it.' The solution to this problem is, surely, to provide the regulatory commissions with the additional resources required" (pp. 153–4). Nevertheless, the addition of new services raises a number of regulatory issues, some of which are discussed in the next section.

## 11.2. **Sustainability under partial regulation**

Partial regulation usually comes about in one of two ways: Multiproduct firms that are subject to price and entry regulations in all their markets have these regulations lifted in a

---

2 For a discussion of these issues in the context of railroad diversification, see Eads (1974). He argued that redeployment of assets increased efficiency and did not drain firms of cash or managerial talent.

proper subset of the markets. Alternatively, multiproduct firms are permitted to enter new, unregulated markets through diversification. In either case, new policies are required that can address the different incentive structures for these partially regulated firms. In this section, we reconsider sustainability as it applies to partially regulated firms, and we examine separation procedures that represent a common approach to regulating these firms.

### *Partial regulation, product mix, and sustainability*

If a totally regulated, multiproduct firm is partially deregulated, will it continue with the same set of products? Will it drop some of the products now subject to competition? Will it diversify into new products? The answers to these questions can be related to questions of sustainability, although now we need to examine whether or not a firm is sustainable under partial regulation (SUPR). Are the conditions necessary for a firm to be sustainable also necessary for a firm to be SUPR? For instance, if a firm is SUPR, does this mean that it must be producing efficiently, earning zero profit, and avoiding cross-subsidies? The answer is no, and this is a problem for regulators. Partial deregulation may mean that the market force keeping an unregulated firm in check, namely, contestability, will not keep a partially regulated firm in check. Consequently, monitoring partially regulated firms is becoming one of the more important dilemmas confronting regulators. Here we shall introduce some of the problem's dimensions.

Using our usual notation, consider a multiproduct firm producing output vector $q = (q_1, \ldots, q_n)$ at prices $p = (p_1, \ldots, p_n)$. Demand for the $i$th good is written $q_i(p)$ and is assumed to be continuously differentiable, with $\partial q_i/\partial p_i < 0$ and $\partial q_i/\partial p_j > 0$ for $i, j = 1, \ldots, n, i \neq j$. Thus, the $n$ goods are weak gross substitutes. The firm's total cost is given by the continuously differentiable function $C(q)$, defined for $q \geq 0$, and with marginal costs denoted $\mathrm{MC}_i \equiv \partial C(q)/\partial q_i, i = 1, \ldots, n$.

Initially, the firm is assumed to have a monopoly in all markets. Profit is given by

$$\pi(p) \equiv pq(p) - C(q(p)) = \sum_{i \in N} p_i q_i(p_i) - C(q_1(p), \ldots, q_n(p)) \tag{11.1}$$

where $N$ is the set of all $n$ goods. $\pi(p)$ is continuous, by continuity of the demand and cost functions, and is assumed to be strictly concave, with a unique maximum attained at $p^*$ such that $\pi(p^*) > 0$. The firm is regulated in all markets by a single regulator. Regulation is effective by constraining the firm to zero profit and preventing entry into all markets. Whether or not the monopolist is sustainable is immaterial in this initial setting. Regardless of how inefficient the monopolist may be or the extent of cross-subsidization across products, new firms cannot compete if the regulator is effective in disallowing entry. However, if the no-entry policy is relaxed in a proper subset of the $n$ markets, sustainability becomes an issue for the partially regulated monopolist.

For convenience, order the goods so that the set of markets $R = \{1, \ldots, r\}$ continues to be regulated, while the set of markets $N - R = \{r + 1, \ldots, n\}$ is deregulated. The price vector for the monopolist is denoted by $p^m = (\overline{p}_1^m, \ldots, \overline{p}_r^m, p_{r+1}^m, \ldots, p_n^m)$, where the bar notation indicates that prices in the first $r$ markets are set by the regulator, perhaps after some review process. At this point we shall not specify how these prices are set, but sustainability of the monopolist will certainly be dependent on the method used. A firm that attempts to enter one or more of these unregulated markets charges prices $p^e$ and has the same production technology available to it as does the monopolist. If the monopoly is invulnerable to all potential entry, then it is said to be SUPR.

> *Definition:* The monopoly price vector $p^m = (\overline{p}_1^m, \ldots, \overline{p}_r^m, p_{r+1}^m, \ldots, p_n^m)$ is sustainable under partial regulation if and only if, given the regulated prices $\overline{p}_i^m \in R$, $p_S^e y_S^e - C(y_S^e) < 0$ and $\pi(p^m) \geq 0$ for all $S \subseteq N - R$, $p_S^e < p_S^m$, $y_S^e \leq q^S(p_S^e, p_{N-S}^m)$.

This definition is based on the Panzar and Willig definition of sustainability (see Section 7.3), the principal difference being that firms can enter markets only in $N - R$; they are barred by regulatory fiat from entry into markets in $R$. A successful entrant must undercut the monopolist's price in one or more of the markets open for entry and earn nonnegative profit. Note, too, that an entrant need serve only a portion of market demand.

To go further in examining SUPR, assumptions are needed on the behavior of the firm and regulator, particularly regarding how the regulated prices are set. With total regulation, we usually assume that the regulator holds the firm to zero profit. The equivalent action in a partially regulated setting would seem to be that the firm can choose any prices in the unregulated markets, whereas prices in the regulated markets must yield zero profit in those regulated markets. But separating the regulated and unregulated markets for the purpose of determining profit is impossible where common costs are involved; so another assumption about regulatory behavior is needed. The assumption used initially will be that after partial deregulation, price and entry constraints are lifted in markets $r + 1, \ldots, n$; but prices are assumed to remain at their original levels, and regulatory entry barriers continue in force in markets $1, \ldots, r$. This would seem to be a natural starting point for the regulator, particularly because information requirements are minimal.

The monopolist, with newfound latitude after deregulation, attempts to maximize profit subject to the set prices in the regulated markets. However, the monopolist is assumed to be aware of potential entrants, and he attempts to choose prices that will deter entry. The monopolist's problem can be written

$$\max_{p_{r+1}, \ldots, p_n} \pi^m = \sum_{i=1}^{r} \overline{p}_i^m q_i^m(\overline{p}_R^m, p_{N-R}^m)$$

$$+ \sum_{i=r+1}^{n} p_i^m q_i^m(\overline{p}_R^m, p_{N-R}^m) - C(q_R^m(\cdot), q_{N-R}^m(\cdot)) \quad (11.2)$$

subject to

$$p_S^e y_S^e < C(y_S^e) \quad \text{for all } S \subseteq N - R,$$
$$p_S^e < p_S^m, \text{ and } y_S^e \le q^S(\overline{p}_R^m, p_{N-R-S}^m, p_S^e)$$

If a solution to this problem exists with $\pi^m \ge 0$, then the monopolist is SUPR. The constraints ensure that the monopolist will not choose prices that can be successfully undercut by entrants.

We can now examine several properties of the SUPR concept. First, a sustainable price vector is SUPR. This point is obvious from the definition of each. A sustainable price vector makes the monopolist invulnerable to potential entrants in any set of markets, $S \subseteq N$. This same price vector makes it invulnerable to potential entrants in any proper subset of markets $S \subseteq N - R$, where entry is permitted under partial regulation.

A necessary condition for a price vector to be sustainable is that the monopolist's profit be zero. Positive profit would allow another firm to drive out the monopolist by duplicating its operations while charging slightly lower prices. Because entry is not allowed in all markets, such duplication is not possible under partial regulation, and zero profit is not a necessary condition for SUPR. In fact, if a totally regulated natural monopoly using a sustainable price vector is partially deregulated, as described earlier, then the natural monopoly will be SUPR and will earn positive profit.[3] But if the natural monopoly is not sustainable, then it may or may not be SUPR, depending on which of the markets become deregulated.

Another necessary condition for sustainability of a monopoly is that it be a natural monopoly. Unfortunately, this is not true for SUPR. A regulatory policy that grants protection to a firm from entrants in some markets may end up protecting an inefficient market structure. Moreover, the extent of the inefficiency can be substantial. We cannot even rule out the possibility that a monopolist with a superadditive cost function will be SUPR,

3 This follows by a continuity argument on the revenue and cost functions.

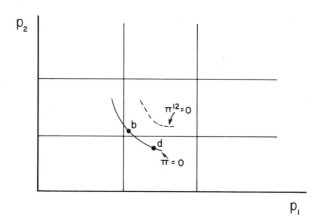

Figure 11.2. SUPR and nonnatural monopolies.

which is evident in Figure 11.2.[4] If the solid arc represents the undominated set of prices yielding zero profit, point *d* will be SUPR if market one is regulated and market two unregulated. No entrant in market two can undercut the monopoly price and make nonnegative profit; in market one, an entrant could make positive profit at the monopolist's price, but entry here is disallowed.

A firm that is not a natural monopoly and has the undominated, zero-profit contour given by the dashed arc in Figure 11.2 is not SUPR. Regardless of which market is protected from entry by regulators, the firm cannot find a price vector such that the other, contestable market is invulnerable. Thus, there is a limit to the degree of inefficiency that might mistakenly be protected

4 The two-product firm in Figure 11.2 is not a natural monopoly, and the zero-profit locus does not pass southwest of the area where single-product firms are viable. Constructing a numerical example of two single-product firms and one two-product firm with a superadditive cost function yielding a picture like Figure 11.2 is not difficult. At point *b*, we have $p_1q_1(p_1) - C(q_1, 0) > 0$, $p_2q_2(p_2) - C(0, q_2') > 0$, and $p_1q_1(p_1) + p_2q_2(p_2) - C(q_1, q_2) = 0$. Combining these yields $C(q_1, 0) + C(0, q_2) < C(q_1, q_2)$, which is necessary for superadditivity: so a single firm is more costly than multiple firms.

through partial regulation. In the two-product case pictured, sufficient conditions for a firm not to be SUPR are

$$[MC_2 - MC_2^0] \frac{\partial q_2}{\partial p_1} +$$
$$\left[ MC_1 - \frac{C(q_1, q_2) - C(0, q_2)}{q_1} \right] \frac{\partial q_1}{\partial p_1} > q_1 \quad (11.3)$$

where $MC_2^0 = \partial C(0, q_2)/\partial q_2$, plus a second condition with the subscripts 1 and 2 reversed in (11.3). Condition (11.3) is derived in the Appendix to this chapter.

Studying (11.3) reveals the properties that contribute to a firm not being SUPR. In the first term on the left side, $\partial q_2/\partial p_1$ is positive by the weak gross-substitute assumption. Therefore, a positive bracketed term contributes to the desired result. This condition follows if there are negative cost complementarities in production, or marginal cost rises as new products are added. Similarly, because $\partial q_1/\partial p_1 < 0$, a negative second bracketed term contributes to the desired result. This bracketed term is the rate of change of average incremental cost (Panzar and Willig, 1977b); therefore, declining average incremental cost favors the firm not being SUPR.[5] An intuitive explanation for this result goes as follows: Suppose the firm is charging a relatively low price in the regulated market and finds itself vulnerable to entrants in the unregulated market. If permitted, the firm will raise the regulated price in order to increase regulated revenues, which then will permit a lower price in the unregulated market. However, this strategy may fail if the greater output sold in the unregulated market can be produced only at ever-increasing costs (the negative cost complementarities), and the advantage of large-scale production is eroded in the regulated market as output in that market decreases with the higher price (the declining average incremental cost).

The point of this exercise is to illustrate that a firm may need

---

5 The reader can compare (11.3) with (7.31), a sufficient condition for a two-product natural monopoly to be sustainable.

to exhibit rather strong nonnatural monopoly properties before we can be certain that it is not SUPR. In turn, this implies that partial regulation may be a means of protecting inefficient production. But even if the partially regulated firm is a natural monopoly, we are likely to observe positive profit and possibly cross-subsidies. The fundamental problem is in the partial-regulation approach. If a firm is a natural monopoly and only some of its markets are contestable, opening those markets to competition may mean only higher profit for the monopoly, with little, if any, entry. Alternatively, if a firm is not a natural monopoly, or if it once was but no longer is owing to new technologies, then partial regulation should be abandoned in favor of total deregulation. A third possibility is that the set of outputs for which the firm is a natural monopoly has shrunk owing to new technologies. In this case, the previously mentioned problems can be avoided by restricting the firm to produce only those goods for which it is a natural monopoly.

The framework can also be used to illustrate the consequences of two approaches to rate-making when entry is allowed in one market (Cicchetti, 1986). Under what Cicchetti labels *flexible regulated pricing,* core customers (buyers of product 1) share in the gains going to stockholders from sales of product 2. Let the total cost be

$$TC = wL_1 + wL_2 + rK$$

The revenue requirements (and thus the price) of product 1 depend on the firm's performance in market two:

$$p_1 q_1 = wL_1 + rK - \beta(p_2 q_2 - wL_2)$$

Here, $\beta$ is the share of net revenue from product 2 (revenue less directly attributable costs) applied to reducing revenue requirements of product 1. The firm can be viewed as maximizing profits subject to this pricing constraint.

Whether the price of the regulated service goes up or down depends on the initial rate structure and strength of demand for product 2. If the firm does not face regulatory constraints in this market, it has the capability (and incentive) to maximize the net contribution from sales. Under rate-base regulation, production costs may not be minimized, for two reasons: the standard A-J outcome for product 1 and the incentive to reduce costs of producing product 2, increasing the firm's market share in the unregulated market. Brennan (1987) examines the situation with no sharing of net revenue ($\beta = 0$) for a special case in which revenue requirements equal $p_1q_1 = c_1q_1 + F$, and the firm is a price-taker in the unregulated market. The production technology is such that

$$C(q_1, q_2) = F + c_1q_1 + c_2(F, c_1)q_2,$$
$$\partial c_2/\partial c_1 < 0, \ \partial c_2/\partial F < 0 \tag{11.4}$$

Within this technology, the greater the fixed or marginal cost of producing the regulated output, the lower the marginal cost of producing the unregulated output. Regulatory concern centers around two potential impacts: (1) Core customers buying the regulated service may pay more than necessary. (2) Competitors in the unregulated market lose market share to the multiproduct firm. Thus, flexible regulated pricing does not solve the problem of inefficient input and output mixes.

Cicchetti also introduces the concept of *partially deregulated pricing.* Under this regime, the multiproduct firm accepts all the risks and bears all the costs of the shared capacity. Revenue requirements amount to total variable costs: $p_1q_1 = wL_1$. With an effective revenue constraint established for core customers, returns in market two accrue to the firm. Of course, now the firm has a tendency to underinvest in capacity. Both types of deregulation provide incentives to market the second (unregulated) product aggressively, and each provides some protection for core customers. The efficiencies of the two alternative ways to constrain $p_1$ warrant further research.

Evaluation of entry raises a number of issues. Mankiw and Whinston (1986) analyze entry in terms of private incentives and social efficiency impacts. Excessive entry (and duplication of facilities) can occur when customers are "stolen" from a rival.

However, increased product diversity induces additional customers into the market – and only some of the social gains associated with the new product can be captured by the entrant. Thus, whether entry is excessive or suboptimal depends on the relative strengths of these two factors. The products used to illustrate sustainability under partial regulation could be independent or have nonzero cross-elasticities. Rivalry among strong natural monopolies could yield too many or too few products, depending on the size of the fixed costs, product substitutabilities, and the nature of the rivalry. For a regulator to make the socially optimal entry decisions requires substantial information.

### Separations procedures

In Section 3.6 we introduced fully distributed cost (FDC) pricing, which is an example of a separations procedure. In that case, a multiproduct firm was charged with allocating its total costs, including common costs, over its various products in an effort to ensure that revenue from the sale of each product would cover its allocated cost. Thus, the products were separated from one another. The same concept has been applied when a regulated firm diversifies into unregulated markets. Regulators usually require that the firm separate its regulated business from its unregulated business to ensure that no cross-subsidies occur.

In telecommunications, the problem arises when firms are required to separate costs among local, intrastate, and interstate services to establish rates. This process for telephones dates back to 1930, when the U.S. Supreme Court decided that separation of telephone revenues and costs "is essential to the appropriate recognition of the competent governmental authority in each field of regulation."[6] Since then, vast amounts of time have been spent devising and revising separations procedures. In a 100-page 1971 *Separations Manual* developed by the National Association of Regulatory Utility Commissioners (NARUC), one can find cost allocations based on length of telephone conversations,

6 *Smith* v. *Illinois Bell Telephone Co.,* 282 U.S. 133 (1930).

number of telephone connections, square feet of office space, and even telephone-pole costs allocated according to the miles of aerial wire supported. NARUC also publishes a lengthy *Electric Utility Cost Allocation Manual* (1973). Here, emphasis is placed on cost allocation "for electric utilities operating under more than one regulatory commissioner's jurisdiction ... in order to prevent inconsistent or incompatible action possibly damaging to either the public or the utility" (p. ix).

As we indicated in Chapter 3 and elsewhere, when there are common costs, allocation or separations procedures are hopelessly arbitrary approaches to rate-making that can lead to undesirable prices and cross-subsidies. In addition, there is the danger that among regulators, separations procedures may foster an unwarranted feeling of accomplishment. Sweeney (1982) explores the problems with separations procedures in a framework similar to that used by Braeutigam (1980) in his study of FDC pricing (see Chapter 3). Sweeney considers a firm that is partially regulated by an agency that requires revenues from each product in the regulated set to cover no more than the respective allocated costs. As in the previous section, we assume that products in the set $R = (1, \ldots, r)$ are regulated, whereas those in the set $N - R = (r + 1, \ldots, n)$ are not. To account for the common costs that the regulation is to allocate, we write the cost function for the firm as

$$\sum_{i=1}^{r} C_i(q_i) + \sum_{i=r+1}^{n} C_i(q_i) + F$$

where $C_i(q_i)$ is the direct cost for product $i$, and $F$ is the common cost. Each product in $R$ must cover no more than its direct cost plus its share of common cost, or

$$p_i q_i(p) \leq C_i(q_i(p)) + \alpha_i F \tag{11.5}$$

where $\alpha_i$ is the common-cost allocator for product $i$. We expect that $0 < \alpha_i < 1$, meaning that each regulated product must cover some part of common cost, and $\Sigma \alpha_i < 1$ (for $i = 1$ to $r$) because some common cost gets allocated by regulators to the unregulated products.

Several different allocations are considered by Sweeney, but we shall confine ourselves to just one, which will be sufficient to illustrate the important results. We assume that $\alpha_i$ is a differentiable function of the outputs in $R$,

$$\alpha_i = \alpha_i(q_1, \ldots, q_r) \tag{11.6}$$

with partials

$$\frac{\partial \alpha_i}{\partial q_i} > 0, \qquad i = 1, \ldots, r \tag{11.7}$$

$$\frac{\partial \alpha_i}{\partial q_j} < 0, \qquad i, j = 1, \ldots, r, \, i \neq j \tag{11.8}$$

Thus, as the $i$th output increases, more of the common cost is allocated to the $i$th output, and less is allocated to all other outputs in $R$. The monopolist's problem can be written as

$$\max_{p_1, \ldots, p_n} \pi = \sum_{i=1}^{r} [p_i q_i(p) - C_i(q_i)]$$
$$+ \sum_{i=r+1}^{n} [p_i q_i(p) - C_i(q_i)] - F \tag{11.9}$$

subject to

$$p_i q_i(p) - C_i(q_i(p)) - \alpha_i(q(p))F \leq 0, \qquad i \in R \tag{11.10}$$

$$0 \leq p_i \leq \hat{p}_i, \qquad i \in N \tag{11.11}$$

where $\hat{p}_i$ is an upper bound on price, or the price that would drive demand to zero. The difference between this problem and the problem presented by (11.2) is important. In the earlier problem, the prices in markets $1, \ldots, r$ were set by the regulator, and the monopolist could choose only the prices in markets $r + 1, \ldots, n$. In effect, the regulator adopted a separations procedure, which we left unspecified, and using that procedure she set prices that

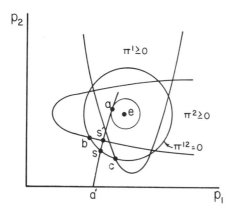

Figure 11.3. Pricing and separations procedures.

ostensibly satisfied some regulatory goal. However, in this problem, a separations procedure is specified, and then the monopolist is free to set all $n$ prices within the confines of the procedure. A priori, we cannot say which approach is preferable without further specifying the information available to both the monopolist and the regulator. More research in this area will be required before effective policies can be implemented.

Returning to the problem given by (11.9)–(11.11), Sweeney derives two important results using the Kuhn–Tucker conditions. Rather than provide details, we can sketch these results graphically. Figure 11.3 is the familiar picture of the profits available to a two-product natural monopoly and to two single-product independent firms. As shown here, the natural monopoly is sustainable owing to the location of arc $bc$ along the zero-profit contour; the point $e$ is the unconstrained profit maximum. Also, the figure is drawn with interdependent demands.

Assuming that market one (two) is the regulated (unregulated) market, the solution to problem (11.9)–(11.11) can be represented by point $a$. Curve $aa'$ represents constraint (11.10), which

Sweeney shows to have the general shape illustrated. The monopolist maximizes profit along this constraint by locating at the highest isoprofit contour that has at least one point in common with $aa'$. This common point is $a$, which is sustainable only if entry into market two is limited. Sweeney's two results are that prices at point $a$ are dominated and that price in the unregulated market exceeds the unconstrained profit-maximizing price corresponding to point $e$. These results obviously do not bode well for this separations approach: We end up with prices such that one or more of them can be lowered to improve welfare without decreasing the monopolist's profit, and we also end up with high prices in unregulated markets. Sweeney explains these results by noting that because regulated products are permitted to return a "fair share" of the common-cost output, reductions in unregulated markets allow more of the common cost to be shifted, via (11.8), to regulated markets. As a result, greater profits are earned in these regulated markets.

In one sense, these results may appeal to regulators. The prices are high in the unregulated markets, thereby reducing the likelihood that there are cross-subsidies from the regulated markets. Also, competitors in the unregulated markets will be pleased, because the monopolist apparently is not relying on profits from the regulated markets to conduct predatory pricing in their markets. In fact, referring again to Figure 11.3, we can see that a single-output firm can successfully enter market two given the monopolist's choice of point $a$. In other words, point $a$ is not SUPR. This turns out to be true in general: The solution to problem (11.9)–(11.11) is not SUPR. Accordingly, the monopolist's prices will be undercut in at least some of the unregulated markets, perhaps even driving the monopolist out entirely. The advantages of natural monopoly production are then lost, and the regulator's optimism proves short-lived.

The monopolist may not behave passively toward potential entrants, however. If he is aware of the potential entrants' and of his competitors' technologies, then he can append constraints from problem (11.3) to the problem in (11.9)–(11.11). Now he prices according to the separations procedures, while at the same time preventing entry by ensuring that the unregulated prices are not too high. In Figure 11.3, the monopolist constrained to operate along $aa'$ by the separations procedure is SUPR along $ss'$. To maximize profit, he will choose point $s'$, the solution to problem (11.9)–(11.11) after (11.3) is appended.

### Cost allocation and rate-of-return regulation

In a similar framework, Sweeney also examines a situation in which the multiproduct monopolist is subject to rate-of-return regulation in several different regulatory jurisdictions. Because jurisdictions may allow varying rates of return, this will influence the firm's decision regarding capital inputs. If the allocation of joint costs follows (11.6)–(11.8) across the markets, the firm maximizes overall profit by shifting capital costs from low-return jurisdictions to high-return jurisdictions. Sweeney shows that this shifting is achieved via output reductions (and price increases) in the market with the low allowed rate of return.

To pursue the combined effects of cost allocation and rate-of-return regulation further, capital and labor inputs can be introduced into the analysis. A source of economies of scope arises when a multiproduct firm makes use of a joint input (Baumol et al., 1982) (see Chapter 4). If the joint input is capital, then a simple extension of the A-J rate-base analysis will identify an incentive for investors to set up two separate firms to produce the outputs, despite the cost savings from a multiproduct firm. That is, profit for the multiproduct firm is less than the sum of profits when firms operate independently, with no shared use of the joint input. As an extreme example, consider a situation in which a large firm produces peak electricity, while a slightly smaller firm produces only off-peak electricity. Each has its own rate base on which its allowed return will be calculated. It is unlikely that regulators will permit such duplication of facilities. A single firm serving both the peak and off-peak periods will need no more capacity than either of the two separate firms and therefore will have a lower rate base on which to enjoy a return.[7]

To examine incentives for a regulated two-product firm that adheres to FDC allocations, consider the neoclassical production functions

$$q_i = f^i(K, L_i) \quad \text{for } i = 1, 2$$

where $K$ is a joint input used in producing both outputs. The formulation is essentially the same as the peak-load pricing model with a neoclassical production function (see Section 5.1). The gains to joint production can be substantial – reducing the under-utilized capacity that would arise in separate firms. For the welfare-maximizing firm, we find that if revenues do not cover costs, and demands are independent, the Ramsey pricing rules from Section 5.1 are

$$\frac{p_1 - w/f_L^1}{p_1} e_1 = \frac{p_2 - w/f_L^2}{p_2} e_2$$

and

$$\frac{p_1 f_K^1 + p_2 f_K^2 - r}{p_1 e_1 + q_2 e_2} = \left[ \frac{-\lambda}{\mu + \lambda} \right] \frac{1}{e_1 e_2}$$

where $\lambda$ and $\mu$ are the Lagrangian multipliers for the firm's budget constraint and the economy-wide income constraint, respectively, and $w$ and $r$ replace $b$ and $\beta$, respectively. Recall that the latter constraint ensures that total expenditures in the economy do not exceed total income.

---

7  Rozek (1984) presented a model of a multiproduct firm that even overcapitalized when $s < r$, a result quite contrary to the intuition from the A-J model. However, the regulator does not separate the capital used in producing monopoly output, $q_1$, from that actually used in producing $q_2$, sold in a competitive market. Grace (1986a) presents a model of a less myopic regulatory process and examines the impacts of alternative cost-allocation procedures when there is jointness in production. With $s < r$, the tendency for undercapitalization is reduced, but not reversed, in Grace's model.

The resulting prices yield an implicit joint-cost allocator, $\alpha_R$, which can be incorporated into total cost as

$$w(L_1 + L_2) + \alpha_R rK + (1 - \alpha_R)rK = \text{TC}$$

Moreover, if profit is zero, we have total cost equal to total revenues:

$$\text{TC} = \text{TR} = p_1 q_1 + p_2 q_2$$

These can be decomposed into direct costs and a share of fixed (capital) costs:

$$p_1 q_1 = wL_1 + \alpha_R rK$$
$$p_2 q_2 = wL_2 + (1 - \alpha_R)rK$$

Because we know that $p_i q_i > wL_i$, $i = 1, 2$, from Section 5.1, the value of the Ramsey capacity-cost allocator depends on the relative demand elasticities, the marginal-value product of capital, and the marginal-value product of the variable input for each product. The resulting prices need bear no relation to FDC prices, where the FDC allocator depends on variables such as relative output or relative directly attributable costs.

The derivation of $\alpha_R$ illustrates the importance of cost-allocation mechanisms in the context of regulation. A strong case can be made that analyses of A-J-type constraints must be supplemented by the cost-allocation considerations raised by Wellisz (1963). He showed how procedures used in natural-gas transmission distorted the seasonal output mix, as peak consumption was underpriced. Similarly, Grace (1986a) has explored the implications of regulatory practices in telecommunications – where the FCC approved allocations of the local-network cost to local and long-distance users of the network. Instead of focusing on elasticities and cost conditions, regulators have tended to allocate a greater percentage of joint local-network costs to long-distance users in an attempt to hold local rates down.

Although we lack adequate information for determining whether or not actual allocations track the implicit Ramsey (or some distributionally weighted Ramsey) allocator, the choice of $\alpha$ can lead to perverse results. For example, suppose regulators want to raise the price of output 1 to increase revenues, while they lower the price for output 2. They will tend to allocate a greater proportion of capacity costs to the former market. Grace shows that when there are large returns to scale for output 1, an increase in the allocation to that output (compared with $\alpha_R$) raises price in the short run. With lower output of $q_1$, the long-run derived demand in market one for the joint input is reduced – possibly outweighing the increased demand in the other market. Thus, a lower level for the joint input could be chosen by the regulated firm – ultimately hurting the consumers of product 2 (who were being "favored" by a relatively lower allocation). The theoretical possibility is not proof that past regulatory policies have in fact sacrificed efficiency unnecessarily. Nevertheless, the example illustrates the need to take the input-mix adjustments into account when trying to influence the output mix via cost-allocation procedures. Cabe (1988) does this in a general model of rate-of-return regulation and cost allocation by making the allocation mechanism endogenous. He shows that by manipulating the allocator, the regulator can reduce the firm's ability to overcapitalize. The allocator requires prices that can obtain only at fairly efficient levels of capital.

If the costs of capital differ in the various jurisdictions ($r_1 \neq r_2$), or the allowed rates of return differ ($s_1 \neq s_2$), then the potential input and output-mix distortions become even more complicated. For now, we note only that the rate of return is only one instrument used in the regulatory process. The specification of a cost allocator for a jointly used input can have significant impacts on the output mix and costs. Empirical studies can overestimate or underestimate the impacts of rate-base regulation if they do not incorporate the role of cost-allocation regulation.

### 11.3 Deregulation and residual regulation

Complete elimination of regulatory constraints is seldom politically feasible and may be inefficient. Yet, in a number of industries, giving firms greater price and product-mix flexibility can reduce the costs of regulation. Many issues are raised by such residual regulation, including appropriate criteria for price floors and price ceilings. For example, in the case of long-distance telecommunications, the FCC has limited price reductions by AT&T. Low prices benefit consumers, but harm competitors; so the latter have strong incentives to constrain the dominant firm's pricing behavior. Allegations of predatory (below-cost) pricing for some products are accompanied by concerns of monopolistic pricing for other products (or consumers) that must provide revenues "above costs" if the firm is to earn at least a competitive rate of return. If technological change or an increased awarenees of regulatory costs makes deregulation seem desirable in an industry, principles for evaluating price flexibility are needed for the transition period.[8] In some industries in the past, entry has been viewed as excessive; so this political justification for government intervention is reviewed here in the context of deregulation.

### Price floors for residual regulation

Several criteria have been used to evaluate price floors. One approach is simply to use FDC prices. Prices that are below fully distributed or fully allocated costs are viewed as predatory by some people, but as indicated in Chapters 3 and 7, FDC prices provide a poor standard for promoting either efficiency or equity. Arbitrary accounting allocation of unattributable costs is a pointless exercise. As Baumol (1983) points out, other firms that would like to see higher prices can find cost-allocation techniques that put the regulated firm at a competitive disadvantage. For

8 Of course, such residual regulation has direct and indirect costs; so the development of pricing rules does not imply that complete deregulation should not be considered. AT&T spent $380 million on legal fees during the decade prior to the 1984 divestiture. During the following three years, participants may have spent another $75 million for lawyers and consultants who worked on pricing and product-mix issues associated with implementing the decree (*Wall Street Journal,* April 4, 1987). Apparently divestiture has not diminished regulatory activity.

example, competitive haulers of steel, feathers, and platinum will want the railroad to allocate costs of the shipped good according to weight, volume, and market value, respectively.

A marginalist approach to price floors has a much stronger claim to efficiency. Areeda and Turner (1975) argued in an antitrust contest that so long as price is greater than or equal to marginal cost, it should not be viewed as predatory. They suggested that average variable cost (AVC) can be used as a proxy when calculating marginal cost proves difficult. However, short-run and long-run marginal costs will generally differ, calling into question the use of AVC for determining least-cost providers in the long run. Also, this criterion may fail because of second-best considerations, such as those noted in Section 3.5. Furthermore, if rivals exit the market, subsequent price increases will raise questions about the welfare content of the Areeda–Turner approach. Their rule allows a range of acceptable prices, without considering how allocative efficiency might vary over this range.

A third approach for evaluating a price floor, *compensatory pricing,* takes into account the incremental costs and revenues of a product (or of serving a particular consumer group). Consider a multiproduct firm producing $n$ outputs:

$q_1$ = output of product 1

$\hat{q}$ = vector of outputs of products $2, \ldots, n$, $\hat{q} = (q_2, \ldots, q_n)$

$\hat{q} + \Delta\hat{q}$ = vector of outputs demanded (because of complementarity or substitution) if $q_1 = 0$

$C(q_1, \hat{q})$ = total-cost function

$R(q_i, \hat{q}) = p_1 q_1 + \hat{p}\hat{q}$ = total-revenue function

Baumol (1983) defines

gross incremental cost of $q_1 = C(q_1, \hat{q}) - C(0, \hat{q})$

net incremental cost of $q_1 = C(q_1, \hat{q}) - C(0, \hat{q} + \Delta\hat{q})$

gross incremental revenue $= R(q_1, \hat{q}) - R(0, \hat{q})$

net incremental revenue $= R(q_1, \hat{q}) - R(0, \hat{q} + \Delta\hat{q})$

If cross-elasticities of demand between $q_1$ and the other products are zero, and no cost complementarities exist between $q_1$ and the other products, then we can compare $p_1$ and the average incremental cost (AIC) to determine if $p_1$ is "too low." That is, if

$$p_1 \geq [C(q_1, \hat{q}) - C(0, \hat{q})]/q_1 = \text{AIC}$$

then

$$p_1 q_1 \geq C(q_1, \hat{q}) - C(0, \hat{q})$$

If the foregoing relationship holds, the price is compensatory rather than predatory; it receives no cross-subsidy from other products.

Baumol (1983) emphasizes that this standard for pricing $q_1$ is based foremost on fairness (distributive equity) toward the supplier's *other* consumers. The objective is to avoid burdening other consumers with costs incurred to serve the buyers of $q_1$. Nevertheless, there would be efficiency losses if lower prices were required for $q_1$. Pricing below the incremental-cost floor would exclude more efficient suppliers from the market. Baumol would also consider requiring that potentially predatory prices remain in effect after a competitor exits the industry.

If $q_1$ is a substitute (or complement) for the other products, the *net*-incremental-revenue test is appropriate – so lost (increased) revenues and avoided (additional) costs associated with the other products are taken into account. Under an overall-profit ceiling, consumers of the other products will make up the reduction in net profits if

$$R(q_1, \hat{q}) - R(0, \hat{q} + \Delta\hat{q}) \geq C(q_1, \hat{q}) - C(0, \hat{q} + \Delta\hat{q})$$

Also, recall the point made by Faulhaber (1975) and examined in Chapter 7. Passing the net-incremental-profit test for each $q_i$ is necessary but not sufficient for the absence of a cross-subsidy. The test must also be imposed on every combination of the $q_i$'s.

For example, if a telephone system serves three communities, A, B, and C, each alone must pass the net-incremental-profit test, and each coalition of communities, (A, B), (A, C), (B, C), and (A,

B, C), must also pass the test. It is important that the latter coalition pass the test to ensure revenues sufficient to cover total cost. Supposed a line connects A and B, and the incremental cost of calls from A to B is low, and that from B to A is also low. If prices for calling exactly cover their low individual incremental costs, there is no contribution for replacing the line.[9] So the revenue-sufficiency criterion need not be met even if each individual product meets the net-incremental-profit test: "It follows that in order to pass an appropriate test of compensatory pricing, the incremental revenue of each product and every combination of products must contribute net incremental revenues which exceed the corresponding net incremental costs, including the costs of any incremental capital and the normal rate of return on that incremental capital" (Baumol, 1983, p. 187).

### Price ceilings for residual regulation

The setting of an upper bound on price has been a subject of discussion in several previous chapters. Ramsey pricing offers one mechanism for determining prices to different consumer groups, but regulators still will need to check for cross-subsidization. Average stand-alone cost could be used as an upper bound. Although the cost to a specialized firm in producing only $q_1$ does not incorporate gains from economies of scope, the ceiling price of $q_1$ based on stand-alone cost still serves as an equity criterion. The price is no higher than it would be if the group produced for itself. Furthermore, if the stand-alone ceiling is violated, either excess profit will be earned or noncompensatory prices will be charged for other products – inducing a misallocation. To see that the total revenue from a price $\hat{p}$ is no greater than the stand-alone cost of $\hat{q} + \Delta\hat{q}$ (when $q_1 = 0$), we first assume that $p_1$ is compensatory. The net incremental revenue from $q_1$ is greater than or equal to the net incremental cost:

$$p_1 q_1 - \hat{p}\Delta\hat{q} \geq C(q_1, \hat{q}) - C(0, \hat{q} + \Delta\hat{q})$$

9 Note that a multiproduct firm producing goods with stochastic demands can appear to be engaging in cross-subsidization for the purpose of predatory pricing when it is only reducing overall firm risk (Gilligan and Smirlock, 1983).

Because $p_1q_1 + \hat{p}\hat{q} = C(q_1, \hat{q})$, we can subtract this equation from the foregoing inequality to obtain

$$\hat{p}(\hat{q} + \Delta\hat{q}) \leq C(0, \hat{q} + \Delta\hat{q})$$

That is, the total revenue generated if $q_1$ is not produced is less than or equal to the stand-alone cost of $\hat{q} + \Delta\hat{q}$. If regulators are willing to provide managers with some pricing flexibility, this approach to price ceilings has positive efficiency and equity implications.

### Destructive competition

Regulatory interest in price floors does not stem only from a concern that without such constraints, predatory pricing can cause efficient competitors to exit the market and subsequently result in excessive prices. Price-floor regulation has also been justified in terms of *destructive competition,* which is alleged to arise in certain circumstances. In industries with substantial fixed costs and chronic excess capacity, the presence of fluctuating market demand may cause price to fluctuate widely over the business cycle and for much of the time drive price below average total cost for the firms in the industry. According to this scenario, minimum necessary profits may not be earned over the cycle as demand alternatively presses against and falls short of industry capacity. Secular declines in demand can be especially problematic. In the short run, each company will strive to cover a portion of overhead costs by price-shading, and none will cease operations until all are near the brink of collapse. Conversely, an industry whose members operate numerous plants of widely varying efficiencies and with a high variable-cost component can adapt more smoothly to demand downturns, because less efficient plants will be closed down long before the most efficient plants are threatened with failure.

Industrial structures that result in wide price fluctuations are viewed by some as justifying government intervention. Of course, industries with relatively high variability in returns will be expected to experience higher returns on average. Because capital markets operate so as to transfer risk to those willing to bear it, the greater risks and returns can be borne voluntarily by investors. However, often there is a parallel social concern for the wages of employees in the industry. Thus, intervention has sometimes stemmed from the distributional consequences of competition, deterioration of product quality, and high variability of prices.

It is possible to distinguish between destructive competition and predatory behavior. As Kahn (1971, vol. I, p. 173) describes it, destructive competition occurs when price is far below average total costs for a very long time. The prerequisite conditions in an industry for such an occurrence are (1) sunk costs as a high percentage of total cost, (2) long and sustained periods of excess capacity, and (3) sellers too small in relation to the total size of the market to act collusively in order to avoid competition that drives price down to marginal cost. These three conditions in conjunction with price instability, typically caused by inelastic supply in the short run, may result in all of the firms (or a large portion) in an industry failing to cover their total costs, including a normal return on investment. Wages may fall dramatically in slump times.

Destructive competition is therefore *not strategic,* in the sense that rival firms target each other for elimination by deliberately cutting prices or by adding excess capacity, hence earning lower incomes. Rather, it is a structural occurrence that is endogenous to the whole industry; it emanates not from firm-specific strategic behavior but from intense competition, imperfect foresight, and slow exit. Whether or not regulation that limits entry and tries to prop prices up really enhances welfare is another issue. Because we are focusing on the natural monopoly justification for regulation, we shall not critique the destructive-competition rationale for govenment intervention. Economists have tended to be skeptical of this justification for price regulation used in the securities and trucking industries. Subsequent deregulation in some of these industries has yielded significant economies and price reductions. For example, the Securities and Exchange Commission's deregulation of securities transactions is generally viewed as greatly benefiting investors. The industry now provides a wide range of price–risk options unavailable prior to deregulation.

### Impact of selective rate changes

With deregulation, selective rate increases and decreases will differentially affect various consumer groups. Consumers with few substitutes are likely to face higher prices unless potential entry holds prices down. Alternatively, consumers who have been subsidizing others in the past will tend to have prices that reflect the cost of serving them. The incidence of winners and losers from deregulation depends on past price patterns and the new options available to suppliers and demanders.

In some cases, deregulation might result in greater inefficiencies than before. For example, if two gas pipelines compete for business in one city, but are monopolists in smaller towns located on other portions of their routes, deregulation could result in selective rate reductions to compete with each other in the city they jointly serve. Under complete pipeline deregulation, the monopolized markets would face higher prices than before.

Whether or not deregulation results in a welfare improvement depends on the net impact of price increases and decreases and associated cost changes. Because of declining long-run average costs for these pipelines, all prices are not initially equal to marginal costs – in either the larger city or the smaller towns. If the regulators are following the pricing rules developed in Section 3.4, then initially we have complex Ramsey rules in effect. Under those rules for rivalry among strong natural monopolies, the price should not be relatively lower in the competitive market. Deregulation can be expected to disrupt the Ramsey pricing, with prices dropping in the large city (competitive market) and increasing in the small towns (markets in which there are no substitutes available).

Furthermore, if the natural gas is used in the monopolized markets to produce goods that compete with those produced in the "favored" city, inefficiencies arise at the level of secondary competition. The locations of firms using the intermediate good are distorted by relatively inefficient pricing. Kahn (1971, vol. I, pp. 159–80) discusses the impact of selective rate reductions in the face of competition when there are no inherent advantages to the favored location. Resources are devoted to transporting the intermediate good (here, natural gas) to the large city. Unless there are economies of agglomeration, this production pattern represents an uneconomic diversion of service away from markets served by pipeline monopolies (where price is far above marginal cost) toward the "competitive" market (where the rivals fight for business).

Kahn draws several lessons from his analysis of rivalry between firms with similar technologies. First, suppliers with the lowest long-run marginal cost ought to serve the market. Kahn notes that if all prices cannot be equal to long-run marginal cost, the simple Ramsey rule promoting efficiency supports selective rate increases to consumers with inelastic demands. However, if competitors have similar cost structures, selective (competitive) price reductions in those markets need not be efficient.

One advantage of deregulation, however, is that it tends to stimulate cost reductions and encourage the exploration of demand elasticities. The complex Ramsey rules require complete information on cost functions, the direction of technological change, demand elasticities, and demand growth. Under deregulation, enhanced economic incentives for innovative efficiency can outweigh short-run inefficiencies resulting from the behavior described earlier. With deregulation, identifying which firm (or location) has economic advantages is a task involving trial and error. Unless chronic excess capacity (and duplication of facilities) is likely to result, a strong case can be made that this task should be left to the marketplace, rather than to administrative procedures.

### 11.4. Expansion of the product line

This section develops principles to be used in evaluating the impacts of new regulated and unregulated products on consumers and on efficiency. Why would an unregulated single-product firm decide to produce another product? If there were entry barriers in the production of the second product, subadditivity in the production of two products would imply that given adequate demands for the goods, the unregulated firm could increase profits by expanding its product line. Furthermore, consumers of the second good would be better off than when not having the product at all. Whether consumers of the first good would be better off would depend on cost and demand interdependencies. With regulation, a similar result emerges, although the type of regulation (rate-of-return, markup, etc.) can affect incentives to merge or add products. We have seen that when there are savings from the exploitation of multiproduct economies, a regulated firm can benefit consumers even by entering a competitive market. First we consider the case of two rate-base-regulated natural monopolies and examine additional incentives for these firms to merge.

Peles and Sheshinski (1976) provide a simple demonstration of how two single-product natural monopolies subject to separate rate-of-return constraints will, in general, find it advantageous to merge. They analyze a situation in which there are neither economies of scale nor demand interdependences: The incentive for merger arises from regulation, not from real resource savings. The argument goes as follows: Consider two firms under rate-base regulation, so that the A-J input-mix distortions are present. Firms 1 and 2 have both overcapitalized (to $K_1^*$ and $K_2^*$, respectively) and earn the allowed rate of return, $s$, on their rate bases. If the firms merge, they are still subject to the same overall regulatory constraint. The marginal-revenue products of capital used in the production of the two goods will, in general, differ. The merged firm has an option previously unavailable to the single-product firms: The total capital stock, $K_1^* + K_2^*$, can be reallocated between production of the two goods to the good with the higher elasticity of the marginal-revenue product of capital. Profit from the combined operations is greater than the sum of the separate profits earned prior to merger. The output mix is altered toward the product with the more elastic marginal-revenue product function.

Of course, now the realized return is greater than allowed; so the merged firm further expands capital – driving down the realized return. The resulting changes in relative outputs and input usage have a straightforward explanation: The new entity has an additional degree of freedom previously unavailable to the single-product firms.

Peles and Sheshinski also show that the integrated regulated firm uses excessive capital inputs in the production of each output. The full welfare consequences of merger are not clear, however. If demands are independent, the outcome depends on the relative capital intensities of the products, elasticities of substitution between inputs, and product demand elasticities. These factors determine the marginal-revenue products of capital, which establish the output levels of the separate firms and the merged firm.

If A-J biases do not arise, the merger of two regulated natural monopolies producing different products can enhance total welfare if Ramsey prices can now be adopted. Initially, if each firm is pricing at average cost, then, after merger, the combination company can use Ramsey pricing – benefiting consumers of the good with the relatively elastic demand. If the goods are not independent, cross-elasticities can be taken into account in the calculation of Ramsey prices. The sum of consumer surplus and profits is greater after merger. Thus, the demand side can be the source of economies for multiproduct firms.

Others have emphasized a different impact of merger – reduced incentives to keep costs down when rivals join together. Stevenson (1982) noted that even a regulated rival puts downward pressure on prices: "We cannot say that ever-increasing competitive fervor will result in continual reduction in X-efficiency. But we can say that the statement, 'Competition does not matter' with respect to X-inefficiency is not justified" (p. 64).[10] Of

10  X-efficiency considerations relate to whether or not the firm is operating on the production isoquant. According to A-J, the input-mix distortion raises costs, but at least the firm is technologically efficient. However, if absence of rivalry leads to managerial shirking, the firm will be off the production isoquant. This point is addressed in Section 12.4.

course, such negative impacts of merger may be more than outweighed by gains from economies of scope.

When considering the impact of a merger, the fundamental trade-off is between resource savings and the possible creation of market power (Williamson, 1968). Waterson (1983) provides an analysis of merger impacts in the absence of regulation. If the firm produces only one product, its cost function is taken to be

$$C(1) = cq_i + F$$

A firm producing two products has a cost function

$$C(2) = cq_1 + cq_2 + 2F(1 - e/2), \qquad 1 > e > 0$$

The economies-of-scope parameter, $e$, can range from 0 to 1, with the latter implying that the fixed cost of supplying two products is the same as for supplying one.

Waterson uses a Cournot framework to compare merger outcomes under different parameter values, showing that if the cross-elasticity of demand is low relative to own-price elasticities, the savings from economies of scope can outweigh the costs of monopoly power. Similar conclusions emerge when comparing the regulation of two firms with the regulation of the merged firm. Now, not only are economies of scope attained, but also pricing can be directed toward maximizing consumer surplus subject to revenues covering costs. Resource savings are achieved, and Ramsey pricing can be practiced if the products are for the same regulatory jurisdiction.

The possibility of jurisdictional disputes raises a number of important issues for firms operating in several states. Regulators in one state will not, in general, be willing to reduce consumer welfare from product 1 even if it is far less than the increase for product 2's consumers residing in another state. Of course, transfer mechanisms could make both sets of consumers better off, but we noted the difficulties associated with tax and transfer mechanisms in Chapter 2. Also, capital serving one consumer group is not always easily disentangled from that serving another: Backup electricity-generating capacity may serve several states, and the local telephone network serves local and long-distance callers. If allowed returns are not equal across jurisdictions, multiproduct firms may have incentives to allocate capacity to jurisdictions with the higher returns. Furthermore, in some situations, regulators may disallow capital in the rate base, as when a jointly owned nuclear plant is determined to be unnecessary by a state commission.

## 11.5. Vertical integration

Firms often carry on activities in both the production and distribution processes. Such vertical integration raises the same set of regulatory issues considered in the previous sections: transfer pricing, possible predatory pricing, cross-subsidization benefiting unregulated markets, output-mix alterations, and input-mix distortions. Incentives to integrate vertically can be classified into a number of categories, including technical interdependences, market failures, structural imperfections, innovation and planning, and uncertainty about input supply. Although some of these incentives will be examined here, the reader is referred to Blair and Kaserman (1983) for a thorough discussion of these issues. In general, the incentives that apply depend on the market structure and production functions prevailing in the upstream and downstream industries. With regard to social welfare, it is possible that private incentives exist to integrate vertically even when it is socially undesirable. Some of the welfare consequences of integration, both positive and negative, are examined in this section.

The relevant production functions can be represented by the following taxonomy. Assume that the firm initially produces $q_2$. If there are economies of scope in the production of $q_2$ and $q_1$, where $q_1$ is both an output and an input, the firm can achieve efficiencies by vertical integration backward into a variable input or a capital input. Alternatively, it can resort to vertical integration forward into the production of a product using $q_2$ as a variable input or as a fixed input. This simple taxonomy introduces four possibilities when moving from a single-product firm to a two-product firm. The way in which regulators treat a firm that integrates vertically can influence the input and output mixes. Will both products be regulated? Will price comparisons be used to ensure that inappropriate transfer pricing does not arise? How are the gains to joint production to be shared by consumers of the two products? To better understand basic technological trade-offs, we describe the sources of the cost savings from vertical integration.

### Technical interdependencies

Cost savings from integration often are the results of technical interdependencies. For example, sometimes resources can be saved if two stages of a production process are in close proximity with respect to time and location. Alternatively, the input for one process may be a by-product or output of another. Reductions in the cost of production through achievement of technological efficiencies unambiguously increase the welfare of society, ceteris paribus. At the same level of output, resources are released for use in other sectors.

Technological interdependencies often arise in the context of the need for compatibility standards, where components of a product require particular engineering features for the final product to operate properly. Integration may be required to properly handle these interdependencies. Katz and Shapiro (1985) characterize incompatibility as involving a network externality; they focus on the importance of consumer expectations and producer reputations in the relevant markets. The absence of coordination can lead to underprovision or overprovision of compatibility. Farrell and Saloner (1985) apply a similar network model to situations in which firms will have different gains if they adopt a new technology that is incompatible with current products. Their analysis of inertia, information asymmetries, and bandwagon effects yields further insights into the efficient development of technical standards. Vertical integration may enhance the prospects for compatibility – but the efficiency impacts are not necessarily positive Berg (1988).

Other examples of technical interdependencies abound. One could label internal R&D as a kind of vertical integration made desirable by technical linkages. Contracting R&D work outside the firm would be inefficient in many situations. The issues raised by this option were explored in the previous chapter. In the cable-TV industry, some early cable-TV companies were owned by holding companies that also manufactured cable. And today, some cable companies have moved into the production of programming. In communications, AT&T has been vertically integrated into manufacturing through Western Electric. The gains to joint specification of product characteristics and systems requirements made Western Electric a relatively low cost supplier. With the manufacturer placed in closer contact with ultimate consumers, products can be better tailored to match demand. In competitive markets, the most efficient degree of integration can be expected to emerge via pressures for cost reduction. The technical interdependencies inviting integration are more difficult to evaluate under regulation, given entry restrictions and constraints on rates of return.

### Additional incentives

Resource savings can arise from a number of circumstances. For example, market failures can be attenuated through vertical integration. When both supplier and buyer have some monopoly power, haggling costs may be incurred between supplier and buyer over the terms of contracts. Alternatively, even under competition, specification of performance characteristics for complex products is no easy matter. In a static environment, these costs can be avoided through integration or long-term contracts. But in a dynamic setting, integration may be preferred over long-term contracts or a string of short-term contracts. Integration may harmonize interests and permit an efficient decision process to be used.

Also, vertical integration may facilitate the identification of different demand elasticities, making price discrimination feasible. In particular, the necessity of the non-resale condition makes vertical integration potentially attractive to achieve price discrimination. A firm faced with two sets of downstream industries demanding the good could vertically integrate into industry one, thus giving it greater discretion in pricing the good to industry two. The essence of price discrimination by means of vertical integration is that the internal price to integrated subsidiaries must be below the price charged to other firms. Integration into the industry with more elastic demand must occur for price discrimination to be sustainable (Perry, 1978). Such a possibility will be of concern to regulators, although price discrimination can enhance efficiency.

Another category commonly dealt with in the economics literature is that of structural imperfections in the markets. Vertical integration can prove to be profitable to *both* a downstream firm and upstream firm when one or both of the firms wield some monopoly power. Depending on the particular imperfection being analyzed, society as a whole may also benefit from vertical integration in the presence of market imperfections.

Regulatory policy in the face of vertical integration must also address the problem of risk-bearing when regulated utilities integrate backward into the production of their inputs. For example, cases arise in which regulated gas-pipeline companies try to integrate into the search for supplies of natural gas, or when electric utilities integrate into the transportation of energy inputs, oil and coal. The risk surrounding the regulated firm probably increases when it decides to get in the business of oil-and-gas exploration. The cost of capital to the firm depends on risk, and therefore regulators may be pressured to alter the allowed rate of return. What are the efficiency and equity implications of integration in that scenario? Should consumers be forced to pay a higher price as a result of the increase in $s$? Is it possible that the reduced risk from an assured input supply and savings in transactions costs will outweigh the increased risk if there is an unfavorable change in the firm's asset portfolio?

Another problem regulators face with backward integration by utilities is the possibility that input prices charged internally may be inflated, with the higher costs simply being passed on as a legitimate operating expense to consumers. Dayan (1975) notes that the intent of the integration might be to improve the profitability of the input-supplier at the expense of consumers. By charging itself a high transfer price for the input, the vertically integrated firm can inflate its average costs. Completely passive regulation will result in the profit-maximizing monopoly price. The regulated division earns only $s$, but the input-supply division appropriates the full monopoly profit. In fact, with such control, the input distortion disappears, because maximum profits arise when the monopolist minimizes production costs.

To prevent such profiteering, regulators may either prohibit backward integration by natural monopolies or allow integration and regulate the input-suppliers. The first approach results in the loss of potential economies from integration (discussed already), and the second approach imposes regulation on a division in a potentially competitive industry. Not only does this increase the costs of regulation, but also it opens up the possibility of extending input biases to another stage of production. A third possibility might be to allow integration and, if there is competition in the input market, have regulators periodically compare the integrated input-supplier's prices with other nonintegrated input-suppliers' prices to ensure that the input prices to the regulated firm are not unjustifiably higher. Such comparisons become difficult when unique inputs with many characteristics are involved.

## 11.6. Determining the benefits from deregulation

An analysis of regulation must, at some point, address the matter of incentives for deregulation. Many of the most important issues facing policy-makers today arise in the context of technological change, in which new cost structures make entry feasible. Issues are also raised by demand growth, where larger markets imply that the cost function for any single firm supplying the market is not subadditive. Alternatively, public perceptions of the net gains to regulation can change, placing pressure on leg-

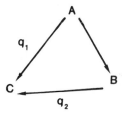

Figure 11.4. Route structure.

islators and regulators to modify regulatory procedures and give greater flexibility to firms.

The timing of policy change often is driven more by anecdotal evidence and industrial experience than by the development of elegant mathematical models. Yet the insights gleaned from these models provide explanations of how different market structures and demand circumstances determine corporate behavior and industry performance. We have already identified inefficiencies that arise under regulations requiring FDC pricing or from cost-plus procedures. The reduction of such misallocations could be achieved through better regulation, but if the costs of achieving improved procedures are high, total (or partial) deregulation may be a better alternative.

### Real resource savings

Let us consider an example of deregulation that results in real welfare gains. Suppose a firm has the characteristics of a natural monopoly, but changes in demand or cost structures alter the benefits of continued regulation. If the firm can be prevented from expending resources on protecting monopoly rents, net gains will be available to society. Figure 11.4 depicts a network that will be used to illustrate the impact of deregulation for a firm for which continued regulation would result in inefficient production methods.

Consider a regulated firm operating on two transportation routes, AC and BC. The linear structure arose out of a system of entry regulation – rather than from a process directed toward cost minimization. For simplicity, let us assume that there is no traffic between the AB segment; under regulation, $q_1$ and $q_2$ are produced. As Morrison and Winston (1985) point out, under deregulation the firm can (1) abandon a route (like route AC), (2) maintain the same route structure (status quo), or (3) adopt a hub-and-spoke structure, routing AC traffic through B. The profits associated with the three options are as follows:

$$(1) \qquad \pi^1 = p_2 q_2 - C(0, q_2)$$
$$(2) \qquad \pi^2 = p_1 q_1 + p_2 q_2 - C(q_1, 0) - C(0, q_2)$$
$$(3) \qquad \pi^3 = p_1 q_1^* + p_2 q_2 - C(q_1^*, q_2)$$

Here, $p_i$ are assumed constant across alternatives (limit pricing), and $q_1^* < q_1$, because being rerouted increases travel time, reducing traffic. The choice between (2) and (3) depends on the possible loss of revenue from increased inconvenience for consumers and cost savings from economies of scope. The economies of scope depend on economies of vehicle size versus the cost of rerouting traffic (which depends on distance and on the need for more elaborate facilities at hubs, for handling the forwarding functions).

Morrison and Winston argue that deregulation has allowed firms in air (and trucking) freight transport to adopt hub-and-spoke operations that maintain service to low-density routes. Such spoke routes permit individual firms to realize economies of vehicle size on their high-density routes. Rail and bus, on the other hand, have remained with linear routes, because significant rerouting reduces demand because of the increase in travel time. Although both air transport and trucking firms would be expected to abandon low-density routes, intermodal coordination can preserve some service.

Morrison and Winston noted that underlying economies, not regulatory agencies, determine the route structures in a competitive, unregulated environment. They found that increases in departure frequencies were the single most important source of welfare gains to airline deregulation, their major finding being that "in 1977 dollars, the welfare increase for all travelers is $5.7 billion. Decomposing this welfare change [they] find the average welfare change per passenger trip due to fare changes is $4.04, to travel time changes is −$0.96, and to frequency changes is $8.00" (Morrison and Winston, 1985, p. 57). Earlier studies had characterized regulation as yielding excessive fares and service-quality competition. Deregulation was projected to result in reduced service (including less frequent departures). As it turned out, deregulation enabled more efficient hub-and-spoke route structures, which, according to Morrison and Winston, was a much more important result of deregulation than was competitive fare reductions. Under the previous regime, airlines were unable to totally restructure their own routes. Rather, piecemeal expansion occurred in response to demand growth in particular routes – and then only with approval by the CAB.

### Sunk costs and the regulatory transition

The issues raised by deregulation include the time period that regulators will allow for adjustments by sellers and buyers. Should there be flash deregulation or some managed transition during which participants in the market are "protected" from competition? Calls for the regulatory transition tend to come from previously protected producers if entry is easy and the regulated firms have substantial sunk costs. Also, if entry barriers are high, sunk costs in durable goods by consumers may limit their competitive options under full deregulation. In such cases, those with short-run inelastic demands for the service will seek protection from price increases. Thus, there will be pleas by suppliers or consumers for continued regulation, for continued mandatory service, and for limitations in allowed price ranges.

Gaskins and Voytko (1981) have catalogued the problems of transition. They note that production inefficiencies can be avoided if the duration and extent of "special" treatment are known and certain. Only if regulators limit the possibility of policy reversals will firms make the investment and output decisions consistent with competition. Furthermore, transition side payments (via direct subsidies or regulation-mandated transfers) can reduce the inevitable disruption that arises when regulated prices or returns are left to market determination.

Meyer and Tye (1985) identify two different regulatory transitions raising different fairness and efficiency considerations and requiring different policies. In a situation of easy entry and minimal commitments tying particular consumers to particular vendors, the contestable-markets model is applicable. No residual regulation is needed to protect consumer interests. The bankruptcy of particular vendors may cause dislocations, but at least the elimination of inefficiencies accompanies such adjustments: "Indeed, complaints about deregulation are more likely to originate with the factors of production – labor and capital – for deregulation can often mean erosion of a previously privileged position. . . . But from the standpoint of consumer (or shipper) interests alone, a prompt, almost immediate, transition would seem advisable" (p. 50).

The second situation involves limited entry possibilities, with some consumer groups having sunk costs or commitments tying them to specific vendors for some period of time. Inelastic demands associated with sunk investments at particular locations can be subjected to monopoly exploitation. Ramsey pricing rules based on relative short-run elasticities raise questions of fairness. Claims of injustice arise as price discrimination emerges. As Meyer and Tye state, "it should never be forgotten that in a market economy, whenever prices for any activity rise disproportionately above the underlying cost fundamentals, business ingenuity (in the form of new or altered technologies, product and location substitutions, etc.) is quickly applied to finding ways to do with less" (p. 50). They are concerned with price differentials including investments that do not prove to be economic in the long run. Thus, they are skeptical of using Ramsey pricing when our knowledge of short- and long-run demand elasticities is so limited, particularly when R&D investments will alter those elasticities.

Electricity, natural-gas, telecommunications, and transportation markets all face some distruptions due to competitive pressures. Cicchetti (1986) has noted that regulators might follow a fourfold approach toward these industries:

1. Allow competitive entry when efficiencies are not lost by the regulated firm.
2. Encourage marginal-cost pricing, unbundle service offerings, and incorporate peak-load and cost-causation considerations into rate designs.
3. Permit coalitions of consumers or large customers to negotiate contracts (so that prices take into account long-run demand elasticities).
4. Avoid inefficient wheeling of electricity, bypass of networks, and carriage of products.

Similarities among industries that traditionally have been regulated suggest that lessons can be learned from deregulation efforts to date. Until recently, the energy, telecommunications, and transportation industries had prices established for bundled services, based on embedded (or historical) costs. The implicit contract between consumers and their traditional suppliers involved an obligation to serve and a commitment to continued consumption. Several of these industries had vertically integrated structures involving production, transmission (or carriage), and distribution to final demanders; so deregulation opens up the possibility of entry at various stages of production and raises issues of access to transmission facilities. Also, time-of-use patterns in these industries often reflect sensitivity to weather and economic conditions. When storage is costly, peak demands drive production capacity.

The traditional utility industries also have significant differences. Investor-owned electric utilities have tended to be more vertically integrated than gas-delivery systems or transportation companies. The electrics tend to own generation, transmission, and distribution facilities (Joskow and Schmalensee, 1983). Similarly, prior to the AT&T divestiture, vertical integration characterized much of telecommunications. Sunk costs play different roles for the various industries. When such costs are significant, difficult problems are raised by consumers leaving their traditional suppliers.

Contractual commitments and traditions of cooperation within the industries also affect regulatory leverage over the phase-in of competitive pressures. For example, long-term commitments and liabilities affect the industries to different degrees. The Federal Energy Regulatory Commission has abrogated some take-or-pay contracts for gas pipelines, but corresponding contracts for electricity tend to be under state jurisdiction. Similarly, interutility coordination and pooling arrangements complicate the introduction of competition into many markets.

Depending on the industry, this issue arises in different degrees. When a vertically integrated firm controls resources or capacity to which another firm would like competitive access, regulators are faced with developing standards for determining the terms for access to a so-called essential facility. As Tye (1987) notes, public policy "has differed significantly, varying paradoxically from mandatory requirements for open interconnection in the once-closed telecommunications industries to an extremely permissive policy by the ICC that has permitted massive cancellations of the open competitive access that previously had prevailed in the rail industry under strict regulation" (p. 337). Electricity-transmission facilities and natural-gas-transmission pipelines are two other examples of facilities for which access issues arise. The efficiency implications of requiring access depend on the degree of monopoly power exercised by the owner of the facility.

In each of these situations, regulatory rules determine the equilibrium output mix and incentives for entry (or exit). In the case of electricity, utilities want to be reimbursed by users of their transmission lines, and they view cogenerators and municipal utilities with excess capacity as competitive threats. Although some of these suppliers are small (and thus electricity price-takers), others are strong natural monopolies locally. Since 1983, the Federal Energy Regulatory Commission has been experimenting with partial deregulation of price and sales of bulk power in the Southwest.[11] Such interstate deregulation leads to competition and increased wheeling. Studies are under way to determine if there are net efficiencies from deregulation. In general, access to and payments for transmission services determine the extent of competition. If FDC methods are applied to historical (embedded) costs to determine the price of transmission services, the resulting prices will deviate from marginal costs. It is unlikely that appropriate second-best outcomes are approximated by current transmission prices.

Similar issues arise in railroads and telecommunications. Transshipment along a rival's track may be needed for a firm to provide end-to-end service. The ICC regulated charges for shipments hauling, which in turn determined transportation patterns for goods. Such fees can be viewed as regulatory instruments for achieving efficiency, although in practice they have tended not to promote least-cost provision of rail transportation.

Similar mechanisms for transferring funds have become institutionalized in telecommunications separations and settlements procedures. In the past, such transfers were directed primarily at covering costs of a shared input – the local network. However, carrier access charges to AT&T, MCI, US Sprint, and others now could be used to affect long-distance rivals differentially. The competitive impacts are nontrivial. For example, in 1986, access charges composed over half of AT&T's total costs. The burden on long-distance callers is also substantial. For the nation, interstate and intrastate contributions to local exchanges reached $11 billion (Kahn and Shew, 1987, p. 195).

Cicchetti's two approaches to rate-making in these industries,

---

11 Over the next decade or so, deregulation, or at least partial deregulation, of the U.S. electric-power industry may become a reality. Joskow and Schmalensee (1983) take an exhaustive look at the potential for competitive markets to supplant regulation in the generation, transmission, and distribution systems.

partially regulated pricing and flexible regulated pricing, have different implications for risk-bearing and thus will affect the cost of capital to the traditional utility. Under flexible pricing, those consumers with inelastic demands may pay more, but they also will share in gains from sales to competitive markets. Price flexibility will allow the firm to avoid stranded capacity – such scenarios are especially likely when there is substantial technological change. Alternatively, caps can be placed on prices to captive consumers, with gains from sales to competitive markets accruing to shareholders. Unbundling transportation from the product (or service) is important under both scenarios, because competitive access to shared (bottleneck) facilities provides incentives for firms to keep costs and prices down.

## 11.7. Summary

The formulation of appropriate regulatory strategies when product mixes change and new competitive pressures emerge requires substantial information regarding costs and demands. The two-product case illustrated the nature of the pricing and entry issues arising under partial regulation. The initial price structure was shown to determine the impact of eliminating pricing and entry restrictions for one market. Similarly, a single-product monopolist will find it profitable to add a product line if the cost function is subadditive. The key question is whether or not revenues from the regulated sector can be used to subsidize the unregulated sector. Even if a firm is sustainable under partial regulation (SUPR), it need not be producing efficiently, earning zero profit, or avoiding cross-subsidies. Monitoring a partially regulated firm raises a number of problems. For example, a policy of partial regulation may protect a relatively high cost multiproduct firm. Complex separations procedures for revenues and costs overlie the regulatory process, increasing the possibilities for input- and output-mix distortions. Potential impacts go beyond inefficiencies associated with variants of FDC pricing. One example showed how price in both regulated and unregulated markets could be dominated by other price structures that covered costs. Such developments call into question the long-run viability of such structures. The economic literature on cost allocation opens up many fruitful avenues for further research.

Potential problems of cross-subsidization and predatory pricing mean that regulators will require substantial information to evaluate utility behavior. Thus, price ceilings and price floors are two instruments used during a regulatory transition to greater pricing flexibility. We have seen that determining gains to deregulation requires careful analysis of the cost and price structures that emerge in a competitive environment.

The topics covered in this chapter are still in the process of being analyzed systematically. Vertical integration and diversification complicate regulatory oversight responsibilities. Given the complexity of the issues raised by multiproduct firms that are partially regulated, we cannot expect to find mathematical formulations that would yield conclusions of yes or no. We do know that technological opportunities and demands are changing – altering the gains to traditional regulation.

For example, telecommunications is in the midst of a major restructuring. The AT&T divestiture reflects judicial, legislative, and regulatory frustration with trying to deal with competitive and noncompetitive services in the context of regulation. The associated dismemberment of the industry giant, with the creation of the regional operating companies, has involved transition costs and consumer dislocations. Whether or not the current partial-regulation/handicapping arrangement in long distance is a good one has been questioned by many; see, for example, MacAvoy and Robinson (1983, 1985). Nevertheless, the judgment that regulation could not keep up with industry developments probably was correct. We shall see if minidivestitures will be called for at the regional level in a decade or so. Under such a restructuring of the industry, provision of the dial tone (POTS, plain old telephone service) would become separated from the pretty awesome new services (PANS) under development.

A similar set of issues faces electric-power and gas-distribution utilities. Joskow and Schmalensee (1983) document the difficulties associated with estabilishing competition in the generation of electricity, but given permissive regulation, technology will determine if the gains ultimately outweigh the costs of further pricing and entry flexibility. Conservation subsidiaries, cogeneration ventures, and nontraditional product lines are raising further questions for regulators. The principles developed in this chapter serve as a starting point for considering the extent to which monopoly expansion into nontraditional product lines will require greater emphasis on nontraditional regulation.

### Appendix

Our objective is to derive a sufficient condition for a two-product monopoly *not* to be SUPR. In Figure 11.2, this will be true if the dashed $\pi^{12} = 0$ isoprofit contour for the two-product firm never cuts below the lower segment of the $\pi^2 = 0$ contour or to the left of the left segment of the $\pi^1 = 0$ contour. In turn, this follows if

$$p_1 q_1(p_1, p_2) > C(q_1(p_1, p_2), 0) \tag{11A.1}$$

and

$$p_2 q_2(p_1, p_2) > C(0, q_2(p_1, p_2)) \tag{11A.2}$$

for all undominated $p_1$ and $p_2$ such that

$$p_1 q_1(p_1, p_2) + p_2 q_2(p_1, p_2) = C(q_1, p_2), q_2(p_1, p_2)) \tag{11A.3}$$

Let us consider what this implies for $p_1$ first. Dropping function arguments for convenience, from (11A.2) and (11A.3) we have

$$p_1 q_1 < C(q_1, q_2) - C(0, q_2) \tag{11A.4}$$

or product 1 covers less than its marginal cost. We rewrite this last expression as

$$p_1 < \frac{C(q_1, q_2) - C(0, q_2)}{q_1} \tag{11A.5}$$

We can view both sides of (11A.5) as functions of $p_1$. At $p_1 = 0$, the inequality holds because the right side is clearly positive. As we increase $p_1$ from zero, if the partial derivative of the right side is no less than 1 (which is the slope of the left-side function), the inequality must continue to hold. This condition on the partial of (11A.5) is

$$[MC_2 - MC_2^0] \frac{\partial q_2}{\partial p_1} + \left[ MC_1 - \frac{C(q_1, q_2) - C(0, q_2)}{q_1} \right] \frac{\partial q_1}{\partial p_1} > q_1$$

(11A.6)

where $MC_2^0 = \partial C(0, q_2)/\partial q_2$. If an analogous result holds for $p_2$, that is, starting from (11A.4) and deriving a condition similar to (11A.6), then the two-product monopoly cannot be SUPR. Condition (11A.6) is reproduced as (11.4) in the chapter.

# 12

# Alternatives to traditional regulation

We have examined the justification for government regulation of natural monopolies. Part I of this volume outlined the pricing principles for these monopolies that would promote economic efficiency. We also indicated a number of regulatory pricing methods whose properties deviate significantly from the efficient principles. In Part II we have seen that regulation may be rooted more in the politics of groups competing for public favors than in the goal of economic efficiency. Moreover, there have been numerous studies pointing out regulatory failures in terms of output and input inefficiencies. An obvious question, then, is whether or not there are alternatives to traditional forms of regulation that may work better. Can the inefficiencies that seem to be inherent in traditional regulation be mitigated by improving regulatory procedures? In the first four sections of this chapter, we study four categories of alternatives: (1) public ownership, (2) franchising, (3) regulating quality, and (4) incentive schemes. In the latter section, we see that the regulators' problems are even more difficult than those that have been described earlier in the book, because the information needed to do a good job of regulating usually is unavailable. Section 12.5 provides a conclusion.

## 12.1. Public ownership

If regulation of private natural monopolies results in inefficient production techniques and output prices, then one solution might be to socialize these monopolies: change the ownership mode from private to public. However, this proposal raises the hackles of many consumers, producers, and regulators for reasons that extend beyond the domain of economic analysis. Such an action would seem to strike at the very foundation of the free-enterprise system. As Meyer (1975b) suggests, "one can scarcely find a topic which summons such heated discussion as the controversy over public versus private ownership of productive resources, particularly for utilities such as electric power, natural gas, and communication" (p. 391).

The economist's role in this broad debate should remain, however, the more narrow, less emotional one of assessing the relative merits of private versus public ownership based on efficiency criteria. Are publicly owned firms more efficient than privately owned firms? If so, can the source of inefficiency among private firms be credited to the regulatory process? If so, can the process be improved to alleviate the inefficiency? If not, what are the economic costs of adhering to a private-ownership mode? On the other hand, if private ownership is more efficient, what are the costs of allowing public ownership? As usual, the answers are not simple, and they require careful analysis of those industries in which there is a mix of public and private natural monopolies.

Several authors have assessed the relative efficiency of public versus private ownership in the electric-power industry. In an early attempt, Meyer (1975b) estimated cost functions for the generation, transmission, distribution, and maintenance costs of electric power. He chose 30 private and 30 public utilities for his sample, using a dummy variable in the cost function to distinguish the two. Although his results indicated that private utilities had statistically significant higher average costs than did public utilities, the source of the discrepancy could not be determined. That is, whether the higher costs were due to the ownership mode or regulatory influence was left unanswered. In addition, although Meyer corrected for scale economies across the utilities in his sample, he was unable to correct for two other factors that may have influenced his results: Publicly owned utilities often are associated with (1) different technologies, in particular, a higher percentage of hydroelectric power, and (2) lower costs of capital.

In a subsequent study, Pescatrice and Trapani (1980) corrected for the different technologies by using only fossil-fuel plants in their sample, and they included input prices in their estimated cost functions. Prices were omitted in the Meyer estimates. They also corrected for the vintage of the generating equipment and confined their estimates to generating costs only, because comparable data were not available for other costs across both the 33 public and 23 private utilities. These authors' results indicated a statistically significant and sizable cost differential between the two types of utilities, with private firms having the higher costs. This result is consistent with that of Meyer, but Pescatrice and Trapani were able to draw more conclusions as a result of correcting for technology and input prices. They argued that the estimated cost differential "would be predicted if regulation of private firms is effective and public firms minimize cost, or, if the cost distortion due to the regulatory effect is greater than that induced by public ownership and the absence of profit incentive" (p. 274). Then, using estimates of input demands, these authors found evidence of cost-minimizing behavior by public firms, and they concluded that the cost differentials were suggestive of inefficiencies caused by regulation of privately owned utilities.

More recently, Atkinson and Halvorsen (1986) have used a broader approach to the issue of private versus public ownership. They argue that in addition to distinguishing among firms according to ownership, one must distinguish those that are regulated from those that are not, and those in competitive output markets from those in monopolistic output markets. Theoretical and empirical models typically examine only one of these three dichotomies, leading to model misspecifications and misinterpretation of results. For example, Alchian (1965) and subsequent authors have argued that public ownership will be less efficient because managers of public firms have more latitude in pursuing non-profit-maximizing objectives. Yet their hypothesis was not supported by the data of Meyer or Pescatrice and Trapani. The reason may be that regulation was not held constant.[1]

Based on a utility-maximizing model of managerial behavior, Atkinson and Halvorsen estimate cost and input demand functions that use shadow prices for inputs, as opposed to actual prices. These shadow prices allow for all types of departures from cost efficiency, including those due to regulatory constraints or utility-maximizing behavior that may be associated more with publicly owned firms. Their estimates are for steam generation of electric power only, where output is a function of capital, labor, and fuel. The data are taken from 123 private and 30 public firms. To correct for competitive conditions, only firms that were monopolies in their service area were used. Their results indicate that the two types of utilities do not differ in regard to cost efficiency. Moreover, their technique allows them to go further and conclude that both types of utilities are inefficient, causing a 2.4 percent increase in costs.[2]

The three studies discussed here provide mixed results regarding relative efficiencies of private and public ownership. Adding other studies does not clarify the picture. For example, Neuberg (1977) and Färe, Grosskopf, and Logan (1983) find public electric utilities to be more efficient, but DiLorenzo and Robinson (1982) find no significant difference. These results are summarized by Atkinson and Halvorsen (1986), along with three studies of public and private ownership of water utilities, where one study showed greater efficiency through public ownership, one reported greater efficiency through private ownership, and one found no significant difference.[3] In addition, Caves and Christensen (1980) found no evidence of differences in performance in the Canadian

---

1 However, as indicated earlier, Pescatrice and Trapani do take this into account by also testing for cost-minimizing behavior on the part of public firms.
2 These results are consistent with the Atkinson and Halvorsen (1980) work mentioned in Chapter 9 on the input biases for electric utilities.
3 See Bruggink (1982), Crain and Zardkoohi (1978), and Feigenbaum and Teeples (1983).

railroad industry. Thus, the debate over public and private ownership will no doubt continue, with each camp able to cite results in support of its cause.

### 12.2. Competition for the market via a franchise

The idea of franchising is that consumers can simply award to one firm an exclusive right to produce and sell a particular good in a particular market. The firm that receives the right or franchise is one of many bidders who compete for the franchise by offering to sell the good to consumers at a specified price. The bidder offering the lowest price is awarded the franchise. If the cost of collusion among the bidders is prohibitively high, then competition among them should drive the price down to average cost (for a single output firm). There is no need to have a regulator. This idea is associated with Demsetz (1968), who argued that simply because scale economies will lead to a single supplier, this does not mean that a profit-maximizing monopoly price need follow. The events that lead from scale economies to the monopoly price are not clearly stated in the literature, and the bidding process could be used to ensure a more acceptable outcome.[4]

### *Justifications for regulation revisited*

On one hand, the usefulness of franchising as an alternative to traditional regulation depends on the industry in question, as we shall show. On the other hand, the usefulness of Demsetz's arguments was that they questioned the incomplete justification usually given for the regulation of firms. That is, regulation was said to be justified simply by the existence of a natural monopoly. A firm that possesses a production technology that gives rise to scale economies purportedly will become, via some ill-explained process, a monopoly that will charge a monop-

---

4  Telser (1969) noted that the bidding process eliminates monopoly prices, but does not ensure marginal-cost prices. Demsetz (1971) responded by emphasizing that negotiations and proper contract specifications can achieve economic efficiency and that regulation does not yield marginal-cost prices either.

olistic price and produce an inefficiently low output. Therefore, it must be regulated. Demsetz questioned this theory, insisting that the production technology alone is insufficient to justify regulation. He criticized the theory of natural monopoly by "constructing an example that is free from irrelevant complications, such as durability of distribution systems, uncertainty, and irrational behavior, all of which may or may not justify the use of regulatory commissions but none of which is relevant to the theory of natural monopoly; for this theory depends on one belief only – price and output will be at monopoly levels if, due to scale economies, only one firm succeeds in producing the product" (p. 57).

This idea is important because Demsetz's work underscores the point made in Chapters 2 and 7: Production technology alone does not justify regulation; instead, the industry must be viewed within its market environment and within applicable institutional arrangements before regulation can be deemed warranted. His conclusion is in keeping with Tables 2.1 and 7.1, which summarized the criteria for justifying regulation for single-product and multiproduct firms, respectively. Implicit in these tables are that firms behave as profit-maximizers, that product quality can be accurately assessed by consumers, and that uncertainty about future costs and quality is absent. Explicit in these tables is the firm's production technology, in addition to whether or not there are barriers to entry into the market. In sector (2.2) of Table 7.1, for example, we see that a weak natural monopoly that is sustainable need not be regulated when there are no barriers to entry (and product quality is known with certainty, and firms are profit-maximizers). Demsetz seems to be referring to this type of situation when he argues for supplanting regulation with franchising. In addition, this reasoning is consistent with the arguments of Baumol, Panzar, and Willig (1982) for the power of contestable markets to ensure efficient outcomes without regulation. Indeed, these authors credit Demsetz as one of the forerunners of contestability theory.

However, if, say, sector (1.1) of Table 7.1 is applicable, then regulation is justified in order to ensure against inefficient monopoly outcome. But the justification is not merely that the firm is a natural monopoly (i.e., it has a subadditive cost function); rather, one or more of the "irrelevant complications" alluded to by Demsetz are present. These complications include durable distribution systems, barriers to entry, and difficulties in assessing quality that when added to the subadditive cost function, justify regulation.

### Criteria for franchise contracts

Williamson (1976) enumerates a number of the complications arising with important natural monopolies that eliminate the possibility of franchising as a replacement for regulation. Four of the major complications include (1) the initial award criteria, (2) execution of the franchise, (3) price–cost relationships, and (4) a lack of bidding parity. In examining these complications, it becomes apparent that there are parallels between them and the implicit and explicit criteria in Table 7.1 (such as assessable quality, barriers to entry, and lack of uncertainty).

For franchising to work, the initial determination of the winning bidder must be based on well-specified criteria. At a minimum, criteria will include the price of the good and its quality. Thus, consumers must assess varying price–quality packages, and they must have the ability and time to do so. If there are multiple outputs or periodic demands, with peak and off-peak periods, then a vector of price–quality relationships must be assessed. Considering electricity, for instance, consumers must assess varying loss-of-load probabilities and must be able to establish trade-offs between these and their attached prices. There is some evidence that this is already done at the individual consumer's level with the fuse systems described in Chapter 6. Moreover, aggregation of preferences for the reliability–price trade-off is necessary: There are complex technical questions, such as choosing between two bidders who offer identical reliability–price packages, but who propose to meet the reliability standards with different technologies. For example, one might choose high-performance (low-performance) equipment, with little (extensive) backup equipment.

In awarding the franchise, the duration of the contract must be specified. Long-term contracts have the advantage of security for the supplier, who may then be more apt to employ durable, economical capital. But during the execution of the contract, what can be done if the quality of service falls below that specified at the outset? The consumers must have some recourse to punish or evict the supplier who does not abide by the contract. Short-term contracts have the advantage that as problems arise, they can be addressed quickly. However, if eviction is possible, then the nature of the long-term contract is unclear. Costly litigation may ensue over the contract terms. And who is to monitor quality and determine when the contract has been violated?

How is price to be set? Should it be a markup over cost, in which case incentives for holding down costs are questionable? Should there be a limit on profit or the rate of return, in which case all the problems associated with these forms of regulation reappear? Also, in a world of uncertainty, there will be changing technologies, shifts in demands, labor-union negotiations, and inflation, all of which suggest that once-and-for-all prices are impractical. Prices will require ongoing assessments and adjustments.

Finally, how does one ensure that at the contract-renewal stage there will be a host of new bidders who will all be on equal footing with the current supplier. The new bidders have no capital in place, but to avoid the wasteful duplication of resources that a single supplier is supposed to avoid, a new bidder must have access to the existing capital should he win the franchise. The existing supplier must be required to sell the capital to the new supplier, but at what price? What is the fair value of the capital, and who determines this value? Was the capital purchased competitively at the outset, and were any kickbacks involved? What depreciation method should be used in determining the fair value? If satisfactory answers cannot be found to these questions, then new bidders may not be on equal footing, which is to say that barriers to entry exist.

These complications make apparent the need for some type of organization to run negotiations between consumers and suppliers. The organization should have engineering, legal, accounting, and economic expertise in order to understand the complex issues. It would be responsible for establishing franchise-award criteria and prices, monitoring quality, and valuing the supplier's capital. Also, because the transactions costs of consumers independently negotiating with suppliers would be prohibitive, there will be economies associated with having standardized contracts between the supplier and consumers that can be enforced by this organization (see the discussion of Goldberg in Section 8.1). All of these complications can be traced to the organization's imperfect information. Nevertheless, the organization must make decisions and provide incentives for efficiency in a world where perfect information does not exist (see Section 12.4). In short, the organization is the same as a regulatory commission.

### 12.3. **Regulating quality**

The qualities of natural monopoly goods, like those of almost all goods, are endogenous variables. The firm or industry may set qualities, or they may be set according to some agreement between firms and regulators. In Chapter 6, reliability of service was determined endogenously in both profit-maximizing and welfare-maximizing frameworks, and because reliability is a measure of quality, this analysis provided an example of how quality might be set in the power industry. However, except for Chapter 6, quality has been exogenous in the analyses throughout this book. In outlining the justification for regulation in Tables 2.1 and 7.1, quality was implicitly held constant. Quality has received relatively little attention in both the theoretical literature and empirical literature on regulation. This neglect is unfortunate, because quality is as important as price in determining welfare. It occupied a central role in showing in the last section how franchising creates problems in some industries. Furthermore, it is influenced directly and indirectly by regulatory activities.[5] A better understanding of this influence could improve the regulatory process. In this section, we provide an example of how regulation can be used to address quality, and then we discuss some quality issues in a general, theoretical framework.

### Quality incentives: rail service

Baumol (1975) offers a story about how a regulatory agency, the Interstate Commerce Commission (ICC), adopted an innovative program that was designed to directly influence quality. Although the particulars are specific to passenger rail service, the general approach may be useful in other regulated industries as well. The story begins with Amtrak, which is a retailer in the business of providing passenger rail service. Amtrak purchases the service from major railroads and then sells the service to consumers. Amtrak does not operate the trains or maintain the right-of-way. The original terms set by the ICC had Amtrak compensating the railroads for the marginal cost of operating passenger trains, with no contribution to the railroads' common costs. The railroads were not pleased with this arrangement. From their perspective, if they were to receive only marginal cost from all services, a deficit would ensue, because they considered themselves to be strong natural monopolies. However, Amtrak was also disgruntled, because they were bound to pay the marginal cost regardless of consumer demand and regardless whether or not low-quality service drove away passengers.

When the contract between Amtrak and the Pennsylvania Central Railroad was up for renegotiation in 1973, Penn Central wanted the passenger service's fully distributed costs covered. Amtrak counterproposed that prices should be dependent on the

5 The actual goal of 1-day-in-10-years loss-of-load probability very likely is the result of long-term interactions between firms and regulators, but also is influenced by other, less direct regulatory instruments. An example would be how rate-of-return regulation may encourage a firm to overcapitalize in the form of excessive capital-intensive reliability (see Section 9.3).

quality of service. After the details were worked out, Penn Central agreed to the following terms: If service quality was outstanding, the railroad would be allowed to enjoy positive profit. Quality was to be measured by punctuality, comfort, and economy. Any cost savings were to be kept by the railroad, at least until a new contract was written. These contracts were to be rewritten at specified intervals.

Most of the incentive money was to be based on punctuality, which was relatively easy to define and monitor. A train was to be considered on time if it fell behind schedule no more than 5 minutes per 100 miles, with a 30-minute maximum. In the New York–Boston service, for example, each percentage point above 20% that trains were on time would mean that the railroad would receive $35,000. Comfort was to be measured by observing the frequency with which cars were cleaned, with $50 penalties assessed for cars not recently cleaned. Finally, the railroad was to receive incentive payments for keeping certain percentages of cars and locomotives in working order. All in all, this contract represented a radical departure from the traditional modes of regulating the rails. It illustrates how formal incentives can be incorporated into the regulatory process.

Many state regulating commissions have adopted similar plans. In order to create rewards for cost-minimizing behavior and penalties for inefficient behavior, the output price is not linked to costs incurred in the short run. Over the long run, regulators set prices on the basis of efficient costs. Of course, finding easily defined performance measures that can be controlled by the regulated firm is not simple, especially because we want to limit subjectivity in their application and to avoid manipulation by either the firm or regulators. Michigan initiated such a program in 1977, with Florida following in 1980. The Florida program creates a generating-performance incentive factor (GPIF), based on the average heat rate of base-load electricity generators and the availability of units. The computed value of the GPIF determines the sizes of penalties and rewards (Johnson, 1985, p. 44). There are problems with both incentive programs, because perverse incentives can be created for the firm to achieve a target at very high costs, which are also passed on to consumers. Nevertheless, well-designed programs can promote efficiency, as the Amtrak example illustrates.

### A theoretical model of optimum quality determination

The theoretical treatments of product quality have mostly addressed questions of how differing market structures and information can affect quality.[6] Because the work of Spence (1975) captures many of the basic issues, in spite of being an oversimplified view of regulatory processes, we use his framework to illustrate how regulation can affect quality. Let $x$ be a continuous measure of the quality of a product produced by a single-product firm. Using our usual notation, demand can be written as

$$q = q(p, x) \tag{12.1}$$

and inverse demand becomes

$$p = p(q, x) \tag{12.2}$$

As (12.1) and (12.2) demonstrate, demand depends on the quality provided by the firm, and we assume that larger values of $x$ imply better quality. Because quality is also costly to provide, the firm's cost function is written as

$$C(q, x) \tag{12.3}$$

which is the cost of producing $q$ units, each of quality $x$.

Using (12.1)–(12.3), we can write consumer surplus as

$$CS = \int_0^q p(u, x) \, du - qp(q, x) \tag{12.4}$$

and profit as

$$\pi = qp(q, x) - C(q, x) \tag{12.5}$$

---

6 See, for example, Schmalensee (1970), Swan (1971), Levhari and Peles (1973), Spence (1975), Nakao (1982), Shapiro (1982), Kambhu (1982), Rogerson (1983), and Gal-Or (1983).

The demand and cost functions are assumed to be twice differentiable in both arguments. We will be interested in comparing profit-maximizing solutions to welfare-maximizing solutions, where welfare is

$$W = \mathrm{CS} + \pi \qquad (12.6)$$

The firm has three decision variables: price, quantity, and quality. We initially assume that the firm chooses quantity and quality, and price then follows via the demand function.

In comparing the maxima of (12.5) and (12.6), the firm chooses quantity so that

$$p = C_q - qp_q \qquad (12.7)$$

to maximize profit, and

$$p = C_q \qquad (12.8)$$

to maximize welfare, where $C_q$ is the marginal cost of output, and subscripts denote partial derivatives. The difference between (12.7) and (12.8) represents the usual monopoly exploitation of price and output. That is, the profit-maximizer sets marginal revenue equal to marginal cost, whereas the welfare-maximizer sets price equal to marginal cost.

To maximize profit with respect to quality, the first-order condition is

$$\frac{\partial \pi}{\partial x} = qp_x - C_x = 0 \qquad (12.9)$$

and the first-order condition for a welfare maximum is

$$\frac{\partial W}{\partial x} = \int_0^q p_x \, du - C_x = 0 \qquad (12.10)$$

Because (12.9) and (12.10) will generally differ, quality will not be optimally set by the profit-maximizer. To see the difference, rewrite (12.10) as

$$\frac{\partial W}{\partial x} = \int_0^q p_x \, du - qp_x + \frac{\partial \pi}{\partial x} \qquad (12.11)$$

We know that $\partial\pi/\partial x = 0$ for a profit maximum; therefore, if $\int_0^q p_q\,du - qp_x$ is positive (negative) at the profit-maximizing solution, quality is being set too low (high). Concentrating on the former possibility, we know that if

$$\frac{1}{q}\int_0^q p_x\,du > p_x \tag{12.12}$$

then quality is set too low by the profit-maximizer. Now, $p_x$ is the marginal valuation of quality by the marginal consumer, and $(1/q)\int_0^q p_x\,du$ is the average valuation of quality (at the margin) over all consumers in the market. Thus, if the average exceeds the marginal valuation, the profit-maximizer sets quality too low. (Spence points out that if $p_{xq} < 0$, then the average will exceed the marginal valuation.) The profit-maximizer responds to the marginal consumer, not to the inframarginal consumers, as would a welfare-maximizer.

### Regulation and quality

To introduce regulation into the model, suppose that the regulator specifies a price, and then the firm chooses quality. This process is similar to many of the forms of regulation encountered throughout this book. For this process to make sense, it must be the case that the regulator cannot observe or assess quality without significant increases in regulatory costs. Otherwise the regulator could simply set the quality level as well. Thus, the regulator maximizes welfare (12.6) over all $p$, for some initial value of $x$. The solution yields an optimum price, $p^*$, which is communicated to the firm. The firm, in turn, maximizes profit (12.5) over all $x$, given $p^*$. An iterative process is established whereby the regulator may choose a new price based on the firm's choice of quality; then the firm chooses a new quality based on the new price, and so forth. A type of duopoly game ensues in which the choice variables are price for one player and quality for the other. If an equilibrium exists, it will depend on the assumption made about each player's conjectures. We can develop reaction paths for both the regulator and firms by assuming Cournot conjectures. In this case, the firm believes that the regulator will not

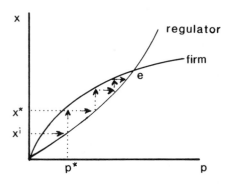

Figure 12.1. Cournot equilibrium for price and quality.

change price once quality is set, and the regulator believes that the firm will not change quality once price is set.[7]

In Figure 12.1, Cournot reaction paths are shown for the regulator and firm that lead to an equilibrium at *e*. The regulator takes the initial quality, $x^i$, and maximizes welfare by selecting price $p^*$. The firm then takes $p^*$ and maximizes profit by selecting quality $x^*$. The iteration process is shown by the arrows, which converge to the stable equilibrium point *e*. As with most reaction functions, it would be possible to construct paths that would yield unstable or no equilibrium points. The Cournot assumption is certainly naive in this setting, because it is probably not a reasonable description of behavior for either participant. Indeed, the regulator's task is to react to the firm's action, and of course the firm recognizes this. In addition, a point like *e* may not be optimum from either player's perspective, and Pareto-superior outcomes probably are possible in which both profit and welfare can be increased. Consequently, neither player will have an interest in point *e*.

7 The reaction function for the firm is determined by maximizing profit over $x$ for a fixed $p$ and then inverting the first-order condition (assuming $d^2\pi/dx^2 \neq 0$) to obtain $x(p)$. Comparative statics can then be used to obtain $dx/dp$, which is the slope of the reaction path. A similar procedure for the regulator yields $dp/dx$.

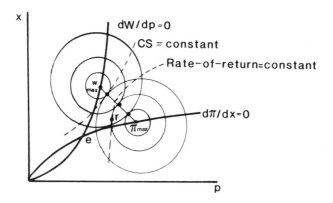

Figure 12.2. Pareto-optimum price–quality solutions.

In Figure 12.2, isoprofit contours surrounding $\pi_{max}$ and iso-welfare contours surrounding $W_{max}$ are added to the picture. The contract curve giving all Pareto-optimum points between the regulator and firm is the line $W_{max}\pi_{max}$. Again, $dW/dp = 0$ and $d\pi/dx = 0$ are the Cournot reaction paths for the regulator and firms, respectively. The Cournot equilibrium is point *e*, and a Stackelberg equilibrium can also be located in the usual manner (not displayed).

The problem for the regulator is to devise an incentive scheme that will lead the firm to the contract curve, preferably close to $W_{max}$. Spence discusses the possibility of confining the firm to a locus of points at which consumer surplus is constant. Any such locus will be tangent to both an isoprofit locus and an isowelfare locus as it passes through the contract curve. This follows because $W = CS + \pi$. The firm then has an incentive to move along the curve of constant consumer surplus to the contract curve, resulting in a Pareto optimum. One curve of constant consumer surplus is shown in Figure 12.2.

Unfortunately, informational problems are likely to rule out this approach. First, the regulator must be able to measure quality unambiguously. We noted the difficulty with doing this regarding reliability of service in Chapter 6, and other forms of quality will present equally vexing measurement problems. Second, the regulator must determine how consumer surplus changes with changes in quality. All inframarginal consumers will be affected by these quality changes; yet information about the effects simply is not conveyed in the usual price and quantity data. One possibility might be to experiment with consumer surveys to assess attitudes toward varying reliabilities.

It should be noted that rate-of-return regulation cannot be ruled out as an instrument for achieving reasonable quality levels. Letting capital be expressed as $K(q, x)$, where $K$ is the number of capital units needed to produce $q$ output units of quality $x$, Spence shows that the rate-of-return constraint confines the firm to a curve that is positively sloped and tangent to an isoprofit contour. One such curve is illustrated in the figure, although there is a family of curves, each associated with an allowed return. The firm will locate at point $r$, because profit is greater there than at any other point on the curve. The contract curve is not attained in this case, but Spence shows that the constraint forces the capital stock to be larger than it would be otherwise, and this will improve quality if the provision of quality is capital-intensive. Such a scenario is consistent with previous results in Chapter 9, where it was shown that rate-of-return-regulated electric utilities may achieve high reliability levels through heavy use of capital. Empirical analysis of telecommunications by Branch (1979) also supports this point.[8]

The complexities of regulating both price and quality in the context of oligopolistic rivalry are explored by VanderWeide and Zalkind (1981). Their model uses Cournot assumptions to examine the impacts of price and entry deregulation on product quality. How quality enters the production and demand functions determines the outcome, along with how regulation gave rise to

---

8  Branch (1979) found a positive relationship between realized rate of return and modernization expenditures for 17 AT&T operating companies for 1960–75. Such expenditures represent discretionary outlays on efficiency and innovation implementation, improving service quality.

the initial industry equilibrium. The general topic offers many fruitful areas for further research.

## 12.4. Regulatory incentive schemes

The incentive scheme described earlier for passenger rail service was novel in that it focused on quality. Most schemes that have been used or proposed have focused on prices and profits, and they can be traced back as far as 1855. At that time, a scheme referred to as the *sliding scale* (Bussing, 1936) allowed gas firms in England to pay dividends that were inversely proportional to the price of gas. Sliding-scale schemes have been tried in the United States as well, and a review of them can be found in Trebing (1963). Recently, Nebraska, Vermont, and some other states have turned to price caps instead of rate-base regulation – protecting customers in core telephone markets and providing flexibility in competitive markets. The FCC is considering the price-cap approach in FCC Docket 87-313 to enhance incentives for cost reduction. In this section, we briefly discuss some of the recently proposed schemes that can be related to concepts developed throughout this book.

### *X-efficiency and partial-adjustment mechanisms*

Optimal managerial effort clearly depends on the rewards to keep costs down. The concept of X-inefficiency has been applied to situations in which the firm is not producing on a production isoquant. Parish and Ng (1972) show that the losses from operating off the production isoquant (and therefore inside the neoclassical production possibility frontier) vanish when the following are considered: First, the cost of increasing efficiency must be included in the analysis. Second, leisure and other nonpecuniary rewards produced within the firm must be considered goods. Third, employees and managers must bear the full cost of substituting these goods for monetary rewards. The cost of monitoring behavior and disciplining those who shirk must be taken into account. Otherwise, motivation is taken to be a free good. Much of what Leibenstein (1966) labels X-efficiency can be accounted for by the standard neoclassical production function that includes a recognition of resource costs of reducing such inefficiencies. On the other hand, if managers engage in expense-preference behavior, or if the attenuation of property rights alters the rewards to risk-taking activity, non-cost-minimizing behavior may be observed. The extensive literature on the firm's internal relationships is summarized by Waterson (1988, pp. 38–61); external and internal constraints are affected by the possibility of takeover, managerial bonus schemes, shareholder information, and employee incentives.

Cross (1970) was concerned with X-efficiency and argued that lax management, outdated production methods, and sloppy cost control were responsible for serious inefficiencies in public utilities. He proposed a price incentive scheme that allows the firm to enjoy a portion of any cost reduction it generates through improved efficiency. In particular, price is set according to

$$p = \beta + \alpha(C/q)$$

where $\beta$ is a base, and $\alpha$ is the sharing rate (presumably between 0 and 1). Consequently, if the firm lowers its average cost from one period to the next, price is reduced by a portion of the savings. The firm enjoys part of the savings in higher profit, and consumers enjoy part of the savings in lower prices. Thus, instead of the lags considered by Bailey (see Section 9.2), regulators manipulate $\beta$ and $\alpha$.

However, it is not clear how this scheme would work in a multiproduct setting, where average cost is not defined, and changes in the product mix arise over time. In addition, it does require that the regulator have knowledge of average cost. Thus, many of the problems inherent in rate-of-return regulation persist, where costs must be defined and then allowed or disallowed by the regulator (see Section 8.2).

Holthausen (1979) has proposed an alternative scheme that is used in conjunction with rate-of-return regulation. A target profit level, $\pi_t$, is defined as the profit the firm would realize if it earned exactly its allowed rate of return. The profit received by the firm is $\pi_t$ plus a percentage of the difference between the actual profit, $\pi_a$, and target profit. Thus, the firm receives

$$\pi = \pi_t + \beta(\pi_a - \pi_t)$$

where $0 \leq \beta \leq 1$. If the actual profit exceeds the target profit, the firm is permitted to retain $\beta$ times the excess. If the regulator sets the allowed rate of return equal to the cost of capital, so that $\pi_t = 0$, then the firm's incentive is to maximize actual profit and keep $\beta$ dollars for each one dollar earned. Also, if actual profit is less than the target profit, the regulator will have to pay a subsidy to the firm. This possibility is a major drawback, and Holthausen discusses other options for this event. The author also shows that overcapitalization in the manner of the A-J effect still occurs, although here the changes in capital with respect to changes in the allowed return are in the opposite direction from those of the A-J model.

Before adopting this scheme, further study will be required to compare its welfare effects to those for schemes in which $\pi_t$ is simply set to zero. The major advantage of the proposed scheme would appear to be that the regulator has influence over the capital stock of the firm through its use of the allowed return in $\pi_t$. But because setting the allowed return greater than the cost of capital implies overcapitalization, it is not clear how welfare is affected by using this instrument.

Another hybrid incentive scheme has been proposed by Loeb and Magat (1979). They suggest that subsidies can be mixed with franchising in a decentralized regulatory process. The idea is that the firm and regulator have knowledge of the firm's demand curve (only a single output firm is considered), but only the firm has cost information. The firm sets price and collects the corresponding revenues. Then *all* consumer surplus is awarded to the firm in the form of a subsidy from the regulator. Obviously the firm will have an incentive to set price equal to marginal cost, because this will maximize welfare, and the firm will receive all of the consumer surplus. The result will be the same as if the firm were a perfect price-discriminator. Note that the regulator requires no cost data.

Franchising enters to extract the excess profit as follows. In contrast to the previous franchising process described in Section 12.2, where the award was given to the bidder offering to sell output at the lowest price, here the award is given to the bidder offering to pay the largest lump sum for the franchise. Because bidders know how the subsidy scheme operates, the value of the subsidy will be capitalized into the offers, and the regulator will receive from the winning bidder what it needs to subsidize the firm. Regulators then can redistribute the subsidy back to consumers via lump-sum transfers. If some rough estimate of average cost is initially available, then an upper bound on price can be established, with the firm getting only the incremental change in consumer surplus. The subsidy and subsequent redistribution will be less than if total consumer surplus were involved.

How does this scheme compare to the former franchising scheme in Section 12.2? In those situations in which the former franchising scheme will work, this scheme should also work. In neither case does the regulator require knowledge of costs, and only in the latter scheme does the regulator require knowledge of demand. An advantage of the latter scheme, however, is that price is set to marginal cost instead of average cost, so that welfare is maximized.

In many important industries, the former franchising scheme would not work because of the complications alluded to in Section 12.2: (1) the initial award criteria, (2) execution of the contract, (3) price–cost relationships, and (4) bidding parity at contract renewal. Would the Loeb–Magat scheme fare any better in addressing these complications? With the possible exception of (3), the answer is probably no. Issues still arise regarding how to monitor quality, how bidders offering the same quality with differing producing techniques are compared, and how capital should be valued at recontracting stages. However, setting and monitoring price may be easier tasks. At least for cost reductions, the firm will have an incentive to lower prices to match lower marginal costs, because it knows a subsidy will follow. Of course, the details on when the subsidy is paid, or how the subsidy is to be collected without a whole new bidding process, are not clear.

This approach has been extended by Vogelsang (1987) to two-part tariffs that replace subsidies as the mechanism for obtaining additional revenue. The service is divided into access and use. One of the two outputs, access, may involve an externality – if individual valuations depend on the number of customers who are part of the network. Vogelsang develops an iterative process in which the incentive mechanism allows the firm to obtain the approximate welfare gain caused by the price changes from the previous period. Under reasonable assumptions and stationary conditions, the process converges to optimal two-part tariffs, where price tends toward marginal cost. When the number of consumers is affected by the fixed fee, a second-best result emerges. Although the approach obviates the need for external subsidies, unless the bidding process is effective, the firm (rather than consumers) will tend to capture the benefits from efficient pricing.

### A scheme for Ramsey prices

The next scheme we discuss is especially designed for multiproduct strong natural monopolies from whom information is limited; under certain conditions it results in Ramsey prices. The scheme was proposed by Vogelsang and Finsinger (1979), who note that the firm knows demand elasticities and cost functions better than the regulators do, and the firm is in a better position to "calculate and implement welfare maximizing prices. But why should they? We see three possible reasons for them to do so" (p. 158). The first reason these authors offer is that the firm's managers may hold humanitarian interests, but this motive is quickly dispensed with. Second, the firm may be susceptible to competitive entry, and welfare-maximizing (Ramsey) prices may stave off entrants. This possibility was discussed earlier in Section 7.4. Third, the regulator could force the firm to implement welfare-maximizing prices. Then the question is how to calculate prices without duplicating the firm's management. The authors' solution goes as follows:

The regulator's objective is to maximize welfare, given by consumer surplus plus profit, subject to a break-even constraint. Ramsey prices are therefore the regulator's goal. The firm's objective is to maximize profit, and it has full knowledge of its demand and cost functions. The cost function exhibits decreasing ray average costs, so that marginal-cost pricing will create a deficit (hence, the firm is a strong natural monopoly). The regulator knows total cost, prices, and quantities in the current period, period $j$, and she requires that all demand must be served at the prevailing price. Finally, the regulator defines a feasible price set for the next period, period $j + 1$, as follows:

$$P_{j+1} = \{p \mid pq_j - C(q_j) \leq 0\} \qquad (12.13)$$

where $q_j$ is the vector of the observed quantities in the current period. The firm maximizes profit in period $j + 1$ subject to (12.13).

To illustrate the process, we use the numerical example first used in Chapter 7 for a two-product firm. Repeating the relevant equations here for convenience, the firm's cost function is

$$C(q_1, q_2) = 5q_1 + 4q_2 - 0.3q_1q_2 + 24 \qquad (7.35)$$

and the two demand functions are

$$y^1 = -0.5p_1 + 10 \qquad (7.36)$$

and

$$y^2 = -1.4p_2 + 20 \qquad (7.37)$$

Using this information, we construct Figure 12.3. The ellipse is the zero-profit locus, and maximum profit is approximately 50.4, where $p_1 \approx 11.3$ and $p_2 \approx 8.5$. Ramsey prices are given by point $R$, which corresponds to point $R$ in Figure 7.3. Here, $p_1 \approx 4.0$ and $p_2 \approx 3.8$.

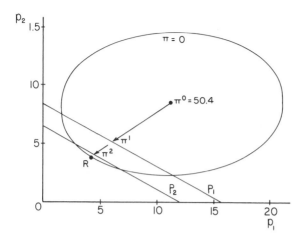

Figure 12.3. A regulatory adjustment process.

We start by assuming that regulation is completely ineffective, and the firm maximizes profit, given by

$$\pi = p_1 y^1 + p_2 y^2 - C(q_1, q_2)$$

which yields (approximately) $\pi^0$, as depicted in Figure 12.3. The regulator notes the initial quantities and cost at this solution, which are $q_1^0 \approx 4.4$, $q_2^0 \approx 8.1$, and $C(q_1^0, q_2^0) \approx 67.6$, and then imposes a constraint on allowed prices in the next period. The set of allowable prices is

$$P_1 = \{p \mid 4.4p_1 + 8.1p_2 - 67.6 \leq 0\} \tag{12.14}$$

which uses the initial quantities and cost. Then the firm maximizes profit again, but this time subject to (12.14). Graphically, this means that the new solution must lie on or below the line denoted $P_1$ in Figure 12.3, which is simply the set of points defined by (12.14). Profit-maximizing prices will be located on $P_1$, and the reader can verify that the solution to the constrained maximization problem is at $\pi_1$, where $p_1 \approx 6.1$ and $p_2 \approx 5.1$.

In the second period, then, profit has decreased and quantities and cost have increased, to $q_1 \approx 7.0$, $q_2 \approx 12.9$, and $C(7.0, 12.9) = 83.5$. Using this information, the regulator imposes the next period's constraint:

$$P_2 = \{p \mid 7.0p_1 + 12.9p_2 - 83.5 \leq 0\} \qquad (12.15)$$

which is also depicted as a straight line in Figure 12.3. The firm again must maximize profit, now subject to $P_2$, resulting in the solution $\pi_2$ on $P_2$ in the figure. The process continues, period after period, and the firm approaches point $R$. Ramsey prices are reached in the limit. Vogelsang and Finsinger provide a formal proof of the convergence of this process to Ramsey prices, along with several qualifications.

The beauty of this process is apparent. First, it works for a multiproduct firm. Second, the regulator needs to observe only current quantities and costs (although defining costs is as difficult as in other schemes). Third, consumer surplus was never introduced into the analysis. This point is perhaps the most intriguing aspect of the process, because Ramsey prices, the result of maximizing consumer surplus plus profit, are reached without introducing consumer surplus.

How does the process succeed? First, consider the constraint, which always allows nonnegative profit. But how? The firm is selling quantities that yield positive profit when the constraint is imposed. The regulator tells the firm it can continue to sell these quantities and incur the same cost, but it must lower prices to obtain zero profit. Naturally, lower prices will mean even greater quantities and greater costs. But by decreasing ray average cost, the new prices, although lower, generate sufficient revenues to exceed these costs by enough to still yield positive profit. Second, during each period in the process, welfare increases by at least the previous period's profit. In these authors' words, the constraint is "set in such a way that the sum of all consumers in period $j$ could acquire the quantities they bought in period $j - 1$ at just $\pi^{j-1}$ less than what they actually paid in period $j - 1$. If, however, in period $j$ they choose to buy $q_j \neq q_{j-1}$, then in terms of consumer surplus . . . they must be at least as well off with $q_j$ as with $q_{j-1}$." (p. 164). Because consumer surplus increases by at least $\pi^{j-1}$, and the firm makes positive profit in period $j$, total welfare increases. Third, the final outcome must be a Ramsey optimum, because the process continues as long as profit is positive. But this profit is added to consumer surplus in subsequent periods, and the process does not stop until the firm exhausts all profit, or consumer surplus is at a maximum. When it is at a maximum, profit is zero, and this outcome defines Ramsey prices.[9]

### Strategic behavior

The Vogelsang and Finsinger (V-F) scheme has desirable properties owing to its minimal information requirements and final outcome. But these appealing results are susceptible to strategic behavior; in particular, the regulator can be duped by the firm. Sappington (1980) has shown that because the regulator has no knowledge of the firm's technology (other than that ray average costs are decreasing), the firm can add waste to the total cost observed by the regulator during one period, in order to enjoy a higher price in the next period. This is easily illustrated in Figure 12.4, which depicts the demand and cost curves for a single-product firm. To make things simple, average and marginal costs are assumed constant, and demand is linear. Suppose that in the first period, the firm charges the monopoly price $p_m$ and enjoys profit given by area $p_m abp_w$. If the firm does not engage in strategic behavior, and the regulator employs the V-F constraint (12.13), it is easy to see that in the second period the firm must charge price $p_w$, which is the Ramsey price. Thus, after only one period the desired result is obtained; consumer surplus is maximized, and profit is zero.

---

9 An alternative explanation for why the process results in Ramsey prices centers around the Ramsey formula $(p - \text{MC})\partial q/\partial p = -kq$ that we derived in Chapter 3. For profit maximization, the same formula holds with $k = 1$. The normal to the welfare surface is $-q$. Thus, the formula implies that at the optimum, the normal to the surface $\{p \mid \pi(p) = 0\}$ and the demand vector $q$ are collinear. See Vogelsang and Finsinger (1979) for more detail.

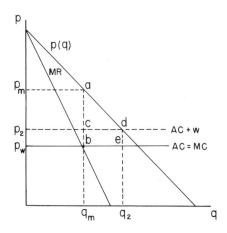

Figure 12.4. Strategic behavior in the Ramsey price scheme.

Next, we admit strategic behavior by having the firm add waste, $w$, to its per-unit cost. Sappington defines waste as simply costs incurred above the minimum cost required to produce a given output. Now the firm can satisfy constraint (12.13) by charging a price in the second period above the true AC. Suppose the firm charges $p_2$ in period 2, and at the same time rids itself of the waste. The firm's total profit is $p_m acp_2$ in period 1 plus the discounted value of $p_2 dep_w$ in period 2. Comparing this profit to the profit in the absence of strategic behavior ($p_m abp_w$), we can say that strategic behavior is advantageous, if in terms of areas,

$$p_m acp_2 + \beta[p_2 dep_w] > p_m abp_w \tag{12.16}$$

where $\beta$ is the firm's discount factor for period-2 profit. After slight manipulation, (12.16) can be written as

$$\beta[cdeb] > [1 - \beta][p_2 cbp_w]$$

or

$$\beta[p_2 - p_w][q_2 - q_m] > [1 - \beta][p_2 - p_w]q_m \tag{12.17}$$

Finally, (12.17) simplifies to

$$\beta > q_m/q_2$$

which is Sappington's sufficient condition for strategic behavior to be worthwhile. Thus, if the firm's discount factor is sufficiently large (i.e., its discount rate sufficiently small), it will behave strategically by adding waste, which reduces period-1 profit but allows a greater overall profit. The result is similar to Sweeney's analysis (1981) of incentives to delay the introduction of cost-saving technologies under markup regulation (discussed in Section 10.2). Increases in the duration of regulatory lag reduce the incentives to incur unnecessary costs in the early periods, because the present value of the future gains is diminished.

This simple example underscores the naiveté inherent in most of the modeling literature that has attempted to capture regulatory processes. In Part I of this book, we derived optimum regulatory pricing policies, but they were based on the assumption that the regulator had full knowledge of demand and the firm's costs. (Chapter 6 was an exception, in that demand was random, and the regulator knew the density function.) However, unless the regulator should decide to completely duplicate the firm's management, a wasteful endeavor, the firm is much more likely to know this information than is the regulator. Consequently, the regulator must rely on the firm to report the information needed to implement an optimum regulatory policy. Moreover, the regulator must hope that the firm is reporting truthfully and non-strategically, even when it may be in the firm's best interest to do otherwise.

Recent literature has begun to address the regulator's problem under conditions of uncertainty and asymmetry of information between the firm and the regulator. The techniques employed represent a significant departure from past studies and can generally be categorized as principal-and-agent analyses. These were discussed briefly in Chapter 8. To reiterate, principal-and-agent analyses have been used to study a wide range of problems involving incentive structures. The literature is composed largely of theoretical derivations of optimum incentives given varying assumptions on risk behavior and information asymmetries. Typically, the principal receives some form of output from an agent in her employ. The agent must expend effort to produce the output. The agent's raison d'être is that he possesses better information about production than does the principal, or he possesses specialized skills not possessed by the principal. The principal attempts to design incentives that will encourage the agent to expend the effort necessary to maximize output from given resources.

The natural interpretation in regulation has the firm as the agent and the regulator as the principal. The principal's objective is to maximize some measure of social welfare, while the firm is interested in maximizing profit. Thus, the regulator's and firm's objectives are divergent, as are the principal's and agent's objectives when the agent does not want to expend the effort needed to fulfill the principal's objective. The regulator must induce the firm to employ its superior knowledge of demand and cost in the social interest. We now outline important results that have been obtained in the principal-and-agent literature as they apply to natural monopoly regulation.

### Asymmetric information: principals and agents

Consider again the regulator's fundamental dilemma. In keeping with most of the models described in Part I, we assume that her goal is to maximize the sum of consumer surplus and firm profit. To accomplish this, the regulator must dictate a price structure to the firm, because the firm's objective of profit maximization would call for a very different structure. But dictating the correct structure requires that the regulator have full information on demand and cost, and without duplicating management she can obtain this information only from the firm. There are at least two difficulties here: (1) The firm may have the information in only a probabilistic sense. (2) The firm may have an incentive to distort the information.

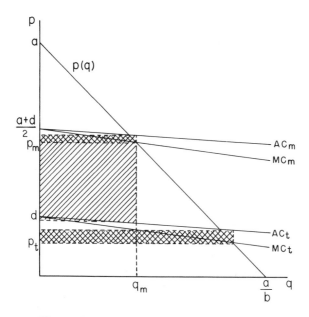

Figure 12.5. Misreporting firm costs.

To explore this incentive, refer to Figure 12.5, which depicts the firm's demand curve and its true average-cost ($AC_t$) and marginal-cost ($MC_t$) curves. An ideal result would have the regulator dictate price $p_t = MC_t$ and then subsidize the firm by an amount equal to the lower crosshatched area. The subsidy that might come from the access fee of a two-part tariff (assuming zero income elasticity; see Chapter 4) or general taxes would allow the firm to break even. Suppose, however, that the regulator knows only the demand curve, and the firm knows that the regulator will follow the policy just described. What costs will the firm report? To provide a specific answer, suppose that the inverse demand function for the firm's output is

$$p = a - bq \qquad (12.18)$$

and true costs are

$$C_t = dq - cq^2/2$$
$$\text{AC}_t = d - cq/2 \qquad (12.19)$$
$$\text{MC}_t = d - cq$$

where parameters $a$, $b$, $c$, and $d$ are all positive, with $a$ and $d$ as shown in Figure 12.5. Again, if the firm reports costs given by (12.19), it earns zero profit. But if the firm knows that it can successfully misreport, it will. For simplicity, suppose the firm considers misreporting only parameter $d$; that is, the firm reports $d' = md$, or

$$C_m = d'q - cq^2/2$$
$$\text{AC}_m = d' - cq/2 \qquad (12.20)$$
$$\text{MC}_m = d' - cq$$

Obviously, if $m \neq 1$, the firm is misreporting. Note that we are assuming that regulatory audits of actual expenses are unable to detect misreporting – perhaps because of the difficulty of identifying costs associated with other (perhaps unregulated) product lines.

The problem for the firm is to

$$\max \pi = p(q)q - C(q) + s$$

subject to

$$p(q) = \text{MC}_m \qquad (12.21)$$
$$s = C_m(q) - p(q)q$$

where $s$ is the subsidy from the regulator. The first constraint represents the price-equals-marginal-cost policy, and the second constraint represents the break-even subsidy policy. The first constraint can be written, in view of (12.20) and (12.18), $a - bq = md - cq$, or

$$q = (md - a)/(c - b) \qquad (12.22)$$

Then, substituting the two constraints into the objective function in (12.21) yields the problem

$$\max_{m} \pi = C_m(q) - C(q)$$
$$= (mdq - cq^2/2) - (dq - cq^2/2) \qquad (12.23)$$
$$= (m - 1)dq$$
$$= (m - 1)d(md - a)/(c - b)$$

Provided the second-order condition for a maximum is satisfied (which will follow if the demand and the marginal-cost curves intersect in the positive quadrant as in Figure 12.5), the first-order condition can be solved to obtain

$$m = \frac{a + d}{2d}$$

If $m \neq 1$ (or $a \neq d$), the firm misreports marginal and average costs to be

$$AC_m = md - \frac{c}{2}q = \frac{a + d}{2} - \frac{c}{2}q$$

$$MC_m = md - cq = \frac{a + d}{2} - cq$$

These costs are illustrated in Figure 12.5, where, under misreporting, the regulator sets price to $p_m$ and the subsidy equal to the upper crosshatched area. The firm earns profit equal to the hatched plus upper crosshatched areas, and there is a deadweight loss due to misreporting.

Recognizing the firm's incentive to misreport its cost when it has an information advantage, Baron and Myerson (1982) explore optimum regulatory strategies. They assume that an efficient auction among potential suppliers for a franchise is not possible, and so the Loeb–Magat-type incentive scheme described earlier in this section is not possible. Thus, the regulator must deal with a single supplier in the manner described in this subsection. In their model, both the regulator and the firm are cognizant of demand, but cost information is asymmetric. Cost is given by $C(q, \theta)$, where $q$ is output and $\theta$ is a technological parameter that is known by the firm, but is a random variable with known density for the regulator. The regulator receives a cost report from the firm, after which she must determine whether or not the firm should produce at all, and if so, she must determine the output price and a subsidy that will ensure nonnegative profit.

A major challenge for the regulator is to induce the firm to not misreport its costs. Hence, the price and subsidy determined by the regulator must be such that the firm will have no incentive to misreport. A regulatory policy that achieves this is said to be an incentive-compatible policy. Baron and Myerson confine the regulator's choice of policies to incentive-compatible policies by appealing to the revelation principle. This principle is instrumental in designing a solution to their problem and is used in most of the problems in the recent regulatory-incentives literature. The idea is that the regulator can always induce the firm to be truthful by assuring the firm that it will do as well by reporting the truth as it would if it misreported. More generally, the revelation principle implies that any outcome that can be achieved through a policy that induces misreporting can also be achieved through some other incentive-compatible policy.

By way of example, refer again to Figure 12.5. Suppose the policy is that the regulator sets price equal to the reported marginal cost and sets the subsidy equal to the resulting deficit. The regulator will hope that the firm reports $MC_t$ and $AC_t$, but we already know that an optimum strategy for the firm, given the stated regulatory policy, is to report $MC_m$ and $AC_m$. The regulator then sets price equal to $p_m$, the subsidy to the upper crosshatched area, and the firm makes a substantial profit, with society suffering a substantial deadweight loss. To induce truthful revelation, the regulator can ask the firm to report its true costs, and then base the price and subsidy on the firm's optimum strategy given the true costs. In other words, the regulator calculates $MC_m$ and $AC_m$ after the firm reports $MC_t$ and $AC_t$, and then the regulator sets $p = MC_m$ and the subsidy according to $AC_m$. The firm has no incentive to misreport, because it can do no better. Reporting higher costs would actually reduce the realized profit. Of course, in terms of welfare, the final outcome is the same as if the firm had misreported under the previous regulatory policy, although now the firm has truthfully reported.

The optimum policy derived by Baron and Myerson obviously differs from the policy just described, because the latter policy does no better in welfare terms than allowing the firm to use a profit-maximizing price and subsidy. In an optimum policy, price exceeds the reported marginal cost. This reported marginal cost is the true cost owing to the incentive-compatability constraint appended to the regulator's welfare-maximizing problem. Thus, price will always exceed the efficient-price-equals-marginal-cost solution. Output is below efficient levels because this reduces the number of units on which the firm can exercise a cost advantage. The extent of the distortion between the efficient and actual outputs will depend on the regulator's beliefs about how likely it is that the firm has lower costs than are reported.

The resultant welfare loss due to the inefficient price can be blamed on the firm's information advantage. Offsetting this advantage is costly to society. That is, ensuring an incentive-compatible policy requires a constraint on the welfare-maximizing problem, and as with any binding constraint, the welfare-maximum solution can be no greater than it would be in the absence of the constraint. The subsidy can be thought of as a reward to the firm for truthful reporting. These authors show that a well-designed subsidy decreases (increases) with reported costs when the regulated price is below (above) the unregulated monopoly price. They explain this by noting that the difference between the regulated and unregulated prices "tends to give the firm some incentive to misrepresent its costs in order to obtain a price closer to the monopoly price. The [subsidy] then must vary with . . . reported cost . . . so as to offset this incentive" (p. 922).

Sappington (1983) advances the asymmetric-information literature by admitting more general cost structures in a multiproduct setting. This allows him to compare an incentive-compatible policy to a straightforward Ramsey pricing policy and also to address the issue of cross-subsidies. In his model, there is a finite number of fixed and variable cost configurations that the firm might incur, depending on the state of nature realized, and the regulator designs a policy that consists of a menu of price-subsidy pairs, one for each possible cost configuration. The firm must make a binding choice on which price-subsidy pair or cost configuration to select. The regulator might intentionally induce the firm to choose an inefficient technology to better limit the firm's rents from its private information. As in the model of Baron and Myerson, there is an incentive-compatibility constraint on the regulator's welfare problem that recognizes that the firm will choose the best strategy for itself given its cost configuration. Just as the optimum price for Baron and Myerson deviated from marginal cost, so the prices for Sappington deviate from the Ramsey prices for most states of nature.

Roughly, products with relatively high (low) marginal costs tend to be priced above (below) cost, and therefore cross-subsidies will tend to favor products with relatively low marginal costs. The actual pricing formulas are complex, however, and the reader should refer to Sappington for more details. In addition, the reader can find other complex incentive schemes that deal with the same fundamental problem between the regulator and firm in Baron and Besanko (1984) and Laffont and Tirole (1986). The latter work is ably summarized by Joskow and Schmalensee (1986).

As we have indicated, in the foregoing models, demand is known by both the firm and regulator, whereas only the firm knows the costs. Realistically, we would expect the firm to have better knowledge of both demand and cost, although modeling this situation would be considerably more difficult. A first step would be to reverse the previous models and assume that cost is common knowledge but demand is known only by the firm. Riordan (1984) addresses the problem and assumes that the regulator must stipulate an output price before demand is known. This is similar to the earlier studies of pricing under stochastic demand (see Chapter 6), where price and capacity were chosen before demand was known, resulting in positive probabilities of excess demand or excess supply. The added difficulty here is that the firm may have an incentive to misreport demand to the regulator in an effort to increase profit. Accordingly, the pricing rules established in Chapter 6 are not incentive-compatible.

Riordan proceeds to design an incentive-compatible scheme whereby the firm sets price and receives a subsidy from the regulator that is negatively related to this price. Using notation from Chapter 6, where a fixed-coefficient technology was used, with $b$, $\beta$, and $Z$ being unit operating cost, unit capacity cost, and capacity, respectively, the subsidy is simply

$$s(p) = \begin{cases} -[p - b - \beta]Z & \text{for } p \geq b \\ 0 & \text{for } p < b \end{cases}$$

Under this scheme, once demand is known to the firm, it can do no better than to set price equal to $b$ when there is excess supply, and set price to equate demand with capacity otherwise. As demonstrated in Chapter 6, these prices will maximize social welfare; consequently, they are incentive-compatible. (Refer to Figure 6.3 to understand why this subsidy discourages the firm from selecting socially nonoptimum prices.)

### Awarding franchises revisited

Awarding natural monopoly franchises in the manner of Demsetz has been a recurring theme in this chapter. Loeb and Magat coupled franchising with a lump-sum subsidy equal to all consumer surplus to show that the firm that won the franchise in an auction would charge a price equal to marginal cost and pay a fee for the franchise that would bring its profit down to zero. The fee would then be distributed to consumers. In their analysis, cost was known to the firm only, and demand was known to both the firm and regulator. Baron and Myerson adopted the same asymmetric-information assumption, but they assumed that there was only one potential supplier, so that an auction was ineffective. Consequently, the Loeb–Magat scheme would not be desirable, because the firm would get all the consumer surplus and pay virtually nothing for the franchise. From the consumers' perspective, that would be worse than simply allowing the firm to behave as an unregulated monopolist. Thus, Baron and Myerson considered having the firm report its costs, and then price could be set accordingly. But this resulted in the possibility of misreporting owing to the asymmetric information – a possibility that did not arise for Loeb and Magat because of the effective auction.

Let us return now to the case in which an auction may be effective, although not perfect as it is in the model of Loeb and Magat. Suppose that during the auction, bidders are uncertain as to what the operating costs will be for the one who wins the franchise. The regulator, too, is uncertain, although she and all bidders are aware of demand. Riordan and Sappington (1987) have examined this situation: The auction is won by the highest bidder, who is essentially the bidder predicting the lowest operating costs. The fee paid for the franchise and the subsequent subsidy to the firm depend on the size of the winning bid. Once again, the revelation principle ensures that bidders will be truthful in reporting their predicted costs.

Riordan and Sappington's results can be summarized as follows: Optimum prices will be set in excess of marginal costs, thus creating distortions, and these distortions will be independent of the number of bidders. They explain these results by noting that the regulator is confronted with two incentive problems: (1) She must be alert to the possibility of bidders biasing their predicted costs upward during the auction, and for this she adjusts the franchise fee. (2) She must be alert to the possibility of the franchise winner exaggerating actual costs, which will become known after the auction, and for this she adjusts the subsidy and price. Interestingly, there are cases in which this scheme will duplicate the Loeb–Magat results, but only when bidders are identical ex ante, or when there are many bidders. Generally, however, the franchise fee will not recover all of the profit to be earned by the firm winning the franchise. The reader should refer to Riordan and Sappington for greater detail on the nuances of this scheme.

The studies on incentive schemes and asymmetric information represent a cutting edge in the theoretical analysis of regulating natural monopolies. The literature is young, and as it matures, we would hope that useful and practical prescriptions will emerge. Joskow and Schmalensee (1986) point out that thus far the work has "not produced a neat set of cookbook rules that can be readily applied with available empirical information to develop optimal or even good incentive mechanisms" (p. 24). This disappointing fact, they argue, is probably due to the inherent difficulty of a problem that includes uncertainty, asymmetric information, and strategic behavior. The encouraging fact, however, is that the theory of regulation is advancing as yesterday's models give way to those that more accurately reflect the regulatory environment.

### Incentive regulation

Although the incentives literature has not produced "neat cookbook rules," economists have provided insights into optimum regulatory policies. Joskow and Schmalensee (1986) draw eight general conclusions for electric utility regulation from the principal-and-agent literature and regulatory practice in the United States:

1. Pure cost-plus reimbursement mechanisms are seldom optimal. Regulatory lag provides some incentives for efficiency, but decoupling allowed revenue from reported accounting costs is desirable. For example, the fuel adjustment clause has been modified in a number of states: Lags, partial adjustment, and the use of fuel price indices (rather than actual prices paid) can increase incentives to search, negotiate, and use forward markets.

2. The incentive mechanism should depend on underlying economic conditions. For example, increases in uncertainty require movement away from fixed-price contracts or price caps. There will be a trade-off between periodic redesign of such schemes and allowing enough time for them to have impacts. If the plan is subject to frequent regulatory modification, the utility can begin to behave strategically – altering the terms of future revenue schedules.

3. Compensation schemes should focus on comprehensive

measures of performance rather than on single indices – such as generating-unit reliability or production heat rates (Johnson, 1985). Indices capturing only part of utility performance might be maximized to the detriment of ratepayers. For example, the Florida PSC disallows "excessive" expenditures on an individual component of total costs, nonfuel operating and maintenance (O&M) expenses, on the basis of comparisons with a benchmark. Although, in principle, the benchmark is used only to "flag" potential problems, rational utility managers will redirect resources toward lowering O&M outlays. Inappropriate choice of the benchmark, such as use of the consumer price index (CPI), can further distort utility decisions as managers attempt to meet unrealistic constraints. Undue emphasis on the electricity-generating-unit availability, the time to dial tone, or consumer complaints about particular service features could raise total costs disproportionately relative to associated benefits.

4. Developments not under managerial control should result in neither rewards nor penalties to the utility. If underlying economic cost and demand conditions result in high risks to investors, then the rate of return should reflect those risks. Determining whether or not stockholders should bear the higher costs associated with unforeseen events, such as an accident shutting down a nuclear plant, raises much tougher issues than those associated with marginal risks. Separating unforeseen events from managerial effort is highly problematic, because the dollars involved will trigger time-consuming investigations and contradictory testimony from expert witnesses. Regulatory responses to such situations will have a significant impact on the ability of firms to attract capital in the future.

5. The long-run financial viability of the firm must not be jeopardized by the incentive mechanism. Over time, the utility must be able to cover costs. Thus, the cost-recovery schedule must have symmetric rewards and penalties. If it is applied only when it will keep prices down, and then is modified if it appears that prices will rise, the objectives of the mechanism will be thwarted. For example, the Mississippi PSC approved a specific incentive

program in August 1986 – and suspended it one month later when the provisions implied a rate increase (Joskow and Schmalensee, 1986, p. 43).

6. A firm commitment to sticking with the incentive mechanism may be difficult to obtain. Thus, the political acceptability of the likely rewards or penalties needs to be factored into the allowed revenue schedule. The Mississippi incident illustrates this point. All participants should be aware of the possible range of outcomes and accept the program in terms of how cost savings will be shared by the utility and customers. Tests using alternative scenarios would help ensure that politically unacceptable outcomes would be avoided – giving credibility to the incentive program.

7. Implementation of new schemes requires that they can easily be compared with traditional regulatory procedures. Cost-accounting systems still will need to be maintained given that the schemes will initially be viewed as experimental. Often, these accounting systems are not informative for purposes of rate design, but they can provide documentation for gauging some impacts of the program.

8. Perfection will be achieved neither by current regulatory arrangements nor by new incentive programs. However, we would like to be able to avoid the more obvious limitations of traditional regulation noted in various sections throughout this book. Because adoption of alternative mechanisms could result in greater incentives for cost minimization, such programs should be given some priority by both utilities and commissions. Regulation need not be a zero-sum game.

Price caps are being considered by both state and federal regulatory commissions as incentive-enhancing mechanisms. Under a CPI–$X$ plan, the regulated firm is constrained so that a weighted average of its prices increases by no more than the consumer price index (CPI) less $X$ percent (expected productivity advancement). Implementation of such a scheme raises a number of issues, including whether to use the CPI or another index of input prices over which the firm has no control. Advocates of a price-cap approach argue that it provides incentives for cost minimization and cost reductions (along the lines of Bailey's regulatory-lag model), that it protects core customers from monopoly pricing, and that managerial and regulatory administrative burdens are reduced.

Vogelsang (1988) notes that the continuation of such a capping system would require revisiting the issue of the firm's achieved rate of return periodically – yielding a modified version of the V-F adjustment mechanism: "Some of the desirable properties of the original V-F mechanism extend to these long-run price caps. In particular, if the regulated firm tries to maximize profits it will choose individual prices within a capped average such that total consumer welfare (expressed as consumer surplus) will increase over time. At the limit consumer surplus will converge to the maximum attainable at normal profit levels for the regulated firm" (p. v). Ramsey prices result if a set of reasonable assumptions hold. The key point is that price caps alone will lead to a crisis situation – as consumers or the firm find the long-term application of a static formula unacceptable. However, if the overall profitability of the firm is all that is measured and reviewed, arbitrary cost allocations on a service-by-service basis are avoided.

### 12.5. Concluding remarks

In a sense, we have now completed a loop within these 12 chapters. We started by outlining why firms should be regulated, and we anchored the criteria for regulation in economic efficiency. Then we discussed various pricing methods that could be used to achieve economic efficiency (through their ability to track marginal costs) and to thwart unwarranted entry by new firms. We have demonstrated how Ramsey pricing promotes efficiency and how nonlinear prices can be utilized to reduce deadweight losses and contribute to the achievement of equity. We have seen that peak-load pricing under certainty and uncertainty can also yield improvements in resource allocation. These pricing schemes offer potentially significant economic efficiency gains relative to the fully allocated cost methods used in most regulatory jurisdictions. The links to sustainable prices were also investigated to show the appropriate conditions for entry regulation.

After leaving this ideal world, with its optimal regulatory behavior, we examined the real world to see how firms are actually regulated. In comparing the two worlds, we saw that there clearly is a gap between what should be done and what is done. The real world displays behavior that recognizes political constituencies, self-interests, and equity issues more than it emphasizes economic efficiency. Furthermore, regulatory constraints can increase costs and inefficiently alter the output mixes of natural monopolies. Potential distortions raise the cost of regulation and reduce the gains from intervention. The addition of technological change to the story leads to further problems – related to appropriate regulatory lags and alternative ways to promote innovative efficiency. Changes in the output mix, vertical integration, and entry into unregulated markets are three other behaviors that regulators must monitor. Deregulation makes economic sense when the justifications for government controls become weakened by economic change. However, the neat conceptual frameworks that take complex cost structures and demand cross-elasticities fully into account are not easy to estimate empirically.

The alternatives to traditional regulation offer techniques that might help to close the gap between the ideal and real worlds. Good alternatives should place economic efficiency at the forefront. But do these or other alternatives have a chance of adoption? Innovative alternatives like those suggested by Vogelsang and Finsinger seemingly could be implemented in a mechanical fashion without being overwhelmed by political tugs-of-war and subjective commission judgments. And this would seem to be precisely what is needed to move the regulatory process in the right direction. But lessons from the principal-and-agent literature suggest that the problems are complex owing to asymmetric information and incentives for strategic behavior. Because implementation requires the support of the very groups that are waging the tug-of-war, no group is likely to let go of its end of the rope to accept an alternative without knowing full well what that alternative means for its well-being. Unfortunately, this knowledge is elusive, because translating rigorous economic analysis to definitive policies is not done with precision. The task of convincing noneconomists to adopt a new policy whose implications may not be fully understood even by the economist borders on hopelessness.

Nevertheless, we make progress through studies of the regulatory process. We expect that the ideas covered in this book will be slowly diffused throughout the halls of government and industry. Hopefully, when books on natural monopoly regulation appear in the next decade or so, there will be less of a gap between the ideal and how regulation actually operates.

One can make a case that the opportunity cost of past regulatory strategies has been high because of induced inefficiencies. In addition, many current policies do not seem to address the problem of fairness in a comprehensive manner. Some would conclude that the principle of specialization and division of labor supports the concept of regulators targeting efficiency rather than fairness, letting welfare agencies deal with income distributional concerns. Others would ask only that favored groups be given benefits directly – so that such assistance is made explicit in the regulatory process, rather than being camouflaged in various accounting conventions. Given changing technologies, alterations in product mixes, and the production interdependencies of the traditional natural monopoly industries, it is difficult to justify a regulation-as-usual approach to our important energy, transportation, and telecommunications sectors.

# References

The following abbreviations are used in the references:

| | |
|---|---|
| *A.E.R.* | *American Economic Review* |
| *Bell J.* | *Bell Journal* |
| *Eca* | *Economica* |
| *E.I.* | *Economic Inquiry* |
| *E.J.* | *Economic Journal* (also used as a combination, e.g., *Southern E.J.* = *Southern Economic Journal*) |
| *Energy J.* | *Energy Journal* |
| *Etrica* | *Econometrica* |
| *I.E.R.* | *International Economic Review* |
| *J.E.* | *Journal of Econometrics* |
| *J.E.I.* | *Journal of Economic Issues* |
| *J.E.L.* | *Journal of Economic Literature* |
| *J.E.T.* | *Journal of Economic Theory* |
| *J.I.E.* | *Journal of Industrial Economics* |
| *J.L.E.* | *Journal of Law and Economics* |
| *J.P.E.* | *Journal of Political Economy* |
| *J. Pub. E.* | *Journal of Public Economics* |
| *L.E.* | *Land Economics* |
| *L.C.P.* | *Law and Contemporary Problems* |
| *O.E.P.* | *Oxford Economic Papers* |
| *P.F.Q.* | *Public Finance Quarterly* |
| *Q.J.E.* | *Quarterly Journal of Economics* |
| *R.L.E.* | *Research in Law and Economics* |
| *Rand J.* | *Rand Journal of Economics* (formerly *Bell J.*) |
| *R.E. Stats.* | *Review of Economics and Statistics* |
| *R.E. Studs.* | *Review of Economic Studies* |
| U.P. | University Press (e.g., Cambridge U.P. = Cambridge University Press) |

Acton, J. P. 1982. "An Evaluation of Economists' Influence on Electric Utility Rate Reforms," *A.E.R.,* 72, 114–19.

and Mitchell, B. M. 1983. "Welfare Analysis of Electricity Rate Charges," in S. V. Berg (ed.), *Innovative Electric Rates,* pp. 195–226. Lexington, MA: Lexington Books.

Alchian, A. A. 1965. "Some Economics of Property Rights," *Il Politico,* 30, 816–29.

Alessio, F. J., Heckerman, D. G., and Wenders, J. T. 1976. "An Analysis of the Benefits and Costs of Electric Generation Reliability," unpublished manuscript, U. of Arizona.

Anderson, R., and Bohman, M. 1985. "Short- and Long-Run Marginal Cost Pricing: On Their Alleged Equivalence," *Energy Economics,* 7, 279–88.

Archer, S. H. 1981. "The Regulatory Effects on Cost of Capital in Electric Utilities," *Public Utilities Fortnightly,* 107(59), 36–9.

Areeda, P., and Turner, D. F. 1975. "Predatory Pricing and Related Practices under Section 2 of the Sherman Act," *Harvard Law Review,* 88, 697–733.

Arrow, K. 1962. "Economic Welfare and the Allocation of Resources for Inventions," in R. R. Nelson (ed.), *The Rate and Direction of Inventive Activity,* pp. 609–25. Princeton, NJ: Princeton University Press.

Arzac, E. R., and Edwards, F. R. 1979. "Efficiency in Regulated and Unregulated Firms: An Iconoclastic View of the Averch-Johnson Thesis," in M. A. Crew (ed.), *Problems in Public Utility Economics and Regulation,* pp. 41–54. Lexington, MA: Lexington Books.

Asbury, J. G., and Mueller, R. O. 1977. "Solar Energy and Electric Utilities: Should They Be Interfaced?" *Science,* 195, 445–50.

Atkinson, A. B., and Waverman, L. 1973. "Resource Allocation and the Regulated Firm: Comment," *Bell J.,* 4, 283–7.

Atkinson, S. E., and Halvorsen, R. 1980. "A Test of Relative and Absolute Price Efficiency in Regulated Utilities," *R.E. Stats.,* 62, 81–8.

1986. "The Relative Efficiency of Public and Private Firms in a Regulated Environment: The Case of U.S. Electric Utilities," *J. Pub. E.,* 29(3), 281–94.

Auerbach, A. J., and Pellechio, A. J. 1978. "The Two-Part Tariff and Voluntary Market Participation," *Q.J.E.,* 92, 571–87.

Averch, H., and Johnson L. L. 1962. "Behavior of the Firm Under Regulatory Constraint," *A.E.R.,* 52, 1052–69.

Awh, R. Y., and Primeaux, W. J., Jr. 1985. "Managerial Discretion and Expense Preference Behavior," *R.E. Stats.,* 67, 224–31.

Bailey, E. E. 1972. "Peak-Load Pricing under Regulatory Constraint," *J.P.E.,* 80, 662–79.

1973. *Economic Theory of Regulatory Constraint.* Lexington, MA: Lexington Books.

1978. "Innovation and Regulation," *J. Pub. E.,* 3, 285–95.

1981. "Contestability and the Design of Regulatory and Antitrust Policy," *A.E.R., Papers and Proceedings,* 71, 178–83.

and Baumol, W. J. 1984. "Deregulation and the Theory of Contestable Markets," *Yale Journal on Regulation,* 2, 111–38.

and Coleman, R. D. 1971. "The Effect of Lagged Regulation in an Averch-Johnson Model," *Bell J.,* 2, 278–92.

and Friedlaender, A. 1982. "Market Structure and Multiproduct Industries," *J.E.L.,* 20, 1024–48.

and Malone, J. C. 1970. "Resource Allocation and the Regulated Firm," *Bell J.,* 1, 129–142.

and Panzar, J. C. 1981. "The Contestability of Airline Markets During the Transition to Deregulation," *L.C.P.,* 44, 125–46.

and White, L. J. 1974. "Reversals in Peak and Off-Peak Pricing," *Bell J.,* 5, 75–92.

Barclay, P., Gegax, D., and Tschirhart, J. 1987. "The Economics of Industrial Cogeneration, Regulatory Policy," working paper, University of Wyoming.

Barke, R. P., and Riker, W. H. 1982. "A Political Theory of Regulation with Some Observations on Railway Abandonments," *Public Choice,* 39(1), 73–106.

Baron, D. P., and Besanko, D. 1984. "Regulation, Asymmetric Information, and Auditing," *Rand J.,* 15, 447–70.

and DeBondt, R. R. 1979. "Fuel Adjustment Mechanisms and Economic Efficiency," *J.I.E.,* 27, 243–61.

and Myerson, R. B. 1982. "Regulating a Monopolist with Unknown Costs." *Etrica* 50, 911–30.

and Taggart, R. A., Jr. 1977. "A Model of Regulation Under Uncertainty and a Test of Regulatory Bias," *Bell J.,* 8, 151–67.

1980. "Regulatory Pricing Procedures and Economic Incentives," in M. A. Crew (ed.), *Issues in Public Utility Pricing and Regulation,* pp. 27–49. Lexington, MA: Lexington Books.

Baseman, K. C. 1981. "Open Entry and Cross-Subsidization in Regulated Markets," in G. Fromm (ed.), *Studies in Public Regulation,* pp. 329–60. Cambridge, MA: M.I.T. Press.

Baumol, W. J. 1975. "Payment by Performance in Rail Passenger Transportation: An Innovation in Amtrak's Operations," *Bell J.,* 6, 281–98.

1977. "On the Proper Cost Tests for Natural Monopoly in a Multiproduct Industry," *A.E.R.,* 67, 809–22.

1981. "Comment on Open Entry and Cross-Subsidization in Regulated Markets," in G. Fromm (ed.), *Studies in Public Regulation,* pp. 361–4. Cambridge, MA: M.I.T. Press.

1983. "Minimum and Maximum Pricing Principles for Residual Regulation," in A. L. Danielsen and D. R. Kamerschen (eds.), *Current Issues in Public-Utility Economics,* pp. 177–96. Lexington, MA: Lexington Books.

Bailey, E. E., and Willig, R. D. 1977. "Weak Invisible Hand Theorems on the Sustainability of Prices in Multiproduct Monopoly," *A.E.R.,* 67, 350–65.

and Bradford, D. F. 1970. "Optimal Departures from Marginal Cost Pricing," *A.E.R.,* 60, 265–83.

and Braunstein, Y. M. 1977. "Empirical Study of Scale Economies and Production Complementarity: The Case of Journal Publication," *J.P.E.,* 85, 1037–48.

Fischer, D., and ten Raa, T. 1979. "The Price–Iso Return Locus and Rational Rate Regulation," *Bell J.,* 10, 648–58.

and Klevorick, A. K. 1970. "Input Choices and Rate-of-Return Regulation: An Overview of the Discussion," *Bell J.,* 1, 162–90.

Panzar, J. C., and Willig, R. D. 1982. *Contestable Markets and the Theory of Industry Structure.* New York: Harcourt Brace Jovanovich.

and Willig, R. D. 1981. "Fixed Costs, Sunk Costs, Entry Barriers and Sustainability of Monopoly," *Q.J.E.,* 96, 405–31.

1986. "Contestability: Developments since the Book," *O.E.P.,* 38, Suppl., 9–36.

Bawa, V. S., and Sibley, D. S. 1980. "Dynamic Behavior of a Firm Subject to Stochastic Regulatory Review," *I.E.R.,* 21, 627–42.

Becker, G. 1976. "Toward a More General Theory of Regulation: Comment," *J.L.E.,* 19, 245–48.

Benson, B. L. 1984. "Rent Seeking from a Property Rights Perspective," *Southern E.J.,* 51, 388–400.

Berg, S. V. 1981a. "Load Management: Rationing vs. Peak Load Pricing," *Energy J.,* 2, 89–98.

1981b. "PURPA and Benefit Cost Analysis for Innovative Rates," *Public Utilities Fortnightly,* 108(8), 21–30.

1983a. "Power Factors and the Efficient Pricing and Production of Reactive Power," *Energy J.,* 4, 93–102.

(ed.) 1983b. *Innovative Electric Rates: Issues in Cost–Benefit Analysis.* Lexington, MA: Lexington Books.

1988. "Duopoly Compatibility Standards with Partial Cooperation and Standards Leadership," *Information Economics and Policy,* 3, 35–53.

and Roth, W. E. 1976. "Some Remarks on Residential Electricity Consumption and Social Rate Restructuring," *Bell J.,* 7, 690–8.

and Savvides, A. 1983. "The Theory of Maximum kW Demand Charges for Electricity," *Energy Economics,* 5, 258–66.

Bergson, A. 1972. "Optimal Pricing for a Public Enterprise," *Q.J.E.,* 86, 519–44.

Berkowitz, M. K. 1977. "Power Grid Economics in a Peak Load Pricing Framework," *Canadian Journal of Economics,* 10, 621–36.

Bernstein, M. H. 1955. *Regulating Business by Independent Commission.* Princeton, NJ: Princeton U.P.

Bessen, S. M. 1974. "The Economics of the Cable Television 'Consenses'," *J.L.E.,* 7, 39–52.

Blair, R. D., and Kaserman, D. L. 1983. *Law and Economics of Vertical Integration and Control.* New York: Academic Press.

Kaserman, D. L., and Pacey, P. L. 1985. "A Note on Purchased Power Adjustment Clauses," *Journal of Business,* 58, 409–17.

Boiteux, M. 1960. "Peak-Load Pricing," *Journal of Business,* 33, 157–79 (originally in French, reprinted from *Cahiers du séminaire d'Econométrie,* 1951).

1971. "On the Management of Public Monopolies Subject to Budgetary Constraints," *J.E.T.,* 3, 219–40 (originally in French, reprinted from *Etrica,* January 1956, 22–40).

Bolter, W. G., et al. 1984. *Telecommunications Policy for the 1980s: The Transition to Competition.* Englewood Cliffs, NJ: Prentice-Hall.

Bonbright, J. C. 1961. *Principles of Public Utility Rates.* New York: Columbia U.P.

Boulding, K. E. 1948. *Economic Analysis,* 3rd ed. New York: Harper.

Boyes, W. J. 1976. "An Empirical Examination of the Averch-Johnson Effect," *E.I.,* 14, 25–35.

Braeutigam, R. R. 1979. "Optimal Pricing with Intermodal Competition," *A.E.R.,* 69, 38–49.

1980. "An Analysis of Fully Distributed Cost Pricing in Regulated Industries," *Bell J.,* 11, 182–96.

1981. "The Regulation of Multiproduct Enterprises by Rate of Return, Markup, and Operating Ratio," *R.L.E.,* 3, 15–38.

1984. "Socially Optimal Pricing with Rivalry and Economies of Scale," *Rand J.,* 15, 127–34.

1986. "The Industrial Cogeneration of Electricity: An Investigation of Incentives and Efficiency," working paper, Northwestern University.

and Quirk, J. P. 1984. "Demand Uncertainty and the Regulated Firm," *I.E.R.,* 25, 45–60.

Branch, B. 1979. "Quality of Service and the Allowed Rate of Return: American Telephone and Telegraph," *Journal of Economics and Business,* 32, 86–8.

Braverman, A., Gruasch, J. L., and Salop, S. 1983. "Defects in Disneyland: Quality Control as a Two-Part Tariff," *R.E. Studs.,* 50, 121–31.

Breen, W. J., and Lerner, E. M. 1972. "On the Use of $\beta$ in Regulatory Proceedings," *Bell J.,* 3, 612–21.

Brennan, M. J., and Schwartz, E. S. 1982. "Consistent Regulatory Policy under Uncertainty," *Bell J.,* 13, 506–21.

Brennan, T. J. 1987. "Cross-Subsidization and Discrimination by Regulated Monopolists," U.S. Department of Justice, Antitrust Division, Economic Analysis Group discussion paper EAG 87-2.

Breyer, S. G. 1982. *Regulation and Its Reform.* Cambridge, MA: Harvard U.P.

and MacAvoy, P. W. 1974. *Energy Regulation by the Federal Power Commission.* Washington, DC: Brookings Institution.

Brigham, E. F., and Tapley, C. 1986. "Public Utility Finance," in E. I. Altman (ed.), *Handbook of Corporate Finance,* pp. 16.1–16.45. New York: Wiley.

Broadman, H. G., Montgomery, W. D., and Russell, M. 1985. "Field Price Deregulation and the Carrier Status of Natural Gas Pipelines," *Energy J.,* 6, 127–39.

Brock, G. W. 1981. *The Telecommunications Industry: The Dynamics of Market Structure.* Cambridge, MA: Harvard U.P.

Brock, W. A., and Dechert, W. D. 1985. "Dynamic Ramsey Pricing," *I.E.R.,* 26, 569–91.

Brown, G., Jr., and Johnson, M. B. 1969. "Public Utility Pricing and Output under Risk," *A.E.R.,* 59, 119–28.

Brown, M. 1966. *On the Theory and Measurement of Technological Change.* Cambridge U.P.

Brown, R. S., Caves, D. W., and Christensen, L. R. 1979. "Modelling the Structure of Costs and Production for Multiproduct Firms," *Southern E.J.,* 46, 256–73.

Brown, S. J., and Sibley, D. S. 1986. *The Theory of Public Utility Pricing.* Cambridge U.P.

Bruggink, T. H. 1982. "Public Versus Regulated Private Enterprise in the Municipal Water Industry: A Comparison of Operating Costs," *Quarterly Review of Economics and Business,* 22(1), 111–25.

Buchanan, J. M. 1966. "Peak Loads and Efficient Pricing: Comment," *Q.J.E.,* 80, 463–71.

Burgess, G., and Paglin, M. 1981. "Lifeline Electricity Rates as an Income Transfer Device," *L.E.,* 57, 41–7.

Burness, H. S., Montgomery, W. D., and Quirk, J. P. 1980. "Capital Contracting and the Regulated Firm," *A.E.R.,* 70, 342–54.

Bussing, I. 1936. *Public Utility Regulation and the So-Called Sliding Scale.* New York: Columbia U.P.

Byatt, I. C. R. 1963. "The Genesis of the Present Pricing System in Electricity Supply," *O.E.P.,* 15, 8–18.

Bye, R. T. 1926. "The Nature and Fundamental Elements of Costs," *Q.J.E.,* 39, 30–62.

    1929. "Composite Demand and Joint Supply in Relation to Public Utility Rates," *Q.J.E.,* 44, 40–62.

Cabe, R. 1988. "Two Essays on the Regulation of Multiproduct Firms," Ph.D. dissertation, University of Wyoming.

Calem, P. S., and Spulber, D. F. 1984. "Multiproduct Two Part Tariffs," *International Journal of Industrial Organization,* 2, 105–15.

Callen, J. L. 1978. "Production, Efficiency, and Welfare in the Natural Gas Transmission Industry," *A.E.R.,* 68, 311–23.

    Mathewson, G. F., and Mohring, H. 1976. "The Benefits and Costs of Rate of Return Regulation," *A.E.R.,* 66, 290–7.

Capron, W. M. (ed.) 1971. *Technological Change in Regulated Industries.* Washington, DC: Brookings Institution.

Carlton, D. W. 1977. "Peak Load Pricing with Stochastic Demand," *A.E.R.,* 67, 1006–10.

    1978. "Market Behavior with Demand Uncertainty and Price Inflexibility," *A.E.R.,* 68, 571–87.

Caves, D. W., and Christensen, L. R. 1980. "The Relative Efficiency of Public and Private Firms in a Competitive Environment: The Case of Canadian Railroads," *J.P.E.,* 88, 958–76.

    Christensen, L. R., and Tretheway, M. W. 1984. "Economics of Density versus Economies of Scale: Why Trunk and Local Service Airline Costs Differ," *Rand J.,* 15, 471–89.

Chao, H. 1983. "Peak Load Pricing and Capacity Planning with Demand and Supply Uncertainty," *Bell J.,* 14, 179–90.

Chapman, R., and Waverman, L. 1979. "Risk Aversion, Uncertain Demand and the Effects of a Regulatory Constraint," *J. Pub. E.,* 11, 107–21.

Chappel, H. W., Jr., and Wilder, R. P. 1986. "Multiproduct Monopoly, Regulation, and Firm Costs: Comment," *Southern E.J.,* 52, 1168–74.

Christensen, L. R., and Greene, W. H. 1978. "An Econometric Assessment of

Cost Savings from Coordination in U.S. Electric Power Generation," *L.E.,* 54, 139–55.

Cicchetti, C. J. 1986. "Marketing Strategies for Natural Gas Distributors in the 1990s," National Economic Research Associates.

Gillen, W. J., and Smolensky, P. 1976. *The Marginal Cost and Pricing of Electricity.* Report to NSF on behalf of the Planning and Conservation Foundation, Sacramento, CA.

and Jurewitz, J. L. 1975. *Studies in Electric Utility Regulation.* Cambridge, MA: Ballinger.

Clark, J. M. 1911. "Rates for Public Utilities," *A.E.R.,* 2, 473–87.

1923. *The Economics of Overhead Costs.* University of Chicago Press.

1939. *The Social Control of Business.* New York: McGraw-Hill.

Clark, R. G. 1978. "The Impact of a Fuel Adjustment Clause on the Regulated Firm's Value and Cost of Capital." *Journal of Financial and Quantitative Analysis,* 13, 745–57.

Clemens, E. W. 1950. "Price Discrimination and the Multiple-Product Firm," *R.E. Studs.,* 19, 1–11.

Coase, R. H. 1937. "The Nature of the Firm," *Eca,* 4, 386–405.

1946. "The Marginal Cost Controversy," *Eca,* 13, 169–82.

1970. "The Theory of Public Utility Pricing and Its Application," *Bell J.,* 1, 113–28.

Coldwell, D., III 1979. "The Present State of the Theory of Public Utilities," *Atlantic E.J.,* 7(2), 39–45.

Cole, L. P. 1981. "A Note on Fully Distributed Cost Prices," *Bell J.,* 12, 329–34.

Congressional Budget Office. 1984. *The Changing Telephone Industry: Access Charges, Universal Service, and Local Rates.* U.S. Government: Congress of the United States (June).

Costello, K. W. 1984. "Electing Regulators: The Case of Public Utility Commissioners," *Yale Journal on Regulation,* 1, 83–105.

and Galen, P. S. 1985. "An Approach for Evaluating Utility-Financed Energy Conservation Programs," *Resources and Energy,* 7, 283–304.

Coursey, D., Isaac, R. M., and Smith, V. L. 1984a. "Natural Monopoly and Contested Markets: Some Experimental Results," *J.L.E.,* 27, 91–113.

Isaac, R. M., Smith, V. L., and Luke, M. 1984b. "Market Contestability in the Presence of Sunk (Entry) Costs," *Rand J.,* 15, 69–84.

Courville, L. 1974. "Regulation and Efficiency in the Electric Utility Industry," *Bell J.,* 5, 53–74.

Cowing, T. G. 1976. "The Environmental Implications of Monopoly Regulation: A Process Analysis Approach," *Journal of Environmental Economics and Management,* 2, 207–23.

Crain, W. M., and Ekelund, R. B., Jr. 1976. "Chadwick and Demsetz on Competition and Regulation," *J.L.E.,* 19, 149–62.

and Zardkoohi, A. 1978. "A Test of the Property-Rights Theory of the Firm: Water Utilities in the United States," *J.L.E.,* 21, 395–408.

Cramer, C. A., and Tschirhart, J. 1980. "National and International Electric

Power Pools," in T. Sandler (ed.), *The Theory and Structures of International Political Economy,* pp. 215–34. Boulder, CO: Westview Press.

1983. "Power Pooling: An Exercise in Industrial Coordination," *L.E.,* 59, 24–34.

Crew, M. A. (ed.) 1979. *Problems in Public Utility Economics and Regulation.* Lexington, MA: Lexington Books.

(ed.) 1980. *Issues in Public Utility Pricing and Regulation.* Lexington, MA: Lexington Books.

(ed.) 1982. *Regulatory Reform and Public Utilities.* Lexington, MA: Lexington Books.

and Kleindorfer, P. R. 1971a. "Marshall and Turvey on Peak Loads or Joint Product Pricing," *J.P.E.,* 79, 1369–77.

1971b. "Recent Contributions to the Theory of Marginal Cost Pricing: The Problem of Peak Loads," *E.J.,* 81, 934–6.

1975. "Optimal Plant Mix in Peak Load Pricing," *Scottish J.P.E.,* 22, 277–91.

1976. "Peak Load Pricing with a Diverse Technology," *Bell J.,* 7, 207–31.

1978. "Reliability and Public Utility Pricing," *A.E.R.,* 68, 31–40.

1979a. "Managerial Discretion and Public Utility Regulation,"*Southern E.J.,* 45, 696–709.

1979b. *Public Utility Economics.* New York: St. Martin's Press.

1979c. "Some Elementary Considerations of Reliability and Regulation," in M. A. Crew (ed.), *Problems in Public Utility Economics and Regulation,* pp. 143–65. Lexington, MA: Lexington Books.

1986. *The Economics of Public Utility Regulation.* Cambridge, MA: M.I.T. Press.

Crockett, J. H., Jr. 1976. "Differential Pricing and Interconsumer Efficiency in the Electric Power Industry," *Bell J.,* 7, 293–8.

Cross, J. G. 1970. "Incentive Pricing and Utility Regulation," *Q.J.E.,* 84, 236–53.

Dahl, A. J. 1978. "California's Lifeline Policy," *Public Utilities Fortnightly,* 102(5), 13–22.

Damus, S. 1984. "Ramsey Pricing by U.S. Railroads: Can It Exist?" *Journal of Transport Economics and Policy,* 6, 51–61.

Danielsen, A. L., and Kamerschen, D. R. (eds.) 1983. *Current Issues in Public-Utility Economics: Essays in Honor of James C. Bonbright.* Lexington, MA: D. C. Heath.

(eds.) 1986. *Telecommunications in the Post-Divestiture Era.* Lexington, MA: Lexington Books.

Dansby, R. E. 1979. "Multi-Period Pricing with Stochastic Demand," *J.E.,* 9, 223–37.

Das, S. P. 1980. "On the Effect of Rate of Return Regulation under Uncertainty," *A.E.R.,* 70, 456–60.

Dasgupta, P., and Stiglitz, J. 1980. "Uncertainty, Industrial Structure and the Speed of R&D," *Bell J.,* 11, 1–28.

Daughety, A. F. 1984. "Regulation and Industrial Organization," *J.P.E.,* 92, 932–53.

Davis, B. E., Caccappolo, G. J., and Chaundry, M. A. 1973. "An Econometric

Planning Model for American Telephone and Telegraph Company," *Bell J.*, 4, 29–56.

and Sparrow, F. T. 1972. "Valuation Models in Regulation," *Bell J.*, 3, 544–67.

Davis, E. G. 1973. "A Dynamic Model of the Regulated Firm with a Price Adjustment Mechanism," *Bell J.*, 4, 270–82.

Davis, O. A., and Whinston, A. B. 1965. "Welfare Economics and the Theory of Second Best," *R.E. Studs.*, 32, 1–16.

Dayan, D. 1975. "Behavior of the Firm Under Regulatory Constraint: A Reexamination," *Industrial Organization Review*, 3, 61–76.

De Alessi, L. 1974. "An Economic Analysis of Government Ownership and Regulation: Theory and Evidence from the Electric Power Industry," *Public Choice*, 19, 526–38.

Delaney, J. B., and Honeycutt, T. C. 1976. *An Empirical Analysis of Electric Utility Research and Development Activity.* NR-AIG-002, Office of Nuclear Reactor Regulation, July V-80.

Demsetz, H. 1968. "Why Regulate Utilities?" *J.L.E.*, 11, 55–65.

1971. "On the Regulation of Industry: A Reply," *J.P.E.*, 79, 356–63.

Derthick, M., and Quirk, P. J. 1985. *The Politics of Deregulation.* Washington, DC: Brookings Institution.

DiLorenzo, T. J., and Robinson, R. 1982. "Managerial Objectives Subject to Political Market Constraints: Electric Utilities in the US," *Quarterly Review of Economics and Business*, 22(2), 113–25.

Dimopoulos, D. 1981. "Pricing Schemes for Regulated Enterprises and Their Welfare Implications in the Case of Electricity," *Bell J.*, 12, 185–200.

Dixit, A. K. 1979. "A Model of Duopoly Suggesting a Theory of Entry Barriers," *Bell J.*, 10, 20–32.

Dougan, W. R. 1984. "Railway Abandonments, Cross-subsidies, and the Theory of Regulation," *Public Choice*, 44, 297–305.

Dublin, J. A., and Navarro, P. 1982. "Regulatory Climate and the Cost of Capital," in M. A. Crew (ed.), *Regulatory Reform and Public Utilities*, pp. 141–67. Lexington, MA: Lexington Books.

Dupuit, J. 1844. "De la Mésure de l'Utilité des Travaux Publics," *Annales des Ponts et Chaussés*, 8; reprinted in Arrow and Scitovsky (eds.), *Readings in Welfare Economics*, pp. 255–83. Homewood, IL: Irwin.

Eads, G. C. 1974. "Railroad Diversification: Where Lies the Public Interest?" *Bell J.*, 5, 595–613.

Ebrill, L. P., and Slutsky, S. M. 1984. "Pricing Rules for Intermediate and Final Good Regulated Industries," working paper, University of Florida.

Eckert, R. D. 1981. "The Life Cycle of Regulatory Commissioners," *J.L.E.*, 24, 113–20.

Edwards, F. R. 1977. "Managerial Objectives in Regulated Industries: Expense Preference Behavior in Banking," *J.P.E.*, 85, 147–62.

Ekelund, R. B., Jr., and Higgins, R. S. 1982. "Capital Fixity, Innovations, and Long Term Contracting: An Intertemporal Economic Theory of Regulation," *A.E.R.*, 72, 32–46.

Ely, R. T. 1937. *Outlines of Economics.* New York: Macmillan.

Evans, D. S. (ed.) 1983. *Breaking Up Bell: Essays in Industrial Organization and Regulation.* Amsterdam: North Holland.

and Heckman, J. J. 1983a. "Multiproduct Cost Function Estimates and Natural Monopoly Tests for the Bell System," in D. S. Evans (ed.), *Breaking up Bell,* pp. 253–82. Amsterdam: North Holland.

1983b. "Natural Monopoly," in D. S. Evans (ed.), *Breaking Up Bell,* pp. 127–56. Amsterdam: North Holland.

1984. "A Test for Subadditivity of the Cost Function with an Application to the Bell System," *A.E.R.,* 74, 615–23.

Färe, R., Grosskopf, S., and Logan, J. 1983. "The Relative Performance of Publicly Owned and Privately Owned Electric Utilities," working paper, Department of Economics, Southern Illinois University, Carbondale.

Farrell, J. R., and Saloner, G. 1985. "Standardization, Compatibility and Innovation," *Rand J.,* 16, 70–83.

Farrell, M. J. 1958. "In Defence of Public-Utility Price Theory," *O.E.P.,* 10, 109–23.

Farrer, T. H. 1902. *The State in Its Relation to Trade.* London: Macmillan.

Faulhaber, G. R. 1975. "Cross-Subsidization: Pricing in Public Enterprises," *A.E.R.,* 65, 966–77.

1979. "Peak-Load Pricing and Regulatory Accountability," in M. A. Crew (ed.), *Problems in Public Utility Economics and Regulation,* pp. 133–42. Lexington, MA: Lexington Books.

and Levinson, S. B. 1981. "Subsidy-Free Prices and Anonymous Equity," *A.E.R.,* 71, 1083–91.

Feigenbaum, S., and Teeples, R. 1983. "Public Versus Private Water Delivery: A Hedonic Cost Approach," *R.E. Stats.,* 65, 672–8.

Feldstein, M. S. 1972a. "Equity and Efficiency in Public Sector Pricing: The Optimal Two-Part Tariff," *Q.J.E.,* 86, 175–87.

1972b. "Distributional Equity and the Optimal Structure of Public Prices," *A.E.R.,* 62, 32–6.

Filer, J. E., and Hollas, D. R. 1983. "Empirical Tests for the Effect of Regulation on Firm and Interruptible Gas Service," *Southern E.J.,* 50, 195–205.

Finsinger, J. 1980. "Peak Load Pricing and Rationing Policies," *Zeitschrift für Nationalokonomie,* 40, 169–82.

and Vogelsang, I. 1981. "Alternative Institutional Frameworks for Price Incentive Mechanisms," *Kyklos,* 34, 388–404.

Fishe, R. P. H., and Maddala, G. S. 1982. "Pricing Electricity in an Uncertain Environment," working paper, University of Florida.

Friedlander, A. F., and Due, J. F. 1972. "Tax Burden, Excess Burden, and Differential Incidence Revisited," *Public Finance,* 27.

and Spady, R. H. 1981. *Freight Transport Regulation: Equity, Efficiency and Competition in the Rail and Trucking Industries.* Cambridge, MA: M.I.T. Press.

Friedman, J. 1983. *Oligopoly Theory.* Cambridge U.P.

Friedman, M. 1952. "The Welfare Effects of an Income and Excise Tax," *J.P.E.,* 60, 25–33.

1962. *Price Theory: A Provisional Text.* Chicago: Aldine.

Frisch, R. 1939. "The Dupuit Taxation Theorem," *Etrica,* 7, 145–50.

Fumas, V. S., and Whinston, A. B. 1982. "Subsidy-Free Welfare Games," *Southern E.J.,* 49, 389–405.

Gabel, R. 1969. "The Early Competitive Era in Telephone Communications, 1893–1920," *L.C.P.,* 34, 340–59.

Gabor, A. 1955. "A Note on Block Tariffs," *R.E. Studs.,* 23, 32–41.

Gabszewicz, J. J., Shaked, A., Sutton, J., and Thisse, J. F. 1986. "Segmenting the Market: The Monopolist's Optimal Product Mix," *J.E.T.,* 39, 273–89.

Gal-Or, E. 1983. "Quality and Quantity Competition," *Bell J.,* 14, 508–16.

Gaskins, D. W., and Voytko, J. M. 1981. "Managing the Transition to Deregulation," *L.C.P.,* 44, 9–32.

Gately, D. 1974. "Sharing the Gains From Regional Cooperation: A Game Theoretic Application to Planning Investment in Electric Power," *I.E.R.,* 15, 195–208.

Gegax, D., and Tschirhart, J. 1984. "An Analysis of Interfirm Cooperation: Theory and Evidence from Electric Power Pools," *Southern E.J.,* 51, 1077–97.

Gellerson, M. W., and Grosskopf, S. P. 1980. "Public Utility Pricing, Investment, and Reliability under Uncertainty: A Review," *P.F.Q.,* 8, 477–92.

Gilligan, T. W., and Smirlock, M. L. 1983. "Predation and Cross-Subsidization in the Value Maximizing Multiproduct Firm," *Southern E.J.,* 50, 37–42.

Glaeser, M. G. 1927. *Outlines of Public Utility Economics.*

Glaister, S. 1987. "Regulation through Output Related Profits Tax." *J.I.E.,* 35, 281–96.

Gold, B. 1981. "On Size, Scale, and Returns: A Survey," *J.E.L.,* 19, 5–33.

Goldberg, V. P. 1976. "Regulation and Administered Contracts," *Bell J.,* 7, 426–48.

   1982. "Peltzman on Regulation and Politics," *Public Choice,* 39, 291–7 (and "Reply").

Gollop, F. M., and Karlson, S. H. 1978. "The Impact of the Fuel Adjustment Mechanism on Economic Efficiency," *R.E. Stats.,* 60, 574–84.

Grace, M. F. 1983. "Access and the Demise of Settlements and Separations?" *Public Utilities Fortnightly,* 112, 17–22.

   1986a. *Cost Allocations in a Multiproduct Natural Monopoly: Separation in Telecommunications,* Ph.D. dissertation, University of Florida.

   1986b. "Shared Inputs, Overcapitalization, and Regulation," *Economic Letters,* 22, 381–4.

Gravelle, H. S. E. 1976. "The Peak-Load Problem with Feasible Storage," *E.J.,* 86, 256–77.

Gray, H. M. 1940. "The Passing of the Public Utility Concept," *Journal of Land and Public Utility Economics,* 16, 8–20.

   1976. "The Sharing of Economic Power in Public Utility Industries," in W. Sichel (ed.), *Salvaging Public Utility Regulation,* pp. 5–19. Lexington, MA: Lexington Books.

Griffin, J. M. 1982. "The Welfare Implications of Externalities and Price Elasticities for Telecommunications Pricing," *R.E. Stats.,* 64, 59–66.

Griliches, Z. 1972. "Cost Allocation in Railroad Regulation," *Bell J.,* 3, 26–41.

Groves, T., and Ledyard, J. 1977. "Optimal Allocation of Public Goods: A Solution to the Free Rider Problem," *Etrica,* 45, 783–809.

Hagerman, R., and Ratchford, B. 1978. "Some Determinants of Allowed Rates of Return on Equity to Electric Utilities," *Bell J.,* 9, 46–55.

Hajiran, H., Kamerschen, D. R., and Legler, J. B. 1986. "The Economic and Political Determinants of the Requested–Granted Rate of Return in Public Utility Rate Cases," in A. L. Danielsen and D. R. Kamerschen (eds.), *Telecommunications in the Post-Divestiture Era,* pp. 29–56. Lexington, MA: D. C. Heath.

Hamlen, S. S., Hamlen, W. A., and Tschirhart, J. 1977. "The Use of Core Theory in Evaluating Joint Cost Allocation Schemes," *Accounting Review,* 3, 616–27.

1980. "The Use of the Generalized Shapley Allocation in Joint Cost Allocation," *Accounting Review,* 2, 269–87.

Hamlen, W. A., and Jen, F. 1983. "An Alternative Model of Interruptible Service Pricing and Rationing," *Southern E.J.,* 49, 1108–21.

and Tschirhart, J. 1980. "Solar Energy, Public Utilities, and Economic Efficiency," *Southern E.J.,* 47, 348–65.

Harris, J. E. 1979. "Pricing Rules for Hospitals," *Bell J.,* 10, 224–43.

Harris, M., and Raviv, A. 1981. "A Theory of Monopoly Pricing Schemes with Demand Uncertainty," *A.E.R.,* 71, 347–65.

Harrod, R. 1961. "The Neutrality of Improvements," *E.J.,* June, 300–4.

Hasenkamp, G. 1976a. *Specification and Estimation of Multiple Output Production Functions.* New York: Springer-Verlag.

1976b. "A Study of Multiple-Output Production Functions: Klein's Railroad Study Revisited," *J.E.,* 4, 253–62.

Hausman, W. J., and Neufeld, J. L. 1984. "Time-of-Day Pricing in the U.S. Electric Power Industry at the Turn of the Century," *Rand J.,* 15(1), 116–26.

Hayashi, P. M., and Trapani, J. M. 1976. "Rate of Return Regulation and the Regulated Firm's Choice of Capital–Labor Ratio: Further Empirical Evidence in the Averch-Johnson Model," *Southern E.J.,* 42, 384–98.

Sevier, M., and Trapani, J. M. 1985. "Pricing Efficiency Under Rate-of-Return Regulation: Some Empirical Evidence for the Electric Utility Industry," *Southern E.J.,* 51, 776–92.

Henderson, J. S. 1983. "The Economics of Electricity Demand Charges," *Energy Journal,* 4, 127–40.

Herriott, S. R. 1985. "The Organizational Economics of Power Brokers and Centrally Dispatched Power Pools," *L.E.,* 61, 308–13.

Hicks, J. R. 1932. *The Theory of Wages.* London: Macmillan.

Hirschleifer, J. 1958. "Peak Loads and Efficient Pricing: Comment," *Q.J.E.,* 72, 451–62.

1976. "Toward a More General Theory of Regulation, Comment," *J.L.E.,* 19, 241–4.

Holthausen, D. M. 1979. "A Model of Incentive Regulation," *J.E.,* 12, 61–73.

Hopkinson, J. 1892. "The Cost of Electric Supply," *Transactions of Junior Engineering Society,* 33–46.

Hotelling, H. 1929. "Stability in Competition," *E.J.,* 39, 41–57.

1932. "Edgeworth's Taxation Paradox and the Nature of Demand and Supply Functions," *J.P.E.,* 40, 577–616.

1935. "Demand Functions with Limited Budgets," *Etrica,* 3, 66–78.

1938. "The General Welfare in Relation to Problems of Taxation and Railway and Utility Rates," *Etrica,* 6, 242–69.

Howe, J. W. 1976. "Lifeline Rates – Benefits for Whom?" *Public Utilities Fortnightly,* 98, 22–5.

Intriligator, M. D. 1971. *Mathematical Optimization and Economic Theory.* Englewood Cliffs, NJ: Prentice-Hall.

Isaac, R. M. 1982. "Fuel Cost Adjustment Mechanisms and the Regulated Utility Facing Uncertain Fuel Prices," *Bell J.,* 13, 158–69.

Jackson, R. 1969. "Regulation and Electric Utility Rate Levels," *L.E.,* 45, 372–6.

Jarrell, G. A. 1978. "The Demand for State Regulation of the Electric Utility Industry," *J.L.E.,* 21, 269–95.

Jensen, M. C. 1972. "Capital Markets: Theory and Evidence," *Bell J.,* 3, 357–98.

Johnson, L. L. 1985. *Incentives to Improve Elective Utility Performance.* Santa Monica: Rand Corp.

Jones, F. W. 1983. *Input Biases Under Rate of Return Regulation.* New York: Garland.

Jordan, W. J. 1972. "Producer Protection, Prior Market Structure and the Effects of Government Regulation," *J.L.E.,* 15, 151–76.

1983. "Heterogeneous Users and the Peak Load Pricing Model," *Q.J.E.,* 98, 127–38.

Joskow, P. L. 1972. "The Determination of the Allowed Rate of Return in a Formal Regulatory Hearing," *Bell J.,* 3, 632–44.

1974. "Inflation and Environmental Concern: Structural Change in the Process of Public Utility Price Regulation," *J.L.E.,* 17, 291–327.

1979. "Public Utility Regulatory Policies Act of 1978: Electric Utility Rate Reform," *Natural Resources Journal,* 19, 787–809.

and Jones, D. R. 1983. "The Simple Economics of Industrial Cogeneration," *Energy J.,* 1, 1–22.

and Noll, R. G. 1981. "Regulation in Theory and Practice: An Overview," in G. Fromm (ed.), *Studies in Public Regulation,* pp. 1–65. Cambridge, MA: M.I.T. Press.

and Schmalensee, R. 1983. *Markets for Power.* Cambridge, MA: M.I.T. Press.

1986. "Incentive Regulation for Electric Utilities," *Yale Journal on Regulation,* 4, 1–50.

Just, R. E., Hueth, D. L., and Schmitz, A. 1982. *Applied Welfare Economics and Public Policy.* Englewood Cliffs, NJ: Prentice-Hall.

Kafoglis, M. Z. 1969. "Output of the Restrained Firm," *A.E.R.,* 59, 583–9.

Kahn, A. E. 1968. "The Graduate Fair Return: Comment," *A.E.R.,* 58, 170–3.

1971. *The Economics of Regulation: Principles and Institutions,* Vol. I and Vol. II. New York: Wiley.

1979. "Applications of Economics to an Imperfect World," *A.E.R. Papers and Proceedings,* 69, 1–13.

1983. "Utility Diversification," *Energy J.,* 1, 149–60.

1984. "The Road to More Intelligent Telephone Pricing," *Yale Journal on Regulation,* 1, 139–58.

Kahn, A. E., and Shew, W. B. 1987. "Current Issues in Telecommunications Regulation Pricing," *Yale Journal on Regulation,* 4, 191–256.

Kambhu, J. 1982. "Optimal Product Quality under Asymmetric Information and Moral Hazard," *Bell J.,* 13, 483–92.

Kamerschen, D. R., and Keenan, D. C. 1983. "Caveats on Applying Ramsey Pricing," in A. L. Danielsen and D. R. Kamerschen (eds.), *Current Issues in Public-Utility Economics,* pp. 197–208. Lexington, MA: D. C. Heath.

Kamien, M. I., and Schwartz, N. L. 1982. *Market Structure and Innovation.* Cambridge U.P.

Karlson, S. H. 1986. "Multiple-Output Production and Pricing in Electric Utilities," *Southern E.J.,* 53, 73–86.

Kaserman, D. L., and Tepel, R. C. 1982. "The Impact of the Automatic Adjustment Clause on Fuel Purchase and Utilization Practices in the U.S. Electric Utility Industry," *Southern E.J.,* 48, 687–700.

and Mayo, J. W. 1985. "Advertising and the Residential Demand for Electricity," *Journal of Business,* 58, 399–408.

Katz, M. L. 1983. "Non-uniform Pricing, Output and Welfare under Monopoly," *R.E. Studs.,* 50, 37–56.

1986. "An Analysis of Cooperative Research and Development," *Rand J.,* 17, 527–43.

and Shapiro, C. 1985. "Network Externalities, Competition, and Compatibility," *A.E.R.,* 75, 424–40.

Kay, J. A. 1979. "Uncertainty, Congestion and Peak Load Pricing," *R.E. Studs.,* 46, 601–11.

and Thompson, D. J. 1986. "Privatisation: A Policy in Search of a Rationale," *E.J.,* 96, 18–32.

Keeler, T. E. 1984. "Theories of Regulation and the Deregulation Movement," *Public Choice,* 44, 103–45.

Kendrick, J. W. 1975. "Efficiency Incentives and Cost Factors in Public Utility Automatic Revenue Adjustment Clauses," *Bell J.,* 6, 299–313.

Khanna, S. K. 1982. "Economic Regulation and Technological Change: A Review of the Literature," *Public Utilities Fortnightly,* 110, 35–44.

Klein, B., Crawford, R. G., and Alchian, A. A. 1978. "Vertical Integration, Appropriable Rents, and the Competitive Contracting Process," *J.L.E.,* 21, 297–326.

Klevorick, A. K. 1966. "Graduated Fair Return: A Regulatory Proposal," *A.E.R.,* 56, 477–84.

1971. "The 'Optimal' Fair Rate of Return," *Bell J.,* 2, 122–53.

1973. "The Behavior of a Firm Subject to Stochastic Regulatory Review," *Bell J.,* 4, 57–88.

Knieps, G., and Vogelsang, I. 1982. "The Sustainability Concept Under Alternative Behavioral Assumptions," *Bell J.,* 13, 234–41.

Kolbe, A. L., and Read, J. A., Jr., with Hall, G. R. 1984. *The Cost of Capital:*

*Estimating the Rate of Return for Public Utilities.* Cambridge, MA: M.I.T. Press.

Laffont, J. J., and Tirole, J. 1986. "Using Cost Observations to Regulate Firms," *J.P.E.,* 94, 614–41.

Lancaster, K. J. 1979. "The Problem of the Second Best and the Efficient Pricing of Electrical Power," report prepared by Gordian Associates, New York.

Lapinski, M. 1975. "A Guide to the Sources of the Economics of Regulation Literature," *Public Utilities Fortnightly,* July 17, 95, 21–9.

Lee, L. W. 1980. "A Theory of Just Regulation," *A.E.R.,* 70, 848–62.

Leibenstein, H. 1966. "Allocative Efficiency vs. 'X-Efficiency'," *A.E.R.,* 56(3), 392–415.

Leland, H. E. 1972. "The Theory of the Firm Facing Uncertain Demand," *A.E.R.,* 62, 278–91.

1974a. "Regulation of Natural Monopolies and the Fair Rate of Return," *Bell J.,* 5, 3–15.

1974b. "Production Theory and the Stock Market," *Bell J.,* 5, 125–44.

and Meyer, R. 1976. "Monopoly Pricing Structures with Imperfect Discrimination," *Bell J.,* 7, 449–62.

Levhari, D., and Peles, Y. 1973. "Markets Structure, Quality and Durability," *Bell J.,* 4, 235–49.

Levine, M. E. 1987. "Airline Competition in Deregulated Markets: Theory, Firm Strategy, and Public Policy," *Yale Journal on Regulation,* 4, 393–494.

Lewis, W. A. 1941. "The Two-Part Tariff," *Eca,* 8, 249–70.

1946. "Fixed Costs," *Eca,* 14, 231–58.

Lindahl, E. 1958. "Just Taxation – A Positive Solution," in R. A. Musgrave and R. Peacock (eds.), *Classics in the Theory of Public Finance,* pp. 168–76. London: Macmillan.

Link, A. N. 1977. "A Comment on the Efficient Allocation of Resources in a Regulated and Unionized Monopoly," *Southern E.J.,* 44(2), 383–4.

1978. "Optimal Firm Size for R&D Innovations in Electric Utilities," *Journal of Economics and Business,* 31, 52–6.

Lipsey, R. G., and Lancaster, K. J. 1956. "The General Theory of Second Best," *R.E. Studs.,* 24, 11–32.

Littlechild, S. C. 1970a. "A Game-Theoretic Approach to Public Utility Pricing," *E.I.,* 8, 162–6.

1970b. "Marginal-Cost Pricing with Joint Costs," *E.J.,* 80, 323–35.

1970c. "Peak-Load Pricing of Telephone Calls," *Bell J.,* 1, 191–210.

1975a. "Common Costs, Fixed Charges, Clubs, and Games," *R.E. Studs.,* 42, 117–24.

1975b. "Two-Part Tariffs and Consumption Externalities," *Bell J.,* 6, 661–70.

1983. "The Structure of Telephone Tariffs," *International Journal of Industrial Organization,* 1, 365–77.

and Thompson, G. F. 1977. "Aircraft Landing Fees: A Game Theoretic Approach," *Bell J.,* 8, 186–204.

Locklin, D. P. 1933. "The Literature on Railway Rate Theory," *Q.J.E.,* 47, 167–230.

Loeb, M., and Magat, W. A. 1979. "A Decentralized Method for Utility Regulation," *J.L.E.,* 22, 399–404.

Loehman, E., and Whinston, A. 1971. "A New Theory of Pricing and Decision-making for Public Investment," *Bell J.,* 2, 606–25.

Orlando, J., Tschirhart, J., and Whinston, A. B. 1979. "Cost Allocation for a Regional Wastewater Treatment System," *Water Resources Research,* 15, 193–202.

Lowry, E. D. 1973. "Justification for Regulation: The Case for Natural Monopoly," *Public Utilities Fortnightly,* 28, 1–7.

MacAvoy, P. W. 1979. *The Regulated Industries and the Economy.* New York: Norton.

and Robinson, K. 1983. "Winning by Losing: The AT&T Settlement," *Yale Journal on Regulation,* 1, 1–42.

1985. "Losing by Judicial Policymaking: The First Year of the AT&T Divestiture," *Yale Journal on Regulation,* 2, 225–62.

McChesney, F. S. 1987. "Rent Extraction and Rent Creation in the Economic Theory of Regulation," *Journal of Legal Studies,* 16(1), 101–18.

McCormick, R. E., Shughart, W. F., and Tollison, R. D. 1984. "The Disinterest in Deregulation," *A.E.R.,* 74, 1075–9.

McCraw, T. K. 1984. *Prophets of Regulation: Charles Francis Adams, Louis D. Brandeis, James M. Landis, and Alfred E. Kahn.* Cambridge, MA: Harvard U.P.

McKie, J. W. 1970. "Regulation and the Free Market: The Problem of Boundaries," *Bell J.,* 1, 6–26.

McNicol, D. L. 1973. "The Comparative Statics Properties of the Theory of the Regulated Firm," *Bell J.,* 4, 428–53.

Magat, W. A. 1976. "Regulation and the Rate and Direction of Induced Technical Change," *Bell J.,* 7, 479–96.

Makhija, A. K., and Thompson, H. E. 1984. "Capitalized Interest and the Cost of Money to Electric Utilities," *L.E.,* 60–9.

Mankiw, G. B., and Whinston, M. D. 1986. "Free Entry and Social Inefficiency," *Rand J.,* 17, 48–58.

Marchand, M. G. 1973. "Economic Principles of Telephone Rates under a Budgetary Constraint," *R.E. Studs.,* 40, 507–15.

Marino, A. M. 1978. "Peak Load Pricing under Regulatory Constraint: Two Remarks," *Southern E.J.,* 44, 606–15.

1981. "Optimal Departures from Marginal Cost Pricing: The Case of a Rate of Return Constraint," *Southern E.J.,* 48, 37–49.

Mayo, J. W. 1984. "Multiproduct Monopoly, Regulation, and Firm Costs," *Southern E.J.,* 51, 208–18.

1986. "Multiproduct Monopoly, Regulation, and Firm Costs: Reply," *Southern E.J.,* 52, 1175–8.

Meade, J. E. 1944. "Price and Output Policy of State Enterprise," *E.J.,* 54, 337–9.

Meyer, J. R., Wilson, R. W., Baughcum, M. A., Burton, E., and Caovette, L. 1979. *The Economics of Competition in the Telecommunications Industry.* Boston: Charles River.

———and Tye, W. B. 1985. "The Regulatory Transition," *A.E.R., Papers and Proceedings,* 75, 46–56.

Meyer, R. A. 1975a. "Monopoly Pricing and Capacity Choice under Uncertainty," *A.E.R.,* 65, 326–37.

———1975b. "Publicly Owned versus Privately Owned Utilities: A Policy Choice," *R.E. Stats.,* 57, 391–9.

———1976. "Capital Structure and the Behavior of the Regulated Firm under Uncertainty," *Southern E.J.,* 42, 600–9.

———1979a. "Optimal Nonlinear Pricing Structures: An Application to Energy Pricing," *Applied Economics,* 4, 241–54.

———1979b. "Regulated Monopoly under Uncertainty," *Southern E.J.,* 45, 1121–9.

———and Leland, H. E. 1980. "The Effectiveness of Price Regulation," *R.E. Stats.,* 62, 555–66.

Milon, J. W. 1981. "Alternative Energy Systems and Electric Rate Reform," *Public Utilities Fortnightly,* 107, 15–20.

Mirman, L. J., and Sibley, D. 1980. "Optimal Nonlinear Prices for Multiproduct Monopolies," *Bell J.,* 11, 659–70.

———Samat, D., and Tauman, Y. 1983. "An Axiomatic Approach to the Allocation of a Fixed Cost Through Prices," *Bell J.,* 14, 139–51.

———Tauman, Y., and Zang, I. 1985. "Supportability, Sustainability, and Subsidy-Free Prices," *Rand J.,* 16(1), 114–26.

———1986. "Ramsey Prices, Average Cost Prices and Price Sustainability," *International Journal of Industrial Organization,* 4, 123–40.

Mitchell, B. M. 1978. "Optimal Pricing of Local Telephone Service," *A.E.R.,* 68, 517–37.

———Manning, W. G., Jr., and Acton, J. P. 1978. *Peak-Load Pricing: European Lessons for U.S. Energy Policy.* Cambridge, MA: Ballinger.

Mitnick, B. M. 1980. *The Political Economy of Regulation.* New York: Columbia University Press.

Mohring, H. 1970. "The Peak Load Problem with Increasing Returns and Pricing Constraints," *A.E.R.,* 60, 693–705.

Moore, T. G. 1970. "The Effectiveness of Regulation of Electric Utility Prices," *Southern E.J.,* 36, 365–75.

———1978. "The Beneficiaries of Trucking Regulation," *J.L.E.,* 21, 327–43.

Morgan, M. G., and Talukdar, S. N. 1979. "Electric Power Load Management: Some Technical, Economic, Regulatory and Social Issues," *Proceedings of the IEEE,* 67, 241–313.

Morgan, T. D., Harrison, J. L., and Verkuil, P. R. 1985. *Economic Regulation of Business: Cases and Materials,* 2nd ed. St. Paul, MN: West Publishing.

Morin, R. A. 1985. *Utilities' Cost of Capital.* Arlington, VA: Public Utilities Reports.

Morrison, S. A., and Winston, C. 1985. "Intercity Transportation Route Structures under Deregulation: Some Assessments Motivated by the Airlines Experience," *A.E.R., Papers and Proceedings,* 75, 57–61.

Munasinghe, M., and Gellerson, M. 1979. "Economic Criteria for Optimizing Power System Reliability Levels," *Bell J.,* 10, 353–65.

Murphy, M. M. 1977. "Price Discrimination, Market Separation and the Multi-Part Tariff," *E.I.,* 15, 587–99.

Musgrave, R. A. 1959. *The Theory of Public Finance,* pp. 136–59. New York: McGraw-Hill.

Myers, S. C. 1972. "The Application of Finance Theory to Public Utility Rate Cases," *Bell J.,* 3, 58–97.

Nadiri, M. I., and Schankerman, M. A. 1981. "The Structure of Production, Technological Change and the Rate of Growth of Total Factor Productivity in the Bell System," in T. Cowing and R. Stevenson (eds.), *Productivity Measurement in Regulated Industries,* pp. 219–47. New York: Academic Press.

Nakao, T. 1982. "Product Quality and Market Structure," *Bell J.,* 13, 133–42.

National Association of Regulatory Utility Commissioners. 1971. *Separations Manual.* Washington, DC: NARUC.

National Association of Regulatory Utility Commissioners. 1973. *Electric Utility Cost Allocation Manual.* Washington, DC: NARUC.

Navarro, P. 1982. "Public Utility Commission Regulation: Performance, Determinants, and Energy Policy Impacts," *Energy J.,* 2, 119–39.

Needham, D. 1983. *The Economics and Politics of Regulation: A Behavioral Approach.* Boston: Little, Brown.

Needy, C. W. 1975. *Regulation-Induced Distortions.* Lexington, MA: Lexington Books.

　　1977. "Optimal Distortion Mix for Constrained Profit-Maximization," *E.I.,* 15, 251–68.

Negishi, T. 1960. "Welfare Economics and Existence of an Equilibrium for a Competitive Economy," *Metroeconomica,* 12, 92–7.

Nelson, R. A. 1982. "An Empirical Test of the Ramsey Theory and Stigler-Peltzman Theory of Public Utility Pricing," *E.I.,* 20, 277–90.

　　1984. "Regulation, Capital Vintage, and Technical Change in the Electric Utility Industry," *R.E. Stats.,* 66, 59–69.

Nelson, R. H. 1987. "The Economics Profession and the Making of Public Policy," *J.E.L.,* 25(1), 49–91.

Neuberg, L. G. 1977. "Two Issues in the Municipal Ownership of Electric Power Distribution Systems," *Bell J.,* 8, 303–23.

Neufeld, J. L. 1987. "Price Discrimination and the Adoption of the Electricity Demand Change," *Journal of Economic History,* 21, 693–709.

　　and Watts, J. 1981. "Inverted Block or Lifeline Rates and Micro-Efficiency in the Consumption of Electricity," *Energy Economics,* 3(2), 113–21.

Ng, Y., and Weisser, M. 1974. "Optimal Pricing with a Budget Constraint – The Case of the Two-Part Tariff," *R.E. Studs.,* 41, 337–45.

Nguyen, D. T. 1978. "Public Utility Pricing with Stochastic Demands: A Note," *Applied Economics,* 10, 43–7.

Noll, A. M. 1987. "Bell System R&D Activities: The Impact of Divestiture," *Telecommunications Policy,* June, 161–78.

Noll, R. G. 1971. *Reforming Regulation.* Washington, DC: Brookings Institution.

    1986. "State Regulatory Responses to Competition and Divestiture in the Telecommunications Industry," in R. E. Grieson (ed.), *Antitrust and Regulation,* pp. 165–200. Lexington, MA: D. C. Heath.

Nowell, C., and Tschirhart, J. 1988. "Testing Competing Theories of Regulatory Behavior," working paper, University of Wyoming.

Oi, W. Y. 1971. "A Disney Land Dilemma: Two-Part Tariffs for a Mickey Mouse Monopoly," *Q.J.E.,* 85, 77–96.

Okuguchi, K. 1975. "The Implications of Regulation for Induced Technical Change: Comment," *Bell J.,* 6, 703–5.

Olson, C. V., and Trapani, J. M. III 1981. "Who Has Benefited from Regulation of the Airline Industry," *J.L.E.,* 24, 75–93.

Ordover, J., and Panzar, J. 1980. "On the Nonexistence of Pareto Superior Outlay Schedules," *Bell J.,* 11, 351–4.

Oren, S. S., and Smith, S. A. 1981. "Critical Mass and Tariff Structure in Electronic Communications Markets," *Bell J.,* 12, 467–87.

    Smith, S. A., and Wilson, R. B. 1983. "Competitive Nonlinear Tariffs," *J.E.T.,* 29, 49–71.

Owen, B. M., and Braeutigam, R. 1978. *The Regulation Game: Strategic Use of the Administrative Process.* Cambridge, MA: Ballinger.

Panzar, J. C. 1976. "A Neoclassical Approach to Peak Load Pricing," *Bell J.,* 7, 521–30.

    1980. "Sustainability, Efficiency, and Vertical Integration," in P. Kleindorfer and B. M. Mitchell (eds.), *Regulated Industries and Public Enterprise,* pp. 171–85. Lexington, MA: D. C. Heath.

    1981. "Comment on Open Entry and Cross-Subsidization in Regulated Markets," in G. Fromm (ed.), *Studies in Public Regulation,* pp. 365–9. Cambridge, MA: M.I.T. Press.

    and Sibley, D. S. 1978. "Public Utility Pricing under Risk: The Case of Self-Rationing," *A.E.R.,* 68, 888–95.

    and Willig, R. D. 1977a. "Economies of Scale in Multi-Output Production," *Q.J.E.,* 91, 481–94.

    1977b. "Free Entry and the Sustainability of Natural Monopoly," *Bell J.,* 8, 1–22.

    1981. "Economies of Scope," *A.E.R.,* 71, 268–72.

Parish, R., and Ng, Y. 1972. "Monopoly, X-Efficiency and the Measurement of Welfare Loss," *Eca,* 39, 301–8.

Peles, Y. C., and Sheshinski, E. 1976. "Integration Effects of Firms Subject to Regulation," *Bell J.,* 7, 308–13.

    and Stein, J. L. 1976. "The Effect of Rate of Return Regulation Is Highly Sensitive to the Nature of Uncertainty," *A.E.R.,* 66, 278–89.

Peltzman, S. 1971. "Pricing in Public Enterprises: Electric Utilities in the United States," *J.L.E.,* 14, 109–47.

    1976. "Towards a More General Theory of Regulation," *J.L.E.,* 19, 211–40.

Perrakis, S. 1976. "On the Regulated Price Setting Monopoly Firm with a Random Demand Curve," *A.E.R.*, 66, 410–16.

and Zerbinis, J. 1981. "An Empirical Analysis of Monopoly Regulation Under Uncertainty," *Applied Economics*, 13, 109–25.

Perry, M. K. 1978. "Price Discrimination and Forward Integration," *Bell J.*, 9, 209–17.

Pescatrice, D. R., and Trapani, J. M., III 1980. "The Performance and Objectives of Public and Private Utilities Operating in the United States," *J. Pub. E.*, 13, 259–76.

Petersen, H. C. 1975. "An Empirical Test of Regulatory Effects," *Bell J.*, 6, 111–27.

1982. "Gainers and Losers with Lifeline Electricity Rates," *Public Utilities Fortnightly*, 108, 33–5.

Philips, L. 1983. *The Economics of Price Discrimination*. Cambridge U.P.

Phillips, C. F., Jr. 1984. *The Regulation of Public Utilities: Theory and Practice*. Arlington, VA: Public Utility Reports.

Phillips, O. R., and Battalio, R. C. 1983. "Two Part Tariffs and Monopoly Profits when Visits Are Variable," *Bell J.*, 14, 601–4.

Pigou, A. C. 1913. "Railway Rates and Joint Costs: Comment," *Q.J.E.*, 27, 535–8.

Posner, R. 1969. "Natural Monopoly and Its Regulation," *Stanford Law Review*, 21, 548–643.

1971. "Taxation by Regulation," *Bell J.*, 2, 22–50.

1974. "Theories of Economic Regulation," *Bell J.*, 5, 335–58.

Pressman, I. 1970. "A Mathematical Formulation of the Peak-Load Pricing Problem," *Bell J.*, 1, 304–26.

Primeaux, W. J., Jr. 1977. "An Assessment of X-efficiency Gained Through Competition," *R.E. Stats.*, 59, 105–8.

1978. "Rate Base Methods and Realized Rates of Return," *E.I.*, 16, 95–107.

Filer, J. E., Herren, R. S., and Hollas, D. R. 1984. "Determinants of Regulatory Policies Toward Competition in the Electric Utility Industry." *Public Choice*, 43, 173–86.

and Mann, P. C. 1986. "Regulator Selection Methods and Electricity Prices," *L.E.*, 62, 1–13.

and Nelson, R. A. 1980. "An Examination of Price Discrimination and Internal Subsidization by Electric Utilities," *Southern E.J.*, 47, 84–99.

Ramsey, F. R. 1927. "A Contribution to the Theory of Taxation," *E.J.*, 37, 47–61.

Rees, R. 1968. "Second-Best Rules for Public Enterprise Pricing," *Eca*, 35, 260–73.

Renshaw, E. 1985. "A Note on Equity and Efficiency in the Pricing of Local Telephone Services," *A.E.R.*, 75, 515–18.

Rhoades, S. A. 1980. "Monopoly and Expense Preference Behavior: An Empirical Investigation of a Behavioralist Hypothesis," *Southern E.J.*, 4, 419–32.

Riordan, M. H. 1984. "On Delegating Price Authority to a Regulated Firm," *Rand J.*, 15, 108–16.

and Sappington, D. E. M. 1987. "Awarding Monopoly Franchises," *A.E.R.,* 77, 375–87.

Roberts, K. 1979. "Welfare Considerations of Nonlinear Pricing," *E.J.,* 89, 66–83.

Roberts, R. B., Maddala, G. S., and Enholm, G. 1978. "Determinants of the Requested Rate of Return and the Rate of Return Granted in a Formal Regulatory Process," *Bell J.,* 9, 611–21.

Rogerson, W. P. 1983. "Reputation and Product Quality," *Bell J.,* 14, 508–16.

Rohlfs, J. 1974. "A Theory of Interdependent Demand for a Communications Service," *Bell J.,* 5, 16–37.

Rolph, E. R., and Break, G. F. 1949. "The Welfare Aspects of Excise Taxes," *J.P.E.,* 57, 46–54.

Romano, R. E. 1987. "A Note on Market Structure and Innovation When Inventors Can Enter," *J.I.E.,* 35, 353–8.

Ross, T. W. 1984. "Uncovering Regulator's Social Welfare Weights," *Rand J.,* 15, 152–5.

Rozek, R. P. 1984. "The Over-capitalization Effect with Diversification and Cross Subsidization," *Economics Letters,* 16, 159–63.

Ruggles, N. 1949. "Recent Developments in the Theory of Marginal Cost Pricing," *R.E. Studs.,* 17–18, 107–26.

Russell, M., and Shelton, R. B. 1974. "A Model of Regulatory Agency Behavior," *Public Choice,* 20, 47–62.

Salas Fumas, V., and Whinston, A. B. 1982. "Subsidy-Free Welfare Games," *Southern E.J.,* 49, 389–406.

Salkever, D. S. 1970. "Public Utility Pricing and Output under Risk: Comment," *A.E.R.,* 60, 487–8.

Samuelson, P. A. 1947. *Foundations of Economic Analysis.* Cambridge, MA: Harvard U.P.

1969. "Contrast Between Welfare Conditions for Joint Supply and for Public Goods," *R.E. Stats.,* 51, 26–30.

Sandberg, I. W. 1975. "Two Theorems on a Justification of the Multiservice Regulated Company," *Bell J.,* 6, 346–56.

Sappington, D. E. M. 1980. "Strategic Firm Behavior Under a Dynamic Regulatory Adjustment Process," *Bell J.,* 11, 360–72.

1982. "Optimal Regulation of Research and Development under Imperfect Information," *Bell J.,* 13, 354–68.

1983. "Optimal Regulation of a Multiproduct Monopoly with Unknown Technological Capabilities," *Bell J.,* 14, 453–63.

and Shepherd, W. 1982. "Sustainability, Entry Restriction, and Induced Technological Bias," *Q.R. of Econ. and Bus.,* 22, 43–52.

and Stiglitz, J. E. 1986. "Information and Regulation," in E. Bailey (ed.), *Public Regulation: New Perspectives in Institutions and Policies.* Cambridge, MA: M.I.T. Press.

Sav, G. T. 1977. "R&D Decisions Under Alternative Regulatory Constraints," *Atlantic E.J.,* 5, 73–80.

Scherer, C. R. 1976. "Estimating Peak and Off-Peak Marginal Costs for an Electric Power System: An *Ex Ante* Approach," *Bell J.,* 7, 575–601.

Scherer, F. M. 1980. *Industrial Market Structure and Economic Performance,* 2nd ed. Chicago: Rand McNally.

Schmalensee, R. 1970. "Regulation and the Durability of Goods," *Bell J.,* 1, 54–64.

1979. *The Control of Natural Monopolies.* Lexington, MA: Lexington Books.

1981. "Monopolistic Two-Part Pricing Arrangements," *Bell J.,* 12, 445–66.

Schmookler, J. 1962. "Changes in Industry and in the State of Knowledge as Determinants of Industrial Innovation," in *The Rate and Direction of Inventive Activity,* pp. 195–232. Washington, DC: National Bureau of Economic Research.

Schotter, A., and Schwödiauer, G. 1980. "Economics and Game Theory: A Survey," *J.E.L.,* 18, 479–527.

Scott, F., Jr. 1981. "Estimating Recipient Benefits and Waste from Lifeline Electricity Rates," *L.E.,* 57(4), 536–43.

and Morrell, S. O. 1985a. "Two-Part Pricing for a Multiproduct Monopolist," *E.I.,* 23, 295–307.

1985b. "The Effect of a Fuel Adjustment Clause on a Regulated Firm's Selection of Inputs," *Energy J.,* 6, 117–26.

Seagraves, J. A. 1984. "Regulating Utilities with Efficiency Incentives," *Public Utilities Fortnightly,* 113, 18–23.

Sexton, R. J., and Sexton, T. A. 1987. "Cooperatives as Entrants," *Rand J.,* 18, 581–95.

Shaked, A., and Sutton, J. 1982. "Natural Oligopolies," *Etrica,* 51, 1469–84.

Shapiro, C. 1982. "Consumer Information, Product Quality, and Seller Information," *Bell J.,* 13, 483–92.

1967. "On Balance Sets and Cores," *Naval Research Logistics Quarterly, 14, 435–60.*

Shapley, L. S. 1953. "The Value of an *N*-Person Game," in Kuhn and Tucker (eds.), *Contributions to the Theory of Games,* pp. 307–17. Princeton U.P.

1967. "On Balanced Sets and Cores." *Naval Research Logistics Quarterly,* 14, 453–60.

Sharkey, W. W. 1981. "Existence of Sustainable Prices for Natural Monopoly Outputs," *Bell J.,* 12, 144–54.

1982a. "Suggestions for a Game-Theoretic Approach to Public Utility Pricing and Cost Allocation," *Bell J.,* 13, 57–68.

1982b. *The Theory of Natural Monopoly.* Cambridge U.P.

and Telser, L. G. 1978. "Supportable Cost Functions for the Multiproduct Firm," *J.E.T.,* 18, 23–37.

Shepherd, W. G. 1984. "Contestability vs. Competition," *A.E.R.,* 74, 572–87.

Sherman, R. 1972. "The Rate-of-Return Regulated Public Utility Firm Is Schizophrenic," *Applied Economics,* 4, 23–31.

1977. "Financial Aspects of Rate-of-Return Regulation," *Southern E.J.,* 44, 240–8.

1981. "Pricing Inefficiency Under Profit Regulation," *Southern E.J.,* 48, 475–89.

1985. "The Averch and Johnson Analysis of Public Utility Regulation Twenty Years Later," *Review of Industrial Organization,* 2, 178–94.

1989. *The Regulation of Monopoly.* Cambridge U.P.

and George, A. 1979. "Second-Best Pricing for the U.S. Postal Service," *Southern E.J.,* 45, 685–95.

and Visscher, M. L. 1978. "Second Best Pricing with Stochastic Demand," *A.E.R.,* 68, 41–53.

1979. "Rate-of-Return Regulation and Price Structure," in M. A. Crew (ed.), *Problems in Public Utility Economics and Regulation,* pp. 119–32. Lexington, MA: Lexington Books.

1982. "Rate of Return Regulation and Two Part Tariffs," *Q.J.E.,* 97, 27–42.

Sheshinski, E. 1971. "Welfare Aspects of a Regulatory Constraint: Note," *A.E.R.,* 61, 175–8.

1986. "Positive Second-Best Theory," in K. J. Arrow and M. D. Intriligator (eds.), *Handbook of Mathematical Economics,* Vol. III, pp. 85–101. Amsterdam: North Holland.

Shubik, M. 1982. *Game Theory in the Social Sciences: Concepts and Solutions.* Cambridge, MA: M.I.T. Press.

Sichler, B. J. 1928. "A Theory of Telephone Rates," *L.E.,* 4, 175–88.

Silberberg, E. 1978. *The Structure of Economics: A Mathematical Analysis.* New York: McGraw-Hill.

Simons, H. 1948. *Economic Policy for a Free Society,* Chapter 2. University of Chicago Press.

Smiley, R. H. 1985. "Management Compensation in Regulated Industries," in M. A. Crew (ed.), *Analyzing the Impact of Regulatory Change in Public Utilities,* pp. 111–25. Lexington, MA: Lexington Books.

and Greene, W. 1983. "Determinants of the Effectiveness of Electric Utility Regulation," *Resources and Energy,* 5, 65–81.

Smirlock, M., and Marshall, W. 1983. "Monopoly Power and Expense Preference Behavior: Theory and Evidence to the Contrary," *Bell J.,* 14, 167–78.

Smith, B. A. 1970. "Technological Innovation in Electric Power Generation: 1950–1970," *L.E.,* 46, 336–47.

Smith, V. K. 1974. "The Implications of Regulation for Induced Technical Change," *Bell J.,* 5, 623–32.

1975. "The Implications of Regulation for Induced Technical Change: Reply," *Bell J.,* 6, 706–7.

Smithson, C. W. 1978. "The Degree of Regulation and the Monopoly Firm: Further Empirical Evidence," *Southern E.J.,* 44, 568–80.

and Veendorp, E. C. H. 1982. "The 'Optimum' Degree of Rate of Return Regulation: A Two Sector Analysis," *Southern E.J.,* 48, 733–44.

Solow, R. 1957. "Technical Change and the Aggregate Production Function," *R.E. Stats.,* 39, 312–30.

Sorenson, J. R., Tschirhart, J. T., and Whinston, A. B. 1976. "A Game Theoretic Approach to Peak-Load Pricing," *Bell J.,* 7, 497–520.

1978a. "A Theory of Pricing under Decreasing Costs," *A.E.R.,* 68, 614–24.

1978b. "Private Good Clubs and the Core," *J. Pub. E.,* 10, 77–95.

Spady, R. H. 1979. *Econometric Estimation for the Regulated Transportation Industries.* New York: Garland.

Spann, R. M. 1974. "Rate of Return Regulation and Efficiency in Production: An Empirical Test of the Averch-Johnson Thesis," *Bell J.,* 5, 38–52.

1976. "The Regulatory Cobweb: Inflation, Deflation, Regulatory Lags and the Effects of Alternative Administrative Rules in Public Utilities," *Southern E.J.,* 43, 827–39.

Spence, M. 1975. "Monopoly, Quality and Regulation," *Bell J.,* 6, 417–29.

1977a. "Consumer Misperceptions, Product Failure and Producer Liability," *R.E. Studs.,* 44, 561–72.

1977b. "Nonlinear Prices and Welfare," *J. Pub. E.,* 7, 1–18.

1983. "Contestable Markets and the Theory of Industry Structure: A Review Article," *J.E.L.,* 21, 981–90.

Spremann, K. 1978. "On Welfare Implications and Efficiency of Entrance Fee Pricing," *Zeitschrift für Nationalokonomie,* 38, 231–52.

Squire, L. 1973. "Some Aspects of Optimal Pricing for Telecommunications," *Bell J.,* 4, 515–25.

Starrett, D. A. 1978. "Marginal Cost Pricing of Recursive Lumpy Investments," *R.E. Studs.,* 45, 215–27.

State of New York Public Service Commission. 1977. "Opinion and Order Revising Outstanding Curtailment Plan," No. 77–2, March 11.

Steiner, P. O. 1957. "Peak Loads and Efficient Pricing," *Q.J.E.,* 71, 585–610.

Stevenson, R. 1982. "X-Inefficiency and Interfirm Rivalry: Evidence from the Electric Utility Industry," *L.E.,* 58, 52–66.

Stewart, J. F. 1982. "Economic Efficiency and Automatic Fuel-Cost Adjustment Mechanisms: Theory and Empirical Evidence," in M. A. Crew (ed.), *Regulatory Reform and Public Utilities,* pp. 167–80. Lexington, MA: Lexington Books.

Stigler, G. J. 1946. *Theory of Price.* New York: Macmillan.

1968. *The Organization of Industry.* Homewood, IL: R. D. Irwin.

1971. "The Theory of Economic Regulation," *Bell J.,* 2, 3–21.

1974. "Free Riders and Collective Action: An Appendix to Theories of Economic Regulation," *Bell J.,* 5, 359–65.

and Friedland, C. 1962. "What Can Regulators Regulate? The Case of Electricity," *J.L.E.,* 5, 1–16.

Stolleman, N. C. 1987. "A Comparison of Rate Base Rate-of-Return and Ceiling Price Regulation," GTE paper presented at 15th annual Telecommunications Policy Research Conference.

Strand, S. H. 1980. "Regulatory Boundaries and Efficient Resource Allocations in the Production and Transportation of a Single Good," *Southern E.J.,* 46, 777–91.

Sutton, J. 1986. "Vertical Product Differentiation: Some Basic Themes," *A.E.R., Papers and Proceedings,* 76, 393–8.

Swan, P. L. 1971. "The Durability of Goods and the Regulation of Monopoly," *Bell J.,* 2, 347–57.

Sweeney, G. 1981. "Adoption and Cost-Saving Innovations by a Regulated Firm," *A.E.R.*, 71, 437–47.

1982. "Welfare Implications of Fully Distributed Cost Pricing Applied to Partially Regulated Firms," *Bell J.*, 13, 525–33.

Takayama, A. 1969. "Behavior of the Firm Under Regulatory Constraint," *A.E.R.*, 59, 255–60.

1974. *Mathematical Economics.* Hinsdale, IL: Dryden Press (2nd ed., 1985).

Taussig, F. W. 1913. "Railways Rates and Joint Costs Once More," *Q.J.E.*, 27, 378–84.

1913. "Railway Rates and Joint Costs: Reply," *Q.J.E.*, 27, 687–94.

Taylor, L. D. 1975. "The Demand for Electricity – A Survey," *Bell J.*, 6, 74–110.

1980. *Telecommunications Demand: A Survey and Critique.* Cambridge, MA: Ballinger.

Telser, L. G. 1969. "On the Regulation of Industry: A Note," *J.P.E.*, 77, 937–52.

1971. "On the Regulation of Industry: Rejoinder," *J.P.E.*, 79, 364–5.

Telson, M. L. 1975. "The Economics of Alternative Levels of Reliability for Electric Power Generation Systems," *Bell J.*, 6, 670–94.

Temple, Barker & Sloan, Inc. 1978. "An Evaluation of Four Marginal Costing Methodologies," Report to Electric Power Research Institute.

ten Raa, T. 1984. "Resolution of Conjectures on the Sustainability of Natural Monopoly," *Rand J.*, 15(1), 135–41.

Thomas, G., Whinston, A., and Wright, G. 1972. "A New Approach to Water Allocation Under Uncertainty," *Water Resources Research*, 8, 1151–8.

Tollison, R. D. 1982. "Rent Seeking: A Survey," *Kyklos*, 35, 575–92.

Trebing, H. M. 1963. "Towards an Incentive System of Regulation," *Public Utilities Fortnightly*, 72, 22–7.

1974. "Realism and Relevance in Public Utility Regulation," *J.E.I.*, 8, 209–34.

1976. "The Chicago School versus Public Utility Regulation," *J.E.I.*, 10, 97–126.

1984. "Public Utility Regulation: A Case Study in the Debate over Effectiveness of Economic Regulation," *J.E.I.*, 18, 223–50.

1985. "The Impact of Diversification on Economic Regulation," *J.E.I.*, 19, 463–74.

Tschirhart, J. T. 1980. "On Public Utility Pricing under Stochastic Demand," *Scottish J.P.E.*, 27, 216–34.

and Jen, F. 1979. "Behavior of a Monopoly Offering Interruptible Service," *Bell J.*, 10, 244–58.

Turvey, R. 1968. "Peak Load Pricing," *J.P.E.*, 76, 101–13.

1969. "Marginal Cost," *E.J.*, 79, 282–99.

1970. "Public Utility Pricing and Output under Risk: Comment," *A.E.R.*, 60, 485–6.

1974. "How to Judge when Price Changes Will Improve Resource Allocation," *E.J.*, 64, 825–32.

and Anderson, D. 1975. *Electricity Economics: Essays and Case Studies.* Baltimore: Johns Hopkins U.P.

Tye, W. B. 1987. "Competitive Access: A Comparative Industry Approach to the Essential Facility Doctrine," *Energy Law J.,* 8, 337–79.

VanderWeide, J. H., and Zalkind, J. H. 1981. "Deregulation and Oligopolistic Price–Quality Rivalry," *A.E.R.,* 71, 144–54.

Vardi, J., Zahavi, J., and Avi-Itzhak, B. 1977. "Variable Load Pricing in the Face of Loss of Load Probability," *Bell J.,* 8, 270–88.

Veall, M. R. 1983. "Industrial Electricity Demand and the Hopkinson Rate: An Application of the Extreme Value Distribution," *Bell J.,* 14, 427–40.

Vickrey, W. 1948. "Some Objections to Marginal-Cost Pricing," *J.P.E.,* 56, 218–38.

Visscher, M. 1973. "Welfare-Maximizing Price and Output with Stochastic Demand: Comment," *A.E.R.,* 63, 224–9.

Vogelsang, I. 1987. "A Non-Bayesian Incentive Mechanism Using Two-Part Tariffs," working draft WD-3669-MF. Santa Monica: Rand Corp.

    1988. "Price Cap Regulation of Telecommunications Services: A Long-Run Approach," N-2704-MF. Santa Monica: Rand Corp.

    and Finsinger, J. 1979. "A Regulatory Adjustment Process for Optimal Pricing by Multiproduct Monopoly Firms," *Bell J.,* 10, 157–71.

von Neumann, J. 1947. "The Mathematician," in R. B. Heywood (ed.), *The Works of the Mind,* p. 196. University of Chicago Press.

    and Morgenstern, O. 1944. *Theory of Games and Economic Behavior.* Princeton, NJ: Princeton U.P.

Walker, D. 1955. "The Direct–Indirect Tax Problems: Fifteen Years of Controversy," *Public Finance,* 10, 153–76.

Waterson, M. 1983. "Economies of Scope within Market Frameworks," *International Journal of Industrial Organization,* 1, 223–37.

    1987. "Recent Developments in the Theory of Natural Monopoly," *Journal of Economic Surveys,* 1, 59–80.

    1988. *Regulation of the Firm and Natural Monopoly.* Oxford: Basil Blackwell.

Waverman, L. 1975. "Peak-Load Pricing under Regulatory Constraint: A Proof of Inefficiency," *J.P.E.,* 83, 645–54.

Webb, M. G. 1977. "The Determination of Reserve Generating Capacity Criteria in Electricity Supply Systems," *Applied Economics,* 9, 19–31.

Weingast, B. R., and Moran, M. J. 1983. "Bureaucratic Discretion or Congressional Control? Regulatory Policymaking by the Federal Trade Commission," *J.P.E.,* 91, 765–800.

Weiss, L. W., and Strickland, A. D. 1976. *Regulation: A Case Approach.* New York: McGraw-Hill.

Wellisz, S. H. 1963. "Regulation of Natural Gas Pipeline Companies: An Economic Analysis," *J.P.E.,* 71, 30–43.

Wendel, J. 1976. "Firm–Regulator Interaction with Respect to Firm Cost Reduction Activities," *Bell J.,* 7, 631–40.

Wenders, J. T. 1976. "Peak Load Pricing in the Electric Utility Industry," *Bell J.,* 7, 232–41.

    1986a. "Economic Efficiency and Income Distribution in the Electric Utility Industry," *Southern E.J.,* 52, 1056–67.

1986b. "The Economic Theory of Regulation and the US Telecommunications Industry," working paper. Department of Economics, University of Idaho, Moscow.

1987. *The Economics of Telecommunications: Theory and Policy.* Cambridge, MA: Ballinger.

and Egan, B. L. 1986. "The Implications of Economic Efficiency for U.S. Telecommunications Policy," *Telecommunications Policy,* 10, 33–40.

and Taylor, L. D. 1976. "Experiments in Seasonal-Time-of-Day Pricing of Electricity to Residential Users," *Bell J.,* 7, 531–52.

Westfield, F. M. 1965. "Regulation and Conspiracy," *A.E.R.,* 55, 424–43.

1971. "Innovation and Monopoly Regulation," in W. M. Capron (ed.), *Technological Change in Regulated Industries,* pp. 13–43. Washington, DC: Brookings Institution.

White, L. J. 1972. "Quality Variation when Prices Are Regulated," *Bell J.,* 3, 425–36.

Wilcox, C., and Shepherd, W. B. 1975. *Public Policies Toward Business,* 5th ed. Homewood, IL: Irwin.

Wilder, R. P., and Stansell, S. R. 1974. "Determinants of Research and Development Activity by Electric Utilities," *Bell J.,* 5, 646–50.

Williamson, O. E. 1964. "Managerial Discretion and Business Behavior," *A.E.R.,* 54, 1032–57.

1966. "Peak-Load Pricing and Optimal Capacity under Indivisibility Constraints," *A.E.R.,* 56, 810–27.

1968. "Economies as an Antitrust Defense: The Welfare Tradeoffs," *A.E.R.,* 58, 18–36.

1974. "Peak-Load Pricing: Some Further Remarks," *Bell J.,* 5, 223–8.

1975. *Markets and Hierarchies: Analysis and Antitrust Implications.* New York: Free Press.

1976. "Franchise Bidding for Natural Monopolies – in General and with Respect to CATV," *Bell J.,* 7, 73–104.

Willig, R. D. 1976. "Consumer's Surplus Without Apology," *A.E.R.,* 66, 589–97.

1978. "Pareto-Superior Nonlinear Outlay Schedules," *Bell J.,* 9, 56–69.

1979. "The Theory of Network Access Pricing," in H. Trebing (ed.), *Issues in Public Utility Regulation,* pp. 109–52. East Lansing: Michigan State University.

and Bailey, E. E. 1977. "Ramsey-Optimal Pricing of Long Distance Telephone Services," paper presented at Mt. Bell seminar, Pricing in Regulated Industries, Carefree, AZ.

Wilson, R. 1975. "Informational Economies of Scale," *Bell J.,* 6, 184–95.

Wilson, T. 1945. "Price and Outlay Policy of State Enterprise," *E.J.,* 55, 454–61.

Wiseman, J. 1957. "The Theory of Public Utility Price – An Empty Box," *O.E.P.,* 9, 56–74.

Zajac, E. E. 1970. "A Geometric Treatment of Averch-Johnson's Behavior of the Firm Model," *A.E.R.,* 60, 117–25.

1972. "Note on 'Gold Plating' or 'Rate Base Padding'," *Bell J.,* 3, 311–15.

1978. *Fairness or Efficiency: An Introduction to Public Utility Pricing.* Cambridge, MA: Ballinger.

Zimmer, M. A. 1978. "Empirical Tests of the Averch-Johnson Hypothesis: A Critical Appraisal," in G. S. Maddala, W. S. Chern, and G. S. Gill (eds.), *Econometric Studies in Energy Demand and Supply,* pp. 152–71. New York: Praeger.

Zweifel, P., and Beck, K. 1987. "Utilities and Cogeneration: Some Regulatory Problems," *Energy J.,* 8, 1–15.

# Author index

# Subject index

Accelerated depreciation, 303, 319
Access fee
    discriminating, 121
    under rate-of-return regulation, 335
    uniform, 103
Additive demand, 196, 204, 348
Advertising expenses, 300
Airline industry routes, 79, 470
Airport facilities, 248
Allowable costs, 300
Allowed return, 298, 305, 318, 347–9
Amtrak, 489–90
Anonymously equitable prices, 257
Appropriability of ideas, 389–90
Ash Council, 285
Asymmetric information, *See*
    Principal-and-agent
AT&T, 5, 79, 123, 245, 296–7, 382,
    389–91, 418, 421, 453, 466, 474–
    5, 477, 496
Attributable cost, 92–3, 442
Automatic adjustment clauses
    empirical tests of, 371–3
    and incentives, 365–7
    theoretical model of, 367–71
Average incremental cost, 262–3, 441,
    455
Averch–Johnson (A-J) effect
    and aggregation problems, 354–6
    and biased factor augmentation,
        410, 412–15
    described, 305
    empirical tests of, 340–1

and firm's behavior, 356–9
and merger incentives, 461–2
in multiproduct firm, 333–9
and peak-load pricing, 333–5
and Ramsey prices, 336–9
and regulator's behavior, 359–65
and regulatory lag, 341–5
in single-product firm, 324–33
and stochastic environment, 345–54
and two-part tariffs, 335–6

Backward integration, 467
Banking industry, 359
Barriers to entry, 26, 28–9, 32–3, 44–
    5, 53, 237, 241–3, 484–6
Base load, 173, 188
Bellcore, 391
Bell Laboratories, 389–90, 392
Benefit–cost analysis, 180–3
Bertrand–Nash behavioral
    assumptions, 246–7, 266
Beta coefficients, 318
Bonneville Power Administration,
    220
Book value, 319
Break-even constraint
    with linear prices, 53, 56, 58, 64,
        243
    peak-load pricing with, 162
    under stochastic demand, 206
    and sustainability, 243
    and two-part tariff, 111–17
Bypass, 124